MW01247698

The Official CompTIA® A+® Core 1 and Core 2 Instructor Guide (Exams 220-1001 and 220-1002)

Volume 2

The Official CompTIA® A+® Core 1 and Core 2 Instructor Guide (Exams 220-1001 and 220-1002)

COURSE EDITION: 1.01

Acknowledgements

CompTIA.

James Pengelly, Author

Pamela J. Taylor, Author

Brian Sullivan, Media Designer

Peter Bauer, Content Editor

Thomas Reilly, Vice President Learning

Katie Hoenicke, Director of Product Management

James Chesterfield, Manager, Learning Content and Design

Becky Mann, Senior Manager, Product Development

Notices

DISCLAIMER

While CompTIA, Inc. takes care to ensure the accuracy and quality of these materials, we cannot guarantee their accuracy, and all materials are provided without any warranty whatsoever, including, but not limited to, the implied warranties of merchantability or fitness for a particular purpose. The use of screenshots, photographs of another entity's products, or another entity's product name or service in this book is for editorial purposes only. No such use should be construed to imply sponsorship or endorsement of the book by nor any affiliation of such entity with CompTIA. This courseware may contain links to sites on the Internet that are owned and operated by third parties (the "External Sites"). CompTIA is not responsible for the availability of, or the content located on or through, any External Site. Please contact CompTIA if you have any concerns regarding such links or External Sites.

TRADEMARK NOTICES

CompTIA®, A+®, and the CompTIA logo are registered trademarks of CompTIA, Inc., in the U.S. and other countries. All other product and service names used may be common law or registered trademarks of their respective proprietors.

COPYRIGHT NOTICE

Copyright © 2019 CompTIA, Inc. All rights reserved. Screenshots used for illustrative purposes are the property of the software proprietor. Except as permitted under the Copyright Act of 1976, no part of this publication may be reproduced or distributed in any form or by any means, or stored in a database or retrieval system, without the prior written permission of CompTIA, 3500 Lacey Road, Suite 100, Downers Grove, IL 60515-5439.

This book conveys no rights in the software or other products about which it was written; all use or licensing of such software or other products is the responsibility of the user according to terms and conditions of the owner. If you believe that this book, related materials, or any other CompTIA materials are being reproduced or transmitted without permission, please call 1-866-835-8020 or visit **www.help.comptia.org**.

Table of Contents

Using the Official CompTIA® A+® Core 1 and Core 2 Instructor Guide (Exams 220-1001 and 220-1002)

Welcome to the Instructor

Welcome to the only materials on the market today developed by CompTIA to prepare learners for CompTIA certification exams. You can utilize *The Official CompTIA® A+® Core 1 and Core 2 (Exams 220-1001 and 220-1002)* curriculum to present world-class instructional experiences whether:

- Your students are participating with you in the classroom or virtually.
- You are presenting in a continuous event or in an extended teaching plan, such as an academic semester.
- Your presentation takes place synchronously with the students or asynchronously.
- Your students have physical courseware or are using digital materials.
- You have any combination of these instructional dimensions.

To make the best use of *The Official CompTIA® A+® Core 1 and Core 2 (Exams 220-1001 and 220-1002)* materials in any or all of these dimensions, be sure to review all of the components of the CompTIA CHOICE platform. The CompTIA CHOICE platform is developed and hosted by Logical Operations and has been customized specifically for Official CompTIA Content.

Preparing to Teach

Effectively presenting the information and skills in this course requires adequate preparation in any presentation modality. As such, as an instructor, you should familiarize yourself with the content of the entire course, including its organization and instructional approaches. You should review each of the activities and exercises so you can facilitate them during the learning event. Also, make sure you review the tips for presenting in the different dimensions; these instructor tips are available as notes in the margins of your Instructor Guide.

In addition to the curriculum itself, Microsoft® PowerPoint® slides, data files, and other course-specific support material may be available by downloading the files from the CHOICE Course screen. Be sure to obtain the course files prior to your learning event and make sure you distribute them to your students.

Course Facilitator Icons

Throughout the Instructor Guide, you may see various instructor-focused icons that provide suggestions, answers to problems, and supplemental information for you, the instructor.

Instructor Icon	Instructor Icon Descriptive Text
Show Slide(s)	The **Show Slide** icon provides a prompt to the instructor to display a specific slide from the provided PowerPoint files.
Teaching Tip	The **Teaching Tip** icons provide additional guidance and background that you may want to utilize during specific parts of the course, including lecture, whiteboard sketching, or demonstrations.
Interaction Opportunity	The **Interaction Opportunity** provides suggestions on different ways to engage with students, either through discussions or activities.

Digital Software Updates

Software vendors mentioned in this course may at any time deploy software updates digitally, resulting in changes that may not be reflected dynamically in this course. Stay up to date with product updates and be ready to adapt the material to any changes in the user interface.

Presentation Tips for the *The Official CompTIA® A+® Core 1 and Core 2 (Exams 220-1001 and 220-1002)* Course

Here are some useful tips for presenting the *The Official CompTIA® A+® Core 1 and Core 2 (Exams 220-1001 and 220-1002)* course.

- With the latest revision of the certification exams and corresponding exam objectives, a significant amount of new content has been added to this edition of the course. You might need to employ time-saving techniques, such as asking participants to read some of the content as "homework" and then spending very little classroom time on that content, to ensure that you can cover all of the content included in the course manual.
- If you will have remote participants for your class, it is strongly recommended that you position a camera directly above a work area so that remote students can watch as you or other participants work with the various hardware components throughout the course.
- Throughout the course, when software or applications are being installed or updated that might take considerable time, consider having students start the install or update, then present the related content. You might also consider having the install or update begin before a scheduled classroom break.
- In the troubleshooting topics, you might have to send students out of the physical classroom in order to introduce errors and issues into their devices. For remote participants, you might want to also introduce issues into your devices so that you can demonstrate how to troubleshoot and correct the errors.
- The **Video** icon provides access to different videos that can be incorporated into the course. These videos, developed exclusively for CompTIA by ITPro.TV, provide demonstrations of key activities in the course. These are a good alternative to show if you do not have access to all equipment mentioned in the course.

Course-Specific Technical Requirements

Hardware

For this course, you will need one HOST and one WORKBENCH computer for each student and the instructor, along with some additional components and equipment.

Each HOST computer will run Windows® 10, Hyper-V®, and multiple virtual machines and will need the following minimum hardware configurations:

- 2 GHz multicore x64 CPU with virtualization support
- 8 to 16 GB RAM (More RAM provides better VM performance.)
- 200 GB free disk space (An SSD will provide much better performance than an HDD.)
- DVD-ROM drive
- Ethernet network cards supported by the Windows® host OS (Windows® 10)
- Internet access (Contact your local network administrator.)

 Note: Some activities require web access for the HOST. VMs should not be connected to the Internet or to the physical classroom network.

- Keyboard and mouse (or other pointing device)
- 1,024 x 768 resolution monitor recommended

Each WORKBENCH computer should be capable of running Windows® 10 (1803 build).

Software

For each HOST computer, you will need product ISOs and (where applicable) product keys/ licenses for the following software:

- Windows® 10 x64 Pro/Enterprise Branch 1803 or later with Hyper-V® installed
- Windows® 8.1 Pro/Enterprise x64 Edition
- Windows® 7 Professional/Enterprise x64 Edition SP1 (Build 7601)
- Windows® Server 2016 Standard Edition
- CentOS 7 x64 (A prebuilt VM is provided. You will only need to provide an ISO if you want to demonstrate or run an attended installation of Linux.)

 Note: If you do not have the specific builds available, future versions of Windows® 10 or Server 2016 should not substantially affect the activity steps. However, security and virus definition updates could cause some of the tools used in the activities to fail; if this is the case, disable Windows® Defender. Windows® 7 must have SP1 installed.

For each WORKBENCH computer, you will need:

- Product ISOs and (where applicable) product keys/licenses for Windows® 10 x64 Pro/Enterprise Branch 1803
- CPU-Z (**www.cpuid.com/softwares/cpu-z.html**)

You will also need:

- A variety of peripherals such as keyboards and mice, different kinds of displays and cabling, microphones and speakers, and webcams.
- A variety of upgrade components such as storage drives, graphics adapters, power supplies, and RAM.
- A variety of laptops and mobile devices.
- Cleaning kits, toolkits, and testing equipment such as multimeters and power supply testers.
- Printing and networking equipment.
- IoT/home automation equipment.

Setting Up the Course

A detailed Setup Guide is provided on the **Instructor Resources** tile of the CHOICE Course screen. It includes complete instructions for setting up instructor and student computers to complete all of the hands-on activities in this course.

Presentation Planners

The lesson durations given in the course content are estimates based on a typical class experience. Your presentation timing and flow may vary based on factors such as the size of the class, whether students are in specialized job roles, whether you plan to incorporate videos or other assets from the CHOICE Course screen into the course, and so on.

Because the content can be presented in a continuous flow or separately across a multi-session series, several sample presentation planners are provided on the **Instructor Resources** tile of the CHOICE Course screen. You can use these sample planners to determine how you will conduct the class to meet the needs of your own situation.

About This Course

CompTIA A+ certified professionals are proven problem solvers. They support today's core technologies from security to cloud to data management and more. CompTIA A+ is the industry standard for launching IT careers into today's digital world. It is the only industry recognized credential with performance-based items to prove pros can think on their feet to perform critical IT support tasks in the moment. It is trusted by employers around the world to identify the go-to person in end point management and technical support roles. CompTIA A+ is regularly re-invented by IT experts to ensure that it validates core skills and abilities demanded in the workplace.

The Official CompTIA® A+® Core 1 and Core 2 (Exams 220-1001 and 220-1002) course provides the background knowledge and skills you will require to be a successful A+ technician. It will help you prepare to take the CompTIA A+ Core Series certification examinations (exam numbers 220-1001 and 220-1002), in order to become a CompTIA A+ Certified Professional.

Course Description

Target Student

This course is designed for individuals who have basic computer user skills and who are interested in obtaining a job as an entry-level IT technician. This course is also designed for students who are seeking the CompTIA A+ certification and who want to prepare for the CompTIA A+ Core 1 220-1001 Certification Exam and the CompTIA A+ Core 2 220-1002 Certification Exam.

Prerequisites

To ensure your success in this course, you should have experience with basic computer user skills, be able to complete tasks in a Microsoft® Windows® environment, be able to search for, browse, and access information on the Internet, and have basic knowledge of computing concepts. You can obtain this level of skills and knowledge by taking the following official CompTIA courses:

* *The Official CompTIA® IT Fundamentals+ (Exam FC0-U61)*

Note: The prerequisites for this course might differ significantly from the prerequisites for the CompTIA certification exams. For the most up-to-date information about the exam prerequisites, complete the form on this page: **https://certification.comptia.org/training/exam-objectives**

Course Objectives

In this course, you will install, configure, optimize, troubleshoot, repair, upgrade, and perform preventive maintenance on personal computers, digital devices, and operating systems.

You will:

* Support operating systems.
* Install and configure PC system unit components and peripheral devices.
* Install, configure, and troubleshoot display and multimedia devices.
* Install, configure, and troubleshoot storage devices.
* Install, configure, and troubleshoot internal system components.
* Install, configure, and maintain operating systems.
* Maintain and troubleshoot Microsoft Windows.
* Explain network infrastructure concepts.
* Configure and troubleshoot network connections.
* Manage users, workstations, and shared resources.
* Implement client virtualization and cloud computing.
* Implement physical security.
* Secure workstations and data.

- Troubleshoot workstation security issues.
- Support and troubleshoot laptops.
- Support and troubleshoot mobile devices.
- Install, configure, and troubleshoot print devices.
- Implement operational procedures.

The CompTIA CHOICE Home Screen

Logon and access information for your CHOICE environment will be provided with your class experience. The platform is your entry point to the learning experience, of which this course manual is only one part.

On the Home screen, you can access the Course screens for your specific courses. Visit the Course screen both during and after class to make use of the world of support and instructional resources that make up the learning experience.

Each Course screen will give you access to the following resources:

- **Classroom**: A link to your training provider's classroom environment.
- **eBook**: An interactive electronic version of the printed book for your course.
- **Files**: Any course files available to download.
- **Checklists**: Step-by-step procedures and general guidelines you can use as a reference during and after class.
- **Videos**: Brief videos, developed exclusively for CompTIA by ITPro.TV, provide demonstrations of key activities in the course. These are a good alternative to view if you do not have access to all equipment mentioned in the course.
- **Assessment**: A series of different assessments for each lesson as well as an overall course self-assessment.

Depending on the nature of your course and the components chosen by your learning provider, the CHOICE Course screen may also include access to elements such as:

- LogicalLABs, a virtual technical environment for your course.
- CertMaster Practice, an adaptive knowledge assessment and practice test platform.
- Various partner resources related to the courseware.
- Related certifications or credentials.
- A link to your training provider's website.
- Notices from the CHOICE administrator.
- Newsletters and other communications from your learning provider.
- Mentoring services.

Visit your CHOICE Home screen often to connect, communicate, and extend your learning experience!

How to Use This Book

As You Learn

This book is divided into lessons and topics, covering a subject or a set of related subjects. In most cases, lessons are arranged in order of increasing proficiency.

The results-oriented topics include relevant and supporting information you need to master the content. Each topic has various types of activities designed to enable you to solidify your understanding of the informational material presented in the course. Information is provided for reference and reflection to facilitate understanding and practice.

Data files for various activities as well as other supporting files for the course are available by download from the CHOICE Course screen. In addition to sample data for the course exercises, the course files may contain media components to enhance your learning and additional reference materials for use both during and after the course.

Checklists of procedures and guidelines can be used during class and as after-class references when you're back on the job and need to refresh your understanding.

At the back of the book, you will find a glossary of the definitions of the terms and concepts used throughout the course. You will also find an index to assist in locating information within the instructional components of the book. In many electronic versions of the book, you can click links on key words in the content to move to the associated glossary definition, and on page references in the index to move to that term in the content. To return to the previous location in the document after clicking a link, use the appropriate functionality in your PDF viewing software.

As You Review

Any method of instruction is only as effective as the time and effort you, the student, are willing to invest in it. In addition, some of the information that you learn in class may not be important to you immediately, but it may become important later. For this reason, we encourage you to spend some time reviewing the content of the course after your time in the classroom.

As a Reference

The organization and layout of this book make it an easy-to-use resource for future reference. Taking advantage of the glossary, index, and table of contents, you can use this book as a first source of definitions, background information, and summaries.

Course Icons

Watch throughout the material for the following visual cues.

Student Icon	Student Icon Descriptive Text
	A **Note** provides additional information, guidance, or hints about a topic or task.
	A **Caution** note makes you aware of places where you need to be particularly careful with your actions, settings, or decisions, so that you can be sure to get the desired results of an activity or task.
	Video notes show you where an associated video is particularly relevant to the content. These videos can be accessed through the Video tile in CHOICE.
	Checklists provide job aids you can use after class as a reference to perform skills back on the job. Access checklists from your CHOICE Course screen.
	Additional **Practice Questions** are available in the Assessment tile in your CHOICE Course screen.

Lesson 10
Managing Users, Workstations, and Shared Resources

LESSON INTRODUCTION

Once you have the computer network up and running, you can start to configure it to provide useful services. File and print sharing are key uses of almost every network. When configuring these resources, you have to be aware of potential security issues and understand how to set permissions correctly, to ensure that data is only accessible to those users who really should have been authorized to see it.

Along with permissions, you will also need to manage user accounts on networks. Windows® networks can use local accounts within workgroups or centralized Active Directory® accounts on a domain network. In this lesson, you will learn some basic principles for managing users in both types of environment.

LESSON OBJECTIVES

In this lesson, you will:

- Manage Windows local user and group accounts.

- Configure network shares and permissions.

- Configure accounts and policies in Active Directory domains.

Topic A

Manage Users

EXAM OBJECTIVES COVERED

1002-1.4 Given a scenario, use appropriate Microsoft command line tools.
1002-1.5 Given a scenario, use Microsoft operating system features and tools.
1002-1.6 Given a scenario, use Microsoft Windows Control Panel utilities.
1002-2.6 Compare and contrast the differences of basic Microsoft Windows OS security settings.

Teaching Tip

Make sure learners understand the difference between administrator and standard account types and know the different interfaces for managing user accounts and system rights.

Show Slide(s)

User and Group Accounts (2 slides)

Teaching Tip

Exam candidates should know these group names and permissions.

Managing user accounts and permissions is an important task on any type of network. In this topic, you will learn how group accounts can be used to allocate permissions more easily and use consoles to configure system policies that can improve the security of the computer and network.

USER AND GROUP ACCOUNTS

A user account is the principal means of controlling access to computer and network resources and rights or privileges. The **User Accounts** applet in Control Panel is adequate for creating accounts on a family computer. If you are configuring computers for business use, you might want to use more advanced tools to create group accounts as well as user accounts.

SECURITY GROUPS

A **security group** is a collection of user accounts that can be assigned permissions in the same way as a single user object. Security groups are used when assigning permissions and rights, as it is more efficient to assign permissions to a group than to assign them individually to each user. You can assign permissions to a user simply by adding the user to the appropriate group(s).

Group	Description
Built-in Local Groups	Built-in groups are given a standard set of rights that allow them to perform appropriate system tasks. Starter and Home editions of Windows allow the use of two groups only: • Limited/standard user. • Computer administrator. For Windows Professional/Business, the principal built-in local groups include Administrators, Users, Guests, and Power Users.

Group	Description
Administrators	An Administrator account can perform all management tasks and generally has very high access to all files and other objects in the system. The user created at installation is automatically added to this group. You should restrict use of this type of account, using a regular user account when appropriate, and only log in with administrative privileges for specific tasks.
	When Windows is installed to a new computer, the account actually named "Administrator" is disabled by default. The setup procedure creates an account with administrative privileges in its place.
	Note: *If the computer is not part of a domain, the "Administrator" account is re-enabled in Safe Mode if all other administrative accounts have been deleted or disabled (as a disaster recovery mechanism). Note that the "Administrator" account is not subject to UAC and so should be left disabled if the computer is to be used securely.*
Users	When a new user is created, they are typically added to the standard Users group. The group is able to perform most common tasks, such as shutting down the computer, running applications, and using printers. Ordinary users can also change the time zone and install a local printer, provided there is a suitable driver already installed.
Guests	The Guests group has only limited rights; for example, members can browse the network and Internet and shut down the computer but cannot save changes made to the desktop environment. Generally, you should disable the Guest account (its default condition) and establish a proper user account for each user accessing your system. If the account is enabled, then any user attempting to access your computer who does not hold their own user account, will be connected using the Guest account credentials.
	Note: *The default Guest account is the only member of the Guests group. While the Guest user account is usually disabled, the Guests group is not.*
Power Users	The Power Users group still appears to support legacy applications, but its use is strongly deprecated. The rights allocated to this account type can be abused to allow the user to obtain more powerful Administrator or System privileges. You can read more about issues with using Power Users at **support.microsoft.com/en-us/help/825069/a-member-of-the-power-users-group-may-be-able-to-gain-administrator-ri**.

Group	Description
System Groups	There are a number of other default groups, providing a means to easily configure things like privileges to access remote desktop, backup, event logs, and so on. Windows also includes built-in system groups. Their membership cannot be changed manually, as it is dependent on what users are doing at the time.
	• **Everyone**—All users who access the computer are members of the group Everyone. This includes users who have not been authenticated and who are accessing the computer as a guest.
	• **Authenticated Users**—All users who access the computer and have a valid user account.
	• **Creator Owner**—The Creator Owner group includes the account of the resource owner. Normally, the creator of a resource is the owner, but administrators (and other users who have been allowed to do so) are able to take ownership.
	• **Interactive**—This group contains the user account of the person currently working locally at the computer.
	• **Network**—This group contains the user account(s) of any users currently connected to the computer over a network.
System and Service Accounts	There are also some non-interactive accounts that you should be aware of. Users cannot sign in to these accounts. They are "owned" by the OS (NT_AUTHORITY). They are used to run Windows processes and services:
	• **LocalSystem**—An account with the same, or in some ways better, privileges as the default Administrator account. A process executed using the system account is unrestricted in terms of making changes to the system configuration and file system.
	• **LocalService**—A limited account used to run services that cannot make system-wide changes. LocalService can access the network anonymously.
	• **NetworkService**—An account that has the same privileges as LocalService but can access the network using the computer's machine account's credentials.

LOCAL USERS AND GROUPS

Show Slide(s)

Local Users and Groups (2 slides)

Teaching Tip

Remind learners that these tools are not available in the Home editions.

In Pro, Professional, and Enterprise editions of Windows, the **Local Users and Groups** management console provides an interface for managing both user and group accounts. It is not available in Starter or Home editions.

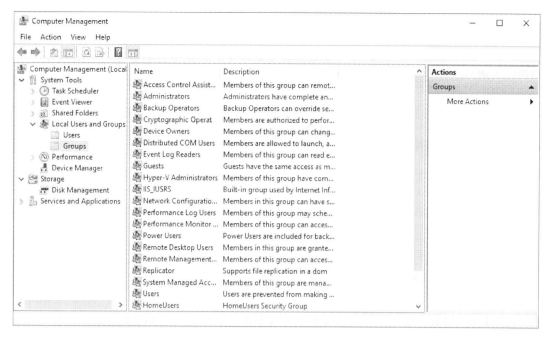

Local Users and Groups management console. (Screenshot used with permission from Microsoft.)

CREATING A NEW USER

To create a user, right-click on or in the **Users** folder and select **New User**. The account can be configured with the following properties:

Setting	Use
Username (required)	The username may be up to 20 characters and cannot contain the characters "/\ [ ] : ; | = , + * ? < > The username must be unique. Usernames are not case sensitive.
Full name (optional)	This should include the first and last name, and any middle initials if required.
Description (optional)	May be used to describe the user's job role.
Password (optional but recommended	Passwords can be up to 128 characters (at least 8 is recommended). Passwords are case sensitive. Avoid passwords that simply use words; include upper and lower case letters, punctuation, and numbers.
User must change password at next logon	A useful way to ensure that an administrator-assigned password is reset by the user when they first access the account.
User cannot change password	Generally, users control their own passwords, but for some user accounts it is preferable for the administrator to control the password.
Password never expires	A useful option which overrides the local security policy to expire passwords after a fixed number of days. This option should be selected for system accounts, such as those used for replication and application services.
Account is disabled	Prevents use of the account. Acts as an alternative to deleting an account.

RENAMING AND DELETING USER ACCOUNTS

To rename a user account, select the account name, then right-click and choose the **Rename** option. A renamed account retains all the properties of the original account and also retains access to system resources.

To delete an account, select the account name and either press the **Delete** key or choose **Delete** from the context menu.

Windows uses a Security ID (SID) to uniquely identify each user and group. A warning message is displayed to remind you that this account identifier is unique. Even if you recreate another account with exactly the same username, the identifier created is still different. The new account cannot assume any access to resources that were assigned to the original.

Disabling an account prevents it from being used, but allows the account to be reactivated if required.

ADDING A USER TO A GROUP

When a user is made a member of a group, the user obtains all the permissions allocated to that group. A user account can be a member of more than one group account. To add a user to a group or remove a user from a group, right-click the group account and select **Properties**.

Configuring members of the Administrators built-in group. (Screenshot used with permission from Microsoft.)

THE net user COMMANDS

You can also manage accounts at the command line using the `net user` command. You need to execute these commands in an administrative command prompt:

- `net user dmartin Pa$$w0rd /add /fullname:"David Martin" /logonpasswordchg:yes`

This example adds a new user account and forces the user to choose a new password at first login.

- `net user dmartin /active:no`

  Disables the `dmartin` account.

- `net user dmartin`

  Show the properties of the `dmartin` account.

- `net localgroup Administrators dmartin /add`

  Add the `dmartin` account to the Administrators local group.

 Note: *Don't confuse* `net user` *commands with* `net use`, *which is for configuring file shares.*

 Note: *To learn more, check the **Video** tile on the CHOICE Course screen for any videos that supplement the content for this lesson.*

 *Access the Checklist tile on your CHOICE Course screen for reference information and job aids on **How to Manage Windows Local Users and Groups**.*

LOCAL SECURITY POLICY

Policies are the most fine-grained means of adjusting registry settings outside of editing the registry directly. Policies can be used to configure almost any aspect of Windows, from the color of the desktop to the number of characters required in a user password.

On a standalone workstation, password and account policies can be configured via the **Local Security Policy** snap-in (`secpol.msc`) located in **Administrative Tools**. You would use this to force users to choose more complex or longer passwords or to prevent users from re-using old passwords.

 Show Slide(s)

Local Security Policy

 Teaching Tip

Remind learners that these tools are not available in the Home editions.

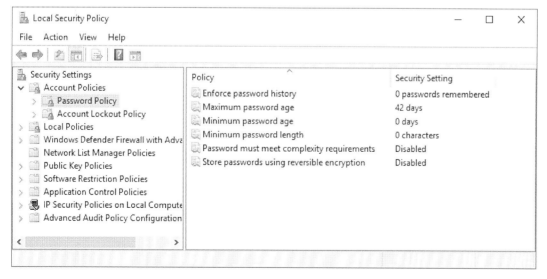

Local Security Policy editor. (Screenshot used with permission from Microsoft.)

A wider range of settings can be configured via the **Local Group Policy** snap-in (`gpedit.msc`). Group policy exposes pretty much the whole of the registry to configuration via a dialog-based interface, rather than editing individual keys through regedit. Policies can be applied to the computer object or to user accounts.

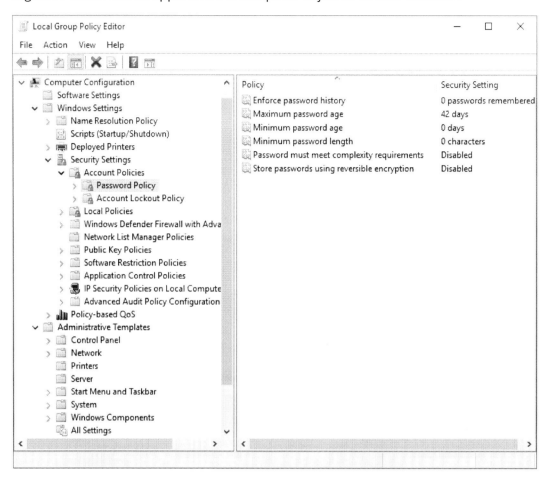

The Local Group Policy editor. You can edit the same security policies here but any other number of computer and user account settings can also be configured. (Screenshot used with permission from Microsoft.)

 Note: The policy editors are not included in the Starter or Home editions of Windows.

SSO AND CREDENTIAL MANAGER

Show Slide(s)

SSO and Credential Manager

Single Sign On (SSO) means that a user only has to authenticate to a system once to gain access to all its resources (that is, all the resources to which the user has been granted rights). An example is the Kerberos authentication and authorization model for Active Directory domain networks. This means, for instance, that a user who has authenticated with Windows is also authenticated with the Windows domain's SQL Server® and Exchange Server services. Another example is the use of a Microsoft account to sign in to Windows and also be signed in to web applications such as OneDrive® and Office365®.

The advantage of single sign-on is that each user does not have to manage multiple user accounts and passwords. The disadvantage is that compromising the account also compromises multiple services.

Note: It is critical that users do not re-use work passwords or authentication information on third-party sites. Of course, this is almost impossible to enforce, so security managers have to rely on effective user training.

CREDENTIAL MANAGER

SSO is not available for many services. Most users do not try to remember each password for every website or network they use. Instead, they use the OS to save (or cache) the password. You can view cached passwords for websites and Windows/network accounts using the Control Panel app **Credential Manager**.

You can remove any credentials that you no longer want to store. Removing a credential may also resolve an authentication or service problem. You can view the plaintext of a web credential but not of a Windows credential.

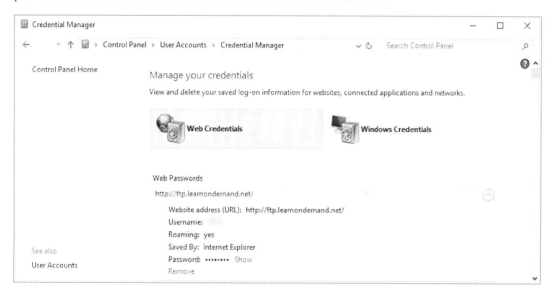

Credential Manager. (Screenshot used with permission from Microsoft.)

Activity 10-1
Discussing Windows User Management

Show Slide(s)

Activity: Discussing Windows User Management

SCENARIO

Answer the following questions to check your understanding of the topic.

1. **Which three principal user security groups are created when Windows is installed?**

   Users, **Administrators**, and **Guests**. You might also include **Power Users**, though use of this group is deprecated. There are also system groups, but users cannot be assigned manually to these. Going beyond the account types listed in the exam objectives, you might include groups such as **Remote Desktop Users**, **Remote Management Users**, or **Backup Operators**.

2. **What tool would you use to add a user to a local security group?**

   You can change the account type between Standard and Administrator via the basic **Users** app, but the **Local Users and Groups** management console is the main tool to use. You could also use the `net` command suite or PowerShell.

3. **True or false? If you delete a user, you can recover the user's permissions and group memberships by creating a new account with the same name.**

   False. Accounts have a unique Security Identifier (SID) that Windows uses to track them. A newly created account would have the same name but a different SID.

4. **How can you ensure that an administrator-set default password for an account is not used permanently?**

   Set the **User must change password at next logon** option in the user account properties.

5. **What is the function of** `secpol.msc`**?**

   It is the image name of the Local Security Policy management console. You can use this to define system security policies, such as password complexity.

Topic B

Configure Shared Resources

EXAM OBJECTIVES COVERED
1002-1.4 Given a scenario, use appropriate Microsoft command line tools.
1002-1.6 Given a scenario, use Microsoft Windows Control Panel utilities.
1002-1.8 Given a scenario, configure Microsoft Windows networking on a client/desktop.
1002-2.6 Compare and contrast the differences of basic Microsoft Windows OS security settings

One of the main uses of networks is for file and printer sharing. As a CompTIA A+ technician, you will often need to configure network shares. It is important that you configure the correct permissions on shares, understanding how share and NTFS permissions interact.

Teaching Tip
Be sure to allocate plenty of time to this topic.

WORKGROUPS

In a **peer-to-peer network**, each computer can be both a server and a client. Each user administers his or her PC and the resources on it. The user can decide to give others access to files on his or her PC or to printers that are attached to it. Under Windows, this type of network is described as a workgroup.

Show Slide(s)
Workgroups

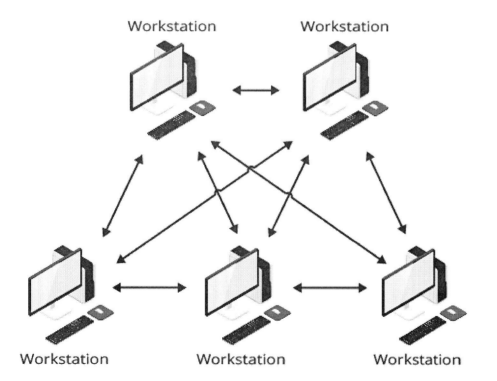

Peer-to-peer network. (Image © 123RF.com.)

A workgroup is quite simple to set up initially, but unreliable and difficult to organize. For example, a user could switch off their machine while someone else was accessing it. There is no good means of deciding who should have access to the network. It is difficult to grow the network, as when a machine or new user is added, all the other machines have to be "informed" about it.

Workgroups are designed to support small groups of users. There is no centralized management of user accounts or of resources, and each machine requires a separate administrator. Desktop operating systems such as Windows can act as servers in a workgroup, but they are restricted in terms of the number of inbound connections they can support.

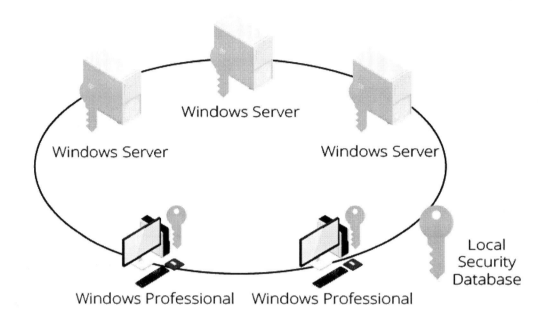

Workgroup security accounts are all stored locally. (Image © 123RF.com.)

 Show Slide(s)

Homegroups

 Teaching Tip

Homegroups are easy enough to set up and use if everything is working, but they do seem prone to going inexplicably wrong at times. The best general troubleshooting approach is to reset everything (including the firewall), ensure all the relevant services and protocols are bound to the adapter (including IPv6), and make sure the date and time are synched correctly.

It can also be worth clearing the HomeGroup cache at C:\Windows \ServiceProfiles \LocalService\AppData \Roaming \PeerNetworking if the network is afflicted with a "ghost" homegroup.

 Note: *Not all real-world networks are completely peer-to-peer or completely client-server. Some networks use a mixture of both approaches.*

As different versions of Windows have been released, Microsoft has implemented different ways for users to set up home networks simply.

 Note: *The workgroup name can be changed using the* **Computer Name** *dialog box from* **System** *properties. The workgroup name is cosmetic, however. It is almost always left set to "WORKGROUP."*

HOMEGROUPS

A **homegroup** is a feature introduced in Windows 7, and continued in Windows 8, to simplify secure access to shared folders and printers on a home network.

The problem with a workgroup network is that there is no centralized database of users. Sharing folders would either require the local user's password to be shared, identical user accounts to be set up and maintained on each machine, or facilitated via the Guest account with no authentication.

Homegroups are secured via a simple password. A computer can only belong to one homegroup at a time. Homegroups can contain a mix of Windows 7 and Windows 8 computers.

To set up a homegroup, open the Network and Sharing Center and select **Choose homegroup and sharing options**.

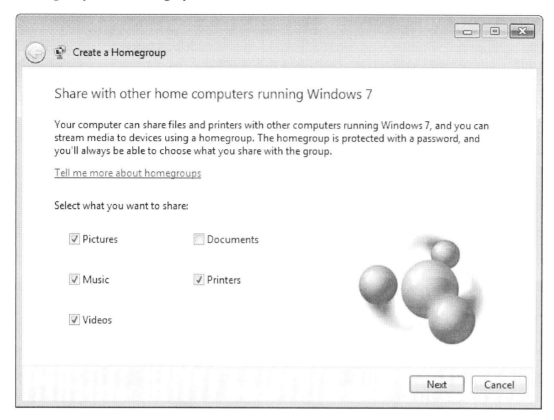

Configuring a homegroup—choosing which resources to share. (Screenshot used with permission from Microsoft.)

 *Note: The network type must be defined as **Home** (Windows 7) or **Private** (Windows 8) or Windows will not allow the creation of a homegroup. Also, IPv6 must be enabled for homegroups to work.*

JOINING A HOMEGROUP

When a homegroup has been configured on a network, you will see a **Join now** button when you are browsing the **Homegroup** object in Explorer. Having joined a group, network users can access shared libraries and folders and choose whether to share their own libraries. Shared homegroup folders are shown via the **Homegroup** object in Explorer, which shows all the user accounts participating in the homegroup.

WINDOWS 10 AND HOMEGROUPS

The early versions of Windows 10 continued to support the homegroup feature. With the release of Windows 10 (1803), support for homegroups was discontinued. Windows 10 (1803) computers cannot create or join a homegroup.

 *Note: At the time of writing, a bug means that homegroup options can still appear in a folder's **Give Access To** shortcut menu. These options do not do anything.*

NETWORK AND SHARING CENTER

Whenever a new network link is detected, Windows prompts you to define it as **Public** or **Private** (Home or Work). The former option disables file and printer sharing and network discovery on the link. On a private network, you can customize the sharing

 Show Slide(s)
Network and Sharing Center (2 slides)

 Teaching Tip
Windows in a home/ workgroup configuration autoconfigures security and firewall settings based on the user's choice of the network type as private (home or office) or public.

options to include printers, disable password-protected sharing, and so on. These options are configured via the **Network and Sharing Center**.

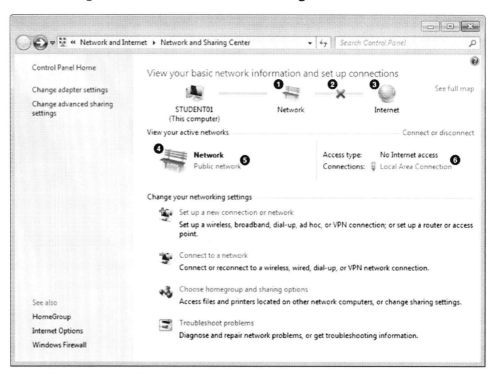

Navigating the Windows 7 Network and Sharing Center—1) Select to view computers on the network; 2) Select a cross to start the troubleshooter; 3) Select to open the web browser; 4) Select the network icon to manage names and locations; 5) Select the link to change the network type; 6) Select the adapter link to view status and configure properties. (Screenshot used with permission from Microsoft.)

In Windows 8 and Windows 10, the network map feature has been dropped and there is no option to change the network location type. This is done via Windows Settings instead. Select **Network & Internet** and then **Ethernet** or **WiFi** as appropriate. Under **Network profile**, select **Public** or **Private**.

 Note: *Note that the "Network profile" options do not appear if UAC is set to the highest "Always notify" level.*

ADVANCED SHARING SETTINGS

From the Network and Sharing Center, select **Advanced sharing settings** to configure the options for each profile. To share files on the network, **Turn on network discovery** and **Turn on file and printer sharing** must both be selected.

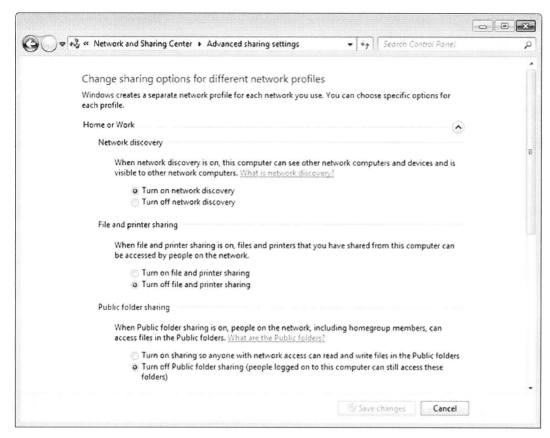

Advanced sharing settings. (Screenshot used with permission from Microsoft.)

Windows has a pre-defined folder for sharing files (the Public folder), which is available to all users of the PC and to network users, if enabled here.

Under **All networks**, you can select **Turn off password-protected sharing** to allow anyone to access any file share configured on the local computer without entering any credentials. This enables the Guest user account, which is normally disabled.

 Note: For password-protected sharing, network users must have an account configured on the local machine. This is one of the drawbacks of workgroups compared to domains. Either you configure accounts for all users on all machines, use a single account for network access (again, configured on all machines), or you disable security entirely.

NETWORK SHARE CONFIGURATION

You can share other folders by right-clicking and selecting **Share with** (Windows 7) or **Give access to** (Windows 10). Select an account, then set the **Permission level** to **Read** or **Read/write** as appropriate.

 Show Slide(s)

Network Share Configuration (6 slides)

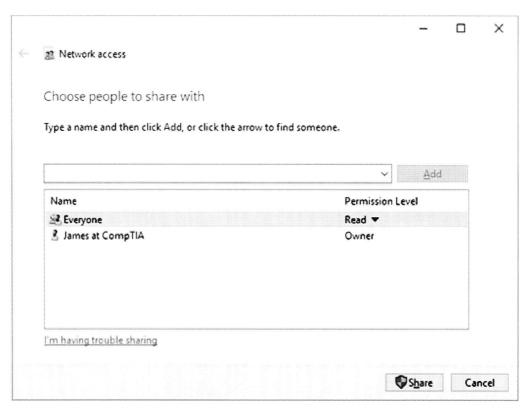

Configuring Advanced Sharing properties. (Screenshot used with permission from Microsoft.)

ADVANCED SHARING

In the folder's property dialog box, you can use the **Share** tab to configure advanced share properties:

- **Share name and optional comment**—the share name identifies the share on the network while the comment can describe the purpose of the share. You can share the same folder multiple times with different names and permissions.
- **Maximum number of users allowed to connect at any one time**—Windows desktop versions are limited to 20 inbound connections. Only Windows Server systems support more connections.
- **Permissions**—choose the groups or users allowed to access the folder and what type of access they have.

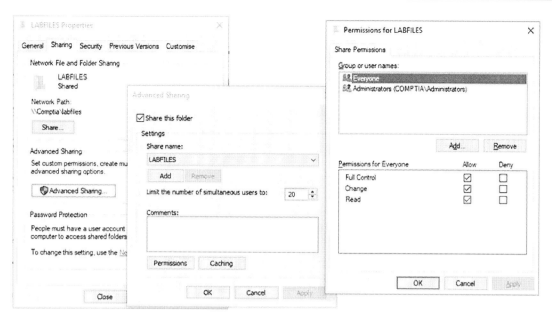

Configuring Advanced Sharing properties—Notice that while Everyone has "Read" permission, the share permissions for Everyone are "Full Control." The "Read" permission is enforced by NTFS security. (Screenshot used with permission from Microsoft.)

Windows provides three levels of share permissions:

- **Full Control**—allows users to read, edit, create, and delete files and subdirectories, and to assign permissions to other users and groups.
- **Change**—this is similar to full control but does not allow the user to set permissions for others.
- **Read**—users are permitted to connect to the resource, run programs, and view files. They are not allowed to edit, delete, or create files.

Most of the time, the shared folder permission is set to **Full Control**. The effective permissions are managed using NTFS security.

MANAGING SHARED FOLDERS

The **Shared Folders** snap-in (available through the Computer Management console) lets you view all the shares configured on the local machine as well as any current user sessions and open files.

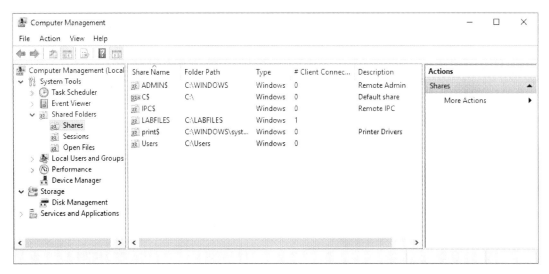

Viewing the Shared Folders snap-in via the Computer Management console. (Screenshot used with permission from Microsoft.)

Teaching Tip

If learners ask about IPC$, explain that the InterProcess Communications (IPC) share isn't used for file system access. Applications implementing SMB use it to make Remote Procedure Calls (RPC) in commands (enumerating shares, reading files, creating files, and so on).

Teaching Tip

"Local share" is wording from a previous version of the exam objectives (that has now been dropped). It is retained here just in case it is used in older questions.

ADMINISTRATIVE SHARES

You can think of the shares configured manually on a computer using the process described previously as local shares. In addition to any local shares created by a user, Windows automatically creates a number of hidden administrative shares, including the root folder of any local drives (C$), the system folder (ADMIN$), and the folder storing printer drivers (PRINT$). Administrative shares can only be accessed by members of the local Administrators group.

 Note: *Note that if you disable password-protected sharing, the administrative shares remain password-protected.*

In fact, if you add a $ sign at the end of a local share name, it will be hidden from general browsing too. It can still be accessed via the command-line or by mapping a drive to the share name.

BROWSING SHARES AND MAPPING DRIVES

In File Explorer, network shares are listed by the server computer under the system object Network. Any network-enabled devices such as wireless displays, printers, smartphones, and router/modems are also listed here. The shortcut menu for Network allows you to open the Network and Sharing Center (via the Properties option) and map or disconnect network drives.

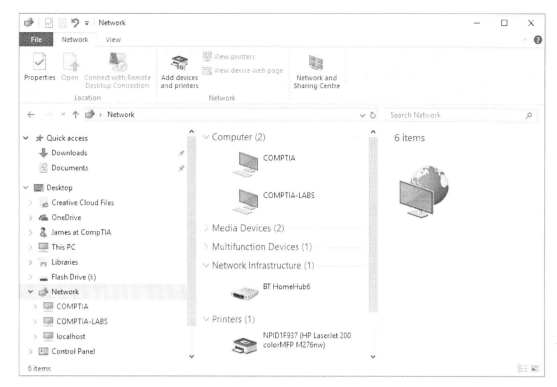

Viewing devices on the network—the LaserJet 200 printer listed here is connected directly to the network. (Screenshot used with permission from Microsoft.)

You can also access a shared folder using Universal Naming Convention (UNC) syntax (***ComputerName*\\Path**), where *ComputerName* is the host name, FQDN, or IP address of the server and Path is the folder and/or file path. Remember that you can view an administrative share this way (if you have the relevant permissions). For example, the path **\\\\COMPTIA\\Admin$** connects to the "Windows" folder on the "COMPTIA" computer.

A **network drive** is a local share that has been assigned a drive letter. To map a share as a drive, right-click it and select **Map Network Drive**. Select a drive letter and keep **Reconnect at sign-in** checked, unless you want to map the drive temporarily. The drive will now show up under Computer or This PC. To remove a mapped drive, right-click it and select **Disconnect**.

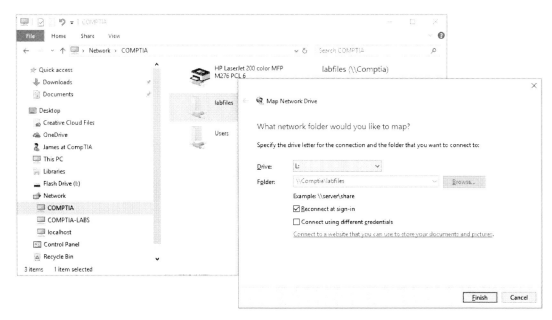

Mapping a network drive. (Screenshot used with permission from Microsoft.)

PRINTER SHARING VERSUS NETWORK PRINTER MAPPING

Many print devices come with an integrated Ethernet and/or Wi-Fi adapter. This means that they can communicate directly on the network. Such a printer can be mapped using the **Add Printer** wizard (from **Devices** and **Printers**). Just enter the IP address or host name of the printer to connect to it.

Any printer directly connected to a computer (whether via USB or direct network connection) can also be shared so that other network users can access it. A local printer is shared on the network via the **Sharing** tab on its **Printer Properties** sheet. To connect to a shared printer, open the server object from **Network** and the printer will be listed. Right-click it and select **Connect**.

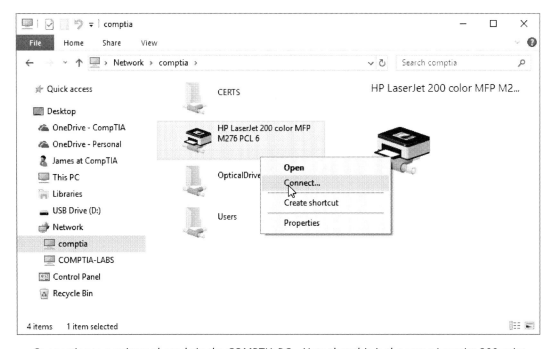

Connecting to a printer shared via the COMPTIA PC—Note that this is the same LaserJet 200 print device as shown earlier but it is being connected to as a shared device, rather than mapped directly. (Screenshot used with permission from Microsoft.)

OFFLINE FILES AND SYNC CENTER

One of the issues with a workgroup is that a computer may get turned off by its user without the user consulting the rest of the workgroup first. There is no centralized control or administration over access to resources. If you need to use files on a network share where the connection is unreliable for any reason, you can use Windows' offline files feature to cache the files in the share on your local computer. To enable this, just right-click the share or mapped drive and select **Always available offline**.

Show Slide(s)

Offline Files and Sync Center

When the connection is restored, any changes between the local cache and the network share are synchronized automatically. If there are any conflicts, these are reported in the **Sync Center** Control Panel applet. You can use the **Resolve** button to choose whether to keep one or both versions.

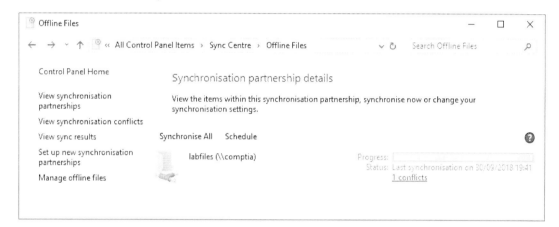

Using Sync Center to resolve file conflicts in an offline folder cache. (Screenshot used with permission from Microsoft.)

THE net COMMANDS

There are several `net` command utilities that you can use to view and configure shared resources on a Windows network. A few of the commands are provided here, but you can view the full list by entering `net /?` You can view help on a specific command by entering `net use /?`

Show Slide(s)

The net Commands

- `net use DeviceName \\ComputerName\ShareName`

  This command will connect to a network resource, such as a folder or printer. For example, to map the DATA folder on MYSERVER to the M: drive, you would enter:
  `net use M: \\MYSERVER\DATA /persistent:yes`

- `net use DeviceName /delete`

  This command removes a connection (`net use * /delete` removes all connections).

- `net view`

  Used without switches, this displays a list of servers on the local network. Use `net view \\Host` to view the shares available on a particular server (where *Host* is an IP address or computer name).

Show Slide(s)

NTFS File and Folder Permissions (8 slides)

Teaching Tip

Exam candidates need to know how share and NTFS permissions interact and about inheritance and ownership.

NTFS FILE AND FOLDER PERMISSIONS

When you configure a network share, you can set share permissions for the accounts allowed to access the share. Share permissions have a number of limitations:

- The resource is only protected when a user connects over the network. Someone gaining access to the local machine would not have the same restrictions.
- The permissions set apply from the root of the share and all subdirectories and files within the share inherit the same permissions.

Systems that use the FAT file system are only able to support share permissions, but with NTFS it is possible to implement a much more comprehensive and flexible system of permissions. NTFS security protects the resource even when it is accessed locally and has a configurable system of propagation and inheritance.

Windows enforces local security on an NTFS volume by holding an Access Control List (ACL) as part of the record for each file and folder stored in the volume's Master File Table (MFT). When a user attempts to access a file or directory, the security system checks which users and groups are listed in the ACL. A list of permissions is then obtained for that user.

Security can be applied to individual files or (more commonly) to folders. When folders are secured, the matter of inheritance needs to be considered.

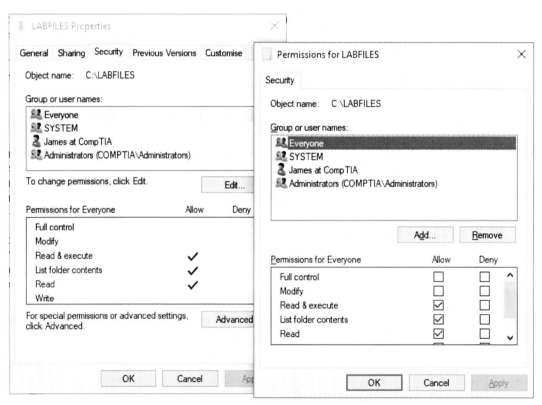

Configuring NTFS permissions via the Security tab for a folder. (Screenshot used with permission from Microsoft.)

CONFIGURING NTFS PERMISSIONS

To configure the NTFS security settings of a file or folder, right-click the object and select **Properties**, then select the **Security** tab. Users that may set permissions are restricted to administrators, users with full control permissions, and the owner of the file or folder.

Permissions that may be applied to folders differ from those that apply to files. The differences are summarized in the following tables. Note that each permission may either be allowed or denied.

Folder Permission	Allows
Read	View files and subfolders including their attributes, permissions, and ownership.
Write	Create new folders and files, change attributes, view permissions and ownership.
List	View the names of files and subfolders.
Read & Execute	Pass-through folders for which no permissions are assigned, plus read and list permissions.
Modify	Read/Execute and Write permissions, as well as the ability to rename and delete the folder.
Full Control	All the above, plus changing permissions, taking ownership, and deleting subfolders and files.

File Permission	Allows
Read	Read the contents of the file and view attributes, ownership, and permissions.
Write	Overwrite the file and view attributes, ownership, and permissions.
Read & Execute	Read permissions, plus the ability to run applications.
Modify	Read/Execute and Write permissions, as well as the ability to rename and delete the file.
Full Control	All the above, plus changing permissions and taking ownership.

 Note: These are available via the basic interface. There are in fact 12 individual permissions that could be applied to a file or folder (select Advanced), but the combinations listed are usually sufficient.

EFFECTIVE PERMISSIONS AND ALLOW VERSUS DENY

Permissions are usually applied at one of three levels:

- For application folders, the read/execute permission is granted to the appropriate group.
- For data areas, the modify or read permission is assigned as appropriate.
- To home directories (personal storage areas on a network), full control is assigned to the relevant user.

A user may obtain multiple permissions from membership of different groups or by having permissions allocated directly to his or her account. Windows analyzes the permissions obtained from different accounts to determine the effective permissions. In this process, it is important to understand that "deny" overrides anything else (in most cases). If an account is not granted an "allow" permission, an implicit deny is applied. This is usually sufficient for most purposes. Explicit deny permissions are only used in quite specific circumstances.

Putting explicit deny permissions to one side, the user obtains the most effective "allow" permissions obtained from any source. For example, if one group gives the user "Read" permission and another group gives the user "Modify" permission, the user will have "Modify" permission.

PERMISSION PROPAGATION AND INHERITANCE

NTFS permissions that are assigned to a folder are automatically inherited by the files and subfolders created under the folder. To prevent this from happening, open the

Security page and select **Advanced**, then select the **Permission** tab. In Windows 7, select the **Change permissions** button to proceed.

Select the **Disable inheritance** button. In Windows 7, there is an **Include inheritable permissions** check box to uncheck rather than a button. Then, choose whether to **Convert inheritable permissions into explicit permissions** (in Windows 7, this is the **Copy** option) or **Remove** inherited permissions. You can then modify the permissions on this folder independently of its parent.

To apply security settings for the current folder to all child objects (permission propagation), check the **Replace all child object permissions with inheritable permissions** box.

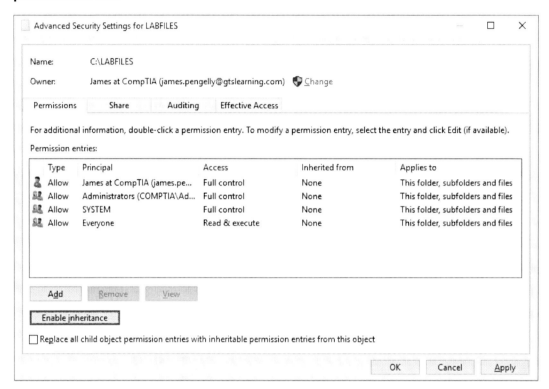

Configuring permissions inheritance on a folder. (Screenshot used with permission from Microsoft.)

 Note: Directly assigned permissions (explicit permissions) always override inherited permissions, including "deny" inherited permissions. For example, if a parent folder specifies deny write permissions but an account is granted allow write permissions directly on a child file object, the effective permission will be to allow write access on the file object.

OWNERSHIP

The owner of a resource can manage that resource in terms of permissions and other attributes. Generally speaking, if a user creates a file, they will own the file. Administrators can assign ownership to some other user (or group). This might be done because the current owner of a resource has been deleted from the user accounts database.

When a folder's ownership details are modified, the administrator can choose to propagate the changes down the tree to subfolders and their contents.

MOVING AND COPYING NTFS FILES AND FOLDERS

The behavior of NTFS permissions when moving and copying files under Windows is summarized in the following table.

Action	Effect
Moving files and folders on the same NTFS volume	Write permission is required for the destination folder and Modify for the source folder. NTFS permissions are retained.
Moving files and folders to a different NTFS volume	Write permission is required for the destination folder and Modify for the source folder. NTFS permissions are inherited from the destination folder and the user becomes the Creator/Owner.
Copying files and folders on the same NTFS volume or different NTFS volumes	Write permission is required for the destination folder and Read for the source folder. NTFS permissions are inherited from the destination folder and the user becomes the Creator/Owner.
Moving files and folders to a FAT or FAT32 partition	Modify permission is required for the source folder. All permissions and NTFS attributes (such as encryption) are lost, as FAT does not support permissions or special attributes.

COMBINING NTFS AND SHARE PERMISSIONS

It is possible to use a combination of share and NTFS permissions to secure resources. The factors to consider include:

- Share permissions only protect the resource when it is accessed across the network.
- NTFS permissions are used to protect the resource from unauthorized local access.
- Disk partitions using the FAT file system can only be protected using share permissions.
- Share permissions are set at the root of the share and all files and subdirectories inherit the same permissions.
- NTFS permissions are used in combination with the share permissions to provide greater flexibility; for example, to place more restrictive permissions at lower levels in the directory structure.
- If both share and NTFS permissions are applied to the same resource, the most restrictive applies (when the file or folder is accessed over the network). For example, if the group "Everyone" has Read permission to a share and the "Users" group is given Modify permission through NTFS permissions, the effective permissions for a member of the "Users" group will be Read.

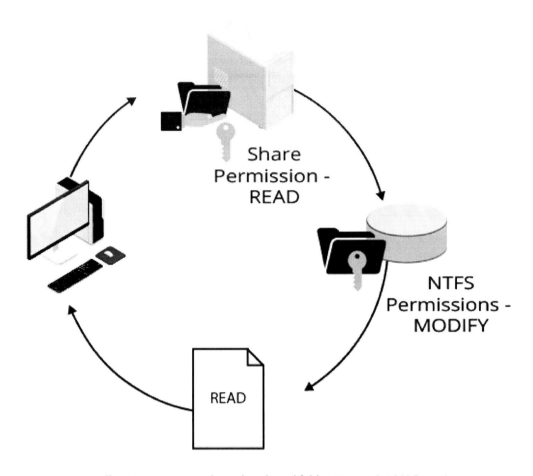

Effective permissions through a shared folder. (Image © 123RF.com.)

In practice, share permissions are always configured as Full Control and the NTFS permissions are used to configure the actual rights.

 Note: *If you do not have sufficient permissions to access or modify a resource, you will see an "Access denied" error message.*

Activity 10-2
Discussing Shared Resource Configuration

Show Slide(s)

Activity: Discussing Shared Resource Configuration

SCENARIO

Answer the following questions to check your understanding of the topic.

1. You are setting up a Windows 10 workstation as a file server for a small office.

   How many computers can connect to the file share at any one time?

   Up to 20 computers.

2. **What is the significance of a $ symbol at the end of a share name?**

   The share is hidden from the file browser. It can be accessed by typing a UNC. The default administrative shares are all configured as hidden.

3. **What basic NTFS permissions do you need to move a file and to copy a file?**

   To move a file, you need Write permissions for the destination folder and Modify permissions for the source folder; to copy a file, you need Write permissions for the destination folder and Read permissions to the source folder.

4. **When you set permissions on a folder, what happens to the files and subfolders by default?**

   They inherit the parent folder's permissions.

5. **If a user obtains Read permissions from a share and Deny Write from NTFS permissions, can the user view files in the folder over the network?**

   Yes (but he or she cannot create files).

6. A user is assigned Read permissions to a resource via his user account and Full Control via membership of a group.

   What effective permission does the user have for the resource?

   Full control—the most effective permissions are applied.

Activity 10-3
Configuring Shared Resources

BEFORE YOU BEGIN
Complete this activity by using Hyper-V Manager and the PC1 (Windows 10) and PC2 (Windows 7) VMs.

SCENARIO
In this activity, you will configure the two client VMs as part of a workgroup and practice creating users and shares.

---

1. Both **PC1** and **PC2** are joined to a domain. To complete this activity, you need to remove **PC2** from the domain and join it to the **WORKGROUP** workgroup.

    a) Start the **PC2** VM, and sign on using the account **515support\administrator** and password **Pa$$w0rd**

    b) Select **Start**, right-click **Computer**, and select **Properties**.

    c) In the **System** applet, under **Computer name, domain, and workgroup settings**, select **Change settings**.

    d) In the **System Properties** dialog box, select the **Change** button.

    e) Select the **Workgroup** option button and type **WORKGROUP** in the box.

    f) Select **OK**.

    g) At the **Computer Name/Domain Name Changes** prompt, select **OK**.

    h) In the **Windows Security** dialog box, enter the user name **administrator** and the password **Pa$$w0rd** and then select **OK**.

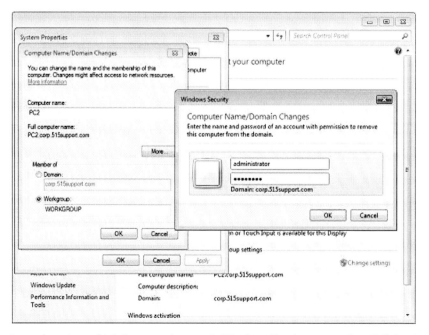

Leaving a domain and joining a workgroup in Windows 7—there are a lot of dialog boxes to click through! (Screenshot used with permission from Microsoft.)

---

i)   When you are prompted by the **Welcome to the WORKGROUP workgroup** dialog box, select **OK**, and then select **OK** again to confirm that a restart is required.

j)   In the **System Properties** dialog box, select the **Close** button.

k)   At the **Microsoft Windows** prompt, select **Restart Now**.

2.   Configure PC1 to join the workgroup by using the **Settings** app.

a)   Start the PC1 VM and sign on using the account **515support\administrator** and password **Pa$$w0rd**

b)   Select the **Start** button, and select the **Settings** icon.

c)   Select **Accounts** and then select the **Access work or school** node.

d)   Select **Connected to 515support AD domain** then select the **Disconnect** button. Confirm the prompt by selecting **Yes**.

e)   Confirm again by selecting **Disconnect**.

f)   In the **Enter alternate account info** box, enter the user name **Admin** with **Pa$$w0rd** and select **OK**.

g)   When you are prompted, select **Restart now**.

3.   Create a standard user account named **Sam** on PC2.

a)   Switch to the **PC2** VM, and sign on using the account **Admin** and password **Pa$$w0rd**

b)   Select **Start**, right-click **Computer**, and select **Manage**.

c)   Expand **Local Users and Groups** and select the **Users** folder.

d)   Right-click **Users** and select **New User**.

e)   In the **User name** box, type **Sam** and then type **Pa$$w0rd** in the **Password** and **Confirm password** boxes.

f)   Uncheck **User must change password at next logon**, and then select the **Create** button.

g)   Select the **Close** button.

h)   Select **Start**, then select the arrow on the **Shut down** button, and select **Log off**.

i)   Select the **Sam** user account icon. Type **Pa$$w0rd** in the password box and then press **Enter**.

4.   Configure anonymous file sharing on **PC1**.

a)   Switch to the **PC1** VM, and sign on using the account **Admin** and password **Pa$$w0rd**

b)   Select the network status icon and select **Network & Internet settings**.

c)   In the **Settings** app, select **Sharing options**.

d)   Under **Guest or Public**, select **Turn on network discovery** and **Turn on file and printer sharing**.

e)   Expand the **All Networks** section.

f)   Select **Turn off password protected sharing**.

g)   Select **Save changes**.

h)   Leave the **Settings** app open.

5.   Examine the changes this setting has made to the Guest account, and observe security group memberships.

a)   Right-click **Start** and then select **Computer Management**.

b)   Expand **Local Users and Groups** and select the **Users** folder.

c)   Observe that the **Guest** account is enabled.

d)   Select the **Groups** folder, and observe the built-in groups.

e)   Right-click **Guests** and select **Properties**.

f)   Verify that the only member is the **Guest** user account.

g)   Select **Cancel**.

h)   Right-click **Administrators** and select **Properties**.

        This group contains the built-in **Administrator** user account. This root-type account should not be used. The **Admin** user was created during setup.

i) Select **Cancel**.

j) Leave the **Computer Management** console open.

6. Create an anonymous read only file share to the **C:\LABFILES** folder on **PC1**.

a) Open **File Explorer** and browse to the **C:** root folder.

b) Right-click the **LABFILES** folder and select **Give access to→Specific people**.

c) From the list box, select the **Everyone** account and select the **Add** button.

d) Verify that the permission level defaults to **Read**.

e) Select the **Share** button.

f) Select **Done**.

Teaching Tip

Optionally, point out that the VMs can communicate without a DHCP server because they are using APIPA.

7. Test the file share by connecting to it from **PC2**.

a) Switch to the **PC2** VM.

b) Open **Windows Explorer** and browse to the share using its UNC path: **\\PC1\LABFILES**.

c) Copy a file from the share to your desktop.

d) Confirm you have read-only permissions by trying to delete a file.

e) Log off from the PC2 VM.

8. Anonymous access is simple to set up, but it is not very secure. In the next part of the activity, you will configure password-protected file sharing and explore some of the difficulties of managing this in a workgroup.

9. Disable anonymous access and test the effect it has on opening the share from PC2.

Teaching Tip

While homegroups are on the exam objectives, Microsoft is dropping support for them, so learners will not work with them in this activity. If learners have time, they can experiment with creating a homegroup by using the **PC2** (Windows 7) and **PC3** (Windows 8.1) VMs.

a) Switch to the **PC1** VM. In the **Settings** app, select **Sharing options**.

b) Expand the **All Networks** section.

c) Select **Turn on password protected sharing**.

d) Select **Save changes**.

e) Switch to the **Computer Management** console and view the **Users** folder.

f) Press **F5** to refresh the view.

g) Verify that the **Guest** account is now disabled.

h) Leave the **Computer Management** console open.

i) Switch to the **PC2** VM, and sign back on as *Sam*

j) Open **Windows Explorer**, and browse to the share by using its UNC path **\\PC1\LABFILES**.

k) Verify that, after a delay, you are prompted to enter credentials.

l) Try to authenticate by using the user name *Sam* and password *Pa$$w0rd*

m) Select **Cancel** to acknowledge each prompt when this fails.

n) Close Windows Explorer.

10. The **Sam** user account is local to PC2. PC1 cannot authenticate the account. To configure password-protected access, create the *Sam* account on **PC1**, using *Pa$$w0rd* as the password.

a) Switch to the **PC1** VM.

b) Select the **Computer Management** console.

c) Right-click **Users** and select **New User**.

d) In the **User name** box, type *Sam*

e) Type *Pa$$w0rd* in the **Password** and **Confirm password** boxes.

f) Uncheck **User must change password at next logon**, and then select the **Create** button.

g) Select the **Close** button.

h) Switch to the **PC2** VM.

i) Open **Windows Explorer**, and browse to the **\\PC1\LABFILES** share.

You should be able to connect this time.

11. Use **PC2** to change Sam's password, and observe the effect on accessing the file share.

    Creating user accounts on each PC is not an efficient use of administrators' time. It is also difficult to keep the account credentials in sync.

    a) On the **PC2** VM, press **Ctrl+Alt+End**, and then select **Change a password**.
    b) Set the new password to **NotPa$$w0rd**
    c) Select **OK**.
    d) Log off and log back on (remembering that the password is now **NotPa$$w0rd**).
    e) Open **Windows Explorer**, and try to browse to the **\\PC1\LABFILES** share.
    f) Verify that after a delay, you are prompted to enter credentials.
    g) Provide the current user name and password, and select **Cancel** for each prompt.
    h) Switch to the **PC1** VM.
    i) In the **Computer Management** console, right-click the **Sam** user account and select **Set Password**.
    j) Observe the warning.

       Resetting a password like this can make encrypted files inaccessible.
    k) Select **Proceed**.
    l) Set the new password to **NotPa$$w0rd** and select **OK**.
    m) Select **OK** at the prompt.
    n) Switch to **PC2**, and verify that you can access the share again.

12. In the last part of this activity, you will investigate the permissions configured on the share. Make the MARKETING subfolder writable by Sam's account. You should do this by configuring NTFS permissions (via the folder's **Security properties** tab).

    a) Switch to the **PC1** VM.
    b) Open **File Explorer**, and browse to the **C:\LABFILES** folder.
    c) Right-click the **MARKETING** folder and select **Properties**.
    d) Select the **Security** tab.
    e) Select the **Edit** button.
    f) In the **Permissions for MARKETING** dialog box, select the **Add** button.
    g) In the **Select Users or Groups** dialog box, type **sam** and then select **Check Names**.

       The name should be resolved to **PC1\Sam** and be underlined.
    h) Select **OK**.

 Note: Remember that this is just the display name. The permission is configured using the account SID.

i) In the **Permissions for MARKETING** dialog box, with the **Sam** account selected in the top box, in the **Permissions for Sam** box, check the **Allow** box for the **Modify** permission.

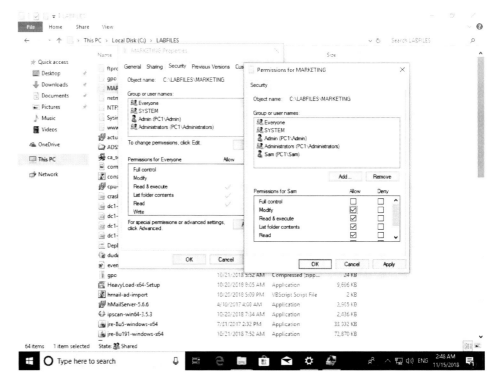

Configuring NTFS permissions. (Screenshot used with permission from Microsoft.)

j) Select **OK**.

k) In the **MARKETING Properties** dialog box, select **OK**.

l) Switch to **PC2**, and verify that you can delete the file in **C:\LABFILES\MARKETING** and create a new file in the folder.

Make sure you understand the permissions that have been configured:

Interaction Opportunity

Be sure to answer any questions that learners have about the effective permissions in place here.

- The LABFILES parent folder NTFS permissions are set to allow the **Everyone** group read permissions. As Sam is automatically part of the **Everyone** system group, these are the permissions that apply to the files and most of the subfolders when Sam tries to access them.
- The MARKETING subfolder gives Sam explicit **Full Control** permissions. When combining the read permission from the parent and the full control permission set here, the most effective permission "wins." This means that Sam has full control over objects in the MARKETING subfolder.

13. If you have time, view the share permissions for the folder, and investigate how they interact with NTFS permissions.

a) Switch to the **PC1** VM.

b) In File Explorer, browse to the C:\ root folder.

c) Right-click the **LABFILES** folder and select **Properties**.

d) Select the **Sharing** tab.

e) Select **Advanced Sharing**.

f) In the **Advanced Sharing** dialog box, select the **Permissions** button.

g) In the **Permissions for LABFILES** dialog box, with the **Everyone** account selected in the top box, in the **Permissions for Everyone** box, uncheck the **Allow** boxes for **Full Control** and **Change**.

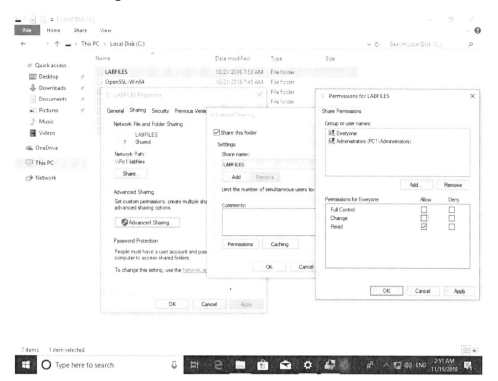

Configuring share permissions. (Screenshot used with permission from Microsoft.)

h) Select **OK**.

i) In the **Advanced Sharing** dialog box, select **OK**.

j) In the **LABFILES Properties** dialog box, select **Close**.

k) Switch to **PC2**, and verify that you cannot delete the file you created in **C:\LABFILES \MARKETING** or create another new file in the folder. Cancel any permission denied error prompts you receive.

Share permissions apply from the root of the share (but only when the file or folder is accessed over the network). When combined with NTFS permissions, the most restrictive permission applies, which is why this step failed. You can't avoid setting share permissions, but really you discount them by setting them to Full Control for all valid users and then configuring NTFS permissions to facilitate whatever security policy you want to apply. You can use NTFS permissions to configure rights for different accounts and have different access levels for individual files and subfolders.

14. If you have time, switch to the **PC1** VM, and view the **Shared Folders** snap-in in the **Computer Management** console.

You can use this console to create and modify shares, view users connected to shares, and view files opened by users. You can also force open files or sessions to close.

15. At the end of each activity, you need to close the VMs and discard any changes you made.

a) From the connection window, select **Action→Revert**.

b) If you are prompted to confirm, select the **Revert** button.

c) Repeat these steps to revert the PC2 VM.

Topic C

Configure Active Directory Accounts and Policies

EXAM OBJECTIVES COVERED
1002-1.4 Given a scenario, use appropriate Microsoft command line tools.
1002-1.8 Given a scenario, configure Microsoft Windows networking on a client/desktop.
1002-2.2 Explain logical security concepts.
1002-2.7 Given a scenario, implement security best practices to secure a workstation.

So far in this lesson, you have managed users and shared resources from a single computer. If you are part of a large organization, you would quickly find that this is a very inefficient way to configure resources. On a network, you can use something called directory-based tools to manage users, groups, and folders.

WINDOWS ACTIVE DIRECTORY DOMAINS

Show Slide(s)

Windows Active Directory Domains

Windows networking provides two kinds of user account: local and domain. **Local accounts** are stored in the **Local Security Accounts database** known as the **Security Account Manager (SAM)**, stored in the registry, as a subkey of HKEY_LOCAL_MACHINE. These accounts are local to the machine and cannot be accessed from other computers. If a user needs access to multiple computers in a workgroup environment, then each computer will need to hold a relevant user account.

Domain accounts are stored in the Active Directory (AD) on a **Windows Server Domain Controller (DC)**. These accounts can be accessed from any computer joined to the domain. Only domain administrators can create these accounts.

ACTIVE DIRECTORY COMPONENTS

Show Slide(s)

Active Directory Components (2 slides)

Teaching Tip

Obviously, there is much more to AD but learners really need to know about DCs, domains, and OUs.

Active Directory is a complex service, with many components. Some of the components that you will encounter as an A+ technician include domain controllers, member servers, and organizational units.

DOMAIN CONTROLLERS

A **domain** is the basic administrative building block in Windows client/server networking. To create a domain, you need one or more Windows servers configured as **domain controllers**.

The domain controllers store a database of network information called **Active Directory**. This database stores user, group, and computer objects. The domain controllers are responsible for providing authentication services to users as they attempt to logon to the network.

The servers are controlled by network administrators, who also define client computers and users permitted to access resources. This network model is centralized, robust, scalable, and secure.

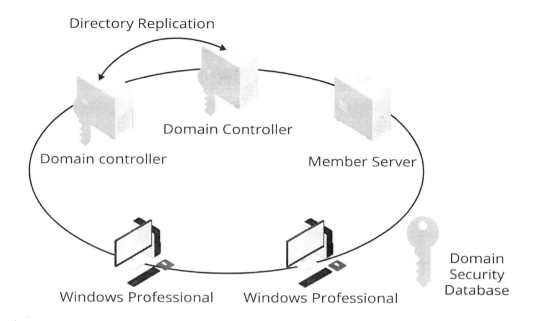

Active Directory security accounts are stored and managed from a domain controller. (Image © 123RF.com.)

MEMBER SERVERS

Member servers are any server-based systems that have been configured into the domain, but do not maintain a copy of the Active Directory database and are, therefore, unable to provide logon services. Because the user validation process consumes resources, most servers are configured as member servers rather than domain controllers. They will provide file and print and application server services (such as Exchange for email or SQL Server for database or line-of-business applications).

ORGANIZATIONAL UNITS

Organizational Units (OUs) provide a way of dividing a domain up into different administrative realms. You might create OUs to delegate responsibility for administering different company departments or locations. For example, a "Sales" department manager could be delegated control with rights to add, delete, and modify user accounts but no rights to change account policies, such as requiring complex passwords or managing users in the "Accounts" OU.

DOMAIN MEMBERSHIP

To fully participate in the benefits of an Active Directory domain, client computers must become members of the domain. Domain membership means:

- The computer has a computer account object within the directory database.
- Computer users can log on to the domain with domain user accounts.
- The computer and its users are subject to centralized domain security, configuration, and policy settings.
- Certain domain accounts automatically become members of local groups on the computer.
- Client computers within the domain allow users to access the network's services.

In Windows 7, Windows 8/8.1, and Windows 10, you can use the **System Properties** dialog box to join a domain. On a Windows 10 PC, you can also use the **Settings** app to join a domain.

 Show Slide(s)

Domain Membership

 Teaching Tip

Exam candidates should know how to perform a domain join.

 Teaching Tip

Note the importance of correctly configured DHCP and AD DNS services to the join process.

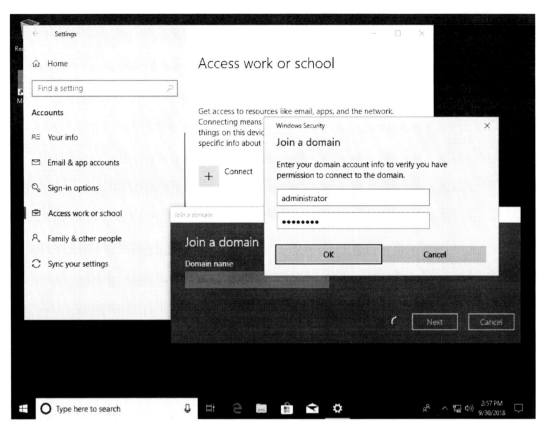

Joining a domain using the Settings app in Windows 10. (Screenshot used with permission from Microsoft.)

Note: *The other option is to join an Azure Active Directory. Azure is essentially a cloud-hosted version of AD.*

Note: *To learn more, check the **Video** tile on the CHOICE Course screen for any videos that supplement the content for this lesson.*

Access the Checklist tile on your CHOICE Course screen for reference information and job aids on How to Join a Domain.

DOMAIN SIGN-IN

Show
Slide(s)

Domain Sign-In

To use services in the domain, the user must sign into the PC using a domain account. The **Other user** option in the sign in screen will provide a domain option if it is not the default. You can also enter a username in the format ***Domain\UserName*** to specify a domain login.

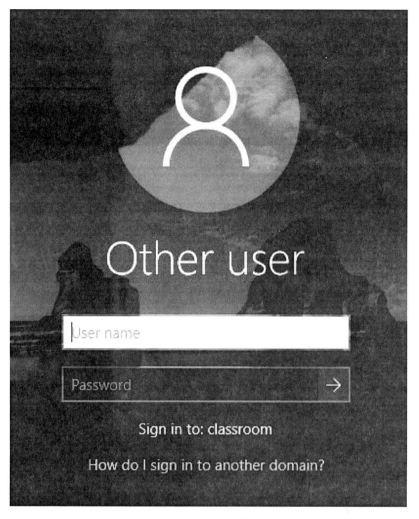

Signing into a domain. (Screenshot used with permission from Microsoft.)

GROUP POLICY OBJECTS

On a standalone workstation, security policies for the local machine and for local accounts are configured via the **Local Security Policy** or **Local Group Policy** snap-in. In an AD domain, they can be configured via **Group Policy Objects (GPOs)**. GPOs are a means of applying security settings (as well as other administrative settings) across a range of computers and users. GPOs are linked to network administrative boundaries in Active Directory, such as domains and OUs.

GPOs can be used to configure software deployment, Windows settings, and, through the use of **Administrative Templates**, custom Registry settings. Settings can also be configured on a per-user or per-computer basis.

A system of inheritance determines the **Resultant Set of Policies (RSoPs)** that apply to a particular computer or user. GPOs can be set to override or block policy inheritance where necessary.

Windows ships with default **security templates** to provide the basis for GPOs (**configuration baselines**). These can be modified using the **Group Policy Editor** or **Group Policy Management Console (GPMC)**. GPOs can be linked to objects in Active Directory using the object's property sheet.

Show Slide(s)

Group Policy Objects (2 slides)

Teaching Tip

Note that the settings are the same as local group policy. The advantage is that you create policies that can be attached to large numbers of accounts rather than configuring them for each account separately.

Teaching Tip

Make sure learners understand the difference between computer and user settings. Also make sure they understand what sort of objects GPOs can be applied to.

Teaching Tip

Point out that computers have accounts in the domain and can be assigned to OUs too.

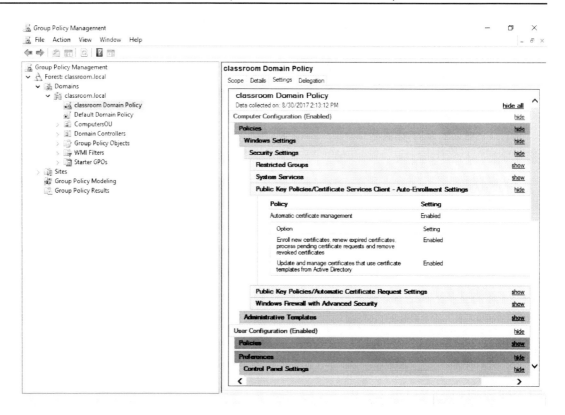

Group Policy Management. (Screenshot used with permission from Microsoft.)

SECURITY POLICY UPDATES

When updating local or group security policies, it is important to be familiar with the use of two command-line tools:

- `gpupdate`—policies are applied at log on and refreshed periodically (normally every 90 minutes). The `gpupdate` command is used to apply a new or changed policy to a computer immediately whereas `gpupdate /force` causes all policies (new and old) to be reapplied. The `gpupdate` command can be used with `/logoff` or `/boot` to allow a sign-out or reboot if the policy setting requires it.

- `gpresult`—displays the RSoP for a computer and user account. When run without switches, the current computer and user account policies are shown. The `/s`, `/u`, and `/p` switches can be used to specify a host (by name or IP address), user account, and password.

BASIC AD FUNCTIONS

Show Slide(s)

Basic AD Functions (2 slides)

Teaching Tip

Though Server Manager provides numerous management consoles, the one to key on is **AD Users and Computers.**

Windows Server versions are quite similar to their desktop equivalent, so Windows Server 2016 shares many of the features of Windows 10. In Windows Server, the **Server Manager** app provides a single location where you can access server management tools. When you install Active Directory on a server, several management consoles are added to the **Tools** menu in **Server Manager**.

Accessing the AD management consoles via Server Manager. (Screenshot used with permission from Microsoft.)

*Note: Logging in locally to the server is burdensome and an increased security risk. More typically, you will install the **Remote Server Administration Tools** (RSATs) to your local computer to connect to the server to make changes.*

ACCOUNT CREATION AND DELETION

The **Active Directory Users and Computers** console allows you to manage users, groups, and Organizational Units. By default, there are some existing containers and OUs to store some of the default accounts created when AD is installed. You can create more OUs to store accounts in. You can use OUs to store accounts that have a similar security or administrative profile.

To create a new user account, right-click in the container or OU where you want to store the account and select **New→User**.

Complete the username fields then in the next dialog box, choose an initial password. The default option is to force the user to select a new password at first sign in.

You can delete a user account by right-clicking the object and selecting **Delete**. Deleting an account is not easy to reverse, though AD does now support a **Recycle Bin** feature. In many circumstances, it may be more appropriate to disable an account. Once an account is disabled, the user is denied access to the network until the administrator re-enables the account.

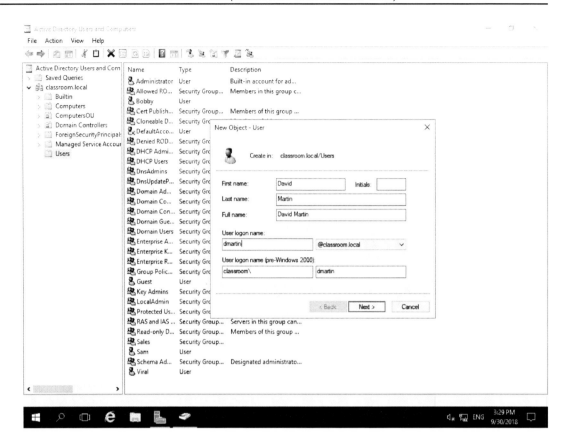

Creating a new user account in AD. (Screenshot used with permission from Microsoft.)

Note: *To learn more, check the* **Video** *tile on the CHOICE Course screen for any videos that supplement the content for this lesson.*

Access the Checklist tile on your CHOICE Course screen for reference information and job aids on How to Create and Delete Domain Accounts.

LOGON SCRIPTS

Show
Slide(s)

Logon Scripts

Logon scripts, also known as login scripts or sign-in scripts, run when a user logs on to a computer. User logon scripts can be assigned to users as part of a **group policy**. Logon scripts can be used to configure the environment for the user—setting environmental variables, setting a home folder, mapping drives to specific server-based folders, and mapping to printers or other resources, for example. A logon script can also be used to ensure that the client meets the security requirements for signing on to the network. For example, if the client has out-of-date software, logon can be denied until the software is updated.

If possible, assign logon scripts to the largest number of users that need the same configuration. A script can be assigned at the domain level, the OU level, or security group level. If a user requires additional or different settings, a logon script can be created for individual users, but that is one more item to maintain.

*Note: To learn more, check the **Video** tile on the CHOICE Course screen for any videos that supplement the content for this lesson.*

Access the Checklist tile on your CHOICE Course screen for reference information and job aids on *How to Manage Logon Scripts*.

HOME FOLDER

A **home folder** is a private network storage area located in a shared network server folder in which users can store personal files. The home folder can be created for domain users through the **Active Directory Users and Computers** tool. Using home folders, administrators can more easily create backups of user files because all of the files are located in one place on a file server. If the administrator doesn't assign a home folder location, the computer will automatically use the **Documents** folder location as the default home folder.

Show
Slide(s)

Home Folder

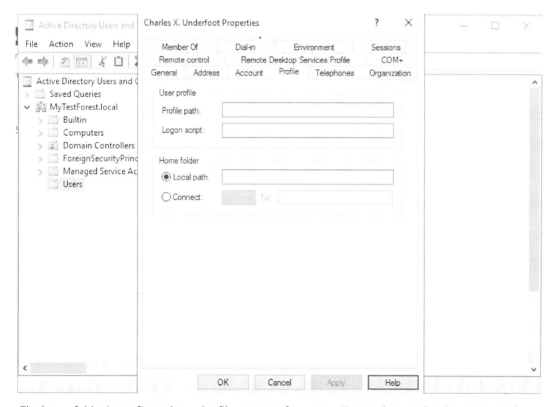

The home folder is configured as a Profile property for a user. (Screenshot used with permission from Microsoft.)

*Note: To learn more, check the **Video** tile on the CHOICE Course screen for any videos that supplement the content for this lesson.*

Access the Checklist tile on your CHOICE Course screen for reference information and job aids on *How to Create Home Folders*.

FOLDER REDIRECTION

Show Slide(s)
Folder Redirection

Teaching Tip
For more detailed information including new and changed functionality, refer to **https:// docs.microsoft.com/e n-us/windows- server/storage/ folder-redirection/ folder-redirection- rup-overview**.

By default, user settings and data files are stored in a local user profile located in the **Users** folder. For users that work on more than one computer, they will have separate profiles on each computer and the data files stored on the first computer are not available on the second computer. Microsoft created a couple of technologies to deal with this issue. One is **folder redirection** and the second is **roaming profiles**. Folder redirection allows an administrative user to redirect the path of a local folder (such as the user's home folder) to a folder on a network share. Roaming profiles redirect user profiles to a network share as well. By using both folder redirection and roaming profiles, the user's data and profile information is available when the user logs into any computer on the network where the network share is located.

BENEFITS OF USING FOLDER REDIRECTION

By having folders redirected from local storage to network storage, administrators can back up user data while backing up network data folders. This ensures that user data is being backed up without relying on users to back up their data.

Another benefit is, by using folder redirection with roaming profiles and the **offline files** feature, users can access network files even if the network is unavailable, if network access is slow, or users are working offline.

*Note: To learn more, check the **Video** tile on the CHOICE Course screen for any videos that supplement the content for this lesson.*

Access the Checklist tile on your CHOICE Course screen for reference information and job aids on How to Configure Folder Redirection.

ACCOUNT LOCKS AND PASSWORD RESETS

Show Slide(s)
Account Locks and Password Resets

If a user account violates a security policy, such as an incorrect password being entered repeatedly, it may be locked against further use. The account will be inaccessible until it is unlocked by setting the option in the **Properties** dialog box on the **Account** tab.

Using the Properties dialog box to unlock a user account. (Screenshot used with permission from Microsoft.)

If a user forgets a password, you can reset it by right-clicking the account and selecting **Reset Password**. You can use this dialog as another way to unlock an account too.

 *Note: To learn more, check the **Video** tile on the CHOICE Course screen for any videos that supplement the content for this lesson.*

 Access the Checklist tile on your CHOICE Course screen for reference information and job aids on How to Unlock Domain Accounts and Reset Passwords.

Activity 10-4

Discussing Active Directory Account and Policy Configuration

Show Slide(s)

Activity: Discussing Active Directory Account and Policy Configuration

SCENARIO

Answer the following questions to check your understanding of the topic.

1.   **What type of computer stores Active Directory account information?**

A Windows server running the Domain Controller (DC) role.

2.   **What are the prerequisites for joining a computer to a domain?**

The computer must be running a supported edition of Windows (Professional, Enterprise, or Ultimate). The computer must be joined to the network with an appropriate IP configuration (typically configured via DHCP) and be able to access the domain's DNS server(s). An account with domain administrative credentials must be used to authorize the join operation.

3.   **True or false? If you want the same policy to apply to a number of computers within a domain, you could add the computers to the same Organizational Unit (OU) and apply the policy to the OU.**

True.

4.   **What is the difference between the `gpupdate` and `gpresult` commands?**

`gpupdate` is used to refresh local policy settings with updates or changes from the policy template. `gpresult` is used to identify the Resultant Set of Policies (RSoP) for a given computer and/or user account.

5.   **In Active Directory, what are the options for running a script each time the user logs on?**

You can specify scripts to run for a number of users by using group policy and attaching the policy to an appropriate container, such as an OU. You can also specify a script manually for each user account via the account properties.

6.   **How do you unlock an AD user account?**

Open **Active Directory Users and Computers**. and locate the user account. Right-click the user object and select **Properties**. Check the **Unlock account** box. Select **OK**.

Activity 10-5
Configuring Active Directory Accounts and Policies

Show Slide(s)

Activity: Configuring
Active Directory
Accounts and Policies

BEFORE YOU BEGIN
In this activity, you will configure accounts and settings on servers and clients within an Active Directory (AD) domain. Take a moment to review the VMs available on the local network.

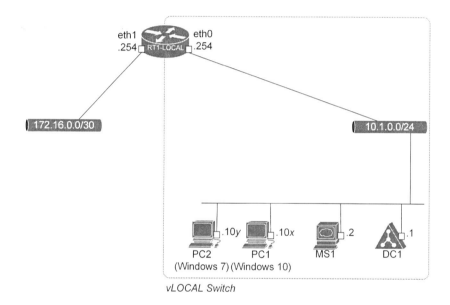

Network environment for the activity.

There are two Windows Server VMs. The **DC1** VM is running Active Directory and DNS and has the IP address 10.1.0.1. The **MS1** VM is running DHCP and has the static address 10.1.0.2. The **PC1** and **PC2** VMs are the Windows 10 and Windows 7 client workstations. Their addresses are dynamically assigned by the DHCP server from the range 10.1.0.101 to 10.1.0.109.

SCENARIO
In this activity, you will look at some of the features of a Windows domain server-based network by configuring a user account, GPO, and folder redirection.

1. Start the VMs to create the network. You do not need to open connection windows for the VMs unless prompted.
   a) In **Hyper-V Manager**, right-click **RT1-LOCAL** and select **Start**.
   b) Right-click **DC1** and select **Start**.
   c) Wait until the DC1 thumbnail shows the logon screen, and then start **MS1**.

   d)   Wait until the MS1 thumbnail shows the logon screen, and then start **PC1** and **PC2**.

   e)   Open a connection window for **PC1**.

   f)   Sign-on using the account ***515support\Administrator*** and password ***Pa$$w0rd***

2.   Investigate the domain's DNS suffix, and test connectivity with the Domain Controller.

   a)   Point to the network status icon.

        The tooltip should identify the connection as **corp.515support.com**. This is the DNS suffix for the domain.

Checking the network status. (Screenshot used with permission from Microsoft.)

        Using a subdomain such as **corp** (**ad** is also popular, but any label can be used) is one way of configuring the namespace for the local AD network. Some companies use the same domain name (**515support.com**) internally and externally. Users only need to use the "simple" domain label (**515support**) to sign on.

   b)   Open a command prompt. Run the command `hostname.`.

        This reports the local machine's name (**PC1**)

   c)   Run `ipconfig` and record the "Connection-specific DNS Suffix" parameter.

   d)   Run the following command: `ping pc1`

        The command automatically appends the DNS suffix to the hostname to use the Fully Qualified Domain Name (FQDN) of **pc1.corp.515support.com**.

   e)   Run the following command: `ping dc1`

        The test should be successful.

   f)   Close the command prompt.

3.   The **PC1** VM has been installed with the Remote Server Administration Tools (RSAT). These allow administrators to configure the domain without having to sign on to the DC locally. Use RSAT to view the domain's DNS server, running on DC1.

   a)   On **PC1**, select **Start→Windows Administrative Tools→DNS**.

   b)   In the **Connect to DNS Server** dialog box, select **The following computer**. Type ***dc1*** and select **OK** .

c) In the **DNS** console, expand **dc1→Forward Lookup Zones→corp.515support.com**.

A Forward Lookup Zone is a list of host names mapped to IP addresses. You can see automatically registered A host records for each VM in the zone. The record contains the IPv4 address assigned by DHCP. Each host name is appended with the domain suffix (**corp.515support.com**) to create a Fully Qualified Domain Name (FQDN). The servers also have IPv6 (AAAA) host records.

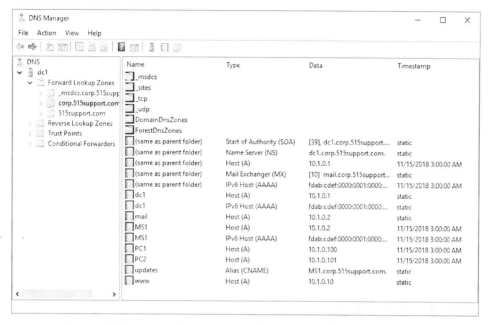

Viewing DNS records. (Screenshot used with permission from Microsoft.)

The **updates** alias record (CNAME) enables a host to be accessed by using a different label.

d) Start the web browser and open **updates.corp.515support.com**.
A web page showing the company's update portal is returned.

e) Switch back to the **DNS** console, and open the **_tcp** folder.

This is one of the folders containing records that support Windows domain services. Clients use these service records to sign on and query the directory. There is a record for LDAP (Lightweight Directory Access Protocol).

f) Close all open windows on the PC1 VM.

4. Use RSAT to create a new domain user account called ***David***, and then add **David** to the **Sales** security group (this has been created for you already).

a) On the **PC1 VM**, select **Start→Windows Administrative Tools→Active Directory Users and Computers**.

b) In the left pane, expand **corp.515support.com→Users**.

c) Right-click **Users** and select **New→User**.

d) In the **New Object – User** dialog box, in the **First name** box, type ***David***

e) In the **User logon name** box, type ***david*** and then select **Next**.

f) In the **Password** and **Confirm password** boxes, type ***Pa$$w0rd***

g) Clear the **User must change password at next logon** box and check the **Password never expires** box. Select **Next** and then select **Finish**.

h) In **Active Directory Users and Computers**, in the main pane, right-click the **David** user account and select **Add to a group**.

i) In the **Enter the object names** box, type ***sales*** then select the **Check Names** button.
The name should be underlined to show that it has been matched to a valid Active Directory object.

j) Select **OK**, then confirm the prompt by selecting **OK** again.

k) Observe that the **Users** folder contains both user and security group accounts. Observe some of the built-in Active Directory security groups, such as **Domain Admins** and **Domain Users**.

l) Locate the **Sales** security group account. Right-click it and select **Properties**. Inspect the **Members** and **Member Of** tabs.

Security groups can both contain user and group accounts and be members of other group accounts. This nesting allows sophisticated permissions systems to be implemented.

m) Select **Cancel**.

In this example, using a group hasn't saved much time. But if you imagine a sales department with a few hundred users who all need the same permissions to be allocated, you can understand why using groups is more efficient and secure than allocating permissions directly to user accounts.

n) View the **ComputersOU** and **Domain Controllers** folders. These are Organizational Unit (OU) containers. They contain the accounts for the domain-joined computers.

The DC is in a separate container to the other computers. This means it is easy to apply different policies to it. Most networks would have separate containers for member servers and client computers too (or even more subdivisions).

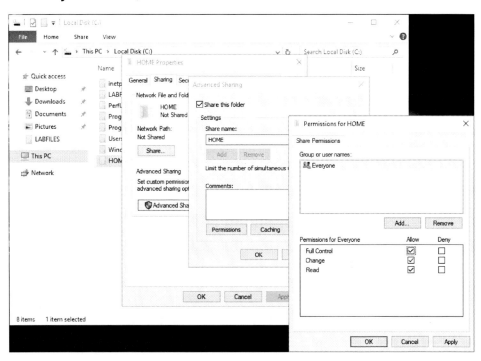 **Teaching Tip**

Optionally, discuss with learners why they are not configuring this folder on the DC.

5. Create a shared folder on **MS1** called *HOME*, and configure the share permissions to give **Full Control** to the **Everyone** group.

a) Open a connection window for **MS1**.

b) Sign on using the account *515support\Administrator* and password *Pa$$w0rd*.

c) Open **File Explorer**, and create a folder named *HOME* in the **C:** root folder.

d) Right-click the **HOME** folder and select **Properties**.

e) Select the **Sharing** tab and then select the **Advanced Sharing** button.

f) Check the **Share this folder** box and then select the **Permissions** button.

g) With **Everyone** selected, check the **Allow** box for **Full Control**.

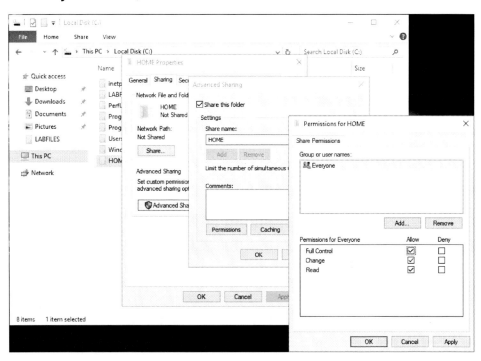

Configuring shared folder permissions. (Screenshot used with permission from Microsoft.)

h) Select **OK**.

i) In the **Advanced Sharing** dialog box, select **OK**. Leave the **HOME Properties** dialog box open.

6. To allow the redirection process to copy each user's folders and keep them private to each user, you need to configure specific permissions on the parent folder and disable inheritance.

a) In the **HOME Properties** dialog box, select the **Security** tab and then select the **Advanced** button.

b) In the **Advanced Security Settings for HOME** dialog box, select the **Disable inheritance** button.

c) At the prompt, select **Convert inherited permissions into explicit permissions on this object**.
This "detaches" the HOME folder from inheriting permission from the C:\ parent folder.

d) Select each **Users (MS1\Users)** entry and select **Remove**.

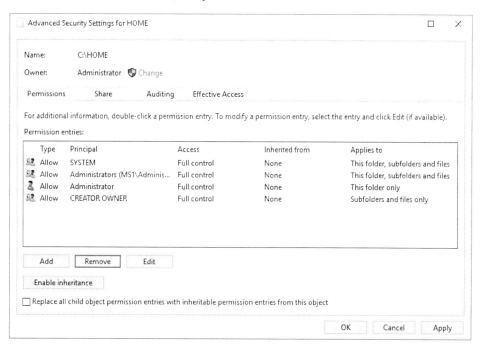

Configuring NTFS permissions on the share. (Screenshot used with permission from Microsoft.)

e) Select the **Add** button.

f) In the **Permission entry for HOME** dialog box, select the **Select a principal** link.

g) In the **Select Users or Groups** dialog box, type *authenticated users* in the box and select **Check Names**.

h) Select **OK**.

i) From the **Applies to** box, select **This folder only**.

j) Select **Show advanced permissions**.

k) Change the selections so that only the following are checked: **Traverse folder / execute file, Read attributes, and Create folders / append data.**

Configuring an NTFS permission entry on the share. (Screenshot used with permission from Microsoft.)

l) Select **OK**.
The effect of these permissions is to allow an authenticated user to create folders within HOME. The folders that get created will NOT inherit these permissions and so will be created with default permissions (full control for the user that created the folder).

m) In the **Advanced Security Settings for HOME** dialog box, select **OK**.

n) In the **HOME Properties** dialog box, select **Close**.

Teaching Tip

You can accomplish this much more easily using Drive Mappings (and mapped drives are not so widely used these days anyway), but the point is to illustrate the use of GPO and logon scripts.

Teaching Tip

Optionally, ask learners to create an OU and move selected users to that, and then apply the policy to the OU, rather than to the domain.

7. Create a logon script to map the folder **\\DC1\LABFILES** as the **L:** drive.

a) Switch to the **PC1** VM.

b) Use the desktop icon to start **Notepad++**.

c) Enter the following command: `net use L: \\DC1\LABFILES / persistent:yes`

d) Select **File→Save**. In the left pane, select **Desktop**. In the **File name** box, type *map.bat* and then select the **Save** button.

8. Create a GPO to run the script, and attach the GPO to the domain.

a) On the **PC1 VM**, right-click the **map** file on the desktop and select **Copy**.

b) Select **Start→Windows Administrative Tools→Group Policy Management**.

c) Expand **Forest→Domains→corp.515support.com**. Right-click **corp.515support.com** and select **Create a GPO in this domain, and Link it here**.

d) In the **New GPO** dialog box, in the **Name** box, type *515 Support Logon Policy*. Select **OK**.

e) Right-click **515 Support Logon Policy** and select **Edit**.

f) In the **Group Policy Management Editor** window, expand **User Configuration→Policies→Windows Settings** and select **Scripts**. Double-click **Logon**.

g) In the **Logon Properties** dialog box, select the **Show Files** button.

h) Right-click in the **Explorer** window and select **Paste** to copy the **map** file to the folder; then, close the Explorer window.

i) In the **Logon Properties** dialog box, select the **Add** button. In the **Add a Script** dialog box, select the **Browse** button. Select **map** and select **Open**.

j)   Select **OK** in the **Add a Script** dialog box and in the **Logon Properties** dialog box.

9.   Configure the folder redirection policy within the current GPO.

   a)   In the **Group Policy Management Editor** window, expand **User Configuration→Policies→Windows Settings→Folder Redirection**.
   b)   Right-click **Documents** and select **Properties**.
   c)   In the **Documents Properties** dialog box, from the **Setting** list box, select **Basic - Redirect everyone's folder to the same location**.
   d)   In the **Root path** box, type **\\MS1\HOME**
   e)   Select **OK**. Confirm the prompt by selecting **Yes**.

10. Test the new policy using the current account on **PC1**.

   a)   On the **PC1** VM, open **File Explorer**.
   b)   Copy some of the files from **C:\LABFILES** into the **Documents** folder.
   c)
   Open a command prompt and run `gpupdate`

   Note the message—you must log off and log back on for folder redirection to be applied.
   d)   Sign out from **PC1**.
   e)   Select **Other user**. Use the user name **515support\administrator** and **Pa$$w0rd** as the password.
   You might notice that sign on seems slower than before. This is because the files you copied to **Documents** are being moved to the **\\MS1\HOME** share.
   f)   Open **File Explorer** and observe the **Sync** icon on the **Documents** folder.

Teaching Tip

If the policies don't get applied, try restarting the VM.

UAC conflicts with network drive mappings, so the L: drive will not appear when you are logged on using a Domain Admin account. If learners switch accounts on PC1 (use **Sam** or **Viral**), then they will see the mapped drive.

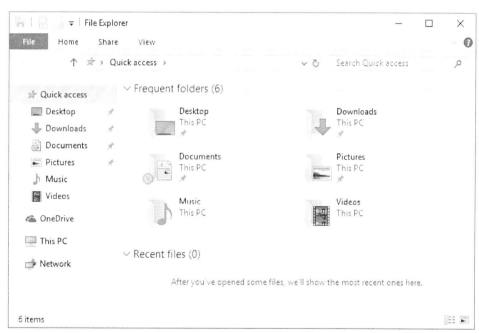

Folder redirection applied to the Documents folder. (Screenshot used with permission from Microsoft.)

   g)   Open the **Sync Center** from **Control Panel**. Are there any errors?
   You will likely see a Status of Ready for first sync.

11. Test the new policy by using the **David** account on **PC2**.

   a)   Open a connection window for the **PC2** VM, and sign in using the account name **David** and password **Pa$$w0rd**
   b)   Open **Explorer** and verify that the **L:** drive is mapped to **\\DC1\LABFILES**.
   c)   Open the **Documents** library, and verify that the **My Documents** folder is set up to sync. Test that you can create and edit a new file in the folder.

d) View the **Sync Center** in **Control Panel**.

Teaching Tip

Note that the author has taken some shortcuts to make the lab simpler. In a production environment, you'd probably give admins access via a permission entry on the root folder (applying to all subfolders).

12. Optionally, switch to the **MS1** VM, and examine the contents of **HOME**.

You should see folders for **Administrator** and **David**. You will not be able to view the contents of these folders because the redirection policy gave users exclusive access.

13. At the end of each activity, you need to close the VMs. You will always discard any changes you made.

a) From the connection window, select **Action→Revert**.

b) If prompted, select the **Revert** button to confirm.

c) On the **HOST**, in the **Hyper-V Manager** console, right-click each VM that is still running and select **Revert**. At the end of the activity, the state of each VM should be listed as **Off**.

Summary

In this lesson, you managed user accounts, workstations, and shared resources. These administrative tasks are critical knowledge for any A+ technician.

What experiences do you have in working with any of the technologies discussed in this lesson?

A: Answers will vary according to the backgrounds of different individuals. Possible experiences include: managing local user accounts on a home PC, configuring network shares, and joining a computer to an AD domain.

Which AD configuration task do you expect to perform most often in your workplace?

A: Answers will vary, but might include creating and disabling accounts, joining computers to domains, or configuring home folders and folder redirection.

 Practice Question: *Additional practice questions are available on the CompTIA CHOICE platform within the **Assessments** tile.*

Lesson 11
Implementing Client Virtualization and Cloud Computing

LESSON INTRODUCTION

As organizations grow in size and scope, there is an increased need for resources, especially when it comes to computing. Virtualization can help ease the growing pains of an organization by providing the opportunity to leverage one computer and one operating system for use over many systems, and save valuable time and resources when it comes to hardware, software, and personnel.

Virtualization is also the technology underpinning cloud computing; one of the dominant trends in networking. Many organizations are outsourcing parts of their IT infrastructure, platforms, storage, or services to a cloud service provider. Virtualization is at the core of cloud service provider networks. As a CompTIA® A+® technician, your customers will expect you to be able to advise on types of cloud deployments and identify some of the configuration issues involved in connecting to cloud services.

LESSON OBJECTIVES

In this lesson, you will:

- Set up and configure a hypervisor and virtual machine guests.
- Identify the purposes and types of cloud services.

Topic A
Configure Client-Side Virtualization

 EXAM OBJECTIVES COVERED
1001-4.2 Given a scenario, set up and configure client-side virtualization.

 Teaching Tip

Make sure learners can distinguish between the types and features of hypervisors and know the different applications of virtualization.

Virtualization separates the elements of the computing environment—the applications, operating system, programs, documents, and more—from each other and from the physical hardware by using an additional software layer to mediate access. Virtualization can provide flexibility and scalability for organizations where the costs for hardware and software and the IT infrastructure needed to maintain them both continue to increase. It can increase resource utilization by allowing resources to be pooled and leveraged as part of a virtual infrastructure, and it can provide for centralized administration and management of all the resources being used throughout the organization.

As a CompTIA A+ technician, you will often be called upon to deploy, configure, and support Virtual Machines (VMs). You need to know about the types, capabilities, and uses of different virtualization technologies.

VIRTUALIZATION

 Show Slide(s)

Virtualization

 Teaching Tip

Make sure learners know the basic components and terminology of virtualization.

When computers based on the microprocessor CPU were first produced, a single computer was designed to run a single operating system at any one time. This makes multiple applications available on that computer—whether it be a workstation or server—but the applications must all share a common OS environment. Some computers were configured with two or more operating systems and could choose the one to load at boot time (multiboot). The operating systems could not be used simultaneously, however.

Dramatic improvements and cost reductions in CPU and system memory technology mean that all but the cheapest computers are now capable of virtualization. **Virtualization** means that multiple operating systems can be installed and run simultaneously on a single computer.

There are many different ways of implementing this and many different reasons for doing it. In general terms, though, a virtual platform requires at least three components:

- Computer(s)—the platform or host for the virtual environment. Optionally, there may be multiple computers networked together.
- Hypervisor or Virtual Machine Monitor (VMM)—manages the virtual machine environment and facilitates interaction with the host hardware and network.
- Guest operating systems or Virtual Machines (VMs)—operating systems installed under the virtual environment. The number of operating systems is generally only restricted by hardware capacity. The type of guest operating systems might be restricted by the type of hypervisor.

The presence of other guest OSs can be completely transparent to any single OS. Each OS "thinks" it is working with a normal CPU, memory, hard disk, and network link. The guest OSs can be networked together or they may be able to share data directly through the hypervisor, though for security reasons this is not commonly implemented.

HYPERVISORS

As noted previously, a hypervisor manages the virtual machine environment and facilitates interaction with the host hardware and network.

Microsoft Hyper-V hypervisor software. This machine is running several Windows and Linux guest operating systems. You can see each is allocated a portion of system memory to use. (Screenshot used with permission from Microsoft.)

Some of the main functions of the hypervisor include:

- Emulation—each guest OS expects exclusive access to resources such as the CPU, system memory, storage devices, and peripherals. The hypervisor emulates these resources and facilitates access to them to avoid conflicts between the guest OSs. The VMs must be provided with drivers for the emulated hardware components.
- Guest OS support—the hypervisor may be limited in terms of the different types of guest operating systems it can support. Virtualization is often used as a means of installing old OSs, such as MS-DOS or Windows 9x, as well as modern versions of Windows and Linux.

> **Note:** *macOS can also be installed as a VM. This breaks the terms of Apple's EULA if the hardware platform is not itself an Apple PC.*

- Assigning resources to each guest OS—for example, if the host computer has 4 GB memory, 1 GB might be required by the host OS, leaving 3 GB to assign to each guest OS. You could have three guests, each configured with 1 GB, for instance. Similarly, each guest OS will take up disk space on the host. Data is saved to virtual disk image files.
- Configuring networking—a hypervisor will be able to create a virtual network environment through which all the VMs can communicate. It will also be able to create a network shared by the host and by VMs on the same host and on other hosts. Enterprise virtual platforms allow the configuration of virtual switches and routers.

Show Slide(s)

Hypervisors (4 slides)

Teaching Tip

The CPU and memory aren't emulated as such. Each VM runs within a protected space within those resources. The view from "inside" the VM is that it has a regular CPU and memory modules to work with.

The hard disk is an image file. Components such as the network adapter are emulated.

- Configuring security—ensures that guests are "contained" and cannot access other VMs or the host except through authorized mechanisms. This is important to prevent data "leaking" from one VM to another, to prevent one compromised VM from compromising others, and to prevent malware from spreading between VMs or from a VM to the host.

One basic distinction that can be made between virtual platforms is between host and bare metal methods of interacting with the computer hardware.

HOST-BASED HYPERVISOR

Teaching Tip

Although Hyper-V looks like it's host-based, it is actually Type 1. When you install Hyper-V as a feature (role in Windows Server), it takes ownership of the computer and flips the current Windows installation into a special "default" VM. This VM is then installed with the management console to configure Hyper-V. Note that this default VM does interact with the file system itself rather than a disk image.

You can also install Windows Server in a Hyper-V only mode, which does "feel" more like a Type 1. The same technology is used in both cases.

The author advises not getting drawn into a debate about whether KVM is Type 1 or Type 2.

In a guest OS (or host-based) system, the hypervisor application, known as a **Type 2 hypervisor**, is itself installed onto a host operating system. Examples of host-based hypervisors include VMware Workstation™, Oracle® VirtualBox, and Parallels® Workstation. The hypervisor software must support the host OS. For example, Parallels Workstation is designed to run on macOS®. You cannot run it on a Windows® PC but you *can* use it to run a Windows VM on macOS.

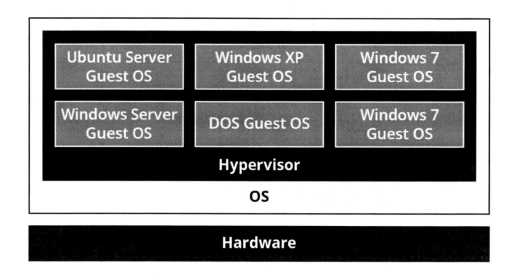

Guest OS virtualization (Type 2 Hypervisor). The hypervisor is an application running within a native OS and guest OSs are installed within the hypervisor.

BARE METAL HYPERVISOR

A bare metal virtual platform means that the hypervisor—called a **Type 1 hypervisor**—is installed directly onto the computer and manages access to the host hardware without going through a host OS. Examples include VMware ESX® Server, Microsoft's Hyper-V®, and Citrix's XEN Server. The hardware need only support the base system requirements for the hypervisor plus resources for the type and number of guest OSs that will be installed. Linux® also supports virtualization through Kernel-based Virtual Machine (KVM). KVM is embedded in the Linux kernel.

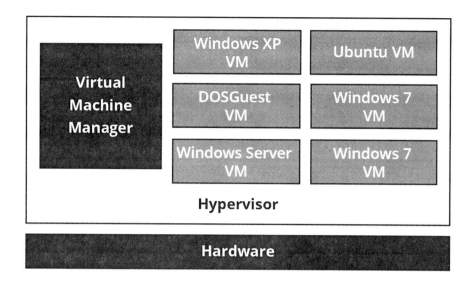

Type 1 "bare metal" hypervisor. The hypervisor is installed directly on the host hardware along with a management application, then VMs are installed within the hypervisor.

Note: If the hypervisor is running in a 64-bit environment, 32-bit guest OSs can still be installed, providing the hypervisor supports them. 32-bit hypervisors will not support 64-bit guest OSs, however.

PROCESSOR SUPPORT AND RESOURCE REQUIREMENTS

CPU vendors have built special instruction set extensions to facilitate virtualization. The Intel technology for this is called **VT-x** (Virtualization Technology) while AMD calls it **AMD-V**. Most virtualization products also benefit from a processor feature called **Second Level Address Translations (SLAT)**, which improves the performance of virtual memory when multiple VMs are installed. Intel implements SLAT as a feature called Extended Page Table (EPT) and AMD calls it Rapid Virtualization Indexing (RVI).

Most virtualization software requires a CPU with virtualization support enabled and performance of the VMs will be impaired if virtualization is not supported in the hardware. Some cheaper CPU models ship without the feature and sometimes the feature is disabled in the system firmware. If specifying a computer that will be used for virtualization, check the CPU specification carefully to confirm that it supports Intel VT-x or AMD-V and SLAT, if necessary.

Multiple CPU resources—whether through **Symmetric Multiprocessing** (SMP) or multiple physical processors, multicore, or HyperThreading—will greatly benefit performance, especially if more than one guest OS is run concurrently.

As mentioned earlier, each guest OS requires sufficient system memory over and above what is required by the host. For example, it is recommended that Windows 7 be installed on a computer with at least 1 GB memory. This means that the host must have at least 2 GB and possibly more. As you can see, if you want to run multiple guest operating systems concurrently, the resource demands can quickly add up. If the VMs are only used for development and testing, then performance might not be critical and you may be able to specify less memory.

Each guest OS also takes up a substantial amount of disk space. The VM's "hard disk" is stored as an image file on the host. Most hypervisors use a "dynamically expanding" image format that only takes up space on the host as files are added to the guest OS. Even so, a typical Windows installation might require 20 GB. More space is required if you want to preserve snapshots. A snapshot is the state of a disk at a particular point-

Show Slide(s)

Processor Support and Resource Requirements (2 slides)

Teaching Tip

Note that the "x" in VT x stands for x86-64. Intel® developed a different 64-bit architecture called Itanium (IA-64). VT-i extensions are for that architecture. VT-x is for the AMD-developed 64-bit architecture, which proved much more successful as it was more compatible with legacy 32-bit code.

in-time. This is useful if you want to be able to roll back changes you make to the VM during a session.

> *Note: In an enterprise environment, you need not be constrained by the local disk resources on the host. Disk images could be stored in a high-speed Storage Area Network (SAN).*

Most hypervisors also allow guest VMs to use the host's adapters (sound card, for instance) and peripherals (input devices, printers, and USB devices, for instance).

VIRTUAL NETWORKS

Show Slide(s)

Virtual Networks (3 slides)

Where multiple virtual machines are running on a single platform, virtualization provides a means for these VMs to communicate with each other and with other computers on the network—both physical and virtual—using standard networking protocols.

The guest operating system running in each virtual machine is presented with an emulation of a standard hardware platform. Among the hardware devices emulated will be one or more network adapters. The number of adapters and their connectivity can typically be configured within the hypervisor.

Within the virtual machine, the virtual adapter will look exactly like an ordinary NIC and will be configurable in exactly the same way. For example, protocols and services can be bound to it and it can be assigned an IP address.

Typically, a hypervisor will implement network connectivity by means of one or more **virtual switches** (or vSwitches using VMware's terminology). These perform exactly the same function as Ethernet switches, except that they are implemented in software rather than hardware.

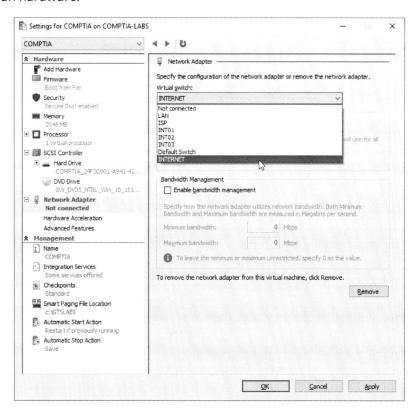

Selecting which virtual switch the network adapter in a VM is connected to. Note that there is also a "Not connected" option. (Screenshot used with permission from Microsoft.)

Connectivity between the virtual network adapters in the guest VMs and the virtual switches is configured via the hypervisor. This is analogous to connecting patch cables between real computers and real switches. Multiple virtual machines may be connected to the same virtual switch or to separate switches. The number of virtual switches supported varies from one hypervisor to another.

In this networking model, the virtual machines and the virtual switch can all be contained within a single hardware platform, so no actual network traffic is generated. Instead, data is moved from buffers in one virtual machine to another.

It is also possible to configure connectivity between the host computer's physical NIC and the virtual switches. This provides a bridge between the virtual switches within the host platform and the physical switches on the network, allowing frames to pass between physical and virtual machines and between the virtual machines and the host.

For example, in Microsoft's Hyper-V virtualization platform, three types of virtual switch can be created:

- **External**—binds to the host's NIC to allow the VM to communicate on the physical network.
- **Internal**—creates a switch that is usable only by VMs on the host and the host itself.
- **Private**—creates a switch that is usable only by the VMs. They cannot use the switch to communicate with the host.

Configuring virtual switches in Microsoft's Hyper-V hypervisor. Most of the switches are private, which means that only the VMs can access them. The selected virtual switch can share the host network adapter, though, allowing communication between the VM and the host and allowing the VM to use the physical network to access the Internet. (Screenshot used with permission from Microsoft.)

Note: *When the VMs are allowed to interact with a "real" network, the host must support a high bandwidth, high availability network link. Any failure of the physical link will affect multiple VMs.*

Show
Slide(s)
Virtual Machines (3 slides)

VIRTUAL MACHINES

In principle, any type of operating system can be virtualized. This includes client OSs and server OSs. Note that some hypervisors have limited support for certain operating systems. For example, Hyper-V only provides support for particular distributions of Linux, though the situation is improving as the Hyper-V Linux Integration Services (LIS) drivers get added to the kernel of more Linux distributions.

There are also many different purposes for deploying a virtual platform. You can make a rough distinction between **client-side virtualization**, deployed to desktop-type machines, and **server-side virtualization.**

CLIENT-SIDE VIRTUALIZATION

Client-side virtualization refers to any solution designed to run on "ordinary" desktops or workstations. Each user will be interacting with the virtualization host directly. Desktop virtual platforms, usually based on some sort of guest OS hypervisor, are typically used for testing and development:

- Virtual labs—create a research lab to analyze viruses, worms, and Trojans. As the malware is contained within the guest OS, it cannot infect the researcher's computer or network.
- Support legacy software applications—if the host computers have been upgraded, software may not work well with the new operating system. In this scenario, the old OS can be installed as a VM and the application software accessed using the VM.
- Development environment—test software applications under different operating systems and/or resource constraints.
- Training—lab environments can be set up so that learners can practice using a live operating system and software without impacting the production environment. At the end of the lab, changes to the VM can be discarded so the original environment is available again for the next student to use.

Teaching Tip

Server consolidation works best where there are large numbers of servers performing the same sort of role—web server farms, for instance.

Note that another use is application virtualization, but this is covered in the "Cloud" topic.

SERVER-SIDE VIRTUALIZATION

For server computers and applications, the main use of virtualization is better hardware utilization through **server consolidation**. A typical hardware server may have resource utilization of about 10%. This implies that you could pack the server computer with another 8 or 9 server software instances and obtain the same performance.

Show
Slide(s)
Security Requirements (3 slides)

SECURITY REQUIREMENTS

Like any computing technology, deploying a virtualization solution comes with security challenges.

Teaching Tip

A lot of virtualization security issues apply to "traditional" client-server networks too.

The problem of rogue VMs has its counterpart in allowing desktops to boot from USB (thereby loading a foreign OS such as live Linux).

GUEST OS SECURITY

Each guest OS must be patched and protected against viruses and Trojans like any other OS. Patching each VM individually has performance implications, so in most environments, a new image would be patched and tested then deployed to the production environment. Running security software (antivirus and intrusion prevention) on each guest OS can cause performance problems. Solutions for running security applications through the host or hypervisor are being developed.

 Note: *Ordinary antivirus software installed on the host will NOT detect viruses infecting the guest OS. Scanning the virtual disks of a guest OS from the host could cause serious performance problems.*

The process of developing, testing, and deploying images brings about the first major security concern with the virtual platform itself. This is the problem of rogue VMs. A **rogue VM** is one that has been installed without authorization. The uncontrolled deployment of more and more VMs is referred to as **VM sprawl**. It's a lot easier to add a guest image to a server than it is to plug a new hardware server into the network!

System management software can be deployed to detect rogue builds. More generally, the management procedures for developing and deploying machine images need to be tightly drafted and monitored. VMs should conform to an application-specific template with the minimum configuration needed to run that application (that is, not running unnecessary services). Images should not be developed or stored in any sort of environment where they could be infected by malware or have any sort of malicious code inserted. One of the biggest concerns here is of rogue developers or contractors installing backdoors or "logic bombs" within a machine image. The problem of criminal or disgruntled staff is obviously one that affects any sort of security environment, but concealing code within VM disk images is a bit easier to accomplish and has the potential to be much more destructive.

HOST SECURITY

Another key security vulnerability in a virtual platform is that the host represents a single point of failure for multiple guest OS instances. For example, if the CPU on the host crashes, three or four guest VMs and the application services they are running will suddenly go offline.

Another point is that running the host at a constantly high level of utilization could decrease the **Mean Time Between Failure (MTBF)** of its components. The MTBF is the number of hours the manufacturer expects that a component will run before experiencing some sort of hardware problem. If hardware is subjected to greater than expected loads, it may fail more often than expected.

A successful **Denial of Service (DoS)** attack on a host machine, host OS, or hypervisor will cause far more damage to the server infrastructure than a DoS on a single web server. As an example, most hypervisors support a disk snapshots feature. Snapshots allow the user to revert to the saved image after making changes. This can be misused to perform DoS by causing the undo files to grow to the point where they consume all the available disk space on the host.

HYPERVISOR SECURITY

Apart from ensuring the security of each guest OS and the host machine itself, a virtual platform introduces an additional layer for the attention of security analysts—that of the hypervisor. At the time of writing, there are few significant exploits, but hypervisor software is subject to patches and security advisories like any other software. As the use of virtual platforms grows, hypervisors will increasingly be the target of attacks.

Another issue is **VM escaping**. This refers to malware running on a guest OS jumping to another guest or to the host. As with any other type of software, it is vital to keep the hypervisor code up-to-date with patches for critical vulnerabilities.

Activity 11-1

Discussing Client-Side Virtualization Configuration

Show Slide(s)

Activity: Discussing Client-Side Virtualization Configuration

SCENARIO

Answer the following questions to check your understanding of the topic.

1. **What is a Type 2 hypervisor?**

   Hypervisor software that must be installed to a host OS. A Type 1 (or bare metal) hypervisor is installed directly on the host PC.

2. **What is a guest OS?**

   An OS installed on a virtual machine running within the virtual environment.

3. **What system resources are most important on a system designed to host multiple virtual machines?**

   The CPU must support virtualization extensions (and ideally be multi-processor or multicore), and there must be plenty of system memory and disk space.

4. **What might you need to install to a guest OS to make full use of a hypervisor's features?**

   The drivers for the emulated hardware (often referred to as an extensions, additions, or integration components).

5. **True or false? VMs can be networked together by using a virtual switch, which is implemented in software by the hypervisor.**

   True.

6. **If users have access to virtualization tools, what network security controls might be required?**

   A VM needs to be subject to network access control and authorization, like any physical computer device. The VMs need to be checked to ensure they are not running malware, for instance.

7. **If you are using a normal antivirus product to protect a VM from malware, should you install the A-V product on the host to scan the VM disk image or on the VM itself?**

   On the VM. The A-V software will not be able to scan the disk image for malware and may lock the file and cause performance problems while trying to perform the scan.

Topic B
Cloud Computing Concepts

 EXAM OBJECTIVES COVERED
1001-2.2 Compare and contrast common networking hardware devices.
1001-4.1 Compare and contrast cloud computing concepts.

One of the latest trends in networking is to outsource part of an organization's IT infrastructure, platforms, storage, or services to a cloud service provider. In this topic, you will identify basic cloud concepts.

CLOUD COMPUTING

The **cloud** has lots of different definitions but generally refers to any sort of IT infrastructure provided to the end user where the end user is not aware of or responsible for any details of the procurement, implementation, or management of the infrastructure. Its internal workings are a "cloud"; the end user is only interested in and pays for the services provided by the cloud.

The **National Institute of Standards and Technology (NIST)** created a standardized definition for cloud computing. This allows consumers to more easily compare services and deployment models from different vendors if they all use the same definition.

The NIST definition states: "Cloud computing is a model for enabling ubiquitous, convenient, on-demand network access to a shared pool of configurable computing resources (e.g., networks, servers, storage, applications, and services) that can be rapidly provisioned and released with minimal management effort or service provider interaction." (**https://nvlpubs.nist.gov/nistpubs/Legacy/SP/ nistspecialpublication800-145.pdf**, section 2.)

NIST identifies five characteristics that are essential in defining something as being cloud computing. These are defined in the following table.

Characteristic	Description
On-demand self service	Consumers can provision services on the fly without interaction with service provider personnel.
Broad network access	Services are available over networks using standard clients, including workstations, laptops, tablets, and smart phones.
Resource pooling	Multiple customers share the service provider's resources in a multi-tenant model. Resources are dynamically assigned as they are needed without regard to where the customer or the resource are located. However, a customer can request resources from a specific location at the country, state, or data-center level. Resources include memory, storage, processing, and network bandwidth.
Rapid elasticity	Resources are automatically provisioned to scale up or down as resources are required by the customer.

 Show Slide(s)
Cloud Computing (2 slides)

 Interaction Opportunity
If time permits, engage learners in a discussion of what their definition of the cloud is.

Characteristic	Description
Measured service	Resources are measured through metering on a per use basis. The metering measurement is based on the type of resource such as storage, processing, bandwidth, or active users. The metering mechanism should be accessible to the customer via a reporting dashboard, providing complete transparency in usage and billing.

BENEFITS OF CLOUD COMPUTING

Show Slide(s)
Benefits of Cloud Computing

Teaching Tip
Quite a few cloud services are not actually pay-per-use. A lot of the SaaS "cloud" services are just subscription services.

There are many benefits to using cloud computing. This includes savings in the cost of infrastructure and support, energy cost savings, rapid deployment, and allowing the customer to make the choices that make the most sense for their organization.

One of the most often cited benefits of implementing cloud computing is that the cloud provides **rapid elasticity**. This means that the cloud can scale quickly to meet peak demand. For example, a company may operate a single web server instance for most of the year, but provision additional instances for the busy Christmas period and then release them again in the New Year.

This example also illustrates the principles of on-demand and pay-per-use—key features of a cloud service (as opposed to a hosted service). On-demand implies that the customer can initiate service requests and that the cloud provider can respond to them immediately. This feature of cloud service is useful for project-based needs, giving the project members access to the cloud services for the duration of the project, and then releasing the cloud services back to the hosting provider when the project is finished. This way, the organization is only paying for the services for the duration of the project.

The provider's ability to control a customer's use of resources through metering is referred to as **measured service**. The customer is paying for the CPU, memory, disk, and network bandwidth resources they are actually consuming rather than paying a monthly fee for a particular service level.

In order to respond quickly to changing customer demands, cloud providers must be able to provision resources quickly. This is achieved through **resource pooling** and virtualization. Resource pooling means that the hardware making up the cloud provider's data center is not dedicated to or reserved for a particular customer account. The layers of virtualization used in the cloud architecture allow the provider to provision more CPU, memory, disk, or network resources using management software, rather than (for instance) having to go to the data center floor, unplug a server, add a memory module, and reboot.

Flexibility is a key advantage of cloud computing. However, the implications for data risk must be well understood when moving data between private and public storage environments. You need to be aware that any point from the server to the end user could be compromised if proper security measures are not taken and adhered to when transferring data over public and private networks.

COMMON CLOUD MODELS

Show Slide(s)
Common Cloud Models

Teaching Tip
NIST defines the deployment models as private, community, public, and hybrid clouds.

In most cases, the cloud (that is, the hardware and/or software hosting the service) will be off-site relative to the organization's users, who will require an Internet link to access the cloud services. There can be different ownership and access arrangements for clouds, which can be broadly categorized as described in the following table.

Cloud Model	Description
Public or multi-tenant	This model is hosted by a third-party and shared with other subscribers. This is what many people understand by cloud computing. As a shared resource, there are risks regarding performance and security.
Hosted private	This model is hosted by a third-party for the exclusive use of one organization. This is more secure and can guarantee a better level of performance, but is correspondingly more expensive. The OpenStack project (**openstack.org**) is one example of a technology you could use to implement your own cloud computing infrastructure.
Private	In this model, the cloud infrastructure is completely private to and owned by the organization. In this case, there is likely to be one business unit dedicated to managing the cloud while other business units make use of it. This type of cloud could be on-site or off-site relative to the other business units. An on-site link can obviously deliver better performance and is less likely to be subject to outages (loss of an Internet link, for instance). On the other hand, a dedicated off-site facility may provide better shared access for multiple users in different locations.
Community	With this model, several organizations share the costs of either a hosted private or fully private cloud.
Hybrid	There will also be cloud computing solutions that implement some sort of hybrid public/private/community/hosted/on-site/off-site solution. For example, a travel organization may run a sales website for most of the year using a private cloud but "break out" the solution to a public cloud at times when much higher utilization is forecast. Google's **Gov Cloud** is another example. This cloud can be used by government branches within the U.S., but it is not available to consumers or businesses.

INTERNAL AND EXTERNAL SHARED RESOURCES

All networks provide a pool of shared resources for use by servers and clients. For example, file servers can provide disk storage resources to client computers in the form of shared folders. Servers themselves can use shared disk storage in the form of Storage Area Networks (SANs). Use of virtualization and hybrid cloud computing solutions allows these shared resources to be provisioned using a mixture of internally owned assets and externally provisioned assets.

Show Slide(s)

Internal and External Shared Resources

CLOUD SERVICE OPTIONS

As well as the ownership model (public, private, hybrid, or community), cloud services are often differentiated on the level of sophistication provided. These models are referred to as **Something as a Service (*aaS)**, where the *something* can refer to infrastructure, network, platform, or software.

Show Slide(s)

Cloud Service Options (2 slides)

Teaching Tip

IaaS is good for organizations with "pockets" of need or for small organizations.

Service Type	Description
IaaS	**Infrastructure as a Service (IaaS)** is a means of provisioning IT resources such as servers, load balancers, and Storage Area Network (SAN) components quickly. Rather than purchase these components and the Internet links they require, you rent them on an as-needed basis from the service provider's data center. In an IaaS arrangement, you are typically billed based on the resources you consume, much like a utility company bills you for the amount of electricity you use.
	IaaS is a bare bones service offering. You will need to configure the components and build the platform on top. Examples of IaaS include Rackspace's CloudServers offering, in which you rent a virtual server running an operating system of your choice. You then install the applications you need onto that virtual server. Other examples include Amazon's Elastic Compute Cloud (EC2) service and Amazon's Simple Storage Service (S3).
SaaS	**Software as a Service (SaaS)** is a different model of provisioning software applications. Rather than purchasing software licenses for a given number of seats, a business would access software hosted on a supplier's servers on a pay-as-you-go or lease arrangement (on-demand). Virtual infrastructure allows developers to provision on-demand applications much more quickly than previously. The applications can be developed and tested within the cloud without the need to test and deploy on client computers.
	Perhaps the most well-known SaaS example is the Salesforce® Customer Relationship Management (**CRM**) service. Other notable SaaS examples are the Zoho suite of applications, Google's applications suite, and Microsoft's Office 365 suite.
PaaS	provides resources somewhere between SaaS and IaaS. A typical PaaS solution would provide servers and storage network infrastructure, but also provide a multi-tier web application/database platform on top, in contrast to Infrastructure as a Service. This platform might be based on Oracle® or MS SQL or PHP and MySQL™.
	As distinct from SaaS, though, this platform would not be configured to actually do anything. Your own developers would have to create the software, such as the CRM or e-commerce application, that runs using the platform.
	The service provider would be responsible for the integrity and availability of the platform components, but you would be responsible for the security of the application you created on the platform. An example is Rackspace's CloudSites offering, in which you rent a virtual web server and associated systems such as a database or email server. Amazon's Relational Database Service (RDS) enables you to rent fully configured MySQL and Oracle database servers.

Operating Systems and Software

Operating Systems

Amazon Machine Images (AMIs) are preconfigured with an ever-growing list of operating systems. We work with our partners and community to provide you with the most choice possible. You are also empowered to use our bundling tools to upload your own operating systems. The operating systems currently available to use with your Amazon EC2 instances include:

Operating Systems		
Red Hat Enterprise Linux	Windows Server	Oracle Enterprise Linux
OpenSolaris	Amazon Linux AMI	Ubuntu Linux
Fedora	Gentoo Linux	Debian
	SUSE Linux Enterprise	

Software

Amazon EC2 enables our partners and customers to build and customize Amazon Machine Images (AMIs) with software based on your needs. We have hundreds of free and paid AMIs available for you to use. A small sampling of the software available for use today within Amazon EC2 includes:

Databases	Batch Processing	Web Hosting
IBM DB2	Hadoop	Apache HTTP
IBM Informix Dynamic Server	Condor	IIS/Asp.Net
Microsoft SQL Server Standard	Open MPI	IBM Lotus Web Content Management
MySQL Enterprise		IBM WebSphere Portal Server
Oracle Database 11g		

Application Development Environments	Application Servers	Video Encoding & Streaming
IBM sMash	IBM WebSphere Application Server	Wowza Media Server Pro
JBoss Enterprise Application Platform	Java Application Server	Windows Media Server
Ruby on Rails	Oracle WebLogic Server	

Amazon's EC2 offers IaaS (Linux or Windows machine images) and PaaS (database and application development environments).

VIRTUAL DESKTOPS

Virtual Desktop Infrastructure (VDI) refers to using a VM as a means of provisioning corporate desktops. In a typical VDI, desktop computers are replaced by low-spec, low-power thin client computers.

When the thin client starts, it boots a minimal OS, allowing the user to log on to a VM stored on the company server or cloud infrastructure. The user makes a connection to the VM using some sort of remote desktop protocol (Microsoft Remote Desktop or Citrix ICA, for instance). The thin client has to find the correct image and use an appropriate authentication mechanism. There may be a 1:1 mapping based on machine name or IP address, or the process of finding an image may be handled by a connection broker.

All application processing and data storage in the **Virtual Desktop Environment (VDE)** or workspace is performed by the server. The thin client computer only has to be powerful enough to display the screen image, play audio, and transfer mouse, key commands and video, and audio information over the network.

All data is stored on the server or in the cloud so it is easier to back up and the desktop VMs are easier to support and troubleshoot. They are better locked against unsecure user practices because any changes to the VM can easily be overwritten from the template image. With VDI, it is also easier for a company to completely offload their IT infrastructure to a third-party services company.

Show
Slide(s)

Virtual Desktops (2 slides)

The main disadvantage is that in the event of a failure in the server and network infrastructure, users have no local processing ability. This can mean that downtime events may be more costly in terms of lost productivity.

VIRTUAL NIC

A virtual machine includes a virtual NIC. However, there will also need to be a physical NIC to get the thin client computer onto the network. These adapters do not have to connect to the same network. The physical NIC might be isolated to a network provisioning the VDI solution. The virtual NIC available from the virtual desktop would connect to the corporate data network and (via the organization's routers) to the Internet.

CLOUD-BASED APPLICATIONS

Show Slide(s)
Cloud-Based Applications

Teaching Tip
Citrix XenApp was formerly MetaFrame / Presentation Server.

Application virtualization is a more limited type of VDI. Rather than run the whole client desktop as a virtual platform, the client either accesses a particular application hosted on a server or streams the application from the server to the client for local processing. This enables programmers and application administrators to ensure that the application used by clients is always updated with the latest code.

Most application virtualization solutions are based on Citrix XenApp. Microsoft has developed an App-V product within its Windows Server range. VMware has the ThinApp product.

OFF-SITE EMAIL APPLICATIONS

Traditionally, most organizations set up and configured their own email server. With cloud computing, the email server can be another off-site service. It might be something like Gmail™ or Yahoo!® Mail. It also might be part of a Office 365 Business Premium, which includes the Exchange email server service. Using an off-site email application to access these off-site email services makes it easier for users to access their mail from multiple devices and locations such as their laptop, desktop, tablet, and smart phone. The mailbox is synchronized so that no matter which device the mail is accessed from, the account accurately indicates which messages have been read, unread, deleted, or moved to other folders.

CLOUD FILE STORAGE

A variety of cloud file storage services are available. These services might be integrated into the Windows File Explorer, or they might have their own dedicated synchronization app, or both. OneDrive® is one cloud file storage service. All Office 365 users receive dedicated storage space for their account. Personal and business OneDrive accounts are separate, but can be linked. OneDrive is integrated into the Windows File Explorer and also has a dedicated OneDrive app that can be installed. OneDrive can also be accessed through a browser. Dropbox™ is another file storage service that can be accessed in the same types of ways. Other cloud file storage services that can be synchronized between all of a user's devices include iCloud® from Apple® and Google Drive™.

In addition to allowing a single user to synchronize content between all of their own devices, the user can also share the cloud storage content with other users. In this case, multiple users can simultaneously access the content to work collaboratively, or they can access it at different times. Each user's changes are typically marked with a flag or color highlighting to indicate who made changes to what content.

VIRTUAL APPLICATION STREAMING

When **virtual application streaming** is implemented, a small piece of the application is typically installed on the end user device. This is just enough of the application for the system to recognize that the application is available to the user. When the user accesses the application, additional portions of the application code are downloaded to the device. Many users only use a small portion of the features available in an application. By downloading only the portions that are being used, the streaming goes quickly, making the user unaware in most cases that the application is being streamed. If additional features are accessed from the application menu, the supporting code for those features is then downloaded. The administrator can configure the streaming application to remove all of the downloaded code, or they can configure it to retain what has been downloaded so it will be faster to load the application the next time the user wants to use it.

CLIENT PLATFORMS

Cloud-based applications can often be deployed for smart cell phones and tablets as well as for laptops and desktops. Typically, the application uses the same base code for all of these platforms, but has additional features that are better supported on laptops and desktops that would be difficult to implement with small screen size, less RAM, and less storage space on a smart phone or tablet. In other instances, the features are the same across all client platforms; it all depends on the features and purpose of the application. By streaming an application or running it in the cloud, much of the memory and storage requirements are eliminated on the client.

CONTAINER VIRTUALIZATION

Container virtualization dispenses with the idea of a hypervisor and instead enforces resource separation at the operating system level. The OS defines isolated containers for each user instance to run in. Each container is allocated CPU and memory resources, but the processes all run through the native OS kernel.

Show Slide(s)
Container Virtualization

These containers may run slightly different OS distributions but cannot run guest OSs of different types (you could not run Windows or Ubuntu® in a RedHat® Linux® container, for instance). Alternatively, the containers might run separate application processes, in which case the variables and libraries required by the application process are added to the container.

One of the best-known container virtualization products is Docker (**docker.com**). Containerization is also being widely used to implement corporate workspaces on mobile devices.

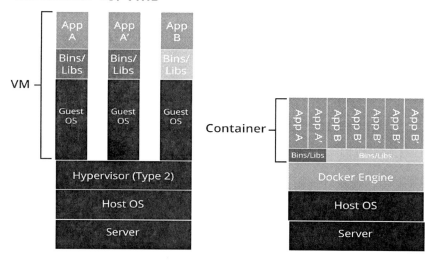

Comparison of Containers versus Virtual Machines.

CLOUD-BASED NETWORK CONTROLLERS

Show Slide(s)

Cloud-Based Network Controllers

When you deploy a network using a mixture of local and cloud-based resources, potentially using different cloud providers, it can be difficult to obtain "visibility" of the whole network from a single management and monitoring interface. For example, you might have an overall network where clients are using multiple wired and wireless local networks to connect, there might be use of Virtual Private Networks (VPNs), some of the organization's servers might be privately controlled, but others might be hosted in the cloud, and so on.

A **cloud-based network controller** allows you to register and monitor some (or perhaps all) of these different component networks, clients, and servers. Cloud-based network controllers (and network controllers generally) depend on **Software Defined Networking (SDN)**. SDN means that network access devices—access points, switches, routers, and firewalls—can be configured using software programs and scripts.

Activity 11-2

Discussing Cloud Computing Concepts

SCENARIO

There has been a lot of talk around the office recently about cloud services. You have heard some other people touting this as the only way to go for storage. In order to be sure of yourself before you join in these conversations, you wrote down some questions and did a little research about them to make sure you know what you are talking about.

1. **How do the five components of cloud computing defined by the NIST work together to provide users with cloud computing services?**

   Resource allocation is provided through rapid elasticity and resource pooling. Resource allocation is requested through on-demand self-service. Broad network access makes the resources available to the user. Measured service enables the provider to meter customer usage and bill the customer accordingly.

2. **Which type of cloud would your organization be likely to use?**

   Answers will vary. Depending on how much control you need over the storage or services provided through the cloud, you might select a private cloud solution as the most secure, and a community cloud solution as the least secure.

3. A cloud service should exhibit rapid elasticity, allow users to access resources on-demand, and pay on a per-use basis.

   What type of service should the provider run to enable these features?

   A measured service with the resources to cope with changing demands.

4. A company has contracted the use of a remote data center to offer exclusive access to Platform as a Service resources to its internal business users.

   How would such a cloud solution be classed?

   Offsite hosted private.

5. When users connect to the network, they use a basic hardware terminal to access a desktop hosted on a virtualization server.

   What type of infrastructure is being deployed?

   Virtual Desktop Infrastructure (VDI).

 Show Slide(s)

Activity: Discussing Cloud Computing Concepts

 Teaching Tip

Consider having learners connect to a free cloud storage site and view the available space and any other information available about the service.

Summary

In this lesson, you examined implementation requirements for client virtualization and cloud computing. The ability to support these and other emerging technologies is very likely to have an impact on the day-to-day responsibilities of an A+ technician.

What types of client-side virtualization technologies does your organization use?

A: Answers will vary, but might include the use of virtual machines to support legacy applications or for training purposes.

What type of cloud computing does your organization use? What other services might you recommend be implemented?

A: Answers will vary, but might include SaaS offerings such as Salesforce Sales Cloud or Office 365. You might suggest infrastructure services be investigated if your organization tends to have fluctuating data storage needs.

 *Practice Question: Additional practice questions are available on the CompTIA CHOICE platform within the **Assessments** tile.*

Lesson 12
Security Concepts

LESSON INTRODUCTION

So far in this course, you have installed and configured PC hardware and software and network devices. Another facet of a CompTIA® A+® technician's duties involves protecting organizational computing assets from attacks. In this lesson, you will identify security threats and vulnerabilities, plus some of the logical and physical controls used to mitigate them.

In today's work environment, cybersecurity is everyone's responsibility. As an A+ technician, you are in the position to identify potential security issues before they become big problems. By identifying security threats and vulnerabilities, as well as some of the controls that can counteract them, you can help keep your organization's computing resources safe from unauthorized access.

LESSON OBJECTIVES

In this lesson, you will:

- Describe logical security concepts.
- Describe physical security threats and vulnerabilities.
- Describe physical security controls.

Topic A

Logical Security Concepts

EXAM OBJECTIVES COVERED
1002-2.2 Explain logical security concepts.
1002-2.7 Given a scenario, implement security best practices to secure a workstation.

 Teaching Tip

This topic aims to give learners an overview of access control systems and the technologies used to implement them.

 Show Slide(s)

Security Basics (2 slides)

 Teaching Tip

"CIA" isn't a content example but it is fundamental to describing the way security systems work.

Logical security refers to the idea that any information or data that is created, stored, and transmitted in digital form is secured to the desired level. This concept applies to many components of the digital world, such as the Internet, cloud-based computing, networks, mobile devices, tablets, laptops, and standard desktop computers.

SECURITY BASICS

Security is the practice of controlling access to something (a resource). Security is always balanced against accessibility; restricting access makes a resource better protected but also less usable. Secure information has three properties, often referred to as the CIA triad:

- **Confidentiality**—this means that certain information should only be known to certain people.
- **Integrity**—this means that the data is stored and transferred as intended and that any modification is authorized.
- **Availability**—this means that information is accessible to those authorized to view or modify it.

Security policies ensure that an organization has evaluated the risks it faces and has put in place controls to mitigate those risks. Making a system more secure is also referred to as **hardening** it. Different security policies should cover every aspect of an organization's use of computer and network technologies, from procurement and change control to acceptable use.

SECURITY CONTROLS

 Show Slide(s)

Security Controls (4 slides)

 Interaction Opportunity

Ask learners if they can think of any other examples.

Security controls are safeguards or prevention methods to avoid, counteract, or minimize security risks relating to personal or company property. For example, a firewall is a type of security control because it controls network communications by allowing only traffic that has specifically been permitted by a system administrator. Security controls can be classified by several criteria, such as by the time that they act relative to a security incident, according to their nature, or by people, technology, and operations/processes. There are different classification schemes, but one way to understand the types of security controls is to consider the following classes:

- Physical controls such as fences, doors, locks, and fire extinguishers.
- Procedural controls such as incident response processes, management oversight, security awareness, and training.
- Logical controls such as user authentication (login) and software-based access controls, antivirus software, and firewalls.
- Legal and regulatory or compliance controls such as privacy laws, policies, and clauses.

LOGICAL SECURITY CONTROLS

Logical security refers to controls implemented in software to create an access control system. The overall operation of an access control system is usually described in terms of three functions, referred to as the AAA triad:

- **Authentication** means one or more methods of proving that a user is who she/he says she/he is.
- **Authorization** means creating one or more barriers around the resource such that only authenticated users can gain access. Each resource has an access control list specifying what users can do. Resources often have different access levels; for example, being able to read a file or being able to read and edit it.
- **Accounting** means recording when and by whom a resource was accessed.

IMPLICIT DENY AND LEAST PRIVILEGE

Logical security is founded on the principle of implicit deny. **Implicit deny** means that unless there is a rule specifying that access should be granted, any request for access is denied. This level of minimal access includes facilities, computing hardware, software, and information.

 Show Slide(s)
Implicit Deny and Least Privilege

This principle can be seen clearly in firewall policies. A firewall filters access requests using a set of rules. The rules are processed in order from top-to-bottom. If a request does not fit any of the rules, it is handled by the last (default) rule, which is to refuse the request.

A complementary principle is that of **least privilege**. This means that a user should be granted rights necessary to perform their job and no more.

 Note: These principles apply equally to users (people) and software processes. Much software is written without regard to the principles of implicit deny and least privilege, making it less secure than it should be.

ENCRYPTION

Many logical security controls depend to some extent on the use of encryption technologies. **Encryption** is an ancient technique for hiding information. Someone obtaining an encrypted document cannot understand that information unless they possesses a key. The use of encryption allows sensitive data to travel across a public network, such as the Internet, and remain private. If the data packets were intercepted and examined, the content would be unreadable.

 Show Slide(s)
Encryption (3 slides)

 Teaching Tip
Encryption isn't called out as a specific objective or example, but many of the security technologies that are examples depend on it.

Ensure that learners are familiar with the different encryption types, examples of encryption algorithms, and the use of digital certificates.

The use of encryption and other digital security techniques provides users with three important security requirements on computer networks: confidentiality, integrity, and authentication. There are three principal types of cryptographic technology: symmetric encryption, asymmetric encryption, and cryptographic hashing. These all have different roles in achieving the goals of confidentiality, integrity, and/or authentication. Often two or more of these three different types are used together in the same product or technology.

 Interaction Opportunity
Point out that symmetric encryption is well suited to confidentiality but not so useful for authentication or integrity. Ask learners to suggest why this is the case (you can't prove a unique identity with a shared key).

SYMMETRIC ENCRYPTION

In symmetric encryption, a single secret key is used to both encrypt and decrypt data. The secret key is so-called because it must be kept secret. If the key is lost or stolen, the security is breached.

 Note: Symmetric encryption is also referred to as single-key or private-key. Note that "private key" is also used to refer to part of the PKI process (discussed shortly), so take care not to confuse the two uses.

The main problem with symmetric encryption is secure distribution and storage of the key. This problem becomes exponentially greater the more widespread the key's distribution needs to be. The main advantage is speed, as symmetric key encryption is less processor intensive than asymmetric encryption.

Symmetric encryption is used to encode data for storage or transmission over a network. The most widely used symmetric encryption technology (or cipher) is the Advanced Encryption Standard (AES). Older ciphers such as Data Encryptions Standard (DES/3DES) and Rivest Cipher (RC) have known weaknesses that make them less suitable for use in modern security systems.

One of the principal measures of the security of an encryption cipher is the size of the key. Early ciphers used between 32- and 64-bit keys. Currently, 1024-bit keys would be selected for general use, with larger keys required for highly sensitive data. The larger the key, however, the more processing is required to perform encryption and decryption.

ASYMMETRIC ENCRYPTION

Teaching Tip

Asymmetric encryption is best suited to authentication.

In asymmetric encryption, if a public key is used to encrypt data, only a mathematically related private key can be used to decrypt it. The private key must be kept a secret known only to a single subject (user or computer). The public key can be widely and safely distributed to anyone with whom the subject wants to communicate, because the private key cannot be derived from the public key. Also, the public key cannot be used to decrypt a message that it has just encrypted.

 Note: A key pair can be used the other way around. If the private key is used to encrypt something, only the public key can then decrypt it. The point is that one type of key cannot reverse the operation it has just performed.

Asymmetric encryption is mostly used for authentication technologies, such as digital certificates and digital signatures, and key exchange. **Key exchange** is where two hosts need to know the same symmetric encryption key without any other host finding out what it is. Symmetric encryption is much faster than asymmetric, so it is often used to protect the actual data exchange in a session. Asymmetric encryption is more complex, taking longer for a computer to process, and so typically only used on small amounts of data, such as the authentication process to set up the session.

Most asymmetric encryption technologies use the **RSA cipher**, named after its designers Ron Rivest, Adi Shamir, and Leonard Adleman.

CRYPTOGRAPHIC HASHES

Teaching Tip

Cryptographic hashing provides the integrity function in most systems. Note that it's not really correct to describe this as encryption. Encryption is a reversible cryptographic process; hashing is a one-way cryptographic process.

A **hash** is a short representation of data. A **hash function** takes a variable-length string (text) as input and produces a fixed-length value (32-bit, for instance) as output. A **cryptographic hash** makes it impossible to recover the original string from the hash value. This technique can be used to prove that a message has not been tampered with (integrity). For example, when creating a digital signature, the sender computes a cryptographic hash of the message and then encrypts the hash with his or her private key. When the recipient receives the message and decrypts the hash, the recipient computes its own hash of the message and compares the two values to confirm they match. Cryptographic hashes are also used for secure storage of data where the original meaning does not have to be recovered (passwords for instance).

Two of the most commonly used cryptographic hash algorithms are **Secure Hash Algorithm** (SHA-1 and SHA-2) and **Message Digest** (MD5). MD5 is the older algorithm and is gradually being phased out of use.

PKI AND CERTIFICATES

Asymmetric encryption is an important part of **Public Key Infrastructure (PKI)**. PKI is a solution to the problem of authenticating subjects on public networks. Under PKI, users or server computers are validated by a **Certificate Authority (CA)**, which issues the subject a digital certificate. The **digital certificate** contains a public key associated with the subject embedded in it. The certificate has also been signed by the CA, guaranteeing its validity. Therefore, if a client trusts the signing CA, they can also trust the user or server presenting the certificate.

The client can then send the server (comptia.org, for example) data (their credit card details, for example) encrypted using the public key, safe in the knowledge that only that particular server will be able to decrypt it (using its private key). A similar technique can be used to encrypt the contents of emails. The sender uses the recipient's public key to encrypt the data with the assurance that only the linked private key can be used to decrypt the data again. PKI can also be used by mobile applications to encrypt any data sent between the client and the server.

Digital certificates are also used for secure authentication to computer networks. The certificate is stored with the private key on a smart card hardware token. To authenticate, the card provides the certificate to the authentication server, which checks that it is valid and trusted. It then uses the public key in the certificate to issue an encrypted challenge to the user. The smart card should be able·to decrypt this challenge using the private key and send an appropriate response.

EXECUTION CONTROL

Authentication and authorization gives subjects the right to sign on to a computer and network and (potentially) to make changes to the system configuration. This places a certain amount of trust in the user to exercise those rights responsibly. Users can act maliciously, though, or could be tricked into an adverse action. **Execution control** refers to logical security technologies designed to prevent malicious software from running on a host. Execution control can establish a security system that does not entirely depend on the good behavior of individual users.

TRUSTED/UNTRUSTED SOFTWARE SOURCES

To prevent the spread of malware such as Trojans, it is necessary to restrict the ability of users to run unapproved program code, especially code that can modify the OS, such as an application installer. Windows uses the system of Administrator and Standard user accounts, along with User Account Control (UAC) and system policies, to enforce these restrictions.

Developers of Windows applications can use digital certificates to perform code signing and prove the authenticity and integrity of an installer package. Linux® also prompts when you attempt to install untrusted software. Software is signed with a cryptographic key. Packages need the public key for the repository in order to install the software. When prompted that you are installing untrusted software, you can either respond that you want to install it anyway or cancel the installation.

Mobile OS vendors use this "walled garden" model of software distribution as well. Apps are distributed from an approved store, such as Apple's App Store or the Windows Store. The vendor's store policies and procedures are supposed to prevent any Trojan-like apps from being published.

There are also third-party network management suites to enforce application control. This means configuring blacklists of unapproved software (allowing anything else) or whitelists of approved software (denying anything else).

Show Slide(s)

PKI and Certificates

Teaching Tip

Don't go into too much detail here; just explain the role of the CA and use of digital certificates.

Note that this example has been simplified. In fact, the public key encrypts a symmetric secret key for the session, rather than encrypting the data exchange directly. This improves performance, as asymmetric encryption works efficiently only on small amounts of data.

Show Slide(s)

Execution Control (5 slides)

Teaching Tip

Point out that you will cover the bulk of best practices (focusing on authentication) in the next topic.

DISABLE AutoRun

One of the problems with legacy versions of Windows is that when an optical disk is inserted or USB or network drive is attached, Windows would automatically run commands defined in an **autorun.inf** file stored in the root of the drive. A typical autorun.inf would define an icon for a disk and the path to a setup file. This could lead to malware being able to install itself automatically.

In modern versions of Windows®, an **AutoPlay** dialog box is shown prompting the user to take a particular action. AutoPlay settings can be configured via a drive's property dialog box. Also, UAC will require the user to explicitly allow any executable code to run. There is a Control Panel applet to configure default AutoPlay actions.

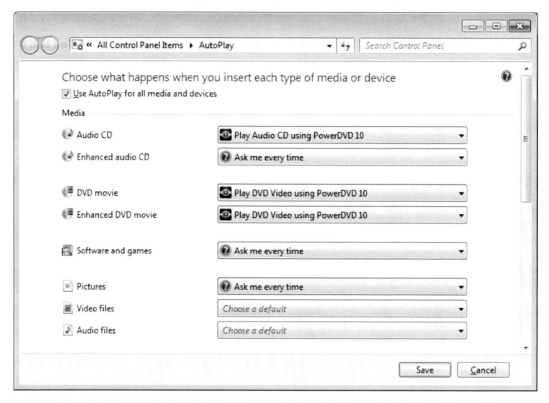

Configuring AutoPlay in Windows 7. (Screenshot used with permission from Microsoft.)

ANTIVIRUS/ANTI-MALWARE

antivirus (A-V) is software that can detect malware and prevent it from executing. The primary means of detection is to use a database of known virus patterns, called definitions, signatures, or patterns. Another technique is to use **heuristic** identification. "Heuristic" means that the software uses knowledge of the sort of things that viruses do to try to spot (and block) virus-like behavior. Most antivirus software is better described as **anti-malware**, as it can detect software threats that are not technically virus-like, including spyware, Trojans, rootkits, and ransomware. It is critical to ensure that the security software is updated regularly.

PATCH MANAGEMENT

It is important to apply critical and security updates for OS and application software. Failing to keep operating systems and software applications up-to-date can cause anything from graphical corruptions when using new video drivers to complete system crashes and vulnerability to malware. That said, there are two approaches to applying updates:

*   Apply all the latest patches to ensure the system is as secure as possible against attacks against flaws in the software.

- Only apply a patch if it solves a particular problem being experienced.

The second approach obviously requires more work, as you need to keep up-to-date with security bulletins. However, it is well recognized that updates can cause problems, especially with software application compatibility. Best practice is to test updates on a non-production system before rolling them out.

 Note: *To check the current build of Windows, run* `winver`. *To check the version number of a particular file, right-click and select **Properties**.*

NAC

Show Slide(s)
NAC (3 slides)

Firewalls are principally deployed to manage access between networks. They control communications by blocking packets based on access rules permitting or denying certain combinations of IP addresses and network ports, or other filtering criteria.

Firewalls cannot control whether a device can connect to a network in the first place. **Defense in depth**, or endpoint security, refers to controls that monitor the security of a network "behind" the perimeter firewall. **Network Access Control (NAC)** allows administrators to devise policies or profiles describing a minimum security configuration that devices must meet to be granted network access. This is called a **health policy**. Typical policies check things such as malware infection, firmware and OS patch level, personal firewall status, and the presence of up-to-date virus definitions. A solution may also be to scan the registry or perform file signature verification. The health policy is defined on a NAC management server along with reporting and configuration tools.

PHYSICAL PORT SECURITY

With wired ports, access to the physical switch ports and switch hardware should be restricted to authorized staff, using a secure server room and/or lockable hardware cabinets. To prevent the attachment of unauthorized client devices, a switch port can be disabled using the management software or the patch cable can be physically removed from the port. Completely disabling ports in this way can introduce a lot of administrative overhead and scope for error. Also, it doesn't provide complete protection as an attacker could unplug a device from an enabled port and connect their own laptop. Consequently, more sophisticated methods of ensuring port security have been developed.

MAC ADDRESS FILTERING

Configuring **MAC filtering** on a switch means defining which MAC addresses are allowed to connect to a particular port. This can be done by creating a list of valid MAC addresses or by specifying a limit to the number of permitted addresses. For example, if port security is enabled with a maximum of two MAC addresses, the switch will record the first two MACs to connect to that port but then drop any traffic from machines with different network adapter IDs that try to connect.

Many devices also support **whitelisting** and/or **blacklisting** of MAC addresses. A MAC address added to a whitelist is permitted to connect to any port, whereas a MAC address on a blacklist is prohibited from connecting to any port.

PORT SECURITY / IEEE 802.1X

The IEEE 802.1X standard defines a **Port-based Network Access Control (PNAC)** mechanism. PNAC means that the switch (or router) performs some sort of authentication of the attached device before activating the port.

Teaching Tip

Make sure learners are familiar with 802.1X terminology: supplicants and authenticators, for instance.

Under 802.1X, the device requesting access is the **supplicant**. The switch, referred to as the authenticator, enables the **Extensible Authentication Protocol over LAN (EAPoL)** protocol only and waits for the device to supply authentication data. Using

EAP, this data could be a simple username/password (EAP-MD5) or could involve using a digital certificate or token. The authenticator passes this data to an authenticating server, which checks the credentials and grants or denies access.

MDM

Show Slide(s)

MDM

Mobile Device Management (MDM) is a class of management software designed to apply security policies to the use of mobile devices in the enterprise. This software can be used to manage enterprise-owned devices as well as **Bring Your Own Device (BYOD)**.

The core functionality of these suites is similar to Network Access Control (NAC) solutions. The management software logs the use of a device on the network and determines whether to allow it to connect or not, based on administrator-set parameters. When the device is enrolled with the management software, it can be configured with policies to allow or restrict use of apps, corporate data, and built-in functions, such as a video camera or microphone.

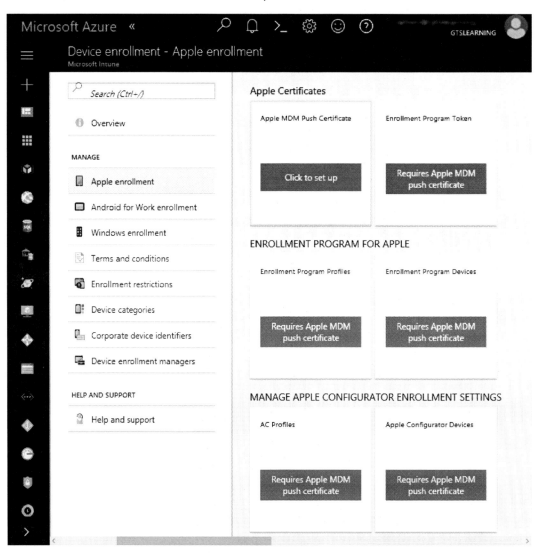

Configuring iOS device enrollment in Microsoft's Intune Enterprise Mobility Management (EMM) suite. Used with permission from Microsoft.

VPN

As well as allowing hosts to connect over wired or wireless local connections, most networks have to allow devices to connect remotely, to support home workers, field workers, branch offices, partners, suppliers, and customers. A remote connection is obviously easier for external attackers to try to exploit than a local one, so remote access must be subject to stringent security policies and controls.

A Virtual Private Network (VPN) connects the components and resources of two (private) networks over another (public) network. A VPN is a "tunnel" through the Internet (or any other public network). It uses special connection protocols and encryption technology to ensure that the tunnel is secure and the user is properly authenticated. Once the connection has been established, to all intents and purposes, the remote computer becomes part of the local network (though it is still restricted by the bandwidth available over the WAN link).

With a VPN, TCP/IP communications are encrypted and then packaged within another TCP/IP packet stream. The VPN hardware or software can encrypt just the underlying data in a packet or the entire packet itself before wrapping it in another IP packet for delivery. If a packet on the public network is intercepted along the way, the encrypted contents cannot be read by a hacker. Such encryption of data or packets is typically implemented by using a protocol suite called **Internet Protocol Security** (IPSec).

A remote access request is only granted if the user authenticates correctly and the account has been given remote (or "dial-in") permission. The client device could also be subject to NAC policy checks before it is allowed to fully join the VPN.

Show Slide(s)

VPN

Activity 12-1
Discussing Logical Security Concepts

Show Slide(s)

Activity: Discussing Logical Security Concepts

SCENARIO

Answer the following questions to check your understanding of the topic.

1. Confidentiality and integrity are two important properties of information stored in a secure retrieval system.

    What is the third property?

    Availability—information that is inaccessible is not of much use to authorized users. For example, a secure system must protect against Denial of Service (DoS) attacks.

2. While you are assigning privileges to the accounting department in your organization, Cindy, a human resource administrative assistant, insists that she needs access to the employee records database so that she can fulfill change of address requests from employees. After checking with her manager and referring to the organization's access control security policy, Cindy's job role does not fall into the authorized category for access to that database.

    What security concept is being practiced in this scenario?

    The principle of least privilege.

3. **What distinguishes a cryptographic hash from the output of an encryption algorithm?**

    An encrypted ciphertext can be decrypted by using the correct key; a cryptographic hash is irreversibly scrambled.

4. **What type of cryptographic algorithm is AES?**

    The Advanced Encryption Standard (AES) is a symmetric encryption cipher. This means that the same key can be used to perform both encryption and decryption operations on a message.

5. **What type of cryptographic key is delivered in a digital certificate?**

    A digital certificate is a wrapper for a subject's public key. The public and private keys in an asymmetric cipher are paired. If one key is used to encrypt a message, only the other key can then decrypt it.

6. John brought in the new tablet he just purchased and tried to connect to the corporate network. He knows the SSID of the wireless network and the password used to access the wireless network. He was denied access, and a warning message was displayed that he must contact the IT Department immediately.

What happened and why did he receive the message?

John's new tablet probably does not meet the compliance requirements for network access. Being a new device, it might not have had updates and patches applied, it might not have appropriate virus protection installed, or it does not meet some other compliance requirement. This caused the system to appear as a non-compliant system to the network, and network access was denied.

7. **What type of network access is facilitated by VPN?**

A Virtual Private Network (VPN) is often deployed to provide remote access to users who cannot otherwise make a physical connection an office network. A remote access VPN means that the user can connect to a private network using a public network for transport. Encryption and authentication are used to make sure the connection is private and only available to authorized users. You might also mention that VPNs can be used to other types of access (such as connecting one network site to another).

Topic B
Threats and Vulnerabilities

 Teaching Tip

This topic tries to give learners an overview of what might threaten network security and what might make the network vulnerable to such threats.

 Show Slide(s)

Vulnerabilities, Threats, and Risks

 Teaching Tip

Emphasize the differences between vulnerabilities, threats, and risks.

 Show Slide(s)

Social Engineering Threats

 Teaching Tip

You can refer learners to Kevin Mitnick's books; Bruce Schneier's website is also a good resource. Point out that social engineering is not only about telephone or personal contact; email and IM are also dangerous because it is so easy to impersonate another user.

It's worth talking about the risks of social networking sites and how much personal information can be exposed through profiles on Facebook, etc.

 Interaction Opportunity

Ask learners if they have experienced social engineering attacks or attempts, and ask them to give examples.

EXAM OBJECTIVES COVERED

1002-2.5 Compare and contrast social engineering, threats, and vulnerabilities.

In this topic, you will distinguish the concepts of threats, vulnerabilities, and controls. By identifying common security threats and vulnerabilities, you will be better equipped to suggest or implement the most effective counteractive measures.

VULNERABILITIES, THREATS, AND RISKS

In IT security, it is important to distinguish between the concepts of vulnerability, threat, and risk:

* **Vulnerability**—a weakness that could be triggered accidentally or exploited intentionally to cause a security breach.
* **Threat**—the potential for a **threat agent** or **threat actor** (something or someone that may trigger a vulnerability accidentally or exploit it intentionally) to "exercise" a vulnerability (that is, to breach security). The path or tool used by the threat actor can be referred to as the threat vector.
* **Risk**—the likelihood and impact (or consequence) of a threat actor exercising a vulnerability.

To understand network security, you need to understand the types of threats that a network is exposed to and how vulnerabilities can be exploited to launch actual attacks.

SOCIAL ENGINEERING THREATS

Much of the focus in computer security is in deterring malicious external and insider threats. Attackers can use a diverse range of techniques to compromise a security system. A pre-requisite of many types of attack is to obtain information about the security system. **Social engineering** refers to means of getting users to reveal this kind of confidential information or allowing some sort of access to the organization that should not have been authorized. A social engineering attack uses deception and trickery to convince unsuspecting users to provide sensitive data or to violate security guidelines. Social engineering is often a precursor to another type of attack.

It is also important to note that gaining access to a network is often based on a series of small steps rather than a single large step. That is, knowing the email address of an employee allows an attacker to search for facts about that user online. This might help target the user with fake messages. A message might be convincing enough to persuade the user to reveal some confidential information or install some malware. The malware allows the attacker to access the network and try to discover the ID of a more privileged account or the location of important data files.

Because these attacks depend on human factors rather than on technology, their symptoms can be vague and hard to identify. Social engineering attacks can come in a variety of methods: in person, through email, or over the phone. Social engineering typically takes advantage of users who are not technically knowledgeable, but it can

Show Slide(s)
Common Social Engineering Exploits

also be directed against technical support staff if the attacker pretends to be a user who needs help.

COMMON SOCIAL ENGINEERING EXPLOITS

Preventing social engineering attacks requires an awareness of the most common forms of social engineering exploits.

IMPERSONATION

Impersonation (pretending to be someone else) is one of the basic social engineering techniques. The classic impersonation attack is for an attacker to phone into a department, claim they have to adjust something on the user's system remotely, and get the user to reveal their password.

Attackers will generally try one of the following methods to make an impersonation attack convincing:

- Intimidate their target by pretending to be someone senior in rank.
- Intimidate the target by using spurious technical arguments and jargon or alarm them with a hoax.
- Coax the target by engaging with them in and putting them at their ease.

Do you really know who's on the other end of the line? (Photo by Uros Jovicic on Unsplash.)

PHISHING AND SPEAR PHISHING

Phishing is a combination of social engineering and **spoofing** (disguising one computer resource as another). The attacker sets up a spoof website to imitate a target bank or ecommerce provider's secure website. The attacker then emails users of the genuine website informing them that their account must be updated, supplying a disguised link that actually leads to their spoofed site. When the user authenticates with the spoofed site, their log on details are captured. Another technique is to spawn a "pop-up" window when a user visits a genuine site to try to trick them into entering their credentials through the pop-up.

Spear phishing refers to a phishing scam where the attacker has some information that makes the target more likely to be fooled by the attack. The attacker might know the name of a document that the target is editing, for instance, and send a malicious copy, or the phishing email might show that the attacker knows the recipient's full name, job title, telephone number, or other details that help to convince the target that the communication is genuine.

PHARMING

Pharming is another means of redirecting users from a legitimate website to a malicious one. Rather than using social engineering techniques to trick the user, however, pharming relies on corrupting the way the victim's computer performs Internet name resolution, so that they are redirected from the genuine site to the malicious one. For example, if mybank.com should point to the IP address w.x.y.z, a pharming attack would corrupt the name resolution process to make it point to IP address a.b.c.d.

TRUST AND DUMPSTER DIVING

Being convincing or establishing trust usually depends on the attacker obtaining privileged information about the organization or about an individual. For example, an impersonation attack is much more effective if the attacker knows the user's name. As most companies are set up toward customer service rather than security, this information is typically easy to come by. Information that might seem innocuous, such as department employee lists, job titles, phone numbers, diary appointments, invoices, or purchase orders, can help an attacker penetrate an organization through impersonation.

Another way to obtain information that will help to make a social engineering attack credible is by obtaining documents that the company has thrown away. **Dumpster diving** refers to combing through an organization's (or individual's) garbage to try to find useful documents. Attackers may even find files stored on discarded removable media.

 Note: Remember that attacks may be staged over a long period of time. Initial attacks may only aim at compromising low-level information and user accounts, but this low-level information can be used to attack more sensitive and confidential data and better protected management and administrative accounts.

SHOULDER SURFING

Shoulder surfing refers to stealing a password or PIN, or other secure information, by watching the user type it. Despite the name, the attacker may not have to be in close proximity to the target. They could use high-power binoculars or CCTV to directly observe the target from a remote location.

TAILGATING

Tailgating (or piggybacking) is a means of entering a secure area without authorization by following close behind the person that has been allowed to open the door or checkpoint. This might be done without the target's knowledge or may be a means for an insider to allow access to someone without recording it in the building's entry log. Another technique is to persuade someone to hold a door open, using an excuse such as "I've forgotten my badge/key."

 Show Slide(s)

Mitigation of Social Engineering Attacks

 Teaching Tip

Another important point is training users to interpret browser warnings about digital certificates accurately. Most users understand that a website is only secure and authenticated if it has a digital certificate and is accessed via the HTTPS protocol. Phishers will attempt to craft a digital certificate for the site to make it more credible.

MITIGATION OF SOCIAL ENGINEERING ATTACKS

Social engineering is best defeated by training users to recognize and respond to such situations.

- Train employees to release information or make privileged use of the system only according to standard procedures.
- Establish a reporting system for suspected attacks—though the obvious risk here is that a large number of false negatives will be reported.
- Train employees to identify phishing-style attacks plus new styles of attack as they develop in the future.
- Train employees not to release any work-related information on third-party sites or social networks (and especially not to reuse passwords used for accounts at work).

Other measures include ensuring documents and information is destroyed before disposal, using multifactor access control, to put more than one or two barriers between an attacker and his or her target, and restricting use of administrative accounts as far as possible.

 Show Slide(s)

Network Footprinting Threats (2 slides)

 Teaching Tip

Exam candidates need to know what information can be obtained via a scanning attack.

NETWORK FOOTPRINTING THREATS

Footprinting is another information-gathering threat, in which the attacker attempts to learn about the configuration of the network and security systems. Footprinting can be accomplished by social engineering attacks. There are also many software-based tools and techniques for gathering information.

 Note: Footprinting describes investigating the overall network and security topology, whereas fingerprinting describes probes that attempt to discover how a particular host is configured.

OPEN PORTS

Network mapping refers to tools that gather information about the way the network is built and configured and the current status of hosts. One approach to protecting a network from unwanted footprinting or fingerprinting is to prevent unauthorized hosts from connecting at all. An "open port" in this sense is an Ethernet port that allows any computer to connect to the switch. Ethernet ports can be physically or administratively disabled to prevent this, though that would not stop an attacker from unplugging an authorized machine and connecting a different one. There are various Network Access Control (NAC) or endpoint security solutions that can require devices to authenticate before network access is granted.

As well as the physical Ethernet port, an "open port" can also refer to a TCP or UDP network application port. **Port scanning** aims to enumerate the TCP or UDP application ports on a host that are accepting connections. The `netstat` tool can be used on Windows and Linux to investigate open connections on the local computer. More advanced probes, such as `nmap`, can discover a good deal more information about a host.

```
C:\Windows\system32>netstat -b -n

Active Connections

  Proto  Local Address          Foreign Address        State
  TCP    192.168.1.110:5806     185.41.10.123:80       CLOSE_WAIT
 [IEXPLORE.EXE]
  TCP    192.168.1.110:5807     185.41.10.123:80       CLOSE_WAIT
 [IEXPLORE.EXE]
  TCP    192.168.1.110:5808     216.58.208.40:443      ESTABLISHED
 [IEXPLORE.EXE]
  TCP    192.168.1.110:5809     216.58.208.40:443      ESTABLISHED
 [IEXPLORE.EXE]
  TCP    192.168.1.110:5810     104.27.151.216:80      CLOSE_WAIT
 [IEXPLORE.EXE]
  TCP    192.168.1.110:5811     104.27.151.216:80      CLOSE_WAIT
 [IEXPLORE.EXE]
  TCP    192.168.1.110:5812     104.27.151.216:80      CLOSE_WAIT
 [IEXPLORE.EXE]
  TCP    192.168.1.110:5813     104.27.151.216:80      CLOSE_WAIT
 [IEXPLORE.EXE]
  TCP    192.168.1.110:5814     104.27.151.216:80      CLOSE_WAIT
 [IEXPLORE.EXE]
  TCP    192.168.1.110:5815     104.27.151.216:80      CLOSE_WAIT
 [IEXPLORE.EXE]
  TCP    192.168.1.110:5816     52.28.192.217:443      ESTABLISHED
 [IEXPLORE.EXE]
  TCP    [fe80::5c9e:8be5:bb3e:f341%4]:2179  [fe80::5c9e:8be5:bb3e:f341%4]:5519
 ESTABLISHED
 [vmms.exe]
  TCP    [fe80::5c9e:8be5:bb3e:f341%4]:3587  [fe80::5cf0:94fe:4f4:a8a%4]:57395
 ESTABLISHED
  p2psvc
 [svchost.exe]
  TCP    [fe80::5c9e:8be5:bb3e:f341%4]:5519  [fe80::5c9e:8be5:bb3e:f341%4]:2179
 ESTABLISHED
 [VmConnect.exe]

C:\Windows\system32>_
```

Displaying open connections with netstat. (Screenshot used with permission from Microsoft.)

When a host running a particular operating system responds to a port scan, the syntax of the response might identify the specific operating system. This fact is also true of application servers, such as web servers, FTP servers, and mail servers. The responses these servers make often include several headers or banners that can reveal a great deal of information about the server.

Ports can be closed by disabling unnecessary or unused protocols, services, and applications. If a service must be run, a port can be blocked on a particular interface or restricted to certain hosts using an Access Control List (ACL) enforced by a firewall.

Port scanning tools are also useful defensive tools because a network administrator needs to ensure that unauthorized ports are not open on the network. These could be a sign of some sort of Trojan or backdoor server. Such tools often try to hide themselves from diagnostic port scans.

EAVESDROPPING THREATS

Show Slide(s)

Eavesdropping Threats

Teaching Tip

If you have time, you might want to demonstrate use of Wireshark.

Eavesdropping (or sniffing) refers to capturing and reading data packets as they move over the network. When an attacker (for example, a malicious user) has gained access to the network, they can use a packet sniffer such as Wireshark® to capture live network traffic. Unless the packets are encrypted, the attacker can gain a lot of information about the way the network is designed as well as intercepting any data transmitted in plaintext.

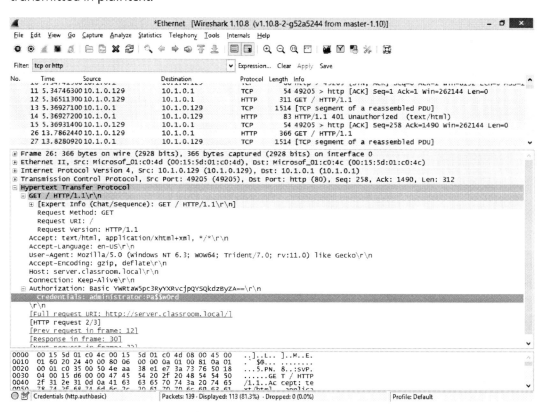

Capturing basic HTTP authentication in Wireshark.

In the first instance, an attack would be limited to data traffic to and from the individual user's computer (as well as broadcast traffic) as network switches will prevent all other traffic from being directed to that computer. However, switches can be subverted by various different types of attack:

- **MAC flooding**—overloading the switch's MAC cache, referred to as the **Content Addressable Memory (CAM) table**, using a tool such as Dsniff or Ettercap to prevent genuine devices from connecting and potentially forcing the switch into "hub" or "flooding" mode.

- **ARP poisoning**—the attacker poisons the switch's ARP table with a false MAC-IP address mapping, typically allowing the attacker to masquerade as the subnet's default gateway.

 Note: *A packet sniffer is a defensive as well as an offensive tool. It can be used to try to detect network intrusions and unauthorized and malicious traffic.*

SPOOFING AND MITM THREATS

 Show Slide(s)
Spoofing and MITM Threats

Having gathered information about a network, an attacker may be able to probe or damage it by launching further attacks. Many of the network, transport, and application protocols in use on private networks and the Internet were designed without any regard for security. Protocols such as TCP or UDP are vulnerable to packet sniffing because they were designed to transmit information in plain text. Devices communicating using these protocols do not typically authenticate with one another, making them vulnerable to spoofing, Denial of Service, and Man-in-the-Middle attacks.

 Show Slide(s)
Password Attacks

SPOOFING AND PACKET/PROTOCOL ABUSE

The term spoofing (or impersonation or masquerade) covers a very wide range of different attacks. Social engineering and techniques such as phishing and pharming are types of spoofing attack. It also possible to abuse the way a protocol works or network packets are constructed to inject false or modified data onto a network. The ARP poisoning attack described earlier is a good example of this. The ARP and DNS protocols are often used as vectors for spoofing attacks.

Spoofing can also be performed by obtaining a logical token or software token. A logical token is assigned to a user or computer when they authenticate to some service. A token might be implemented as a web cookie, for instance. If an attacker can steal the token and the authorization system has not been designed well, the attacker may be able to present the token again and impersonate the original user. This type of spoofing is also called a **replay attack**.

MAN-IN-THE-MIDDLE ATTACK

A **Man-in-the-Middle (MITM)** attack is another specific type of spoofing attack where the attacker sits between two communicating hosts and transparently monitors, captures, and relays all communication between them. Man-in-the-middle attacks are used to gain access to authentication and network infrastructure information for future attacks, or to gain direct access to packet contents.

For example, in an ARP poisoning attack, the attacker sends spoofed ARP messages onto the network to associate his IP address with another host, typically the subnet's default gateway. The rest of the network hosts will then start communicating with the attacker, who will be able to sniff the packets and either send them on to the genuine host (to try to keep the attack covert), send modified versions of the packets, or drop them (performing a Denial of Service attack).

MitM attacks can be defeated using **mutual authentication**, where both server and client exchange secure credentials.

PASSWORD ATTACKS

Computer systems are protected by accounts and accounts are protected by credentials, typically passwords. Passwords can be discovered via social engineering or because a user has written one down. Packet sniffing attacks are often launched with the purpose of obtaining credentials for one or more accounts. If a network protocol uses cleartext credentials, then the attacker's job is done. Most passwords are only

 Teaching Tip
Technically, passwords are not usually encrypted, as encryption implies the possibility of decryption. A password is cryptographically protected using a one-way hash function.

Explain how a password might be vulnerable to these attacks. A password filled with random alphanumeric and symbol characters that is only 6 characters long is far more vulnerable than a 20-character password of words from a dictionary strung together (unless the attacker knows that you like to choose passwords by stringing together x number of words from a dictionary!).

Point out that where web servers are compromised, their password databases are often sold online and accounts protected by weak passwords will be discovered very quickly. If a user has then used the same password for all their online accounts, the security of their "digital identity" is very definitely at risk.

sent over the network or stored on a device using some sort of cryptographic protection, however.

> **Note:** *A password might be sent in an encoded form, such as Base64, which is simply an ASCII representation of binary data. This is not the same as cryptography. The password value can easily be derived from the Base64 string.*

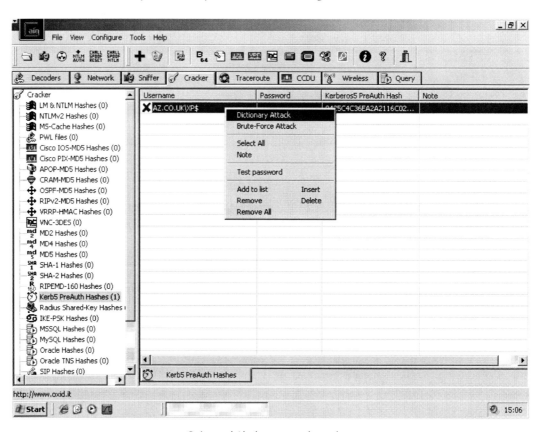

Cain and Abel password cracker.

Either the channel can be protected or the password can be protected (or both). If the channel is encrypted, the attacker has to compromise the encryption keys stored on the server. If the password is protected by a cryptographic hash, the attacker might be able to use password cracking software to decipher it.

TYPES OF PASSWORD ATTACKS

Show Slide(s)

Types of Password Attacks

A cryptographic hash scrambles the data in a way that the original plaintext password is normally unrecoverable. However, the cryptographic hash function might be vulnerable to these types of attacks:

- **Dictionary**—the password cracker matches the hash to those produced by ordinary words found in a dictionary. This could also include information such as user and company names or pet names or any other data that people might naively use as passwords.
- **Brute force**—the software tries to match the hash against one of every possible combination it could be. If the password is short (under 7 characters) and non-complex (using only letters, for instance), a password might be cracked in minutes. Longer and more complex passwords increase the amount of time the attack takes to run.

RAINBOW TABLE ATTACKS

A dictionary attack can be used where there is a good chance of guessing the likely value of the plaintext. **Rainbow tables** refine the dictionary approach. The technique was developed by Phillipe Oechsli and used in his Ophcrack Windows password cracker. The attacker uses a precomputed lookup table of all probable plaintext passwords (derived from the dictionary) and their matching hashes. Not all possible hash values are stored, as this would require too much memory. Values are computed in "chains" and only the first and last values need to be stored. The hash value of a stored password can then be looked up in the table and the corresponding plaintext discovered.

The hash functions used to store passwords can be made more secure by adding salt. Salt is a random value added to the plaintext. This helps to slow down rainbow table attacks against a hashed password database, as the table cannot be created in advance and must be recreated for each combination of password and salt value. Rainbow tables are also impractical when trying to discover long passwords (over about 14 characters). UNIX and Linux password storage mechanisms use salt, but Windows does not. Consequently, in a Windows environment it is even more important to enforce password policies, such as selecting a strong password and changing it periodically.

DENIAL OF SERVICE ATTACKS

A **Denial of Service (DoS)** attack causes a service at a given host to fail or to become unavailable to legitimate users. Typically, DoS attacks focus on overloading a service. It is also possible for DoS attacks to exploit design failures or other vulnerabilities in application software. An example of a physical DoS attack would be cutting telephone lines or network cabling. DoS attacks may simply be motivated by the malicious desire to cause trouble. They may also be part of a wider attack, such as a precursor to a DNS spoofing attack.

DISTRIBUTED DoS (DDoS) ATTACKS/BOTNETS

Network-based DoS attacks are normally accomplished by flooding the server with bogus requests. They rely on the attacker having access to greater bandwidth than the target or on the target being required to devote more resources to each connection than the attacker. There are many different methods of achieving this, often exploiting weaknesses in protocols.

Most bandwidth-directed DoS attacks are **Distributed DoS (DDoS)**. This means that the attacks are launched from multiple compromised systems, referred to as a **botnet**. To establish a botnet, an attacker will first compromise one or two machines to use as "handlers" or "masters." The handlers are used to compromise multiple **zombie** devices with DoS tools (bots). In this way, the attacker can conceal his or her activities. This is also referred to as an asymmetric threat, because the attacker's resources can be far less than those of the victim.

Show Slide(s)

Denial of Service Attacks (4 slides)

Teaching Tip

The defenses against network-based DoS attacks are principally firewalls, IPS, and application patches.

The "Storm Worm" represents a breed of botnet. The control network functions in a "peer-to-peer" manner and the software and control mechanisms are continually updated to evade detection and removal.

Also note that botnets can be leveraged to perform almost any function. In the future, they could be used to brute force encryption keys, for instance. Spam and phishing are probably more typical than DoS.

It's worth stressing the degree to which malware creation has become "professionalized" and now forms a substantial "shadow economy."

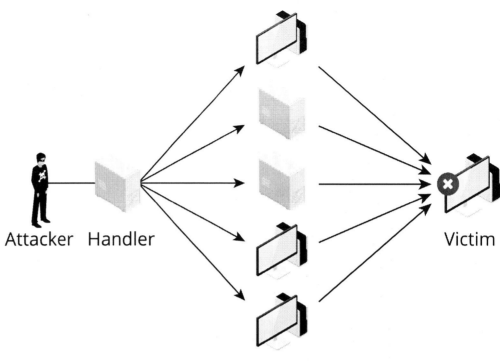

Attacker   Handler

Victim

Zombie/Drone Devices

DDoS attacks using zombies/drones. (Image © 123RF.com.)

Show Slide(s)

Vulnerabilities and Zero-Day Exploits

Teaching Tip

Protection against software exploitation comes from applying security patches (for third-party applications) or secure programming practice (for your own applications).

Discuss zero-day exploits (that is, a software vulnerability that is exploited before a fix becomes available).

Most of these attacks are directed against database-backed websites. Targets include banks, ecommerce, and social networking sites.

The growing use of Software as a Service (online CRM applications, for instance) also poses a tempting target.

Large botnets are necessary to overcome the high bandwidth of targets. The increasing use of "always-on" broadband connections means that attackers can target a large base of naïve home users with the aim of compromising their PCs. Also, any Internet-connected device can potentially be infected and used as a bot. Devices such as webcams that can be configured over the Internet are often vulnerable.

Once the bot is installed, the attacker has a backdoor that gives them access to the device. They can then use the backdoor to install DDoS tools and trigger the zombies to launch the attack at the same time. As well as a single attacker using a botnet, DDoS attacks might be coordinated between groups of attackers. There is growing evidence that nation states are engaging in **cyber warfare** and terrorist groups have also been implicated in DDoS attacks on well-known companies and government institutions. There are also **hacker collectives** who might target an organization as part of a campaign.

VULNERABILITIES AND ZERO-DAY EXPLOITS

Software exploitation means an attack that targets a vulnerability in OS or application software or device firmware. A vulnerability is a design flaw that can cause the application security system to be circumvented or that will cause the application to crash. The most serious vulnerabilities allow the attacker to execute arbitrary code on the system, which could allow the installation of malware. Malicious code that can successfully use a vulnerability to compromise a host is called an "exploit."

Note: This issue does not just affect PCs. Any type of network appliance or device can also be vulnerable to exploits. The risks to embedded systems have become more obvious and the risks posed by unpatched mobile devices and the "Internet of Things" is likely to grow.

Typically, vulnerabilities can only be exploited in quite specific circumstances, but because of the complexity of modern software and the speed with which new versions must be released to market, almost no software is free from vulnerabilities. Most vulnerabilities are discovered by software and security researchers, who notify the vendor to give them time to patch the vulnerability before releasing details to the wider public. A vulnerability that is exploited before the developer knows about it or can release a patch is called a **zero-day** exploit. It is called "zero-day" because the developer has had zero days to fix the flaw. These can be extremely destructive, as it can take the vendor a lot of time to develop a patch, leaving systems vulnerable for days, weeks, or even years.

While some zero-day attacks can be extremely destructive, they are relatively rare. A greater risk is the large number of unpatched or legacy systems in use. An unpatched or non-compliant system is one that its owner has not updated with OS and application patches or installed with A-V and firewall security software. A **legacy** system is one where the software vendor no longer provides support or fixes for problems.

 Note: There is a class of network security software described as Network Access Control (NAC) that scans devices as they attempt to join and use the network and denies access if they are non-compliant with regard to a "system health" or Standard Operating Environment (SOE) policy.

Activity 12-2
Discussing Threats and Vulnerabilities

Show Slide(s)

Activity: Discussing Threats and Vulnerabilities

SCENARIO

Answer the following questions to check your understanding of the topic.

1. **What do all types of social engineering attack have in common?**

   Many different of attacks can be classed as a type of social engineering, but they all exploit some weakness in the way people behave (through manipulation and deception). These weaknesses might arise from politeness and cultural norms, from habitual behavior, or from respect for authority and rank.

2. An attacker crafts an email addressed to a senior support technician inviting him to register for free football coaching advice. The website contains password-stealing malware.

   What is the name of this type of attack?

   A phishing attack tries to make users authenticate with a fake resource, such as a website that appears to be a genuine online banking portal. Phishing emails are often sent in mass as spam. This is a variant of phishing called spear phishing, because it is specifically targeted at a single person, using personal information known about the subject (such as his or her hobbies).

3. **What is the difference between tailgating and shoulder surfing?**

   Tailgating means following someone else through a door or gateway to enter premises without authorization. Shoulder surfing means observing someone type a PIN or password or other confidential data.

4. **What type of software is typically used to perform eavesdropping on an Ethernet network?**

   A packet sniffer or packet capture utility. When combined with software to decode the frames, these can also be called packet analyzers or network monitors.

5. **What attack might be launched to eavesdrop on all communications passing over a local network segment?**

   Address Resolution Protocol (ARP) poisoning or spoofing. This is a type of Man-in-the-Middle attack.

6. An attacker learns that a system policy causes passwords to be configured with a random mix of different characters but that are only five characters in length.

What type of password cracking attack would work best here?

Brute force attacks are effective against short passwords (under seven characters). Dictionary attacks depend on users choosing ordinary words or phrases in a password.

7. What is the difference between a DoS and a DDoS attack?

Denial of Service (DoS) is any type of attack that halts or disrupts a network application or resource. A Distributed Denial of Service (DDoS) is a specific class of DoS attack. It means that the attacker uses multiple hosts to launch the attack. The distributed hosts are usually PCs and other devices (zombies) compromised by malware (bots) controlled by the attacker.

8. With what type of threat is a "zero day" associated?

A zero day is a type of software exploit. You could also say that it is associated with hacking and malware threats. The term arises because an attacker has found a means of exploiting a vulnerability in the software before the software developer has been able to create a patch or fix for the vulnerability.

Topic C

Physical Security Measures

 EXAM OBJECTIVES COVERED
1002-2.1 Summarize the importance of physical security measures.
1002-2.9 Given a scenario, implement appropriate data destruction and disposal methods.

 Teaching Tip

This topic is quite straightforward, so you may prefer to designate it as self-study if time is short.

Physical security refers to the implementation and practice of control methods that are intended to restrict physical access to facilities. One case where physical security is important is when there is a need to control access to physical documents, password records, and sensitive documents and equipment. One successful unauthorized access attempt can lead to financial losses, credibility issues, and legalities. In addition, physical security involves increasing or assuring the reliability of certain critical infrastructure elements such as switches, routers, and servers.

PHYSICAL SECURITY CONTROLS

 Show Slide(s)

Physical Security Controls

Physical security measures means controlling who can access a building or a secure area of a building, such as a server room. One of the oldest types of security is a wall with a door in it (or a fence with a gate). In order to secure such a gateway, it must be fitted with a lock or door access system.

LOCK TYPES

 Show Slide(s)

Lock Types

Door locks can be categorized as follows:

- **Conventional**—a conventional lock prevents the door handle from being operated without the use of a key. More expensive types offer greater resistance against lock picking.
- **Deadbolt**—this is a bolt on the frame of the door, separate to the handle mechanism.
- **Electronic**—rather than a key, the lock is operated by entering a PIN on an electronic keypad. This type of lock is also referred to as cipher, combination, or keyless.
- **Token-based**—a smart lock may be opened using a magnetic swipe card or feature a proximity reader to detect the presence of a wireless key fob or one-time password generator (physical tokens) or smart card.
- **Biometric**—a lock may be integrated with a biometric scanner, so that the lock can be activated by biometric features, such as a fingerprint, voice print, or retina scan. Biometric locks make it more difficult for someone to counterfeit the key used to open the lock.
- **Multifactor**—a lock may combine different methods, such as smart card with PIN.

A secure gateway will normally be self-closing and self-locking, rather than depending on the user to close and lock it.

TURNSTILES AND MANTRAPS

 Show Slide(s)

Turnstiles and Mantraps

Tailgating is a means of entering a secure area without authorization by following close behind the person who has been allowed to open the door or checkpoint. Training and a strict policy can mitigate the sort of instinctive politeness that causes employees to "co-operate" with this type of attack. Effective training should also ensure that employees keep doors locked to protect secure areas, such as server and equipment rooms. Gateways can also have improved physical security, such as CCTV monitoring or the presence of a security guard.

Another option is a turnstile or a mantrap. A **mantrap** is two sets of interlocking doors inside a small space, where the first set of doors must close before the second set opens. If the mantrap is manual, a guard locks and unlocks each door in sequence. In this case, an intercom or video camera is typically used to allow the guard to control the trap from a remote location. If the mantrap is automatic, identification or a key of some kind may be required for each door, and sometimes different measures may be required for each door. Metal detectors are often built in to prevent entrance of people carrying weapons. Such use is particularly frequent in banks and jewelry shops.

SECURITY GUARDS

Human security guards, armed or unarmed, can be placed in front of and around a location to protect it. They can monitor critical checkpoints and verify identification, allow or disallow access, and log physical entry occurrences. They also provide a visual deterrent and can apply their own knowledge and intuition to potential security breaches.

Show Slide(s)

Security Guards

ID BADGES AND SMART CARDS

A photographic ID badge showing name and (perhaps) access details is one of the cornerstones of building security. Anyone moving through secure areas of a building should be wearing an ID badge; anyone without an ID badge should be challenged.

Radio Frequency ID (RFID) badges can be used with proximity badge readers to monitor the location of the subject. When the RFID badge passes a reader (with a range up to about 5 m), it registers a signal and transmits its ID to the management software.

Show Slide(s)

ID Badges and Smart Cards

A contactless smart card reader. (Image © 123RF.com.)

As well as using RFID tracking, smart card badges and key fobs can be programmed with biometric authentication or with some sort of token-generating or certificate-based authentication. This type of badge could be used to open smart locks, as described earlier.

Show
Slide(s)

Entry Control Rosters

ENTRY CONTROL ROSTERS

An electronic lock may be able to log access attempts but if no technological solution is available, a security guard can manually log movement using a sign-in and sign-out sheet. An **entry control roster** requires all visitors to sign in and out when entering and leaving the building. Logging requirements will vary depending on the organization, but should include the following:

- Name and company being represented.
- Date, time of entry, and time of departure.
- Reason for visiting.
- Contact within the organization.

When possible, one single entry point should be used for all incoming visitors. This decreases the risk of unauthorized individuals gaining access to the building and tailgating.

Show
Slide(s)

Physical Security
Controls for Devices

PHYSICAL SECURITY CONTROLS FOR DEVICES

The most vulnerable point of the network infrastructure will be the communications room. This should be subject to the most stringent access and surveillance controls that can be afforded.

CABLE LOCKS AND LOCKING CABINETS

Another layer of security can be provided by installing equipment within lockable rack cabinets. These can be supplied with key-operated or electronic locks.

Rack cabinet with key-operated lock. (Image by Bunlue Nantaprom © 123RF.com.)

Server-class hardware often features physical chassis security (server locks). The chassis can be locked, preventing access to the power switch, removable drives, and USB ports. An attacker with access to these might be able to boot the machine with a different operating system to try to steal data or install malware. If there is no chassis protection and the computer cannot be located in a secure room, another tool is a USB lock. This device engages springs to make it difficult to remove from a USB port unless the key is used. Although they can deter and delay, they are unlikely to prevent a determined attacker.

If installing equipment within a cabinet is not an option, it is also possible to obtain cable hardware locks for use with portable devices such as laptops.

PRIVACY SCREENS

A **privacy screen** prevents anyone but the user from reading the screen. Modern TFTs are designed to be viewed from wide angles. This is fine for home entertainment use but raises the risk that someone would be able to observe confidential information shown on a user's monitor. A privacy filter restricts the viewing angle to only the person directly in front of the screen.

DATA DISPOSAL METHODS

As well as the security of premises, equipment rooms, and devices, physical security measures also need to account for the media on which data is stored. **Remnant removal** refers to decommissioning data storage media, including hard disks, flash drives, tape media, and CDs/DVDs. The problem has become particularly prominent as organizations recycle their old computers, either by donating them to charities or by sending them to a recycling company, who may recover and sell parts. There are at least three reasons that make remnant removal critical:

Show Slide(s)

Data Disposal Methods (3 slides)

Teaching Tip

Stress that a company's reputation is also at risk if it does not have a secure disposal policy enforced. This is especially important if the organization handles confidential personal data, such as a bank or online store.

- An organization's own confidential data could be compromised.
- Third-party data that the organization processes could be compromised, leaving it liable under Data Protection legislation, in addition to any contracts or Service Level Agreements signed.
- Software licensing could be compromised.

The main issue is understanding the degree to which data on different media types may be recoverable. Data "deleted" from a magnetic-type disk such as a hard disk is not erased. Rather, the sectors are marked as available for writing and the data they contain will only be removed as new files are added. Similarly, using the standard Windows format tool will only remove references to files and mark all sectors as useable. In the right circumstances and with the proper tools, any deleted information from a drive could be recoverable.

There are several approaches to the problem of data remnants on magnetic disks.

PHYSICAL DESTRUCTION

A magnetic disk can be mechanically shredded, incinerated, or degaussed in specialist machinery:

Teaching Tip

YouTube hosts any number of videos illustrating these processes. Other sanitation suggestions collated by PC Pro include angle grinder, 12-gauge shotgun, and thermite.

- **Shredding**—the disk is ground into little pieces. A mechanical shredder works in much the same way as a paper shredder.
- **Incineration**—exposing the disk to high heat melts its components.
- **Degaussing**—exposing the disk to a powerful electromagnet disrupts the magnetic pattern that stores the data on the disk surface.

These types of machinery are costly and will render the disk unusable, so it cannot be recycled or repurposed.

> *Note: There are many companies specializing in secure disposal. They should provide a certificate of destruction, showing the make, model, and serial number of each drive they have handled plus date of destruction and the means by which it was destroyed.*

A less expensive method is to destroy the disk with a drill or hammer—do be sure to wear protective goggles. This method is not appropriate for the most highly confidential data as it will leave fragments that could be analyzed using specialist tools.

Optical media cannot be reformatted. Discs should be destroyed before discarding them. Shredders are available for destroying CD and DVD discs.

OVERWRITING/DISK WIPING

If a disk can be recycled or repurposed, destruction is obviously not an option. **Disk wiping** software ensures that old data is destroyed by writing to each location on the media, either using zeroes or in a random pattern. This leaves the disk in a "clean" state ready to be passed to the new owner. This overwriting method is suitable for all but the most confidential data, but is time consuming and requires special software.

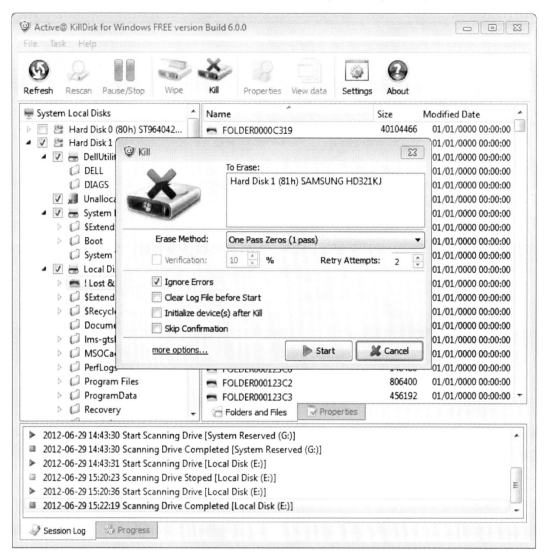

Active KillDisk data wiping software.

LOW LEVEL FORMAT

Most disk vendors supply tools to reset a disk to its factory condition. These are often described as **low level format** tools and will have the same sort of effect as disk wiping software. A "proper" low level format creates cylinders and sectors on the disk. This can generally only be done at the factory. The disk utilities just clean data from each sector; they don't re-create the sector layout.

 Note: *Check with the drive vendor for more information. For example, Seagate describe the tools available at knowledge.seagate.com/articles/en_US/FAQ/203931en.*

Activity 12-3

Discussing Physical Security Measures

Show
Slide(s)

Activity: Discussing
Physical Security
Measures

SCENARIO

Answer the following questions to check your understanding of the topic.

1. Katie works in a high-security government facility. When she comes to work in the morning, she places her hand on a scanning device in her building's lobby, which reads her hand print and compares it to a master record of her hand print in a database to verify her identity.

   What type of security control is this?

   Biometric authentication deployed as part of a building's entry control system.

2. **Why might an ID badge not be restricted to use at doors and gateways?**

   A visible ID badge shows that someone is authorized to move around a particular zone. This means that even if they are able to slip through a door using tailgating or some other method, they can be identified and challenged for not wearing visible ID.

3. **What sort of information should be recorded on an entry control roster?**

   Name and company being represented, date, time of entry, and time of departure, reason for visiting, and contact within the organization.

4. **What is a server lock?**

   A computer in which the chassis can be locked shut, preventing access to physical components.

5. **What type of device would a privacy screen be used to protect?**

   A display device such as a monitor. A privacy screen prevents the display from being observed at any angle other than directly in front of the screen.

6. **What three methods of mechanically destroying a hard disk are most effective?**

   Incineration, degaussing, and shredding. Making the disk unusable by damaging it with a drill or hammer is likely to leave remnants that could in theory be analyzed. Note that degaussing is not effective against SSDs.

Summary

In this lesson, you explored general security concepts. Every organization will have different security requirements based on the type of business they conduct. It is your job to understand those requirements and know how security controls should be implemented to directly support those needs.

What physical security controls have been employed at organizations where you have worked?

A: Answers will vary, but may include door access controls such as keypad or proximity card reader, video monitoring such as video cameras, emergency procedures in case of fire.

What steps has your organization taken to ensure the security of mobile devices? Have you planned ahead in case the devices are lost or stolen? If so, how?

A: Answers will vary, but may include installing anti-malware apps, ensuring users enable screen lock and passcode settings, configuring device encryption, requiring remote wipe capability in case of loss, enabling location services and applications, requiring that users back up their data, and ensuring that all patches and updates are applied.

 Practice Question: *Additional practice questions are available on the CompTIA CHOICE platform within the **Assessments** tile.*

Lesson 13
Securing Workstations and Data

LESSON INTRODUCTION

Ensuring the security of information processing systems isn't an easy job. Sources of vulnerabilities and weaknesses can seem as limitless as the range of threats and attackers poised to try to take advantage of them. As a CompTIA® A+® PC technician, you need to make yourself aware of the latest developments and best practices to use to secure systems.

In thinking about securing those systems, you also need to be aware that your focus cannot just be on the devices or even the users. The data processed by those devices and users is typically the asset that an attacker will be after. Being able to classify and identify data types and know why certain types pose high risks is essential to implementing effective security measures.

LESSON OBJECTIVES

In this lesson, you will:

- Use security best practices to secure a workstation.
- Implement data protection policies.
- Describe data protection processes during incidents.

Topic A

Implement Security Best Practices

 EXAM OBJECTIVES COVERED
1002-2.2 Explain logical security concepts.
1002-2.3 Compare and contrast wireless security protocols and authentication methods.
1002-2.7 Given a scenario, implement security best practices to secure a workstation.

You have seen how logical and physical security controls can be deployed together in an access control system. In this topic, we will focus on best practices regarding authentication and authorization. You need to make sure that the devices attached to your network are only being operated by authorized users. To ensure that, you have to use policies and technologies effectively to protect their account credentials.

AUTHENTICATION

Workstation security is ensured by following best practices. As you have seen, best practices can include things like using antivirus software, configuring a firewall, configuring execution control, and using patch management procedures. These controls are very important but the cornerstone of effective security is an access control system. Accounts on the computer system are configured with permissions to access resources and (for privileged accounts) rights to change the system configuration. To access an account, the user must authenticate by supplying the correct credentials, proving that he or she is the valid account holder.

The validity of the whole access control system depends on the credentials for an account being known to the account holder only. The format of the credentials is called an **authentication factor**. There are many different authentication factors. They can be categorized as something you *know* (such as a password), something you *have* (such as a smart card), or something you *are* (such as a fingerprint). Each has advantages and drawbacks.

SOMETHING YOU KNOW: STRONG PASSWORDS

The typical "something you know" factor is the logon, which comprises a username and a password. The username is typically not a secret (though it's wise to share it as little as possible), but the password must be known only by a single user.

For a system to be secure against attack, strong passwords are required. Hackers often use dictionary files containing popular words and phrases, or they may investigate the background of their target to look for likely passwords. Once a hacker obtains a password, she or he can gain access to a system posing as that person.

The following rules make passwords difficult to guess:

- A longer password is more secure—between 8 and 14 characters is suitable for an ordinary user account. Administrative accounts should have longer passwords.
- No single words—better to use word and number/punctuation combinations.
- No obvious phrases in a simple form—birthday, username, job title, and so on.
- Mix upper and lowercase.
- Use an easily memorized phrase—underscored characters or hyphens can be used to represent spaces if the operating system does not support these in passwords.
- Do not write down a password or share it with other users.

 Teaching Tip
This topic covers a large range of technologies, so be prepared to allocate plenty of time to it.

 Show Slide(s)
Authentication

 Teaching Tip
Exam candidates need to know how these authentication methods are implemented in either hardware or software, or both.

 Show Slide(s)
Something You Know: Strong Passwords

• Change the password periodically.

The main problem with passwords is that they are prone to user error; selecting weak passwords, writing them down, and so on. Some types of behavior can be improved by system policies.

Another concern is password management. A typical user might be faced with having to remember dozens of logons for different services and resort to using the same password for each. This is unsecure, as your security becomes dependent on the security of these other (unknown) organizations. In a Windows domain, password management can be mitigated by applications that are compatible with the Kerberos authentication mechanism used by the domain. This is referred to as single sign on. Users must also be trained to practice good password management—at the least not to re-use work passwords on websites they access in a personal capacity.

Another instance of "something you know" authentication is a password reset mechanism, where to authorize the reset you have to answer with some personal information (childhood friend, city or town of birth, and so on).

BIOS/UEFI PASSWORDS
A system user password is one that is required before any operating system can boot. The system password can be configured by the BIOS or UEFI firmware setup program. A BIOS user password is shared by all users and consequently very rarely configured. It might be used to provide extra security on a standalone computer that does not often require user logon, such as a computer used to manage embedded systems. A PC with UEFI firmware may support pre-boot authentication. This means that the system loads an authentication application to contact an authentication server on the network and allow the user to submit the credentials for a particular user account.

 Note: The system user password just allows the computer to proceed with the boot process. A system/supervisor password protects access to the firmware system setup program. Configuring a user password requires a supervisor password to be set, too.

SOMETHING YOU HAVE: SMART CARDS AND TOKENS
There are various ways to authenticate a user based on something they *have* (a token). A smart card contains a chip that stores the user's account details in a digital certificate. The logon provider uses the certificate to decide if it should trust the card and ensure secure transmission of the credentials. The card must be presented to a card reader before the user can be authenticated. The user must typically also input a PIN or biometric scan. This prevents misuse of lost or stolen cards. It is also possible for the data to be read wirelessly (contactless cards), via **Radio Frequency Identification (RFID)**.

Another token-based technology is the SecurID token, from RSA. A **key fob** generates a random number code synchronized to a code on the server. The code changes every 60 seconds or so. This is an example of a one-time password.

 Show Slide(s)

Something You Have: Smart Cards and Tokens

 Teaching Tip

Near Field Communications (NFC) technologies are also appearing, especially in the smartphone market. Unlike RFID, NFC allows two-way communication and provides the basis of contactless payment systems.

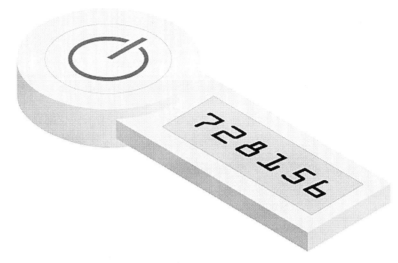

Key fob token generator. (Image © 123RF.com.)

The main concerns with token-based technologies are loss and theft and the chance that the device can be faked. There are also equipment and maintenance costs.

SOMETHING YOU ARE: BIOMETRICS

Show Slide(s)

Something You Are: Biometrics

Something you *are* means employing some sort of biometric recognition system. Many types of biometric information can be recorded, including fingerprint patterns, signature recognition, iris or retina recognition, or facial recognition.

The chosen biometric information (the template) is scanned and recorded in a database. When the user wants to access a resource, he or she is re-scanned and the scan compared to the template. If they match, access is granted.

The main problems with biometric technology are that users find it intrusive and threatening to privacy, setup and maintenance costs, and the chance that the confirmation scan could be spoofed. For example, a facial recognition scan could be fooled by using a photo of the subject. Biometrics can also be prone to false negative and false positives. A **false negative** occurs when the system denies entry when it should allow it. A **false positive** occurs when the system grants entry when it should deny it.

MULTIFACTOR AUTHENTICATION

Show Slide(s)

Multifactor Authentication

An authentication technology is considered "strong" if it combines the use of more than one type of factor (multifactor). Single factor authentication systems can quite easily be compromised: a password could be written down or shared, a smart card could be lost or stolen, and a biometric system could be subject to high error rates.

Two-factor authentication combines something like a smart card or biometric mechanism with "something you know," such as a password or PIN. **Three-factor authentication** combines all three technologies. An example of this would be a smart card with integrated thumb- or fingerprint reader. This means that to authenticate, the user must possess the card, the user's fingerprint must match the template stored on the card, and the user must input a PIN.

Note: Multifactor authentication requires a combination of different technologies. For example, requiring a PIN along with Date of Birth may be stronger than entering a PIN alone, but it is not multifactor.

SOFTWARE TOKENS

Most networks and services require users to authenticate before providing access. The problem is that the user does not want to have to submit his or her credentials every time he or she performs an action. The user expects the system to remember that they have authenticated already. To accommodate this, the system grants a software token to the device or app that the user used to authenticate with. Whenever the user submits a request, the app submits the authorization token as proof that the user is authenticated.

Show Slide(s)
Software Tokens

If the token system is not designed securely, any third-party that is able to obtain the token from the user's device or capture it as it is transmitted over the network will be able to act as that user. This is called a **replay attack**.

Token-based authorization is used on Single Sign On (SSO) networks. One example is the Kerberos authentication and authorization system used for Windows domain logon. On the web, tokens can be implemented using cookies, but JavaScript Object Notation (JSON) Web Tokens (JWT) are now more popular. Software tokens can use digital signing to prove the identity of the issuing server. Tokens should also be designed with mechanisms to prevent replay. This could mean issuing them as "use once" or time-limiting them.

REMOTE AUTHENTICATION

Enterprise networks and ISPs potentially need to support hundreds or thousands of users and numerous different remote and wireless access technologies and devices. The problem arises that each access device needs to be configured with authentication information, and this information needs to be synchronized between them.

Show Slide(s)
Remote Authentication

Teaching Tip

These technologies are widely deployed on wired LANs too, as part of NAC (endpoint) security solutions.

RADIUS

A scalable authentication architecture can be developed using RADIUS. **RADIUS** stands for Remote Authentication Dial-in User Service. Under this protocol, Authentication, Authorization, and Accounting are performed by a separate server (the AAA server). Network access devices, such as routers, switches, wireless access points, or VPN servers, function as client devices of the AAA server. Rather than storing and validating user credentials directly, they pass this data between the AAA server and the user.

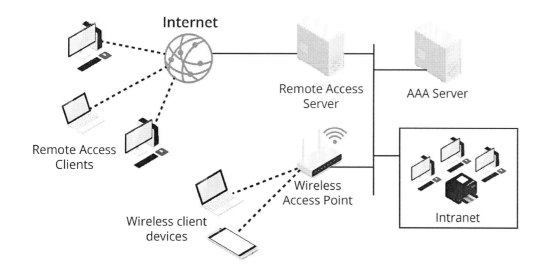

RADIUS. (Image © 123RF.com.)

TACACS+

Terminal Access Controller Access Control System Plus (TACACS+) is a similar protocol to RADIUS but designed to be more flexible and reliable. TACACS+ was developed by Cisco® but is also supported on many of the other third-party and open source RADIUS server implementations. Where RADIUS is often used to authenticate connections by wireless and VPN users, TACACS+ is often used in authenticating administrative access to routers and switches.

Show
Slide(s)

Password and Account
Policies

PASSWORD AND ACCOUNT POLICIES

Despite the availability of multifactor methods, many authentication systems are still based on passwords. This means that good password management is a critical element of network security. Users can be made to choose strong passwords by configuring account policies. There are also more general account policies that can be applied to improve security.

ACCESS CONTROL POLICIES

Most resources in a computer or network environment are protected from unauthorized use by an **Access Control List (ACL)**. An ACL is basically a list of subjects (users or computers) and the privileges they have on the object (or resource). ACLs can be defined for resources such as files and directories or for network connections (a firewall ACL).

The following policies enforce the use of ACLs and ensure that they are effective:

- Requiring passwords (mandatory logon)—when Windows is used for home computers, local user accounts are allowed to be configured without passwords. In a business environment, the security policy will default to requiring the user to sign in with a password.
- Change default admin user—rename default accounts so attackers cannot use known account names to access the system. It can make it harder to "hack" a computer if the identity of the default administrator or root account is concealed. In Windows, this account is disabled by default and replaced with a named account created during setup.
- Change default user passwords—as well as default usernames, appliances ship with a default password, such as "admin" or "password." To secure the device, you must change this when first setting it up.
- Disable guest account—the guest account allows limited access to Windows but is disabled by default. Keep it disabled to prevent unauthorized access to any shared files and folders on the device or system. File permissions can be allocated to the Everyone group account and the guest account is a member of Everyone. This might be overlooked when configuring permissions as the guest account is not typically enabled.
- Restricting user permissions (least privilege)—least privilege is a basic principle of security stating that someone (or something) should be allocated the minimum necessary rights, privileges, or information to perform their role. Users can be configured either as administrators or standard users. Additionally, User Account Control mitigates against exploitation of administrative privileges.

LOCAL SECURITY POLICY AND GROUP POLICY

On a standalone workstation, password and account policies can be configured via the Local Security Policy snap-in (`secpol.msc`) or the Group Policy snap-in (`gpedit.msc`).

Note: These tools are not available on the Basic/Home/Core editions of Windows.

On a Windows domain network, Group Policy Objects (GPO) can be saved as collections of group policy settings.

PASSWORD PROTECTION POLICIES

System policies can help to enforce credential management principles by stipulating particular requirements for users. Password protection policies mitigate against the risk of attackers being able to compromise an account and use it to launch other attacks on the network.

Show Slide(s)

Password Protection Policies

Teaching Tip

Remind learners of the drawbacks of requiring strong passwords. Users can easily forget passwords if they are too complex, but security breaches can occur if passwords are too weak.

It won't be tested on the exam, but you might want to note that a domain can have only one password policy for domain user accounts. Later versions of Windows Server support fine-grained password policies, configured through a different interface.

You might also want to discuss password filters. These are lists of strings that cannot be used as passwords. These can be compiled from databases of well-known passwords and augmented with custom strings (company/department names, user names, etc.). Password filters are supported in Azure AD and protection can be extended to on-premises domains.

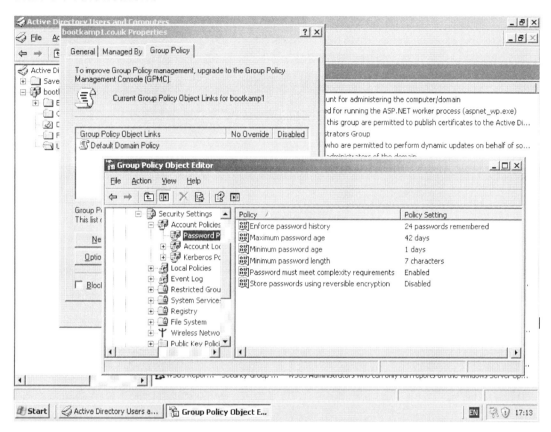

Configuring domain password policy using Group Policy. (Screenshot used with permission from Microsoft.)

The following table provides some examples used by Windows.

Policy	Description
Minimum password length	A minimum acceptable password length is specified.
Password must meet complexity requirements	Enforce password complexity rules—that is, no use of username within password and combination of at least six upper/lower case alpha-numeric and non-alpha-numeric characters. Note that this only applies when passwords are created or changed. Existing passwords are not tested against the policy.
Maximum password age	This configures a password expiration policy. When the time limit is reached, the user is forced to change the password.

Policy	Description
Enforce password history/ Minimum password age	This specifies that a unique password must be used when the user changes the password. The system remembers up to 24 previously used passwords so the minimum password age must be set to a value of 1 or greater to make the policy effective (otherwise users can quickly cycle through a number of passwords to get back to choosing an old favorite).
User cannot change password	This user account setting stops the user from changing his or her account password.
Password never expires	This user account setting can override a system policy set to force a regular password change.

Note: "Password reuse" can also mean using a work password elsewhere (on a website, for instance). Obviously, this sort of behavior can only be policed by "soft" policies.

ACCOUNT RESTRICTIONS

Show Slide(s)
Account Restrictions

To make the task of compromising the user security system harder, account restrictions can also be used. These may be specific to a particular user or applied globally.

Policy	Description
Logon Time Restrictions	For each account on the system, access to the server may be restricted to particular times. Periodically, the server checks whether the user has the right to continue using the network. If the user does not have the right, then an automatic logout procedure commences.
Station Restrictions	User access to the server can be restricted to a particular workstation or a group of workstations.
Concurrent Logons	By default, any user can log on to the domain from multiple workstations. If required, concurrent logons may be restricted to a specific number of connections.
Account Expiration Date	Setting an expiration date means that an account cannot be used beyond a certain date. This option is useful for accounts for temporary and contract staff.
Disable Account	Once an account is disabled, the user is denied access to the server until the network administrator re-enables the account.
Failed Attempts Lockout	The network administrator may specify a maximum number of incorrect logon attempts within a certain period. Once the maximum number of incorrect logons has been reached, the server disables the account. This prevents hackers from trying to gain system access using lists of possible passwords.

DESKTOP LOCK AND TIMEOUT

Show Slide(s)
Desktop Lock and Timeout

One problem with the logon system is that once logged on, the system trusts the workstation implicitly. If a user leaves the workstation unattended, someone else could perform actions as though they were that user (a so-called "lunchtime attack"). To prevent the possibility of this happening, users should be trained to lock the workstation whenever they leave it. The simple means of doing this is to press

Windows+L (every version of Windows puts the menu option for lock screen in a different place). Another way of locking the computer is to set a screensaver-required password. The screensaver can be set to timeout and lock the desktop after a set period of inactivity (no mouse or keyboard input). The user must then input their credentials to resume the session.

 Note: On a domain, a GPO can be configured to enforce the use of password-protected screensavers.

GUIDELINES FOR IMPLEMENTING SECURITY BEST PRACTICES

 *Note: All of the Guidelines for this lesson are available as checklists from the **Checklist** tile on the CHOICE Course screen.*

Show Slide(s)

Guidelines for Implementing Security Best Practices

Here are some best practices to follow for implementing security on workstations and data.

IMPLEMENT SECURITY BEST PRACTICES

Follow these guidelines for implementing security best practices:

- Consider using multifactor authentication.
- Create secure passwords.
- Consider password protecting BIOS/UEFI.
- Take measures to prevent software tokens from being used in replay attacks.
- Consider using RADIUS in VPN implementations and TACACS+ for authenticating administrative access to routers and switches.
- Enforce use of ACLs through Local Security Policy or Group Policy Objects.
- Enforce the use of strong passwords through GPOs.
- Implement account restrictions to make compromising user security harder.
- Require users to lock unattended systems.
- Implement timeouts for unattended systems.

 *Note: To learn more, check the **Video** tile on the CHOICE Course screen for any videos that supplement the content for this lesson.*

Activity 13-1

Discussing Security Best Practices Implementation

Show Slide(s)

Activity: Discussing Security Best Practices Implementation

SCENARIO

Answer the following questions to check your understanding of the topic.

---

1. **What constitutes a strong password?**

   Something easy to remember but difficult to guess. A password should be sufficiently long and mix alphanumeric and punctuation characters and case.

2. **How does a smart card provide authentication?**

   It contains a chip that can store the user's account and credentials securely in a digital certificate that the logon provider trusts. Therefore, possession of the device is confirmation of identity.

3. **Why should use of a smart card be protected by a PIN?**

   To prevent misuse of the card if it is lost or stolen.

4. **What are the drawbacks of biometric authentication technologies?**

   Users find it intrusive, it is relatively expensive (compared to password-based authentication), and there are risks from false positives and false negatives. Some implementations of biometric methods can be vulnerable to spoofing, such as using a photograph to pass through a facial recognition system.

5. **What type of biometric recognition is most suitable for integrating with a laptop computer?**

   Finger or thumbprint readers are generally the simplest type of device. Facial recognition using a built-in camera is also becoming popular.

6. **What general methods can be used to prevent a replay attack against a software token?**

   Using coding techniques to accept a token only once or restrict the timeframe in which a token can be used.

7. **In AAA architecture, what type of device might a RADIUS client be?**

   AAA refers to Authentication, Authorization, and Accounting. When the role is played by a Remote Access Dial-in User Service (RADIUS) server, the server processes authentication and authorization requests. The clients submitting the requests to the server are network access devices, such as routers, switches, wireless access points and VPN servers. The end user devices connecting to them are referred to as supplicants.

8. **What type of account policy can protect against password-guessing attacks?**

A lockout policy (disables the account after a number of incorrect logon attempts).

Topic B

Implement Data Protection Policies

EXAM OBJECTIVES COVERED
1002-1.6 Given a scenario, use Microsoft Windows Control Panel utilities.
1002-2.2 Explain logical security concepts.
1002-2.6 Compare and contrast the differences of basic Microsoft Windows OS security settings.
1002-2.7 Given a scenario, implement security best practices to secure a workstation.
1002-4.6 Explain the processes for addressing prohibited content/activity, and privacy, licensing, and policy concepts.

Teaching Tip

This topic introduces a wide range of terms and technologies, so allow plenty of time to cover it.

An access control system designates which accounts are authorized to view and modify which data files or records. In designing security, however, you always have to think about what might go wrong. What if an attacker can circumvent the access control system somehow? When data that should be kept private is breached, it is almost impossible to recover and re-secure. As a CompTIA A+ technician, it is imperative that you be able to recognize confidential and sensitive data types and understand the mechanisms that can be deployed to keep data secure.

DATA POLICIES

Show Slide(s)

Data Policies

Most organizations process private, confidential, and secret information, recorded in different kinds of documents or data stores. Document management, or more generally **Information Content Management (ICM),** is the process of managing information over its lifecycle, from creation to destruction. At each stage of the lifecycle, security considerations are vital. All employees must be trained to identify different types of confidential, private, and regulated data and follow all policies and security best practices when handling it.

Most documents go through one or more draft stages before they are published and subsequently may be revised and re-published. As a draft or revision, a document will be subject to a workflow, which describes how editorial changes are made and approved. The workflow will specify who are the authors, editors, and reviewers of the document.

As part of the creation process, the document must be classified depending on how sensitive it is. Classification restricts who may see the document contents. Classification is generally divided into several levels, following military usage:

- **Unclassified**—there are no restrictions on viewing the document.
- **Classified (internal use only/official use only)**—viewing is restricted to the owner organization or to third-parties under a Non-disclosure Agreement (NDA).
- **Confidential**—the information is highly sensitive, for viewing only by approved persons within the organization (and possibly by trusted third-parties under NDA).
- **Secret**—the information is too valuable to permit any risk of its capture. Viewing is severely restricted.
- **Top Secret**—this is the highest level of classification.

Confidential, secret, and top-secret information should be securely protected (encrypted) for storage and transmission.

Over its lifecycle, information may change in sensitivity, typically (but not always) becoming less sensitive over time. A document may be downgraded to a lower security level or eventually declassified. In this circumstance, there needs to be a clear process of authorization and notification so that confidentiality is not breached.

Corporate documents such as accounts information, product designs, and sales plans are relatively simple to identify and classify. Companies must also take regard of other types of sensitive information, such as Personally Identifiable Information (PII), software licenses, and Digital Rights Management (DRM) content.

 Note: *While we have discussed documents, the same principles hold for other types of information store, such as records in a database.*

PII

The rise in consciousness of identity theft as a serious crime and growing threat means that there is an increasing impetus on government, educational, and commercial organizations to take steps to obtain, store, and process **Personally Identifiable Information (PII)** more sensitively and securely.

PII is data that can be used to identify, contact, or locate an individual or, in the case of identity theft, to impersonate them. A social security number is a good example of PII. Others include names, date of birth, email address, telephone number, street address, biometric data, and so on.

Some types of information may be PII depending on the context. For example, when someone browses the web using a static IP address, the IP address is PII. An address that is dynamically assigned by the ISP may not be considered PII. These are the sort of complexities that must be considered when laws are introduced to control the collection and storage of personal data.

Employees should be trained to identify PII and to handle personal or sensitive data appropriately. This means not making unauthorized copies or allowing the data to be seen or captured by any unauthorized persons. Examples of treating sensitive data carelessly include leaving order forms with customers' credit card details on view on a desk, putting a credit card number in an unencrypted notes field in a customer database, or forwarding an email with personal details somewhere in the thread.

 Note: *In the European Union (EU), personal data is subject to Data Protection laws, recently updated by the General Data Protection Regulation (GDPR) framework, which make data handlers responsible for compliant collection and storage of personal information. The US does not have comparable legislation though it does operate a "Privacy Shield" scheme for US companies exchanging data with EU ones. While there is no single "data protection" law in the US, there are various Federal and state-level statutes that impact privacy and data collection/processing.*

PII may also be defined as responses to challenge questions, such as "What is your favorite color/pet/movie?" PII is often used for password reset mechanisms and to confirm identity over the telephone. Consequently, disclosing PII inadvertently can lead to identity theft.

PROTECTED HEALTH INFORMATION (PHI)

Protected Health Information (PHI) refers to medical and insurance records, plus associated hospital and laboratory test results. PHI may be associated with a specific person or used as an anonymized or de-identified data set for analysis and research. An anonymized data set is one where the identifying data is removed completely. A de-identified data set contains codes that allow the subject information to be reconstructed by the data provider. PHI trades at high values on the black market, making it an attractive target. Criminals would seek to exploit the data for insurance fraud or possibly to blackmail victims. PHI data is highly sensitive and unrecoverable. Unlike a credit card number or bank account number, it cannot be changed.

 Show Slide(s)

PII (2 slides)

 Teaching Tip

Make sure learners can expand each acronym and identify examples of each regulated data type.

Consequently, the reputational damage that would be caused by a PHI data breach is huge.

PAYMENT CARD INDUSTRY DATA SECURITY STANDARD (PCI DSS)

There are also industry-enforced regulations mandating data security. A good example is the **Payment Card Industry Data Security Standard (PCI DSS)** governing processing of credit card and other bank card payments. It sets out protections that must be provided if cardholder data—names, addresses, account numbers, and card numbers and expiry dates—is stored. It also sets out sensitive authentication data, such as the CV2 confirmation number or the PIN used for the card (not that the cardholder should ever divulge that to a third party).

Regulations such as PCI DSS have specific cybersecurity control requirements; others simply mandate "best practice," as represented by a particular industry or international framework. Frameworks for security controls are established by organizations such as the National Institute of Standards and Technology (NIST).

ACLs AND DIRECTORY PERMISSIONS

Show Slide(s)

ACLs and Directory Permissions

It's easy to overlook the fact that the most important part of a computer system is the data stored on it. A computer is just a tool and is relatively easy to replace. Data could represent days, months, or years of work. Data can be protected against unauthorized access, modification, or deletion by several mechanisms.

A **permission** is a security setting that determines the level of access a user or group account has to a particular resource. Permissions can be associated with a variety of resources, such as files, printers, shared folders, and network directory databases. Permissions can typically be configured to allow different levels of privileges, or to deny privileges to users who should not access a resource.

A permission is usually implemented as an **Access Control List (ACL)** attached to each resource. The ACL contains a number of **Access Control Entries (ACE)**, which are records of subjects and the permissions they hold on the resource. A subject could be identified in a number of ways. On a network firewall, subjects might be identified by MAC address, IP address, and/or port number. In the case of directory permissions in Windows, each user and security group account has a unique Security ID (SID).

Show Slide(s)

Data Encryption

Recall that in Windows, there are two systems of permissions:

Teaching Tip

You might want to note that color coding for encrypted folders is turned off by default in Windows 10. Use the **View** tab in **Folder Options** to enable it.

This course content slightly simplifies the mechanics of EFS. An RSA key pair is used to encrypt and decrypt a File Encryption Key (FEK). The FEK is a key used with a symmetric cipher (AES). A symmetric cipher is used for the actual data encryption because it is much faster. The RSA key pair is used to protect the FEK because it allows the user to be authenticated as the unique key holder.

- File-system permissions enforced by NTFS allow the object owner to set access control to individual files and folders. File-level permissions will prevent any unauthorized access to a file or folder both across the network and locally by prompting all users, including the user who created the file, to enter the correct user name and password for access.
- Share-level permissions only apply when a folder is accessed over a network connection. They offer no protection against a user who's logged on locally to the computer or server containing the shared resource.

Separate permissions at the share level and file level is unique to Windows environments. In Linux, the same set of read, write, and delete permissions are valid at both the local level and across the network.

DATA ENCRYPTION

When data is hosted on a file system, it can be protected by the operating system's security model. Each file or folder can be configured with an Access Control List (ACL), describing the permissions that different users (or user groups) have on the file. These permissions are enforced only when the OS mediates access to the device. If the disk is exposed to a different OS, the permissions could be overridden. To protect data at-rest against these risks, the information stored on a disk can be encrypted.

FILE/FOLDER ENCRYPTION (EFS)

One approach to encrypting file system data is to apply encryption to individual files or folders. The **Encrypting File System (EFS)** feature of NTFS supports file and folder encryption. EFS is only available to use with professional/enterprise editions of Windows.

Without strong authentication, encrypted data is only as secure as the user account. If the password can be compromised, then so can the data. The user's password grants access to the key that performs the file encryption and decryption.

There is also the chance of data loss if the key is lost or damaged. This can happen if the user's profile is damaged, if the user's password is reset by an administrator, or if Windows is reinstalled. It is possible to back up the key or (on a Windows domain) to set up recovery agents with the ability to decrypt data.

To apply encryption, open the file's or folder's property sheet and select the **Advanced** button. Check the **Encrypt contents** box, then confirm the dialog boxes.

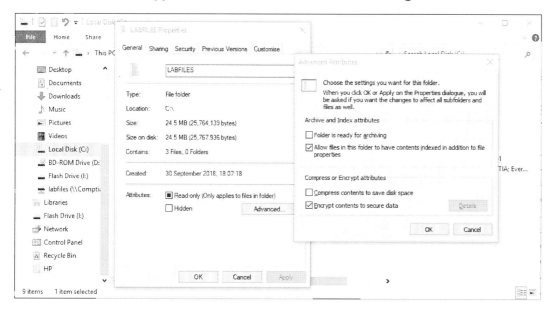

Applying encryption to a folder using EFS. (Screenshot used with permission from Microsoft.)

Folders and files that have been encrypted can be shown with green color coding in Explorer. Any user other than the one that encrypted the file will receive an "Access Denied" error when trying to browse, copy, or print the file.

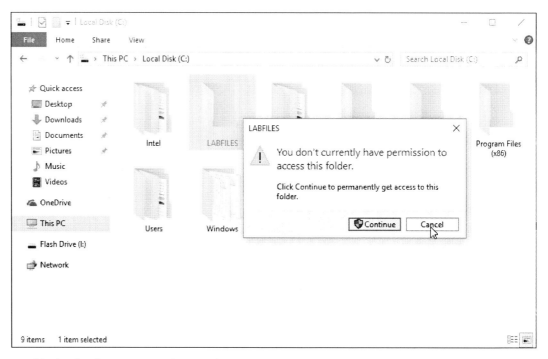

A file that has been encrypted cannot be opened by other users—even administrators. (Screenshot used with permission from Microsoft.)

FULL DISK ENCRYPTION

Show
Slide(s)

Full Disk Encryption

An alternative to file encryption is to use a **Full Disk Encryption (FDE)** product. The **BitLocker** disk encryption product is built into Windows Enterprise editions and is available with Windows 7 Ultimate, Windows 8 Pro, and Windows 10 Professional.

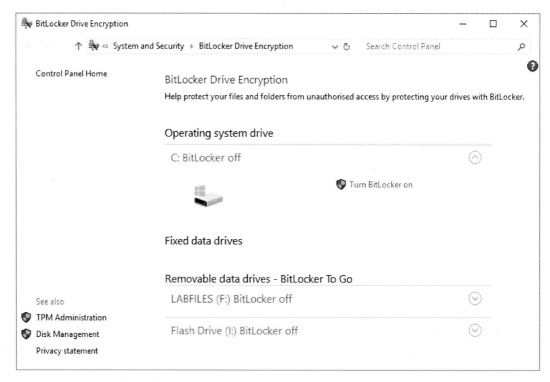

Configuring BitLocker and BitLocker To Go via the Control Panel. (Screenshot used with permission from Microsoft.)

Disk encryption carries a processing overhead but modern computers usually have processing capacity to spare. It is particularly useful for mobile devices, such as laptops, and removable drives. The main advantage is that it does not depend on the user to remember to encrypt data so mitigates the risk of data loss in the case of the theft or loss of the device. Disk encryption also encrypts the swap file, print queues, temporary files, and so on.

BitLocker® can be used with any volumes on fixed (internal) drives. It can also be used with removable drives in its **BitLocker To Go** form.

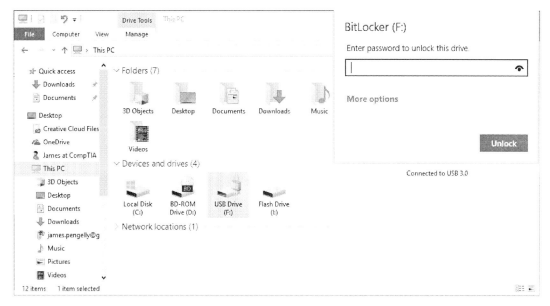

Removable drive protected with BitLocker To Go. (Screenshot used with permission from Microsoft.)

 Note: In older Windows versions (Vista and XP), there was no support for encrypting removable drives. BitLocker To Go Reader is a standalone application that allows USB drives encrypted in Windows 7 or later to be read in Windows XP or Windows Vista. This gives the user read-only access to the files on the drive. They can be copied but this removes the encryption from the copies.

When the data is encrypted, the user must have access to the encryption key to access it. Some disk encryption products, including BitLocker, can make use of a **Trusted Platform Module (TPM)** chip in the computer to tie use of a hard disk to a particular motherboard. The TPM is used as a secure means of storing the encryption key and to ensure the integrity of the OS used to boot the machine. Alternatively, the key could be stored on a removable smart card or on a USB stick. The computer's firmware must support booting from USB for the last option to work.

 *Note: The TPM must be configured with an owner password (often the system password set in firmware). You can manage TPM settings from Windows using the TPM Management snap-in (select **TPM Administration** from the BitLocker applet).*

During BitLocker setup, a recovery key is also generated. This should be stored on removable media (or written down) and stored securely (and separately from the computer). This key can be used to recover the encrypted drive if the startup key is lost.

DATA LOSS PREVENTION (DLP)

In a workplace where mobile devices with huge storage capacity proliferate and high bandwidth network links are readily available, attempting to prevent the loss of data by controlling the types of storage device allowed to connect to PCs and networks can be

 Show Slide(s)
Data Loss Prevention (DLP)

 Teaching Tip
Refer learners to a vendor site such as Symantec for more information about specific DLP product features and implementation guidelines.

impractical. Another option is to use policies or software to prevent data "leakage" or loss by focusing on the data files.

Users must of course be trained about document confidentiality and make sure that they are aware of the insecurity of unencrypted communications. This should also be backed up by Human Resources (HR) and auditing policies that ensure staff are trustworthy. "Soft" measures such as these do not protect against user error or insider threats, however.

Data Loss Prevention (DLP) products scan content in structured formats, such as a database with a formal access control model, or unstructured formats, such as email or word processing documents. DLP software uses some sort of dictionary database or algorithm (regular expression matching) to identify confidential data. The transfer of content to removable media, such as USB devices, or by email, IM, or even social media, can then be blocked if it does not conform to a predefined policy.

Such solutions will usually consist of the following components:

- Policy server—to configure confidentiality rules and policies, log incidents, and compile reports.
- Endpoint agents—to enforce policy on client computers, even when they are not connected to the network.
- Network agents—to scan communications at network borders and interface with web and messaging servers to enforce policy.

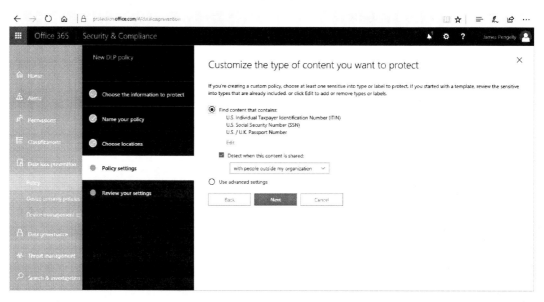

Creating a Data Loss Prevention policy in Office 365. Used with permission from Microsoft.

SOFTWARE LICENSING AND DRM

Show Slide(s)

Software Licensing and DRM (2 slides)

As well as managing use of confidential and sensitive data, you need to consider methods for identifying and removing prohibited content. The acceptable use policies built into most employee contracts will prohibit the abuse of Internet services to download games or obscene content. Employees should also avoid using work accounts for personal communications.

Prohibited content also extends to the installation and use of software. When you buy software, you must accept the license governing its use, often called the **End User License Agreement (EULA)**. The terms of the license will vary according to the type of software, but the basic restriction is usually that the software may only be installed on one computer.

The software is often activated using a product key, which will be a long string of characters and numbers printed on the box or disk case. The product key will generate a different product ID, which is often used to obtain technical support. The product ID is displayed when the application starts and can be accessed using the About option on the Help menu.

A company may have hundreds of employees who need the same software on their computers. Software manufacturers do not expect such companies to buy individual copies of the software for each employee. Instead, they will issue a license for multiple users, which means that the company can install the software on an agreed number of computers for their employees to use.

If a site has a large number of computers, these computers are often networked. This means that software bought under license can be installed onto a network server so that all authorized users can access it without it being installed on each individual computer.

Consider the example of Microsoft Windows. Windows is commercial software, meaning it must be paid for. A condition of installing Windows is accepting the EULA. Microsoft requires you to activate Windows when you install it, which helps them to verify that you are not breaking the terms of the license. There are several different types of license, summarized here:

- **Original Equipment Manufacturer (OEM)**—this is for pre-installed versions of Windows sold with new PCs. The license is not transferable and the software may not be installed on a different PC.
- **Retail**—these personal licenses are subdivided into Full and Upgrade versions of software. The software may be transferred between computers but may only be installed on one computer at any one time. Upgrade versions require a valid license and setup media for a qualifying upgrade product.
- **Volume**—these enterprise licenses are schemes to simplify license administration in larger organizations and businesses.
- **Server**—licensing for servers is different from licensing desktop software. As well as a license for the software installed on the server, **Client Access Licenses (CAL)** are required, based on the number of clients accessing the software services. CALs can be sold per server (limiting the number of simultaneous accesses) or per seat (specifying each unique device or user).

It is illegal to use or distribute unauthorized copies of software (pirate copies). Pirated software often contains errors and viruses as well. Enterprises need monitoring systems to ensure that their computers are not hosting unlicensed or pirated software.

SHAREWARE, FREEWARE, AND OPEN SOURCE APPLICATIONS

Shareware, freeware, and open source licenses are different ways of distributing applications to commercial software:

- **Shareware** is software that you can install free of charge so that you can evaluate it for a limited period. If you decide to continue using the software after this period, you must register it, usually for a fee. When you register the software you often become entitled to extra features and support.
- **Freeware** is software that is available free of charge.

 Note: Even if software is distributed as shareware or freeware, the copyright is still held by the publisher or designer. Both shareware and freeware may still be governed by a license, which may restrict its use (for example, to prevent commercial use of the product or to redistribute or resell it).

- **Open source** is software that also makes the program code used to design it available. The idea is that other programmers can investigate the program and make it more stable and useful. An open source license does not forbid commercial use of applications derived from the original, but it is likely to impose the same conditions on further redistributions.

DIGITAL RIGHTS MANAGEMENT (DRM)

Digital music and video is often subject to copy protection and **Digital Rights Management (DRM)**. When you purchase music or video online, the vendor may license the file for use on a restricted number of devices. You generally need to use your account with the vendor to authorize and deauthorize devices when they change. Most DRM systems have been defeated by determined attackers and consequently there is plenty of content with DRM security removed circulating. From an enterprise's point-of-view, this is prohibited content and they need monitoring systems to ensure that their computers are not hosting pirated content files.

GUIDELINES FOR IMPLEMENTING DATA PROTECTION POLICIES

Show Slide(s)

Guidelines for Implementing Data Protection Policies

Here are some guidelines to follow regarding data protection policies.

IMPLEMENT DATA PROTECTION POLICIES

Follow these guidelines for implementing data protection policies:

- Classify documents based on how sensitive it is.
- Protect PII, PHI, and PCI data.
- Implement permissions as ACLs attached to resources.
- Use full disk, folder, and file encryption.
- Implement a data loss prevention policy.
- Follow all software licensing agreements and DRM.

Activity 13-2

Discussing Data Protection Policies

Show
Slide(s)

Activity: Discussing
Data Protection
Policies

SCENARIO

Answer the following questions to check your understanding of the topic.

1. **Why should PII be classed as sensitive or confidential?**

   Disclosing Personally Identifiable Information (PII) may lead to loss of privacy or identity theft. There may be legal or regulatory penalties for mishandling PII.

2. **What is PHI?**

   Protected Health Information (PHI) is data such as medical records, insurance forms, hospital/laboratory test results, and so on.

3. **True or false? The encryption applied by EFS can be overridden by the local administrator account.**

   False—only the user can decrypt files, via their account password or a backup key. In a Windows domain, administrators can be configured key recovery agents but the local administrator does not have this right automatically. This means that the disk cannot be connected to a different computer to circumvent the protection afforded by encryption.

4. **What is the function of a TPM in relation to Windows' BitLocker feature?**

   A Trusted Platform Module can store the disk encryption key to tie use of the disk to a particular computer.

5. You are advising a customer on purchasing security controls.

   What class of security technology prevents users from sending unauthorized files as email attachments?

   Data Loss Prevention (DLP).

6. **What type of software license is locked to a single hardware device?**

   Original Equipment Manufacturer (OEM).

Activity 13-3
Configuring Data Protection

 Show Slide(s)

Activity: Configuring Data Protection

 Teaching Tip

If the HOST disk subsystem is slow, encrypting the boot volume with BitLocker could take 30-40 minutes. If this is the case, you could leave the VM running and revisit the activity later in the course. Alternatively, ask learners to add a second additional disk (BITLOCKER.VHDX). Copy LABFILES to it and use BitLocker on that volume instead.

BEFORE YOU BEGIN

You will use accounts within an Active Directory (AD) domain, but you will work principally with the PC1 and PC2 VMs.

SCENARIO

In this activity, you will look at how file permissions, folder encryption, and disk encryption can and cannot protect data on removable and fixed disks. You cannot attach USB media to a VM, so you will use a second virtual hard disk (VHD) to simulate a removable drive.

1. Attach a second virtual hard disk to PC1. It does not need to have a large capacity (8 GB is fine).
   a) In the **Hyper-V Manager**, right-click **PC1** and select **Settings**.
   b) Select the **SCSI Controller** node and then, with **Hard Drive** selected in the box, select the **Add** button
   c) Select the **New** button.
   d) In the wizard, select **Next** to begin the wizard.
   e) With **Dynamically expanding** selected, select **Next**.
   f) In the **Name** box, type *REMOVABLE* and in the **Location** box, type *C:\COMPTIA-LABS \TEMP* and then select **Next**.
   g) In the **Size** box, type *8* and then select **Finish**.
   h) Select the **Apply** button.
   i) Leave the **Settings** dialog box open.

2. Enable the virtual Trusted Platform Module (TPM) for PC1, and eject the product disc from the optical drive.
   a) In the **Settings** dialog box, select the **DVD Drive** node.
   b) In the **Media** panel, select **None**.
   c) In the **Settings** dialog box, select the **Security** node.
   d) Check the **Enable Trusted Platform Module** box.
   e) In the **Settings** dialog box, select **OK**.

3. Start the VMs to create the network.
   You do not need to open connection windows for the VMs unless you are prompted to do so.
   a) In Hyper-V Manager, right-click **RT1-LOCAL** and select **Start**.
   b) Right-click **DC1** and select **Start**.
   c) Wait until the DC1 thumbnail shows the logon screen, and then start **MS1**.
   d) Wait until the MS1 thumbnail shows the logon screen, and then start **PC1**. Do **NOT** start PC2.
   e) Open a connection window for **PC1**.
   f) Select the **Other user** icon.
   g) Sign on using the account *515support\Bobby* and password *Pa$$w0rd*

4. Initialize the new disk and format it with NTFS.

   a) Right-click **Start** and select **Disk Management**.

   b) In the **Initialize Disk** dialog, select **OK**.

   c) In the bottom of the window, right-click the **Unallocated** box on **Disk 1** and select **New Simple Volume**.

   d) In the **New Simple Volume Wizard**, select **Next** twice to use all the available space on the disk.

   e) On the **Assign Drive Letter or Path** page, from the list box, select **R** and select **Next**.

   f) In the **File system** box, verify that **NTFS** is selected.

   g) In the **Volume label** box, type *REMOVABLE* and select **Next**.

   h) Select **Finish**.

   i) Close Disk Management.

5. Create an *UNSECURE* folder on the disk, and add some files.

   a) Open File Explorer, and browse to the **R:** drive's root folder.

   b) Right-click and select **New→Folder**. Type *UNSECURE* and press **Enter**.

   c) Create some files in the **UNSECURE** folder.

6. Set NTFS permissions on **UNSECURE** so that only the **Bobby** account has access.

You will use this folder to show that the security properties set here can be overridden.

   a) In File Explorer, browse to the R: drive's root folder.

   b) Right-click the **UNSECURE** folder and select **Properties**.

   c) In the **UNSECURE Properties** dialog box, select the **Security** tab and then select the **Advanced** button.

   d) In the **Advanced Security Settings for UNSECURE** dialog box, select the **Disable inheritance** button.

   e) Select **Convert inherited permissions into explicit permissions on this object**.

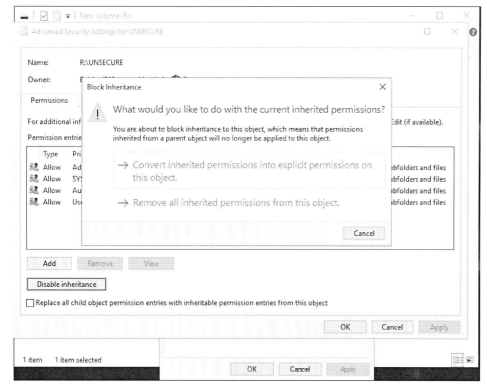

Disabling inherited permissions on a folder. (Screenshot used with permission from Microsoft.)

   f) In the **Advanced Security Settings for UNSECURE** dialog box, select **OK**.

g) In the **UNSECURE Properties** dialog box, select the **Edit** button.

h) Select the **Add** button.

i) In the **Select Users or Groups** dialog box, type ***bobby*** in the box and select **Check Names**. Select **OK**.

j) With the **Bobby** account selected, in the **Permissions for Bobby** box, check the box for **Full control** in the **Allow** column.

k) Select the **Apply** button.

l) In the **Group or user names** box, select **Authenticated Users** and then select the **Remove** button.

m) In the **Group or user names** box, select **Administrators (PC1\Administrators)** and then select the **Remove** button.

n) In the **Group or user names** box, select **Users (PC1\Users)** and then select the **Remove** button.

Edit the permissions entries so that only the Bobby and SYSTEM accounts remain.
(Screenshot used with permission from Microsoft.)

o) Select **OK**.

p) In the **UNSECURE Properties** dialog box, select **OK**.

7. Create a **SECURE** folder on the disk, and add some files.

a) In File Explorer, browse to the R: drive's root folder. Right-click and select **New→Folder**. Type ***SECURE*** and press **Enter**.

b) Create some files in the **SECURE** folder.

8. Apply encryption to the **SECURE** folder. You will use this folder to demonstrate that the information in it can be kept secure, so long as the encryption key is also protected.

a) In File Explorer, browse to the R: drive's root folder. Right-click the **SECURE** folder and select **Properties**. Select the **Advanced** button.

b) Check the **Encrypt contents to secure data** box, and then select **OK**.

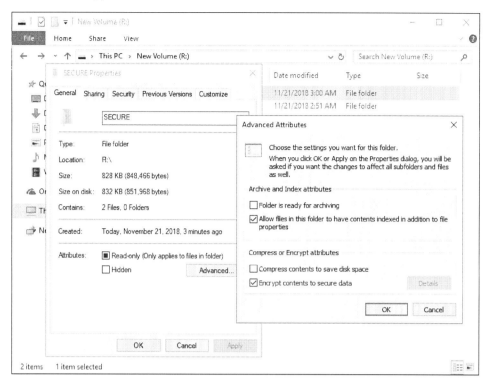

Use an object's advanced attributes dialog to apply EFS encryption. (Screenshot used with permission from Microsoft.)

c) In the **SECURE Properties** dialog box, select the **Apply** button.

d) In the **Confirm Attribute Changes** dialog box, with the **Apply changes to this folder, subfolders and files** option selected, select **OK**.
This may take a few minutes. The progress bar will close when complete.

e) In the **SECURE Properties** dialog box, select the **Advanced** button.

f) Select the **Details** button and view the information in the dialog box.

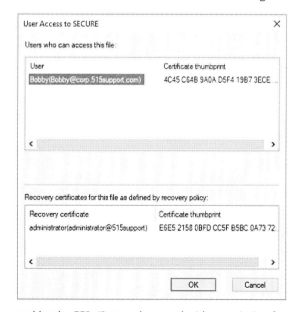

Certificates used by the EFS. (Screenshot used with permission from Microsoft.)

It shows the thumbprint for the certificate that was used to encrypt the folder. The administrator is automatically configured as a recovery agent for the domain network, and can recover the user certificate if lost or damaged.

g) Select **Cancel**.

h) In the **Advanced Attributes** dialog box, select the **OK** button.

i) In the **SECURE Properties** dialog box, select the **OK** button.

j) Optionally, select **View→Options**, select the **View** tab, then check **Show encrypted or compressed NTFS files in color** and select **OK** to show color-coding for encrypted folders.

9. Use BitLocker to encrypt the system disk.

a) Click in the instant search box, and type ***bitlocker***. From the search results, select **Manage BitLocker**.

b) Under **Operating system drive**, select **Turn on BitLocker**.

c) After the progress bar completes, if necessary, select **Next**.

d) Read the warning about backing up files. This is a good idea but you will skip it for this activity. Select **Next**.

e) After the progress bar completes, select **Next**.

f) On the **How do you want to back up your recovery key?** page, select **Save to a file**. Navigate into the **R:\UNSECURE** folder and then select **Save**.

g) In the **BitLocker Drive Encryption** wizard, select **Next**.

h) On the **Choose which encryption mode to use** page, select **Compatible mode** and select **Next**.

i) With the **Run BitLocker system** box unchecked, select **Start encrypting**.

j) Wait for the **C: BitLocker Encrypting** message to change to **C: BitLocker on**. This could take up to 40 minutes. Optionally, browse the options available from the **TPM Administration** link while you are waiting.

10. Shut down PC1, create a checkpoint, and export the VM so you can use the virtual disks in another VM.

a) Shut down the PC1 VM.

b) In Hyper-V Manager, when the **State** changes to **Off**, right-click **PC1** and select **Checkpoint**.

c) In the **Checkpoints** pane, right-click the new checkpoint, and select **Export**.

d) In the **Export Virtual Machine** dialog box, select **Browse**.

e) Select the **C:\COMPTIA-LABS\TEMP** folder, and then select the **Select Folder** button.

f) In the **Export Virtual Machine** dialog box, select **Export**. Wait for the **Status** column to clear.

   You might need to scroll right to view the **Status** column. The export will take about 5 minutes to complete.

Teaching Tip

Make sure students choose the REMOVABLE image from within the PC1 subfolder (not the original REMOVABLE.VHDX file).

11. Imagine that PC1 is a laptop that has just been stolen and that the REMOVABLE disk is a USB thumb drive that was also in the laptop bag that was pilfered by the thief. With PC2 now acting as the thief's computer, what data can be accessed? To find out, attach the disks to **PC2**.

a) In Hyper-V Manager, right-click **PC2** and select **Settings**.

b) Select the **SCSI Controller** node and then, with **Hard Drive** selected in the box, select the **Add** button.

c) Select the **Browse** button, select the **C:\COMPTIA-LABS\TEMP\PC1\Virtual Hard Disks\PC1.vhdx** and then select **Open**. Select **Apply**.

d) Select the **SCSI Controller** node and then, with **Hard Drive** selected in the box, select the **Add** button.

e) Select the **Browse** button. Select **C:\COMPTIA-LABS\TEMP\PC1\Virtual Hard Disks\REMOVABLE.vhdx** and then select **Open**.

f) Select **OK**.

12. Start **PC2**, and use the **Admin** account to gain access to the **UNSECURE** folder.

a) Start the **PC2** VM and open a connection window.

b) When the VM has booted, sign on as **.\Admin** with the password ***Pa$$w0rd***

c) If prompted with the **AutoPlay** dialog box, close the box.

d) Open Windows Explorer, and select the **Computer** object. You should see the foreign Local Disk with its BitLocker encryption symbol and the REMOVABLE disk.

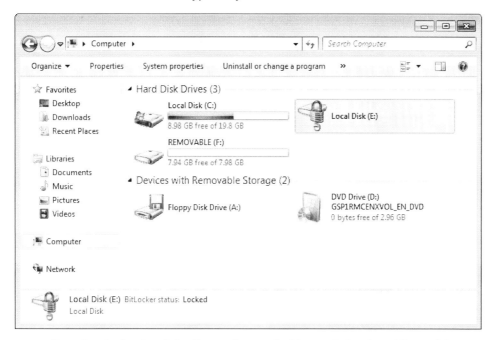

Browsing the foreign disks. (Screenshot used with permission from Microsoft.)

e) Open the **REMOVABLE** drive (this is shown as drive F: in the screenshot). Open the **UNSECURE** folder. At the **You don't currently have permission to access this folder** warning, select **Continue**. Read the error message and select **Close**.

f) Right-click **UNSECURE** and select **Properties**. Select the **Security** tab.

g) Select the **Continue** button.

h) In the **Advanced Security Settings for UNSECURE** dialog box, in the **Change owner to** box, select **Admin (PC2\Admin)**. Check the **Replace owner on subcontainers and objects** box. Select **OK**.

i) In the **Windows Security** dialog box, select **Yes**. Select **OK**.

j) Select **OK**.

k) Browse the contents of the folder. You should be able to view and modify the files you created, but you shouldn't be able to view the recovery key yet.

13. Now, try to view the encrypted folders and drives.

a) Browse to the REMOVABLE drive's root folder and open the **SECURE** folder.

b) Verify that you can view the folder contents. Try to open a file. If a warning dialog box is displayed, select **OK** or **Cancel** to close it.

c) Open the **Computer** object, and double-click the BitLocker drive. Read the message prompting you for the recovery key. Leave this dialog box open.

14. Try to retrieve the recovery key from the REMOVABLE disk, and use it to gain access to the BitLocker volume.

a) Open the REMOVABLE drive's root folder and the **UNSECURE** folder.

b) Right-click the **BitLocker Recovery Key** file and select **Properties**. Select the **Security** tab. Examine the permission entry.

The only reason you don't yet have access to this file is that it was not set to inherit permissions from its parent folder. When you took ownership, the full control permissions were not applied to this object. But as the new owner, you can change the permissions easily.

c) Select the **Edit** button.

d) Select the **Add** button. Type *PC2\Admin* in the box and select **Check Names**. Select **OK**.

e) In the **Permission for BitLocker Recovery Key** dialog box, with the **Admin** account selected, check the **Full control** box in the **Allow** column.

f) Select **OK**.

g) In the **BitLocker Recovery Key properties** dialog box, select **OK**.

h) Open the BitLocker Recovery Key file. Select the value under **Recovery Key** and copy it.

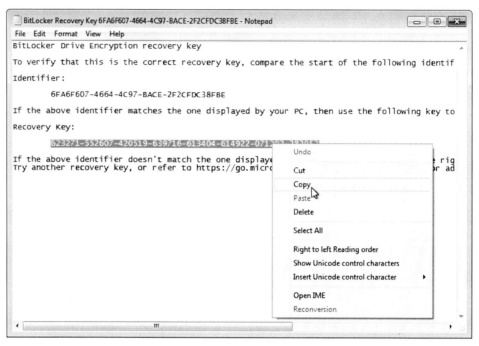

Copying the recovery key. (Screenshot used with permission from Microsoft.)

i) Switch to the **BitLocker Drive Encryption** dialog box, and select **Type the recovery key**.

j) Click in the box and press **Ctrl+V** to paste the key you copied. Optionally, also select **More Information** and verify that the key identification strings match. Select **Next**.

k) Observe the message, but just select **Finish**.

l) Browse the folders and files in the BitLocker volume.

As you have seen, for file permissions to be effective, the disk must remain under the control of its original OS. This type of permissions system is referred to as discretionary, because the security is dependent on ownership. Encryption is non-discretionary, but for it to be effective, you must keep the key (or recovery key) secure. The recovery key should *never* be kept in the same physical location as the encrypted device.

15. You need to revert the changes you made and discard the checkpoint you created. Please complete these steps carefully to ensure the other activities continue to function as expected.

a) On **PC2**, from the connection window, select **Action→Revert**. If you are prompted, select the **Revert** button to confirm.

b) In Hyper-V Manager, select **PC1**. In the **Checkpoints** pane, right-click the **Initial Config** checkpoint and select **Apply**. In the confirmation dialog box, select **Apply**.

c) In the **Checkpoints** pane, right-click the dated checkpoint and select **Delete Checkpoint**. In the confirmation dialog box, select **Delete**.

d) For each of the other VMs that are running, right-click them and select **Revert**.

e) On the HOST, in File Explorer, browse to **C:\COMPTIA-LABS\TEMP** and delete the entire contents of folder.

Topic C
Protect Data During Incident Response

 EXAM OBJECTIVES COVERED
1002-4.6 Explain the processes for addressing prohibited content/activity, and privacy, licensing, and policy concepts.

While you hope that security and data handling policies will be sufficient to protect your computer systems and networks, you also need to consider the situations where those protections fail. To cope with failures of security policy, or attempted breaches of policy, organizations need well-rehearsed incident response procedures to investigate and remediate the breach.

As an IT technician, you will often be involved in identifying and reporting security incidents and potentially in assisting with investigations and evidence gathering. It is important that you understand some of the general principles of effective incident response and forensic investigation procedures.

INCIDENT RESPONSE POLICIES

In the course of performing technical support, you may have to report or respond to security incidents. A security incident could be one of a wide range of different scenarios, such as:

- A computer or network infected with viruses, worms, or Trojans.
- An attempt to break into a computer system or network through phishing or an "evil twin" Wi-Fi access point.
- An attempt to damage a network through a Denial of Service (DoS) attack.
- Users with unlicensed software.
- Finding prohibited material on a PC—illegal copies of copyrighted material, obscene content, or confidential documents that the user should not have access to.

An **incident response policy** sets out procedures and guidelines for dealing with security incidents. The actions of staff immediately following detection of an incident can have a critical impact on these aims, so an effective policy and well-trained employees are crucial. Incident response is also likely to require coordinated action and authorization from several different departments or managers, which adds a further level of complexity.

SECURITY INCIDENT HANDLING LIFECYCLE

The NIST Computer Security Incident Handling Guide special publication SP800-61 identifies the following stages in an incident response lifecycle:

- **Preparation**—making the system resilient to attack in the first place. This includes hardening systems, writing procedures, and establishing confidential lines of communication. It also implies creating incident response resources and procedures.
- **Detection and Analysis**—determining whether an incident has taken place and assessing how severe it might be, followed by notification of the incident to stakeholders.
- **Containment, Eradication, and Recovery**—limiting the scope and magnitude of the incident. The typical response is to "pull the plug" on the affected system, but

 Teaching Tip

Although learners will not be managing incidents, they should understand the overall process and the role of junior technicians in the early stages of incident response and reporting.

Show Slide(s)

Incident Response Policies

this is not always appropriate. Once the incident is contained, the cause can then be removed and the system brought back to a secure state.
- **Post-incident Activity**—analyzing the incident and responses to identify whether procedures or systems could be improved. It is also imperative to document the incident.

INCIDENT RESPONSE DOCUMENTATION

Show Slide(s)
Incident Response Documentation

A serious incident will be a highly pressured scenario. Without adequate preparation, staff will not be able to respond effectively. Without clear policies and guidelines, staff discovering and investigating the incident are more likely to make bad decisions. Without an incident log, different employees will find it harder to coordinate their efforts. If there are no contact lists and lines of communication, information about the incident might be disclosed inappropriately, whether that means senior personnel not being informed or knowledge of the incident becoming public too early.

Preparing for incident response means establishing documented policies and procedures for dealing with security breaches and the personnel and resources to implement those policies. Incident response documentation should also establish clear lines of communication, both for reporting incidents and for notifying affected parties as the management of an incident progresses. It is vital to have essential contact information readily available. Also consider that the incident response personnel might require secure, out-of-band communication methods, in case standard network communication channels have been compromised.

As with any type of procedural documentation, this must also be kept up to date with changes. The procedures should be reviewed periodically (every few months) but events such as staff changes, the deployment of new network or security systems, or changes in the legal/regulatory environment should trigger an immediate review of incident response documents.

FIRST RESPONDERS

Show Slide(s)
First Responders

An **incident** is any event that breaches security policy. Of course, this covers a huge number and variety of different scenarios. In order to prioritize and manage incidents, an organization should develop some method of categorizing and prioritizing them (triage), in the same way that troubleshooting support incidents can be logged and managed.

Larger organizations will provide a dedicated **Computer Security Incident Response Team (CSIRT)** as a single point-of-contact for security incidents so that they can be reported through the proper channels.

The members of this team should be able to provide the range of decision making and technical skills required to deal with different types of incidents. The team needs a mixture of senior decision makers (up to director level) who can authorize actions following the most serious incidents, managers, and technicians (who can deal with minor incidents on their own initiative).

When an incident is detected, it is critical that the appropriate person on the CSIRT be notified so that they can take charge of the situation and formulate the appropriate response (first responder). This means that employees at all levels of the organization must be trained to recognize and respond appropriately to actual or suspected security incidents.

It is also wise to provide for confidential reporting so that employees are not afraid to report insider threats, such as fraud or misconduct. It may also be necessary to use an "out-of-band" method of communication so as not to alert the intruder that his or her attack has been detected.

Note: *An employee (or ex-employee) who reports misconduct is referred to as a whistleblower.*

When notification has taken place, the CSIRT or other responsible person(s) can formulate the response.

DATA AND DEVICE PRESERVATION

Computer **forensics** is the science of collecting evidence from computer systems to a standard that will be accepted in a court of law. It is highly unlikely that a computer forensic professional will be retained by an organization, so such investigations are normally handled by law enforcement agencies. Like DNA or fingerprints, digital evidence is mostly **latent**. Latent means that the evidence cannot be seen with the naked eye; rather, it must be interpreted using a machine or process.

If a forensic investigation is launched (or if one is a possibility), it is important that technicians and managers are aware of the processes that the investigation will use. It is vital that they are able to assist the investigator and that they not do anything to compromise the investigation. In a trial, the defense will try to exploit any uncertainty or mistake regarding the integrity of evidence or the process of collecting it.

Show
Slide(s)
Data and Device
Preservation (2 slides)

COLLECTION OF EVIDENCE

The first phase of a forensic investigation is collection of evidence. The two principal questions here are:

- What evidence must be collected?
- How should the evidence be collected?

Neither question is trivial. A computer system may contain multiple gigabytes (or even terabytes) of data, most of which will not be relevant to the incident. Evidence may only exist in volatile storage (system or cache RAM). If the computer system is not owned by the organization, there is the question of whether search or seizure is legally valid. This may also make it difficult for law enforcement agents to begin an investigation. For example, if an employee is accused of fraud, you must verify that the employee's equipment and data can be legally seized and searched. Any mistake may make evidence gained from the search inadmissible.

The question of "how" is complicated because it is much more difficult to capture evidence from a digital "crime scene" than it is from a physical one. As mentioned, some evidence will be lost if the computer system is powered off; on the other hand, some evidence may be unobtainable until the system *is* powered off. Additionally, evidence may be lost depending on whether the system is shut down or "frozen" by suddenly disconnecting the power.

The general procedure will be as follows:

1. The crime scene must be thoroughly documented using photographs and ideally video and audio. Investigators must record every action they take in identifying, collecting, and handling evidence.

   Note: *Remember that if the matter comes to trial, the trial could take place months or years after the event. It is vital to record impressions and actions in notes.*

2. The investigator should then interview witnesses to establish what they were doing at the scene and also to gather information about the computer system.
3. If possible, evidence is gathered from the live system, including screenshots of display screens and the contents of cache and system memory, using forensic software tools. It is vital that these tools do nothing to modify the digital data that they capture.

4. Forensic tools are used to make a copy of data on the hard drive(s). This is performed using drive imaging rather than file copy methods, so that the copy is made at sector level.
5. A cryptographic hash is made of the collected data. This can be used to prove that the digital evidence collected has not been modified subsequently to its collection.
6. The system is either shut down or powered off.
7. Depending on the strength of evidence required, the physical drives are then identified, bagged, sealed, and labeled using tamper-proof bags. It is also appropriate to ensure that the bags have anti-static shielding to reduce the possibility that data will be damaged or corrupted on the electronic media by Electrostatic Discharge (ESD). Any other physical evidence deemed necessary is also "Bagged and Tagged."

CHAIN OF CUSTODY

Show Slide(s)

Chain of Custody

It is vital that the evidence collected at the crime scene conform to a valid timeline. Digital information is susceptible to tampering, so access to the evidence must be tightly controlled.

A crucial element of the investigation is that each step is documented and (ideally) recorded. This proves that the evidence has been handled correctly and has not been tampered with. Once evidence has been bagged, it must not subsequently be handled or inspected, except in controlled circumstances.

A **Chain of Custody** form records where, when, and who collected the evidence, who has handled it subsequently, and where it was stored. The chain of custody must show access to, plus storage and transportation of, the evidence at every point from the crime scene to the court room. Anyone handling the evidence must sign the chain of custody and indicate what they were doing with it.

Activity 13-4

Discussing Data Protection During Incident Response

Show
Slide(s)

Activity: Discussing
Data Protection During
Incident Response

SCENARIO

Answer the following questions to check your understanding of the topic.

1. **What is incident reporting?**

   The process of identifying security breaches (or attempted breaches and suspicious activity) to security management personnel.

2. **Why are the actions of a first responder critical in the context of a forensic investigation?**

   Digital evidence is difficult to capture in a form that demonstrates that it has not been tampered with. Documentation of the scene and proper procedures are crucial.

3. **What does Chain of Custody documentation prove?**

   Who has had access to evidence collected from a crime scene and where and how it has been stored.

4. The contract ended recently for several workers who were hired for a specific project. The IT department has not yet removed all of those employees' login accounts. It appears that one of the accounts has been used to access the network, and a rootkit was installed on a server. You immediately contact the agency the employee was hired through and learn that the employee is out of the country, so it is unlikely that this person caused the problem.

   What actions do you need to take?

   You need to create an incident report, remove or disable the login accounts, isolate the infected server and possibly any user computers that communicate with the server, and remove the rootkit from the server. In terms of wider security policies, investigate why the temporary accounts were not disabled on completion of the project.

Interaction
Opportunity

Some learners might find this question more challenging. Consider working through the proper response with them to be sure they identify all the actions required.

Summary

In this lesson, you implemented and described many concepts and techniques that can be used to establish the desired level of security for data and workstations within an organization. Every organization will have different security requirements based on the type of business they conduct. It is your job to understand those requirements and know how security controls should be implemented to directly support those needs.

Which security best practices do you feel are the most important? Which are the minimum measures that should be taken? Does your organization implement good security practices?

A: Answers will vary, but may include following a company's security policy, entering a password that meets strong password requirements, and installing antivirus software on workstations.

Have you had experience with security incidents such as data breaches? What might have been done differently to further protect the data that was put at risk?

A: Answers will vary, but may include establishing clear incident response policies, appointing key personnel to act as first responders, and training IT personnel in basic data and device preservation techniques.

 *Practice Question: Additional practice questions are available on the CompTIA CHOICE platform within the **Assessments** tile.*

Lesson 14
Troubleshooting Workstation Security Issues

LESSON INTRODUCTION

For all that you try to configure workstation security according to best practices—securing user accounts, installing antivirus software, updating with patches, and encrypting data—there will be times when those procedures fail to work properly and you have to deal with malware infection. As a CompTIA® A+® PC technician, it is essential that you be able to identify types of malware, the symptoms of malware infections, and the steps to take to remove malicious code and prevent it from re-infecting computers and networks.

LESSON OBJECTIVES

In this lesson, you will:

- Detect, remove, and prevent malware infections.
- Troubleshoot common workstation security issues.

Topic A
Detect, Remove, and Prevent Malware

EXAM OBJECTIVES COVERED

1002-2.4 Given a scenario, detect, remove, and prevent malware using appropriate tools and methods.
1002-3.3 Given a scenario, use best practice procedures for malware removal.

Teaching Tip

Exam candidates should be able to distinguish types of malware and know how to use antivirus software.

Show Slide(s)

Computer Viruses and Worms

Teaching Tip

Exam candidates should be familiar with this terminology and with the different types of threats.

Explain that, in most cases, malware types are not mutually exclusive and that they are usually built and delivered as a combination of attacks.

Malware is a catch-all term to describe malicious software threats and social engineering tools designed to vandalize or compromise computer systems. In this topic, you will learn to describe different malware threats and operate antivirus software to protect the computer against infection and remediate infections.

COMPUTER VIRUSES AND WORMS

Computer **viruses** are programs designed to replicate and spread amongst computers. They produce a wide variety of symptoms on a PC and, in extreme cases, can cause permanent damage or loss of files. There are several different types of viruses, and they are generally classified by the different ways they can infect the computer (the vector). For example:

- **Boot sector viruses**—these attack the boot sector information, the partition table, and sometimes the file system.
- **Firmware viruses**—these are targeted against the firmware of a specific component, such as the drive controller. Such viruses are often only used in highly directed attacks, as the firmware is specific to particular models of drive, the firmware code is difficult to obtain and compromise, and executing the firmware update without the user realizing it is tricky.
- **Program viruses**—these are sequences of code that insert themselves into another executable program. When the application is executed, the virus code becomes active.
- **Script viruses**—scripts are powerful languages used to automate OS functions and add interactivity to web pages. Scripts are executed by an interpreter rather than self-executing. Most script viruses target vulnerabilities in the interpreter.
- **Macro viruses**—these viruses affect Office documents by using the programming code that underpins macro functionality maliciously.

What these types of viruses have in common is that they must infect a host file. That file can be distributed through any normal means—on a disk, on a network, or as an attachment through an email or instant messaging system.

Email attachment viruses—usually program or macro viruses in an attached file—often use the infected host's electronic address book to spoof the sender's address when replicating. For example, Alice's computer is infected with a virus and has Bob's email address in her address book. When Carlos gets an infected email apparently sent by Bob, it is the virus on Alice's computer that has sent the message.

Viruses are also categorized by their virulence. Some viruses are virulent because they exploit a previously unknown system vulnerability—a "zero-day" exploit. Others employ particularly effective social engineering techniques to persuade users to open the infected file. An infected email attachment with the subject "I Love You" is one of the best examples of the breed.

While the distinguishing feature of a virus is its ability to replicate by infecting other computer files, a virus can also be configured with a payload that executes when the virus is activated. The payload can perform any action available to the host process. For example, a boot sector virus might be able to overwrite the existing boot sector, an application might be able to delete, corrupt, or install files, and a script might be able to change system settings or delete or install files.

WORMS

Worms are memory-resident malware that replicate over network resources. Unlike a virus, a worm is self-contained; that is, it does not need to attach itself to another executable file. They typically target some sort of vulnerability in a network application, such as a database server. The primary effect of a worm infestation is to rapidly consume network bandwidth as the worm replicates. A worm may also be able to crash an operating system or server application (performing a Denial of Service attack). Also, like viruses, worms can carry a payload that may perform some other malicious action (such as installing a backdoor).

TROJAN HORSES AND SPYWARE

Other types of malware are not classed as viruses as they do not necessarily try to make copies of themselves within another "host" process. They can be just as much of a security threat as viruses, however. A **Trojan Horse**—or, more simply, just "Trojan"—is a program (usually harmful) that is packaged as something else. For example, you might download what you think is a new game, but when you run it, it also installs a keylogger and starts sending a transcript of whatever you type to a host on the Internet. There is also the case of rogueware or scareware fake antivirus, where a web pop-up displays a security alert and claims to have detected viruses on the computer and prompts the user to initiate a full scan, which installs the attacker's Trojan.

Many Trojans function as **backdoor** applications. Once the Trojan backdoor is installed, it allows the attacker to access the PC, upload files, and install software on it. This could allow the attacker to use the computer in a botnet, to launch Denial of Service (DoS) attacks or mass-mail spam. Trojans are also used by attackers to conceal their actions. Attacks or spam appear to come from the corrupted computer system.

SPYWARE AND KEYLOGGERS

Spyware is a program that monitors user activity and sends the information to someone else. It may be installed with or without the user's knowledge. Aggressive spyware or Trojans known as "keyloggers" actively attempt to steal confidential information by capturing a credit card number by recording key strokes entered into a web form, for example. Another spyware technique is to spawn browser pop-up windows to try to direct the user to other websites, often of dubious origin.

 Show Slide(s)

Trojan Horses and Spyware (5 slides)

 Teaching Tip

A lot of attention is now placed on convergent threats. For example, crackers gather "farms" of zombies (or botnets) infected with Trojans and rent them out to spammers, who in turn put phishing Trojans in their spam. MessageLabs estimates the value of a farm of 1000 bots at $50/week. The SpamThru Trojan is a good example (this actually installs a virus scanner, which will remove other viruses!).

Rogueware is the source of one of the few major security incidents to have affected macOS users. Some Trojans depend on flaws in the OS to infect the computer; others use social engineering techniques.

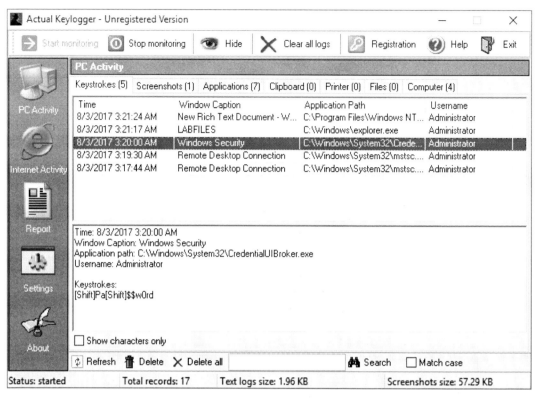

Actual Keylogger—Windows software that can run in the background to monitor different kinds of computer activity (opening and closing programs, browsing websites, recording keystrokes, and capturing screenshots). (actualkeylogger.com)

Note: Spyware doesn't have to depend on executable programs installed locally. Script and server-side programs on websites can be used to track a user's Internet history through use of cookies and information reported to the site by the browser.

ROOTKITS

Many Trojans cannot conceal their presence entirely and will show up as a running service. Often the service name is configured to be similar to a genuine process to avoid detection. For example, a Trojan may use the filename `run32dll` to masquerade as `run32dll`. One class of backdoor that is harder to detect is the **rootkit**. A rootkit is a set of tools designed to gain control of a computer without revealing its presence. They are so-called because they execute with root or system-level privileges. The general functions of a rootkit will be as follows:

- Replace key system files and utilities to prevent detection and eradication of the rootkit itself.
- Provide a backdoor channel for the rootkit handler to reconfigure the PC, steal information, or install additional spyware or other malware remotely.
- Evade antivirus software by infecting firmware code.

Rootkits may also be deployed as part of Digital Rights Management (DRM) and copy protection mechanisms. Infamously, Sony released a music player for its Extended Copy Protection CDs that also installed a rootkit.

RANSOMWARE

Ransomware is a type of malware that tries to extort money from the victim. One class of ransomware will display threatening messages, such as requiring Windows® to be reactivated or suggesting that the computer has been locked by the police because it was used to view child pornography or for terrorism. This may block access to the computer by installing a different shell program but this sort of attack is usually relatively trivial to fix. Another class of ransomware attempts to encrypt data files on any fixed, removable, and network drives. If the attack is successful, the user will be unable to access the files without obtaining the private encryption key, which is held by the attacker. If successful, this sort of attack is extremely difficult to mitigate, unless the user has up-to-date backups of the encrypted files.

WannaCry ransomware. Wikimedia Public Domain image.

 Note: Most ransomware will be capable of encrypting removable drives too so backup devices should not be left attached routinely. A cloud-based backup might offer a better alternative, but if the credentials for the cloud file server are cached, the ransomware is likely to be able to encrypt those, too.

Ransomware uses payment methods such as wire transfer, Bitcoin, or premium rate phone lines to allow the attacker to extort money without revealing his or her identity or being traced by local law enforcement.

SOURCES OF MALWARE INFECTION

 **Show Slide(s)**

Sources of Malware Infection

There are numerous sources of malware infection, but the main ones are:

- Visiting "unsavory" websites with an unpatched browser, low security settings, and no antivirus software.
- Opening links in unsolicited email.
- Infection from another compromised machine on the same network.
- Executing a file of unknown origin—email attachments are still the most popular vector, but others include file sharing sites, websites generally, attachments sent via chat/Instant Messaging, AutoRun USB sticks and CDs, and so on.
- Becoming victim to a "zero-day" exploit (that is, some infection mechanism that is unknown to software and antivirus vendors).

Show
Slide(s)

Antivirus Software

ANTIVIRUS SOFTWARE

Antivirus software (A-V) uses a database of known virus patterns (definitions) plus **heuristic** malware identification techniques to try to identify infected files and prevent viruses from spreading. "Heuristic" means that the software uses knowledge of the sort of things that viruses do to try to spot (and block) virus-like behavior.

Typically, the software is configured to run automatically when a user or system process accesses a file. The antivirus software scans the file first and blocks access if it detects anything suspicious.

The user can then decide either to try to disinfect the file, quarantine it (block further access), or delete it. Another option might be for the user to ignore the alert (if it is deemed a false positive, for instance) and exclude the file from future scans.

The A-V scanner also runs at boot-time to prevent boot sector viruses from infecting the computer. Most types of software can also scan system memory (to detect worms), email file attachments, removable drives, and network drives.

The latest "antivirus" software is usually "anti-malware" software, and includes routines and signatures to detect and block Trojans, rootkits, ransomware, and spyware.

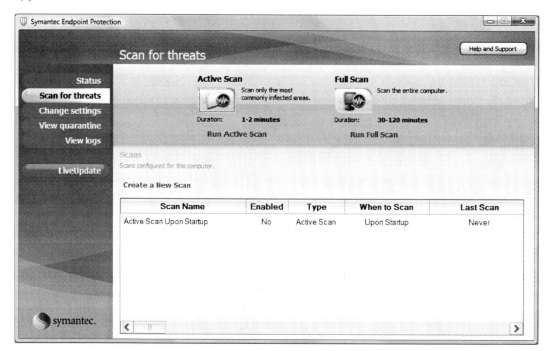

Symantec Endpoint Protection malicious software protection.

Antivirus software can be purchased either as personal security suites, designed to protect a single host, or network security suites, designed to be centrally managed from a server console. Most antivirus software is designed for Windows PCs and networks, as these are the systems targeted by most virus writers, but software is available for Linux® and macOS® as well.

Some of the major vendors are Symantec™ (including the Norton™ brand), McAfee®, Trend Micro™, Kaspersky™, ESET® (NOD32®), and Bitdefender™.

· Antivirus updates must be managed as they are made available. Antivirus engine updates can include enhancements, bug fixes, or new features being added to the software engine, improving the manner in which the software operates. Updates can be implemented automatically or manually depending on the software. Automatic updating refers to software that periodically downloads and applies updates without any user intervention, whereas manual updating means that a user must be involved to either initiate the update, download the update, or at least approve installation of the update.

BEST PRACTICES FOR MALWARE REMOVAL

CompTIA has identified a seven-step best practice procedure for malware removal:

1. Identify and research malware symptoms.
2. Quarantine infected systems.
3. Disable **System Restore** (in Windows).
4. Remediate infected systems:
   - Update anti-malware software.
   - Scan and use removal techniques (Safe Mode, Pre-installation environment).
5. Schedule scans and run updates.
6. Enable **System Restore** and create restore point (in Windows).
7. Educate end user.

These steps are explained in more detail in the remainder of this topic.

Show Slide(s)

Best Practices for Malware Removal

MALWARE RESEARCH

There are several websites dedicated to investigating the various new attacks that are developed against computer systems. Apart from the regular IT magazines, some good examples include **cert.org**, **sans.org**, **schneier.com**, and **grc.com**. The SANS "Top 20" critical security controls is one of the most useful starting points (**sans.org/top20/**). Antivirus vendors also maintain malware encyclopedias ("bestiaries") with complete information about the type, symptoms, purpose, and removal of viruses, worms, Trojans, and rootkits.

Show Slide(s)

Malware Research

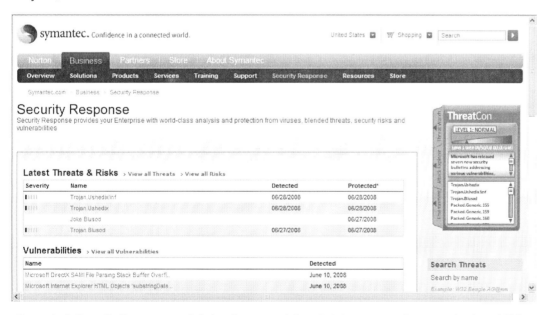

Symantec's Security Response portal showing current threat status, recent viruses and vulnerabilities, and search options for the malware database.

QUARANTINE AND REMEDIATION OF INFECTED SYSTEMS

Following the seven-step procedure, if symptoms of a malware infection are detected, the next steps should be to apply a quarantine, disable **System Restore**, and then remediate the infected system.

Show Slide(s)

Quarantine and Remediation of Infected Systems (2 slides)

QUARANTINING INFECTED SYSTEMS

Malware such as worms propagate over networks. This means that one of the first actions should be to disconnect the network link. Infected files could have been uploaded to network servers or cloud services, though these systems should have server-side scanning software to block infected files.

Move the infected system to a physically or logically secure work area. To remediate the system, you might need network access to tools and resources but you cannot risk infecting the production network. You should also ensure that the infected computer is not used until it has been cleaned up.

Once the infected system is isolated, the next step is to disable System Restore and other automated backup systems, such as File History. If you are relying on a backup to recover files infected by malware, you have to consider the possibility that the backups are infected, too. The safest option is to delete old system restore points and backup copies, but if you need to retain them, try to use antivirus software to determine whether they are infected.

Also consider identifying and scanning any removable media that has been attached to the computer. If the virus was introduced via USB stick, you need to find it and remove it from use. Viruses could also have infected files on any removable media attached to the system while it was infected.

The main tool to use to try to remediate an infected system will be antivirus software, though if the software has not detected the virus in the first place, you are likely to have to use a different suite. Make sure the antivirus software is fully updated before proceeding. This may be difficult if the system is infected, however. It may be necessary to remove the disk and scan it from a different system.

REMEDIATING INFECTED SYSTEMS

If a file is infected with a virus, you can (hopefully) use antivirus software to try to remove the infection (cleaning), quarantine the file (the antivirus software blocks any attempt to open it), or erase the file. You might also choose to ignore a reported threat, if it is a false positive, for instance. You can configure the action that software should attempt when it discovers malware as part of a scan.

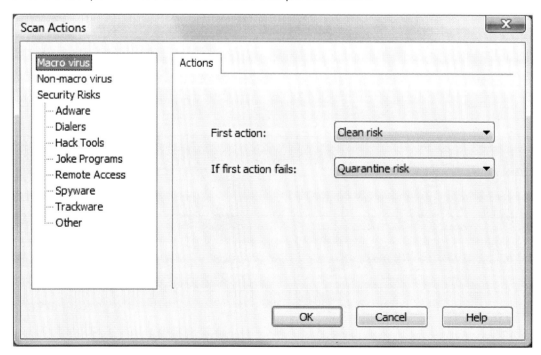

Configuring scan remediation options.

Most of the time the software will detect the virus and take the appropriate action. If you cannot clean a file, and have a backup copy, use it to restore the file. Check the files you restore to make sure that your backups are not infected.

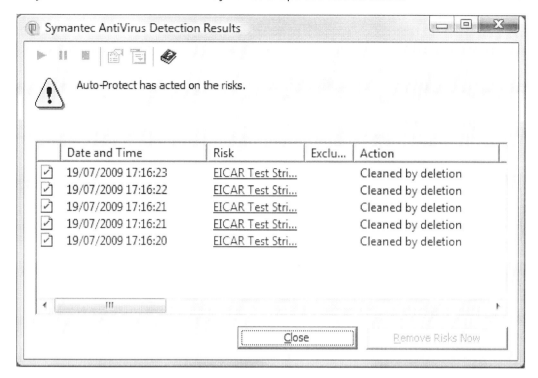

Detecting and remediating a virus infection.

Another option is to remove the virus manually. For assistance, check the website and support services for your antivirus software. In some cases, you may have to follow a further procedure to remove the virus or Trojan Horse:

- Use Task Manager or `taskkill` to terminate suspicious processes.
- Execute commands at a command prompt terminal and/or manually remove registry items using `regedit`.
- Use `msconfig` to perform a safe boot or boot into Safe Mode, hopefully preventing any infected code from running at startup.
- Boot the computer using the product disk and use the Windows Recovery Environment (WinRE) to run commands from a "clean" command environment. Another option, as mentioned previously, is to remove the disk from the infected system and scan it from another system, taking care not to allow cross-infection.

> **Note:** *The CompTIA exam objectives mention the recovery console. This is a precursor to WinRE, used by the Windows 2000 and Windows XP versions. Recovery console presents a limited subset of the commands normally available at a Windows command prompt and does not provide as many tools as WinRE.*

Antivirus software will not necessarily be able to recover data from infected files. Also, if a virus does disrupt the computer system, you might not be able to run antivirus software anyway and would have to perform a complete system restore. This involves reformatting the disk, reinstalling the OS and software (possibly from a system image snapshot backup), and restoring data files from a (clean) backup.

> **Note:** *Windows 8 and Windows 10 support a "refresh" reinstallation mode that wipes desktop applications but preserves user data files, personalization settings, and Windows Store apps. This might be of use in removing malware.*

Show
Slide(s)

Malware Infection
Prevention (2 slides)

MALWARE INFECTION PREVENTION

Once a system has been cleaned, you need to take the appropriate steps to prevent re-infection.

CONFIGURING ON-ACCESS SCANNING

Almost all security software is now configured to scan on-access. **On-access** means that the A-V software intercepts an OS call to open a file and scans the file before allowing or preventing it from being opened. This reduces performance somewhat but is essential to maintaining effective protection against malware.

> *Note: When configuring antivirus software, it is vital to configure the proper exceptions. Real-time scanning of some system files and folders (notably those used by Windows Update) can cause serious performance problems.*

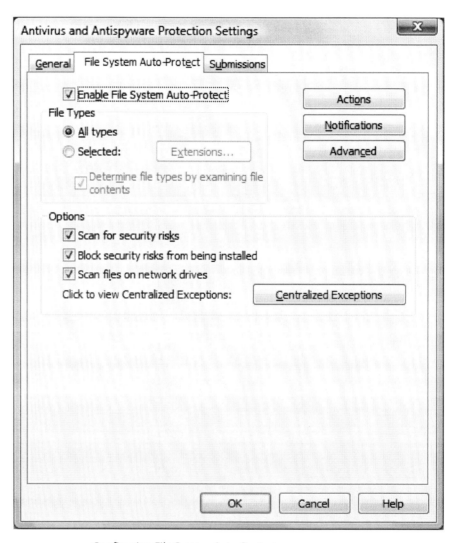

Configuring File System Auto-Protect on-access scans.

> *Note: Antivirus software depends on services to run properly—make sure that these are not disabled.*

CONFIGURING SCHEDULED SCANS

All security software supports scheduled scans. These scans can impact performance, however, so it is best to run them when the computer is otherwise unused. Symantec

Endpoint Protection performs an "Active Scan" at startup, but the user can define any type of scan to run to a schedule of their own choosing.

You also need to configure the security software to perform malware pattern and antivirus engine updates regularly.

Configuring a scheduled scan.

DNS CONFIGURATION

DNS spoofing allows attackers to direct victims away from the legitimate sites they were intending to visit and towards fake sites. As part of preventing reinfection, you should inspect and re-secure the DNS configuration.

- Flush the local DNS cache to clear out any potentially malicious entries. In Windows, you can use `ipconfig /flushdns` to do this.
- Check the HOSTS file for spoofed entries—mappings in the HOSTS file are loaded into the DNS cache and can override other name resolution methods, depending on how the system is configured. Malware often tries to corrupt the file to insert malicious entries. In Windows, the file is stored in **%SYSTEMROOT% \System32\drivers\etc\hosts**. In Linux, it is located in **/etc/hosts**. These files should generally be empty, though there may be commented (#) text.
- In Windows, check the priority order for name resolution services is set as per network policies. The priority order is set in the registry key **HKLM→SYSTEM→CurrentControlSet→Services→Tcpip→ServiceProvider**.
- Validate the DNS resolvers set as primary and secondary in the client's IP configuration (use `ipconfig /all`).

- Check these local DNS resolver services to make sure they are operating normally and are configured according to policy. You may also want to flush the cache on these servers. You could also test name resolution with `nslookup` to compare results of queries performed by your local DNS infrastructure with results obtained from a trusted Internet DNS provider. Google's public DNS servers (8.8.8.8 and 8.8.4.4) are quite widely used, for instance. Another option is Quad9, sponsored by IBM. Quad9 has a special focus on blocking domains known to host malicious content. There is a filtered service (9.9.9.9 and 149.112.112.112) and a non-secured service (9.9.9.10 and 149.112.112.10).
- Check that where you are forwarding queries, these queries are being sent to legitimate DNS servers on the Internet. Most organizations use their ISP's servers. Ensure that queries are reaching the intended servers and are not being redirected to a rogue DNS.

SOFTWARE FIREWALLS

If malware was able to run with administrative privileges, it may have made changes to the software (host) firewall configuration. An unauthorized port could potentially facilitate reinfection of the machine. You should inspect the firewall policy to see if there are any unauthorized changes. Consider resetting the policy to the default.

ENABLING SYSTEM RESTORE

If you disabled **System Restore** and automatic backups, you should re-enable them as part of the recommissioning process. Create a fresh restore point or system image and a clean data backup. As a final step, complete another antivirus scan; if the system is clean, then remove the quarantine and return it to service.

GUIDELINES FOR REDUCING MALWARE EFFECTS

Show Slide(s)

Guidelines for Reducing Malware Effects

*Note: All of the Guidelines for this lesson are available as checklists from the **Checklist** tile on the CHOICE Course screen.*

Consider the following guidelines to help reduce the effects of malware.

REDUCE THE RISK AND IMPACT OF MALWARE

The following guidelines can help reduce the risk and impact of malware:

- Carry out regular backups that allow data to be recovered, in case of loss due to a virus infection. Do not leave the backup device attached to the host. This minimizes the risk of the backup files becoming infected.
- Apply operating system and application security patches.
- Do not allow users to bring in their own software programs. If necessary, measures such as removing (or disabling) removable drives can be used. Windows-based systems also allow the administrator to determine who can run new programs, install new software, or download files from the web. Use these rights effectively.
- Install and use an antivirus package. The virus package must be kept up-to-date with updated signatures (or definitions), since viruses are continually being developed and the latest signatures offer the most protection.
- Select antivirus software that scans automatically (on-access). This provides much more reliable protection against web and email attachment threats.
- Configure filtering on the messaging server—this will prevent most of the unsolicited messages (spam) arriving at the server from getting to the users' mailboxes.

- Do not log on with administrative privileges except where necessary. Limit administrative privileges to a few, selected accounts. Keep passwords for these accounts secure.
- Educate users about not running attachments—and supplement this with procedures that will prevent files, such as executables and Office macros, from being allowed to run. This could be accomplished (for instance) by only allowing digitally signed code to be executed.
- Audit system events (such as logons) and review logs for unusual activity.
- Establish a procedure for recovery following virus infection to minimize the spread and effect of a virus.
- Routine procedures, such as applying critical and security patches to the OS and applications and updating virus definitions and malware threats in antivirus software, should be automated where possible or performed according to a strict schedule.
- Try to find time to monitor security developments so that you are aware of new threat types and strategies or "zero-day" vulnerabilities (flaws that have not been fixed by a patch).
- The organization needs to develop and enforce effective policies, backed up by disciplinary procedures to supplement training and education programs. The efforts of a single support technician are unlikely to make much difference. Training and educating can be more problematic, and you may well have to overcome resistance from end users accepting responsibility for security.

 *Note: To learn more, check the **Video** tile on the CHOICE Course screen for any videos that supplement the content for this lesson.*

Activity 14-1

Discussing Detecting, Removing, and Preventing Malware Infections

Show Slide(s)

Activity: Discussing Detecting, Removing, and Preventing Malware Infections

SCENARIO

Answer the following questions to check your understanding of the topic.

1. **What are the principal characteristics of Trojan malware?**

   Trojan malware is named after the Trojan Horse. This myth involved Greek warriors hidden in a wooden horse presented as a gift to the city of Troy. The Trojans wheeled the horse into the city and left it unguarded. At night, the Greek warriors slipped out, opened the gates, and let the Greek army in to ravage the city. A Trojan is malware disguised as legitimate software. Most Trojans establish a backdoor so that use of the computer can be subverted by a remote handler.

2. **What general class of malware is crypto-malware an example of?**

   Crypto-malware is a type of ransomware. The malware encrypts files on the target and then demands a ransom be paid to release the key that can decrypt them again.

3. **Why might you need to use a virus encyclopedia?**

   Typically, if a virus cannot be removed automatically, you might want to find a manual removal method. You might also want to identify the consequences of infection—whether the virus might have stolen passwords, and so on.

4. **Why must antivirus software be kept up-to-date regularly?**

   While there are certain heuristic techniques, a scanner is most effective when it can detect viruses that it recognizes. The virus update contains details about new or changed virus threats. If the update is not made, it is quite unlikely that these viruses will be detected if they infect your system.

5. **What type of file scan offers best protection for ordinary users?**

   On-access scans. These might reduce performance somewhat but very few users would remember to scan each file they use manually before opening.

6. **What would be the purpose of quarantining an infected file, rather than deleting it?**

   If antivirus software cannot clean a file, you may still want to investigate alternative methods of recovering data from the file. Quarantine means the antivirus software blocks access without actually removing the file from the file system.

7.   Why is DNS configuration a step in the malware remediation process?

Compromising domain name resolution is a very effective means of redirecting users to malicious websites. Following malware infection, it is important to ensure that DNS is being performed by valid servers.

8.   What sort of training should you give to end users to reduce the risk of infections?

Not to disable security applications and to be wary of emailed links, file attachments, removable media, and websites from unproven sources.

Activity 14-2
Using Antivirus Software

Show Slide(s)

Activity: Using Antivirus Software

Teaching Tip

The labfiles.iso disc image contains files such as the EICAR test string (embedded in setup.exe), Cain, and Netcat.

Show Slide(s)

One of the issues with security software is the tendency to overload administrators with alerts. Not all warnings are relevant to all environments. Point out that, as students have no Internet access in this activity, they cannot use a Microsoft account for enhanced security. Most software requires a period of tuning and adjustment so that when alerts are displayed, they reflect real priorities.

BEFORE YOU BEGIN
Complete this activity using Hyper-V Manager and the PC1 (Windows 10) VM.

SCENARIO
Windows ships with an anti-malware product named Windows Defender. In this activity, you will evaluate the product and test that it detects some known threats.

1. Start **PC1** and view the Windows Defender Security Center.
   a) Start the **PC1** VM and sign on using the account **Admin** and password **Pa$$w0rd**
   b) On the taskbar, in the notification area, select **Show hidden icons** and then select the **Windows Defender** icon.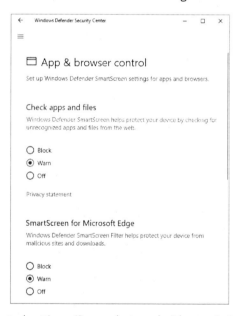
   c) In the **Account protection** alert, select **Dismiss**.
   d) Select **App & browser control**, and observe the settings for **SmartScreen**.

App & browser control settings. (Screenshot used with permission from Microsoft.)

This enforces an execution control that prevents known malicious code from running.
   e) Scroll down and select **Exploit protection settings**.

   If malicious code is run by the user, it still has to find a way to exploit or compromise a target process in the OS, usually by manipulating the way the process uses system memory. The system settings shown here are processor features designed to make it harder for malicious code to do this.
   f) If necessary, select the **Open Navigation** icon or maximize the **Windows Defender Security Center** Settings window, and then select **Device security**.

You can see from the **Core isolation** feature that the OS is aware that it is running as a VM. You should also see a **Secure boot** option enabled. This prevents unknown OSs from being installed to the device. The **Standard hardware security not supported** message indicates that no Trusted Platform Module (TPM) is present.

g) In the **Windows Defender Security Center** Settings app, select **Device performance & health**.

There should be no issues detected. Some systems will display a **Fresh start** option to reinstall Windows from here.

h) In the **Windows Defender Security Center** Settings app, select **Family options**.

This contains a link to a site where you can configure parental controls.

2. View the options for the antivirus components of Windows Defender.

a) In the **Windows Defender Security Center** Settings app, select **Virus & threat protection**.

Although no status alerts are displayed, no scan has been run and no updates have been obtained. If over-reporting of alerts is one issue with security software, under-reporting can also represent a serious problem. To be fair, this VM setup with no Internet or server management is not typical of most deployments. Defender would display an alert if it could reach the Internet and discover that updates were available. You might notice an alert about updates after running a scan.

b) Select the **Scan Now** button to start a scan. While the scan is running, review the other settings.

c) Select **Virus & threat protection settings**.

"Real-time protection" means that Defender is configured for on-access scanning.

d) Select **Manage Controlled folder access**.

While Windows folders are protected by default, you might enable this option to try to prevent crypto-malware from encrypting your profile folders.

e) Select the **Back** button. Scroll down the **Virus & threat protection settings** page. Observe the **Exclusions** option.

You would use this to prevent Defender scanning a particular folder or file.

f) Select the **Back** button. Select **Virus & threat protection updates**.

You can see the date of the last definition update here.

g) Select the **Back** button. Check to see if the scan has finished.

It should not detect any threats.

3. Optionally, open the **odysseus.iso** disc image and view the Defender response.

 Note: Depending on the security policy in place in the training center, the odysseus.iso file might not be available for you to use.

a) In the VM connection window, select **Media→DVD Drive→Insert Disk**.

b) Browse to the **C:\COMPTIA-LABS\LABFILES** folder. Select **odysseus.iso** and select **Open**.

c)   Open File Explorer and browse to the **This PC** object. Double-click the **DVD Drive** icon.

A User Account Control (UAC) warning is shown because a setup.exe process is trying to execute. The process' image file is unsigned (the publisher is listed as unknown).

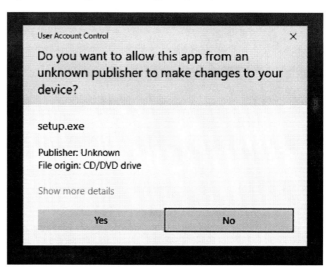

UAC warning that the publisher of the executable file cannot be verified. (Screenshot used with permission from Microsoft.)

d)   You would not normally proceed, but for this activity, select **Yes**.

e)   View the notifications generated by Windows Defender. You may need to select **See full history** under **Quarantined threats**.

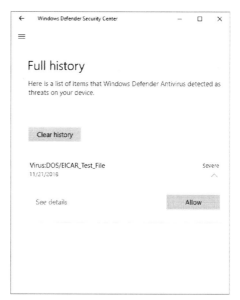

Threats quarantined by Windows Defender. (Screenshot used with permission from Microsoft.)

EICAR (**eicar.org**) is not actually a virus. It is a string that properly configured virus scanners should detect as a virus.

f)   In File Explorer, right-click the **DVD Drive** and select **Scan with Windows Defender**.

The scan should discover an additional threat. Cain (**oxid.it**) is a well-known tool for sniffing and cracking passwords.

g)   In File Explorer, right-click the **DVD Drive** and select **Open**.

There are some additional utilities that Windows Defender does not identify as threats but some security software might. ActualKeylogger (**actualkeylogger.com**) can record keystrokes and take screen captures covertly. Ncat is an implementation of the remote access tool Netcat (**nmap.org/ncat**).

h) Right-click **autorun.inf** and select **Open**.

This file sets the setup.exe process to run without an interactive window (using the / verysilent switch). Older versions of Windows might have allowed the file to run on insertion of the DVD, but autoplay settings and UAC prevent that from happening in Windows 10.

4. Are you confident that Windows Defender blocked the Trojan completely? Optionally, investigate the VM to see if there are any other changes. Some things may only become apparent if you restart the VM.

5. At the end of each activity, you need to close the VMs. You will always discard any changes you made.

   a) From the connection window, select **Action→Revert**.

   b) If prompted, select the **Revert** button to confirm.

Interaction Opportunity

If learners complete this step, here is what they should find:

- Inspecting **Apps & Features** will reveal the presence of **Odysseus**. The Trojan has modified the Registry so that it runs Netcat at startup.

- After a restart, the nc.exe (Netcat) process will run and try to open a listener. This will be blocked by the firewall, however.

- Learners can view the **nc.exe** process in Task Manager and may be able to track down the ini script that launches at startup.

- Also point out that the installer didn't generate any logs (this has to be activated via a policy).

Topic B

Troubleshoot Common Workstation Security Issues

EXAM OBJECTIVES COVERED
1002-2.2 Explain logical security concepts.
1002-3.2 Given a scenario, troubleshoot and resolve PC security issues.

Interaction Opportunity

As you discuss these symptoms, ask participants to share their experiences with security issues.

As with many areas of computer support, your responsibility for computer security does not end as soon as the security measures are implemented. As with printing, networking, hardware, and software, it is your responsibility to your users and clients to ensure proper security functions on an ongoing basis as well as to correct security problems that might compromise your systems or prevent users from accessing the resources that they need. The information and skills in this topic should help you troubleshoot any security issues that arise and restore your organization's security functions.

COMMON SYMPTOMS OF MALWARE INFECTION

Show Slide(s)

Common Symptoms of Malware Infection

A virus's payload can be programmed to perform many different actions and there are, besides, many different types of malware. Consequently, there can be very many different symptoms of malware infection.

PERFORMANCE SYMPTOMS

When the computer is slow or "behaving oddly," one of the things you should suspect is malware infection. Some specific symptoms associated with malware include:

- The computer fails to boot or experiences lock ups.
- Unexpected or threatening messages or graphics appear on the screen.
- Performance at startup or generally is very slow.
- Network performance is slow or Internet connections are disrupted.

Any sort of activity or configuration change that was not initiated by the user is a good reason to suspect malware infection. Of course, all these things can have other causes, too. If you identify these symptoms, run an antivirus scan. If this is negative but you cannot diagnose another cause, consider quarantining the system or at least putting it under close monitoring.

> **Note:** *If a system is "under suspicion," do not allow users with administrative privileges to sign in to it, either locally or remotely. This reduces the risk that malware could compromise a privileged account.*

APPLICATION CRASHES AND SERVICE PROBLEMS

One of the key indicators of malware infection is that security-related applications, such as antivirus, firewall, and Windows Update, stop working. You might also notice that applications or Windows tools (Notepad for instance) stop working or crash frequently.

Software other than Windows is often equally attractive for malware writers as not all companies are diligent in terms of secure coding. Software that uses browser plug-ins is often targeted; examples include Adobe's Reader® software for PDFs and Flash®

Player. If software from a reputable vendor starts crashing (faulting) repeatedly, suspect malware infection and apply the quarantining/monitoring procedures described earlier.

FILE SYSTEM ERRORS AND ANOMALIES

Another "red flag" for malware infection is changes to system files and/or file permissions.

- The file system or individual files are corrupted or deleted.
- Date stamps and file sizes of infected files change.
- Permissions attributes of files change, resulting in "Access Denied" errors.
- New executable files (EXEs and DLLs) appear in system folders. They may have file names that are very close to valid programs (notpad.exe).

These sorts of issues are less likely to have other causes so you should quarantine the system and investigate it closely.

EVENT VIEWER

The system, application, and security logs may be of use in detecting malware that is attempting to remain concealed. You can inspect these log files using Event Viewer. High numbers of audit failures in the security log or unexpected Windows Installer events are the types of thing that warrant further investigation. The log will also list application and service crash events, which may reveal some sort of malware infection.

WEB BROWSER SECURITY ISSUES

Malware often targets the web browser. Remember that malware is not always destructive. Malware such as adware and spyware is designed with commercial or criminal intent rather than to vandalize the computer system.

Common symptoms of infection by spyware or adware are pop-ups or additional toolbars, the home page or search provider changing suddenly, searches returning results that are different to other computers, slow performance, and excessive crashing (faults). Viruses and Trojans may spawn pop-ups without the user opening the browser.

 Note: The lines between useful utilities, adware, and spyware are not completely clear-cut, but if something is there that the user (or IT department) did not explicitly sanction, then it's best to get rid of it.

Another symptom is **redirection**. This is where the user tries to open one page but gets sent to another. Often this may imitate the target page. In adware, this is just a blunt means of driving traffic through a site, but spyware may exploit it to capture authentication details.

 Note: If a user experiences redirection, check the HOSTS file for malicious entries. HOSTS is a legacy means of mapping domain names to IP addresses and is a popular target for malware. Also verify which DNS servers the client is configured to use.

TROJANS, ROOTKITS, AND BOTNETS

Malware that tries to compromise the PC will try to create a communications channel with its "handler." If the firewall is still working, you may see unfamiliar processes or ports trying to connect to the Internet.

 Note: Remember that the most powerful malware can disguise its presence. For example, the netstat *utility shows ports open on the PC. A rootkit may replace* netstat *with a modified version that does not show the ports in use by the rootkit.*

 Show Slide(s)

Web Browser Security Issues (2 slides)

 Teaching Tip

Point out that a lot of redirection attempts are based on corrupting DNS.

One use of Trojans and rootkits is to scan other hosts for weaknesses and launch Denial of Service (DoS) attacks against networks. Most ISPs monitor the use of scanning tools and will warn you if they detect their use coming from your IP address.

 Note: Trojans and rootkits are likely to try to disguise their presence. New breeds of rootkit try to occupy firmware, for instance, so that not even disinfecting the file system or re-formatting the hard drive will remove them. Sometimes the only way to diagnose such infections is to examine network traffic from the infected PC from a different machine.

VIRUS ALERT HOAXES AND ROGUE ANTIVIRUS

Hoax virus alerts are quite common. They are often sent as mass emails as a prank. Most advise you to forward the "alert" to everyone in your address book. Some hoax virus alerts describe a number of steps that you "must take" to remove the virus—following these steps may cause damage to your computer. Use legitimate portals to research malware.

Rogue antivirus is a particularly popular way to disguise a Trojan. In the early versions of this attack, a website would display a pop-up disguised as a normal Windows dialog box with a fake security alert, warning the user that viruses have been detected. As browsers and security software have moved to block this vector, cold calling vulnerable users claiming to represent Microsoft support has become a popular attack.

DIGITAL CERTIFICATE ISSUES

Show Slide(s)

Digital Certificate Issues (4 slides)

Websites and program code are very often made trustworthy by proving the site or code author's identity using a **digital certificate**. The certificate is a wrapper for the public key in a public/private key pair. The public key enables a client to read the certificate holder's signature, created using an encryption mechanism. As that signature could only have been made with the linked private key, and the private key should be known only to the holder, if the user trusts the certificate, then the user can trust the website or program code.

The issue then is how the user is able to trust the certificate. Most certificates are issued and vouched for by a third-party called a **Certificate Authority (CA)**. The CA adds its own signature to the site certificate. The user can validate the CA's signature, because the CA's root certificate is installed on the computer.

Root certificates have to be trusted implicitly, so it would obviously be highly advantageous if a malicious user could install a bogus root certificate and become a trusted root CA. Installing a trusted root certificate usually requires administrative privileges. On a Windows PC, most root certificate updates are performed as part of Windows Update or installed by domain controllers or administrators as part of running Active Directory. There have been instances of stolen certificates and root certificates from CAs being exploited because of weaknesses in the key used in the certificate.

When you browse a site using a certificate, the browser displays the information about the certificate in the address bar:

- If the certificate is valid and trusted, a padlock icon is shown. Click the icon to view information about the certificate and the Certificate Authority guaranteeing it.

Browsing a secure site: 1) Check the domain name as highlighted in the address bar; 2) Only enter confidential data into a site using a trusted certificate; 3) Click the padlock to view information about the certificate holder and the CA that issued it and optionally to view the certificate itself.

- If the certificate is highly trusted, the address bar is colored green. High assurance certificates make the website owner go through an even more rigorous identity validation procedure.
- If the certificate is untrusted or otherwise invalid, the address bar might show a color-coded alert and the site is blocked by a warning message. If you want to trust the site anyway, click through the warning.

 There is a problem with this website's security certificate.

The security certificate presented by this website was not issued by a trusted certificate authority.
The security certificate presented by this website has expired or is not yet valid.

Security certificate problems may indicate an attempt to trick you or intercept any data you send to the server.

We recommend that you close this webpage and do not continue to this website.

 Click here to close this webpage.

 Continue to this website (not recommended).

 More information

Untrusted certificate warning. (Screenshot used with permission from Microsoft.)

Note: Digital certificates are also used to verify the identity of software publishers. If a certificate has not been issued by a one of the trusted root CAs, Windows will warn you that the publisher cannot be verified when you try to install an add-on or other type of application.

EMAIL ISSUES

Spam is unsolicited email messages, the content of which is usually advertising pornography, miracle cures for various personal conditions, or bogus stock market tips and investments. Spam is also used to launch phishing attacks and spread viruses and worms. Spam needs to be filtered before it reaches the user's inbox. Most email applications now ship with junk mail filters or you can install a filter at the organization's mail gateway. These filters need to be kept up-to-date in order to protect against the latest spamming techniques.

 Show Slide(s)
Email Issues

 Interaction Opportunity
Ask learners how often they have retrieved legitimate messages from a junk folder.

Note: Host-based spam filters are fine for home users but enterprise networks will usually deploy a mail gateway to filter spam and scan message for malware before it reaches the company's internal mail servers.

If the filter tags a message as spam, it posts it to a "Junk" email folder and no notification is displayed to the user. The user can inspect the junk folder manually to retrieve any legitimate messages that have been blocked by accident (false positives).

The main problem with **email filtering** is that it can block genuine messages too, leading to missed communications. Some filters may support detection levels so that where the scan is not certain the message is spam, it may hold it and send a blocked notification to the user's inbox.

As well as detecting spam automatically, these tools allow the user to blacklist known spammer domains or to whitelist known safe senders.

Email file attachments are frequently used as a vector for malware. As well as deploying filtering to detect such messages as spam, most A-V software can scan message attachments for malware before they can be opened.

In addition to being a vector for infection, spam may be a symptom of malware infection. One of the main criminal uses of Trojans is to install spamming software on the "zombie" PC. The software starts sending out spam emails. The software may do this surreptitiously to avoid detection; that is, it does not try to send thousands of messages at a time, but a few messages every hour. Because the Trojan may have infected thousands or millions of PCs (a botnet), it is capable of delivering huge quantities of spam.

If a computer's email is hijacked in this way, the user is likely to receive bounces, non-deliverable messages, automated replies from unknown recipients, or messages from users regarding the spam that has been sent. This does not always indicate malware infection, however; it could simply be that the spammer has spoofed the user's email address. If the volume is large, they may receive complaints from other networks and from their ISP. You can use various websites—**mxtoolbox.com** is one example—to check whether your organization's public IP address appears on any blacklist.

GUIDELINES FOR TROUBLESHOOTING COMMON WORKSTATION SECURITY ISSUES

Show Slide(s)

Guidelines for Troubleshooting Common Workstation Security Issues (3 slides)

Consider the following guidelines when troubleshooting common workstation security issues.

TROUBLESHOOT COMMON WORKSTATION SECURITY ISSUES

Follow these guidelines for troubleshooting common workstation security issues:

- Symptoms of malware infection might include:
  - Performance issues such as failure to boot, lock ups, slow performance, or strange messages or images on screen.
  - Frequent application crashes and service problems.
  - Changes to system files or changes to file permissions.
  - Event log entries showing a high number of audit failures or application and service crash events.
- Web browsers are frequent targets for malware delivery.
  - May be adware or spyware.
  - Might redirect users to a site that imitates the site the user attempted to access.
  - As compromised PC attempts to communicate with handler, unfamiliar processes or ports show up in firewall log files.
  - Hoax virus alerts requesting users to forward the message, or messages including steps to remove the virus with the steps doing the actual damage.

- Rogue antivirus disguises Trojans.
- Check for compromised CAs.
- Verify the padlock icon is shown in browsers for secure sites and that the address bar is not maroon, which would indicate an untrusted, insecure site.
- Check the Junk email folder to ensure legitimate emails are not improperly flagged.
- Make sure users understand the potential issues in running email file attachments.

Activity 14-3
Discussing Troubleshooting Common Workstation Security Issues

Show Slide(s)

Activity: Discussing Troubleshooting Common Workstation Security Issues

SCENARIO
Answer the following questions to check your understanding of the topic.

1. Early in the day, a user called the help desk saying that his computer is running slowly and freezing up. Shortly after this user called, other help desk technicians who overheard your call also received calls from users who report similar symptoms.

   Is this likely to be a malware infection? If so, what type of malware would you suspect?

   It is certainly possible. Software updates are often applied when a computer is started in the morning so that is another potential cause but you should investigate and log a warning so that all support staff are alerted. It is very difficult to categorize malware when the only symptom is performance issues. You might say a virus or worm as the malware is non-stealthy. However, it is equally possible that performance issues could be a result of a badly written Trojan or a Trojan/backdoor application might be using resources maliciously (for DDoS, Bitcoin mining, spam, and so on).

Interaction Opportunity

Emphasize that there is no one "right" answer, and encourage learners to speculate on the cause.

2. **Why might a PC infected with malware display no obvious symptoms?**

   If the malware is used with the intent to steal information or record behavior, it will not try to make its presence obvious. A rootkit may be very hard to detect even when a rigorous investigation is made.

3. You receive a support call from a user who is "stuck" on a web page. She is trying to use the **Back** button to return to her search results, but the page just displays again with a pop-up message.

   Is her computer infected with malware?

   If it only occurs on certain sites, it is probably part of the site design. A script running on the site can prevent use of the **Back** button. It could also be a sign of adware or spyware though, so it would be safest to scan the computer using up to date anti-malware software.

4. Another user calls to say he is trying to sign on to his online banking service, but the browser reports that the certificate is invalid.

   Should the bank update its certificate, or do you suspect another cause?

   It would be highly unlikely for a commercial bank to allow its website certificates to run out of date or otherwise be misconfigured. You should strongly suspect redirection by malware or a phishing/pharming scam.

5. Your company's static IP address has been placed on a number of anti-spam blacklists.

    Could this be the result of external fraud or do you need to investigate your internal systems for malware?

    It would be very unusual for someone to be able to insert your IP address into multiple blacklists. You should suspect that malware is being used to send spam from your network.

Show Slide(s)

Activity: Identifying Security Protection Methods

Teaching Tip

Suggested answers might include:

- For physical security: verifying employees have IDs showing, that building access is limited or monitored, and that locks are used as needed.

- For digital security: ensuring that users have only the access needed to files and folders, and that passwords are secure and changed regularly.

- For anti-malware security: verifying that anti-malware is installed on devices that will connect to the network and that virus definitions are up-to-date.

- For firewalls: configuring firewalls to enable users to get where they need to go, but that unauthorized users cannot get into the network.

- For strong passwords: verifying that only strong passwords can be used on the network, and that users don't make their password available to others.

- For email filtering: setting up filtering to allow only business related messages to get through into user's mailboxes.

Activity 14-4

Identifying Security Protection Methods

SCENARIO

The IT department security team has invited members from various departments, including PC Support, HR, Marketing, and Software Development, to join them in reviewing and updating the security documents for the organization. You were selected to represent the PC Support team on the committee.

You received an email outlining the topics for the next meeting. You want to write down some ideas you think are important to include, and write down your justification for including the items. Be sure to take into consideration everything you have learned so far about security.

1. Fill in the table with the information you feel is important to discuss during a meeting about security protection methods.

Item	Details to Discuss	Justification
Physical security		
Digital security		
Anti-malware software		
Firewalls		
Strong passwords		
Email filtering		

2. Share your table with the class. See which items you all included and if there are important items you should have included.

Summary

In this lesson, you performed troubleshooting on workstation security issues such as malware, web browser and digital certificate issues, and email issues. In your role as an A+ technician, you will be advising and supporting users in multiple areas surrounding computing devices, so using the guidelines and procedures provided in this lesson will enable you to provide the required level of support to users.

Which best practice for minimizing the effect of malware do you think is most important?

A: Answers will vary, but might include keeping antivirus software and signature files updated, or user awareness training.

How might you recognize a possible spyware or adware infection on a workstation?

A: Answers will vary, but might include the appearance of pop-ups or additional toolbars, or unexpectedly being redirected to a different web page.

 Practice Question: Additional practice questions are available on the CompTIA CHOICE platform within the Assessments tile.

Lesson 15

Supporting and Troubleshooting Laptops

LESSON INTRODUCTION

As a CompTIA® A+® technician, you will require a robust knowledge of portable computing principles. In this lesson, the focus will be on laptops and how they differ from desktop systems in terms of features, upgrade/repair procedures, and troubleshooting.

LESSON OBJECTIVES

In this lesson, you will:

- Use laptop features.
- Install and configure laptop hardware.
- Troubleshoot common laptop issues.

Topic A
Use Laptop Features

 EXAM OBJECTIVES COVERED
1001-1.3 Given a scenario, use appropriate laptop features.
1001-3.1 Explain basic cable types, features, and their purposes.
1001-3.9 Given a scenario, install and configure common devices.

One of the most prevalent mobile devices in today's workplaces has to be the laptop computer. As a CompTIA A+ technician, you will be asked to select and configure laptops for different business and leisure uses. In this topic, you will focus on features that distinguish different laptop models and laptops from desktop computers.

LAPTOPS

 Show Slide(s)

Laptops

 Teaching Tip

Laptop hardware and mobile devices form a significant part of the 220-1001 exam objectives. Try to source examples of laptops and expansion options such as port replicators and docking stations to pass around as you discuss laptop features.

 Teaching Tip

Point out that screen sizes range from about 11 inches to about 17 inches. Those laptops with 11 to 14 inch screens are considered ultraportable, whereas laptops with screens over 15.5 inches are considered desktop replacements.

A **laptop** is a complete portable computer system. Laptops have specialized hardware designed especially for use in a portable chassis and can run on battery or AC power. Laptops use the same sort of operating systems as desktop PCs, however, and have many upgradeable or replaceable components.

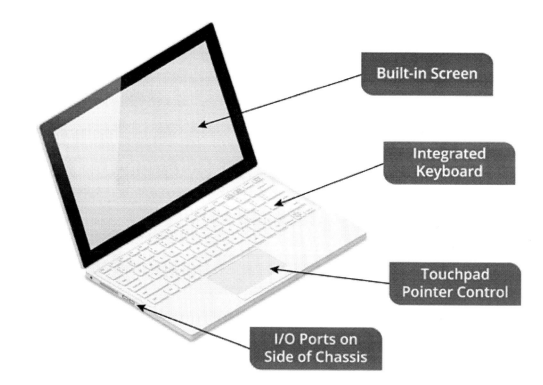

Distinctive features of a laptop computer, including the built-in screen, integrated keyboard, touchpad pointer control, and I/O ports (on both sides and rear of chassis). (Image © 123RF.com.)

Like desktops, laptops come in many different models and specifications. You could broadly categorize laptops as follows:

- **Entry Level/Budget**—basic model (often with home or business versions) featuring average components and a trade-off between features and portability.
- **Ultraportable**—very small and light machines offering extended operating time on battery power. The trade-off here is smaller screen size, lower capacity drives, and fewer peripherals.
- **Desktop Replacement**—a powerful machine with similar performance, capacity, and peripherals to a desktop PC. The trade-off is that these machines are less portable and less able to run for long on battery power.
- **Media Center**—portable home entertainment systems, featuring large screens, storage capacity, media features (such as TV tuner, video recording, and surround sound), and components capable of running the latest games.
- **Gaming Laptop**—an increasingly popular class of machine. ATI and NVIDIA are producing more graphics adapters designed for laptops, though they cannot quite match the power of desktops built for gaming.

Although laptops can use peripheral devices, the basic input and output devices are provided as integrated components.

TOUCHPADS

Almost all laptops use **touchpads** as the primary pointing device. Moving a finger over the touch-sensitive pad moves the cursor and tapping it issues a click. Touchpads also come with buttons and scroll areas to replicate the function of a mouse's scroll wheel. Most touchpads now support multi-touch or using gestures, such as a pinch to zoom the display.

 Show Slide(s)

Touchpads

 Teaching Tip

If learners query the use of "almost," tell them that some laptops use a device called a point stick (IBM TrackPoint) instead of or as well as a touchpad. Lenovo still produces ThinkPad laptops with a point stick.

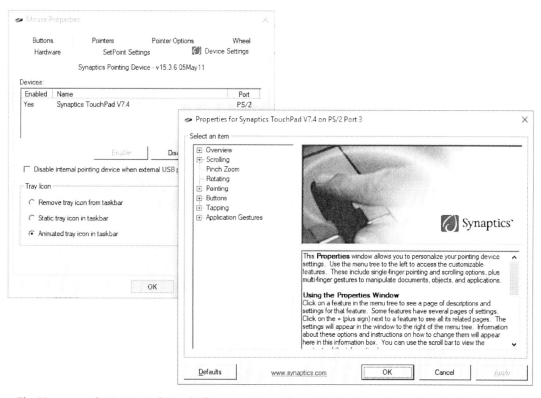

The Mouse applet in Control Panel allows you to configure both mice and touchpads—installing the vendor's driver makes extra configuration settings available.

In Windows®, the touchpad can be configured using the **Mouse** applet in Control Panel. Installing the manufacturer's driver will make the device-specific options available, such as configuring scroll areas or gesture support.

*Note: When you are using a touchpad, it is easy to brush the pad accidentally and for this to be interpreted as a click event. If this happens a lot, adjust the sensitivity setting or completely disable the **Tap to click** functionality.*

KEYBOARDS

 Show Slide(s)
Keyboards (2 slides)

 Teaching Tip
Identifying the purpose of a function key by the icon can sometimes be challenging. If laptops are deployed in your classroom environment, you might consider having learners try out some of the special function keys.

Apart from being flatter and more compact, a laptop keyboard is similar to a desktop keyboard. The main difference is the Function (Fn) keys operate using the **Fn** key with the top row of numerals.

 Note: Actually, many desktop keyboards also include function keys to support use as an external keyboard for a laptop. If not being used with a laptop, these keys can be mapped to perform different functions.

A laptop keyboard with function and media control keys across the top.

These Function (Fn) keys perform laptop-specific functions indicated by distinctive icons. Typical functions include:

- **Display**—toggle the video feed between the built-in laptop display, the built-in display and an external monitor (dual display), and an external monitor only.
- **Screen orientation**—some tablet/laptop hybrids have rotatable screens while others can be used in tablet mode and can switch the screen orientation automatically between portrait and landscape modes depending on how the device is being held. A screen orientation function key will allow you to choose whether to lock the screen in one orientation.
- **Wireless/Bluetooth/Cellular/GPS**—toggle the radio for Wi-Fi, Bluetooth®, cellular data, and/or Global Positioning System (GPS) on and off. Each of these settings might be separately configurable or be selectively disabled via different toggle states and indicators. There is often an airplane mode toggle to completely disable all wireless functions.
- **Volume**—adjust the sound up, down, or off (mute).
- **Screen brightness**—dim or brighten the built-in display.
- **Keyboard backlight**—illuminate the keys (useful for typing in low light).
- **Touchpad**—sometimes the touchpad can interfere with typing, causing the cursor to jump around. A touchpad toggle allows you to enable or disable it as required.
- **Media options**—this allows control over audio and video playback, such as stop, pause, fast forward, and rewind controls, or skipping between tracks.

Depending on the size of the chassis, a laptop keyboard may not support a numeric keypad. In this case, some of the ordinary keys may function as a keypad in conjunction with **NumLock** or the **Fn** key.

 Note: One issue to watch out for in laptop keyboards and chassis designs is flex, where the board buckles slightly when keys are pressed. None of the input devices on a laptop are really suitable for sustained use. An external keyboard and/or mouse can of course be connected using a USB or wireless port.

CONFIGURATION OF KEYBOARD SETTINGS

In Windows, you use the **Keyboard** applet in Control Panel or Windows Settings to configure options such as the repeat rate and sensitivity for keys. The vendor driver may make additional settings available for configuring function keys.

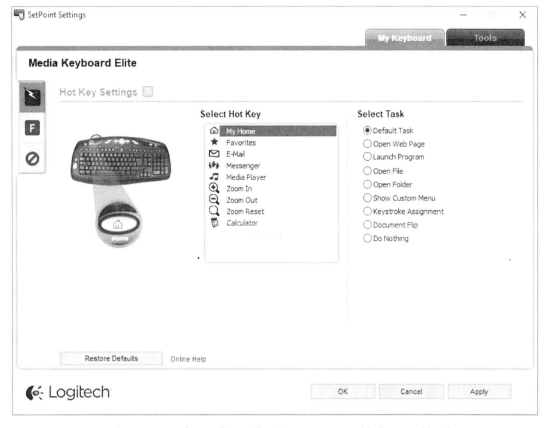

Logitech SetPoint software for configuring programmable keys and hot keys.

DISPLAYS AND TOUCHSCREENS

Most modern laptop displays are also **touchscreens** of one kind or another. Some can be used with a stylus as well as (or instead of) finger touch.

Another important point to note about the laptop display screen is that it holds the antenna wires for the Wi-Fi adapter. These are connected to the adapter via internal wiring.

Show Slide(s)

Displays and Touchscreens (2 slides)

ROTATING OR REMOVABLE SCREENS

Some laptops are based on tablet hybrid form factors where the touchscreen display can be fully flipped or rotated between portrait and landscape orientations. Another approach, used on Microsoft's Surface® tablets, is for the keyboard portion of the laptop to be detachable and for the screen to work independently as a tablet.

> *Note: In Windows 10, tablet mode for the Start Screen is selected automatically (by default) on hybrid devices. For example, removing the keyboard from a Microsoft Surface tablet or folding the screen of an HP X360 device over through 360 degrees puts Windows 10 into tablet mode. You can use Windows 10 settings to manually select tablet mode and to configure these automatic behaviors.*

TOUCHSCREEN CONFIGURATION

In Windows, touchscreen options are configured using the **Tablet PC Settings** and **Pen and Touch** applets.

Use the Tablet PC Control Panel applet to set up or calibrate a touchscreen. (Screenshot used with permission from Microsoft.)

You can use **Tablet PC Settings** to calibrate the display and set options for orientation and left- or right-handed use, and you can use **Pen and Touch** to configure gesture settings, such as using tap-and-hold to trigger a right-mouse click event.

EXPANSION OPTIONS

Show Slide(s)

Expansion Options

Teaching Tip

Options such as RJ-45 and optical disc drives are starting to be omitted from laptops, especially the ultraportable models.

Laptops ship with standard wired ports for connectivity. The ports are usually arranged on the left and right edges. Older laptops might have ports at the back of the chassis. There will be at least one video port for an external display device, typically HDMI or DisplayPort/Thunderbolt, but possibly VGA or DVI on older laptops. There will also be a number of USB Type A ports and one or more USB Type C ports on a modern laptop, one of which may also function as a Thunderbolt port.

Other standard ports include microphone and speaker jacks and RJ-45 (Ethernet) for networking. Finally, a laptop might come with a memory card reader.

USB provides a simple means of adding or upgrading an adapter without having to open the laptop chassis. USB adapters (or "dongles") can provide a wide range of functionality:

- **USB to RJ-45**—provide an Ethernet port for a laptop or mobile device. Ultrathin laptops often omit a built-in RJ-45 port as it is too tall to fit in the chassis.

USB to Ethernet adapter. (Image © 123RF.com.)

- **USB to Wi-Fi/Bluetooth**—this might be used to upgrade to a better Wi-Fi standard than the laptop's built-in adapter. Most dongles will also function as a Bluetooth adapter. Some Wi-Fi dongles are compact but those lacking large antennas may not perform well; the drawback of large antennas is, of course, that they protrude significantly.
- **USB Optical Drive**—most ultraportable laptops no longer feature optical drives as they cannot fit within the ultrathin chassis.

PORT REPLICATORS

A **port replicator** usually attaches to a special connector on the back or underside of a portable computer. It provides a full complement of ports for devices such as keyboards, monitors, mice, and network connections. A replicator does not normally add any other functionality to the portable computer.

Show
Slide(s)

Port Replicators

A port replicator. (Image by Elnur Amikishiyev © 123RF.com.)

DOCKING STATIONS

A **docking station** is a sophisticated port replicator that may support add-in cards or drives via a media bay. When docked, a portable computer can function like a desktop machine or use additional features, such as a full size expansion card.

Show
Slide(s)

Docking Stations

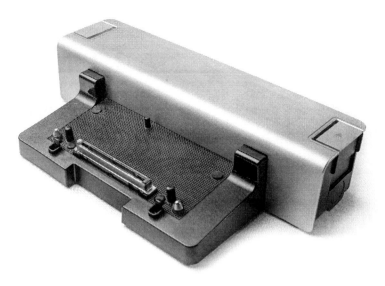

A laptop docking station. (Image by Luca Lorenzelli © 123RF.com.)

Note: *Most port replicators and docking stations use proprietary connectors. There are USB versions but their performance can be a bit erratic.*

PHYSICAL LOCKS

Show
Slide(s)

Physical Locks

Being so portable makes laptops easy devices to steal. Many cable locks are available to chain the laptop to a desk. These are typically either key or combination operated. If key operated, make sure you record the key code in case you need to get a replacement.

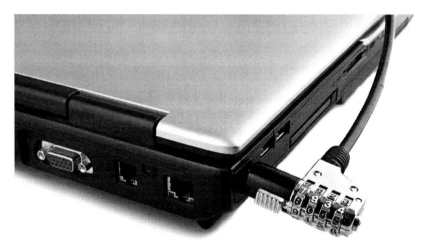

Kensington laptop locks. (Image by © 123RF.com.)

Most laptops come with a connection point for a Kensington lock in the chassis.

Activity 15-1

Discussing Laptop Features

Show Slide(s)

Activity: Discussing Laptop Features

SCENARIO

Answer the following questions to check your understanding of the topic.

Interaction Opportunity

If you have a range of different laptop computers available, ask learners to:

- Identify the external components such as the keyboard, display, track point, or touchpad.
- Identify what the function keys do.
- List expansion options and external ports.

1. **What feature would you expect to find on a modern touchpad, compared to older models?**

   Support for multi-touch.

2. **True or false? Touchpad settings would be configured via the Touch applet in Windows Control Panel.**

   False—the touchpad is configured via tabs in the **Mouse** applet.

3. **What two display settings would you expect to be able to control via a laptop's Fn keys?**

   Screen brightness, and toggling the output between the built-in screen and external display.

4. **What device would you use to extend the functionality of a laptop while sitting at a desk?**

   A docking station is used to extend functionality (allowing use of additional drives or adapters) but you could also mention a port replicator, which extends the number of connectivity options.

5. **What connectivity issue is resolved by providing a USB-to-RJ-45 dongle?**

   Ethernet/wired network connectivity.

6. **What is the brand name of the standard cable lock security system for laptops?**

   Kensington.

Topic B

Install and Configure Laptop Hardware

EXAM OBJECTIVES COVERED
1001-1.1 Given a scenario, install and configure laptop hardware and components.
1001-1.2 Given a scenario, install components within the display of a laptop.
1001-5.5 Given a scenario, troubleshoot common mobile device issues while adhering to the appropriate procedures.

There will be situations where dealing with external components won't completely address the issues or problems a user is having with his or her laptop. You will need to be able to install and configure internal laptop hardware components.

LAPTOP DISASSEMBLY PROCESSES

Show Slide(s)
Laptop Disassembly Processes

When it comes to performing upgrades or replacing parts, there are some issues specific to laptops that you should be aware of.

Note: Only open a laptop to access internal components if it is no longer under warranty or if you are an authorized technician for the laptop brand.

HAND TOOLS AND PARTS

Laptops use smaller screws than are found on desktops. You may find it useful to obtain a set of jeweler's screwdrivers and other appropriate hand tools. It is also much easier to strip the screws—remove the notch for the screwdriver—take care and use an appropriately sized screwdriver!

You need to document the location of screws of a specific size and the location and orientation of ribbon cables and other connectors. It can be very easy to remove them quickly during disassembly and then to face a puzzle during reassembly.

Note: A useful tip is to take a photo of the underside of the laptop and print it out. As you remove screws, tape them to the relevant point in your picture. This ensures you will not lose any and will know which screw goes where. Photograph each stage of disassembly so you know where to re-fit cables and connectors.

As with a desktop, organize parts that you remove or have ready for installation carefully. Keep the parts away from your main work area so that you do not damage them by mistake. Keep static-sensitive parts, such as the CPU, memory, and adapter cards, in anti-static packaging.

FORM FACTORS AND PLASTICS/FRAMES

Many laptops are built using proprietary components and scope for customization and upgrade is fairly limited. However, as laptops have become cheaper and more popular, there are more vendors offering "bare bones" laptops and compatible components.

The laptop chassis incorporates the motherboard, power supply, display screen, keypad, and touchpad. The plastics or aluminum frames are the hard surfaces that cover the internal components of the laptop. They are secured using either small screws or pressure tabs. Note that screws may be covered by rubber or plastic tabs.

Make sure you obtain the manufacturer's service documentation before commencing any upgrade or replacement work. This should explain how to disassemble the chassis and remove tricky items, such as plastic bezels, without damaging them. You should only perform this work if a warranty option is not available.

LAPTOP FRUs

Laptops have fewer field replaceable units (FRUs) than desktops. That said, laptop components and designs have become better standardized. Using components sourced from the laptop vendor is still recommended, but basic upgrade options, such as memory and disks, have become much simpler as it reduces warranty support costs for the vendors.

Some FRUs can be accessed easily by removing a screw plate on the back cover (underside) of the laptop. This method generally provides access to the disk drive, optical drive, memory modules, and possibly Mini PCIe adapters such as Wi-Fi cards and modems. The connectors can usually be flipped up and down to allow easy insertion and removal.

MASS STORAGE FOR LAPTOPS

Laptops use the same kind of mass storage devices as PCs:

- Hard Disk Drive (HDD)—magnetic disk technology offering low cost per gigabyte storage.
- Solid State Drive (SSD)—flash memory technology offering much faster performance and less weight and power consumption. SSDs are now the mainstream choice for laptops.
- Hybrid—an HDD with a large (8 GB+) cache of flash memory, offering a performance boost compared to basic HDDs.

A laptop typically supports one internal mass storage device only, with extra storage attached to an external port. The internal drive can usually be accessed via a panel, but you may have to open the chassis on some models.

Laptop mass storage drives are usually 2.5" form factor though sometimes the 1.8" form factor is used. Compared to 3.5" desktop versions, magnetic 2.5" HDDs tend to be slower (usually 5400 rpm models) and lower capacity. Within the 2.5" form factor, there are also reduced height units designed for ultraportable laptops. A standard 2.5" drive has a z-height of 9.5 mm; an ultraportable laptop might require a 7 mm (thin) or 5 mm (ultrathin) drive.

 Show Slide(s)
Laptop FRUs

 Teaching Tip
There's an optional activity for disassembling a laptop, but if you do not have the resources to allow learners to do this (individually or in groups), you might want to demonstrate the process yourself.

Laptops are a lot cheaper than they used to be! But perhaps not that cheap.

 Show Slide(s)
Mass Storage for Laptops

A laptop HDD with SATA interface. (Image © 123RF.com.)

Magnetic and hybrid drives use ordinary SATA data and power connectors, though the connectors on the drive mate directly to a port in the drive bay, without the use of a cable. 1.8" drive bays might require the use of the Micro SATA (μSATA or uSATA) connector.

SSD flash storage devices can also use the SATA interface and connector form factors but could also use an adapter or memory card-like interface:

- mSATA—an SSD might be housed on a card with a Mini-SATA (mSATA) interface. These cards resemble Mini PCIe cards but are not physically compatible with Mini PCIe slots. mSATA uses the SATA bus, so the maximum transfer speed is 6 Gbps.
- M.2—this is a new set of form factors for mini card interfaces. An M.2 SSD usually interfaces with the PCI Express bus, allowing much higher bus speeds than SATA. M.2 adapters can be different lengths (42 mm, 60 mm, 80 mm, or 110 mm) so you should check that any given adapter will fit within the laptop chassis. 80 mm (M.2 2280) is the most popular length for laptop SSDs.

 Note: *The specific M.2 form factor is written as 22 nn, where nn is the length. "22" refers to the card width, all of which are 22 mm.*

LAPTOP RAM

 Show Slide(s)

Laptop RAM

Laptop DDR SDRAM is packaged in small modules called **Small Outline DIMM (SODIMM)**. Both DDR and DDR2 use 200-pin packages, but the key position for DDR2 is slightly different to prevent insertion in a slot designed for DDR. DDR3 uses a 204-pin SODIMM module whereas DDR4 modules have 260 pins.

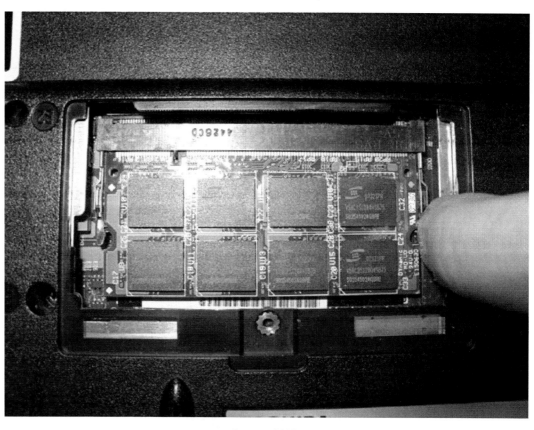

Laptop RAM.

The memory is typically fitted into slots that pop-up at a 45° angle to allow the chips to be inserted or removed. Sometimes one of the memory slots is easily accessible via a panel but another requires more extensive disassembly of the chassis to access.

Note: There are a couple of other laptop memory module form factors, including Mini-DIMM and Micro-DIMM. These are smaller than SODIMM and used on some ultraportable models. Always check the vendor documentation before obtaining parts for upgrade or replacement.

ADAPTER CARDS FOR LAPTOPS

Depending on the design, adapters for modems, wireless cards, and SSD storage cards may be accessible and replaceable via screw-down panels. Note that there are a number of adapter formats, notably Mini PCIe, mSATA, and M.2, none of which are compatible with one another.

You can obtain "wireless" mini PCIe or M.2 adapters for laptops that will provide some combination of Wi-Fi, Bluetooth, and/or cellular data (4G LTE) connectivity. Remember that when upgrading this type of adapter, you need to re-connect the antenna wires used by the old adapter or install a new antenna kit. The antenna wires are usually routed around the screen in the laptop's lid. The antenna connections can be tricky and are quite delicate, so take care.

If installing an adapter with cellular functionality, remember to insert the SIM as well.

 Show Slide(s)
Adapter Cards for Laptops

 Teaching Tip
Point out any expansion cards in use on the laptops in the classroom.

OPTICAL DRIVES FOR LAPTOPS

Laptops use slimline optical drive units. The unit is typically accessible from the bottom panel. As with a hard drive, the unit mates with a fixed SATA data and power connector at the back of the drive bay. You will typically need to replace the device with the same Original Equipment Manufacturer (OEM) part, or at least the same caddy design.

 Note: Optical drives are of decreasing relevance to mobile computing. It is more cost-effective to use an external drive as a replacement. You might want to consider replacing an optical drive with a second hard drive. The hard drive must be fitted to a caddy that fits the optical drive bay.

 *Note: To learn more, check the **Video** tile on the CHOICE Course screen for any videos that supplement the content for this lesson.*

 Show Slide(s)
Optical Drives for Laptops

 Access the Checklist tile on your CHOICE Course screen for reference information and job aids on How to Upgrade Laptop System Components.

LAPTOP CPU AND MOTHERBOARD UPGRADES

The CPU is generally upgradeable as long as the new device is supported by the motherboard.

 Note: Some laptop CPUs—those that use Ball Grid Array (BGA) sockets—are soldered to the motherboard and, therefore, are not upgradeable.

The CPU is covered by a heatpipe, rather than a heat sink. This is a long, flat metal strip that conducts heat toward the fan. Otherwise, it is locked into place in much the same way as a desktop CPU.

There will be few occasions when it is economical to replace the system board itself. If you do need to do so, detach the stand-offs that hold the board to the chassis. If upgrading the system board, you will probably also need to update the chipset driver

Show Slide(s)
Laptop CPU and Motherboard Upgrades

(or notebook system software) and allow Windows to discover the new device using Plug-and-Play.

Show Slide(s)

Laptop Video Card Upgrades

LAPTOP VIDEO CARD UPGRADES

Laptops often use an integrated graphics adapter that is part of the system chipset or CPU, especially at the lower end of the market. Integrated graphics can be advantageous in terms of battery life and cooling. However, as laptops get used more and more as desktop replacements, particularly as game machines, dedicated graphics becomes important. Cheaper graphics adapters may also feature a limited amount of onboard memory (or none at all). In this scenario, they share system memory with the CPU. Obviously, this decreases the amount of system memory available.

Few laptop video cards are actually upgradeable, though they may be replaceable. This is because high-end cards tend to have specific power and cooling requirements and a modular approach is not possible given the limited space available.

Show Slide(s)

Laptop Component Replacement

LAPTOP COMPONENT REPLACEMENT

There are other components that you may need to replace to effect repairs. In most cases, you will need to source "like-for-like" replacements to ensure the proper fit.

Show Slide(s)

Laptop Display and Digitizer Replacement

LAPTOP DISPLAY AND DIGITIZER REPLACEMENT

A built-in laptop display will be one of three types:

- LCD (TFT) with fluorescent backlight—this has been the standard display technology for the last few years. The backlight is a fluorescent bulb that illuminates the image, making it bright and clear. An inverter supplies the correct AC voltage to the backlight from the laptop's DC power circuits.
- LCD with LED backlight—manufacturers are increasingly switching to this technology. LED backlights do not require an inverter.
- OLED—this technology is expensive at the screen size required by laptops and there are issues with power draw and battery life. Consequently, OLED has not really established itself as a mainstream choice for laptop displays.

Teaching Tip

A few vendors experimented with OLED screens on laptops, but it is not widely used. OLED is used more often with top-end mobile and TV displays.

When a laptop has a touchscreen display, it will also have a **digitizer** fitted. The digitizer is sandwiched between a layer of glass and the LCD display. Analog signals are created when you tap or swipe the surface of the display. The digitizer is connected to the laptop with a flexible digitizer cable. A grid of sensors is activated when you tap or swipe the screen. The information from the sensors is sent through the digitizer cable to a circuit that converts the analog signal to a digital signal.

If you need to replace a display, digitizer, or inverter, make a very careful record of how the existing unit is connected to the video card and system board, including the routing of any cables.

Note: Replacing these components is relatively tricky and upgrading them can be even more complex. Make sure you get specific information or advice for the model of laptop you are servicing.

Show Slide(s)

Laptop Speaker Replacement

LAPTOP SPEAKER REPLACEMENT

To replace laptop speakers, you will need to disassemble the laptop to the system board. Make sure you obtain replacement speakers that are compatible with your laptop model. Remove the old speakers and fit the new ones, remembering to connect the audio cable.

LAPTOP INPUT DEVICE REPLACEMENT

Laptop input devices include keyboards, touchpads, webcams, microphones, and smart card readers.

Show Slide(s)

Laptop Input Device Replacement

KEYBOARDS AND TOUCHPADS

When you are replacing components like the keyboard and touchpad, you will almost always need to use the same parts. Each part connects to the motherboard via a data cable, typically a flat ribbon type. Accessing the parts for removal and replacement might require complete disassembly or might be relatively straightforward—check the service documentation.

> **Note:** *If you are upgrading the keyboard or touchpad (rather than replacing the same part), you may need to install a new driver and configure settings via the Mouse and Keyboard applets.*

WEBCAMS AND MICROPHONES

Almost all laptops come with built-in webcams and microphones. The webcam is normally positioned at the top of the display with an LED to show whether it is active.

> **Note:** *Laptop users are understandably worried about the privacy implications of built-in webcams. If the laptop is infected with malware, it is usually possible for the malware to enable the webcam without activating the LED.*

The microphone will be positioned somewhere on the laptop chassis. There will also be microphone and speaker 3.5 mm jacks for the connection of a headset or external speakers.

SMART CARD READERS

A smart card reader is a feature of enterprise laptops supporting authentication using digital smart cards. You will typically need to replace this with the same OEM part. The laptop will probably need to be completely disassembled to access the device. It is connected to the system board by a data cable.

LAPTOP POWER SUPPLIES

Portable computers can work off both building power and battery operation.

Show Slide(s)

Laptop Power Supplies

Teaching Tip

Not all AC adapters and batteries are created equal. Point out that the size and shape of DC jacks and laptop batteries varies greatly even between laptop models from the same manufacturer.

AC ADAPTERS

To operate from building power, the laptop needs a power supply that can convert from the AC (Alternating Current) supplied by the power company to the DC (Direct Current) voltages used by the laptop's components. The power supply is provided as an external **AC adapter**.

AC adapters are normally universal (or auto-switching) and can operate from any 110-240 VAC 50/60 Hz supply (check the label to confirm). Some adapters (notably some sold with US machines) are fixed-input (for instance, they only work with a 115 VAC supply or have to be manually switched to the correct input).

An AC adapter for an HP laptop. (Image by Olga Popova © 123RF.com.)

 Note: Plugging a fixed-input 240 V adapter into a 110 V supply won't cause any damage (though the laptop won't work), but plugging a fixed-input 110 V adapter into a 240 V supply will.

 Note: When you are using a laptop abroad, in addition to a universal AC adapter, you will also need a power plug adapter to fit the type of socket used in that country. It is also best to get a surge protector designed for the voltage used in the country too. This helps to protect the laptop from damage.

AC adapters are also rated for their power output (ranging from around 65-120 W). Again, this information will be printed on the adapter label. Output (W) is calculated by multiplying voltage (V) by current (I). A larger output will be able to power more peripheral devices.

The power output of adapters and batteries can vary, so using an adapter designed for an ultra-mobile model probably won't work with a desktop replacement, even if it's the same brand. A 90 W adapter should be sufficient for most uses, but always check the documentation carefully. If you need to replace the power supply, it is best to get the manufacturer's recommended model, though universal AC adapters are available. These typically ship with a number of DC power connectors, which vary quite widely in size. They also have variable voltage settings. You must set the voltage correctly before plugging it in.

 Note: Most laptops will display a message at boot time if an underpowered AC adapter or battery is present.

DC JACK REPLACEMENT

It is relatively common for the DC jack to fail. The port can become loose over time or the jack itself can become separated from the motherboard. Replacing a DC jack means disassembling the laptop, de-soldering and removing the old jack, then soldering the new jack into place. Most laptop DC jacks are specific to the manufacturer and even the laptop model.

Replacement DC jack—the part is soldered to the motherboard via the contact pin seen on the right. (Image by Sergey Kolesnikov © 123RF.com.)

BATTERY POWER

Laptop computers use removable, rechargeable Lithium ion (Li-ion) battery packs. Li-ion batteries have good storage capacity and hold their charge well. They are typically available in 6, 9, or 12 cell versions, with more cells providing for a longer charge.

Before inserting or removing the battery pack, you must always turn the machine off and unplug it from the AC wall outlet. A portable battery is usually removed by releasing catches on the back or underside of the laptop.

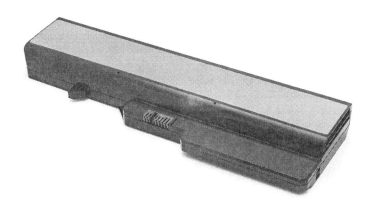

A removable laptop battery pack. (Image by cristi180884 © 123RF.com.)

A portable computer's battery can be charged in three ways:

- Plug the computer into an AC wall outlet with the computer turned off. This method is called a quick charge. It takes a couple of hours to fully charge a flat battery.
- Charge the battery while the computer is plugged into an AC wall outlet and turned on. This method is called a trickle charge. Trickle charging is slower because the primary use of power is for operating the PC, rather than for charging the battery. It can take several hours to charge a battery while the machine is turned on.
- Use a battery charger. This method charges the battery while it is not in the computer, but involves purchasing an extra charging unit.

To maximize battery life, different battery types require different charging regimes. Always consult the manufacturer's instructions for obtaining optimal battery life for a specific product. Modern Li-ion batteries should not be allowed to fully discharge, as this reduces battery life. They benefit from regular charging and have circuitry to prevent over-charging. However, some degree of caution should be exercised when leaving batteries to recharge unattended (for example, overnight) as this circuitry has been known to fail. Do not leave a battery charger close to flammable material and ensure there is plenty of ventilation around the unit.

Li-ion batteries are also sensitive to heat. If storing a Li-ion battery, reduce the charge to 40% and store at below 20° C.

Note: *Li-ion batteries hold less charge as they age and typically have a maximum usable life of around 2-3 years. If you charge a battery and the run time is substantially decreased, you may need to purchase a new battery.*

Note: *To learn more, check the **Video** tile on the CHOICE Course screen for any videos that supplement the content for this lesson.*

Activity 15-2

Discussing Laptop Hardware Installation and Configuration

Show Slide(s)

Activity: Discussing Laptop Hardware Installation and Configuration

SCENARIO

Answer the following questions to check your understanding of the topic.

1. **What is the process for installing memory in a laptop?**

    Verify that the DDR version of the upgrade module is supported by the motherboard. Take anti-static precautions. Locate the memory slot, which is usually accessed via a panel on the back cover. Move the connector up to 45° and insert the memory card, taking care to align it correctly. Push the card flat again.

2. **What type of standard adapter card might be used to connect internal FRU devices to the motherboard of a laptop?**

    Mini-PCIe, mSATA, or M.2.

3. **What distinguishes a magnetic hard drive designed for a laptop from one designed for a PC?**

    Laptop drives are 2.5" (or sometimes 1.8"), rather than 3.5". They also tend to be slower (5,400 rpm, rather than 7,200 or 10,000 rpm) and lower capacity. The largest at the time of writing is 5 TB, so this may not be a limiting factor in practice.

4. A user reports that when they plug in anything to a USB port on the laptop, the device is not recognized by the system.

    Is this something you can easily repair?

    Typically, the processor, the DC jack, and USB ports are attached directly on the board and cannot be replaced without replacing the whole laptop motherboard. If the other USB ports are functional, a USB hub could provide additional ports.

5. Several laptops need to be replaced in the next fiscal cycle, but that doesn't begin for several months. You want to improve functionality as much as possible by upgrading or replacing components in some of the laptops that are having problems.

Which items are most easily replaced in a laptop?

The fixed drive, system memory (RAM), and plug-in wireless card will be the easiest upgradable components to install. If items need repairing, fans, the screen, the battery, touchpad, and the keyboard should be straightforward to replace, if you can obtain compatible parts.

Activity 15-3
Installing and Configuring Laptop Hardware

BEFORE YOU BEGIN

Read the following notes carefully before you start:

- Create a clean work environment with plenty of working space.
- Gather all necessary tools and equipment. A notepad and pen will be useful for making diagrams and notes.
- Implement anti-static and safety procedures.
- Make sure that the laptop is powered off and disconnected from building and battery power before proceeding.
- Always take time and care.
- Always place static-sensitive equipment such as processors and memory in anti-static bags.

SCENARIO

In the first part of the activity, you will disassemble a laptop using these steps as your guidelines. Check with your instructor for any extra instructions. Your instructor may not want you to completely disassemble the laptop due to the risk of breaking plastics, etc. If so, make a note now of which step you are to stop at.

In the second part of the activity, you will reassemble a laptop, working from the notes made by your partner.

---

1.   Shut down Windows and turn off your laptop.

2.   Disconnect all peripherals (keyboard, mouse, and monitor), removable storage (media bay or memory card), and power cables from the system unit. Place these in a tidy manner under your workbench (or wherever your instructor tells you to).

3.   Remove the laptop battery and store it safely. Hold down the laptop power button for 30 seconds.

4.   With the lid shut, flip the laptop and use your notepad and pen to make a diagram of the existing layout of cut-out panels and drives, plus their screw locations.

     Some screws may be covered by caps or rubber feet.

5.   Remove each cut-out and its component, making a careful note of how to reconnect any wires and cables attached to adapter cards. Carefully put each component in an anti-static bag and the screws in a container, using a system to identify which screw is used at any given location.

6.   If you are continuing from here, release the screws that secure the chassis and the plastics (palm rest and touchpad assembly). Carefully put the screws in a container, using a system to identify which screw is used at any given location.

 Show Slide(s)

Activity: Installing and Configuring Laptop Hardware

 Teaching Tip

Clearly, this activity depends on having several laptops available for disassembly. Arrange learners in groups if necessary.

Ensure that learners read the notes before they begin, and that they implement safety precautions and anti-ESD kits.

If you do not want learners to completely disassemble the laptop, you could ask them to stop at removing easily accessible cards and drives, for instance. Clearly explain how far they should progress.

As learners are working through the steps, move around the room, offering advice and ensuring that learners are not damaging any components.

Emphasize that nobody should reboot a laptop until you have checked the reassembly. Point out and correct any errors that are dangerous, but let learners troubleshoot and fix any other issues.

7. Flip the laptop over again, and open the lid. Remove the plastic bezel at the top of the keyboard. This might be difficult but take care not to snap it. When lifting the bezel, take care to discover whether any cables are connected to it. If there are, unplug them and make a note of how they should be re-attached.

8. Remove the keyboard by releasing the screws that secure it, then unplugging the ribbon cable. Record how the cable should be reattached, then store the components.

9. Disconnect the LCD cable and LCD power connector connecting the display to the motherboard. There is also likely to be a cable connecting the radio antenna (running around the screen) to the wireless adapter. Again, make a careful note of how to reconnect these components.

10. Remove the LCD panel, taking care to handle and store it safely, as it is fragile.

11. Locate any remaining cables preventing disassembly of the top panel (touchpad, audio connectors, and power button, for instance) taking care to note how they should be reconnected.

12. Remove any internal drive cages or heat pipes covering the components you want to inspect. As with a desktop, make a careful note of how fan power connectors are attached.

     Note: *This concludes the first part of the activity.*

13. When you and your partner have completed the first part of the activity, swap places and completely reassemble your partner's laptop. Allow them to access any notes and diagrams you have made, and tell them of any particular difficulties you had during disassembly.

14. Reboot the laptop that you just reassembled. If it does not reboot, or if there are errors when you try to resolve the problem, ask your instructor for guidance.

Topic C

Troubleshoot Common Laptop Issues

 EXAM OBJECTIVES COVERED
1001-5.5 Given a scenario, troubleshoot common mobile device issues while adhering to the appropriate procedures.

Part of your duties as a CompTIA A+ technician will be helping users when they encounter problems with their mobile devices. In this topic, you will troubleshoot issues with laptop hardware and associated mobile app issues.

COMMON LAPTOP ISSUES

The same basic approach to troubleshooting applies for laptops as it does for desktop PCs, though there are some issues specific to laptops and other portable devices that you should be aware of.

- Display issues, including problems with built-in display devices, touchscreens, and external displays.
- Power and cooling issues.
- Input and output device issues.
- Communication and connectivity issues.
- Issues with GPS and location services.
- OS and app issues, such as performance problems and unresponsive apps.

DISPLAY ISSUES

Display issues include:

- **Problems with a built-in display.** When you are troubleshooting a laptop display, you will often need to take into account the use of the integrated display and/or an external display and how to isolate a problem to a particular component, such as either display, the video card, or a display toggle.

  The components most likely to fail on an older LCD screen are the backlight and inverter. The backlight is a fluorescent bulb that illuminates the image, making it bright and clear. The inverter supplies the correct AC voltage to the backlight. If the display has been flickering or if the image is very dim, but still present, suspect a problem with the backlight or inverter rather than the LCD itself. As you may know if you have fluorescent lighting at home, the inverter is more likely to fail than the tube itself.

  Many laptops now use LED arrays for the backlight. As these work off DC power, there is no inverter.

  The LCD is only likely to need replacing if it gets physically damaged.

 Note: As well as the display itself, it is fairly common for the plastics around the case to get cracked or broken and for the hinges on the lid to wear out. The plastics are mostly cosmetic (though a bad break might expose the laptop's internal components to greater risks) but if the hinges no longer hold up the screen, they will have to be replaced.

 Show Slide(s)
Common Laptop Issues

 Teaching Tip
This topic focuses on troubleshooting laptops, but there are content overlaps with other parts of the course that deal with troubleshooting smartphone and tablet issues, as well as troubleshooting Wi-Fi issues as part of networking.

 Interaction Opportunity
Discuss the issues raised in this topic, and consider asking learners to brainstorm other issues and solutions.

 Show Slide(s)
Display Issues

The backlight, inverter, or screen on a laptop can be replaced by unscrewing the plastic bezel (the screws will be concealed by rubber stoppers). Take care not to damage the connectors once the panel has been freed from its housing.

- **Problems with a touchscreen.** Common touchscreen issues include:
  - Touchscreen is not responsive.
  - Touchscreen doesn't act as expected.
- **Problems with an external display.** External display issues include:
  - No image on external display.
  - Wrong image on external display.
  - External display image is too large or too small.

GUIDELINES FOR TROUBLESHOOTING DISPLAY ISSUES

Show Slide(s)

Guidelines for Troubleshooting Display Issues (2 slides)

*Note: All of the Guidelines for this lesson are available as checklists from the **Checklist** tile on the CHOICE Course screen.*

Here are some guidelines for troubleshooting display issues.

TROUBLESHOOT BUILT-IN DISPLAY ISSUES

Consider these guidelines when you need to troubleshoot built-in display issues:

- Determine whether the source of the problem is the integrated display, an external display, or other component of the display subsystem.
  - First check that the video card is good by using an external monitor. Toggle the appropriate **Fn** key—usually **Fn+4** or **Fn+8**. Alternatively, there should be a very dim image on the LCD if the graphics adapter is functioning but the backlight/ inverter has failed.
  - Ensure the laptop is switched to using the built-in display again. Check that power management settings are not set to an energy saving mode that disables or dims the backlight.
  - Check that a cutoff switch (a small plastic pin near the hinge connecting the LCD to the rest of the chassis) is not stuck. When it is depressed, power to the backlight is switched off.
  - If all these tests are negative, the backlight, inverter, or cable has failed. If the backlight flickers (or has been flickering before complete failure), there's more likely to be a problem with the inverter. An inverter can be tested using a bulb or multimeter, but at this point you will probably need to book the laptop in for repair or use it with an external monitor only.
- Check for physical damage. If the display is damaged (if it has been bent or dented, for example), this can cause pixelation problems—areas of the image break down with mis-coloring, blockiness, or jaggedness.
- Check the resolution. LCDs are best used at the native resolution. Any other resolution will produce some distortion in the image, which isn't a sign of a fault in the screen itself. Also, fast changing images (such as those produced by video playback) can produce artifacts on low quality screens.
- Check the driver. When updating the driver for a display adapter, check whether the laptop vendor has released their own driver. Laptops often contain OEM (Original Equipment Manufacturer) versions of graphics adapters and you need to use the system vendor's driver rather than the retail driver.

TROUBLESHOOT TOUCHSCREEN ISSUES

Consider these guidelines when you need to troubleshoot touchscreen issues such as unresponsive or misbehaving touchscreens:

- Verify that the touchscreen is clean.
- Look for evidence that the laptop might have been dropped or severely damaged.
- Try using the device in a different location in case some source of electromagnetic interference (EMI) is affecting the operation of the touchscreen.
- If the laptop has just been serviced, check that the right wires are still connected in the right places for the digitizer to function. Remember to ask "What has changed?"
- If you cannot identify an obvious physical problem, you should attempt to rule out a software problem before suspecting a more serious hardware problem.
  - In many cases, a restart may solve the problem.
  - In Windows, you can also try uninstalling the touchscreen driver and reinstalling the device, using the latest driver if possible.
  - You could also try running the calibration utility.

 Note: *Removing a faulty digitizer from an existing display can be tricky. It might be cheaper to replace the whole unit, depending on the cost of parts.*

TROUBLESHOOT EXTERNAL DISPLAY ISSUES

Consider these guidelines as you troubleshoot external display issues such as no image or wrong image on an external display, or if the external display image is too large or too small:

- A keyboard toggle switch cuts the display between built-in only, both simultaneously, and external only. Verify this switch is set properly.
- Windows display settings control whether the external display duplicates or extends the built-in one. If there is no external image and the toggle button is set correctly, after checking other obvious things (Is the external display switched on? Is it in power-saving mode? Is it set to the correct input mode? Is the cable connected?), check that the resolution for the external display is appropriate.
- Look for updated drivers for the graphics adapter and laptop chipset (system software).
- Try a different display unit and/or cable to rule out hardware problems.

 Note: *If the external display is connected via a cable, try using a different (known good) cable. If the display is using a wireless connection, such as Miracast or Wi-Fi Direct, check that both device and display support the same standards.*

POWER AND COOLING ISSUES

Power and cooling issues include battery issues, AC power issues, and overheating.

Show Slide(s)

Power and Cooling Issues

- **Battery issues.** If you are working from the battery, first check that it is inserted correctly and seated properly in its compartment. Also check whether the battery contacts are dirty. You can clean them by using alcohol preps or even just a dry cloth.

  An LED may be present to indicate when the laptop is running on battery power or an LED may simply show when a battery is being charged. If the battery is properly inserted and still does not work, it is most likely completely discharged. If the battery will not hold a charge, it could be at the end of its useful life. You can test this by using a "known good" battery; if this does not work, then there is something wrong with the power circuitry on the motherboard.

  Properly caring for the battery not only prolongs battery life, but also mitigates health and safety risks. Using an incorrect battery charging cable or exposing a battery to harsh environmental conditions, such as extreme heat, can result in an explosion.

- **Short battery life.** As batteries age, the maximum charge they can sustain decreases, so short battery life will usually indicate that the battery needs replacing. If the battery is not old or faulty, you could suspect that an app is putting excessive strain on the battery. In Windows 10, you can use the **Settings** app to identify whether an app is having an adverse effect on battery life.

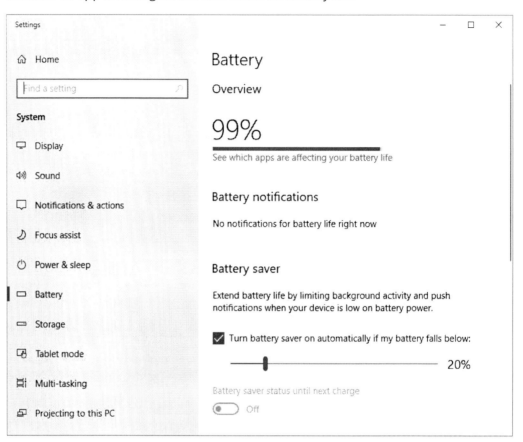

Battery status and notifications in Windows 10. (Screenshot used with permission from Microsoft.)

- **Swollen batteries.** If you notice any swelling from the battery compartment, discontinue use of the laptop immediately. Signs that the battery has swollen can include a device that wobbles when placed flat on a desk or a deformed touchpad or keyboard. A swollen battery is usually caused by overcharging, indicating some sort of problem with the battery's charging circuit, which is supposed to prevent overcharging. If a device is exposed to liquid, this could also have damaged the battery.

Li-ion batteries are designed to swell to avoid bursting or exploding but great care must be taken when handling a swollen battery to avoid further damage that may cause it to burst or explode. It may also be a fire hazard and/or leaking hazardous chemicals—do not allow these to come into contact with your skin or your eyes. If the battery cannot be released safely and easily from its compartment, contact the manufacturer for advice. You should also contact the manufacturer for specific disposal instructions. A swollen battery should not be discarded via standard recycling points unless the facility confirms it can accept batteries in a potentially hazardous state.

Note: Problems with batteries and AC adapters often occur in batches. Make sure you remain signed up to the vendor's alerting service so that you are informed about any product recalls or safety advisories.

- **AC power issues.** AC power issues usually surface as problems with a battery not charging, slow performance, devices not functioning. error messages, and spontaneous rebooting.
- **Overheating.** Overheating can be a considerable problem with laptops due to their compact size and integrated design. The components are all within close proximity and can generate and trap a lot of heat.

  Dust trapped in cooling passages acts as an insulator and can prevent proper cooling, possibly resulting in overheating. Excessive heat should be avoided in such devices as it can shorten the life of components.

  The bottom surface of the laptop gets quite hot when improperly ventilated. This can easily happen when laptops are put on soft surfaces, on people's laps, or in places where there is not enough room between the vents and a wall. Sometimes people will get careless and unwittingly cover the vents with books, mouse pads, etc.

  There are several cooling methods and considerations used to keep the devices within a safe heat range for operation:

  - Laptop CPUs are engineered to draw less power and thus run cooler than their similarly rated desktop counterparts.
  - Fans are used to move the hot air out from the inside of the laptop case.
  - Limit the use of the laptop battery as much as possible. The battery itself can be a heat source.
  - Laptop cooling (or chiller) pads are accessories that are designed to sit under the laptop to protect a user from getting a burn from a device overheating. The cooler is placed underneath the laptop to move the air away from the device.

 Note: To learn more, check the **Video** *tile on the CHOICE Course screen for any videos that supplement the content for this lesson.*

GUIDELINES FOR TROUBLESHOOTING POWER AND COOLING ISSUES

Here are some guidelines for troubleshooting power and cooling issues.

 Show Slide(s)

Guidelines for Troubleshooting Power and Cooling Issues (2 slides)

TROUBLESHOOT BATTERY ISSUES

Some simple guidelines for acceptable battery maintenance include:

- Follow manufacturer instructions on the proper charging and discharging of the battery.
- Use the battery charger provided by the manufacturer or an approved replacement charger.
- Never expose the battery to fire or water or drop, throw, or jolt the battery.
- Only use the recommended battery for your device.
- Make use of power management features included with your device/OS to prolong battery life.

TROUBLESHOOT AC POWER ISSUES

Consider these guidelines as you troubleshoot AC power issues:

- If there is a power problem, first establish how the laptop should be operated and confirm that this procedure is being followed. For example, some laptops require that a battery be present, even on AC power.
- If you experience problems working from AC power, first test the outlet with a "known good" device (such as a lamp). Next check that an LED on the AC adapter is

green; if there is no LED, check the fuse on the plug and if available, try testing with a "known good" adapter.

- If this does not work, inspect the DC socket on the laptop for any sign of damage. You could also check the AC adapter using a multimeter.

 Note: Most adapters contain a circuit breaker to prevent overloads. If this trips, it will be a few minutes before the adapter will work again.

- Sometimes AC adapters can get mixed up. If an underpowered adapter is used—for example, a 65 W adapter is plugged into a 90 W system—the laptop BIOS will display a warning at boot time.
- As with desktops, spontaneous reboots may indicate a power problem, though a more likely cause is overheating. Another possibility is that peripherals are trying to draw down too much power.
- Try disconnecting drives from the media bays or USB then re-booting to see if the problem is fixed. Note that larger 3.5" hard drives and external CD/DVD writers will typically require their own power supply, even if connected via USB.

TROUBLESHOOT COOLING ISSUES

Consider these guidelines as you troubleshoot cooling issues:

- Because laptops do not have the air circulation that desktop PCs do, it is important to keep the device air ducts clean.
- In servicing laptops, it is a good practice to regularly blow dust from the cooling passages using compressed air or vacuum it with an electronics vacuum. When using compressed air to clean the inside of the laptop, you must be cautious of the internal components. It is easy to damage other components inside the laptop while cleaning.

INPUT AND OUTPUT DEVICE ISSUES

 **Show Slide(s)**
Input and Output Device Issues

Here are some common issues you might encounter with laptop input and output devices:

- **Input devices.** The main problem with keypads tends to be stuck keys.

  Be aware that the Function (Fn) keys can often be used to disable devices, such as the wireless adapter. Each device will have an LED on the chassis showing whether it is enabled or not.

  If the laptop does not have a separate keypad, users may become confused when NumLock is active and the keys go to numeric input.

  Another issue is with using an external keyboard and experiencing problems with the Function key being locked. This can typically be solved by turning off NumLock on the external keyboard.

  Another problem is where the touchpad is configured to be too sensitive and typing causes vibrations that move the cursor. Examples include the pointer drifting across the screen without any input or a "ghost cursor" jumping about when typing.

- **Sound and speaker issues.** On a laptop, problems can arise with the onboard speakers and with external speakers, resulting in no sound or distorted sound.

 Note: To learn more, check the Video tile on the CHOICE Course screen for any videos that supplement the content for this lesson.

GUIDELINES FOR TROUBLESHOOTING INPUT AND OUTPUT DEVICE ISSUES

Here are some guidelines for troubleshooting input and output device issues.

 Show Slide(s)

Guidelines for Troubleshooting Input and Output Device Issues

TROUBLESHOOT INPUT AND OUTPUT DEVICE ISSUES

Consider these guidelines as you troubleshoot input and output device issues:

- If there is debris under a key, try cleaning with compressed air.
- If the laptop has been serviced recently and the keyboard has stopped working, check that the connector has not been dislodged as some service operations require the keyboard to be removed.

 Note: Removing a key on a laptop keyboard can be a risky proposition. They are typically not the type of key where the key cap is in a peg, which you find on full-sized keyboards. Laptop keys are usually floating on a dual-hinge mechanism, usually plastic, that will easily break if you attempt to remove it forcefully. Refer to the manufacturer's instructions when attempting to fix a key on the keyboard.

- If a device that is activated via a function key is not working, check that it has not been disabled by accident.
- If the wrong characters appear when you type, check the NumLock status indicator if available.
- For touchpad issues, install up-to-date drivers and configure input options to suit the user. Many laptops now come with a **Fn** key to disable the touchpad.

 Note: Conversely, mouse problems can often arise following the installation of updates or version upgrades. Try to identify "what changed?" when troubleshooting problems like this.

- If no sound is played from the onboard speakers:
  - Check that the volume controls have not been turned all the way down or that sound has not been muted. Remember that on a laptop there may be function or multimedia keys to control the volume.
  - Check that the correct playback device is configured in Windows (using the **Sound** applet in Control Panel). The applet includes a utility that can test the speaker setup.
  - If you cannot locate a configuration problem, try connecting external speakers or a headset to identify whether the problem may be with the internal speaker unit.
  - If there is no sound from either type of output, suspect a problem with the sound card or internal wiring.

 *Note: To learn more, check the **Video** tile on the CHOICE Course screen for any videos that supplement the content for this lesson.*

COMMUNICATION AND CONNECTIVITY ISSUES

Wi-Fi and Bluetooth connectivity issues on a laptop can be approached in much the same way as on a PC. Problems can generally be categorized as either relating to "physical" issues, such as interference, or to "software" configuration problems.

 **Show Slide(s)**

Communication and Connectivity Issues

- Remember that wireless devices need power.
- Wireless devices can often experience difficulties following the laptop being put into sleep or hibernation mode.
- If there are intermittent connectivity problems, be aware that wireless input and communications devices can experience trouble with interference.

Note: The radio antenna wire for a mobile will be built into the case (normally around the screen).

GPS AND LOCATION SERVICES

Here are some issues you might encounter with GPS and location services:

- GPS and other wireless functions do not seem to work at all, or they work only intermittently.
- GPS does not usually work well indoors as the satellite signals lack the power to penetrate dense construction material. Most devices use a combination of GPS and the **Indoor Positioning System (IPS)**, which uses information from nearby Wi-Fi hotspots, to provide location services.

GUIDELINES FOR TROUBLESHOOTING COMMUNICATION AND CONNECTIVITY ISSUES

Here are some guidelines for troubleshooting communication and connectivity issues.

 Show Slide(s)

Guidelines for Troubleshooting Communication and Connectivity Issues

TROUBLESHOOT COMMUNICATION AND CONNECTIVITY ISSUES

Consider these guidelines when you are troubleshooting issues with communication and connectivity:

- If there is a problem with wireless, Bluetooth, or cellular data/GPS:
  - Verify that the adapter is enabled.
  - Check the status of function key toggles on a laptop or use the notification shade toggles on a mobile device to check that something like airplane mode has not been enabled.
  - Different wireless functions may be toggled on or off selectively or collectively.
  - If the laptop has been serviced recently and wireless functions have stopped working, check that the antenna connector has not been dislodged or wrongly connected.
- If a wireless device such as a Bluetooth mouse or keyboard that has been working stops, it probably needs a new battery.
- If you experience problems restoring from hibernate or sleep mode, try cycling the power on the device or reconnecting it and check for updated drivers for the wireless controller and the devices.
- If you are experiencing intermittent connectivity issues:
  - Try moving the two devices closer together.
  - Try moving the devices from side-to-side or up-and-down.
  - Consider using a Wi-Fi analyzer to measure the signal strength in different locations to try to identify the source of interference.
- If there is a problem with the Global Positioning System (GPS):
  - Check that the GPS receiver is enabled and that the laptop is not in airplane mode.
  - Ensure that Location Services are enabled for the device.
  - Verify that each app has been granted permission to use the service. If the app does not prompt for permission if it has not been granted, try uninstalling and reinstalling the app.

 *Note: To learn more, check the **Video** tile on the CHOICE Course screen for any videos that supplement the content for this lesson.*

OS AND APP ISSUES

Although this topic covers common laptop hardware issues, you should also be aware of some problems that can arise from OS and app issues.

Show Slide(s)
OS and App Issues

- Slow performance.
- Unresponsive devices and apps.
- Email issues. Users often want to send confidential email with the assurance that only the recipient can read it. To do this, the recipient sends the sender a digital certificate and the sender uses the public key in that certificate to encrypt the message. The recipient then uses another part of the certificate (the private key) to decrypt the message. If the certificate is missing or not recognized, the device will be unable to decrypt the email.

GUIDELINES FOR TROUBLESHOOTING OS AND APP ISSUES

Here are some guidelines for troubleshooting OS and app issues.

Show Slide(s)
Guidelines for Troubleshooting OS and App Issues

TROUBLESHOOT OS AND APP ISSUES

Consider these guidelines as you troubleshoot OS and app issues on a laptop:

- For slow performance issues:
  - A Windows laptop might suffer from slow performance for the same reasons as a PC and you should approach troubleshooting in the same way.

    Slow performance on a mobile device is likely either to be caused by an app that requires a higher system specification or by running too many apps. Mobile devices are designed to manage system requirements without intervention from the user, but it may be worth closing all apps in case there is a fault in one that has not been detected.
- For unresponsive apps and devices: If an app or the mobile device as a whole is not responding—for example, if the screen is frozen or if apps are not loading—or performing very slowly, the best solution is usually to perform a reset.
  - App reset: use this if a particular app is not responding. In iOS®, double-click **Home** twice to open the multitasking toolbar then tap-and-hold the app and click the **Stop** icon that appears when it starts jiggling. In Android™, you can manage an app's cached data and access a Force Stop option through **Settings→Applications→Manage Applications**.
  - Restart/"soft" reset/power cycle: essentially rebooting the device (without losing any settings or data). Holding the **Sleep/Wake/Power** button down for a few seconds brings up a menu prompting the user to turn off the device. When troubleshooting, leave the device powered off for a minute then restart by holding the **Sleep** button again.
  - Forced restart: if the touchscreen is not responding to input and you cannot perform a power cycle normally, you can force the device to turn off. On an Android device, hold down the **Sleep/Wake/Power** button for 10 seconds; in iOS, hold **Home**+**Sleep** for 10 seconds.
  - Factory reset/erase: this deletes any user data and settings and puts the device in its "vanilla" factory state. In iOS, use **Settings→General→Reset→Erase All Content and Settings**. In Android, select **Settings→Backup & reset→Factory data reset**.

Teaching Tip
Point out that iPhones with no Home key have more complex forced restart sequences. The current method (for iPhone 8 and newer) is **Volume Up→Volume Down→Press and hold Power**.

> *Note: These procedures can vary from device-to-device so always check the instructions. If you cannot get an ordinary screen in Android, check the vendor documentation for the hardware buttons to use to get to a boot recovery screen (from a powered off state, **Power+Volume Down** is typical). iOS can be booted in recovery mode by holding the **Home** button when connecting the device to iTunes over USB.*

- For email issues, use the email client or encryption program's support documentation to find out how to install or locate the appropriate certificate.

> **Note:** *To learn more, check the **Video** tile on the CHOICE Course screen for any videos that supplement the content for this lesson.*

Activity 15-4
Troubleshooting Common Laptop Issues

Show Slide(s)

Activity: Troubleshooting Common Laptop Issues

SCENARIO

Answer the following questions to check your understanding of the topic.

1. You are troubleshooting a laptop display.

   If the laptop can display an image on an external monitor but not the built-in one, which component do you know is working, and can you definitively say which is faulty?

   The graphics adapter is working. The problem must exist either in the cabling to the built-in screen or with a screen component, such as an inverter, backlight, or the display panel itself. Further tests will be required to identify which (though it may be quicker to replace the whole screen assembly).

2. You received a user complaint about a laptop being extremely hot to the touch.

   What actions should you take in response to this issue?

   Overheating can be a sign that dust and dirt is restricting the necessary airflow within the device, so start by cleaning the ventilation duct with compressed air, and then make sure that the device is getting proper air circulation around the outside of the case.

3. A user complains that their Bluetooth keyboard, which has worked for the last year, has stopped functioning.

   What would you suggest is the problem?

   The batteries in the keyboard have run down—replace them.

4. A user working in graphics design has just received a new laptop. The user phones to say that performance with the graphics program in the office is fine but dismal when he takes the laptop to client meetings.

   What could be the cause?

   The laptop could be using reduced performance settings to conserve battery life.

5. A laptop user reports that they are only getting about two hours of use out of the battery compared to about three hours when the laptop was first supplied to them.

What do you suggest?

Batteries lose maximum charge over time. It may be possible to recondition the battery or to use power saving features, but the only real way to restore maximum battery life is to buy a new battery.

6. A laptop user is complaining about typing on their new laptop. They claim that the cursor jumps randomly from place-to-place.

What might be the cause of this?

The user could be touching the touchpad while typing, or vibrations could be affecting the touchpad. Update the driver, or reduce the sensitivity/disable touch and tap events.

Summary

In this lesson, you performed support and troubleshooting routines on laptop computers. Familiarity with using various laptop features and technologies, as well as installing, configuring, and troubleshooting laptop components and behavior, will no doubt contribute to your success as an A+ support technician.

In your professional experience, have you supported laptop computers? If not, what kind of experience do you have with using them?

A: Answers will vary: experience levels can range from no experience at all to power users who are very comfortable with using laptops and the technologies used with them.

Of the common laptop issues discussed in this lesson, which do you expect to encounter most often? Briefly explain your response.

A: Answers will vary, but might include dealing with display issues, particularly in situations where users use their laptops at the office and on the road, where different external monitors need to be taken into account.

 *Practice Question: Additional practice questions are available on the CompTIA CHOICE platform within the **Assessments** tile.*

Lesson 16

Supporting and Troubleshooting Mobile Devices

LESSON INTRODUCTION

Mobile devices are everywhere today. Because of their portability and powerful computing capabilities, they are prominent in most workplaces. So, as a certified CompTIA® A+® technician, you will be expected to configure, maintain, and troubleshoot mobile computing devices. With the proper information and the right skills, you will be ready to support these devices as efficiently as you support their desktop counterparts.

LESSON OBJECTIVES

In this lesson, you will:

- Describe characteristics of mobile devices.
- Connect and configure mobile device accessories.
- Configure network connectivity for mobile devices.
- Support mobile apps.
- Secure mobile devices.
- Troubleshoot mobile device issues.

Topic A
Mobile Device Types

EXAM OBJECTIVES COVERED
1001-1.4 Compare and contrast characteristics of various types of other mobile devices.

Interaction Opportunity

There are no hands-on activities for this topic, but if you can arrange for sample devices for learners to look at, that will boost their understanding.

Show Slide(s)

Mobile Devices

Driven by the iPhone® and iPad®, the last few years have seen a huge uptake in the use of mobile devices. In some instances they have replaced traditional computer form factors (laptop and desktop) for day-to-day tasks, such as messaging/email and browsing the web. In this topic, you will learn about the smartphone and tablet form factors and about other types of portable computing technologies.

MOBILE DEVICES

As an A+ technician, your primary focus is likely to be on the more traditional system hardware components and laptop technologies. However, you might also be asked to support devices in the mobile computing realm. Not only has mobile technology reached a new level of performance and portability, but also the use of these devices is on the rise every day. As a certified A+ technician, you will be expected to understand how these devices work and how they should be deployed within the workplace.

Mobile devices such as smartphones and tablets are based on one of three operating systems (Apple® iOS®, Android™, or Windows Mobile®) and a store-based software ecosystem, which allows for third-party apps to be downloaded to add functionality to the device. The main distinction between a smartphone and tablet is the size of the device, rather than its functionality.

The major smartphone and tablet vendors are Apple and Samsung. Other vendors include LG, Google™, HTC, Huawei, Motorola/Lenovo, Microsoft®, Nokia, Sony, and Amazon™.

SMARTPHONES

Show Slide(s)

Smartphones

A smartphone is a device with roughly the same functionality as a personal computer that can be operated with a single hand. Previous handheld computers, known as Personal Digital Assistants (PDA), and earlier types of mobile phones with some software functionality (feature phones), were hampered by clumsy user interfaces. Modern smartphones use touchscreen displays, making them much easier to operate.

Most smartphones have a screen size between 4.5" and 5.7". Leading smartphones provide high resolution screens. For example, the iPhone X has a resolution of 2436x1125.

Smartphones have fast multicore CPUs, anywhere between 2 and 6 GB system memory, and 16 GB+ flash memory storage. They come with features such as premium front and back digital cameras, input sensors like accelerometers, and Global Positioning System (GPS) chips. They can establish network links using Wi-Fi and a cellular data plan.

Typical smartphone form factor. (Image © 123RF.com.)

TABLETS

Prior to the iPad, tablet PCs were usually laptops with touchscreens. The iPad defined a new form factor; smaller than a laptop and with no physical keyboard. Tablets tend to be sized at around either 10" or 7" screens. Tablets use a range of screen resolutions, depending on the price. Microsoft's Surface® 4 tablet features a resolution of 2736x1824.

Show Slide(s)

Tablets

An example of a tablet. (Image © 123RF.com.)

Many Windows® mobile devices adopt a hybrid approach where a laptop can be converted into a tablet by flipping the screen. Microsoft's Surface Pro tablet is available with a detachable keyboard, which can also function as a cover for the screen. Other vendors are also producing hybrid devices that can function as both a laptop and a tablet.

Network links are mainly established using Wi-Fi, although some tablets come with a cellular data option, too.

PHABLET

Phablets sit between smartphones and tablets in terms of size and usability. The name is a portmanteau of Phone and Tablet. They were first popularized by Samsung with their successful Note devices. Phablets have screen sizes between 5.5" and 7". These devices often come with a stylus which can be used for note taking, sketching, and annotations.

Phablets always come with cellular data and a connection to the phone system, as well as Wi-Fi.

MOBILE DEVICES VS. LAPTOPS

Show Slide(s)
Mobile Devices vs. Laptops

Laptops and smartphones/tablets/hybrids are obviously all classes of portable or mobile devices, but you should be aware of the factors that distinguish them.

Factor	Description
Processors	CPUs and their chipsets for smartphones and tablets are often based on the ARM (Advanced RISC Machine) microarchitecture, such as the Apple A, Samsung Exynos, and NVIDIA Tegra derivatives. RISC stands for Reduced Instruction Set Computing. RISC microarchitectures use simple instructions processed very quickly. This contrasts with Complex (CISC) microarchitectures, which use more powerful instructions but process each one more slowly. Intel's PC/laptop CPU microarchitecture is CISC with RISC enhancements (micro-ops).
	As well as the computing power to keep up with increasingly complex apps and games available for these devices (many models are now dual- or quad-core and some use 64-bit CPUs), mobile CPUs must deliver power and thermal efficiency to maximize battery life to an even greater extent than laptops.
System memory	Tablet RAM (a low power DDR SDRAM variant) works much as it does in a PC or laptop to store instructions for the OS when it loads plus any apps the user starts.
Storage	Solid State Drives (flash memory) are used for mass storage rather than hard disks (though this is increasingly the case for laptops and PCs, too).
Component replacements/ upgrades	Many of the hardware components of a laptop can be fixed and replaced when issues arise. There are few field-serviceable parts in a smartphone or tablet. What makes it difficult to repair a tablet is that the parts are soldered and not socketed. Many components are glued into place to keep them stable. When something breaks, in most cases, the entire device needs to be replaced. Similarly, components in a tablet are not upgradeable.
Operating System	Laptops can run a number of different operating systems, including versions from Microsoft®, Linux®, and UNIX®. Smartphones and tablets can only run the OS that the device was manufactured to run (iOS, Android, or Windows).

Interaction Opportunity
If learners point out that if an iOS device is jailbroken, it is usually possible to install Android or Linux on it, discuss how that would put the device outside of the mainstream support environment.

MOBILE DISPLAY/TOUCH INTERFACE

A **touchscreen** allows the user to control the OS directly by swiping or tapping with a finger (or with a stylus) rather than using navigation buttons or a scroll wheel.

Modern mobile devices use capacitive touchscreens. These capacitive displays support **multitouch**, meaning that gestures such as "sweeping" or "pinching" the screen can be interpreted as events and responded to by software in a particular way. Newer devices are also starting to provide **haptic feedback**, or touch responsiveness, making virtual key presses or gestures feel more "real" to the user. On the latest models, screens feature **light sensors** to dim and brighten displays based on ambient conditions. Some devices also feature an eye tracking display to scroll up and down based on where the user is looking.

The touchscreen itself is covered by a thin layer of scratch-resistant, shock-resistant tempered glass, such as Corning's Gorilla Glass. Some users may also apply an additional screen protector. If so, these need to be applied carefully (without bubbling) so as not to interfere with the touch capabilities of the screen.

Apple uses its own version of shatter resistant glass on its current models which is coupled with its branded Retina Display. Other manufacturers utilize Samsung-derived displays, whereas Samsung's flagship phone utilizes a *curved* **OLED** display.

Most mobile devices can be used either in portrait or landscape orientation. A component called an **accelerometer** can detect when the device is moved and change the screen orientation appropriately. There will actually be three accelerometers to measure movement along three axes. Newer devices may use both accelerometers and **gyroscopes** to deliver more accurate readings. As well as switching screen orientation, this can be used as a control mechanism (for example, a driving game could allow the tablet itself to function as a steering wheel).

On some devices, these sensors can be calibrated via a utility that uses a predetermined pattern of movement to calibrate the sensor.

MOBILE DEVICE FORM FACTORS

Mobile devices are even less likely than laptops to have field serviceable parts. The electronics will be densely packed and often soldered or glued together. Most will require return to the manufacturer to replace failed components such as a battery, display screen, or storage device.

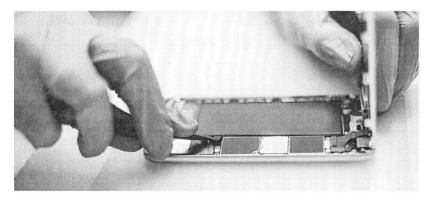

Mobile handset with cover removed—note the slot for the SIM card in the top-right and that the battery is accessible but not designated as user-removable. (Image by guruxox © 123RF.com.)

Some mobiles have a user-replaceable battery, accessed by removing the cover. There will also be a port for a Subscriber Identity Module (SIM) card for GSM-based or 4G LTE cellular access. This may also be fitted by removing the case. Refer to the device documentation for instructions on removing the case. Always power off the device before opening the case.

Show Slide(s)

Mobile Display/Touch Interface

Teaching Tip

Mobile devices with foldable screens are likely to appear through 2019/2020. Some other sensors used in mobile devices include:

- Magnetometer—supports compass-based functionality.
- Barometer—measures air pressure (detect altitude and weather conditions).
- Proximity sensor—disables touch when you hold the phone to your ear to make a call.
- Heart rate monitor—some devices have a dedicated LED; others use the camera.
- Infrared (IR) camera—allows thermal imaging. This also prevents face recognition systems being tricked with a photo.

Show Slide(s)

Mobile Device Form Factors

*Caution: While it would usually void the warranty to further disassemble the device, there may be some circumstances in which you want to replace a part yourself. The best guide to doing so is a website hosting gadget "teardown" videos and repair guides, such as **ifixit.com**.*

Show Slide(s)

E-Readers

E-READERS

Unlike a tablet, an **e-reader** is designed for the sole purpose of reading digital books and magazines (with perhaps the option to add annotations). E-readers use **electrophoretic ink (e-ink)** technology to create an **Electronic Paper Display (EPD)**. Compared to the LED or OLED display used on a tablet, an EPD has low power consumption but facilitates high contrast reading in a variety of ambient light conditions. In typical conditions, these screens do not need to use a backlight, saving power and extending battery life. It is not unusual to get several days of usage on a single charge for these devices. Like most tablets and smartphones, an e-reader is charged using a USB cable.

An example of an e-reader device. (Image © 123RF.com.)

E-readers are manufactured for major book retailers such as Amazon and Barnes and Noble. They have Wi-Fi connectivity to download e-books directly from the retailer's webstore.

Show Slide(s)

Wearable Technology

WEARABLE TECHNOLOGY

Electronics manufacturing allows a great deal of computing power to be packed within a small space. Consequently, computing functionality is being added to wearable items, such as watches, bracelets, and eyeglasses.

SMART WATCHES

Smart watches have risen in popularity in recent years. Current competing technologies are based on the Android Wear OS, Samsung's Tizen OS, and Apple iOS, each with their own separate app ecosystems. A smart watch is likely to be customizable with different watch faces and wrist straps.

An example of a smart watch. (Image © 123RF.com.)

Most smart watches use Bluetooth® to pair with a smartphone. They are able to display key information at a glance (emails, messages, and social media status, for instance), allowing the user to better interact with the phone. Some newer smart watches are starting to appear with their own Wi-Fi connectivity, allowing use of the watch without proximity to a paired phone.

As well as helping with personal information management, many smart watches come with health features. Technologies bundled include heart rate monitors via Infrared (IR) sensors, accelerometers to measure sleeping patterns and movement for exercise, plus cameras and IR sensors to operate devices such as TVs.

FITNESS MONITORS

As the name suggests, fitness monitors focus on exercise and health uses rather than a range of computing tasks. This makes them cheaper devices than smart watches. They usually connect via Wi-Fi or Bluetooth to send data to a mobile app or PC software for analysis. Some feature a GPS tracker to allow runners to map their exercise accurately.

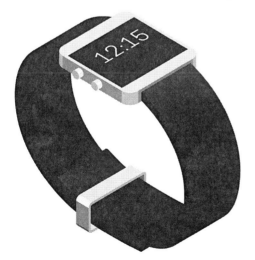

Example of a wearable fitness monitor. (Image © 123RF.com.)

Features of fitness monitors might include:

* Pedometer to count the steps taken during a specified period of time.
* Accelerometer to measure the intensity of the workout.
* Heart rate and blood pressure monitors.
* A calculation of the number of calories burned.

VR/AR HEADSETS AND SMART GLASSES

A Virtual Reality (VR) headset is designed to replace what you can see and hear in the real world with sights and sounds from a game or conferencing app generated by software. There are tethered VR headsets that connect to a computer as a peripheral device, but it is also possible to use a smartphone with a headset to get the VR experience.

Mobile VR headsets, such as Samsung Gear or Google Daydream View™, only work with selected (premium) smartphone models. These headsets contain lenses that split the smartphone display into a stereoscopic image, giving the illusion of depth. The headsets also come with a motion controller to allow you to interact with objects in the VR environment.

 Note: *There are also standalone mobile VR headsets, such as the Oculus Go. This contains a basic smartphone (without cellular capability) embedded in the headset. Apple does not make a VR headset for the iPhone (at the time of writing), but there are third-party options.*

Augmented Reality (AR) is a somewhat similar technology to VR. Rather than provide a completely simulated environment, AR projects digital artifacts onto "ordinary" reality. This could be as simple as providing context-sensitive notes, messages, or advertising or as complex as generating digital avatars within the real world. This latter technique is exploited by popular smartphone camera games, such as Pokémon Go, which enables you to locate collectible cartoon characters in unlikely real world locations through your smartphone camera. Another use case is an app like Samsung's AR Emoji, which transforms people captured in the viewfinder in various unsettling ways.

There are also some AR devices, though they have not gained a very large market yet. Smart glasses were pioneered by Google with their Google Glass range and Google is rumored to be working on a more sophisticated AR headset (codenamed Google A65 at time of writing). Other AR-like devices are made by Microsoft (HoloLens®) and AiR for industrial applications.

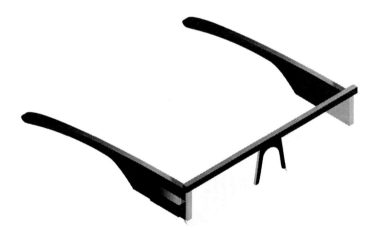

Example of smart glasses. (Image © 123RF.com.)

Network connectivity and pairing with other mobile devices is provided by Wi-Fi and/or Bluetooth. Most AR headsets or smart glasses also come with a camera, and there are issues arising due to the potential invasion of privacy or breach of confidentiality such a relatively concealed recording device could pose.

Input methods allowing the user to control the software running on the glasses include buttons, eye tracking, natural language voice input, plus gesture controls.

GPS NAVIGATION DEVICES

A **Global Positioning System (GPS)** chip is built into most smartphones and many tablets and other smart devices, but there are also dedicated GPS navigation devices (also called sat navs, for "satellite navigation"). These come in 5-6" models aimed both at in-vehicle use and smaller clip-on devices for walkers and cyclists. GPS devices combine providing an accurate geolocation system with map and local traffic information to allow users to plot routes and help them follow a route with turn-by-turn navigation advice. Some devices use over-the-air radio to provide live traffic information; other models have to be tethered to a smartphone to use its data plan. Most are touchscreen-operated with many models also supporting voice control.

 Show Slide(s)

GPS Navigation Devices

Activity 16-1
Discussing Mobile Device Types

Show Slide(s)

Activity: Discussing Mobile Device Types

Teaching Tip

If possible, provide learners with an array of the devices covered in this topic, including tablets, wearable devices, e-Readers, and GPS devices. If you don't have a lot of devices, point out that many of the features of these mobile devices can be found on most smartphones.

Discuss features and connectivity options for the different devices. For instance, which devices can be used standalone, and which must be tethered to a computer or smartphone for updates?

SCENARIO
Answer the following questions to check your understanding of the topic.

---

1. **What are the principal characteristics of the phablet form factor?**

   A phablet is essentially a smartphone with a screen size of more than approximately 5.5" but less than about 7". Phablets can make voice calls and use cellular data, while many tablets are limited to Wi-Fi connectivity.

2. **What is the relevance of ARM to smartphones?**

   Advanced RISC Machines (ARM) produce the CPU designs most widely used in smartphones.

3. **True or false? Smartphones use a type of memory technology that works both as system memory and as persistent storage.**

   False—like PCs, smartphones use a variant of DDR for system memory. This is volatile storage so a flash memory device is used for persistent storage.

4. **What is meant by wearable technology?**

   Wearable technology is devices that the user doesn't need to hold (as they are affixed to the wearer via a band or clip) to provide uninterrupted interaction between computer and network systems and the user. Examples include Virtual Reality (VR) headsets, smartwatches (such as Apple's iWatch), and fitness monitors like FitBit.

5. **What technology gives an e-Reader better battery life than a tablet?**

   The e-Ink display works without backlighting, producing little to no heat through resistance and better energy efficiency.

Topic B

Connect and Configure Mobile Device Accessories

EXAM OBJECTIVES COVERED
1001-1.5 Given a scenario, connect and configure accessories and ports of other mobile devices.
1001-2.7 Compare and contrast Internet connection types, network types, and their features.

Mobile devices gain much of their functionality by being able to connect to the user's regular computer. By making the files available on the mobile device, they can continue working on the files from a mobile device. Being able to connect the mobile device back to the computer might require additional accessories. In this topic, you will examine the connection types and accessories used for mobile devices.

WIRED CONNECTIONS FOR ACCESSORIES

Although mobile devices are designed to be self-contained, there is the need to attach peripheral devices, connect to a computer, or attach a charging cable

APPLE DOCK AND LIGHTNING CONNECTORS

Older Apple devices use a proprietary 30-pin dock connector, enabling connections to various peripheral devices. The dock is also used to charge the battery. A dock-connector to USB cable facilitates connections to a USB bus (that is, to a PC), though not the connection of USB devices such as hard drives to the iPhone/iPad.

On the latest Apple devices, the 30-pin dock connector is replaced by an 8-pin Lightning® connector (also proprietary). The Lightning connector is reversible (can be inserted either way up). There are various Lightning converter cables to allow connections to interfaces such as HDMI, VGA, and SD card readers.

USB CONNECTORS

Android-based devices usually have a Micro-B USB port for charging and connectivity. You might find older devices using the Mini-B USB port. New devices are quickly adopting the USB-C connector. One issue for Android is that there is no standard way of positioning the connectors, so connections to devices such as speaker or charging docks tend to have to use a cable .

WIRELESS CONNECTIONS FOR ACCESSORIES

Short-range wireless connectivity is often a better option for mobile devices than wired connections.

BLUETOOTH

Bluetooth is used for so-called Personal Area Networks (PAN) to share data between devices and connect peripheral devices to hosts, such as smartphones and tablets. Bluetooth is a radio-based technology but it is designed to work only over close range. Bluetooth is quoted to work at distances of up to 10 meters (30 feet) for Class 2 devices or 1 meter (3 feet) for Class 3 devices. Devices supporting the Bluetooth 2.0—

Teaching Tip

This topic recaps some of the peripheral technologies used with PCs. Focus on their use on the different mobile platforms. You will also look at some of the accessories available for mobile devices.

Show Slide(s)

Wired Connections for Accessories

Teaching Tip

Remind learners that detailed information about connection Interfaces Is found elsewhere in the course. Focus your presentation on which interfaces are used by different devices.

Show Slide(s)

Wireless Connections for Accessories (2 slides)

Interaction Opportunity

Ask learners to locate settings for Bluetooth and tethering on their own mobile devices.

Enhanced Data Rate (EDR)— standard have a maximum transfer rate of 3 Mbps; otherwise, the maximum rate is 1 Mbps.

 Note: Bluetooth 3 supports a 24 Mbps HighSpeed (HS) mode, but this uses a specially negotiated Wi-Fi link rather than the Bluetooth connection itself.

Bluetooth needs to be enabled for use via device settings. You may also want to change the device name—remember that this is displayed publicly. Opening the settings page makes the device discoverable to other Bluetooth-enabled devices.

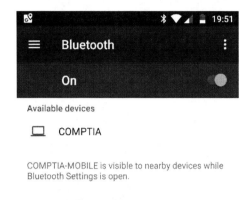

Enabling Bluetooth on an Android device. In this figure, the Android device is named "COMPTIA-MOBILE." "COMPTIA" is a nearby Windows PC with Bluetooth enabled.

NFC

An increasing range of smartphone models have **Near Field Communications (NFC)** chips built in. NFC allows for very short range data transmission (up to about 20 cm/8 in) to activate a receiver chip in the contactless credit card reader. The data rates achievable are very low but these transactions do not require exchanging large amounts of information.

NFC allows a mobile device to make payments via contactless Point-of-Sale (PoS) machines. To configure a payment service, the user enters their credit card information into a Mobile Wallet app on the device. The wallet app does not transmit the original credit card information, but a one-time token that is interpreted by the card merchant and linked backed to the relevant customer account. There are three major Mobile Wallet apps: Apple Pay, Android Pay, and Samsung Pay. Some PoS readers may only support a particular type of wallet app or apps.

As with Bluetooth, NFC can be enabled or disabled via settings. The device must be unlocked to initiate a transaction.

InfraRed (IR)

Many mobile devices are also equipped with an **infrared (IR)** sensor or **blaster**. This is not used for data connections as such but does allow the device to interact with appliances such as TVs and set-top boxes. An app on the device can be installed to allow the mobile device to be used as a remote control for the appliance.

TETHERING AND MOBILE HOTSPOTS

Tethering refers to using a mobile device's cellular data plan to get Internet access on a PC or laptop (or other device). Not all carriers allow tethering and some only allow it as a chargeable service add-on. Connect the device to the PC via USB or Bluetooth, then configure tethering settings through the **Settings→Network** menu.

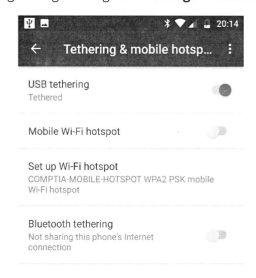

Configuring tethering on an Android phone. The device in this figure is connected to the PC over USB, but you could use Bluetooth too.

If you want to provide access to more than one device, you can enable the **Mobile Hotspot** setting. Configure the device with the usual settings for an access point (network name, security type, and passphrase) and then other devices can connect to it as they would any other WLAN.

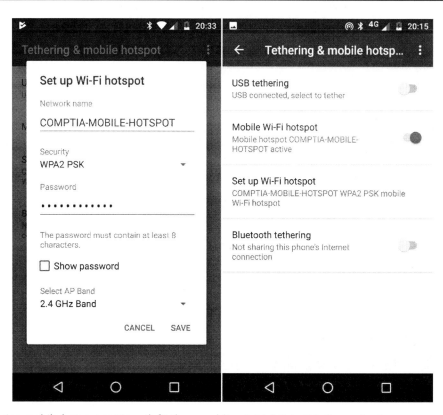

Configuring mobile hotspot settings (left) then enabling it (right). In this figure, hosts can connect to the "COMPTIA-MOBILE-HOTSPOT" network and use the device's cellular data plan to get Internet access.

COMMON MOBILE DEVICE ACCESSORIES

Some popular peripheral options for mobile devices include the following:

Show Slide(s)

Common Mobile Device Accessories

Teaching Tip

3.5 mm headphone jacks are being phased out of mobile device designs. Users have to connect to the Lightning or USB-C port. Converter stub cables for 3.5 mm headphones can be obtained.

Peripheral	Description
External keyboard	As the touchscreen keyboards can be quite small and difficult to use, an external keyboard facilitates any extended typing work.
Headset	Provides audio input/output. As well as being useful for the phone function, some devices support voice recognition. There will usually be an audio connector for headsets or they can be connected via Bluetooth.
Speaker dock	Allows the device to play audio through external speakers. These can be connected either via the data port, the 3.5 mm audio jack, or more commonly through Bluetooth.
Game pad	Allows the use of a console-type controller (with joystick, cursor pad, and action buttons) with compatible mobile game apps. The game pad will come with some sort of clip to place the smartphone in. It must then be connected via USB or Lightning or paired with the device over Bluetooth. The functionality of the joystick and buttons is configured through each app individually.
Micro-SD (Secure Digital) slot	Allows the device's internal storage to be supplemented with a removable memory card.

DOCKING STATIONS

As modern smartphones develop, manufacturers have been able to include processing power to rival some desktops and sometimes even replace them altogether. A smartphone docking station connects the device to a monitor and input devices (keyboard and mouse).

Example of a smartphone dock. (Image © 123RF.com.)

PROTECTIVE COVERS AND WATERPROOFING

Although they are made from relatively tough components, mobiles are still prone to damage from dropping, crushing, scratching, or immersion. Rigid or rubber protective covers mitigate this risk a little. Covers can also often function as a stand so that the device can be placed upright on a desk. Many smartphone users also just like to personalize their phone with a cover.

A screen protector is a thin but tough film designed to provide extra protection for the display without compromising touch sensitivity.

Some cases are able to provide a degree of waterproofing. Some mobile devices are designed to be inherently waterproof. Waterproofing is rated on the **Ingress Protection (IP) scale**. A case or device will have two numbers, such as IP67. The first (6) is a rating for repelling solids, with a 5 or 6 representing devices that are dust protected and dust proof, respectively. The second value (7) is for liquids, with a 7 being protected from immersion in up to 1 m and 8 being protected from immersion beyond 1 m.

 Note: If dust protection is unrated, the IP value will be IPX7 or IPX8.

CREDIT CARD READERS

For devices with the appropriate port, a credit card reader can be added to a tablet or smartphone. This enables mobile vendors, such as those at festivals or street vendors, to take credit card payments without having a network cable or phone line connected to the credit card reader.

MOBILE POWER

Obviously, smartphones and tablets are primarily designed to work from battery power but can be plugged into building power via the charging cable and adapter. Some devices come with removable battery packs but these are very much the exception rather than the rule. Most vendors try to design their devices so that they will support "typical" usage for a full day without charging.

The charging speed that can be expected depends on what kind of USB connection is available:

- USB over Type A/B ports and power adapters can supply up to 2.5 W (500 mA at 5 V) for USB 2 or 4.5 W (900 mA at 5 V) for USB 3.
- **Quick Charge (QC)** adapters can deliver up to 18 W over USB Type A/B ports.
- Computer ports and charging adapters using USB-C can nominally supply up to 100 W (5 A at 20 V). Not all devices will be able to draw power at that level, though.
- Wireless charging (by induction) pads and stands can supply up to 15 W. Most wireless charging devices are based on the Qi standard developed by the Wireless

Power Consortium. Some chargers may be capable of charging multiple devices simultaneously.

- Portable charging banks provide a larger battery, such as 10,000 or 20,000 milliamp hours (mAh), than is found in a typical phone. This allows the phone to be charged from the power pack two or three times before the power pack itself needs recharging. The output of these devices ranges from 2.1 A to about 5 A.

*Note: If connected to a computer (or a laptop running on AC power) the device will **trickle charge**, which takes longer (try disconnecting other USB devices to improve charge times using this method). Also, the Quick Charge standard imposes a phased charging regime to protect battery lifetime (overcharging can reduce the maximum possible charge more quickly). If power is available, the battery is **fast-charged** to 80% and then trickle charged.*

As the battery ages, it becomes less able to hold a full charge. If it is non-removable, the device will have to be returned to the vendor for battery replacement.

*Note: To learn more, check the **Video** tile on the CHOICE Course screen for any videos that supplement the content for this lesson.*

Access the Checklist tile on your CHOICE Course screen for reference information and job aids on How to Connect and Configure Mobile Device Accessories.

Activity 16-2

Discussing Mobile Device Accessory Connection and Configuration

SCENARIO

Answer the following questions to check your understanding of the topic.

1. **What type of peripheral port would you expect to find on a current generation smartphone?**

   For Apple devices, the Lightning port. For Android and Windows, it will be USB—either Micro Type B or Type-C.

2. **How would you upgrade storage capacity on a typical smartphone?**

   If the smartphone supports removable flash cards such as Micro-SD, you can add a larger card. Otherwise, the components in these devices are not field replaceable, so there are no upgrade options.

3. **What technology do smartphones use to facilitate payment at points of sale?**

   Near Field Communications (NFC) allows the user to touch a receiver for the phone to pass card data to a point of sale terminal.

4. **True or false? An IP67-rated smartwatch could be considered risk-free for wear while swimming in an indoor pool.**

   False—IP67 rates immersion up to 1 m (for up to 30 minutes), so wearing a device while swimming would be a significant risk.

 Show Slide(s)

Activity: Discussing Mobile Device Accessory Connection and Configuration

 Teaching Tip

Optionally, as an additional activity, provide learners with a variety of mobile device accessories and cables that will work with the mobile devices they have. Examples could include:

- Chargers.
- Screen protectors and case covers.
- Docking stations.
- USB and Lightning cables and display adapters.

Consider also including some cables or accessories that will not work with the devices they have. You could also provide containers labeled with the various mobile devices, and have learners place the accessories and cables in the appropriate container after they verify that the accessory or cable works with the device they have.

Topic C

Configure Mobile Device Network Connectivity

EXAM OBJECTIVES COVERED

1001-1.6 Given a scenario, configure basic mobile device network connectivity and application support.
1001-2.7 Compare and contrast Internet connection types, network types, and their features.
1001-3.9 Given a scenario, install and configure common devices.

In this topic, you will examine some of the features and methods used to connect mobile devices to networks and the Internet.

CELLULAR DATA NETWORKS

Cellular data means connecting to the Internet via the device's cell phone radio and the handset's cellular network provider. The data rate depends on the technology supported by both the phone and the cell tower (3G or 4G, for instance). When a mobile device uses the cellular provider's network, there are likely to be charges based on the amount of data downloaded. These charges can be particularly high when the phone is used abroad (referred to as roaming) so it is often useful to be able to disable mobile data access.

 Teaching Tip

A lot of the technologies discussed here have been already covered—you are just considering them in the context of mobile devices.

 Show Slide(s)

Cellular Data Networks (4 slides)

 Teaching Tip

Ask learners which type of cellular network their phones connect to.

 Interaction Opportunity

Ask learners why they might want or need to turn Wi-Fi or cell network connections on and off. Reasons might include being on an airline that doesn't allow cell phone use, being in a corporate environment where cell phones are not allowed to connect to the wireless network, forcing the device to use one network or the other when both are available.

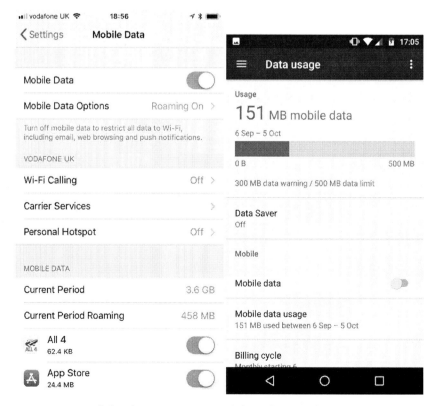

Cellular data options in iOS (left) and Android (right).

The indicator on the status bar at the top of the screen shows the data link in use. A device will usually default to Wi-Fi if present and show a signal strength icon. 📶 / ◺ A device using a cellular data network may show a strength icon for a 4G network 📶 / ◺ or the type of data network (H+ for HSPA+ for instance).

The cellular data connection can usually be enabled or disabled via the notification shade but there will also be additional configuration options via the **Settings** menu. You can usually set usage warnings and caps and prevent selected apps from using cellular data connections.

MOBILE HOTSPOTS AND TETHERING

As explained earlier, tethering means connecting another device to a smartphone or tablet via USB or Bluetooth so that it can share its cellular data connection. You can also share the link by configuring the smartphone or tablet as an access point, turning it into a personal or mobile hotspot.

Configuring an iPhone to work as a mobile hotspot.

CELLULAR RADIOS

A **cellular radio** makes a connection using the nearest available transmitter (cell or base station). Each base station has an effective range of up to 5 miles (8 km). The transmitter connects the phone to the mobile and landline telephone networks. Cellular radio works in the 850 and 1900 MHz frequency bands (mostly in the Americas) and the 900 and 1800 MHz bands (rest of the world). There are two main cellular radio network types, each developing different standards for the "generations" of cellular data access (2G, 3G, and so on). **Global System for Mobile Communication (GSM)** is deployed worldwide while **Code Division Multiple Access (CDMA)** is adopted by carriers in the Americas.

Note: Just to confuse things, GSM radios now use a type of CDMA technology too. In its technical sense, CDMA is a means of exchanging radio signals, it's just that the term "CDMA" has become a handy label to distinguish these networks from GSM. Within the US, Sprint and Verizon use CDMA while AT&T and T-Mobile use GSM.

GSM NETWORKS AND SIM CARDS

GSM works with a **Subscriber Identity Module (SIM) card**. The user adds the card to the device and the card obtains all the information it needs to connect to the network, including a phone number, radio frequency bands to use, and information about how to connect when roaming in different countries. Updates to this information are "pushed" to the card by the network provider so there is never a need to perform a manual update.

Interaction Opportunity

If learners have smartphones or cellular tablets, have them locate the label with the various numbers on it.

Under GSM, a handset is identified by an **International Mobile Station Equipment Identity (IMEI)**. It is used by the GSM network to identify valid devices and can be used to stop stolen phones from accessing the network, regardless of the SIM used.

This number is usually printed on a label in the battery compartment on a mobile phone. If it is a sealed case, then the number will be found on the back or bottom of the device. You can also access the IMEI number by dialing ***#06#** and it will display the IMEI on the device screen. Any phone connected to a GSM network must have the IMEI number stored in the **Equipment Identity Register (EIR) database**. If a phone is reported as being lost or stolen, the IMEI number is marked to be invalid in the EIR.

A SIM card is registered to a particular user and can be transferred between devices. The user is identified by an **International Mobile Subscriber Identity (IMSI)** number. The number is stored on the SIM card in the format:

- Three-digit mobile country code.
- Two-digit mobile network code.
- Up to 10 digit mobile station identification number.

Note: The IMEI number identifies the device. The IMSI number identifies the subscriber.

An unlocked handset can be used with any type of SIM card from the user's chosen network provider; a locked handset is tied to a single network provider.

CDMA NETWORKS

CDMA locks the handset to the original provider and does not require any sort of SIM card. Handsets are identified by a **Mobile Equipment ID (MEID)**. Information that the cellular radio needs to connect to the network is provided as **Preferred Roaming Index (PRI)** and **Preferred Roaming List (PRL)** databases.

Note: Handsets from CDMA providers might come with a SIM card but the SIM card is to connect to 4G networks, which are all GSM-based. A handset might also have a SIM card to support roaming when traveling internationally as CDMA networks are not widespread outside the Americas.

*Note: To learn more, check the **Video** tile on the CHOICE Course screen for any videos that supplement the content for this lesson.*

Access the Checklist tile on your CHOICE Course screen for reference information and job aids on How to View IEMI and IMSI Numbers.

BASEBAND UPDATES AND RADIO FIRMWARE

A **baseband update** modifies the firmware of the radio modem used for cellular, Wi-Fi, Bluetooth, NFC, and GPS connectivity. **Radio firmware** in a mobile device contains an operating system that is separate from the end-user operating system (for example, Android or iOS). The modem uses its own baseband processor and memory, which boots a **Realtime Operating System (RTOS)**. An RTOS is often used for time-sensitive embedded controllers, of the sort required for the modulation and frequency shifts that underpin radio-based connectivity.

The procedures for establishing radio connections are complex and require strict compliance with regulatory certification schemes, so incorporating these functions in the main OS would make it far harder to bring OS updates to market. Unfortunately, baseband operating systems have been associated with several vulnerabilities over the years, so it is imperative to ensure that updates are applied promptly. These updates are usually pushed to the handset by the device vendor, often as part of OS upgrades. A handset that has been jailbroken or rooted might be able to be configured to prevent baseband updates or apply a particular version manually, but in the general course of things there is little reason to do so.

Note: **Jailbreaking** *and* **rooting** *mean circumventing the usual operation of the mobile OS to obtain super-user or root administrator permissions over the device.*

Show Slide(s)

Baseband Updates and Radio Firmware

WI-FI NETWORKS AND HOTSPOTS

Not all mobile devices support cellular radios, but every smartphone and tablet supports a Wi-Fi radio.

In Android, you can use the notification shade to select a network or open the Wi-Fi settings menus.

Show Slide(s)

Wi-Fi Networks and Hotspots (2 slides)

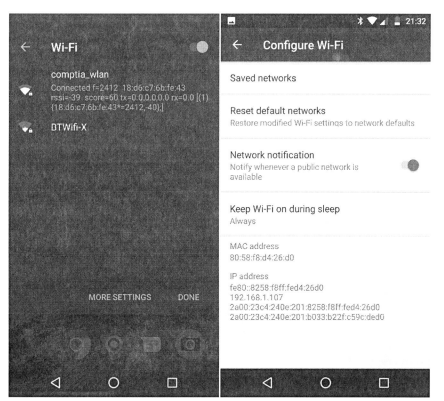

Using Android to join a Wi-Fi network (left). The device's network address can be checked using the Advanced Settings page (right).

In iOS, Wi-Fi networks can be setup via **Settings→Wi-Fi**. Either select the network name (if it is being broadcast) and credentials or manually configure the SSID and security level (WEP, WPA, or WPA2, for instance).

A **hotspot** is a location served by some sort of device offering Internet access via Wi-Fi. There are many ways to implement a hotspot:

- A business may set up an open access point to allow public access (or require payment via a captive portal).
- A smartphone or tablet might be configured to share its cellular data connection (a personal hotspot).
- A "Mi-Fi" mobile broadband device is one dedicated to providing a personal hotspot service.

When you are using a public hotspot, anyone else joined to the wireless network and the owner of the hotspot can easily intercept traffic passing over it. Consequently, users need to be careful to use SSL/TLS (with a valid digital certificate) to send confidential information to and from web servers and mail clients. Another option is to use a Virtual Private Network (VPN) to protect the browsing session.

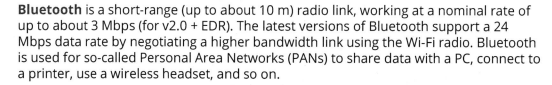

Access the Checklist tile on your CHOICE Course screen for reference information and job aids on How to Enable or Disable Network Connections on Mobile Devices.

Show Slide(s)
Mobile VPN Configuration

MOBILE VPN CONFIGURATION

A Virtual Private Network (VPN) uses a protocol such as **IPSec** or **Secure Sockets Tunneling Protocol (SSTP)** to create a **tunnel** through a carrier network. The contents of the tunnel can be encrypted so that no one with access to the carrier network (such as open access point) can intercept information passing through the VPN.

A **mobile VPN** is one that can maintain the VPN link across multiple carrier networks, where the IP address assigned to the mobile device may change often. The Mobile VPN app assigns a virtual IP address to connect to the VPN server, then uses any available carrier network to maintain the link. It is also capable of sustaining the link when the device is in sleep mode. Mobile VPNs are usually implemented as third party apps on both Android and iOS devices.

Show Slide(s)
Bluetooth (3 slides)

Teaching Tip

This is one of those technologies that was covered earlier. Take this opportunity to describe key points of using Bluetooth to connect mobile devices.

BLUETOOTH

Bluetooth is a short-range (up to about 10 m) radio link, working at a nominal rate of up to about 3 Mbps (for v2.0 + EDR). The latest versions of Bluetooth support a 24 Mbps data rate by negotiating a higher bandwidth link using the Wi-Fi radio. Bluetooth is used for so-called Personal Area Networks (PANs) to share data with a PC, connect to a printer, use a wireless headset, and so on.

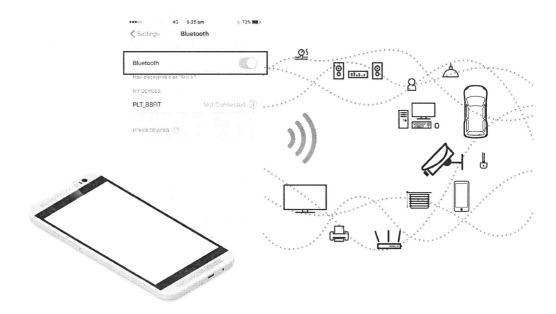

Bluetooth pairing.

In iOS, Bluetooth devices are configured via **Settings→General→Bluetooth**. Switch Bluetooth on to make the device discoverable and locate other nearby devices. In Android, you can access Bluetooth settings via the notification shade.

In Windows, you can manage Bluetooth Devices using the applet in Control Panel or

Windows Settings and the Bluetooth icon in the notification area. The pairing system should automatically generate a passkey when a connection request is received. Input or confirm the key on the destination device and accept the connection.

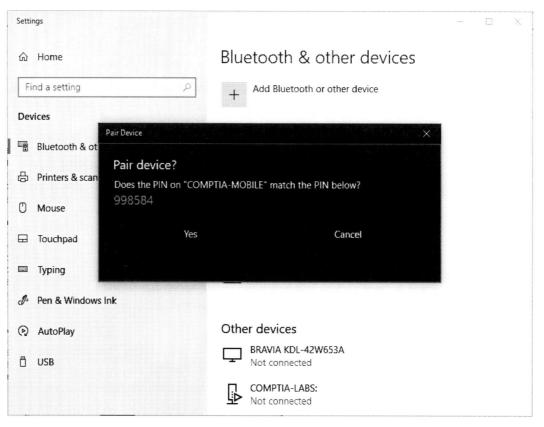

Pairing a Windows 10 computer with a smartphone. (Screenshot used with permission from Microsoft.)

To test the connection, you can simply try use the device—check that music plays through Bluetooth headphones, for example. If you are connecting a device and a

Windows PC, you can use the Bluetooth icon 🅱 or `fsquirt` command to launch the Bluetooth File Transfer Wizard and enable sending or receiving of a file.

If you cannot connect a device, check that it has been made discoverable. Another option is to make the computer visible to Bluetooth devices (so that you can initiate a connection from the device rather than from Windows). You should also check that the PC is configured to allow connections (and that the Bluetooth radio is turned on).

If you make a computer discoverable, check the pairing list regularly to confirm that the devices listed are valid.

If you still cannot add or use Bluetooth devices, check that the **Bluetooth Support Service** is running. Also, consider using **Device Manager** to disable power management settings on the Bluetooth adapter and the problematic Bluetooth device.

Note: *To learn more, check the **Video** tile on the CHOICE Course screen for any videos that supplement the content for this lesson.*

Access the Checklist tile on your CHOICE Course screen for reference information and job aids on How to Enable Bluetooth.

AIRPLANE MODE

Each type of wireless radio link can be toggled on or off individually using the **Control Center** (swipe up from the bottom in iOS) or **notification shade** (swipe down from the top in Android). For example, you could disable the cellular data network while leaving Wi-Fi enabled to avoid incurring charges for data use over the cellular network. Most airlines prevent flyers from using radio-based devices while onboard a plane. A device can be put into **airplane mode** to comply with these restrictions, though some carriers insist that devices must be switched off completely at times such as take-off and landing. Airplane mode disables all wireless features (cellular data, Wi-Fi, GPS, Bluetooth, and NFC). On some devices, some services can selectively be re-enabled while still in airplane mode.

 Show Slide(s)

Airplane Mode (2 slides)

 Interaction Opportunity

Ask learners to view the options for toggling radio services on their own mobile devices.

iOS iPhone (left) and Android phone (right) with Airplane (Aeroplane) mode enabled.

 Show Slide(s)

Email Configuration Options (4 slides)

EMAIL CONFIGURATION OPTIONS

One of the most important features of mobile devices is the ability to receive and compose email. The settings are configured on the device in much the same way you would set up a mail account on a PC. For example, in iOS, open **Settings→Mail, Contacts, Calendars** then select **Add Account**.

 Teaching Tip

Point out that the precise mechanism for setting up accounts varies between iOS and different kinds of Android and between versions.

COMMERCIAL PROVIDER EMAIL CONFIGURATION

Most mobile devices have integrated provider configurations that allow the OS to **autodiscover** connection settings. Autodiscover means that the mail service has published special Domain Name System (DNS) records that identify how the account for a particular domain should be configured. Many autodiscover-enabled providers will be listed on the device. Choose the mail provider (Exchange, Gmail™, Yahoo!®, Outlook®, iCloud®, and so on) then enter your email address and credentials and test the connection.

 Teaching Tip

The main point is that an autodiscover-enabled service can be configured with just the email address and password.

Interaction Opportunity

Ask learners what email options they have set up on their own mobile devices. Do they have corporate and personal accounts configured on the same phone? Encourage discussion about the pros and cons of doing this.

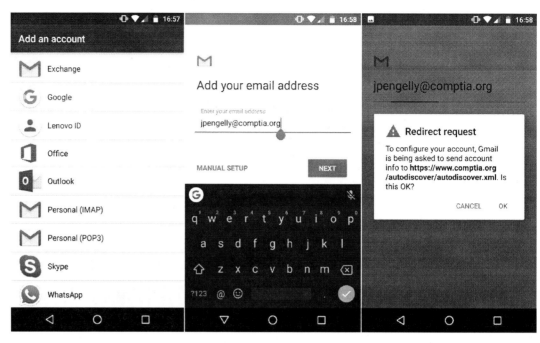

Configuring an autodiscover-enabled Exchange mail account in Android.

CORPORATE AND ISP EMAIL CONFIGURATION

Teaching Tip

Stress the importance of only using SSL-enabled mail services.

Exchange is usually an integrated provider option and clients can autodiscover the correct settings. To manually configure an **Exchange ActiveSync** account you need to enter the email address and user name (usually the same thing) and a host address (obtain this from the Exchange administrator) as well as a password and the choice of whether to use **SSL** (most Exchange servers will require SSL). There is often also a field for domain but this is usually left blank.

 Note: *If there is a single "Domain\User Name" field, prefix the email address with a backslash: \me@company.com.*

If you are connecting to an **Internet Service Provider (ISP)** or **corporate mail gateway** that does not support autodiscovery of configuration settings, you can enter the server address manually by selecting **Other**, then inputting the appropriate server addresses:

- Incoming mail server—**Internet Mail Access Protocol (IMAP)** or **Post Office Protocol (POP3)**.

   Note: *Choose **IMAP** if you are viewing and accessing the mail from multiple devices. POP3 will download the mail to the device, removing it from the server mailbox. Note that Exchange doesn't use either POP3 or IMAP (though it can support them) but a proprietary protocol called **Messaging Application Programming Interface (MAPI)**.*

- Outgoing mail server—**Simple Mail Transfer Protocol (SMTP)**.
- Enable or disable **Secure Sockets Layer (SSL)**.

   Note: *SSL protects confidential information such as the account password and is necessary if you connect to mail over a public link (such as an open Wi-Fi "hotspot"). Note that you can only enable SSL if the mail provider supports it.*

- Ports—the secure (SSL enabled) or unsecure ports used for IMAP, POP3, and SMTP would normally be left to the default. If the email provider uses custom port settings, you would need to obtain those and enter them in the manual configuration.

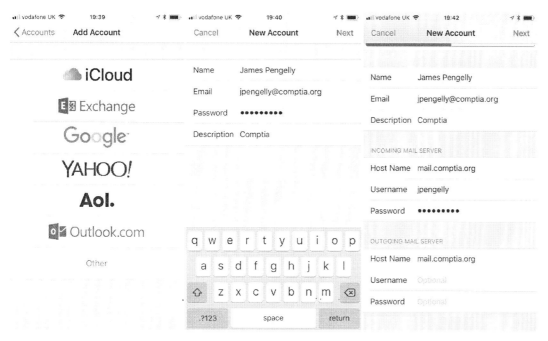

Configuring an email account manually in iOS.

S/MIME

Connecting to email servers by using secure ports ensures that the password you use to connect is protected by encryption. It does not provide "end-to-end" encryption of the messages you send, however. Encryption of an actual email message by using digital certificates and digital signatures ensures that a message can be read only by the intended recipient, that the identity of the sender is verified, and that the message has not been tampered with. The main difficulty is that both sender and recipient must agree to use the same (or compatible) encryption products. There are two main standards: **Pretty Good Privacy (PGP)** and **Secure Multipart Internet Mail Extensions (S/MIME)**. Both provide similar sorts of functions but use different mechanisms to trust digital identities.

Both PGP and S/MIME work with digital certificates and public/private key pairs. It is important to understand the two different ways these key pairs are used in an asymmetric encryption system:

- When you sign a message, you use your private key to validate who you are and give the public key related to that private key to anyone you want to communicate with. The public key allows the recipient to verify who you are.
- When you want people to send you messages that only you can read, your public key is used by the sender to encrypt the message. Once encrypted, only your private key can decrypt it (your public key cannot be used to reverse the encryption).

The **encryption keys** are stored and exchanged using digital certificates. Each mobile OS has a store for certificates, and for email encryption to work properly, the correct certificates and root certificates must be available to the application. In most scenarios, these would be added to the device using **Mobile Device Management (MDM)** software.

 Teaching Tip

Emphasize the difference between connection security (between the email client and local server) and end-to-end message authentication, integrity, and confidentiality (between sender and recipient). Discuss other communication services that provide end-to-end encryption, such as WhatsApp, Silence (SMSSecure), and Signal.

Note: *To learn more, check the* **Video** *tile on the CHOICE Course screen for any videos that supplement the content for this lesson.*

Access the Checklist tile on your CHOICE Course screen for reference information and job aids on How to Configure Email Accounts.

Activity 16-3

Discussing Mobile Device Network Connectivity Configuration

Show Slide(s)

Activity: Discussing Mobile Device Network Connectivity Configuration

SCENARIO

Answer the following questions to check your understanding of the topic.

1. **Why would a user be likely to disable cellular data access but leave Wi-Fi enabled?**

    To avoid data charges (especially when using the device abroad).

2. **What is tethering?**

    Tethering is the use of a smartphone as an Internet connectivity hub. It can share its Internet connection with a computer via either a cable, Bluetooth, or Wi-Fi.

3. **What serial number uniquely identifies a particular handset?**

    International Mobile Station Equipment Identity (IMEI) for handsets from GSM providers or Mobile Equipment ID (MEID) from CDMA providers.

4. **What is the function of a smartphone's baseband processor?**

    The baseband system is usually dedicated to providing radio modem functions, acting as an interface with the cell tower, access point, or other radio source to transmit signals.

5. **How do you configure an autodiscover-enabled email provider on a smartphone?**

    Just select the provider then enter the email address. If the account is detected, you will be prompted for the password.

6. **True or false? S/MIME is used to configure a secure connection to a mailbox server, so that your password cannot be intercepted when connecting over an open access point.**

    False—S/MIME is for encrypting messages. SSL/TLS is used to secure connections.

Activity 16-4
Configuring Bluetooth

**Show
Slide(s)**

Activity: Configuring
Bluetooth

**Teaching
Tip**

Provide learners with
two Bluetooth devices,
such as a laptop with
Bluetooth capability
and a smartphone, a
smartphone and a
Bluetooth headset or
speaker, or have
learners pair up to
connect their own
mobile devices. Be
prepared to guide
learners through this
activity, provide access
to device
documentation, and
assist as needed.

**Interaction
Opportunity**

Ask learners which
accessories they use
with their personal
mobile devices, and
which accessories their
organizations might
use.

SCENARIO

Personal Area Networks (PAN) are widely used to provide connectivity for wireless peripherals, as well as Internet connection tethering and personal hot spots. In this activity, you will practice using Bluetooth to configure a PAN.

---

1. Access the settings on the mobile device to determine which wireless connection methods are supported on your mobile device.

    Note: Your instructor will provide you with documentation or help guide you through this activity. As mobile devices vary widely, step-by-step directions would not necessarily apply to the devices available to you.

2. Create a Bluetooth connection between two Bluetooth capable devices.
   a) Enable Bluetooth on the mobile device by using the system settings.
   b) Enable pairing on the device.
   c) On your mobile device, find a device for pairing.
   d) Once the device is found, it will ask for a PIN code.
       Depending on the type of device, the PIN code will be sent via a text, or will be a standard code, such as "0000" used for wireless headsets.
   e) Verify that a connection message has been displayed.
   f) Test the connection by using the two devices together to either transfer data, answer or make a call, or play music.

Topic D

Support Mobile Apps

 EXAM OBJECTIVES COVERED
1001-1.7 Given a scenario, use methods to perform mobile device synchronization.
1001-3.9 Given a scenario, install and configure common devices.

Data synchronization is the process of automatically merging and updating common data that is stored on multiple devices. For example, a user can access his or her email contacts list from both his or her mobile device and his or her laptop computer. Synchronization is established when the devices are either connected via a cable or wirelessly, or over a network connection. In this topic, you will identify methods and best practices for managing accounts and apps and synchronizing mobile devices.

MOBILE ACCOUNT SETUP

Most mobile devices have a single user account, configured when the device is used for the first time (or re-initialized). This account is used to manage the apps installed on the device by representing the user on the app store. iOS requires an Apple ID while an Android device requires either a **Google Account** or a similar vendor account, such as a **Samsung Account**. This type of account just requires you to select a unique ID (email address) and to configure your credentials (pattern lock, fingerprint, face ID, and so on). Accounts can also be linked to a cellphone number or alternative email address for verification and recovery functions.

 Note: Multi-user capability is more useful on tablet devices (for use in the classroom, for instance) than on smartphones. Android has some multi-user functionality. Apple makes classroom deployment software available, but otherwise iOS is single user per device.

As well as managing the app store, the account can be used to access various services, such as an email account and cloud storage.

The user can set up sub-accounts for services not represented by their Apple ID or Google Account, such as a corporate email account. Each app can set up a sub-account, too. For example, your device might have accounts for apps such as Facebook or LinkedIn®.

Account settings allow you to choose which features of a particular account type are enabled to synchronize data with the device. You can also add and delete accounts from here.

 Show Slide(s)
Mobile Account Setup

 Interaction Opportunity
Poll learners to see which smartphone store account types are most popular: Apple, Google, Samsung, or Microsoft?

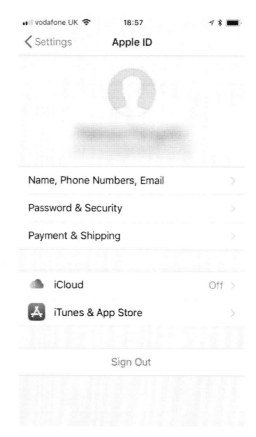

iOS supports a single Apple ID account per device. (Screenshot courtesy of Apple.)

MOBILE APPLICATIONS AND APP STORES

Show Slide(s)

Mobile Applications and App Stores (2 slides)

Interaction Opportunity

Learners should know how to check permissions and use the install/uninstall/ update features of app stores. Ask them to view app permission settings on their own devices.

Teaching Tip

It's not on the objectives, but you could also spend some time on adding/ moving icons on the home screens if you think it would be useful.

Apps are installable programs that extend the functionality of the mobile device. An app must be written and compiled for a particular mobile operating system (Apple iOS, Android, or Windows).

iOS APPS

Apps are made available for free or can be bought from the **App Store**. Apps have to be submitted to and approved by Apple before they are released to users. This is also referred as the **walled garden model** and is designed to prevent the spread of malware or code that could cause faults or crashes. Apps can use a variety of commercial models, including free to use, free with in-app purchases, or paid-for.

Third-party developers can create apps for iOS using Apple's **Software Development Kit (SDK) Xcode** and the programming language **Swift**. Xcode can only be installed and run on a computer using macOS®.

Note: There is also an Apple Developer Enterprise program allowing corporate apps to be distributed to employees without having to publish them in the App Store.

Apple's App Store and app permission settings. This app is already installed, but an update is available.

ANDROID APPS

Android's app model is more relaxed, with apps available from both Google Play™ and third-party sites, such as Amazon's app store. The Java-based SDK (Android Studio) is available on Linux, Windows, and macOS. Apps are supposed to run in a sandbox and have only the privileges granted by the user.

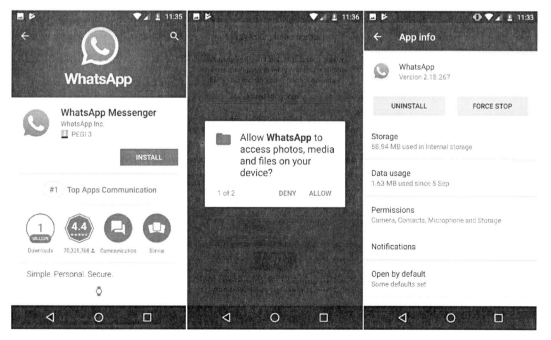

Use the Play Store to install an app (left), grant the app permissions (middle), and review permissions and other settings (right).

An app will normally prompt when it needs to obtain permissions. If these are not granted, or if they need to be revoked later, you can do this via the app's **Settings** page.

Android also allows third-party or custom programs to be installed directly via an **Android Application Package (apk)** file, giving users and businesses the flexibility to directly install apps (**sideload**) without going through the storefront interface. An APK file contains all of that program's code, including .dex files, resources, assets, certificates, and manifest files. Similar to other file formats, APK files can be named almost anything, as long as the file name ends in .apk.

TYPES OF DATA TO SYNCHRONIZE

Show Slide(s)

Types of Data to Synchronize

Interaction Opportunity

Consider asking participants to brainstorm additional data types.

Mobile device synchronization (sync) refers to copying data back and forth between different devices. This might mean between a PC and smartphone or between a smartphone, a tablet, and a PC. Many people have multiple devices and need to keep information up-to-date on all of them. If someone edits a contact record on a phone, they want the changes to appear when they next log into email on their PC.

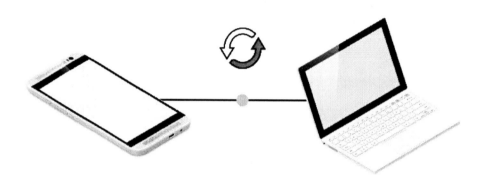

Data synchronization. (Image © 123RF.com.)

There are many different types of information that users might synchronize and many issues you might face dealing with synchronization problems.

CONTACTS

A **contact** is a record with fields for name, address, email address(es), phone numbers, notes, and so on. One issue with contacts is that people tend to create them on different systems and there can be issues matching fields or phone number formats when importing from one system to another using a file format such as **Comma Separated Values (CSV)**. **vCard** represents one standard format and is widely supported now. Maintaining a consistent, single set of contact records is challenging for most people, whatever the technology solutions available!

CALENDAR

A calendar item is a record with fields for appointment or task information, such as subject, date, location, and participants. Calendar records have the same sort of sync issues as contacts; people create appointments in different calendars and then have trouble managing them all. Calendar items can be exchanged between different services using the iCalendar format. Another (fairly minor) issue is that the reminders tend to go off on all devices at the same time.

EMAIL

Most email systems store messages on the server and the client device is used only to manage them (IMAP, Exchange, and web mail, for instance). There can often be sync issues, however, particularly with deletions, sent items, and draft compositions.

PICTURES, MUSIC, AND VIDEO

The main sync issue with media files tends to be the amount of space they take up. There might not be enough space on one device to sync all the files the user has stored. There can also be issues with file formats; not all devices can play or show all formats.

DOCUMENTS

As with media files, documents can use many different formats (Microsoft Word, PDF, plain text, Open XML, and so on). Users editing a document on different devices may have trouble with version history, unless the changes are saved directly to the copy stored in the cloud.

E-BOOKS

There are many apps for purchasing or borrowing **e-books** and **e-magazines** or **e-newspapers**. Often the formats used by different merchants are not interoperable, so multiple e-readers may be required. An e-reader will usually track where you have read to in an e-book, so if you open it on a different device, you can pick up on the page you left off. There are also often facilities for making annotations.

LOCATION DATA

Modern services add **geolocation** data to pretty much everything. If you use a map or travel planner while signed into the service, your location history is likely to have been recorded, unless you have selected an opt-out.

SOCIAL MEDIA DATA

The apps used to manage our **online social lives** store pretty much all information in the cloud, using local storage for cache only, so the view of your online life from your phone is likely to be pretty much the same as from your PC.

APPLICATIONS

When you purchase an app from a store, it will be available across all devices you sign in on, as long as they are the same platform. If you have a Windows PC and an Apple iPhone, you will find yourself managing two sets of apps. Most of them will share data seamlessly, however (the social media ones, for instance). Apple has introduced a family sharing feature to allow apps to be shared between different Apple IDs within the same family.

BOOKMARKS

A **bookmark** is a record of a website or web page that you visited. Browsers keep an automatic history of bookmarks and you can also create a shortcut (or favorite) manually.

PASSWORDS

Both iOS and Android will prompt you to save passwords when you sign in to apps and websites. These passwords are cached securely within the device file system and protected by the authentication and encryption mechanisms required to access the device via the lock screen.

These cached passwords can be synchronized across your devices using cloud services. You have to remember that anyone compromising your device/cloud account will be able to access any service that you have cached the password for.

Show Slide(s)

Synchronization Methods (3 slides)

SYNCHRONIZATION METHODS

Historically, data synchronization would most often take place between a single smartphone and desktop PC. You might use the PC to back up data stored on the smartphone, for instance, or to sync calendar and contact records. Nowadays, it is much more likely for all our devices to be connected via cloud services. If given permission, the device OS backs up data to the cloud service all the time. When you sign in to a new device, it syncs the data from the cloud seamlessly.

iOS SYNCHRONIZATION METHODS

iOS can synchronize with a Windows or Mac computer via the iTunes® program. As with any software, you need to ensure that the computer meets the requirements to install the sync software. The system requirements for these programs are not typically onerous, however. At the time of writing, the principal system requirements for iTunes are a 1 GHz PC with 512 MB RAM, 400 MB free disk space, and Windows 7 or later or any Mac running OS X® or macOS 10.8.5 or later.

The software may install background services and require these to be running to facilitate connections. For example, iTunes requires the Apple Mobile Device Service to communicate with devices and the Bonjour service to enable some features, such as sharing media libraries.

Using iTunes to sync data between an iPhone and a PC.

Once iTunes is installed, the device can be connected to the computer via a USB cable (with an Apple Dock or Lightning connector at the iPhone end) or via a Wi-Fi link.

The software allows the user to choose what to synchronize with the device. Users can also use iTunes as a means of purchasing apps to be sent to their mobile devices.

Another feature of iTunes is the ability to back up, recover, and reinstall firmware on the phone. It is also used to activate the device at the first use.

Apple has also the iCloud service, which allows synchronization of devices via a cloud storage facility so that all iOS devices owned by a user with the same ID can share data, photos, music, and contacts.

ANDROID SYNCHRONIZATION METHODS

Android-based phones are primarily set up to sync with Google's Gmail email and calendar/contact manager cloud services.

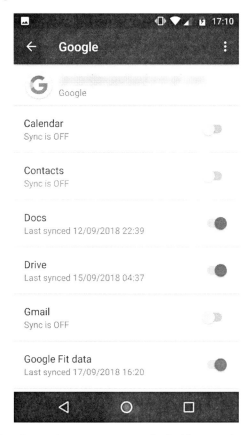

Account settings for the Google master account on an Android smartphone. This account is used for the Play Store and to sync data with other cloud services, but not email, contacts, or calendar.

You can usually view an Android phone or tablet from Windows over USB or Bluetooth and use drag-and-drop for file transfer (using the Media Transfer Protocol). Some Android vendors have utilities for synchronization similar to iTunes, such as Samsung Kies for Samsung phones.

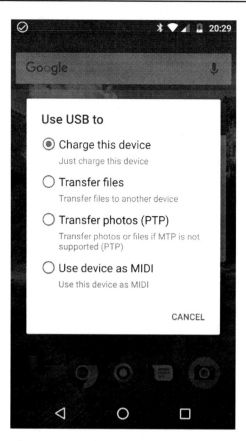

Connecting an Android smartphone to a Windows PC over USB. You can choose whether to allow some sort of data transfer as well as charge the battery. If you enable data transfer, the device's file system will be made available via File Explorer.

The app doubleTwist provides a means of synching with an iTunes library, and there are various other third-party apps for synching with other programs or using protocols such as File Transfer Protocol (FTP).

MICROSOFT AND THIRD-PARTY SYNCHRONIZATION METHODS

Microsoft makes a whole range of cloud services available with a Microsoft account, including free storage space on OneDrive and email/calendar/contact management on Outlook.com. There is also the cloud-based Office suite Office365 with word processing, spreadsheet, and presentation software (amongst others).

Apple, Google, and Microsoft obviously make it easy to use "their" cloud services on "their" devices, but all produce apps for the different platforms, so you can (for example) run OneDrive on an iPhone if you want. There are also third-party cloud sync and storage services, most notably Dropbox™. You should check the vendor's website for any software requirements for installing the desktop app. For example, Dropbox's desktop app runs on Windows 7 or later, macOS 10.9 or later, Ubuntu™ 14.04 or later, or Fedora 21 or later. There are additional requirements for a supported file system (NTFS, HFS/APFS, or ext4, respectively) and in Linux™, for the presence of various libraries and supporting packages.

SYNCHRONIZING TO AUTOMOBILES

Most new automobiles come with in-vehicle entertainment and navigation systems. The main part of this system is referred to as the **head unit**. If supported, a smartphone can be used to "drive" the head unit so the navigation features from your smartphone will appear on the display (simplified for safe use while driving) or you could play songs stored on your tablet via the vehicle's entertainment system. The technologies underpinning this are **Apple CarPlay** and **Android Auto**. Typically, the smartphone has to be connected via USB. Both CarPlay Wireless and Android Auto Wireless have been released, and at time of writing, are supported by a few in-vehicle systems.

MUTUAL AUTHENTICATION FOR MULTIPLE SERVICES

Most service providers want to obtain as much personal data as they can and are consequently hungry for us to register accounts with their apps and websites. Equally, though, many service providers recognize that users don't want to be continually creating multiple accounts on multiple apps or sites and that registration can be a barrier to a user choosing to continue to use the app.

What the CompTIA exam objectives describe as **Mutual authentication for multiple services (SSO [Single Sign On])** means that one service accepts the credentials from another service. This is more usually described as **federated identity management**. For example, you could sign into a popular newspaper app using your Facebook credentials. In this scenario, the newspaper does not process the sign in itself and your password is not passed to the newspaper app. Instead, the newspaper app relies on Facebook's web services to authenticate the account and provide authorization information, which the newspaper app then uses to identify you as a previous customer or user.

A true single sign-on environment means that you authenticate once to access many services. This model is typical of enterprise networks and their email, database, and document management applications. Mobile device apps supporting a true single sign-on environment would usually take the device credentials. For example, when you associate your iPhone with an Apple ID (say, david.martin@apple.com) and unlock it, an SSO newspaper app on that iPhone would identify that you are signed in as david.martin@apple.com and load the appropriate profile for you automatically, without requiring you to sign in again. Not many third party apps actually integrate with SSO in this way, but the vendor cloud services work on this basis. For example, when you sign in to Google, you are signing in to email, maps, YouTube, search, and so on.

*Note: To learn more, check the **Video** tile on the CHOICE Course screen for any videos that supplement the content for this lesson.*

Access the Checklist tile on your CHOICE Course screen for reference information and job aids on How to Support Mobile Apps.

Show Slide(s)

Mutual Authentication for Multiple Services

Teaching Tip

The content example probably doesn't actually intend to cover mutual authentication, which is usually taken to mean something completely different (a server authenticating with a client at the same time as the client authenticates with a server).

Activity 16-5
Discussing Mobile App Support

Show Slide(s)

Activity: Discussing Mobile App Support

SCENARIO
Answer the following questions to check your understanding of the topic.

1. **Why must a vendor account usually be configured on a smartphone?**

   A vendor account, such as an Apple, Google, or Samsung account, is required to use the app store.

2. **What is sideloading?**

   Installing a mobile app without going through the app store. Android supports sideloading through the APK package format. Sideloading is not officially supported on iOS devices.

3. **Which types of data might require mapping between fields when syncing between applications?**

   Contacts and calendar items.

4. **What software is used to synchronize data files between an iOS device and a PC and what connection methods can it use?**

   iTunes. It can work over USB (with a USB-to-Apple cable) or Wi-Fi.

5. **How might an app register users without implementing its own authentication process?**

   Through federated identity management, or as the user sees it, a "Sign in with..." feature. If the user's sign-in with the identity service (Google or Facebook, for example) is cached on the device, this will enable Single Sign On (SSO) with supported apps. This could also be referred to as mutual authentication, of a kind (the app and the sign-in provider must authorize one another).

Topic E
Secure Mobile Devices

EXAM OBJECTIVES COVERED
1002-2.8 Given a scenario, implement methods for securing mobile devices.

Mobile devices can be used for multiple functions within the professional workplace. Knowing that, you must be able to provide basic level support to your users, including configuring security settings.

POPULAR SECURITY CONTROLS FOR MOBILE DEVICES

It is critical that the organization's mobile device security practices be specified via policies, procedures, and training. Although you always want your practices specified via policies and procedures, it is particularly important with respect to mobile devices, because these devices tend to be forgotten or overlooked. They don't reside, or "live," in the workplace in the same way as, for example, a desktop computer, and they won't necessarily be there when virus databases are being updated, patches are being installed, files are backed up, and so on. Procedural and technical controls to manage these mobile devices mitigate the risk that they may introduce vulnerabilities in the company's network security.

There are two principal challenges when it comes to mobile device security: portability and capacity:

- **Portability**—devices that are portable are easy to lose or to steal or to sneak into somewhere they should not be allowed.
- **Capacity**—while great for consumers, the capacity and ease of portability of flash media, removable hard drives, smartphones, and tablets is a big problem for information security. A typical removable hard drive or Network Attached Storage (NAS) device or even a smartphone can copy down the contents of a workstation or even a server in a few minutes. Because they use USB or network ports, it is difficult to prevent the attachment of such devices.

The problems, therefore, surround the fact that because of their portability and capacity, mobile devices can be both targets of attack and the means by which an attack can be accomplished. You have to protect the data on your mobile devices from being compromised, and you have to protect the data in any of your systems from being removed by mobile devices.

> **Note:** *One of the most important steps you can take to maintain security of mobile devices is to not leave the devices unattended.*

MOBILE DEVICE ACCESS CONTROL

The majority of smartphones and tablets are single-user devices. Access control can be implemented by configuring a password or PIN and screen lock. iOS does not support multiple user accounts at all. Later versions of Android support multiple user accounts on both tablets and smartphones.

Show Slide(s)
Popular Security Controls for Mobile Devices

Teaching Tip
This topic starts to look at the mobile objectives and content examples from the Core 2 exam objectives.

Show Slide(s)
Mobile Device Access Control (3 slides)

SCREEN LOCKS AND BIOMETRIC AUTHENTICATION

If an attacker is able to gain access to a smartphone or tablet, they can obtain a huge amount of information and the tools with which to launch further attacks. Apart from confidential data files that might be stored on the device, it is highly likely that the user has cached passwords for services such as email or remote access VPN and websites. In addition to this, access to contacts and message history (SMS, text messaging, email, and IM) greatly assists social engineering attacks.

Consequently, it is imperative that data stored on the device be encrypted and access to the device protected by a **screen lock**.

Configuring a screen lock means that a password/passcode (or at the very least a PIN) is required to use the device. There are also "join-the-dots" **pattern locks**, which are also referred as **swipe locks**.

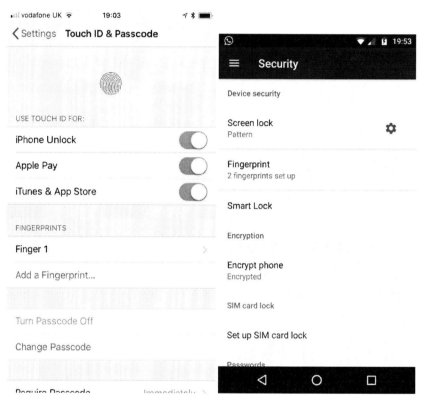

Configuring screen lock options in iOS (left) and Android (right).

 Note: *Pattern passcodes have several drawbacks. The smudge pattern may remain visible on the surface, making it much easier to guess or copy. Swipe patterns are also quite easy to observe over someone's shoulder.*

All but the cheapest device models now include a **fingerprint sensor** to provide a **biometric authentication** method. Apple refers to this feature as **Touch ID**. The user sets up a template fingerprint scan, which is converted to a unique hash and stored within a secure cache on the device (enrollment). To authenticate, the user touches the reader and the device re-computes the hash; if it matches the stored value, then access is granted.

Another biometric mechanism is the **face lock**, with the hash being computed from a picture of the user's face rather than a scan of their fingerprint. This has the advantage of being able to use a standard device (the camera) rather than a special sensor. Apple refers to their system as **Face ID**.

Note: Biometric methods tend to suffer from high error rates, including false negatives (where the sensor does not identify the scan as valid) and false positives (where the sensor validates a scan it should not have). A passcode is also configured as a backup authentication method.

LOCKOUT POLICY AND REMOTE WIPING

The screen lock can also be configured with a **lockout policy** or (put another way) a policy to restrict **failed login attempts**. This means that if an incorrect passcode is entered, the device locks for a set period. This could be configured to escalate—so the first incorrect attempt locks the device for 30 seconds while the third locks it for 10 minutes, for instance. This deters attempts to guess the passcode.

Another option on some phones is the support for **remote wipe** or a **kill switch**. This means that if the handset is stolen, it can be set to the factory defaults, disabled, and/or cleared of any personal data. Some utilities may also be able to wipe any plug-in memory cards, too. The remote wipe could be triggered by a number of incorrect passcode attempts or by enterprise management software.

Other features include backing up data from the phone to a server first and displaying a "Lost/stolen phone—return to XX" message on the handset.

 **Interaction Opportunity**
Ask learners if they have experience with any remote wipe apps for mobile devices.

Most corporate messaging systems come with a Remote Wipe feature, allowing mail, calendar, and contacts information to be deleted from mobile devices.

The OS vendors now often supply the same services, such as Apple's **Activation Lock** or Google's **Device Protection**.

A thief can (in theory) prevent a remote wipe by ensuring the phone cannot connect to the network, then hacking the phone and disabling the security, but this requires some expertise. Even in those cases, services such as **Activation Lock** work in the device firmware, preventing restores or the disabling of location services.

MOBILE DEVICE AND DATA RECOVERY

If a mobile device is lost or stolen, there are mechanisms to use to try to effect its recovery and to prevent any misuse or loss of data stored on the device.

GPS, GEOTRACKING, AND LOCATOR APPLICATIONS

Most smartphones and many tablets are now fitted with Global Positioning System (GPS) receivers. GPS is a means of determining a receiver's position on the Earth based on information received from GPS satellites. The receiver must have line-of-sight to the

 Show Slide(s)
Mobile Device and Data Recovery (2 slides)

 Teaching Tip
Share any stories from the news or your life, or ask learners to share stories about how locator apps have helped locate and recover mobile devices.

GPS satellites. As GPS requires line-of-sight, it does not work indoors. **Indoor Positioning Systems (IPS)** work out a device's location by triangulating its proximity to other radio sources, such as Wi-Fi access points or Bluetooth beacons.

Knowing the device's position (**geotracking**) also allows app vendors and websites to offer location-specific services (relating to search or local weather, for instance) and (inevitably) advertising. You can use **Location Services** settings to determine how visible your phone is to these services.

As well as supporting maps and turn-by-turn instructions, **Location Services** can be used for security to locate a lost or stolen device. Such **Find My Phone** or **locator applications** are now a standard service for all the major mobile OSes. Once set up, the location of the phone (as long as it is powered on) can be tracked from any web browser.

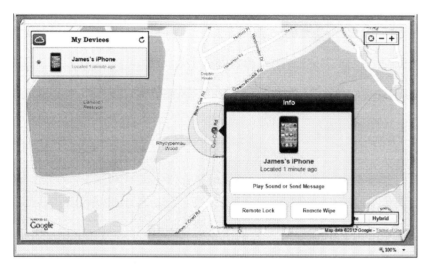

You can use the iCloud and Find My Phone apps to locate an iOS device and remotely lock or wipe it (or send the current holder a polite message to please return it ASAP).

Note: If a mobile device has a locator app installed and the device is lost or stolen, some apps allow the user to remotely enable features in the app. One feature that can be quite useful is enabling the camera on the phone. It has been reported that sometimes the thief has been captured using the photos taken in this manner.

FULL DEVICE ENCRYPTION

All but the earliest versions of mobile device OSes for smartphones and tablets provide **full device encryption**. The purpose of device encryption is to prevent anyone in possession of the device being able to circumvent the mobile OS's access controls and read the raw data stored on the flash memory components. If that raw data is encrypted (and the attacker cannot retrieve the encryption key from the device), then the information remains inaccessible.

In iOS, there are various levels of encryption.

- All user data on the device is always encrypted but the key is stored on the device. This is primarily used as a means of wiping the device. The OS just needs to delete the key to make the data inaccessible rather than wiping each storage location.
- Email data and any apps using the **Data Protection** option are also encrypted using a key derived from the user's passcode. This provides security for data in the event that the device is stolen. Not all user data is encrypted; contacts, SMS messages, and pictures are not, for example.

In iOS, Data Protection encryption is enabled automatically when configuring a password lock on the device.

In Android, encryption is enabled via **Settings→Security**. Android uses full-disk encryption with a passcode-derived key. When encryption is enabled, it can take some time to encrypt the device.

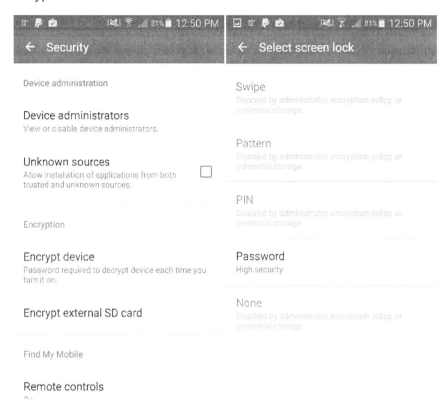

Encryption options in Android OS.

 Note: *The encryption key is derived from the PIN or password. In order to generate a strong key, you should use a strong password. Of course, this makes accessing the device each time the screen locks more difficult.*

 Note: *With the release of Android Nougat, full device encryption is being deprecated in favor of file-level encryption.*

REMOTE BACKUP APPLICATIONS

Most mobile OS devices are configured with a user account linked to the vendor's cloud services (iCloud for iOS, Google Sync for stock Android, and OneDrive for Microsoft). The user can then choose to automatically back up data, apps, and settings to the cloud. A user may choose to use a different backup provider (OneDrive on an Android phone, for instance) or a third-party provider, such as Dropbox.

As well as cloud services, a device can be backed up to a PC. For example, iOS supports making backups via the iTunes program. A third option is for Mobile Device Management (MDM) software to be configured to back up user devices automatically.

MULTIFACTOR AUTHENTICATION AND AUTHENTICATOR APPLICATIONS

Authentication methods are stronger when they are combined. There are four main types of "factor" describing different authentication methods:

- **Something you know**—such as a password or pass code or swipe pattern.

Show Slide(s)

Multifactor Authentication and Authenticator Applications

- **Something you are**—such as your fingerprint or face.
- **Something you have**—such as a unique digital token or smart card.
- **Somewhere you are**—use of a device or service might be tied to your geolocation.

Multifactor authentication means using two different methods. Requiring a user to enter a password and then a PIN is not multifactor.

Mobile device unlock methods are almost always single factor because no one wants to go through the bother of multifactor authentication every time the device is used. A user might configure two alternative methods of unlocking the device, such as configuring face lock and a pattern lock, but this is not multifactor authentication.

Multifactor authentication is often used with online services. For example, when using a new device with a web service or app such as email or online storage, many vendors encourage the use of **2-step verification**. 2-step verification means that as well as a password for the service, you register a phone or alternative email address. When you use a new computer or device to access the service, the **authenticator application** sends a code in the form of a **One Time Password (OTP)** to your phone. You must then supply the account user name and password and the OTP code to authenticate.

This reduces the risk that someone who has discovered your password could access your account, because the computer they are using is not one recognized by the service.

 Note: The OTP is computed in such a way that it can only be used once (and often has to be used within a limited time frame).

MOBILE DEVICE POLICIES

Show Slide(s)

Mobile Device Policies (3 slides)

Interaction Opportunity

If learners are working for one or more companies, encourage them to share any mobile device policies they have to follow.

Mobile Device Management (MDM) is a class of enterprise software designed to apply security policies to the use of smartphones and tablets in business networks. This software can be used to manage corporate-owned devices as well as **Bring Your Own Device (BYOD)**. BYOD means allowing employees to use their private smartphones and tablet devices to access corporate data.

A key feature of MDM is the ability to support multiple operating systems, such as iOS, Android, and the various iterations of Windows and Windows Mobile. A few MDM suites are OS-specific (such as Apple Configurator) but the major ones, such as AirWatch (**www.air-watch.com**), Symantec (**www.symantec.com**), and Citrix Endpoint Management (**www.citrix.com**), support multiple device vendors.

PROFILING SECURITY REQUIREMENTS

The MDM software logs use of a device on the network and determines whether to allow it to connect or not, based on administrator-set parameters. This process can be described as **onboarding**.

When the device is enrolled with the management software, it can be configured with policies to allow or restrict use of apps, corporate data, and built-in functions such as a video camera or microphone. Policies can also be set to ensure the device patch status is up-to-date, that antivirus software is present and updated, and that a device firewall has been applied and configured correctly.

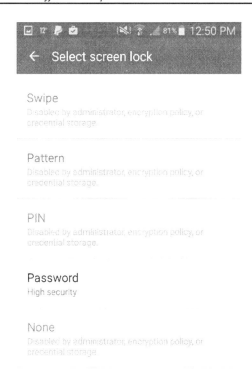

Policy has disabled swipe, pattern, and PIN access, forcing use of a complex password.

A company needs to create a **profile of security requirements** and policies to apply for different employees and different sites are areas within a site. For example, it might be more secure to disable the camera function of any smartphone while onsite but users might complain that they cannot use their phones for video calls. A sophisticated security system might be able to apply a more selective policy and disable the camera only when the device is within an area deemed high risk from a data confidentiality point-of-view. Some policies can be implemented with a technical solution; others require "soft" measures, such as training and disciplinary action.

TRUSTED AND UNTRUSTED APP SOURCES

A **trusted app source** is one that is managed by a service provider. The service provider authenticates and authorizes valid developers, issuing them with a certificate to use to sign their apps and warrant them as trusted. It may also analyze code submitted to ensure that it does not pose a security or privacy risk to its customers (or remove apps that are discovered to pose such a risk). It may apply other policies that developers must meet, such as not allowing apps with adult content or apps that duplicate the function of core OS apps.

The mobile OS defaults to restricting app installations to the linked store (App Store for iOS and Play for Android). Most consumers are happy with this model but it does not work so well for enterprises. It might not be appropriate to deliver a custom corporate app via a public store, where anyone could download it.

Apple operates an enterprise developer program to solve this problem. The enterprise developer can install a profile with their security credentials along with the app. This is normally handled by an MDM suite. The user then chooses to trust the app via **Settings→General→Profiles**. It is also possible to sideload enterprise apps via iTunes and a desktop PC.

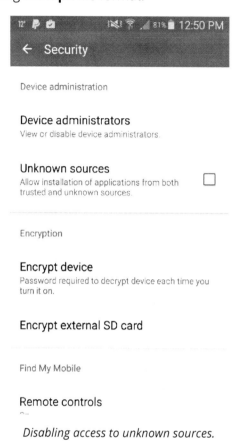

The Play store has a private channel option and Google runs an Android for Work program for enterprise developers.

Android allows for selection of different stores and installation of untrusted apps from any third party, if the user chooses the third party or unknown sources option. This allows a greater degree of customization but also makes the device vulnerable to attacks. With unknown sources enabled, untrusted apps can be downloaded from a website and installed using the **.apk** file format.

Disabling access to unknown sources.

MOBILE DEVICE SECURITY SOFTWARE

Show Slide(s)

Mobile Device Security Software

Mobile devices can use the same classes of security software as PCs and laptops to harden against malware, software exploits, or network exploits.

ANTIVIRUS/ANTI-MALWARE AND FIREWALLS

Modern smartphones are computers in their own right and as such are vulnerable to software exploits as well as being targets of malware and viruses, especially if an untrusted app source has been configured. **antivirus apps** have become popular in the Android app market especially after some publicized cases of viral infection on Android devices. Some mobile antivirus software scans only installed apps and ignores plug-in flash memory cards. There is also a problem with the limited user base and the emerging natures of mobile OS threats and vulnerabilities. This makes it difficult to create pattern databases of known threats and use heuristics (machine learning) to identify new threats.

Another class of security software is the **app scanner**. These are designed to monitor the permissions allocated to apps and how they are using (or abusing) them. There are also **firewall apps** for mobile devices. These can be used to monitor app activity and prevent connections to particular ports or IP addresses. One issue for firewalls is that they must be able to control other apps and therefore logically work at a higher permission level (root). Installing an app with root access is challenging, however. "No-root" firewalls work by creating a Virtual Private Network (VPN) and then controlling app access to the VPN.

Apple has traditionally been relaxed about the need for third-party security solutions, such as antivirus or firewalls. Consequently, there are few iOS security apps.

PATCHING/OS UPDATES

Keeping a mobile OS and its apps up-to-date with patches (and ideally new OS versions) is as critical as it is for a desktop computer. The install base of iOS is generally better at applying updates because of the consistent hardware and software platform. Updates for iOS are notified by an alert on wake and delivered via **Settings→General→Software Update**. App updates are indicated via red notifications on the app icon and delivered via the **Updates** page in the app store.

Android patches are more reliant on the device vendor as they have to deliver the patch for their own "flavor" of Android. Support for new OS versions can also be mixed. Android uses the notification shade to deliver updates. You can also go to **Settings→About→System updates**.

Activity 16-6

Discussing Mobile Device Security

Show Slide(s)

Activity: Discussing Mobile Device Security

SCENARIO

Answer the following questions to check your understanding of the topic.

---

1. **How can the use of mobile devices by employees affect the security of an organization as a whole?**

   Mobile devices can function much like regular computers; therefore, when they are used to send and receive corporate emails and to access systems and data within the corporate network, they are a vulnerability. If a mobile device is lost or stolen, it could be used to access sensitive data or launch attacks. Mobile devices should be secured just as any other system on the corporate network.

2. **What two types of biometric authentication mechanism are supported on smartphones?**

   Fingerprint recognition and facial recognition.

3. **What might a locator application be used for?**

   To identify the location of a stolen phone (or, perhaps, members of one's family) and to provide localized services (movies, restaurants, etc).

4. **What technology mitigates against an online account being accessed from an unknown device?**

   Two-step verification—the site sends a code to a registered phone or alternative email address, prompting the user to verify the validity of the device.

5. **What is MDM?**

   Mobile Device Management (MDM) is a class of management software designed to apply security policies to the use of smartphones and tablets in the enterprise.

6. **True or false? Updates are not necessary for iOS devices because the OS is closed source.**

   False—closed source just means that the vendor controls development of the OS. It is still subject to updates to fix problems and introduce new features.

Topic F
Troubleshoot Mobile Device Issues

EXAM OBJECTIVES COVERED
1002-3.4 Given a scenario, troubleshoot mobile OS and application issues.
1002-3.5 Given a scenario, troubleshoot mobile OS and application security issues.

You can use similar troubleshooting techniques as for PCs and laptops to resolve issues on mobile device operating systems and applications. One difference is that apps, operating system, and hardware are tightly integrated in mobile devices such as smartphones and tablets. You may need to troubleshoot all three components in order to determine which one is actually causing the issue.

MOBILE OS TROUBLESHOOTING TOOLS

When you are troubleshooting a mobile OS, you need to know how to find configuration options and perform different types of device resets.

ADJUSTING SETTINGS

In iOS, configuration settings are stored under the **Settings** app. There are settings for both the core OS and for individual apps. In Android, the **Settings** app can be added to the home screen or accessed via the **Cog** icon in the notification shade.

CLOSING RUNNING APPS

A mobile OS performs sophisticated memory management to be able to run multiple applications while allowing each app to have sufficient resources and preventing an app from consuming excessive amounts of power and draining the battery. The memory management routines shift apps between foreground (in active use), background (potentially accessing the network and other resources), and suspended (not using any resources).

Both iOS and Android show a "multitasking" list of apps that the user has opened. This multitasking list doesn't actually mean that the app is loaded into memory, however. In Android, you can remove an app from the list by pressing the multitasking button (a square or rectangle) then swiping the app left or right off the screen. Doing this won't have any impact on performance.

If an app is actually unresponsive, it can be closed via the **force stop** option.

- In Android, open **Settings→Apps**. Tap an app, then select the **Force Stop** option to close it or the **Disable** option to make it unavailable.
- In iOS, clearing an app from the multitasking list also force stops it. Double tap the **Home** button then swipe the app up off the screen.

Teaching Tip

Note that mobile troubleshooting is covered on both Core 1 and Core 2 exams. The content examples on Core 1 are more weighted towards laptop troubleshooting and were covered elsewhere.

Core 2 duplicates some of the Core 1 content examples but is more exclusively focused on mobile OS troubleshooting (though quite a few of the symptoms are hardware-related).

Show Slide(s)

Mobile OS Troubleshooting Tools

Teaching Tip

These explicit content examples have actually been removed in the new exam objectives, but learners should still know reset procedures to recover from faults such as "frozen system."

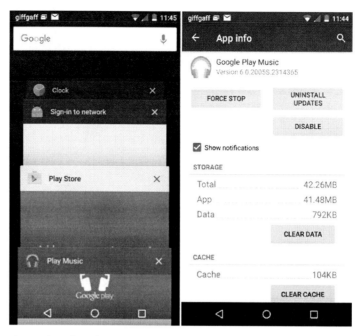

In Android, tap the multitasking button (bottom-right) to view open apps, then swipe left or right to remove them; use the Force Stop option in app settings to fully close an app.

Teaching Tip

You might want to mention that the terms used to speak about mobile reboots and resets are not always consistent. In usage with PCs, a soft reboot (or warm boot) means invoking the OS to perform the shutdown and restart procedure. A hard reboot (or cold boot) means holding down the power button to cut the power if the OS has stopped responding. On mobile devices, the term "soft reset" is used to mean powering off the device and then powering it back on again. As "hard reset" is quite widely used to mean a factory reset; we have used the term "forced restart" to mean cutting the power to force a reboot. Emphasize that the term "hard reset" could be used either to mean a forced restart or a factory default reset, depending on the context.

UNINSTALL/REINSTALL APPS

Another stock response to an app issue is to uninstall then reinstall it.

- To uninstall an iOS app, tap-and-hold it until it wiggles, then press the **X** icon and confirm by pressing **Delete**. You cannot uninstall default apps. To return the screen to normal, press the **Home** button. You can also delete apps from **Settings** or from **iTunes**.
- In Android, use **Settings→Apps** to uninstall (completely remove) or disable (prevent from running) apps. You can also long-press an icon on the home screen then drag it to the **Uninstall** icon (dragging it to **Remove** just hides the app icon).

Apps can be reinstalled via the store (without having to pay for them again!).

REBOOTING A MOBILE DEVICE

Just as turning it off and on again is the tried and trusted method of "fixing" a computer, a reboot can resolve many software-related issues on a mobile device. Users generally leave their mobile devices in a sleep state. Powering the device off closes all applications and clears any data from RAM. Data and settings stored in the device are not affected. This kind of **soft reset** is usually effective in restoring unresponsive or frozen systems and is one of the first things to try when faced with a malfunctioning app or slow performance. It is also used after the installation of some apps.

- On iOS, holding the **Sleep/Wake** button down for a few seconds brings up a menu prompting the user to swipe so the device can be shut down. When you are troubleshooting, leave the device powered off for a minute, and then restart by holding the **Sleep** button again. If the touchscreen is unresponsive, you can perform a forced restart by pressing the **Sleep/Wake** and **Home** buttons for 10 seconds. The screen will go black then the device will restart. When performing a forced restart, unsaved data in current use may be lost.
- On Android, to power off, hold the **Power** button for a few seconds to bring up the **Power Off** prompt. If the touchscreen is unresponsive, a forced restart can often be performed by holding the **Power** button for 10 seconds, though some Android devices use a different key combination for this. You can also boot an Android

device to Safe Mode by tap-and-holding the **Power Off** message. Safe Mode disables third-party apps, but leaves core services running.

FACTORY DEFAULT RESET

A **factory default reset** removes all user data, apps, and settings. The device will either have to be manually reconfigured with a new user account and apps reloaded, or restored from a backup configuration. When you are performing a factory reset, ensure that the device has a full battery charge or is connected to an external power source.

- To factory reset an iOS device, connect it to a PC or Mac running **iTunes**. You can use the **Update** button on the device's summary page to try to reinstall iOS without removing user data. If this does not work, use the **Restore** button to perform a factory reset. If the **Update** or **Restore** buttons are not available, use the force soft restart method described earlier while the device is connected to **iTunes**.
- For Android, you should check for specific instructions for each particular device. On stock Android, you can initiate a reset from the **Backup and Reset** section of **Settings**. If the device will not boot normally, you can enter recovery mode using some combination of the power and volume buttons.

 Note: Some vendors may use the term "hard reset" to mean a factory reset.

 Note: You might be required to sign in immediately after performing a factory restore to protect against theft of the device or your account information. Make sure you have the account credentials available and do not attempt a factory reset within 72 hours of changing your account password.

GUIDELINES FOR USING MOBILE TROUBLESHOOTING TOOLS

 *Note: All of the Guidelines for this lesson are available as checklists from the **Checklist** tile on the CHOICE Course screen.*

 Show Slide(s)
Guidelines for Using Mobile Troubleshooting Tools

Here are some guidelines to help you use mobile troubleshooting tools.

USE MOBILE TROUBLESHOOTING TOOLS

Consider these guidelines for using mobile troubleshooting tools:

- Adjust settings for the core OS and for apps.
- Close running apps that are consuming too much power and draining the battery or those that are unresponsive.
- Uninstall apps that are no longer needed or reinstall apps after replacing a device or after previously uninstalling an app.
- Try a soft reset for devices that are frozen or unresponsive. If that doesn't work, use a forced restart.
- Perform a factory default reset when reissuing the mobile device to another user or preparing it for disposal.

MOBILE OS ISSUE TROUBLESHOOTING

Like any other computer, mobile devices can have their own issues that need diagnosing and fixing.

 Show Slide(s)
Mobile OS Issue Troubleshooting

DIM DISPLAY

One of the common issues is a **dim display**. This usually happens when the user has set the **backlight** to its lowest setting (and disabled automatic light adjustment) or the phone is set to conserve power by auto dimming the light. To adjust, open **Display** settings and select the automatic brightness option or adjust the slider.

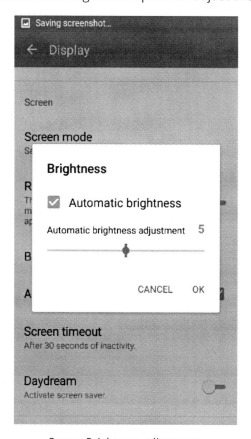

Screen Brightness adjustment.

It is also worth checking for third-party power management apps or the use of a battery-saver mode or profile that automatically dims the backlight to conserve power.

TOUCHSCREEN UNRESPONSIVE OR INACCURATE

If the touchscreen is unresponsive or does not register touches at the correct coordinates, first check for obvious hardware issues (dirt, grease, or cracks). If a screen protector is fitted, check that it is securely adhered to the surface and that there are no bubbles or lifts.

If you can rule out simple hardware causes, unresponsive touch input can be an indication of resources being inadequate (too many open apps) or badly written apps that hog memory or other resources. A soft reset will usually fix the problem in the short term. If the problem is persistent, either try to identify whether the problem is linked to running a particular app or try freeing space by removing data or apps. Windows devices and some versions of Android support re-calibration utilities, but if you cannot identify another cause, then you are likely to have to look at warranty repair.

EXTERNAL MONITOR ISSUES

Screen sharing can be enabled via an adapter cable. If there is a problem, you should try to rule out a bad cable first.

Mobiles can also connect to wireless displays or reception dongles. The principal issue here is that the various wireless standards (Miracast/Wi-Fi Direct, Intel WiDi, Apple AirPlay, Google Chromecast, and Amazon Fire TV) are not interoperable so you need to ensure both the broadcast and reception devices are using the same technology. You also need to rule out the usual potential sources of wireless interference.

 Note: Miracast is based on Wi-Fi Direct, which is less proprietary than the other standards but there are lots of interoperability problems between "Miracast-compatible" devices. The TV vendors all have different names for it (SmartShare, Screen Mirroring, Display Mirroring, and so on).

SOUND ISSUES

If no sound is playing from the device speakers, first check that the volume controls are not turned all the way down and that the mute switch is not activated. Next verify that the device is not in a silent/no interruptions mode. If the problem is restricted to a particular app, check whether it has its own volume controls. If you cannot identify a software issue, check that the device is not configured to use external speakers. These could be connected via a cable or by Bluetooth.

OVERHEATING

Devices have protective circuitry that will initiate a shut down if the internal temperature is at the maximum safe limit.

Handheld devices use passive cooling and so can become quite warm when used intensively. Also make sure that the device is not left sitting in direct sunlight. If a handheld device becomes unusually hot, suspect a problem with the battery. There may be a utility that you can use to access battery status information. You can also use an app to monitor the battery temperature and then compare that to the operating limits. Generally speaking, approaching 40°C is getting too warm.

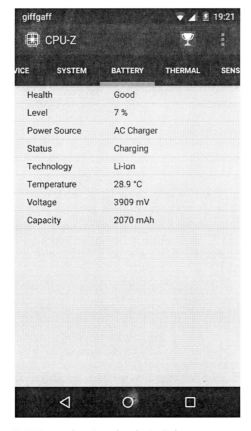

CPU-Z app showing the device's battery status.

If a device overheats repeatedly, check for apps with consistently high CPU utilization. If the device is a few years old, consider the possibility that the battery is failing. Monitor the device during charging cycles; if it overheats, then discontinue use and have it inspected at a repair center.

 Note: *If you have any reason to suspect that a device is prone to overheating, do not leave it to charge unattended.*

GUIDELINES FOR TROUBLESHOOTING MOBILE OS ISSUES

 Show Slide(s)

Guidelines for Troubleshooting Mobile OS Issues (2 slides)

Here are some guidelines to help you troubleshoot mobile OS issues.

TROUBLESHOOT MOBILE OS ISSUES

Consider these guidelines as you troubleshoot the following mobile OS issues:

- **Dim display**. Open the **Display** settings and adjust the automatic brightness option or adjust the brightness slider. Check for apps that dim the backlight to conserve power.
- **Unresponsive or inaccurate touchscreen**. Check for issues with the screen, that any screen protectors are not damaged or incorrectly applied. Check that there are adequate resources available. Use a re-calibration utility if no other cause for the issue is found.
- **Issues with external monitor**. Verify that the cable is good. Verify that a casting dongle (Google Chromecast, Miracast, AirPlay, Amazon Fire, etc) is configured correctly between the device and the mobile device.
- **Sound issues**. Verify volume controls are set correctly. Verify silent mode is not enabled. Check volume controls within the app. Verify it is not configured to use external speakers through a cable or Bluetooth.
- **Overheating**. Determine if the device is being used intensively. Use a battery monitor to view battery status information. Keep device away from direct sunlight or other heat sources.

MOBILE APP ISSUE TROUBLESHOOTING

 **Show Slide(s)**

Mobile App Issue Troubleshooting (3 slides)

As noted previously, with a mobile device it can be difficult to identify when a problem might be caused by the hardware, the OS, or a particular app.

APPS NOT LOADING

Sometimes the user cannot open a series of apps. This is common when apps have been moved or installed to a flash memory card. If the card is removed, malfunctions, or has been wiped, it will cause the user to lose access to that app. Apps can usually be reinstalled from the preferred app store without having to repurchase again.

Missing apps on an Android phone.

Other issues could be some sort of file corruption. Try uninstalling and reinstalling the app; if the problems persist, consider a factory reset.

> *Note: Also consider that Mobile Device Management (MDM) software might prevent an app or function from running in a certain context. Security policies might prevent use of the camera within the corporate office, for instance, and any app that requires the camera might then fail to start.*

APP LOG ERRORS

As consumer-level devices, iOS and Android do not support simple log viewing tools. An app could choose to display its own logs to the user if required, but an app requires root-level permissions to view system logs or the logs of other apps.

Android supports a developer mode, enabled via **Settings** (access **System→About phone** and tap **Build number** seven times), which can show additional diagnostic information when using apps or making network connections. You can also output debugging information over USB. You can use this in conjunction with the SDK to retrieve system logs. Also, on most Android handsets, you can dial ***#*#4636#*#*** to open the status page.

You can view an iOS device's logs from a macOS computer with the Xcode developer tools installed.

SLOW PERFORMANCE

As phones get older, their performance naturally degrades as apps are updated to provide more functionality and features. In order to enable these extra features, they require more memory, space, and CPU power. This results in greater battery utilization and a decrease in performance. As space is reduced and the phone is used more intensively, this can lead to an increase in the amount of errors and corruptions.

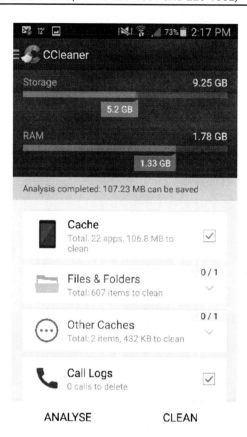

Regular clean with CCleaner.

If soft resets are not working, consider performing a factory reset. When restoring apps and data from backup, try to be selective in choosing what is restored. There are also various apps dedicated to performance optimization and maintenance.

You should also consider any recently installed apps. Having many apps that run some sort of monitoring or connectivity check in the background or apps that display real-time content in a home screen widget will impact performance. You should also check that there is sufficient space left on the flash memory storage.

Note: Vendors try to support device models for as long as possible, but it is frequently the case that major (or sometimes minor) version updates can quite severely impact performance if applied to older devices. Unfortunately, vendors tend not to provide a rollback option for version updates. You can only report the issue and hope the vendor supplies a fix.

BATTERY LIFE

Smartphone batteries degrade over time with each charge and recharge cycle so some decrease in performance is to be expected. Some mobile devices have replaceable batteries but for most models this will be a warranty service operation.

CPU and GPU intensive apps such as games and video playback will drain the battery quickly. A battery charge might be degraded by a faulty or malicious app utilizing high powered peripherals such as GPS, network connections, or even the microphone and camera. You can get information about battery usage via **Settings→More→Battery** in Android or **Settings→Battery** in iOS.

Battery Analyzers for iOS and Android with option to conserve battery.

It might be appropriate to uninstall the app. Alternatively you might be able to restrict the app from running in the background. In iOS, configure this via **Settings→General→Background App Refresh**. In Android, a battery saver mode can be applied automatically when the charge level drops to a certain percentage or you can apply it manually. To configure it, select **Settings→Battery**. Tap the top-right ellipse button for the settings menu and select **Battery saver**.

Keeping your device up-to-date with the latest patches and OS version also ensures optimum operation and battery life conservation.

GUIDELINES FOR TROUBLESHOOTING MOBILE APP ISSUES

Here are some guidelines to help you troubleshoot mobile app issues.

TROUBLESHOOT MOBILE APP ISSUES

Consider these guidelines as you troubleshoot the following mobile app issues:

*   If an app is not loading, verify that it wasn't installed on a memory card that is not in the mobile device. Verify that the app is not corrupted; uninstall and reinstall the app.
*   Examine app log files to determine if the issue can be tracked down in the log file.
*   Put the device in developer mode to access log files:
    *   Android devices: **System→About phone** and tap **Build number** seven times or dial ***#*#4636#*#***.
    *   iOS devices: Connect the device to a macOS computer with the Xcode developer tools installed.
*   Slow performance can be caused by newer apps requiring more resources than are available, reduced battery life, and lack of free storage space. Check that recently installed apps are functioning correctly and are not running in the background.

Show Slide(s)

Guidelines for Troubleshooting Mobile App Issues

- Battery life degrades over time. Keep the OS up-to-date to ensure optimum operations and battery life conservation.

MOBILE WIRELESS ISSUE TROUBLESHOOTING

Show Slide(s)

Mobile Wireless Issue Troubleshooting

Teaching Tip

Refer learners back to the topic on network troubleshooting as well.

Networking is another area where problems occur frequently. On a mobile device, that means troubleshooting wireless connections of different types (Wi-Fi, Bluetooth, or cellular radio). To approach these problems, try to establish whether there is a configuration error or some sort of hardware/interference problem.

TROUBLESHOOTING INTERFERENCE ISSUES

Radio signals can be affected by the distance between the broadcast and reception antennas and by interference from other devices or by barriers such as thick walls or metal. On a mobile, you should also consider that a low battery charge will weaken the signal strength.

You can troubleshoot issues with Wi-Fi signal strength using a Wi-Fi Analyzer app installed on the device. Most apps can record the settings in a particular location so that you have a baseline reading to compare to. If the signal varies from the baseline, check what interference sources might have been introduced.

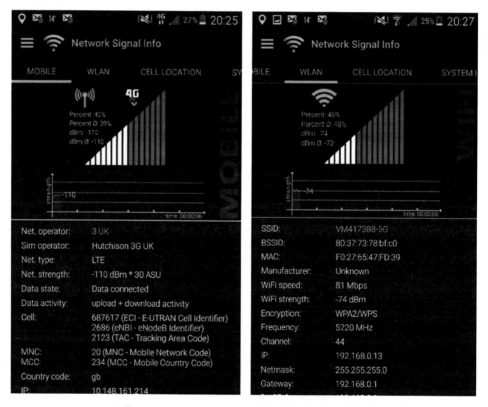

Cell Tower Analyzer (left) and Wi-Fi Analyzer (right).

A similar utility (**Cell Tower Analyzer** or **GSM Signal Monitor**) can be used to analyze cellular radio signals, which use different frequencies to Wi-Fi. An app might combine both functions.

TROUBLESHOOTING WIRELESS CONFIGURATION ISSUES

If there is no Wi-Fi, cellular, or Bluetooth connectivity, first check that the device is not in airplane mode or that the particular radio has not been disabled. Next use **Settings** to verify that the network parameters or Bluetooth pairing information is correct. Try removing the network or Bluetooth pair and reconnecting.

With Wi-Fi, verify that the access point supports the same 802.11 standard as the device. For example, an access point configured to use 802.11ac only will not be accessible to a smartphone with an 802.11n adapter. The access point must be put into compatibility mode.

If you can rule out any other configuration errors, consider obtaining an OS or firmware update for the device or for the access point. Research any known issues between the access point and the model of device.

GUIDELINES FOR TROUBLESHOOTING MOBILE WIRELESS ISSUES

Here are some guidelines to help you troubleshoot mobile wireless issues.

Show Slide(s)
Guidelines for Troubleshooting Mobile Wireless Issues

TROUBLESHOOT MOBILE WIRELESS ISSUES

Consider these guidelines as you troubleshoot the following mobile wireless issues:

- **Interference issues**: Use a Wi-Fi Analyzer app to check for interference and signal strength.
- **Configuration issues**:
  - Verify that the device is not in airplane mode.
  - Verify that a particular radio service has not been disabled.
  - Use **Settings** to verify that configuration parameters are correctly configured.
  - Verify that the Wi-Fi access point supports the same standard as the mobile device.

 Note: *If none of these are the issue, determine if an OS or firmware update is needed.*

MOBILE DEVICE SECURITY TROUBLESHOOTING

As mentioned previously, antivirus software for mobile OS is available but not always that reliable, as new threats and exploits are emerging all the time. You should be alert to general symptoms of malware.

Show Slide(s)
Mobile Device Security Troubleshooting (2 slides)

UTILIZATION SYMPTOMS

Malware or rogue apps are likely to try to collect data in the background. They can become unresponsive and might not shut down when closed. Such apps might cause excessive **power drain** and **high resource utilization**. Another telltale sign of a hacked device is reaching the **data transmission overlimit** unexpectedly. Most devices have an option to monitor data usage and have limit triggers to notify the user if the limit has been reached. This protects from large data bills but should also prompt the user to check the amount of data used by each application in order to monitor their legitimacy.

Unauthorized location tracking can give away too much sensitive information to third parties. Many apps collect location data; not many explain clearly what they do with it. Most app developers will just want information they can use for targeted advertising, but a rogue app could use location data to facilitate other crimes, such as domestic burglary.

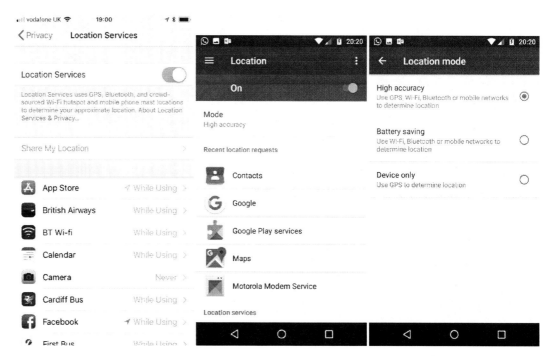

Location services in iOS (left) and Android. Note the option to configure location mode/accuracy.

 Note: *Criminals don't necessarily need to hack a device to get location information. If someone posts pictures online, most will be tagged with location information. A criminal can quite easily get information about where someone lives and then identify when they are on vacation from social media. Users should be trained to strip* **geotagging** *information (or all* **metadata**) *from images before posting them online.*

Location Services can be turned off completely but this will stop many apps from working. You can disable location services on an app-by-app basis, too.

Mobile OSes, like other operating systems, potentially have vulnerabilities that can be exploited to allow an attacker **unauthorized root access**. Root is an account with system-level access to every process running in the OS. If an attacker has this type of access, they can even remotely activate the camera and microphone. With corporate and government installations, this could cause a security breach of sensitive data. The recommendation is to disable and cover cameras and microphones when in sensitive areas. Some companies and government buildings prevent usage of mobile devices in such areas to avoid **unauthorized camera and microphone usage**.

Good patch and upgrade management is required to keep the OS current and up to date.

USER BEHAVIOR ISSUES

System security is not just compromised by malware and hackers. Careless use and failure to follow security best practices cause users to put themselves and the data stored on their devices at risk.

When a user needs to connect to the Internet, it can be tempting to use any available open hotspot, especially if the hotspot has the name of a major brand. An open hotspot set up with malicious intent can harvest a huge amount of information. Any data passing over the access point can be intercepted, unless it is protected by encryption (an HTTPS website, an SSL-enabled mail server, or a Virtual Private Network, for instance). There have also been instances where attackers have been able to exploit faults in the certificate-handling processes of the OS and gained the ability to intercept encrypted traffic too.

There are apps and OS settings that autoconnect to service providers' hotspots. These should be secure, if you trust the service provider to operate a secure network. If the user notices unintentional behavior, however, such as connecting to a Wi-Fi network without prompting or the Wi-Fi radio turning itself on, suspect a rogue app.

 *Note: In the context of troubleshooting security issues, if the signal from wireless equipment drops unexpectedly or users experience slow data speeds, you might also suspect some sort of **jamming** or **Denial of Service (DoS)** attack. An attacker might try to block the signal from a legitimate access point to try to trick users into connecting to a **rogue access point** or **evil twin**.*

Unintended Bluetooth pairing is when anonymous devices are allowed to pair with Bluetooth-enabled devices. Once paired, a rogue device could access most of the data and functions on the target device. Bluebugging, for instance, exploited a firmware flaw to allow an attacker to monitor and place telephone calls. Most devices only turn Bluetooth discoverable mode on for a limited amount of time to minimize the risk of rogue pairing events. Bluetooth should be disabled completely when not in use. Also consider the possibility that a rogue app could be changing Bluetooth settings.

SYSTEM LOCKOUT AND UNAUTHORIZED ACCOUNT ACCESS

A user can be **locked out** if the device has been disabled either by means of the user forgetting the passcode or remotely by **Find My Phone** type software if the device is reported stolen. There are a number of ways to re-enable the device. Usually the user has to wait a certain amount of time to try again or use the recovery tool in iTunes (iOS devices) to restore the device.

 Note: Lost and stolen devices can expose sensitive corporate data. Data containers mitigate this issue by isolating business data from personal data. A data container creates a virtual environment when the app is launched. Using this virtual environment, the user accesses corporate emails and other corporate data. The app creates an encrypted data store, and the user is not permitted to copy data from outside the container or to move data from within the container. This keeps the business data isolated and secure.

If an online account becomes locked and the user has not been making the logon attempts, suspect attempted **unauthorized account access**. Various data breaches have provided hackers with mountains of authentication credentials and personal information to use to try to access email accounts. Once an email account is compromised, the hacker can typically access any other online account that is not protected by secondary authentication, such as 2-step verification.

Whenever a website or service suffers a data breach and leaks personal files/data, it should notify users immediately. Users need to be alert to the possibility of the theft of their personal information and deploy good security practices, such as not using the same password for two different websites and changing passwords regularly.

TROUBLESHOOTING EMAIL PROBLEMS

When you are troubleshooting an email problem, verify that the user's credentials and the email server parameters are set correctly (server type, location (IP or URL), port number, and SSL enable/disable). One typical problem with corporate email is where a password change is enforced on the enterprise network but the mobile device has not been updated with the new password.

Users often want to send confidential email with the assurance that only the recipient can read it. To do this, the recipient sends the sender a digital certificate and the sender uses the public key in that certificate to encrypt the message. The recipient then uses another part of the certificate (the private key) to decrypt the message.

If the certificate is missing or not recognized, the device will be unable to decrypt the email. Use the email client or encryption program's support documentation to find out how to install or locate the appropriate certificate.

GUIDELINES FOR TROUBLESHOOTING MOBILE DEVICE SECURITY ISSUES

Show Slide(s)

Guidelines for Troubleshooting Mobile Device Security Issues (2 slides)

Here are some guidelines to help you troubleshoot mobile device security issues.

TROUBLESHOOT MOBILE DEVICE SECURITY ISSUES

Consider these guidelines as you troubleshoot the following mobile device security issues:

- If there is a huge power drain or high resource utilization, check for malware or rogue apps.
- Check for unauthorized location tracking.
- Remove geotagging information or metadata from images posted online.
- Ensure users are not engaging in behavior that makes their devices vulnerable to attack.
- If using settings that allow automatic connection to service provider hotspots, verify that the hotspot and device are using trusted, secure connections.
- Ensure unintended Bluetooth pairing is not allowed.
- Ensure users are locking the device when unattended.
- Install apps or enable OS features that allow the phone to be locked and/or wiped if it is lost or stolen.
- Verify that email passwords changed on the enterprise network are replicated to the mobile device.
- When sending and receiving encrypted emails with a digital certificate, use the email client or encryption program's support documentation to install or locate the appropriate certificate.

 *Note: To learn more, check the **Video** tile on the CHOICE Course screen for any videos that supplement the content for this lesson.*

Activity 16-7
Troubleshooting Mobile Device Issues

Show Slide(s)

Activity: Troubleshooting Mobile Device Issues

SCENARIO
Answer the following questions to check your understanding of the topic.

1. **True or false? A factory reset preserves the user's personal data.**

    False. Restoring to factory settings means removing all user data and settings.

2. **What is the first step to take when an app no longer loads?**

    Try restarting the device. If that does not work, uninstall and then reinstall the app.

3. Your organization has several tablet devices that are loaned out as needed when employees are traveling. Some users have reported problems getting the Bluetooth keyboard to work with one of the tablets.

    What should you do?

    There are a couple of issues that can cause Bluetooth connectivity problems. First, check whether the device batteries need replacing. Another possibility is that the tablet might need a system update. Finally, the devices might not have been set to discoverable mode. For security purposes, only enable discovery mode on your mobile device when want a Bluetooth device to find your device; otherwise, keep that setting disabled. The Bluetooth settings must be configured to allow devices to connect to the mobile device. This is also referred to as pairing.

4. A user reports that the touchscreen on his mobile device is not responding properly.

    What questions should you ask, and what steps might you take to resolve the issue?

    You should ask if the touch screen is greasy, wet, or dirty. If it needs cleaning, remind the user to use only a soft cloth moistened with eye glass cleaner to gently wipe the screen. If cleaning is not an issue, ask if it appears to be scratched, cracked, or otherwise damaged. If so, make arrangements to have the touch screen replaced. If there is no visible damage, recalibrate the screen for the user, and check for updates.

5. **What is a Wi-Fi Analyzer used for?**

    A Wi-Fi Analyzer is used to check connectivity issues with wireless. It can check for less congested channels.

6. **What are the causes of severe battery drain?**

The display, radio, and CPU are the components that draw the most power. If an app is overutilizing these resources, it could be faulty, badly written, or this could be a sign of malware activity.

Summary

In this lesson, you worked with mobile computing devices. You examined mobile device technologies, including smartphones, tablets, wearable devices, and more. As an A+ technician, you will need to be able to expertly support and troubleshoot mobile devices.

In your professional experience, have you supported mobile devices? If not, what kind of experience do you have with them?

A: Answers will vary: experience levels can range from no experience at all to power users that are very comfortable with mobile devices.

What type of technical support do you think will be expected of an A+ technician as mobile devices become even more prominent within the workplace?

A: Answers will vary, but will most likely include implementing security methods and synchronizing organizational data with mobile devices.

 *Practice Question: Additional practice questions are available on the CompTIA CHOICE platform within the **Assessments** tile.*

Lesson 17

Installing, Configuring, and Troubleshooting Print Devices

LESSON INTRODUCTION

Despite predictions that computers would bring about a paperless office environment, the need to transfer digital information to paper or back again remains as strong as ever. Therefore, printing is still among the most common tasks for users in almost every home or business environment. As a CompTIA® A+® certified professional, you will often be called upon to set up, configure, and troubleshoot printing environments, so you will need to understand printer technologies as well as know how to perform common printer support tasks.

As a professional support technician, you might be supporting the latest cutting-edge technology, or you might be responsible for ensuring that legacy systems continue to function adequately. So, you must be prepared for either situation and be able to provide the right level of support to users and clients. Having a working knowledge of the many printer technologies and components will help you to support users' needs in any technical environment.

LESSON OBJECTIVES

In this lesson, you will:

- Maintain laser printers.
- Maintain inkjet printers.
- Maintain impact, thermal, and 3D printers.
- Install and configure printers.
- Troubleshooting print device issues.
- Install and configure imaging devices.

Topic A

Maintain Laser Printers

EXAM OBJECTIVES COVERED
1001-3.6 Explain the purposes and uses of various peripheral types.
1001-3.11 Given a scenario, install and maintain various print technologies.

Before you can provide the right level of support, you must fully understand how these systems are used in a production environment. You need to understand how the various components work within a printer to provide the desired outputs. In this topic, you will identify components of, and the print process for, laser printer technologies.

PRINTER TYPES

Show Slide(s)

Printer Types

A **printer** is a device that produces text and images from electronic data onto physical media such as paper, photo paper, and labels. A printer output of electronic documents is often referred to as **hard copy**. Printers employ a range of technologies; the quality of the print output varies with the printer type and generally in proportion to the printer cost.

Interaction Opportunity

Ask learners what types of printers and MFDs they have experience with, and what capabilities were available on the devices.

A **printer type** or **printer technology** is the mechanism used to make images on the paper. The most common types for general home and office use are **inkjet** (or **ink dispersion**) and **laser**, though others are used for more specialist applications. Some of the major print device vendors include HP, Epson, Canon, Xerox, Brother, OKI, Konica/Minolta, Lexmark, Ricoh, and Samsung.

There are many types of printers. Each type of printer, and each printer from different manufacturers, implements the printing process slightly differently. All of the printers will have the following common components:

- A connection to computing devices.
- A mechanism for creating text and images.
- A paper feed mechanism.
- Paper input and output options.

Each of these will be discussed in detail throughout this lesson.

PRINTER FEATURES

Show Slide(s)

Printer Features

The following criteria are used to select the best type and model of printer.

SPEED

The basic speed of a printer is measured in Pages Per Minute (ppm). You will see different speeds quoted for different types of output (for example, pages of monochrome text will print more quickly than color photos).

INTERFACES

Almost all printers support USB, but printer models designed for workgroups also support network connections, usually at a higher cost than standard models. Wireless connections may also carry a price premium.

IMAGE QUALITY

The basic measure of image quality is the maximum supported resolution, measured in dots per inch (dpi). Printer dots and screen image pixels are not equivalent. It requires multiple dots to reproduce one pixel at acceptable quality. Pixel dimensions are typically quoted in pixels per inch (ppi) to avoid confusion. Vertical and horizontal resolution are often different, so you may see figures such as 2400x600 quoted. The horizontal resolution is determined by the print engine (that is, either the laser scanning unit or inkjet print head); vertical resolution is determined by the paper handling mechanism.

The minimum resolution for a monochrome printer should be 600 dpi. Photo-quality printers start at 1200 dpi.

Resolution is not the only factor in determining overall print quality, however (especially with color output). When evaluating a printer, obtain samples to judge text and color performance.

 Note: Image quality needs to be matched to use. The best quality will be correspondingly expensive. Always request sample sheets when evaluating a printer.

PAPER HANDLING

Paper handling means the type of paper or media that can be loaded. It may be important that the printer can handle labels, envelopes, card stock, acetate, and so on. The amount of paper that can be loaded and output is also important in high volume environments. Overloaded output trays will cause paper jams. If the output tray is low capacity, this could happen quite quickly in a busy office.

 Teaching Tip
Point out that the paper path varies between manufacturers, with some using a straight-through paper path and others using a U-shaped paper path.

TOTAL COST OF OWNERSHIP (TCO)

TCO is the cost of the printer over its lifetime, including the cost of replacement components and consumables. It is important to know how a printer will be used to work out TCO.

OPTIONS

Options might include additional memory, duplex (double-sided) printing, large format (A3 and greater), binding, and so on. These may be fitted by default or available for additional purchase as optional extras.

MULTI-FUNCTION DEVICE (MFD)

An **MFD** is a piece of office equipment that performs the functions of a number of other specialized devices. MFDs typically include the functions of a printer, scanner, fax machine, and copier. However, there are MFDs that do not include fax functions. Although the multifunction device might not equal the performance or feature sets of the dedicated devices it replaces, multi-function devices are very powerful and can perform most tasks adequately and are an economical and popular choice for most home or small-office needs.

 Show Slide(s)
Laser Printers

 Teaching Tip
Laser and inkjet printers are by far the most common types of general-use printers. Other printer types tend to have more specialized applications. Exam candidates need to know the steps in the laser print process, what the main components are, and how they interact.

LASER PRINTERS

A laser printer is a printer that uses a laser beam to project (or "draw") a latent image onto an electrically charged drum; toner adheres to the drum and is transferred onto the paper as the paper moves through the mechanism at the same speed the drum rotates. The toner is fixed using high heat and pressure, creating a durable printout that does not smear or fade.

Laser printers are one of the most popular printer technologies for office applications because they are cheap (both to buy and to run), quiet, and fast, and they produce high quality output. There are both grayscale and color models.

LASER PRINTER IMAGING PROCESS

Show Slide(s)

Laser Printer Imaging Process (2 slides)

Teaching Tip

Ideally, use an old toner cartridge with a built-in drum to show to learners as you explain the function of each component.

In the laser printing process, laser printers print a page at a time using a combination of electrostatic charges, toner, and laser light. The laser print process follows the steps detailed in the following sections.

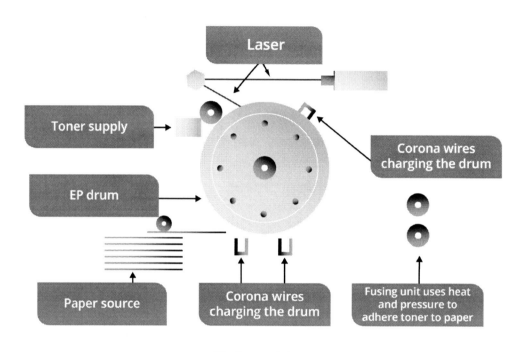

The laser print process.

PROCESSING

Like most printers, laser printers produce their printed output in a series of dots. The computer encodes the page in a printer language and sends it to the printer. The printer's formatter board processes the data to create a bitmap (or **raster**) of the page and stores it in the printer's RAM.

The entire laser printer cycle takes place in one smooth sequence but, since the circumference of the drum that processes the image is smaller than a sheet of paper, the process must be repeated 2-4 times (according to size) to process a single page.

CHARGING (CONDITIONING)

The **electrostatic photographic (EP) drum**, or **imaging drum** is conditioned by a corona wire powered by a high voltage power supply assembly. The corona wire applies a uniform -600 V electrical charge across the drum's surface. A laser printer has a power supply capable of generating very high voltages. It converts the supplied current to optimal AC and DC voltages for specific components, such as the corona wire.

Note: The charging corona is also referred to as the primary corona. On most modern printers, the function of the charging corona wire is actually performed by a metal roller with a rubber coating—the Primary Charge Roller (PCR).

EXPOSING (WRITING)

The surface coating of the photosensitive drum loses its charge when exposed to light. A laser neutralizes the charge that was applied by the corona wire selectively, dot-by-dot and line-by-line, as the drum rotates. The laser-scanning assembly houses a small, low-power laser, similar to that used in an optical drive. As the laser receives the image information, it fires a short pulse of light for each dot in the raster. The pulsing light beam is reflected by a rotating polygonal mirror through a system of lenses onto the photosensitive drum. The drum ends up with a whole series of raster lines with charge/no-charge areas that represent an **electrostatic latent image** of the image to be printed.

DEVELOPING

Laser (and photocopier) toner is composed of a fine compound of dyestuff and either wax or plastic particles. The toner is fed evenly onto a magnetized roller (the **developer roller**) from a hopper.

The developer roller is located very close to the photosensitive drum. The toner carries the same negative charge polarity as the drum, which means that, under normal circumstances, there would be no interaction between the two parts. However, once areas of charge have been selectively removed from the photosensitive drum by the laser, the toner is attracted to them and sticks to those parts of its surface. The drum, now coated with toner in the image of the document, rotates until it reaches the paper.

TRANSFERRING

The paper transport mechanism includes components such as gears, pads, and rollers that move the paper through the printer. Paper loaded into a tray should be held by **media guides**. The printer uses sensors from the guides to detect the paper type. Different trays may support different types, sizes, and thicknesses of media. Pickup components lift a single sheet of paper from the selected input tray and feed it into the printer. To do this, a **pickup roller** turns once against the paper stack, pushing the paper into a **feed** and **separation roller** assembly (the manual feed tray uses a **separation pad** rather than rollers). This assembly is designed to allow only one sheet to pass through.

Interaction Opportunity

The exam objectives refer to "separate pads," but should refer to separation pads. If you have a laser printer, ask learners to inspect it to identify the location of the paper transport mechanism, toner cartridge/drum assembly, and fuser assembly.

Pickup, feed, and separation rollers on an HP 5Si laser printer.

When the paper reaches the **registration roller**, a signal tells the printer to start the image development process. When the drum is ready, the paper is fed between the photosensitive drum and the high voltage **transfer roller** (or secondary corona). The transfer roller applies a positive charge to the underside of the paper. This causes the toner on the drum to be attracted to the paper. As the paper leaves the transfer assembly, a **static eliminator** strip (or **detac corona**) removes any remaining charge from the paper, which might otherwise cause it to stick to the drum or curl as it enters the fuser unit.

FUSING

From the drum and transfer assembly, the paper passes into the **fuser assembly**. The fuser unit squeezes the paper between a hot roller and a pressure roller so that the toner is fused, or melted, onto the surface of the paper. The hot roller is a metal tube containing a heat lamp; the pressure roller is typically silicon rubber. The heat roller has a Teflon coating to prevent toner from sticking to it.

CLEANING

To complete the printing cycle, the photosensitive drum is cleaned to remove any remaining toner particles using a **cleaning blade**, roller, or brush resting on the surface of the drum. Any residual electrical charge is removed using either a discharge (or **erase lamp**) or the **primary charge roller**.

DUPLEX PRINTING AND PAPER OUTPUT PATH

When the paper has passed through the fuser, if a **duplexing assembly** unit is installed, it is turned over and returned to the developer unit to print the second side. Otherwise, the paper is directed to the selected output bin using the exit rollers.

If there is no auto duplex unit, the user can manually flip the paper stack. When duplex mode is selected for the print job, the printer pauses after printing the first side of each sheet. The user must then take the printed pages and return them (without changing the orientation) to the same input paper tray. Once this is done, the user resumes the print job.

COLOR LASER PRINTERS

Color laser printers, once very highly priced and positioned at the top end of the market, are becoming more affordable, with medium quality, entry-level models priced competitively against inkjet equivalents. Color lasers use separate color toner cartridges (Cyan, Magenta, Yellow, and Black) but employ different processes to create the image. Some may use four passes to put down each color; others combine the colors on a **transfer belt** and print in one pass.

LED PRINTERS

A traditional laser printer uses a laser with a rotating mirror and prisms to scan across each raster line. An **LED printer** uses a fixed array of tiny Light Emitting Diodes (LED) to create the light pulses for each dot in each scan line. Vendors claim that with fewer moving parts, LED printers can be more reliable than lasers, but damage to the LED array is expensive to repair. LED printers are usually much lighter than laser printers, however, and print speeds can be a bit faster.

LASER PRINTER MAINTENANCE TASKS

As devices with moving parts and consumable items that deplete quickly, printers need more maintenance than most other computer devices. Printers generate a lot of dirt—principally paper dust and ink/toner spills—and consequently require regular cleaning. Consumable items also require replacing frequently under heavy use. To keep them working in good condition requires a regular maintenance schedule and user training.

Show Slide(s)

Laser Printer Maintenance Tasks (6 slides)

Teaching Tip

Point out that the best source of information on when and how to perform maintenance on any printer is to refer to the manufacturer's documentation.

One of the first steps in maximizing the lifetime of a printer is to train users to treat it with sufficient care and attention. Depending on the environment, users might be expected to perform basic maintenance tasks—such as reloading paper and changing cartridges. Typical problems include:

- Overloading input trays or output trays (not collecting completed jobs promptly).
- Using unsuitable media—for example, card stock or labels in an auto-feed tray.
- Using creased, folded, or dirty paper.
- Breaking trays or covers.
- Inserting ink or toner cartridges incorrectly.

It is also easy for users to be confused by settings such as default paper size, form-to-tray assignment, duplex printing, printing to labels or envelopes, collating multiple copies, and dealing with paper jams.

 Note: For best results and to stay within warranty, use branded supplies designed for the specific model of printer.

Most laser printers benefit from regular, routine maintenance to ensure optimum print quality.

LOADING PAPER

The printer will report when a tray runs out of paper. When loading new paper, remember the following guidelines:

- Use good quality paper designed for use with the model of printer that you have and the printing function.
- Do not overload a paper tray.
- Do not use creased, dirty, or damp paper.
- Refer to the instruction manual when loading non-standard print media, such as transparencies or envelopes. Make sure this type of material is oriented correctly to avoid wasting stocks.

You will also need to deal with paper jams. The printer's status panel will indicate what area of the printer is jammed. Check the instruction manual to find out how to remove any components that might prevent you from removing the paper.

 *Note: **Do not allow a jammed page to rip!** If a page is stuck in the fuser or developer unit, look for a release mechanism or lever.*

REPLACING THE TONER CARTRIDGE

Laser printer toner is a fine powder made of particles of iron, carbon, and resin. Laser printers require a toner cartridge, which is a single, replaceable unit that contains toner as well as additional components used in image production. You will need to maintain a supply of the proper toner cartridges for your printer model. Refill or recycle empty toner cartridges; do not dispose of them in regular trash.

Users can change toner cartridges, but everyone should follow proper handling procedures, which are usually printed right on the cartridge. When toner is low, the printer will display a status message advising you of the fact. Frugal departments may continue printing until the actual output starts to dip in quality. Removing the cartridge and rocking gently from front-to-back can help to get the most out of it.

To replace the toner cartridge, remove the old cartridge by opening the relevant service panel and pulling it out. Place the cartridge in a bag to avoid shedding toner everywhere. Color lasers will usually have four cartridges for the different colors, which can be replaced separately.

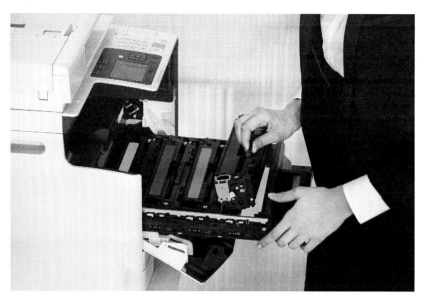

Accessing the toner cartridge on a printer. (Image by Andriy Popov © 123RF.com.)

Take the new cartridge and remove the packing strips as indicated by the instructions. Rock the cartridge gently from front-to-back to distribute the toner evenly. Insert the cartridge, close the service panel, turn on, and print a test page.

If possible, dispose of old cartridges by recycling them.

 Note: *The replacement cartridge often incorporates both toner and the photosensitive drum. An integrated toner cartridge/drum unit is light-sensitive. If you remove it, place it in its storage bag or in a dark area. Remove the cartridge for as short a time as possible.*

CLEANING A PRINTER

The manufacturer's recommendations for cleaning and maintenance must always be followed, but the following guidelines generally apply:

- Unplug the printer before cleaning or performing routine maintenance.
- Use a damp cloth to clean exterior surfaces.
- Do not use volatile liquids such as thinners or benzene to clean the interior or exterior of the printer. Use only approved cleaning solutions or solvents specifically designed for the job.
- The inside of the printer may be hot—take care.
- Wipe dust and toner away with a soft cloth. DO NOT use an ordinary domestic vacuum cleaner. Toner is conductive and can damage the motor. Toner is also so fine that it will pass straight through the dust collection bag and back into the room. Use an approved toner safe vacuum if necessary.

 Note: *Do not use compressed air or an air blaster to clean a laser printer!* *You risk blowing toner dust into the room, creating a health hazard. Compressed air should only be used in a controlled environment with appropriate safety masks and goggles.*

- If toner is spilled on skin or clothes, wash it off with COLD water. Hot water will open the skin's pores and push the toner into the skin.
- Use IPA (99% Isopropyl Alcohol solution) and non-scratch, lint-free swabs to clean rollers. Take care not to scratch a roller.
- Check the manufacturer's recommendations for replacing the printer's dust/ozone filters (if fitted).

CALIBRATING A PRINTER

Calibration is the process by which the printer determines the appropriate print density or color balance (basically, how much toner to use). Most printers calibrate themselves automatically. If print output is not as expected, you can often invoke the calibration routine from the printer's control panel or its software driver.

REPLACING THE MAINTENANCE KIT

A **maintenance kit** is a set of replacement feed rollers, new transfer roller, and a new fuser unit. The feed rollers guide paper through the printer assembly. When they begin to wear out, paper jams become more frequent. Wear on the fuser or rollers is also evidenced by consistent marks on print output or excess toner "blobs" appearing on sheets.

Replacement of the maintenance kit is guided by the printer's internal record of the number of pages that it has printed (copy count). The printer's status indicator will display the message "Maintenance Kit Replace" at this point.

Before replacing the kit, turn off the printer, disconnect from the power, open the service panels, and allow it to cool (the fuser unit becomes extremely hot and may cause burns). Remove the old fuser and rollers and clean the printer. Install the fuser and new rollers (don't forget to remove the packing strips), following the instructions carefully.

An example of a maintenance kit with feed rollers, new transfer rollers and a new fuser unit. (Image by Inga Tihonova © 123RF.com.)

Once you have replaced the maintenance kit, start the printer up and print a test page to check functionality. Use the property sheet or the printer's control panel menu (for example, the Configuration menu on an HP printer) to reset the page count to zero.

As with toner cartridges, try to use a recycling program to dispose of the fuser unit in an environmentally responsible manner.

Note: To learn more, check the **Video** tile on the CHOICE Course screen for any videos that supplement the content for this lesson.

Access the Checklist tile on your CHOICE Course screen for reference information and job aids on How to Maintain Laser Printers.

Activity 17-1
Discussing Laser Printer Maintenance

Show Slide(s)

Activity: Discussing Laser Printer Maintenance

SCENARIO

Answer the following questions to check your understanding of the topic.

---

1. **Why is a laser printer better suited to most office printing tasks than an inkjet?**

   Laser printers are much faster, quieter, and better quality (the pages do not smear) than inkjets at this type of output. They also have lower running costs.

2. **What makes the power supply in a printer different to that used in a PC?**

   A PC's Power Supply Unit (PSU) only needs to generate voltages up to 12 V DC. The charging and transfer corona wires/rollers in a laser printer require much higher voltages. To apply a 600 V charge to the drum, for instance, the corona wire must be charged to 1000 V.

3. **How is the imaging drum in a laser printer charged?**

   Applying a uniform high charge to the photosensitive drum using the primary corona wire or roller.

4. **What is the removal of the charge from the photosensitive drum by a laser called?**

   Laser imaging or writing.

5. **What is the process of image transfer?**

   Passing paper between the photosensitive drum and the secondary or transfer corona wire or roller. This attracts the toner from the drum to the paper.

6. **What must you do before installing a new toner cartridge into a printer?**

   Remove the packing strips. The printer should also be turned off, and the old cartridge should be removed and placed into a sealed bag for recycling.

7. **Which components are provided as part of a laser printer maintenance kit?**

   The main component is a new fuser assembly. The kit will also usually contain a transfer/secondary charge roller plus paper transport rollers for each tray (pickup rollers and a new separation pad).

Topic B

Maintain Inkjet Printers

 EXAM OBJECTIVES COVERED
1001-3.11 Given a scenario, install and maintain various print technologies.

 Teaching Tip

Inkjets are more likely to be used in a SOHO environment, though there are large-format models for professional printing, too. Again, focus on the print process and typical maintenance tasks.

 Show Slide(s)

Inkjet Printers

 Interaction Opportunity

The expansion of K in CMYK is the subject of some controversy. If you want to stir the pot, it might be worth noting that in French, there is no mention of any "key plate," the acronym being CMJN(oir).

 Show Slide(s)

Inkjet Printer Imaging Process

Inkjets are often used for good-quality color output and domestic use. Inkjets are typically cheap to buy but expensive to run, with high cost consumables such as ink cartridges and high-grade paper. Compared to laser printers, they are slower and often noisier, making them less popular in office environments, except as a cheap option for low volume, good quality color printing.

INKJET PRINTERS

An inkjet—or more generally ink dispersion—printer forms images by firing microscopic droplets of liquid ink out of nozzles mounted together on a carriage assembly that moves back and forth across the paper. The printer can use heat or vibrations to release the ink.

Color images are created by combining four inks, referred to as **CMYK** (Cyan, Magenta, Yellow, and Black [K]). The inks are stored in separate reservoirs, which may be supplied in single or multiple cartridges.

> **Note:** *The "K" in CMYK is usually explained as standing for "key," as in a key plate used to align the other plates in the sort of offset print press used for professional color printing in high volumes. It might be more helpful to think of it as "blacK," though.*

There are many types of inkjet printers, ranging from cheaper desktop models, through "prosumer" high quality photo printers, to large format, commercial print solutions. Higher quality printers feature additional ink colors (light magenta and light cyan). These help to produce a wider range of colors (gamut).

INKJET PRINTER IMAGING PROCESS

Inkjets work by firing microscopic droplets of ink (about 50 microns in size) at the paper. The process creates high quality images, especially when specially treated paper is used, but they can be prone to smearing and fading over time.

An inkjet print head is composed of a series of very small holes or nozzles, behind which can be found a reservoir of ink. Under normal conditions, the ink cannot flow though the nozzles because the gap is very small, and the ink reservoir is kept at a pressure slightly below that of the ambient pressure. Characters are formed when a small controlled amount of ink is forced through voltage-charged deflection plates and onto the paper. By synchronizing this action with the movement of the print head across the paper, text and images can be built up in a series of differently shaded or colored dots.

Inkjet printers are line printers—where laser printers are page printers—because they build up the image line-by-line (or at least, row-by-row). A stepper motor moves the print head across the page, advancing a tiny amount each time. On some types of printer, ink is applied when the print head moves in one direction only (unidirectional); on others, ink is applied on both the "outward" and "return" passes over the page (bidirectional). When a line or row has been completed, another stepper motor advances the page a little bit and the next line or row is printed.

If the printer has been idle for some time (or when it is first started up), it applies a cleaning cycle to the print head to remove any dried or clogged ink. This means pushing ink through all the print heads at once then wiping it away into a waste ink collector. The cleaning cycle can also be invoked manually through the printer control panel or driver.

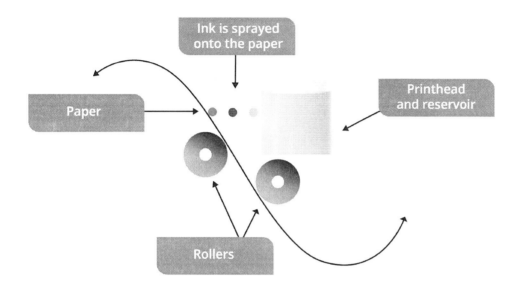

The inkjet printing process.

COMPONENTS OF INKJET PRINTERS

There are two main Ink Delivery Systems (IDS). The charge (or **piezoelectric**) method is used by Epson. The **thermal** method is used by HP, Canon (who refer to it as **Bubblejet**), and Lexmark. Each of these four vendors has licensed their inkjet technology to several other vendors or produce re-branded versions of their printers.

 Show Slide(s)

Components of Inkjet Printers (2 slides)

THERMAL PRINT HEADS

With the thermal method, the ink at the nozzle is heated, creating a bubble. When the bubble bursts, it sprays ink through the nozzle and draws more ink from the reservoir. In general, thermal inkjet print heads are cheaper and simpler to produce, but the heating elements have a relatively short life. Most thermal printers use a combined print head and ink reservoir. When the ink runs out, the print head is also replaced.

 Teaching Tip

If you have inkjet printer internals you can have learners examine without the covers, that could be useful.

PIEZOELECTRIC PRINT HEADS

In the Epson design, the nozzle contains a piezoelectric element, which changes shape when a voltage is applied. This acts like a small pump, pushing ink through the nozzle and drawing ink from the reservoir.

INK CARTRIDGES

Inkjet print heads are often considered consumable items. Often this is unavoidable because the print head is built into the **ink cartridge**, as is the case with most (but not all) thermal print heads. Epson piezoelectric print heads are non-removable and designed to last as long as the rest of the printer components.

As well as containing ink, the ink reservoir has sensors to detect the level of ink remaining. A color printer has at least four ink reservoirs (Black, Cyan, Magenta, and Yellow). The four ink reservoirs may come in a single cartridge or there may be separate cartridges for black and colored ink or each ink may come in its own cartridge.

Ink cartridges. (Image by © 123RF.com.)

CARRIAGE SYSTEM

The print head is moved back and forth over the paper by a carriage system. This comprises a stepper motor (to drive the system), a pulley and belt (to move the print head), a guide shaft (to keep the print head stable), and sensors (to detect the position of the print head). A flat ribbon data cable connects the print head to the printer's circuit board.

There may also be a lever used to set the platen gap or the printer may adjust this automatically depending on driver settings. The platen gap is the distance between the print head and the paper. Having an adjustable platen gap allows the printer to use thicker media.

The carriage mechanism in an inkjet printer. (Image by Erik Bobeldijk © 123RF.com.)

PAPER HANDLING AND DUPLEXING ASSEMBLY

Most inkjets only support one paper path, with single input and output trays, though some have automatic duplexers, and some may have accessory trays. Printers are generally split between models that load from the top and output at the bottom and those that have both input and output bins at the bottom and turn the paper (an "up-and-over" path).

The paper pickup mechanism is quite similar to that of a laser printer. Paper is fed into the printer by an **AutoSheet Feeder (ASF)** mechanism. A **load roller** turns against the paper stack to move the top sheet while a **separation roller** prevents more than one sheet entering.

When the paper is sufficiently advanced, it is detected by a sensor. Feed rollers and sensors then ensure the paper is positioned correctly for printing to begin. The stepper motor controlling the paper feed mechanism advances the paper as the print head completes each pass until the print is complete.

The eject rollers then deliver the paper to the **duplexing assembly** (if installed and duplex printing has been selected) or the output bin. Some inkjets with a curved paper path may have a "straight-through" rear panel for bulkier media.

INKJET PRINTER MAINTENANCE TASKS

Inkjets do not usually handle such high print volumes as laser printers, so maintenance focuses on paper stocking and replacing or refilling ink cartridges, which always seem to run down very quickly. Manufacturers recommend not trying to clean inside the case as you are likely to do harm for no real benefit. The outside of the printer can be cleaned using a soft damp cloth.

LOADING PAPER

Inkjets tend to have smaller paper trays than laser printers and so can need restocking with paper more often. Most inkjets can use "regular" copier/laser printer paper but better results can be obtained by using less absorbent premium grades of paper stock, specifically designed for inkjet use. Often this type of paper is designed to be printed on one side only—make sure the paper is correctly oriented when loading the printer.

As with laser printers, you will also need to clear paper jams. With an inkjet, it is usually easy to see exactly where the paper has jammed. If the sheet will not come out easily, do not just try to pull it harder—check the instruction manual to find out how to release any components that might prevent you from removing the paper.

REPLACE INKJET CARTRIDGES

When the inkjet's driver software determines that a cartridge is empty, it will prompt you to replace it. Check the printer's instruction manual for the correct procedure.

OTHER INKJET MAINTENANCE OPERATIONS

Two other operations may be required periodically.

- **Print head alignment**—if output is not aligned correctly, use the print head alignment function from the printer's property sheet to calibrate the printer. This is typically done automatically when you replace the ink cartridges.
- **Print head cleaning**—a blocked or dirty nozzle will show up on output as a missing line. Use the printer's cleaning cycle (accessed via the property sheet or control panel) to try to fix the problem. If it does not work, there are various inkjet cleaning products on the market.

Show Slide(s)
Inkjet Printer Maintenance Tasks

Teaching Tip
Point out that inkjets especially should be used with specially formulated paper to avoid problems with output quality (smearing, rippling, and so on).

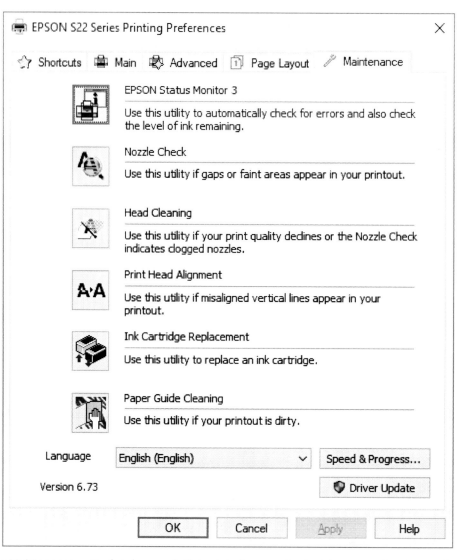

Use the Maintenance or Tools tab on an inkjet printer's property sheet to access cleaning routines and calibration utilities.

Note: *To learn more, check the **Video** tile on the CHOICE Course screen for any videos that supplement the content for this lesson.*

Access the Checklist tile on your CHOICE Course screen for reference information and job aids on *How to Maintain Inkjet Printers*.

Activity 17-2
Discussing Inkjet Printer Maintenance

SCENARIO

Answer the following questions to check your understanding of the topic.

Show
Slide(s)

Activity: Discussing
Inkjet Printer
Maintenance

1. **Which inks are typically used in the color printing process?**

   Cyan, Magenta, Yellow, and Black (CMYK). Do be aware that some printers can use more inks. For example, a 6-color printer might add Light Cyan and Light Magenta inks, or Orange and Green inks (hexachrome).

2. **What two types of print heads are used by inkjet printers?**

   Thermal and piezoelectric. The thermal type is also known by Canon's Bubble Jet trademark because of the way the print head creates an ink bubble by heating. Most other printer vendors use thermal technology but Epson printers use their piezoelectric pump-like process.

3. You have been asked to perform basic maintenance on an inkjet printer. One of the users noticed that the colors are not printing correctly and that the bottom of some letters are not printing.

   What would you do?

   Try using the printer's built-in cleaning cycle, and then replacing the ink cartridge. If these do not work, try using an after market cleaning product. Try using the printer properties sheet to check for print head alignment, color settings, and other settings.

4. **Can inkjet printers use plain copy paper?**

   Yes, but this type of paper will not produce the best results. It is better to use paper designed for inkjets. There are different grades of inkjet paper. Higher-grade paper allows for glossy photo printing.

5. **What is an ASF?**

   An AutoSheet Feeder (ASF) allows the printer to load a sheet of paper from a tray, using pickup rollers to move the sheet and a separation pad to make sure only a single sheet is fed at one time.

Topic C

Maintain Impact, Thermal, and 3D Printers

 EXAM OBJECTIVES COVERED
1001-3.11 Given a scenario, install and maintain various print technologies.

Laser and inkjet printers are widely deployed but there are a number of other printer types that are better optimized for certain tasks. In this topic, you will learn about thermal, impact, and 3D printer types.

IMPACT PRINTERS

An **impact printer** strikes an inked ribbon against paper to leave marks. One common type is the **dot matrix** printer, which uses a column of pins (also called print wires) to strike the ribbon.

Desktop dot matrix printers are no longer very widely deployed, but they are still used for specialist functions such as printing invoices or pay slips, on continuous, tractor-fed paper. Portable models are still widely used for printing receipts.

 Teaching Tip

Learners are less likely to have encountered these printer types already, so allow plenty of time to explain the features and uses of these devices.

 Show Slide(s)

Impact Printers

Teaching Tip

Other types of impact printers include daisy wheel and line printer. Learners shouldn't need to know about these.

 Interaction Opportunity

Ask learners if they have encountered any impact printers, and if so, what they were used for.

Example of a dot matrix printer. (Image © 123RF.com.)

COMPONENTS OF IMPACT PRINTERS

Impact printers are composed of a ribbon cartridge, rollers, and pins for moving paper through the printer, a printhead composed of a number of electromagnetic pins, and some optional components, which might include a paper tray, an output tray, and a support for sheet-fed paper.

Show Slide(s)
Components of Impact Printers

IMPACT PRINTER CONSUMABLES

Impact printers can be used with either plain, carbon, or **tractor-fed** paper:

- **Plain paper** is held firmly against the moving roller (the platen) and pulled through the mechanism by friction as the platen rotates. A cut sheet feeder may be added to some printers to automate the process of providing the next page.
- **Carbon paper** (or **impact paper**) is used to make multiple copies of a document in the same pass (hence carbon copy, or "cc"). A sheet of carbon paper is inserted between each sheet of plain paper and when the print head strikes, the same mark is made on each sheet.
- **Tractor-fed** paper is fitted with removable, perforated side strips. The holes in these strips are secured over studded rollers at each end of the platen. This type of paper is more suitable for multi-part stationery as there is less chance of skewing or slippage since the end rollers fix the movement of the paper.

PAPER FEED MECHANISMS

Impact printers can use either tractor feed when printing on continuous-roll impact paper, or **friction feed** when printing on individually cut sheets of paper. Tractor feed uses pairs of wheels with pins evenly spaced around the circumference at a set spacing. Continuous-roll paper with matching holes in the edges fits over the pins. The wheels turn and pull the paper through the printer. There are usually just two wheels, but there might be additional wheels or pin guides that the paper is latched to. There is usually a lever or other setting on the printer that needs to be engaged in order to use the tractor feed.

Friction feed uses two rollers placed one on top of the other. The rollers turn to force individual cut sheets of paper or envelopes through the paper path. This is used to print on individual sheets of paper (cut-sheet paper) and envelopes. Be sure to set the printer lever or other setting to the cut-sheet mode when printing using friction feed.

IMPACT PRINTER RIBBONS

An impact printer will also have some form of replaceable ribbon. Older-style printers used to have a two-spool ribbon. However, most units now have a cartridge device that slots over or around the carriage of the print head. These integrated ribbons simplify the design of the printer because they can be made as a complete loop moving in one direction only. The two-spool design requires a sensor and reversing mechanism to change the direction of the ribbon when it reaches the end.

When the ribbon on an impact printer fails to produce sufficiently good print quality, the ribbon-holder and contents are normally replaced as a whole. Some printers can use a re-usable cartridge.

IMPACT PRINTER IMAGING PROCESS

In a dot matrix printer, the pins are contained in the **print head**, which is secured to a moving carriage that sweeps across the paper. The pins are fired by coils of wire called solenoids. When a coil is energized, it forms a strong electromagnet that causes the metal firing pin to move sharply forwards, striking the ink-bearing **ribbon** against the paper. A strong permanent magnet moves the pins back into their resting position immediately after firing.

Show Slide(s)
Impact Printer Imaging Process

Note: Do not touch the print head after using the printer. The print head can become very hot, even after short periods of use.

The output quality of a dot-matrix printer is largely governed by the number of pins in the print head. Most modern printers use 9-pin or 24-pin print heads. The latter offer a much-improved print quality. More sophisticated printers may use 48-pin print heads, although if you require this level of quality, an inkjet or laser printer may be a better option.

A platen gap lever is often fitted to printers capable of printing on multi-part stationery. This lever adjusts the gap between the print head and the platen to accommodate different thickness of paper. Incorrect adjustment of the platen gap can cause faint printing (gap too wide) or smudging (too narrow). On more sophisticated printers, the platen gap is adjusted automatically.

IMPACT PRINTER MAINTENANCE TIPS

 **Show Slide(s)**
Impact Printer Maintenance Tips

When you are loading a tractor-fed impact printer with paper, ensure that the holes in the paper are engaged in the sprockets and that the paper can enter the printer cleanly. Ensure that the lever is in the correct position for friction feed or tractor feed as appropriate for the media being used. Follow the manufacturer's instructions to replace the print head or ribbon cartridge. Take care, as the print head may become very hot during use.

 Access the Checklist tile on your CHOICE Course screen for reference information and job aids on How to Maintain Impact Printers.

THERMAL PRINTERS

 Show Slide(s)
Thermal Printers

 Teaching Tip
"Thermal" covers a lot of different printer technologies, but you will focus on direct thermal printers.

A **thermal printer** is a general term for any printer that uses a heating element to create the image on the paper with dye, ink from ribbons, or directly with pins while the feed assembly moves the media through the printer. There are several types of thermal printers that use significantly different technologies and are intended for different uses. The **dye sublimation** print process can be used for photo quality output and **thermal wax transfer** printers can be used as an alternative to color laser printing, but the most common type of thermal printer you are likely to have to support is the **direct thermal** printer.

A direct thermal receipt printer. (Image © 123RF.com.)

Portable or small form factor direct thermal transfer printers are used for high volume barcode and label printing and also to print receipts. Such devices typically support 200-300 dpi, with some models able to print one or two colors. Print speeds are measured in inches per second.

COMPONENTS OF THERMAL PRINTERS

Most direct thermal print devices require special **thermal paper** that contains chemicals designed to react and change color as it is heated by the **heating element** within the printer to create images.

In the **feed assembly** on a direct thermal printer, paper is friction-fed through the print mechanism by a stepper motor turning a rubber-coated roller. Paper and labels may be fanfold or roll format.

Show Slide(s)

Components of Thermal Printers

DIRECT THERMAL PRINTER IMAGING PROCESS

Direct thermal printers have a heating element with heated pins that create an image directly onto special thermal paper.

Show Slide(s)

Direct Thermal Printer Imaging Process

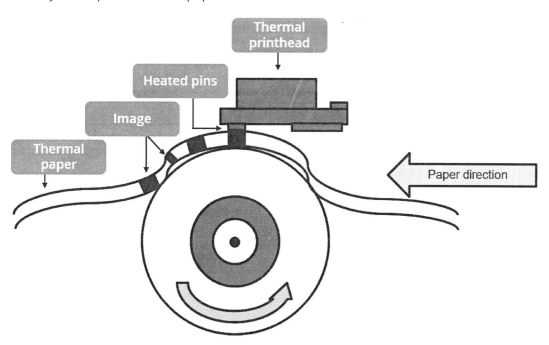

Direct thermal print process.

THERMAL TRANSFER PRINTER MAINTENANCE TIPS

Thermal printers are often used in cash registers and for printing labels. Both of these uses require the printer to be available at all times, and to keep up availability, you should perform regular maintenance.

Show Slide(s)

Thermal Transfer Printer Maintenance Tips

When you are replacing the paper roll, you need to obtain the specific size and type for the brand and model of thermal printer you are using. The process is usually quite simple—just open the printer case, insert the roll, keeping the shiny print side facing outwards, then ensure that the end of the paper in held in place by the print head when closing the case again.

In receipt registers, the cashier rips the paper across the serrated teeth to give the receipt to the customer. This can lead to a build-up of paper dust in the printer from tearing off receipts. It can also lead to bits of paper debris becoming lodged in the mechanism if a clean slice is not made and bits of leftover paper fall into the printer.

Label printers can end up with sticky residue inside the printer. If labels are not loaded correctly, they can separate from the backing while being fed through the printer. You will need to ensure users know how to properly load the labels and how to clean up if labels get stuck inside the printer.

Use a vacuum or soft brush to remove any paper debris. Use a swab and appropriate cleaning fluid, such as Isopropyl Alcohol (IPA), to clean the print head (heating element) or any sticky residue inhibiting the feed mechanism. Alternatively, you can often purchase cleaning cards to feed through the printer to clean the print head safely. Only use cleaning cards when required, though, as they can be abrasive and wear down components.

 Access the Checklist tile on your CHOICE Course screen for reference information and job aids on How to Maintain Thermal Printers.

3D PRINTERS

 Show Slide(s)

3D Printers

 Interaction Opportunity

It's probably not practical to attempt a demonstration of 3D printing, but if you do have the equipment available and enough spare class time, learners will certainly benefit from it.

A **3D print process** builds a solid object from successive layers of material. The material is typically some sort of plastic but there are printer types that can work with rubber, carbon fiber, or metal alloys too. The range of materials that can be used is expanding quickly.

3D printing has very different use cases to printing to paper. It is most widely used in manufacturing, especially to create "proof of concept" working models from designs. The range of other applications is growing, however. For example, 3D printing can be used in healthcare (dentistry and prosthetics), clothing, and to make product samples and other marketing material.

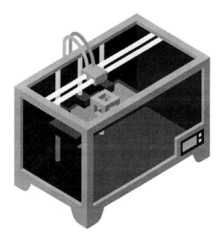

A 3D printer. (Image © 123RF.com.)

3D PRINTER IMAGING PROCESS

 Show Slide(s)

3D Printer Imaging Process

The **3D printer** imaging process begins with either a scan created by a **3D scanner** or by creating an object using **3D modeling software**. From either of these methods, you end up with a 3D model created in software and saved to a 3D model format.

This model is then **sliced** with **slicing software** into horizontal layers. The slicing software might be contained in the 3D modeling software or within the 3D printer. The result is a print job specifying how each layer in the finished object is to be deposited.

The sliced model is then fed to the 3D printer over a USB or Wi-Fi connection, or by inserting an SD card containing the file into the printer. The printer then melts the filament and extrudes it onto the build surface, creating layer upon layer based on the slices. The extruder (and sometimes the build bed) is moved as needed on X/Y/Z axes to create the build.

COMPONENTS OF 3D PRINTERS

There are several types of 3D printers. **Fused filament fabrication (FFF)**, also known as **fused deposition modeling (FDM)**, lays down layers of filament at high temperature. As layers are extruded, adjacent layers are allowed to cool and bond together before additional layers are added to the object. The main components in an FDM 3D printer are:

Show Slide(s)
Components of 3D Printers

- **Print bed/build plate**—a flat glass plate onto which the material is extruded. The bed is usually heated to prevent the material from warping. The bed must be leveled for each print job—this is usually automated, but cheaper printer models require manual calibration. It is very important that the printer frame be strong and rigid enough to keep the bed as stable as possible. Any vibration will result in poor quality printing.
- **Bed/build surface**—a sheet placed onto the base plate to hold the object in position while printing, but also allow its removal on completion. The bed surface material may need to be matched to the filament material for best results.
- **Extruder**—the equivalent of a print head in an inkjet. A motor in the extruder draws filament from the "cold end" through to the nozzle (or "hot end"), where it is melted and squirted onto the object. Different size nozzles can be fitted to the extruder.
- **Gears/motors/motion control**—enable precise positioning of the extruder.
- **Fan**—cools the melted plastic where necessary to shape the object correctly.

The printer must be installed to a suitable environment. A stable, vibration-free floor and dust-free, humidity-controlled surroundings will ensure best results.

 Note: 3D printing involves several possible safety risks. Components work at high temperatures, and use of sharp tools such as scrapers and finishing knives is required. Ideally, the 3D print facility should be accessible only to trained users.

FILAMENT

The "ink" for a 3D printer is supplied as a spool of **filament**. Filament is provided either as 1.75 mm or 3 mm diameter. As noted earlier, there are various different filament materials. The two most popular plastics are Polylactic Acid (PLA) and Acrylonitrile Butadiene Styrene (ABS). Most printers can use a range of filament materials but it is best to check compatibility if a specific "exotic" is required for a project. Each material operates at different extruder and print bed temperatures.

To change a filament, the extruder must be heated to the appropriate temperature. Pull as much of the old filament out as possible—taking care not to burn yourself—then push the new filament through. Do not start printing until all of the old filament has been pushed out.

Filament spools require careful storage once opened. They should be kept free from heat and humidity.

3D PRINTER MAINTENANCE TIPS

3D printers require maintenance specific to the type of printing done. These printers do not print on paper, so have very different maintenance needs and consumables than traditional printers. Among the maintenance tasks you need to perform are:

Show Slide(s)
3D Printer Maintenance Tips

- Remove any leftover filament from nozzles.
- Clean any residual plastic from the platform, nozzles, and other areas. There could also be glue left on the glass if your print process uses glue.

- If the documentation says to, apply grease to the moving parts that move the extruder on the X/Y/Z axes.
- Check tubes in the feeder mechanism to see if they need to be cleaned or replaced.
- Examine couplers to see if they have been damaged by the heat produced during the print process.
- Make sure only approved materials are used when printing.
- Check whether there are new versions of firmware available for the printer and whether you should apply them to the printer.

OTHER 3D PRINTER TYPES

Show Slide(s)

Other 3D Printer Types

Teaching Tip

For more information on comparing 3D print processes, refer to **https://www.sd3d.com/fff-vs-sla-vs-sls/**.

There are two other common types of rapid prototype 3D printing.

Prototype	Description
SLA	**Stereolithography (SLA)** uses liquid plastic resin or **photopolymer** to create objects which are cured using an ultraviolet laser. Excess photopolymer is stored in a tank under the print bed. The print bed lowers into the tank as the object is created. A liquid solvent removes uncured polymer after the model is finished.
SLS	**Selective laser sintering (SLS)** fuses layers together using a pulse laser. The object is created from a powder and lowered into a tank as each layer is added. The powder can be plastic or metal.

 Access the Checklist tile on your CHOICE Course screen for reference information and job aids on How to Maintain 3D Printers.

Activity 17-3

Discussing Impact, Thermal, and 3D Printer Maintenance

SCENARIO

Answer the following questions to check your understanding of the topic.

 Show Slide(s)

Activity: Discussing Impact, Thermal, and 3D Printer Maintenance

1. **What type of printer technology is a dot matrix printer?**

   It is commonly described as an impact printer.

2. **What types of paper/stationery can dot matrix printers use that laser and inkjet printers cannot?**

   Multi-part or continuous tractor-fed stationery and carbon copy paper.

3. **Where are you must likely to encounter thermal printers?**

   Direct thermal printers are typically used as handheld receipt printers. There are other thermal printer types. For example, dye sublimation printers are often used for photo printing.

4. You have been asked to perform basic maintenance on a printer in the Research and Development area. The dot matrix printer used to create shipping documents seems to be printing lighter than normal, and one of the pins seems to not be connecting near the center of the print head as there are blank areas in some letters and images.

   What maintenance should you perform?

   Using the steps in the printer documentation, replace the ribbon in the printer and clean the print head. If this does not fix the problem, replace the print head.

5. A thermal printer used to create labels for parts bins, kits, and boxes is jammed due to a label coming loose during printing.

   How should you resolve this problem?

   Open the printer and locate the label that came off the backing. Remove the label and if there is any sticky residue, clean it with isopropyl alcohol (IPA) applied to a swab. Ensure the roll of labels is properly loaded and that there are no loose labels that might come loose again.

6. **What do you need to create objects with an FDM-type 3D printer?**

   You will need spools of filament, usually made of some type of plastic, to create 3D objects on a print bed or build surface.

7. **What considerations for locating a 3D printer do you have to make?**

The 3D print process is sensitive to movement and vibration, so the printer must be located on a firm and stable surface. The process can also be affected by dust and the ambient temperature and humidity (especially variations and drafts). Finally, some printer types are fully exposed so there is some risk of burns from the high-heat elements. Ideally, the printer should not be accessible to untrained staff.

Topic D

Install and Configure Printers

EXAM OBJECTIVES COVERED
1001-3.10 Given a scenario, configure SOHO multifunction devices/printers and settings.
1001-3.11 Given a scenario, install and maintain various print technologies.

Because printers are such a fundamental component of almost every computing environment, it is almost guaranteed that you will be asked to set up and configure printing on devices, no matter what professional environment you are working in. Although the different technologies used in various printer types affect maintenance and troubleshooting, the type of printer does not substantially affect the way it is installed and configured in an operating system such as Windows or shared on a network. The skills you will learn in this topic should prepare you to install and configure a wide range of printer types efficiently and correctly.

WINDOWS PRINTERS

Windows applications that support printing are typically **WYSIWYG** (What You See Is What You Get), which means that the screen and print output are supposed to be the same. To achieve this, several components are required:

- The **print driver** provides an interface between the print device and Windows.
- Support for one or more **print languages** determines how accurate the output can be.
- The **technology** used by the printer determines the quality, speed, and cost of the output.

> *Note: There is a distinction between the software components that represent the printer and the physical printer itself. The software representation of the printer may be described as the "printer object," "logical printer," or simply "printer." Terms relating to the printer hardware include "print device" or "physical printer." Be aware that "printer" could mean either the physical print device or the software representation of that device. Pay attention to the context in which these terms are used.*

WINDOWS PRINT PROCESS

Display and print functions for compatible applications are handled by the **Windows Presentation Foundation (WPF)**. A WPF print job is formatted and spooled as an **XML Print Specification (XPS)** file in the printer's spool folder (%SystemRoot% \System32\Spool\Printers\).

This spool file is then processed by the printer's device driver. It may either be output directly to an XPS-compatible print device or rendered using a different **Page Description Language (PDL)**, such as HP Printer Control Language or Adobe® PostScript®, and converted to a **raster**, or dot-by-bot description of where the printer should place ink.

Teaching Tip
This topic shifts the focus from printer hardware to connecting to the printer from Windows, configuring printer options and preferences, and managing network printing.

Show Slide(s)
Windows Printers

Teaching Tip
This content goes a bit beyond what is explicitly called out in the exam objectives, but it should be useful for learners to understand the different components involved.

Show Slide(s)
Windows Print Process (2 slides)

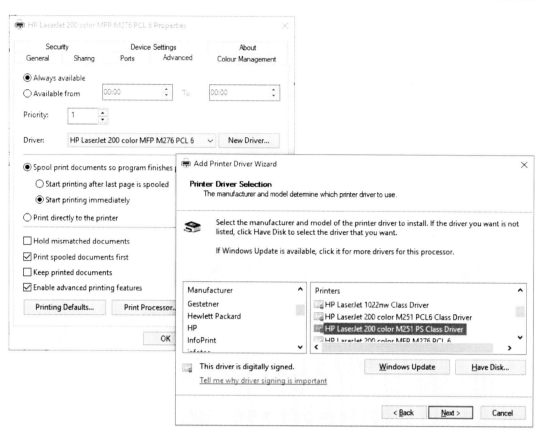

A print device might support more than one PDL—this HP printer supports both Printer Control Language (PCL) and PostScript (PS). (Screenshot used with permission from Microsoft.)

The **print monitor** transmits the print job to the printer and provides status information. Most print devices have their own memory and processor, enabling the print job to be transmitted more quickly and reliably. If a problem is encountered during printing, the print device sends a status message back to the print monitor, informing the user.

Applications and print devices that do not support WPF use the older **Graphics Device Interface (GDI)** print process. Under GDI, the print file can be spooled in one of two formats:

- **EMF (Enhanced Metafile)**—a small, efficient, printer-independent file type. As the file is smaller, it is written to disk more quickly, therefore freeing up resources. The printer must support EMF for this to work.
- **RAW**—this file type differs depending on your printer. RAW files must be formatted for the printer at the spooling stage, therefore it will take longer to spool the file and the file will be larger. The RAW spool format is a useful troubleshooting tool.

Users can also print to network printers. In this case, a redirector service on the local computer passes the print job from the locally spooled file to the spooler on the print server (the computer to which the network printer is connected). Note that a driver for the network device must be installed locally.

FEATURES OF PAGE DESCRIPTION LANGUAGES

PDLs support the following features:

- **Scalable fonts**—originally, characters were printed as bitmaps. This meant that the character could only be printed at sizes defined in the font (a bitmap font consists of a number of dot-by-dot images of each character at a particular font size). Scalable fonts are described by vectors. A **vector font** consists of a description of how each character should be drawn. This description can be scaled up or down to different font sizes. All Windows printers support scalable TrueType or OpenType fonts. OpenType is an extension of TrueType, developed jointly by Microsoft and Adobe. OpenType offers portability between Windows and Mac OS®, better character (Unicode) support, and more advanced typographic options. PostScript compatible printers will also support PostScript outline fonts.

- Color printing—the color model used by display systems is different to that used by printers (**additive** versus **subtractive**). An additive model combines differently colored transmitted light (Red, Green, and Blue, for instance) to form different shades. A subtractive model works using the reflective properties of inks: Cyan, Magenta, and Yellow plus Black ink for "true" blacks. A color model provides an accurate translation between on-screen color and print output and ensures that different devices produce identical output.
- **Vector graphics**—as with fonts, scalable images are built from vectors, which describe how a line should be drawn, rather than providing a pixel-by-pixel description, as is the case with bitmap graphics.

VIRTUAL PRINTERS

There may be circumstances where you do not want to send a print job to a physical print device. Using a virtual printer means that the output is either a file containing instructions in some **page description language** or **bitmap image data**. Some of the reasons users might need to print to a virtual printer include:

- Sending a document from their computer to a fax server.
- Creating a document that cannot be purposely or inadvertently changed.
- Making the document content available outside of the application which originally created the document.
- Combining multiple documents into a single document.
- Testing how the document will appear when printed on paper from a physical printer.

When you are using a virtual print option, there may be a choice of file formats for the output:

- **Print to file**—this creates a file that can subsequently be sent to the print device. It basically means saving a copy of the file that would normally be spooled by the printer. This may be used in conjunction with the PostScript print language. Note that the output files are typically very large.
- **Print to PDF**—the Portable Document Format (PDF) was created by Adobe and later published as an open standard as a device-independent format for viewing and printing documents. Print (or export) to PDF functionality is available in many software applications.
- **Print to XPS**—as noted earlier, the XML Print Specification is the print language supported by Windows. An XPS format file should be printable on modern Windows-compatible printers.
- **Print to image**—some applications support directing the output to a bitmap image file format, such as PNG or JPEG. Vector text and art will be converted to a fixed resolution format.

Show Slide(s)
Virtual Printers

Interaction Opportunity
Find out whether any learners use virtual printers and if so, what they use them for. If they don't currently use them, see if they can think of reasons why they might recommend them to users.

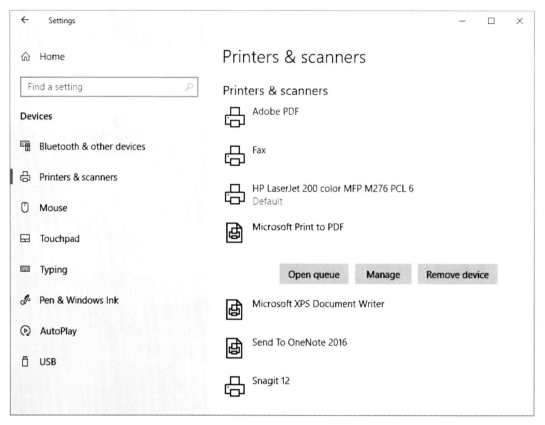

Windows 10 includes Print to PDF and XPS Document Writer virtual printers by default. (Screenshot used with permission from Microsoft.)

 Note: *The PC in the previous figure also has Adobe PDF, Send to OneNote, and SnagIt virtual printers installed.*

LOCAL PRINTER CONNECTIONS

 Show Slide(s)
Local Printer Connections

As with other PC peripherals, USB is now the dominant printer interface.

USB PORTS

 Teaching Tip

Discuss what connectivity options would be standard, which are required for older devices, and which are typically only available at extra cost.

The parallel (LPT) port is no longer part of the exam objectives, but you might want to refer briefly to it so that learners understand the term.

To install a USB printer, connect the device plug (usually a Type B connector) to the printer's USB port and the Type A host plug to a free port on the computer. In most cases, Windows will detect the printer using Plug-and-Play and install the driver automatically. You can confirm that the printer is successfully installed and print a test page using the Devices and Printers or Settings applet.

Even though USB connections are powered, you will still need to connect the printer to mains power as it will draw down more power than USB can supply. Portable printers may have a battery supply.

In the following figure, notice that there is an option to print a test page. In the properties dialog box for the printer, you can see that the printer is connected via USB.

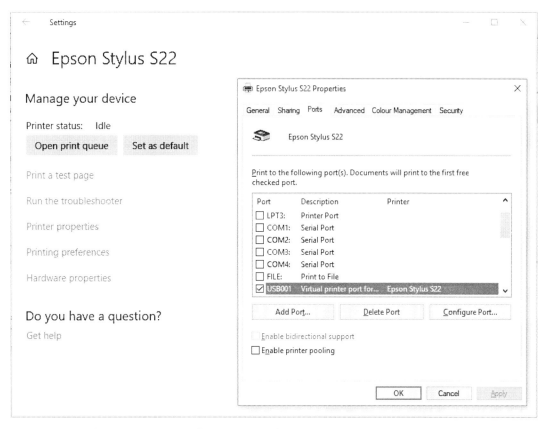

Using Windows Settings to verify printer installation. (Screenshot used with permission from Microsoft.)

ETHERNET

Some printers come equipped with a network adapter and RJ-45 port and can be connected directly to an Ethernet switch. Client devices can then either connect directly to the print device via its Internet Protocol (IP) address or the device can be managed and shared via a network print server.

SERIAL PORT

The serial (RS-232 or COM) port is a legacy port and does not support the bandwidth required by modern desktop printers. Certain Point-of-Sale (PoS) barcode printers and older impact printers are interfaced by serial ports, however.

Connect such a printer using an appropriate "null modem" serial cable; either 9-pin to 9-pin or 25-pin to 9-pin, depending on the printer model. Serial port drivers are unlikely to support Plug-and-Play, so you will need to complete the installation using the Device Setup wizard, selecting the appropriate COM port and driver. You may also need to configure custom COM port settings (via the **Ports** tab in the printer's property dialog box). Check the printer's setup guide for specific cable and connector requirements and installation procedures.

 Teaching Tip

Point out that older printers might also have a Centronix parallel port and require a parallel cable to connect to a parallel port on the printer.

WIRELESS PRINT DEVICE INTERFACES

A cable-free connection to a printer offers a more flexible solution. Most wireless interfaces are built into the printer. Wi-Fi may be available as an installable upgrade. Another option is to connect a wireless print server via the printer's USB port. The two principal wireless printer interfaces are Bluetooth and Wi-Fi.

Bluetooth uses radio communications and supports speeds of up to 3 Mbps. It does not require line-of-sight and supports a maximum range of 10 m (30 feet), though signal strength will be very weak at this distance. To connect via Bluetooth, ensure that the printer is configured as discoverable, then use the **Bluetooth** applet in Control Panel or the **Devices** page in Windows Settings to add the device.

Wi-Fi (802.11) supports higher transfer rates. The printer should be configured with the appropriate WLAN settings (SSID and IP configuration) via its control panel. The main configuration choices are as follows:

- 802.11 standard—the printer's wireless adapter will support a particular 802.11 standard (a, b, g, n, or ac). Other devices connecting to it must support the same standard and be configured with the same security settings.

- Infrastructure versus ad hoc—in infrastructure mode, the printer would be configured to connect to an access point and client connections would also be mediated by the access point. In ad hoc mode, client devices would connect directly to the printer.

Using the printer control panel to join a Wi-Fi network (infrastructure mode).

Ad hoc is a specific mode of peer-to-peer connection associated with legacy standards (802.11a/b/g). You are more likely to encounter devices supporting **Wi-Fi Direct/Wireless Direct**. With Wi-Fi Direct, the server device supports a software-implemented access point to facilitate connections to client devices.

Once the Wi-Fi link is established, you should then be able to connect to the printer from Windows like any other network printer.

PRINTER DRIVERS

Show Slide(s)

Printer Drivers

Operating system printer drivers must be installed for a printer to function correctly. If the device is not detected automatically, the printer port can be selected, and drivers can be installed using the **Devices and Printers** applet or the **Windows Settings** app.

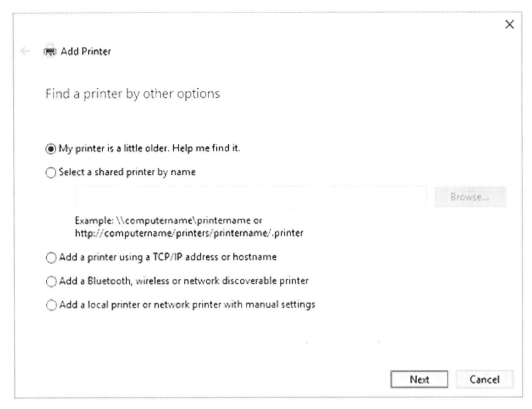

Add Printer Wizard—select a manual configuration if Windows does not detect the printer automatically. (Screenshot used with permission from Microsoft.)

Once the driver has been installed all applications will use it to send output to the printer. To test that the printer has installed correctly, open the **Printer Properties** dialog box (right-click the printer icon in the **Devices and Printers** applet) and select the **Print Test Page** button on the **General** tab.

 Note: Installing a new driver requires elevation (UAC). On a domain network, administrators can install approved drivers to designated servers then use group policy to allow standard users to install local printers using those drivers.

 Note: Make sure you obtain a 32-bit or 64-bit driver as appropriate. Many older print devices have become unusable as the vendor has not developed a 64-bit driver for them. If no up-to-date driver is available from Microsoft, download the driver from the printer vendor's website, extract it to a folder on your PC, then use the Have Disk option to install it.

CONFIGURATION SETTINGS

Print devices are configured and managed via the **Devices and Printers** folder (Windows 7 and 8) or the **Settings** app (Windows 10). The layout of these apps is slightly different, but they present similar options—view the print queue, open properties and preferences, set a default printer, start a troubleshooter, and so on.

 Show Slide(s)
Configuration Settings (2 slides)

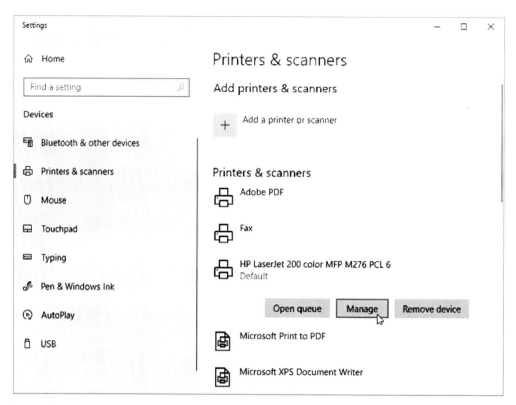

Viewing the print queue and configuring preferences through the Printers and Scanners Settings app page. (Screenshot used with permission from Microsoft.)

There are two main configuration dialog boxes for a local printer: **Printer Properties** and **Printing Preferences**.

 Note: *To adjust some device properties and options, you may have to select* **Run as administrator** *then* **Printer Properties** *or* **Printing Preferences** *as appropriate.*

PRINTER PROPERTIES

A printer's **Properties** dialog box allows you to manage configuration settings for the printer object and the underlying hardware, such as updating the driver, printing to a different port, sharing and permissions, setting basic device options (such as whether a duplex unit is installed), and configuring default paper types for different feed trays.

The **About** tab contains information about the driver and the printer vendor and may include links to support and troubleshooting tips and utilities.

 Note: *The options available for printing preferences and the layout of these dialog boxes is partly vendor-specific.*

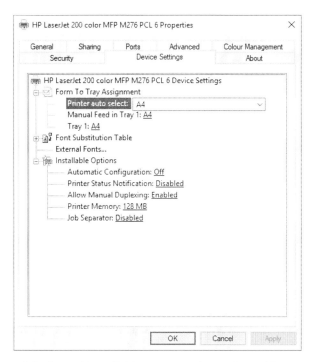

This HP printer allows defaults and installable options to be configured here. (Screenshot used with permission from Microsoft.)

PRINTING PREFERENCES

The **Preferences** dialog box sets the default **print job** options, such as the type and orientation of paper or whether to print in color or black and white.

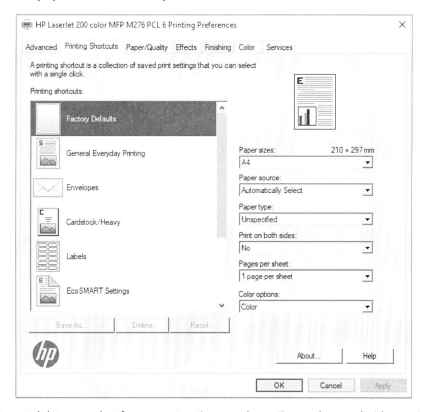

The shortcuts tab lets you select from preset option templates. (Screenshot used with permission from Microsoft.)

These settings can also be changed on a per-job basis by selecting the **Properties** button in the application's **Print** dialog box. Alternatively, the printer may come with management software that you can use to change settings.

PAPER/QUALITY

The **Paper/Quality** tab allows you to choose the type of paper stock (size and type) to use and whether to use an economy or draft mode to preserve ink/toner. You can also use the **Color** tab to select between color and grayscale printing.

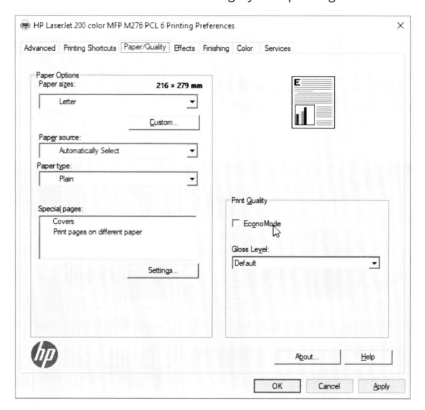

Use the Paper/Quality tab to configure the paper type and whether to use a reduced ink/toner economy mode. (Screenshot used with permission from Microsoft.)

FINISHING

The **Finishing** tab lets you select output options such as whether to print on both sides of the paper (duplex), print multiple images per sheet, and/or print in portrait or landscape orientation.

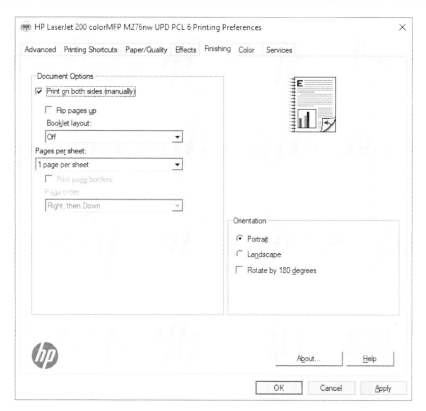

The Finishing tab allows you to select duplex output (this printer allows only manual duplex, where the stack must be flipped by the user and reinserted into the paper tray manually). (Screenshot used with permission from Microsoft.)

COPY COUNT AND COLLATED PRINTS

You can change the copy count and collation options using the **Advanced** tab.

Print and collation options in Word. (Screenshot used with permission from Microsoft.)

A **collated** print job is one where all pages of the first copy are printed, followed by all pages of the second copy, and so on. If the **uncollated** option is selected, then all copies of page 1 are printed first, followed by all copies of page 2, and so on.

PRINTER SHARING AND NETWORKING

Show Slide(s)

Printer Sharing and Networking (2 slides)

Teaching Tip

This is an important section. Make sure exam candidates can distinguish between connecting to a printer directly over the network and connecting to a printer object shared via a Windows computer.

There are two main options for sharing a printer on the network:

*   Windows printer sharing
*   Hardware print server sharing

WINDOWS PRINT SERVER CONFIGURATION

An administrator can share any locally installed printer via its **Sharing** tab in the **Properties** dialog box. **Locally installed** means that Windows communicates with the print device directly over the relevant port. It does not matter whether the port is wired (USB, serial, or Ethernet) or wireless (Bluetooth or Wi-Fi). Drivers for different operating systems can also be installed locally so that clients can obtain the appropriate driver when they connect to the print share.

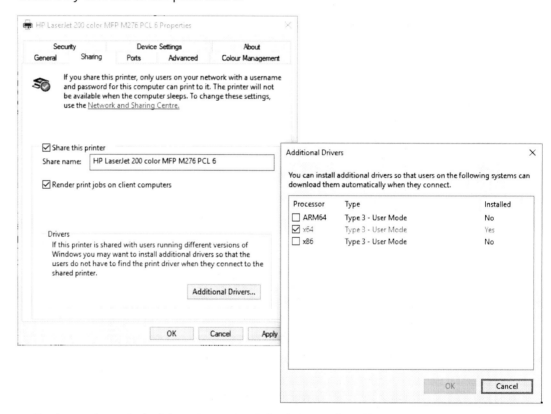

Sharing a printer via the Printer Properties dialog box. Use the Additional Drivers button from the Sharing page to install drivers for operating systems other than the host print server. (Screenshot used with permission from Microsoft.)

 Note: *When you configure sharing, only one PC should be designated as the server for any one print device. If multiple PCs try to act as the server for the same print device, the result will be confusion.*

If the network has clients running a mix of different operating systems, you need to consider how to make a printer driver available for each supported client. If the printer supports a "Type 3" driver, you need only add x86 (32-bit Windows) and/or x64 (64-bit Windows) support. For earlier "Type 2" drivers, each specific Windows version requires its own driver.

Note: Windows 8 and 10 add support for Type 4 drivers. These are designed to move towards a print class driver framework, where a single driver will work with multiple devices. Where a specific print device driver is required, the client obtains it from Windows Update rather than the print server.

SHARED PRINTER CONNECTIONS

An ordinary user can connect to a network printer (assuming that the printer administrator has given them permissions to use it). One way of doing this is to browse through the network resources using the **Network** object in **File Explorer**. Open the server computer hosting the printer, then right-click the required printer and select **Connect**.

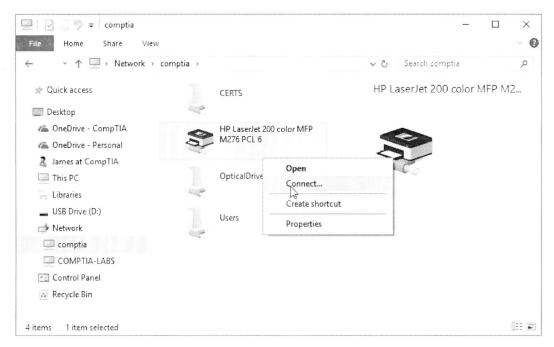

Connecting to a network printer via File Explorer. (Screenshot used with permission from Microsoft.)

INTEGRATED HARDWARE PRINT SERVERS/NAS

Some printers come with integrated or embedded print server hardware and firmware, allowing client computers to connect to them over the network without having to go via a server computer. You can also purchase print servers or use a solution such as a Network Attached Storage (NAS) appliance that supports print sharing. Many wireless Internet routers can be configured to work as a NAS/print server solution.

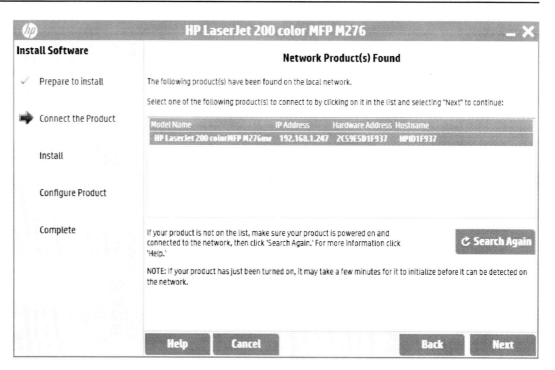

Installing a network printer using a vendor tool. The printer has been connected to the network via an Ethernet cable and been assigned an IP address by a DHCP server.

 Note: *You can also purchase external print servers, such as HP's Jetdirect, that connect to a USB port on the printer and to the network via a standard port.*

In place of a standard network card, a printer could be fitted with a Wi-Fi wireless adapter to make it available in a wireless network.

A network printer needs to be configured so that it has a valid address. On an IP network, you might set the printer to obtain an address automatically via a Dynamic Host Configuration Protocol (DHCP) server or configure it with a static IP address and subnet mask. The printer will need to communicate with computers over one or more Transmission Control Protocol (TCP) or User Datagram Protocol (UDP) network ports. If a network connection cannot be established, verify that these ports are not being blocked by a firewall or other security software.

Most printers provide a mechanism for locally configuring the printer. Usually, this is by means of a menu system which you navigate by using an LCD display and adjacent buttons or a touchscreen on the front of the printer.

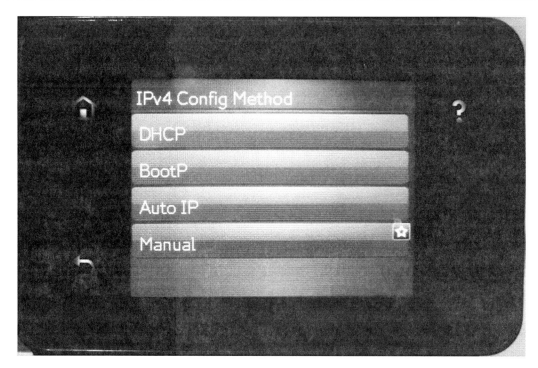

Setting the IP address configuration method via the printer's control panel.

This method is suitable for small office environments where you have few printers to manage. It is also useful in troubleshooting situations when the printer is inaccessible from the network. However, the printer vendor will usually supply a web-based utility to discover and manage their printers, whereas more advanced management suites are available for enterprise networks.

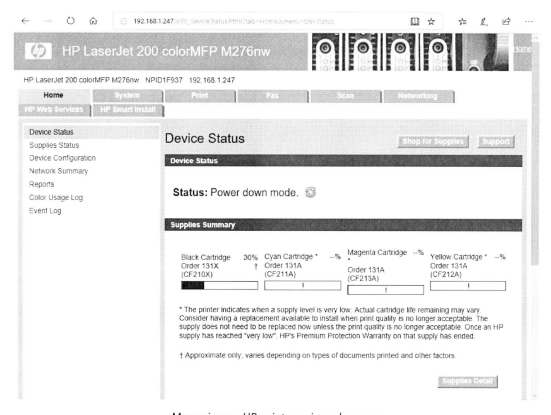

Managing an HP printer using a browser.

CLOUD AND REMOTE PRINTING

A networked printer can also be made available over the web using the HyperText Transfer Protocol (HTTP) and Internet Printing Protocol (IPP). For example, on an HP printer, you can use the management console to enable web services. This allows users to print to the device via HP's ePrint Center using a specially configured print path for the printer (identified by an email address). Alternatively, you could use third-party software, such as Google's Cloud Print™, which can connect to cloud-ready printers or support cloud printing for legacy devices.

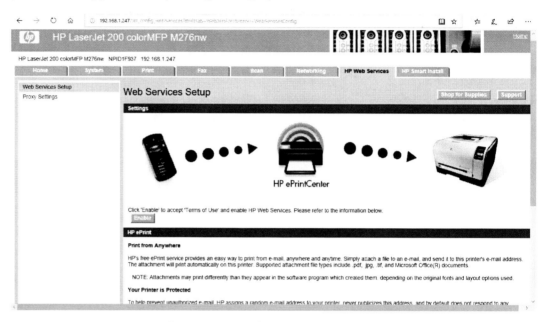

Configuring ePrint web services on an HP printer.

Users can send documents to the printer by logging into the cloud service. There are apps to support mobile devices as well as PCs and laptops.

Bonjour/AirPrint

You may also want to configure a network printer to support clients other than Windows. One option is to enable the **Bonjour** service to allow macOS PCs and iOS mobile devices to connect by using Apple **AirPrint**.

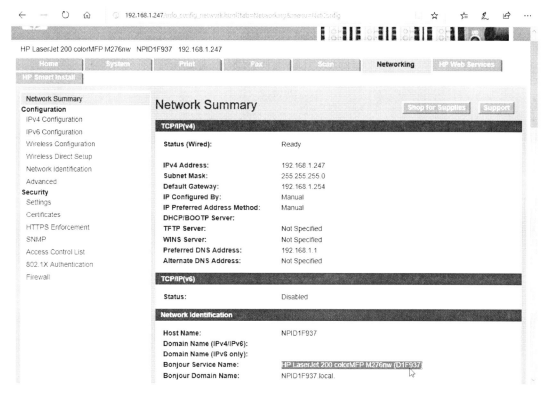

Bonjour services have been configured on this printer allowing macOS and iOS devices to connect to it wirelessly (using Apple AirPrint).

Bonjour is the server part of the solution, while AirPrint provides the client connectivity. Through Bonjour, users can locate printers and file servers. It uses DNS service records to locate the devices offering print and file sharing services. AirPrint is part of the macOS and iOS operating systems and supported by most third-party applications and apps.

The printer can be used from iOS when connected to the same network.

DATA PRIVACY AND SECURITY ISSUES

Show Slide(s)
Data Privacy and Security Issues

You should be aware of some of the data privacy and security issues exposed by shared printers:

- **Hard drive caching**—most printers have a local storage device to use to cache print files. Someone with access to the device could be able to recover confidential information from the hard drive cache.
- **User authentication**—it may be necessary to prevent unauthorized use of a network or cloud-based printer. In a Windows network, the permissions system can be used to control access to the printer. Cloud-based services can also be configured to require user authentication.
- **Data privacy**—jobs sent over a network (such as via a cloud or remote print service) could potentially be intercepted and read, copied, or modified.

 *Note: To learn more, check the **Video** tile on the CHOICE Course screen for any videos that supplement the content for this lesson.*

 Access the Checklist tile on your CHOICE Course screen for reference information and job aids on How to Install and Configure Printers.

Activity 17-4

Discussing Printer Installation and Configuration

Show Slide(s)

Activity: Discussing Printer Installation and Configuration

SCENARIO

Answer the following questions to check your understanding of the topic.

1. **When you are purchasing a new printer, what would you need to decide between as you evaluate connections?**

   Almost all new printers use USB, so the main consideration would be whether you needed support for a wireless or Ethernet connection.

2. You use three Windows applications that need to print to a Canon BJC-4300 printer.

   How many printer drivers must you install?

   One. Applications rely on the operating system to mediate access to devices. They do not need their own drivers.

3. You are setting up a print server and want to enable access for the widest range of Windows 7 machines possible.

   Should you install separate drivers for the Home and Enterprise editions?

   No—there is no difference between editions in this regard. You do need to install drivers for x86 (32-bit) and x64 (64-bit) versions, though.

4. **What tool can you use to confirm that basic print functionality is available?**

   Print a test page by using the option in the setup wizard or on the **General** tab of the **Printer Properties** dialog box.

5. You have installed an automatic duplex unit in an office laser printer.

   What configuration setting would you change to make the unit available for print jobs?

   From **Devices and Printers** or **Settings**, select **Printer Properties** and then select the **Device Settings** tab. Select the **Duplex Unit** setting and select **Installed**.

6. **True or false? When you print 10 copies of an uncollated job, 10 copies of page one are printed, followed by 10 copies of page two, then 10 copies of page three, and so on.**

   True.

7. **True or false? To enable printer sharing via Windows, the print device must be connected to the Windows PC via an Ethernet or Wi-Fi link.**

   False—any print device can be shared via printer properties. The print device can be connected to the Windows print server over USB, Bluetooth, Ethernet, or Wi-Fi. Other clients connect to the printer via the share, however, so the Windows PC must be kept on to facilitate printing.

8. **What configuration information does a user need to use a print device connected to the same local network?**

   The print device's IP address or host name. You might note that vendor utilities can search for a connected device on the local network, so "None" could also be a correct answer.

9. **What service should a network print device run to enable an Apple iPad to use the device over Wi-Fi?**

   The Bonjour service.

Activity 17-5
Installing and Configuring Printers

BEFORE YOU BEGIN

Complete this activity on your WORKBENCH PC. Check with your instructor for extra instructions.

SCENARIO

In the first part of this activity, you will compare and contrast various printers and print processes. There are several printers that are currently not deployed in your organization that are being stored in the IT department inventory cages. In order to determine which ones you will need when the time comes to replace currently deployed printers, you want to examine these printers to identify the features of each. You will then fill out a chart to identify which printers have which features.

In the second part of this activity, you will install and configure a printer. If a physical printer is not available, you can install a PostScript driver, which can be used to create print files that can be sent to any PostScript print device.

1. Examine the printers available to you, then fill out the following table. (Use the space on the bottom half of the page if necessary.)

Printer Type	Creates Images Using	Connection Method	Paper Handling Mechanism

2. Install a physical print device. If necessary, install the printer's driver software before connecting the print device.

   Your instructor will provide you with a print device and the necessary cabling.

Show Slide(s)
Activity: Installing and Configuring Printers

Teaching Tip
Printing is an important topic on the exam, so if at all possible try to arrange for some actual printers for learners to install and use.

You will probably need to arrange learners in groups, with one driving the PC and a partner or two watching.

If you have time and enough print devices, ask learners to uninstall and disconnect the printer, then swap the devices around.

Teaching Tip
Make sure you have a variety of printer types, so learners can examine the printers to identify the similarities and differences between them.

Interaction Opportunity
If time is available, have learners briefly discuss the similarities and differences among the available printer types.

Teaching Tip
Point out that this is the first step in the installation portion of the activity.

a) If the printer comes with setup software that guides you through the installation process, follow the guided setup process.

b) Connect the power cable to an electrical outlet and switch on the print device.

c) Connect the printer cable to the appropriate port on the PC.

You should hear a notification chime. Windows should locate the driver files and install the printer.

d) Click in the **Instant Search** box and type *printers*. Select the **Printers & scanners** link.

e) If your printer is not listed, select **Add a printer or scanner**.

f) If the printer is still not located, select the **The printer or scanner I want isn't listed** link.

g) Try the **My printer is a little older option** first. If this does not work, try **Add a local printer or network printer with manual settings**.

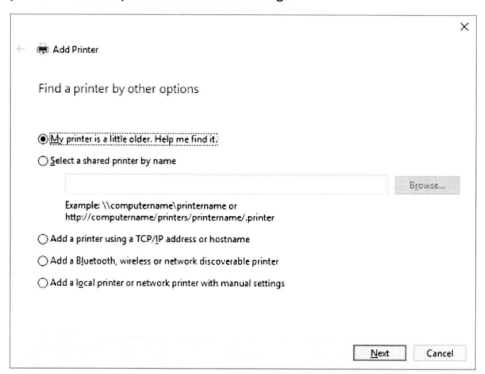

The Add Printer wizard—the wizard will usually detect any local or network printers available. (Screenshot used with permission from Microsoft.)

3. Install a driver to support Print to File.

If a physical print device is not available, you can install a printer driver configured to output to a file.

a) Click in the **Instant Search** box and type *printers*. Select the **Printers & scanners** link.

b) Select **Add a printer or scanner**. When it appears, select the **The printer or scanner I want isn't listed** link.

The **Add Printer** wizard starts.

c) Select **Add a local printer or network printer with manual settings** and select **Next**.

d) From the **Use an existing port** box, select **FILE** and select **Next**.

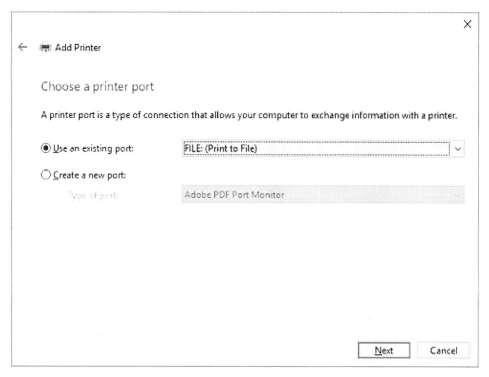

Configuring a printer to direct output to a file, rather than a device port. (Screenshot used with permission from Microsoft.)

e) From the **Manufacturer** box, select **Microsoft**, and then from the **Printers** box, select **Microsoft PS Class Driver**.

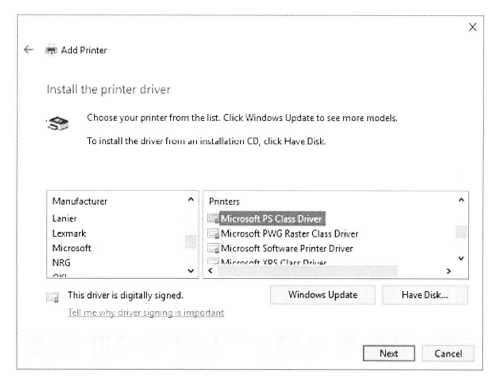

Selecting a printer make and model manually. (Screenshot used with permission from Microsoft.)

f) Select **Next**.

g) Select **Next**.

h)   Accept the default **Printer name** and select **Next**.

The printer driver files will be installed.

i)   Select **Do not share this printer**, then select **Next**.

j)   Select **Finish**.

4.   Pause the print queue.

a)   If necessary, open **Printers & scanners** again.

b)   Observe the message on the printer indicating that it is the default.

c)   Select the printer and then select the **Manage** button.

This shows status information and presents configuration options.

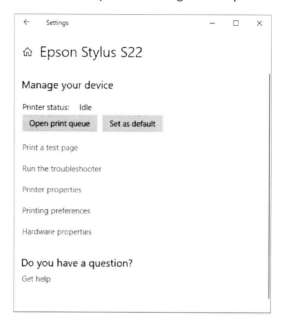

Device settings for an Epsom inkjet printer. (Screenshot used with permission from Microsoft.)

d)   Select **Open print queue** to open the print queue.

e)   Select **Printer→Pause Printing**.

 Note: You will not be able to pause a virtual printer (when printing to a file).

f)   Leave the print queue open.

5.   View the print device's preferences, and configure it to use draft mode output.

a)   Switch back to the **Printers & scanners** app, and select **Printing preferences**.

b)   Configure the following options (most options will not be available if you configured the Print to File option):

• Paper size: select **Letter**.

• Paper type: select **plain paper** in the auto-feeder tray.

• Print quality: set to **Draft/300 dpi**.

c)   Select **OK**.

6.   Print a test page.

a)   Right-click the printer and select **Printer properties**.

 *Note: Select **Printer properties** not **Hardware properties**, as the latter option opens a different dialog box (Device Manager properties).*

b) Look through the options on the various tabs, then select the **General** tab and select **Print Test Page**. If you are printing to a file, save the file as ***test.oxps*** in the **Documents** folder.

c) Select **Close** to dismiss the message. Select **OK** to close the dialog box.

7. View the print queue and the printer's spool folder.

a) Switch to the print queue and observe the job waiting for the print device to come online.

Observing the print queue. (Screenshot used with permission from Microsoft.)

b) In Explorer, open **C:\Windows\System32\Spool\PRINTERS**. If necessary, select **Continue** at the UAC prompt to get access to the folder. Observe the spooled job.

c) Open another Explorer window and browse the **C:\COMPTIA-LABS\LABFILES** folder. Right-click the **comptia-logo.jpg** picture and select **Print** then confirm with **Print** again. If you are printing to a file, save it as ***sample.oxps*** in the **Documents** folder.

d) Verify that the spooled files are listed in the **PRINTERS** folder.

e) Verify that the printer is correctly loaded with paper.

f) In the print queue, right-click the **Full page photo** job and select **Pause**. Select **Printer→Pause Printing**.

g) When the job has printed, collect it from the printer.

h) Look at the spooled files again—verify that they are now either 0 KB or deleted.

i) Switch back to the print queue, right-click the **Full page photo** job, and select **Cancel**. Confirm by selecting **Yes**.

j) Check the **PRINTERS** folder again—the spooled files should no longer be displayed.

k) If you are printing to a file, browse the XPS format documents created in the **Documents** folder.

8. Uninstall the printer.

a) Disconnect the printer from the port and switch it off.

b) Look at **Printers & settings**.

The printer should be listed as offline.

c) Select the printer and select **Remove device**. Select **Yes** to confirm.

d) Verify that another printer (if present) is automatically selected as the new default.

e) If you installed the printer software, open **Settings→Apps→Apps & features**. Select the printer software and select **Uninstall**. Work through the remaining prompts to remove the software.

Topic E

Troubleshoot Print Device Issues

EXAM OBJECTIVES COVERED
1001-5.6 Given a scenario, troubleshoot printers.

Teaching Tip

As with other troubleshooting topics, remind learners to apply the CompTIA troubleshooting methodology as they consider specific symptoms.

Show Slide(s)

Printer Connectivity Troubleshooting

Teaching Tip

Run through these scenarios with learners so that they understand the appropriate response to each.

As a support professional, you will be well aware that one of the most unpleasant problems for users is being unable to print. If users need hard copies of documents and the systems do not work, it can be very frustrating. Users will look to you to identify and resolve their problems quickly, so you will need to recognize common issues and to correct them efficiently when they occur.

PRINTER CONNECTIVITY TROUBLESHOOTING

Printers are usually simple devices to troubleshoot, as in most cases there will be an error message or code displayed on the printer's control panel telling you exactly where the error lies. You may need to look the error code up in the printer documentation to confirm what it means. Use the error code to guide your troubleshooting efforts.

USING PRINTER LOGS

You could also check for multiple failed jobs in the print server's log. For example, in Windows, use Event Viewer to open the **Applications and Services→Microsoft→Windows→Print Service→Operational** log.

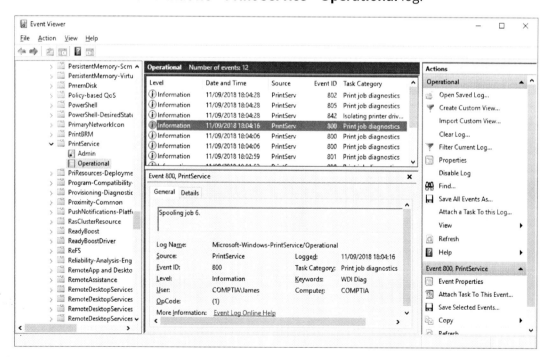

Viewing print service informational messaging—any errors would appear here, too. (Screenshot used with permission from Microsoft.)

Note: *You need to right-click to enable the **Print Service—Operational** log before it starts recording events. Consider creating an administrative alert for error events so that you can be warned of and investigate problems quickly.*

You may also be able to collect error logs from the device itself. Management software will be able to retrieve these logs and report them to a centralized console. Alternatively, you can view them manually using a vendor-supplied tool, such as the management URL for this HP printer.

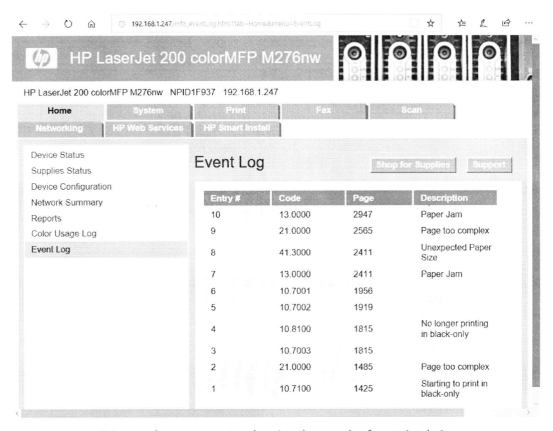

Using a web management tool to view the event log for a print device.

GENERAL TROUBLESHOOTING APPROACH

In the absence of any error code or descriptive error log, remember to test obvious things first:

- Is the printer switched on and loaded with paper?
- Is there sufficient ink or toner?
- Is the connection between the printer and PC good?
- Can you print a test page by using the printer's control panel and from within Windows?

 Show Slide(s)
General Troubleshooting Approach

Also check environmental conditions—a printer may malfunction if it overheats. Check that there is plenty of space around the printer for air to circulate (especially around the vents on the printer case) and that the environment is not excessively hot.

Remember to ask: "What has changed?" It is important to establish whether something has never worked or has just stopped working. If something never worked, then there has been an installation error; if something has stopped working, look for a configuration change or maintenance issue.

Note: Also remember that Windows has several built-in troubleshooting tools, one of which covers printer problems.

GUIDELINES FOR TROUBLESHOOTING PRINT DEVICE ISSUES

 Show Slide(s)
Guidelines for Troubleshooting Print Device Issues

 *Note: All of the Guidelines for this lesson are available as checklists from the **Checklist** tile on the CHOICE Course screen.*

Consider these guidelines as you troubleshoot printing problems in Windows.

NO IMAGE ON THE PRINTER DISPLAY

If there is no image on the printer display but the printer's power LED is lit:

- Verify that the printer has not gone into a power-saving sleep cycle. Pressing the power button or pressing the touchscreen will generally wake the printer.
- Try powering down the printer. Remove the power cord and any peripheral cables, and leave the printer switched off and unplugged for at least a minute. Then reconnect and restart the printer.
- If these steps do not resolve the issue, there is likely to be a hardware fault.

NO CONNECTIVITY

If documents do not print or if you see "Not available" messages relating to the printer you want to use:

- Verify that the printer is switched on and "online." A printer can be taken offline quite easily by pressing the button on the control panel. Often this happens by accident. A printer may also go offline because it is waiting for user intervention or because it has received corrupt print job data.
- Also check the connection between the host PC and printer. Make sure connectors are secure, that the network configuration is correct, or that there are no sources of interference blocking a wireless link, for instance.

 Note: Remember, cycling the power is a time-honored response to most troubleshooting scenarios involving end-user devices.

PRINT QUEUE AND SPOOLER TROUBLESHOOTING

 Show Slide(s)
Print Queue and Spooler Troubleshooting (3 slides)

A **backed-up print queue** means that there are lots of jobs pending but not printing. This might occur because the printer is offline or out of paper or ink/toner. It could also occur because of an error processing a particular print job. If a particular job will not print:

- Open the **Devices and Printers** applet or Windows **Settings** to access the printer and open its print queue. Try restarting the job (right-click the document name and select **Restart**). You need permission to **Manage Documents** on the printer object to restart or cancel jobs.
- If that does not work, delete the print job and try printing it again.
- Many problems, including "Low memory" or "Out of memory" errors, can also be solved by cycling the power on the printer and clearing a backed up print queue.

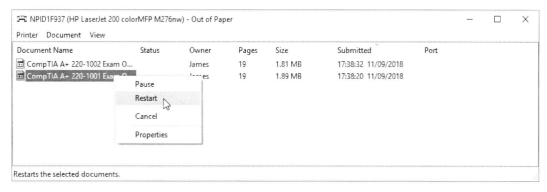

Use the print queue to manage jobs—in this instance, you should be loading the printer with some paper, rather than trying to restart the print job. (Screenshot used with permission from Microsoft.)

If you cannot delete a job (if the print queue is backed up or stalled), you will need to stop the **Print Spooler** service.

1. Open the **Computer Management** console, then expand **Services and Applications** and select **Services**.

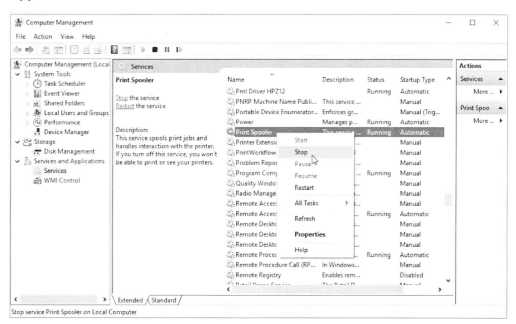

Managing the spooler service using the Computer Management console. (Screenshot used with permission from Microsoft.)

2. Right-click the **Print Spooler** service and select **Stop**.
3. Use Explorer to delete the spooled file from **%SystemRoot%\System32\Spool \Printers**. There will be a *.SPL file (the print job) and possibly a *.SHD file (status information), too.
4. Start the **Print Spooler** service again.

Alternatively, you can use `net` commands to manage the spooler service. Enter the commands `net stop spooler` and `net start spooler` in the **Run** dialog box or at a command prompt.

Another option is to try using different spool settings. Spool settings can be configured on the **Advanced** tab of the **Properties** dialog box. You might want to change these settings if there are problems spooling jobs. This page also lets you set the spooled file type between EMF and RAW (select **Print Processor**). In the **Printer Properties** dialog box, change the spool settings as follows, testing after each change:

*   Change the spool data format to **RAW**.

- Turn off spooling (select **Print directly to printer**).

Also verify that there is plenty of free disk space on the volume hosting the spooler.

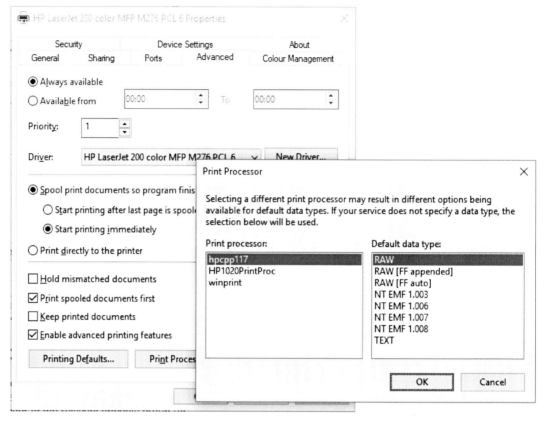

Spool and Print Processor settings in Printer Properties.

PERMISSION ISSUES TROUBLESHOOTING

Show Slide(s)

Permission Issues Troubleshooting

There are several scenarios where permission issues can affect a user's ability to print documents.

ACCESS DENIED

If a user is accessing a printer that has been shared over a network, an **Access Denied** message means that the user account has not been configured with permission to print documents. Add the user to the relevant security group (or add the relevant security group or user object to the printer).

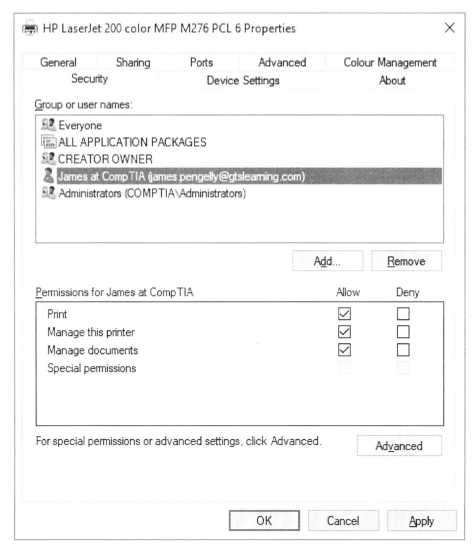

Configure print device permissions on the Security tab in the Printer Properties dialog box.

If the permissions are correct, verify that security software is not causing a problem by trying to scan the spool folder, and verify the permissions on the spool folder itself. You might also investigate the disk hosting the printer spool to ensure there is no problem there.

UNABLE TO INSTALL PRINTER

If a user cannot install a printer, it is likely to be because their account does not have sufficient permissions to install the printer driver. This sort of operation will normally have to be performed by an administrator, though it is possible to configure network security policies that allow users to install printers with signed drivers.

If the problem is not related to permissions, verify that you are attempting to install a driver for the correct version and type of Windows. In particular, remember that 32-bit printer drivers will not work with a 64-bit edition of Windows.

Also verify that the print spooler service is started.

 Note: There's also the possibility that existing printer drivers are interfering with the one you're trying to install. Uninstall these other drivers, then try installing the new one. If you need these older drivers for other printers, try removing them from the default printer status, then install the new printer driver as the default.

Show
Slide(s)

Driver and Garbled
Output Issues

DRIVER AND GARBLED OUTPUT ISSUES

If a print job contains high-resolution graphics or multiple pages and printing is very slow, bear in mind that the printer may not have sufficient resources to handle the job and may display an error such as **Low memory** or **Out of memory**.

- Try clearing the print queue and sending the job again or cycling power on the printer.
- If there are persistent problems with printing from a specific application, check the vendor's troubleshooting website to determine if a driver update will fix the problem.

Use the printer's property sheet to print a test page. If the test page prints successfully, then the problem is related to the print function of a particular application. Try printing a different file from the same application; if this works, then you know that the problem is specific to a particular file. If the test page does not print, try using the printer's control panel to print it. If this works, there is some sort of communication problem between the print device and Windows.

One of the first options when trying to remedy most types of software print problem is to update the driver to the latest version or use a different driver (PostScript instead of PCL, for instance). Also check that the correct job options have been set (media type, input tray, duplex printing, monochrome or color, economy mode, and so on). Remember that print properties set through the application (by selecting **File→Print→Properties→Print Setup**) override those set as the default (either through the Printer object in Windows or through the device's control panel).

If a print job is garbage (if it emits many pages with a few characters on each or many blank pages):

1. Cancel the print job.
2. Clear the print queue.
3. Cycle the power on the printer (leaving it off for 30 seconds to clear the memory).
4. Try to print again.

If the problem persists, update the printer driver and check that the printer is set to use the correct control language (PCL or PostScript). You can also try changing the spool type from EMF to RAW or disabling spooling.

If printing is slow, use the **Advanced** property page to choose the **Start printing immediately** option. You can try changing the spool format from RAW to EMF.

If the characters in a document are different from those expected or if strange characters appear in an otherwise normal print, check that **fonts** specified in the document are available on the PC and/or printer. The software application should indicate whether the specified font is available or whether it is substituting it for the nearest match.

To view fonts installed on the computer, open the **Fonts** applet in Control Panel/ Windows **Settings**. Each font family (such as Arial) often comes with a number of variants (such as Bold or Italic). If you open a font icon, a preview of the font at different sizes is shown. If a font is not shown here, use the **File** menu to locate and install it. Fonts are usually located in **C:\Windows\Fonts**, but some font manager applications may store fonts in another location.

Note: Most fonts require a license—you should not copy them between computers without making the proper licensing arrangements.

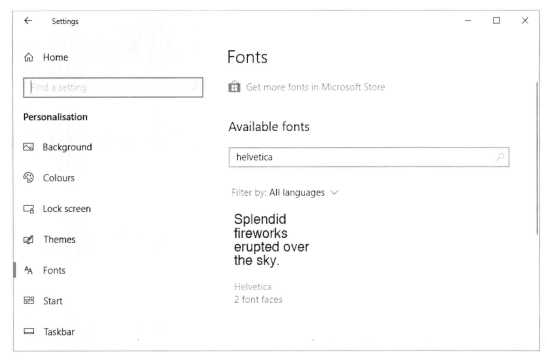

If characters do not appear correctly, check that the proper fonts are installed. (Screenshot used with permission from Microsoft.)

A PostScript printer may use internal fonts in preference to those installed on the PC. Check **Printing Preferences** to confirm that the printer is not using font substitution.

GENERAL PRINT DEFECT RESOLUTION

If a job prints from Windows but the output is smudged, faded, or arrives with unusual marks (print defects), the problem is likely to be a printer hardware or media fault. This section describes some of the common faults likely to be encountered. Always consult the manufacturer's documentation and troubleshooting notes.

Show Slide(s)

General Print Defect Resolution

Note: Working inside any electrical equipment, especially a laser printer, can be dangerous. If the cause of a problem is not easily found, you must seek advice from a qualified source. You should never defeat a safety interlock in order to operate a printer with protective covers removed.

A **paper jam** is one of the most frequently occurring printer problems.

Fixing a paper jam is usually quite straightforward. The key point is to gain proper access to the stuck page. Do not use force to try to remove a sheet as you may cause further damage. Most sheets will pull free from most parts of the printer, but if a page is stuck in the fuser unit of a laser printer, you must use the release levers to get it out. Pulling the paper forcibly through the fuser can damage the rollers and, if the paper rips, leave paper debris on them.

If paper jams are frequent, you need to diagnose the problem, rather than simply fix the symptom each time. Most paper jams arise because the media (paper or labels) are not suitable for the printer or because a sheet is creased, folded, or not loaded properly in the tray. There could be a problem with a roller, too. Identify whether or not the jam occurs in the same place each time, and take appropriate preventive maintenance (clean or replace the part).

The printer control panel should identify the location of the paper jam.

If paper is not feeding into the printer or if the printer is feeding multiple sheets at the same time, verify that it is loaded in the tray properly and that it is of an appropriate weight (not too thick or thin). If you can discount a media problem, try changing the pickup rollers. In a laser printer, these are part of the maintenance kit.

 Note: *Fan the edge of a paper stack with your thumb to separate the sheets before loading the tray. Do not overdo this however—you can generate a static charge that will hold the sheets together.*

LASER PRINTER PRINT DEFECTS

Show Slide(s)

Laser Printer Print Defects

The causes of print defects tend to be specific to the technology used by the imaging process. The following defects are common in laser printers:

- **Faded or faint prints**—if a simple cause such as the user choosing an option for low density (draft output) can be discounted, this is most likely to indicate that the toner cartridge needs replacing.
- **Blank pages**—as noted earlier, this is usually an application or driver problem, but it could indicate that a toner cartridge has been installed without removing its packing seals. Alternatively, if these simple causes can be discounted, this could also be a sign that the transfer roller (or secondary corona wire) is damaged (the image transfer stage fails).
- **Skewed output**—verify that the paper is inserted correctly and that media guides are well-positioned (not too tight and not too loose).
- **White stripes**—this indicates either that the toner is poorly distributed (give the cartridge a gentle shake) or that the transfer roller is dirty or damaged.
- **Black stripes or whole page black**—indicates that the primary transfer roller is dirty or damaged or that the High Voltage Power Supply to the developer unit is malfunctioning.
- **Toner specks**—if the output is "speckled," loose toner may be getting onto the paper. Clean the inside of the printer using an approved toner vacuum.
- **Persistent marks**—streaks, vertical or horizontal lines, and other marks that appear in the same place (referred to as repetitive defects) are often due to dirty

feed rollers (note that there are rollers in the toner cartridge and fuser unit, too) or a damaged or dirty photosensitive drum.

- **Toner not fused to paper**—if the output smudges easily, this indicates that the fuser needs replacing.
- **Wavy or wrinkled output**—make sure the paper is inserted correctly (try turning the stack over).
- **Ghost images**—this is a sign that the photosensitive drum has not been cleaned properly. The drum is smaller than the size of a sheet of paper, so if the image is not completely cleared it will repeat as a light "ghost" or dark "shadow" image farther down the page. Images may also appear from previous prints. Try printing a series of different images and see if the problem resolves itself. If not, replace the drum/toner cartridge.
- **Wrong color/color cast**—if prints come out in the wrong color (for example, if the whole print has a magenta tint), ensure that the toner cartridges have been installed in the correct location (for instance, that a Magenta cartridge hasn't been installed in the Cyan slot). Also ensure that there is sufficient toner in each cartridge. If there is a cast or shadow-like effect, one or all of the cartridges, rollers, or transfer belt are probably misaligned. Try reseating them and then run the printer calibration utility, and print a test page to verify the problem is solved.
- **Color missing**—if a color is completely missing, try replacing the cartridge. If this does not solve the issue, clean the contacts between the printer and cartridge.
- **Paper jams**—if the media and pickup rollers are good and if the jam occurs within the drum assembly but before the image is fused, the cause could be a faulty Static Eliminator Strip. Normally, this removes the high static charge from the paper as it leaves the transfer unit. If the strip fails, the paper may stick to the drum or curl as it enters the fuser unit.

*Note: To learn more, check the **Video** tile on the CHOICE Course screen for any videos that supplement the content for this lesson.*

INKJET AND DOT MATRIX PRINT DEFECTS

Defects in inkjet and dot matrix output tend to be concentrated around print head and media issues.

Show Slide(s)

Inkjet and Dot Matrix Print Defects

INKJET PRINTERS

Lines running through printouts indicate a dirty print head or blocked ink nozzle, which can usually be fixed by running a cleaning cycle. Most other print quality problems (output that smears easily, wavy or wrinkled output, or blurry output) is likely to be a media problem. As with laser printers, persistent marks on output probably indicate a dirty feed roller. If the print head jams, the printer will probably display a status message or show a flashing LED. Try turning the printer off and unplugging it then turning it back on. Inconsistent color output indicates that one of the ink reservoirs is running low (or that a print head for one of the color cartridges is completely blocked). If a document does not print in color, check that color printing has actually been selected.

DOT MATRIX PRINTERS

Lines in the output indicate a stuck pin in the print head. Output can also be affected by the platen position. The platen adjusts the gap between the paper and the print head to accommodate different paper types. Incorrect adjustment of the platen gap can cause faint printing (gap too wide) or smudging (too narrow). On more sophisticated printers, the platen gap is adjusted automatically. Use an Isopropyl Alcohol solution to clean the print head if necessary.

Activity 17-6
Troubleshooting Printer Issues

 Show Slide(s)

Activity: Troubleshooting Printer Issues

SCENARIO

Answer the following questions to check your understanding of the topic.

1. A user reports that the printed output is not up to the usual standards for her printer. You will need to resolve this issue so she can print her report.

   What is the overall process for troubleshooting this issue?

   Print out a test page to see if you can reproduce the problem the user reported. If you see the same problem as reported by the user, identify the print defect, based on the type of printer, to resolve the problem. Document the steps you took to resolve the problem.

2. **If print jobs do not appear at the printer and the queue is clear, what could you try first to solve the problem?**

   Cycle the power on the printer.

3. **Where on disk is the print file spooled in Windows?**

   %SystemRoot%\System32\Spool\Printers.

4. You need to restart the Print Spooler service on a Windows 7 machine. You have logged on as Administrator.

   What are your next steps?

   Right-click **Computer** and select **Manage**. Select **Services and Applications→Services**. Right-click **Print Spooler** and select **Restart**.

5. **How would you track down the source of a paper jam?**

   Check the error message reported by the printer (this may be shown on the printer's console). It may indicate the location of the stuck pages. Otherwise, visually inspect the various feed and output mechanisms.

6. **What should you do if you cannot delete a job stuck in the print queue?**

   Stop the print spooler service, delete the spooled file, then restart the spooler.

7. Paper is jamming in an inkjet printer.

   What could be causing this?

   The paper might not be loaded squarely, there might be too much paper loaded into the tray, or the paper is creased or dirty.

8. **What effect does a worn photosensitive drum have on printing?**

   Faint printing.

9. A laser printer is producing white stripes on the paper.

   What could be causing this?

   Poorly distributed toner or a damaged/worn transfer corona wire. If the secondary corona does not apply a charge evenly across the paper, less toner is attracted from the drum to the part of the sheet where charging failed. Note that if there are repetitive white or black marks (rather than stripes) that do not smudge, the issue is more likely to be dirt or grease on the drum.

10. **What effect does a dirty primary corona wire have on laser printing?**

    It leaves black stripes on the paper. If the charging corona does not apply the correct charge evenly to the drum, toner is attracted to the place where the charging failed, creating a black stripe all the way down the page.

Show Slide(s)

Activity: Maintaining and Troubleshooting Printers

 Teaching Tip

Make as many print devices and cleaning/maintenance kits and parts available as possible. Arrange learners in groups where necessary.

Troubleshooting Ideas:

- Connection Problem (Laser or Inkjet)—partially disconnect the cable at either end or use a doctored connector (simpler with old parallel ports [block off or disconnect any of pins 3-9] or RJ-45) to create a connectivity problem.
- "Cleaning" Issue (Laser Printer)—put tape over the HVPS contacts between the printer and toner cartridge.
- Supplies low (Any)—replace the print medium with worn out ink cartridge, toner cartridge, or ribbon.
- Paper Jam (Laser Printer)—use some Blu Tack to create paper jams at different points in the paper path.
- Economy Mode (Laser or Inkjet)—change printer default settings to use Draft/Economy mode and print a page.
- Print Density (Laser Printer)—change the print density to the lowest (or highest setting), making prints of graphics unusually dark or light.

Activity 17-7

Maintaining and Troubleshooting Printers

SCENARIO

Depending on the equipment available, in this activity, you will complete some routine maintenance and troubleshooting of printers.

1. Read the printer service documentation provided by your instructor carefully.

2. Complete a maintenance cycle on a print device. For example, on a laser printer, complete the following tasks:
   a) Remove the toner cartridge and maintenance kit components from the laser printer.
   b) Clean the laser printer using the approved products available.
   c) Replace the maintenance kit components and toner cartridge.

3. Print a test page using the printer's configuration panel. If available, print the configuration page, too.

4. Depending on the facilities available in your training center, your instructor will create one or more printer issues to troubleshoot. For each scenario, record what you think the problem is and what action you should take. After confirming with the instructor, complete your plan to resolve the problem.
   a) Issue #1
      Problem: _____
      Action: _____
   b) Issue #2
      Problem: _____
      Action: _____
   c) Issue #3
      Problem: _____
      Action: _____
   d) Issue #4
      Problem: _____
      Action: _____

Topic F

Install and Configure Imaging Devices

 EXAM OBJECTIVES COVERED
1001-3.6 Explain the purposes and uses of various peripheral types.

Printers are used to create output from a variety of sources. Some of those sources take the form of copying physical documents and photos. Another source might be from a barcode. Some printers include features that allow you to copy or scan an item to bring it into the computer as a file, or to take it directly from the source to output from the printer. In this topic, you will look at a variety of scanning devices.

IMAGING DEVICES

In a previous lesson, you learned about some imaging devices such as digital cameras and webcams. Another type of imaging device is scanners.

 Show Slide(s)
Imaging Devices

SCANNERS

A **scanner** is a digital imaging device, designed to create computer file data from a real-life object. Typically, scanners handle flat objects, like documents, receipts, or photographs. **Optical Character Recognition (OCR)** software can be used to convert scanned text into digital documents, ready for editing. Historically, scanners could be connected using the parallel port or via a SCSI bus. Nowadays, scanners are connected via USB or via an Ethernet network port (RJ-45) or wireless (Wi-Fi/802.11) network.

 Show Slide(s)
Scanners

FLATBED SCANNERS

A **flatbed scanner** works by shining a bright light, usually from a **Cold Cathode Fluorescent Lamp (CCFL)**, at the object, which is placed on a protective glass surface. A system of mirrors reflects the illuminated image of the object onto a lens. The lens either uses a prism to split the image into its component colors (Red, Green, and Blue) or focuses it onto imaging sensors coated with different color filters.

 Show Slide(s)
Flatbed Scanners

There are two main types of imaging sensor: **Charge Coupled Device (CCD)** and **Complementary Metal Oxide Semiconductor (CMOS)**. Most flatbed scanners use CCD-type sensors.

A flatbed scanner. (Image © 123RF.com.)

SHEET-FED AND ADF SCANNERS

Show Slide(s)

Sheet-Fed and ADF Scanners

Contact Image Sensor (CIS)-based scanners use an array of LEDs (Light Emitting Diodes) that strobe between red, green, and blue light to illuminate the image. This is reflected via a rod-shaped lens onto an image sensor. CIS scanners are typically used in **sheet-fed scanners**. In a sheet-fed scanner or the scan component of an **Automatic Document Feeder (ADF)**, rather than passing the scan head under the paper, the paper is passed over a fixed scan head.

This design is much more compact and often used in "all-in-one" type MultiFunction Devices (MFDs).

MULTI-FUNCTION DEVICES

Show Slide(s)

Multi-Function Devices

Teaching Tip

Ask participants what types of MFDs they have experience with, and what capabilities were available on the devices.

A **multi-function device (MFD)** is a piece of office equipment that performs the functions of a number of other specialized devices. MFDs typically include the functions of a printer, scanner, fax machine, and copier. However, there are MFDs that do not include fax functions. Although the multi-function device might not equal the performance or feature sets of the dedicated devices it replaces, multi-function devices are very powerful and can perform most tasks adequately and are an economical and popular choice for most home or small-office needs.

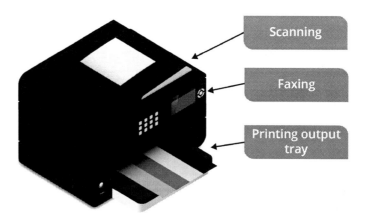

An MFD. (Image © 123RF.com.)

SCAN OPTIONS

When the scanner has been connected to the PC and configured by Plug-and-Play, it should become available to applications that can use the scan interface. Older scanners use **TWAIN**-based software; modern scanners are more likely to use **Windows Image Acquisition (WIA)**. The software will present options for the image output format (PDF or JPEG, for instance) and tools for selecting and correcting the image. Another option may be to use Optical Character Recognition (OCR) software to convert a text image into a computer-editable text document.

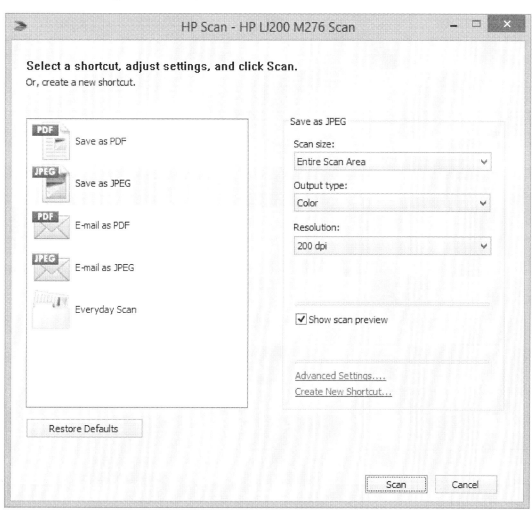

HP Scan image acquisition software.

Some scanners have the options available directly on the printer to specify what format to scan the item as, the resolution, and other options.

BARCODE SCANNERS

A **barcode scanner** is a handheld or pen-shaped device designed to scan barcodes. A barcode is a pattern of different sized parallel bars, typically representing a product number, such as an ISBN, IAN/EAN, or UPC. The reader uses a sensor mechanism (one of a photo diode, laser, or CCD) to read the intensity of light reflected back by the barcode. The reader then reports the number back to application software, which links it to a product database. Barcode scanners are connected to a computer using a USB port.

Show Slide(s)
Scan Options

Teaching Tip
Point out the figure shows options for a specific scanner and that options for other scanners might be different and will be presented in a different dialog box.

Teaching Tip
If learners ask, TWAIN is not an acronym. It's an archaic word meaning "two" or "couple" presented in caps to make it distinctive as the name for the API that was developed for scanner connectivity. Subsequently, someone came up with the expansion "Technology Without An Interesting Name," but that's not an official designation.

Show Slide(s)
Barcode Scanners

Teaching Tip
Some barcode scanners connect to a PC or tablet using PS/2, RS232, serial, or Wi-Fi or other wireless connections.

Teaching Tip
Learners won't need to know this for the exam, but if they ask, the expansions for the acronyms are:

- ISBN—International Standard Book Number.
- IAN/EAN—International/European Article Number, used for retail packaging.
- UPC—Universal Product Code, a particular type of IAN/EAN used more widely in the US and Canada

An example of a barcode scanner. (Image © 123RF.com.)

QR SCANNERS

Show Slide(s)

QR Scanners

Teaching Tip

Ask if anyone has used their smart phone to scan QR codes and where they found the codes. Some might find the codes in Cracker Jacks to play a game, in art museums to get more information about the art piece, or on in-store displays to get additional product information.

Quick Response (QR) codes are a particular type of **2D barcode** that have been widely adopted for consumer-oriented uses. A QR code can be scanned using a smart phone camera, a normal digital camera, or webcam. There is no need to install special barcode scanning hardware. QR code scanning software can identify a QR code image directly from the camera and initiate the appropriate response in software to the information contained in the QR code. This might be to open a website or import a contact record or calendar event.

 Note: *Actually, a camera can be used to scan any type of barcode if the software to identify and interpret the barcode is available.*

An example of a QR code you can scan with a QR scanner installed on your smart phone.

Note: *To learn more, check the* **Video** *tile on the CHOICE Course screen for any videos that supplement the content for this lesson.*

Access the Checklist tile on your CHOICE Course screen for reference information and job aids on How to Install and Configure Imaging Devices.

Activity 17-8

Discussing Imaging Device Installation and Configuration

Show Slide(s)

Activity: Discussing Imaging Device Installation and Configuration

Teaching Tip

If you have a scanner or MFD available, consider asking learners to install it and perform various types of scans (output to PDF, JPEG, and OCR, for instance).

SCENARIO

Answer the following questions to check your understanding of the topic.

1. **What type of connection interface is a scanner most likely to use?**

   All modern scanners will support USB. Some might have an Ethernet network port (RJ-45) or even wireless (Wi-Fi and/or Bluetooth), though this is more typical of Multifunction Devices (MFD) than standalone scanners.

2. **What type of sensor is used to capture an image for conversion to a digital file?**

   Charge Coupled Device (CCD) or Complementary Metal Oxide Semiconductor (CMOS).

3. **What is the function of OCR?**

   Optical Character Recognition (OCR) software can convert a scanned image of text into a digital text file that can be edited in a text editor or word processor.

4. **What type of imaging input device would be most useful for a Point-of-Sale (POS) system?**

   Barcode scanner.

5. **True or false? Any type of smartphone camera can be used to read a QR code.**

   True. The smartphone just needs to capture the image of the Quick Response (QR) code and be installed with software to decode it.

Summary

In this lesson, you supported printers. Because printers enable users to transfer digital information to paper, they are among the most commonly used devices in almost every type of computing environment. As an A+ certified professional, you can use the skills and knowledge from this lesson when you are called upon to install, configure, or troubleshoot printers

When would you recommend to users that they use laser printers? Inkjet printers? Impact printers? Thermal printers?

A: Answers will vary, but will likely include recommending laser printers for high volume needs, inkjet printers for casual low volume use, impact printers when speed rather than quality or the ability to print multi-part forms is needed, and thermal printers for POS terminals.

Which printer maintenance tasks have you performed, on which types of printers? Which maintenance tasks are most important in your organization? Why are they so important?

A: Answers will vary, but may include replacing toner cartridges, cleaning inside and outside of printers, printing a test page, and replacing paper. These tasks are important because they enable users to print when they need to. and they help extend the functional life of the printers.

 Practice Question: Additional practice questions are available on the CompTIA CHOICE platform within the Assessments tile.

Lesson 18

Implementing Operational Procedures

LESSON INTRODUCTION

As a CompTIA® A+® technician, you will be asked to install, configure, maintain, and correct problems with a variety of computer components and software. You will usually be performing this work within the context of a company's operational procedures. You have already explored procedures governing safe working practices, regulated data and content, incident response, and ways of using remote access to handle problems more efficiently.

Other types of operational procedures are designed to ensure the secure and efficient functioning of the IT system. Companies need documentation and change management procedures to keep the use of systems under control, potentially using scripting to ensure standardized configuration changes. They need plans to cope with disasters so that data loss and system downtime is minimized. They need to ensure the physical environment is optimized and does not present any health hazards. This lesson will help you to identify the technologies that underpin these important procedures.

LESSON OBJECTIVES

In this lesson, you will:

- Describe environmental impacts and controls.
- Create and maintain documentation.
- Use change management best practices.
- Implement disaster prevention and recovery methods.
- Describe basic scripting concepts.
- Use proper communication techniques and general professional attitude.

Topic A

Environmental Impacts and Controls

 EXAM OBJECTIVES COVERED
1002-4.3 Given a scenario, implement basic disaster prevention and recovery methods.
1002-4.5 Explain environmental impacts and appropriate controls.

 Teaching Tip

This topic should be straightforward. You may want to designate it for self-study. Focus on power protection in class.

 Show Slide(s)

Power Issues

While you explored personal safety previously, there is also the issue of environmental impacts on computer systems to consider. Computers need stable power supplies and are sensitive to excessive heat. As a CompTIA A+ technician, you must understand the use of controls to ensure the proper environmental conditions for IT systems.

POWER ISSUES

Environmental power problems such as surges, brownouts, and blackouts are caused by failures in the building power supply, rather than failures in the computer's power supply unit, AC adapter, or battery pack.

SURGES

A **surge** is an abrupt but brief change in the value of the voltage. It can last from a few billionths of a second (a transient) to a few thousandths of a second. A **spike** is a powerful surge, such as that caused by a lightning storm. A surge or spike can be caused by high power devices, such as machinery, being turned on or off. Many surges are very small and of too short a duration to cause problems, but some can take the supply several hundred volts over its normal value and cause sufficient interference to a computer's power supply to crash, reboot, or even damage it.

SAGS/BROWNOUTS

Some electrically powered devices require very high starting, or inrush, current. These include items with large motors, such as lifts, washing machines, or power tools, and transformers. When this kind of device is turned on, the large current surge into the device may cause the available voltage within the locality to dip for a brief period, causing a **sag**. Sags may also be caused by the switching of power distribution circuits by the generating companies. A power sag may only last for a few milliseconds but sags of longer than about 10 to 20 milliseconds can cause computer equipment to malfunction. If a sag lasts for longer than a second, it is often called a **brownout**. Overloaded or faulty building power distribution circuits sometimes cause brownouts.

BLACKOUTS

A complete power failure is called a **blackout**. A blackout may be caused by a disruption to the power distribution grid—an equipment failure or the accidental cutting of a cable during construction work, for example—or may simply happen because a fuse has blown or a circuit breaker has tripped.

POWER PROTECTION CONTROLS

 Show Slide(s)

Power Protection Controls (5 slides)

Computing devices of all types, including client systems, network appliances, and servers, require a stable power supply to operate. Electrical events such as voltage spikes or surges can crash computers and network appliances, while loss of power from brownouts or blackouts will cause equipment to fail. A range of power protection devices is available to mitigate these issues.

SURGE PROTECTOR

Passive protection devices can be used to filter out the effects of spikes and surges. The simplest **surge protector** or suppression devices come in the form of adapters, trailing sockets, or filter plugs, with the protection circuitry built into the unit. These devices offer low-cost protection to one or two pieces of equipment. Surge protectors are rated according to various national and international standards, including Underwriters Laboratory (UL) 1449. There are three important characteristics:

- **Clamping voltage**—defines the level at which the protection circuitry will activate, with lower voltages (400 V or 300 V) offering better protection.
- **Joules rating**—the amount of energy the surge protector can absorb, with 600 joules or more offering better protection. Each surge event will degrade the capability of the suppressor.
- **Amperage**—the maximum current that can be carried, or basically the number of devices you can attach. As a general rule of thumb, you should only use 80% of the rated capacity. For example, the devices connected to a 15 A protector should be drawing no more than 12 A. Of course, for domestic wiring, you should take care not to overload the building's power circuits in any case.

LINE CONDITIONERS

Larger industrial power filter units called **line conditioners** or **Power Distribution Units (PDUs)** can be used to protect entire power circuits from the effects of surges or brownouts, but they are unable to remove or reduce the effects of blackouts.

BATTERY BACKUPS AND UPS

Power redundancy means deploying systems to ensure that equipment is protected against blackout events so that both system and network operations can either continue uninterrupted or be recovered quickly. If there is loss of power, system operation can be sustained for a few minutes or hours, depending on load, by using **battery backup**. Battery backup can be provisioned at the component level for disk drives, RAID arrays, and memory modules. The battery protects any read or write operations cached at the time of power loss.

At the system level, an **Uninterruptible Power Supply (UPS)** will provide a temporary power source in the event of complete power loss. The time allowed by a UPS is sufficient to activate an alternative power source, such as a standby generator. If there is no alternative power source, a UPS will at least allow you to shut down the server or appliance properly. Users can save files and the operating system can complete the proper shutdown routines.

Example of a UPS. (Image by magraphics© 123RF.com.)

UPS SIZING

Teaching Tip

Explain why the inverter is needed. The PC's PSU is connected to the UPS and needs AC power to function.

In its simplest form, a UPS comprises a bank of batteries and their charging circuit, plus an inverter to generate AC voltage from the DC voltage supplied by the batteries. The capacity of the battery cells determines the amount of run-time a UPS can supply to any given load. This may range from a few minutes for a desktop-rated model to hours for an enterprise system. The power supplies in the computer equipment are connected to the ports on the UPS, then the UPS is connected to building power. There may also be a USB connection to facilitate monitoring and automated shutdown.

Factors to consider when purchasing a UPS include reliability, cost, uptime, maintenance, and system performance and features. Different UPS models support different power outputs and form factors, such as desktop or rack mounted, depending upon your needs. Determining an appropriate UPS to protect the load from a given system is called **UPS sizing**.

The maximum power rating (and hence cost) of a UPS is determined by the battery specification and the power handling of the inverter and other circuitry. Each UPS is rated according to the maximum VA (power) it can supply without overloading.

UPS Selector

Step 1: Define User Devices > Step 2: User Preferences > Step 3: Recommended Solutions

Compaq ProLiant 1600R

The maximum configuration for this model is described below. Please make any changes relevant to your configuration and user preferences, then submit this form to add this unit to your device list.

System Description

- ❷ Computer type — Mini Tower
- ❷ Monitor type — 14-15 inch LCD
- ❷ Processor type — Alpha 21164
- ❷ Number of Processors — 2
- ❷ No. of populated PCI slots — 0-2 Slots
- ❷ Internal Hard Drives — 6
- ❷ Total External Drives — 0
- ❷ Predominant Hard Drive Type — High RPM hard drive
- ❷ User Site Voltage — ☑ 100 ☑ 120 ☑ 200 ☑ 208 ☑ 230

- ❷ Plug Type: — NEMA 5-15P — To choose graphically click here

- ❷ No. of Power Cords: — 1
- ❷ Quantity — 1

❷ External Peripherals
- ☐ Cable/DSL Modem
- ☐ ISDN Adapter
- ☐ Cable/DSL Router
- ☐ Tape Drive
- ☐ CD/CD-R/CD-RW/DVD/DVD-R

Choosing the UPS—defining the computer and peripherals.

To calculate the required VA rating for a UPS, simply add up the VA ratings of all the equipment to be connected to the unit. These may be calculated by taking the number of watts used by each device and multiplying by 1.67.

> **Note:** *The 1.67 conversion factor is required because the power drawn by a component in a DC circuit is not the same as the power required from the AC circuit. This is caused by the operation of the capacitors in the PC power supply unit.*

Most UPS vendor websites have a configuration wizard, which you can complete to determine what the power output you require is and the UPS models that would suit. You can also specify the maximum duration of battery power (10 minutes, for instance), which enables you to determine how much charge the unit must be able to hold to supply your needs.

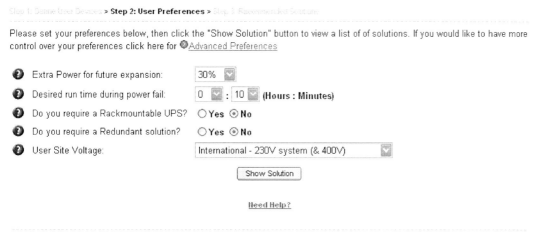

UPS Selector

Step 1: Define User Devices > **Step 2: User Preferences** > Step 3: Recommended Solutions

Please set your preferences below, then click the "Show Solution" button to view a list of of solutions. If you would like to have more control over your preferences click here for ❷ Advanced Preferences

- ❷ Extra Power for future expansion: — 30%
- ❷ Desired run time during power fail: — 0 : 10 **(Hours : Minutes)**
- ❷ Do you require a Rackmountable UPS? — ○ Yes ⦿ No
- ❷ Do you require a Redundant solution? — ○ Yes ⦿ No
- ❷ User Site Voltage: — International - 230V system (& 400V)

[Show Solution]

Need Help?

Defining the power requirements.

Show Slide(s)
Environmental Impacts

Teaching Tip
If you have them, showing examples of the various cleaning products will liven up the presentation for this section.

Interaction Opportunity
Ask learners if they have come across computer components that were in bad condition due to dust and debris. Mention that in different environments, the dust and debris may be more intense depending on the location of the computers.

Show Slide(s)
Dust and Debris

Show Slide(s)
Temperature, Humidity, and Ventilation

Show Slide(s)
General Preventive Maintenance (2 slides)

ENVIRONMENTAL IMPACTS

The environment in which computer equipment is kept can affect its proper operation and lifespan. All electronic equipment should be kept away from extremes of temperature and damp or dusty conditions. Regular inspection and cleaning of a PC's components and inspection of its surroundings may increase the Mean Time Between Failure (**MTBF**) of many components.

DUST AND DEBRIS

Dust (**airborne particles**) is drawn into the computer via ventilation holes. Over time, the dust can form a thick layer over components and ventilation slots, preventing effective heat dissipation. It can clog up peripherals such as keyboards and mice. Dust and smears can make the display hard to read.

Dust can be controlled by cleaning, but you can also deploy controls to ensure that the surrounding environment is clean. Many buildings have environmental control systems with filters that can reduce the amount of dust in the air.

The PC chassis may be designed to protect internal components from airborne particles. For example, fan inlets can be protected by **air or dust filters**. These polyester sheets trap dust on their surface. If using filters, make sure they are cleaned or replaced periodically or they will clog up and prevent air circulating in the PC.

If the environment is particularly dusty, the whole PC can be placed within an **enclosure** with its own air filters and fans.

TEMPERATURE, HUMIDITY, AND VENTILATION

Excessive heat can make a computer unreliable. Computers generate plenty of heat just by running. Obviously a personal computer will be situated in an environment where the temperature is comfortable for humans (around 20°C/68°F). Do check the precise location of the PC though—direct sunlight or proximity to a radiator can cause heat to build up too easily. You must ensure that there is space for air to flow around the case, especially around the ventilation slots.

High humidity—the amount of water vapor in the air—can cause condensation to form. On the other hand, low humidity allows static charges to build up more easily and increases the risk of Electrostatic Discharge (ESD). The ideal level is around 50%.

Condensation can form as a result of sudden warming. When installing new equipment that has just been delivered, it is important to leave it in its packaging for a few hours—depending on the outside temperature—to allow it to adjust to room temperature gradually.

A **Heating, Ventilation, Air Conditioning (HVAC)** system ensures adequate cooling and humidity and dust control within a room or other enclosed space. All air flow into and out of the room is run through ducts, fans, and filters and warmed or cooled to the correct temperature and humidity.

GENERAL PREVENTIVE MAINTENANCE

Regular maintenance can increase the lifespan of equipment, but can also be time-consuming. You may want to consider providing cleaning materials and procedures to users and training them to perform these tasks themselves. To ensure that these tasks are performed regularly, you can also provide them with a schedule as suggested in the following table.

Frequency	Checks
Daily	• Check that nothing is obstructing the ventilation slots of the system unit. • Check that the equipment is installed securely—for example, not positioned near desk edges, no cable trip hazards, no overloaded power points, no damaged cabling, and so on. • Also ensure that there are no liquid hazards (chance of spills).
Weekly	• Clean the exterior of the monitor and system unit. • Clean the keyboard and mouse.
Monthly	• Check that fans are functioning correctly. • Check that all cables are correctly seated and secured to the system unit and peripherals.

It is important to control the build-up of dust (and clean up spills), but it is also important not to use household cleaning products for PC maintenance. Do not blow away dust with your mouth, as moisture may land on electronic components!

 Note: Always power off the computer and disconnect any devices before cleaning them.

MASK AND GLOVES

A **mask** that fits over your mouth and nose should be worn when you are using a compressed air canister, working around toner spills, or working in an otherwise dusty environment. A mask minimizes the risk of inhaling damaging airborne particles. You should also wear latex **gloves** when cleaning up a toner spill.

COMPRESSED AIR

Use a **compressed air blaster** to dislodge dust from difficult to reach areas. Take care with use, however, as you risk contaminating the environment with dust. Ideally, perform this sort of maintenance within a controlled work area and wear an appropriate air filter mask. Also consider wearing safety goggles to minimize the risk of irritating your eyes with dust.

 Teaching Tip

Exam candidates will need to know what materials can and can't be used to clean each type of PC component.

 Note: Do not use compressed air blasters to clean up a toner spill or a laser printer within an office-type area. You will blow fine toner dust into the atmosphere and create a health hazard.

Use caution when working with compressed air. Read the instructions on the can and follow them carefully. Tipping the can too much can cause the propellant to leave the can in liquid form and at sub-freezing temperatures. The freezing could easily damage components, particularly those that may still be hot from use. There is also the issue of the corrosiveness of the chemical damaging components later on. Also, some delicate components on the motherboard can be damaged—literally blown off the board—if compressed air is used too close to a component.

VACUUMS

Use a PC vacuum cleaner or natural bristle brush to remove dust from inside the system unit, especially from the motherboard, adapter cards, and fan assemblies. Home appliances should not be used, as they can produce high levels of static electricity. PC-safe vacuums can often be used to blow air as well as for suction, so they can replace the need for compressed air canisters for blowing dust out of machines.

Sucking the dust up is usually better, though, since blowing the dust can cause it to get onto or into other components.

Note: A PC vacuum can be used to deal with toner spills if the filter and bag are fine enough to contain toner particles. Such vacuums should be labeled "toner safe." Ideally, move the printer to a maintenance room with filters to contain airborne particles. Alternatively, a toner cloth is a special cloth that you stretch that picks up toner particles that are either in the printer or around the printer. Be careful if you are using it inside the printer so that the cloth does not get caught on any components and leave fibers behind.

Show Slide(s)

Peripheral Device and Laptop Maintenance

PERIPHERAL DEVICE AND LAPTOP MAINTENANCE

Peripheral and mobile devices receive the most wear and tear and require the most regular cleaning to keep them working properly.

There are several types of wipes and cloths that you can use to clean displays, keyboards, and other equipment. These use an appropriate cleaning solution for the type of plastic or surface coating that you are cleaning. They should also be non-abrasive and lint-free so that cleaning does not cause scratches or leave behind stray fibers.

MOUSE

Mice suffer from build-up of grease and dust around the buttons and scroll wheel and need regular cleaning. To ensure that the mouse functions correctly, you should use it on a clean, flat surface, such as that provided by a proper mouse mat.

KEYBOARD

Ensure that keyboards are not used in an environment where food and beverages are present, as spillage of these substances can cause the keyboard to malfunction and make it difficult to clean. You can use a compressed air canister, PC vacuum cleaner, or natural bristle brush to clean debris from a keyboard then wipe down the surfaces with a lint-free cloth and approved cleaner. Tightly wound cotton swabs or toothpicks are useful when trying to get dust and debris out from between keys and around buttons or other tight areas.

DISPLAY

The display screen should be kept clean and free of smears to avoid eyestrain when using the computer for prolonged periods. If the screen requires more than dusting, use an approved display screen cleaner, spraying the cleaner onto the cloth or pad, not onto the screen. You can also obtain pre-moistened wipes. You must use approved cleaning products and a non-abrasive cloth to avoid damaging the screen's anti-glare coating. The products are also formulated to provide anti-static protection against further dust buildup. When cleaning the screen, wipe horizontally across the screen and then vertically. Do not forget to clean into the screen corners.

LAPTOP MAINTENANCE ISSUES

Laptops are typically used in dirtier environments than desktops. Despite the name, it is important to encourage users to put the laptop on a firm, flat surface during use, to allow the cooling fan and vent on the bottom to work properly. These vents should be cleaned regularly using a PC-approved vacuum cleaner or compressed air. For actual "laptop" use, it is best to provide a chiller pad or mat to provide air flow and (with active chiller pads) extra USB-powered fans for cooling.

Compressed air can also be used to clean the keyboard. The screen, touchpad, and case can be cleaned using a soft cloth and approved cleaning solution.

DISPOSAL, RECYCLING, AND COMPLIANCE

Even with procedures in place to properly maintain IT equipment, eventually it will need to be decommissioned and either disposed of or recycled. IT equipment contains numerous components and materials that can cause environmental damage if they are disposed of as ordinary refuse.

COMPLIANCE AND GOVERNMENTAL REGULATIONS

In the United States and many other nations, your employer is obligated to comply with governmental regulations that apply to its specific business. The most common regulations are those issued by the federal government, such as the Occupational Safety and Health Administration (OSHA), and state standards regarding employee safety. OSHA-compliant employers must provide:

- A workplace that is free from recognized hazards that could cause serious physical harm.
- Personal protective equipment designed to protect employees from certain hazards.
- Communication—in the form of labeling, Material Safety Data Sheets (MSDSs), and training about hazardous materials.

Your responsibility—to yourself, your employer, your coworkers, and your customers—is to be informed of potential hazards and to always use safe practices.

Protection of the environment is another area that is regulated by the federal and local governments in the United States and many other nations. Many municipalities have regulations that control the disposal of certain types of computer equipment. Your responsibility is to be aware of any environmental controls that are applicable to your workplace, and to be in compliance with those regulations.

Materials safety and environmental legislation require that environmental hazards be disposed of correctly. In the US, environmental matters are the responsibility of the Environmental Protection Agency (EPA).

MSDS DOCUMENTATION

Employers are obliged to assess the risk to their workforce from hazardous substances at work and to take steps to eliminate or control that risk. No work with hazardous substances should take place unless an assessment has been made. Employees are within their rights to refuse to work with hazardous substances that have not been assessed.

Suppliers of chemicals are required to identify the hazards associated with the substances they supply. Some hazard information will be provided on labels, but the supplier must also provide more detailed information on a **Material Safety Data Sheet (MSDS)**.

An MSDS will contain information about:

- Ingredients.
- Health hazards, precautions, and first aid information.
- What to do if the material is spilled or leaks.
- How to recycle any waste product or dispose of it safely.

You may need to refer to an MSDS in the course of handling monitors, power supplies, batteries, laser printer toner, and cleaning products. If handling devices that are broken or leaking, use appropriate protective gear, such as gloves, safety goggles, and an air filter mask.

Show Slide(s)

Disposal, Recycling, and Compliance

Teaching Tip

Point that use of dangerous substances in the workplace and transport and disposal of materials are usually tightly regulated by workplace and environmental legislation. Discuss the legislation relevant to your own country.

Interaction Opportunity

You may want to show and discuss some government websites: **www.epa.gov**, **www.environment-agency.gov.uk**, and **www.environ.ie**.

SAFETY DATA SHEET

Date of issue/Date of revision   **16 July 2018**
Version 9.01

Section 1. Identification

Product name	:	Metal Cleaner
Product code	:	DX579
Other means of identification	:	Not available.
Product type	:	Liquid.

Relevant identified uses of the substance or mixture and uses advised against

Product use	:	Industrial applications.
Use of the substance/ mixture	:	Coating. Paints. Painting-related materials.

An example of MSDS documentation.

Activity 18-1

Discussing Environmental Impacts and Controls

SCENARIO

Answer the following questions to check your understanding of the topic.

 Show Slide(s)

Activity: Discussing Environmental Impacts and Controls

---

1. **What are the principal characteristics of a surge protector?**

   This is a circuit designed to protect connected devices from the effect of sudden increases or spikes in the supply voltage and/or current. Surge protectors are rated by clamping voltage (low values are better), joules rating (higher values are better), and amperage (the maximum current that can be carried).

2. **When you are sizing the load for a UPS, how would you calculate the power used by a PC component?**

   Multiply its Voltage (V) by the Current (I) it draws to calculate power drawn in Watts (W=V*I). You may then need to convert this to a VA rating by multiplying by 1.67. When power is supplied, some is lost through the function of inverters and capacitors. This means that the supply, measured as VA, must exceed the watts drawn by about 70%. This ratio is also described as the Power Factor (PF).

3. **Why should you never use a home vacuum cleaner to clean a PC?**

   Because they generate large amounts of static electricity that may damage sensitive components.

4. **What are the principal environmental hazards to consider when installing PC equipment?**

   Heat and direct sunlight, excessive dust and liquids, and very low or high humidity. Equipment should also be installed so as not to pose a topple or trip hazard.

5. **When might you need to consult MSDS documentation?**

   A Material Safety Data Sheet (MSDS) should be read when introducing a new product or substance to the workplace. Subsequently, you should consult it if there is an accident involving the substance and when you need to dispose of the substance.

Topic B

Create and Maintain Documentation

 EXAM OBJECTIVES COVERED
1002-4.1 Compare and contrast best practices associated with types of documentation.

There are many reasons for creating and maintaining documentation. A big reason is so that in case of a disaster, you already have critical documentation in place that will help you rebuild as quickly as possible. Without detailed documentation, you would have to rely on memory to determine your network layout, which would likely be very time consuming, costly, and ultimately inaccurate. A complete set of configuration documentation will give you a solid base from which you can begin rebuilding individual workstations, servers, and your network.

You should also document organizational policies. By identifying common organizational policies and procedures that deal with computer use, you will be more capable of dealing with compliance issues as they arise and protecting organizational resources.

 Show Slide(s)

Equipment Inventory (2 slides)

 Teaching Tip

Stress the importance of updating configuration baselines and network diagrams following changes.

EQUIPMENT INVENTORY

It is crucial for an organization to have a well-documented inventory of its tangible and intangible assets and resources. This should include all hardware that is currently deployed as well as spare systems and components kept on hand in case of component or system failure. In terms of network management, these will include network appliances (routers, switches, threat management devices, access points), servers, workstations, and passive network infrastructure (cabling and cross-connects).

There are many software suites and associated hardware solutions available for tracking and managing **assets** (or inventory). An asset management database can be configured to store as much or as little information as is deemed necessary, though typical data would be type, model, serial number, asset ID, location, user(s), value, and service information. Tangible assets can be identified using a **barcode label** or **Radio Frequency ID (RFID) tag** attached to the device (or more simply using an identification number). An RFID tag is a chip programmed with asset data. When in range of a scanner, the chip powers up and signals the scanner. The scanner alerts management software to update the device's location. As well as asset tracking, this allows the management software to track the location of the device, making theft more difficult.

For each asset record there should also be a copy of or link to the appropriate vendor documentation. This would include both an invoice and warranty/support contract and support and troubleshooting guidance.

IT **asset management** is the set of management policies that include information about the financial and contractual specifications of all the hardware and software components present in an organization's inventory. Some organizations have exclusive asset management for hardware and software components. As part of inventory management, use the system life cycle to determine whether the items in the inventory need to be retired or replaced. Use proper asset disposal methods when removing assets from inventory. Critical hardware and software inventory provides insurance documentation and helps determine what you need to rebuild the network.

Inventory Entry	Hardware/ Software	Information to Include
Standard workstation	Hardware	A basic description of a standard client workstation. Include minimum requirements and the installed operating system as well as how many workstations of this type are deployed. For workstations that deviate from the norm, be sure to document the deviations.
Specialty workstation	Hardware	A description of any specialty workstations deployed. Include a brief description of their roles and special configurations implemented on them.
Server	Hardware	A list of the basic server hardware configuration and the role of these servers. List their internal hardware and any special configuration settings and software. Include a configuration list for the operating system.
Connectivity hardware	Hardware	A list of all connectivity hardware in as much detail as possible. This includes the device brand and model numbers, but a description of each feature ensures that replacements can be made without research.
Backup hardware	Hardware	Document critical information about backup hardware, such as the vendor and model number of a tape drive, backup hard drives, DVD drives, and network attached storage, if applicable.
Operating system software	Software	All operating system software, including desktop and server operating systems. Include documentation on licensing and copies of the bulk licenses, if possible. Many vendors retain records of software licenses sold to their customers. If this is the case, include this fact in your documentation.
Productivity and application software	Software	Off-the-shelf productivity software, including any applications installed on client devices and servers.
Maintenance utilities	Software	The utilities used to maintain a network, especially backup software and software configuration.
Backup documentation	Software	Records of when backups were made, how frequently to make them, what backups contain, where backups are stored, and credentials needed to restore backups. Document the backup software and version. Special setup and configuration considerations need to be documented, too.

Inventory Entry	Hardware/ Software	Information to Include
Overall asset inventory	Software	If your company maintains an overall asset inventory, attach a copy. Many companies use the inventory as a base to track hardware and maintenance. This usually includes most of the information needed.

NETWORK TOPOLOGY DIAGRAMS

Show Slide(s)
Network Topology Diagrams

Diagrams are the best way to capture the complex relationships between network elements. They are also the most effective means of locating particular items within the network. Diagrams can be used to model physical and logical relationships at different levels of scale and detail. These relationships are described as the **network topology**.

SCHEMATIC BLOCK DIAGRAM

Show Slide(s)
Schematic Block Diagram

A **schematic** is a simplified representation of the network topology. In terms of the **physical** network topology, it can show the general placement of equipment and telecommunications rooms plus device and port IDs without trying to capture the exact position or relative size of any one element. Schematics can also be used to represent the **logical** structure of the network in terms of security zones, VLANs, and subnets.

Schematics can either be drawn manually using a tool such as Microsoft® Visio® or compiled automatically from network mapping software.

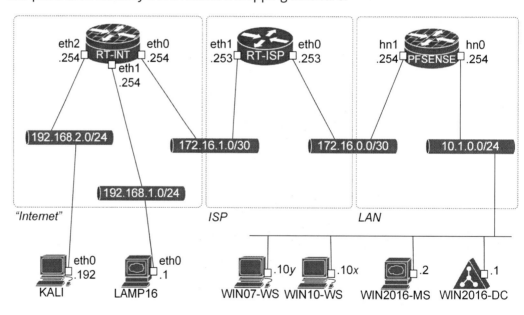

Use a tool such as Visio to create network diagrams.

REFERENCE DOCUMENTATION

Show Slide(s)
Reference Documentation

There are several types of documentation and resources that you might find helpful when you are dealing with common hardware and operating system problems. You can also share documentation and resources with users as a means of assisting and educating them.

Resource	Description
User/installation manuals	User and installation manuals can provide you with basic guidance for installing, configuring, and troubleshooting hardware and software.
	By providing users with various user and installation manuals, users can fix minor issues and problems before requesting additional assistance from a technician. Examples include installing company-specific applications, installing network printers, and mapping drives.
Internet/web-based resources	Internet and web-based resources can provide a wealth of information on installing, configuring, and troubleshooting hardware and software. Many hardware and software manufacturers maintain **knowledge bases (KBs)** and **wikis** to share information about both common and unusual issues that can arise with PC hardware and software.
	Articles written by industry leaders, by support professionals, and by vendors can be a good source of information. Be sure to take into consideration who wrote the article and any verifiable credentials so you can determine the legitimacy of the article content.
	Internet and web-based materials can also provide users with quick reference materials for dealing with everyday issues on their own. Some organizations provide a web page or wiki with user-specific information and reference materials.
Training materials	Most major hardware and software manufacturers provide training materials on how to install and use their products. These materials can be helpful for both new and experienced technicians.
	You can provide training materials for various tasks that users may need to complete on their own, such as virus scans, computer maintenance tasks, and PC clean-up tasks. By providing training materials, you empower users to be proactive in maintaining their systems.

INCIDENT DOCUMENTATION

A piece of software that can be considered part of your support toolkit is a tracking database where incidents that occur can be documented. There are different kinds of incidents, with different reporting requirements. One type of incident is for troubleshooting or support requests. Each support incident will be logged as a job or ticket within the incident management system. The following information will form the core of a job ticket:

Show Slide(s)

Incident Documentation

Information	Notes
Job ID	Job IDs are often referred to as tickets.
Contact	Name, organization, department, email address, telephone number. In a database, the job could be linked to a contact record.
Priority	Assessed from caller's description and customer's service level.

Information	Notes
Problem description	Including information about platform (hardware, OS, application [including version and update number]), and what the user was doing.
Asset	Hardware component or software application associated with the problem, linked to an asset management database.
Details	What was attempted during the first contact.
Follow up	Date and description of follow up actions.
Dates	Dates when the ticket was opened, updated, and closed.

Security incident reporting needs to capture some of the same information but will normally be handled by a dedicated security response team. Reports of actual or suspected security policy violations will initially be processed by a first responder. The report will log the location and time of the incident plus systems affected and the actors and methods used to perform the intrusion. It is important to identify whether any data breach has occurred and what sort of notification must be made for regulatory or compliance purposes. The contents of security incident reports must be kept confidential and access granted on a need-to-know basis only.

Sample incident report.

Accidents represent another type of incident reporting requirement. An **accident** is any instance where a person is injured or computer equipment is damaged due to environmental issues. The report is also used for accidents involving hazardous materials, such as chemical spills, that could have an impact on the environment. Any time an accident occurs at a work site, you should submit an incident report. Reporting these occurrences is often part of company policy and can help provide protection against liability.

Incident documentation might use a simple spreadsheet or database, or it might be a complex help desk management tracking application; it all depends on the needs of your organization. **Incident management** includes the practices and procedures that govern how an organization will respond to an incident in progress.

ORGANIZATIONAL POLICIES

As a vital component of a company's IT infrastructure, employees must understand how to use computers and networked services securely and safely and be aware of their responsibilities. To support this, the organization needs to create written policies and procedures to help staff understand and fulfill their responsibilities and follow best practice.

Show Slide(s)

Organizational Policies

STANDARDS, PROCEDURES, AND GUIDANCE

A **policy** is an overall statement of intent. In order to establish the correct working practices, three different mechanisms can be put in place.

Policy Type	Description
Standard	A standard is a measure by which to evaluate compliance with the policy.
Procedure	A procedure, often referred to as a **Standard Operating Procedure (SOP)**, is an inflexible, step-by-step listing of the actions that must be completed for any given task. Most critical tasks should be governed by SOPs.
Guidelines	Guidelines exist for areas of policy where there are no procedures, either because the situation has not been fully assessed or because the decision making process is too complex and subject to variables to be able to capture it in a procedure. Guidelines may also describe circumstances where it is appropriate to deviate from a specified procedure.

POLICY ENFORCEMENT

It is not enough to just have standards and policies. Your organization and its employees and contractors need to adhere to them as well. For employees and contractors, this requires that they read the standards and policies, and understand that they need to follow them. For the organization, it also needs to follow the standards and policies, regardless of who is acting on the organization's behalf. In addition, the organization may also have regulatory compliance and additional adherence to laws, regulations, guidelines, and specifications relevant to its business. Violations of regulatory compliance regulations often result in legal punishment, including federal fines.

PERSONNEL MANAGEMENT POLICIES

Human Resources (HR) is the department tasked with recruiting and managing the organization's most valuable and critical resource: people. Personnel management policies can be conceived as applying in three phases.

Phase	Description
Recruitment or hiring	Recruitment involves locating then selecting and hiring people to work in particular job roles. Security issues here include screening candidates and performing background checks.
Operation or working	It is often the HR department that manages the communication of policy and training to employees, though there may be a separate training and personal development department within larger organizations. As such, it is critical that HR managers devise training programs that communicate the importance of security to employees.
Termination or separation	Whether an employee leaves voluntarily or involuntarily, termination is a difficult process, with numerous security implications. An employee might be fired, retired, or simply be moving on to another job at another organization.

Operational policies include privilege management, data/information handling, incident response, and use of company devices and services such as Internet access. One function of HR is to draft and communicate these written policies to employees, including any updates to the policies. Another function is to enforce disciplinary measures, perhaps in conjunction with departmental managers.

PASSWORD POLICIES

Teaching Tip

Password policies were covered previously, but they are part of organizational policies, so are mentioned here. Also remind learners that regulated data policies should be considered organizational policies and were covered previously in the course.

A **password policy** defines standards for creating password complexity. It also defines what an organization considers weak passwords and the guidelines for protecting password safety. It specifies standards such as avoiding common passwords, how to create strong passwords, and rules for not using work-related passwords for other sites or services.

ACCEPTABLE USE POLICIES

An **Acceptable Use Policy (AUP)**, or **Fair Use Policy**, sets out what someone is allowed to use a particular service or resource for. Such a policy might be used in different contexts. For example, an AUP could be enforced by a business to govern how employees use equipment and services such as telephone or Internet access provided to them at work. Another example might be an ISP enforcing a fair use policy governing usage of its Internet access services. Enforcing an acceptable use policy is important to protect the organization from the security and legal implications of employees (or customers) misusing its equipment. Typically, the policy will forbid the use of equipment to defraud, defame, or to obtain illegal material. It is also likely to prohibit the installation of unauthorized hardware or software and to explicitly forbid actual or attempted intrusion (snooping). An organization's acceptable use policy may forbid use of Internet tools outside of work-related duties or restrict such use to break times.

AUPs often include policies for the items listed in the following table.

An AUP Policy for	Covers
Rules of Behavior	The equipment used to access the Internet in the workplace is owned by the employer. Many employees expect relatively unrestricted access to Internet facilities for personal use. In fact, employees' use of social networking and file sharing poses substantial risks to the organization, including threat of virus infection or systems intrusion, lost work time, copyright infringement, and defamation. If an employee breaks copyright laws or libels someone using an organization's equipment, the organization itself could be held liable.
	To avoid confusion, an employee's handbook should set out the terms under which use of web browser/email/social networking/P2P software is permitted for personal use, and what penalties infringements could incur. Employers are within their rights to prohibit all private use of Internet services.
	Users should be aware that any data communications, such as email, made through an organization's computer system are liable to be stored within the system, on servers, backup devices, and so on. Consequently, employees should not use computers at work to send personal information, for their own security and privacy if nothing else.
Use of Personally Owned Devices in the Workplace	Portable devices such as smartphones, USB thumb drives, media players, and so on pose a considerable threat to data security as they facilitate file copying. Camera and voice recording functions are other obvious security issues.
	Network access control/endpoint security and data loss prevention solutions can be of some use in preventing the attachment of such devices to corporate networks. Some companies may try to prevent staff from bringing such devices on site. This is quite difficult to enforce, though.

GUIDELINES FOR CREATING AND MAINTAINING DOCUMENTATION

 *Note: All of the Guidelines for this lesson are available as checklists from the **Checklist** tile on the CHOICE Course screen.*

 Show Slide(s)
Guidelines for Creating and Maintaining Documentation (2 slides)

Here are some guidelines to follow when creating and maintaining your documentation.

CREATE AND MAINTAIN DOCUMENTATION
Consider the following guidelines for creating and maintaining documentation:
- Keep an accurate record of the equipment and software within the organization, including:
  - Deployed hardware, both complete systems and components.
  - Deployed software, both applications and operating systems.
  - Spare hardware, both complete systems and components.
  - Software that is not currently installed, both applications and operating systems.
- Use asset tags, either printed barcodes or RFID tags, to track equipment.
- Each asset record should include a copy of or link to the appropriate vendor documentation.

- Document network components through the use of schematic block diagrams showing physical and logical network structure.
- Maintain a library of reference documentation, including:
  - User and installation manuals.
  - Links to Internet and web-based resources.
  - Training materials.
- Document incidents through the use of standardized incident reports.
- Create and maintain organizational policies. This should include:
  - Personnel management policies.
  - Policy on how to handle confidential information.
  - Acceptable use policies.

Activity 18-2

Discussing Documentation Creation and Maintenance

Show Slide(s)
Activity: Discussing Documentation Creation and Maintenance

SCENARIO

Answer the following questions to check your understanding of the topic.

1. What role do barcodes play in managing inventory?

An inventory is a list of assets. To compile a list of assets, you must be able to identify each asset. A barcode label is a good way of doing this. You can use a scanner to link to the asset within the inventory database automatically, avoiding delays and mistakes that might be made by typing an asset ID.

2. What are the two main types of network topology diagrams?

You can create diagrams to show the physical topology or the logical topology. The physical topology shows the location of cabling and ports plus their bandwidth. The logical topology shows IP addresses and subnets plus security controls such as firewalls. There are lots of other types of network topology diagrams, of course, but physical and logical are the two basic distinctions you can make. It is best practice not to try to create a diagram that shows both.

3. What is the purpose of a KB?

A Knowledge Base (KB) is a reference to assist with installing, configuring, and troubleshooting hardware and software. A KB might be created by a vendor to support their products. A company might also create an internal KB, populated with guidelines, procedures, and information from service tickets.

4. What three broad types of incident documentation might a business require?

Incidents can be categorized as support/troubleshooting, security, and accident (whether to personnel or to assets). You should also consider the effect compliance with regulatory or legal requirements has on the documentation that must be kept.

5. While you are answering a service call on a computer that is located in a common area of the office, you come across information showing that some unauthorized websites have been viewed. The activity has been linked to a particular user account.

What is the appropriate action to take?

This is likely to demonstrate a clear breach of Acceptable Use Policies (AUP) and will be the subject of disciplinary action by HR. You should not over-assume or over-react, however. Take care to follow best practices for incident response, such as establishing unambiguous evidence and documenting the entire incident.

Topic C

Use Basic Change Management Best Practices

EXAM OBJECTIVES COVERED
1002-4.2 Given a scenario, implement basic change management best practices.

Practically every technical deployment will face unforeseen issues. The IT project team members should address unexpected changes by using a process that keeps stakeholders informed and that minimizes impact on the overall project, especially the project's timelines and goals.

CHANGE MANAGEMENT

Configuration management means identifying all components of the information and communications technology (ICT) infrastructure (hardware, software, and procedures) and their properties. **Change management** means putting policies in place to reduce the risk that changes to these components could cause service disruption (network downtime).

Show Slide(s)

Change Management

ITIL CONFIGURATION MANAGEMENT MODEL

IT Infrastructure Library (ITIL®) is a popular documentation of good and best practice activities and processes for delivering IT services. Under ITIL, configuration management is implemented using the following elements:

*   Service assets are things, processes, or people that contribute to the delivery of an IT service.
*   A **Configuration Item (CI)** is an asset that requires specific management procedures for it to be used to deliver the service. Each CI must be identified by some sort of label. CIs are defined by their attributes, which are stored in a **Configuration Management Database (CMDB)**.
*   **Baseline** is a fundamental concept in configuration management. The baseline represents "the way it was." A baseline can be a configuration baseline (the ACL applied to a firewall, for instance) or a performance baseline (such as the throughput achieved by a server).
*   A **Configuration Management System (CMS)** is the tools and databases that collect, store, manage, update, and present information about CIs. A small network might capture this information in spreadsheets and diagrams; there are dedicated applications for enterprise CMS.

One of the goals of the CMS is to understand the relationships between CIs. Another is to track changes to CI attributes (and therefore variance from the baseline) over time. The purpose of documentation in terms of change and configuration management is as follows:

*   Identify each component (CI) and label it.
*   Capture each CI and its (relevant) attributes in a CMDB.
*   Capture relationships between CIs. This is best done using diagrams.
*   Capture changes to a CI as a job log and update the CMDB.

DOCUMENTING CHANGES

Each individual system, server, and network component should have a separate document that describes its initial state and all subsequent changes. This document includes configuration information, a list of patches applied, backup records, and even details about suspected breaches. Printouts of hash results, last modification dates of critical system files, and contents of log files may be pasted into this book. System maintenance can be made much smoother with a comprehensive change document. For instance, when a patch is available for an operating system, it typically applies in only certain situations. Manually investigating the applicability of a patch on every possible target system can be very time consuming; however, if logs are available for reference, the process is much faster and more accurate.

 Note: *An example of change management documentation that you can use as a starting point when creating this document for your organization can be found at* **https://www.sans.org/summit-archives/file/summit-archive-1493830822.pdf**.

DOCUMENTED BUSINESS PROCESSES

 **Show Slide(s)**
Documented Business Processes

Depending on the needs of your organization, you might need general business processes to be documented, or you might need every single thing that happens throughout the workday documented. The latter usually applies to businesses that need FDA or other governmental approval to produce and sell goods and services. At the minimum, you should document changes made to systems such as when a new employee comes on board or when an employee leaves and what happens to their hardware and software when those events occur. You will also want to document how various tasks are completed throughout the organization, including how systems are configured, how the network is configured, what criteria is required for making changes to any equipment that is deployed, how and when to replace equipment, and many other aspects of having an organization filled with computing devices.

SOPs AND WORK INSTRUCTIONS

The main difficulty in implementing a workable configuration management system is in determining the level of detail that must be preserved. This is not only evident in capturing the asset database and configuration baseline in the first place, but also in managing **Moves, Adds, and Changes (MACs)** within the organization's computing infrastructure. In terms of computing tasks, a CMS will require that configuration changes be made only when there is a valid job ticket authorizing the change. This means that the activity of all computer support personnel, whether it be installing new devices or troubleshooting, is recorded in job logs. In a fully documented environment, each task will be governed by some sort of procedure. Formal configuration management models often distinguish between two types of procedural documentation:

- A **Standard Operating Procedure (SOP)** sets out the principal goals and considerations (such as budget, security, or customer contact standards) for performing a task and identifies lines of responsibility and authorization for performing it.
- A **Work instruction** is step-by-step instructions for performing an installation or configuration task using a specific product or technology and credentials.

CHANGE MANAGEMENT DOCUMENTATION

To reduce the risk that changes to configuration items will cause service disruption, a documented management process can be used to **plan for change** in a planned and controlled way. Change requests are usually generated when something needs to be corrected, new business needs or processes are identified, or there is room for improvement in a process or system currently in place. The need to change is often described either as reactive, where the change is forced on the organization, or as proactive, where the need for change is initiated internally. Changes can also be categorized according to their potential impact and level of risk (major, significant, minor, or normal, for instance).

In a formal change management process, the need or reasons for change and the procedure for implementing the change is captured in a **Request for Change (RFC)** document and submitted for approval.

Change request documentation should include:

- The purpose of the change.
- The scope of the change.
- A risk analysis of both performing the change and not performing the requested change.
- A documented plan for carrying out the change.
- A method to acquire end-user acceptance that the change was performed to their satisfaction and that the change was properly implemented.
- A **backout plan** in case unforeseen problems arise when the change is made.
- Document all changes that were made.

CHANGE BOARD APPROVAL

The RFC will then be considered at the appropriate level and affected stakeholders will be notified. This might be a supervisor or department manager if the change is normal or minor. Major or significant changes might be managed as a separate project and require approval through a **Change Advisory Board (CAB)**.

PROCESS FOR INSTITUTING CHANGE TO OPERATIONAL POLICIES AND PROCEDURES

Regardless of whether an organization is large enough to require formal change management procedures and staff, the implementation of changes should be carefully planned, with consideration for how the change will affect dependent components. For most significant or major changes, organizations should attempt a trial implementation of the change first. Every change should be accompanied by a rollback (or backout) plan, so that the change can be reversed if it has harmful or unforeseen consequences. Changes should also be scheduled sensitively if they are likely to cause system downtime or other negative impact on the workflow of the business units that depend on the IT system being modified. Most organizations have a scheduled maintenance window period for authorized downtime.

 Show Slide(s)
Process for Instituting Change to Operational Policies and Procedures

When the change has been implemented, its impact should be assessed and the process reviewed and documented to identify any outcomes that could help future change management projects.

GUIDELINES FOR USING CHANGE MANAGEMENT BEST PRACTICES

Here are some best practices to follow regarding change management.

 Show Slide(s)
Guidelines for Using Change Management Best Practices (2 slides)

USE CHANGE MANAGEMENT BEST PRACTICES

Consider these best practices guidelines for using change management:

- Create a separate document for each individual system, server, and network component that describes its initial state and all subsequent changes. This document includes:
  - Configuration information
  - Applied patch list

- Record of backups
- Details about suspected security breaches
- Configuration management using ITIL should be implemented using:
  - Service assets
  - Configuration items
  - Configuration Management Database (CMDB)
  - Baselines
  - Configuration Management System
- Document the need or desire for a change using an RFC document.
- RFCs should be considered at the appropriate level and affected stakeholders notified.
- Major or significant changes might be managed as a separate project and require approval through a Change Advisory Board (CAB).
- Follow documented SOPs and Work Instructions when performing moves, adds, and changes.
- Implementation of changes should be carefully planned, with consideration for how the change will affect dependent components.
- For most significant or major changes, organizations should attempt to trial the change first.
- Every change should be accompanied by a rollback (or remediation) plan.
- Changes should also be scheduled sensitively if they are likely to cause system downtime or other negative impact on workflow.
- When the change has been implemented, its impact should be assessed and the process reviewed and documented to identify any outcomes that could help future change management projects.

Activity 18-3

Discussing Change Management Best Practices

Show
Slide(s)

Activity: Discussing
Change Management
Best Practices

SCENARIO

Answer the following questions to check your understanding of the topic.

1. **Why are documented business processes essential for effective change management?**

   Without documented processes, you do not have a means of measuring or specifying the effects of change. Of course, you could be introducing a change to start using documented business processes! But from that point, any project can be measured and evaluated by the changes it makes to documented procedures. Changes that are supported by documented procedures can also be communicated more clearly to staff.

2. **What are the main components of an RFC?**

   A Request for Change (RFC) sets out the purpose and scope of the proposed change and a documented plan for carrying out the change. Ideally, it should perform a risk analysis of both performing the change and not performing the requested change. It should state the measures by which the change can be judged to have been completed successfully. Ideally, it would also include a backout plan for reversing the change.

3. **What is a change board?**

   A change board is a committee of stakeholders who can approve the planned change.

Topic D

Implement Disaster Prevention and Recovery Methods

EXAM OBJECTIVES COVERED

1002-4.3 Given a scenario, implement basic disaster prevention and recovery methods.

Ensuring that data, applications, client computers, servers, and other network resources are available to users is part of a computer technician's responsibilities. This can be challenging when hardware fails or a natural disaster strikes. In this topic, you will see how to implement measures related to disaster prevention and recovery.

DISASTER PREVENTION AND RECOVERY

Show Slide(s)

Disaster Prevention and Recovery

A disaster could be anything from a fairly trivial loss of power or failure of a minor component to man-made or natural disasters, such as fires, earthquakes, or acts of terrorism. An organization sensitive to these risks will develop an effective, documented **Disaster Recovery Plan (DRP)**. This should accomplish the following:

- Identify scenarios for natural and man-made disasters and options for protecting systems.
- Identify tasks, resources, and responsibilities for responding to a disaster.
- Train staff in the disaster planning procedures and how to react well to change.

When a disaster occurs, the failover recovery plan will swing into action to get the failed part of the network operational as soon as possible. If a disk has failed, swap it out. If a network component has failed, remove and replace or repair the component to provide for high reliability as soon as possible. If data becomes corrupted or lost, utilize your restoration plan to recover the data.

DATA BACKUP AND RESTORATION

Show Slide(s)

Data Backup and Restoration (4 slides)

Teaching Tip

Point out that it is not necessary to back up OS files, but configuration files should be part of the backup.

One of the important tasks you will need to perform as an A+ technician is making sure that users' data and system settings are being backed up in case things go awry.

Data backup is a system maintenance task that enables you to store copies of critical data for safekeeping. Backups protect against loss of data due to disasters such as file corruption or hardware failure. **Data restoration** is a system recovery task that enables you to access the backed-up data. Restored data does not include any changes made to the data after the backup operation. Data backups can be accomplished simply by copying individual files and folders to a local or network location or by using dedicated software and hardware to back up large amounts of data.

Backup operations can be performed at different levels:

- **File level**—this is used to back up user-generated files stored in local profile folders or network shares. Almost all backup software can perform this basic task.
- **Image-level**—this is used to back up an OS and can include third-party software applications, drivers, and custom settings installed under the OS. An image can be used both to restore physical computers and Virtual Machines (VM).

- **Critical applications**—network applications often depend on some sort of database for storage rather than individual file-based storage. Specialist backup software is required to connect to the database. Backups can be made of the whole database or of individual tables and records.

 Note: As well as the application data and settings, make sure you make a backup of product keys and license information. These might be required to restore the application license.

Many devices and user accounts include cloud storage space. If you store your data in a cloud storage site, the onus of performing backups is left to the provider of the cloud space. This data is often also stored on your local storage device, so you have two copies already. Examples include photos and music stored on smart phones being automatically copied to the platform's related cloud storage site such as iCloud® for Apple® devices and Google Drive™ for Android™ devices.

BACKUP MANAGEMENT

The execution and frequency of backups must be carefully planned and guided by policies. Backups are kept back to certain points in time. As backups take up a lot of space, and there is never limitless storage capacity, this introduces the need for storage management routines and techniques to reduce the amount of data occupying backup storage media while giving adequate coverage of the required recovery window. The recovery window is determined by the **Recovery Point Objective (RPO)**, which is determined through business continuity planning.

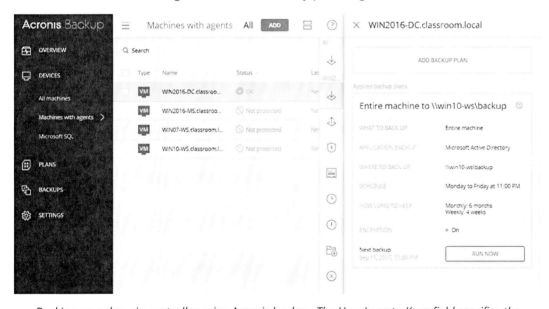

Backing up a domain controller using Acronis backup. The How Long to Keep field specifies the retention period. (Screenshot courtesy of acronis.com.)

Data retention needs to be considered in the short and long term:

- In the short term, files that change frequently might need retaining for version control. Short term retention is also important in recovering from malware infection. Consider the scenario where a backup is made on Monday, a file is infected with a virus on Tuesday, and when that file is backed up later on Tuesday, the copy made on Monday is overwritten. This means that there is no good means of restoring the uninfected file.
- In the long term, data may need to be stored to meet legal requirements or to comply with company policies or industry standards.

A retention policy can either be based on redundancy (the number of copies of each file that should be retained) or on a recovery window (the number of days into the past that should be retained).

BACKUP TYPES

When considering a backup made against an original copy of data, the backup can usually be performed using one of three main types: full, incremental, or differential. In Windows®, a full backup includes all selected files and directories, whereas incremental and differential backups check the status of the archive attribute before including a file. The archive attribute is set whenever a file is modified. This allows backup software to determine which files have been changed and therefore need to be copied.

 Note: *Linux doesn't support a file archive attribute. Instead, a date stamp is used to determine whether the file has changed.*

The following table summarizes the three different backup types.

Type	Data Selection	Backup/Restore Time	Archive Attribute
Full	All selected data regardless of when it was previously backed up	High/low (one tape set)	Cleared
Incremental	New files and files modified since last backup	Low/high (multiple tape sets)	Cleared
Differential	All data modified since the last full backup	Moderate/moderate (no more than 2 sets)	Not Cleared

A typical strategy for a complex network would be a full weekly backup followed by an incremental or differential backup at the end of each day.

- The advantage of using a full daily backup is that one tape set is only required to restore the system.
- The advantage of an incremental backup is that it takes less time to back up, but several tape sets may need to be restored before the system is operational.
- The advantage of a differential backup is the balance of time for both restoring and backing up.

 Caution: *Do not combine differential and incremental backups. Use full backups interspersed with differential backups, or full backups interspersed with incremental backups.*

 Note: *Most software also has the capability to do copy backups. These are made outside the tape rotation system (ad hoc) and do not affect the archive attribute.*

RECOVERY IMAGES

A custom **recovery image** contains the current state of the operating system files, plus all of the desktop applications installed to the boot partition. An image can be used to restore the OS and any critical applications to a workstation or VM in one step. A new image must be created if any additional applications are installed or configuration changes made.

 Teaching Tip

Point out that "refresh" and "reset" mean specific things in Windows. The recovery image isn't at all like a refresh, because it will delete personal files. It's not a reset of vanilla Windows, but it is akin to a factory reset. An OEM recovery image will have the shareware installed by default, so it IS a reset in terms of reverting to a tested build.

If user account profiles are stored on the same partition or drive as the OS, this user data will be included in the image. As images take a relatively long time to create, it is better to back up user data separately using file level backups. User profiles or home folders might be stored on a network file server to make them easier to back up.

BACKUP TESTING

Before you use a backup to restore data, test it to make sure it's reliable. To test the backup:

- Try restoring some of the backed-up data into a test directory, making sure you don't overwrite any data when doing so.
- Configure the backup software to verify after it writes.
- Verify that the backup contains all the required files.
- Test backup devices and media on a regular basis.

OFF-SITE AND LOCAL STORAGE

Typically, the backups you create are stored off-site. If disaster strikes the facility where your servers are located, you won't lose your backup media as well. You might want to keep a set of backup media on site as well, so that you have instant access to the backups in case files are accidentally deleted or corrupted. For off-site storage, you might use a bank safety deposit box for small organizations, or you might contract with a firm that specializes in securely storing backups. Cloud storage services provide an effective means of storing backed up data off-site. Specialist cloud backup providers allow the scheduling and data transfer all to be managed from the cloud console. For on-site storage, consider using a fireproof safe.

Wherever you decide to keep your backups, environmental considerations must be taken into account. Do not store the backups where there is high heat or humidity, which could damage the backup medium. Be sure not to store the backups near equipment with strong magnets that could erase the data and damage the backup media.

BACKUP STORAGE SECURITY

There are various best practices for ensuring security of backup data. They include:

- Authentication of users and backup clients to the backup server.
- Role based access control lists for all backup and recovery operations.
- Data encryption options for both backup transmission and storage.
- Backup of remote clients to a centralized location behind firewalls.
- Default data storage locations must be standardized.
- Create a policy that defines where documents are backed up from.
- Use segregation of duties enforced by policy for all personnel handling backup data.
- Document all access, testing, backup, and restore cycles.

ACCOUNT RECOVERY

Users are likely to have several different accounts to maintain, each with its own password and login name. Frequently, users will forget the password for an account or there may be some sort of fault preventing use of a smart card or biometric credentials. Usually to recover an account password, you will need to input the answers to one or more **challenge questions** and/or receive a token sent to another trusted device or email account.

If password recovery methods do not work, or if the account profile has been deleted or corrupted, you might need to recreate the account or set up a new account then

 Show Slide(s)
Backup Testing

 Interaction Opportunity
Ask if anyone has had experience expecting they were safe because they performed backups, only to find when they went to restore their data, that the backup was not current or was corrupted in some way.

 Show Slide(s)
Off-site and Local Storage (2 slides)

 Interaction Opportunity
Ask learners if their organizations use a third-party storage facility such as Iron Mountain, store backups at another one of their own facilities, or use a bank security deposit box or some other location to store their off-site backups.

 Show Slide(s)
Account Recovery

 Interaction Opportunity
Ask if anyone has needed to use account recovery for any OS, app, or website, and what the experience was like.

import any backed up data and settings to the new account. Windows uses an SID to identify each account in file ACLs. If you recreate an account, it will not have the same SID and you will have to reconfigure file permissions and group memberships.

 Note: If an account profile is corrupted, the key required to decrypt files encrypted using EFS might be lost or damaged. The key is based on the user password. On a domain, you can configure recovery agents with the ability to restore the encryption keys.

GUIDELINES FOR IMPLEMENTING DISASTER RECOVERY AND PREVENTION METHODS

Show Slide(s)

Guidelines for Implementing Disaster Recovery and Prevention Methods (2 slides)

Here are some guidelines to follow to help you implement disaster recovery and prevention.

IMPLEMENT DISASTER RECOVERY AND PREVENTION METHODS

Consider these guidelines when implementing disaster recovery and prevention methods:

- A disaster recovery plan should:
    - Identify scenarios for natural and man-made disasters and options for protecting systems.
    - Identify tasks, resources, and responsibilities for responding to a disaster.
    - Train staff in the disaster planning procedures and how to react well to change.
- Perform backups of data and configuration files on a regular basis. This might be at the file level or the image level. Critical applications should also be backed up.
- Determine the frequency of backups. This might be hourly, daily, weekly, monthly, or some other interval appropriate for the data and information in your organization.
- Determine data retention needs in both the short and the long term.
- Determine whether you need to perform full, incremental, or differential backups.
- Create a custom recovery image for use in restoring a computer.
- Be aware that when you restore data from a backup, the data is only as current as the backup from which you are restoring, so some data might need to be recreated.
- Test backups after they are created.
- Determine where backups will be stored both locally and offsite.
- Document the account recovery methods that will be needed for any systems, applications, or websites used by the organization.

 *Note: To learn more, check the **Video** tile on the CHOICE Course screen for any videos that supplement the content for this lesson.*

Activity 18-4

Discussing Disaster Prevention and Recovery

SCENARIO

Answer the following questions to check your understanding of the topic.

Show
Slide(s)

Activity: Discussing
Disaster Prevention
and Recovery

1. **At which general levels are backups made to facilitate disaster recovery?**

   Backup levels include file, image, and critical application. File level backups allow restoration of user-generated data files in a shared folder or user profile. An image-level backup records a whole installation (OS, third-party software and drivers, and custom settings). This can be used to reinstall a computer or recover a Virtual Machine (VM). A critical application backup saves data and settings kept by a specific software product. This is likely to involve some sort of database backup.

2. **What tests can you perform to ensure the integrity of backup settings and media?**

   You can perform a test restore and validate the files. You can run an integrity check on the media, such as using chkdsk on a hard drive used for backup. Backup software can often be configured to perform an integrity check on each file during a backup operation. You can also perform an audit of files included in a backup against a list of source files to ensure that everything has been included.

3. **For which backup/restore issue is a cloud-based backup service an effective solution?**

   The issue of provisioning an offsite copy of a backup. Cloud storage can also provide extra capacity.

4. **What provisions can you make for account recovery?**

   You might implement a password recovery mechanism for users who have forgotten a password, though this mechanism can itself represent a security risk. You should ensure that profile data is backed up so that it can be restored in the event of file corruption or damage to a disk. If a profile cannot be restored, the account would have to be recreated. This means that the account will have to be reassigned security group memberships and permissions. This is easier if the allocation of those permissions has been well documented in the first place. There may also need to be some provision for configuring a recovery key to restore encrypted data.

Activity 18-5
Configuring Windows Backup

Show Slide(s)

Activity: Configuring
Windows Backup

BEFORE YOU BEGIN
Complete this activity using Hyper-V Manager and the PC1 (Windows 10) VM.

SCENARIO
In this activity, you will look at how File History and Windows Image Backup can be used to facilitate disaster recovery. You cannot attach removable media to the VM, so you will use a second virtual hard disk (VHD) for this activity to simulate a removable drive.

---

1. Attach a second virtual hard disk to **PC1**. Name it ***BACKUP*** and use the default capacity (127 GB).
    a) On the HOST computer, in Hyper-V Manager, right-click **PC1** and select **Settings**.
    b) Select the **SCSI Controller** node and then, with **Hard Drive** selected in the box, select the **Add** button.
    c) Select the **New** button.
    d) On the **Before You Begin** page, select **Next**.
    e) With **Dynamically expanding** selected, select **Next**.
    f) In the **Name** box, type ***BACKUP*** In the **Location** box, type ***C:\COMPTIA-LABS\TEMP*** and then select **Finish**.
    g) In the **Settings** dialog box, select **OK**.

2. Start the VM and sign in as Admin. Initialize the new disk and format it with NTFS.
    a) Start the **PC1** VM and sign on using the account **Admin** and password ***Pa$$w0rd***
    b) Right-click **Start** and select **Disk Management**.
    c) In the **Initialize Disk** dialog box, select **OK**.
    d) In the bottom of the window, right-click the **Unallocated** box on Disk 1 and select **New Simple Volume**.
    e) In the **New Simple Volume Wizard**, select **Next** twice to use all the available space on the disk.
    f) On the **Assign Drive Letter or Path** page, from the list box, select **B** and then select **Next**.
    g) In the **File system** box, verify that **NTFS** is selected. In the **Volume label** box, type ***BACKUP*** and then select **Next**.
    h) Select **Finish**.
    i) Close Disk Management.

3. Turn on File History for the **BACKUP** drive, and configure File History to include the C:\LABFILES folder.
    a) Open the **Documents** folder, and create some Paint files and some text files.
        You will use these as sample data for the backup.
    b) Click in the **Instant Search** box, type ***backup*** and then select **Backup settings** icon from the search results.
    c) In the **Settings** app, select **Add a drive**.

---

d)   In the left pane, select **BACKUP (B:)**.

   *Note: If **Settings** crashes, open it again and re-select the **BACKUP (B:)** drive.*

The **Automatically back up my files** toggle should be switched to **On**.

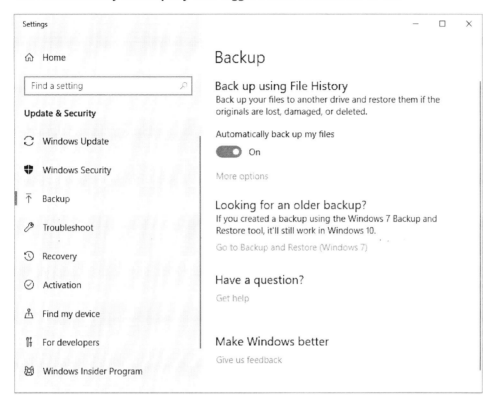

Configuring File History backup. (Screenshot used with permission from Microsoft.)

e)   Select **More options**.
f)   Select **Add a folder**. Select **C:\LABFILES** and then select **Choose this folder**.
g)   Select **Back up now**.
     Leave the **Settings** app open.

4.   Create another File History restore point, and then explore options for restoring files.

a)   Open the **Documents** folder, and then create some more files and edit some of the files you created already.
b)   In the **Settings** app, select **Back up now**.

   *Note: If the backup you started previously is still running, wait for it to finish, then select **Back up now**.*

c)   Click in the **Instant Search** box, type *file history*, and then select the **Restore your files with File History** icon in the search results.

A list of backed up folders is displayed, including LABFILES.

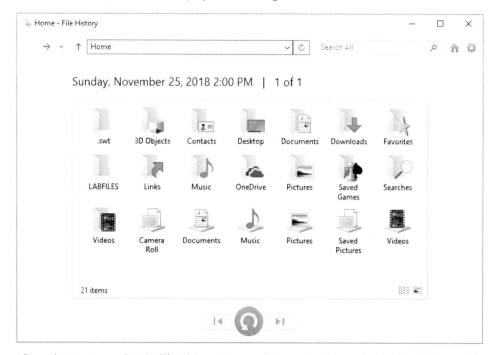

Browsing restore points in File History. (Screenshot used with permission from Microsoft.)

d)   In the **File History** window, open the **Documents** folder (or library).

e)   Use the arrows next to the green **Restore** button to browse the different versions.

f)   Select the earliest version of one of your Paint pictures and select **Restore**.

g)   In the **Replace or Skip Files** dialog box, select **Compare info for both files**.

If this had been a previous file version that had been deleted or damaged, the user could now compare the files and decide which version should be kept.

h)   In the **File Conflict** dialog box, check all the boxes and then select **Continue**.

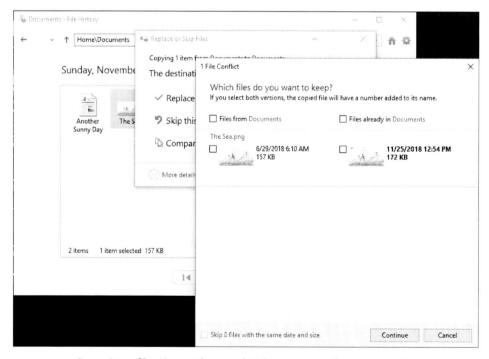

Restoring a file. (Screenshot used with permission from Microsoft.)

5. Create a system image and save it to the **BACKUP** folder.

a) Right-click **Start** and select **Run**. In the box, type ***control /name microsoft.backupandrestore*** and then select **OK**.

You can use the `control` command to open any Control Panel applet, if you know what its name is.

b) Select **Create a system image**.

c) In the **Create a system image** wizard, with **BACKUP (B:)** selected, select **Next**.

d) Select **Start backup**.

It will take a few minutes for the image to be created.

e) When backup is complete, in the **System repair disc** prompt, select **No**.

f) Select **Close**.

g) Optionally, use the **Set up backup** link to view the older Windows backup tool.

This is the interface you would need to use to back up a Windows 7 PC.

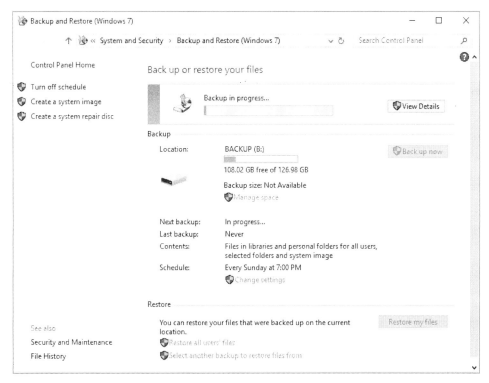

Windows Backup and Restore. This tool is available in Windows 7 and you may prefer to use it in Windows 10 too. (Screenshot used with permission from Microsoft.)

6. Shut down PC1 and then export the VM so that you can use the BACKUP drive in another VM.

a) Shut down PC1.

b) In Hyper-V Manager, right-click the **PC1** VM and select **Checkpoint**.

c) In the **Checkpoints** pane, right-click the new checkpoint and select **Export**.

d) In the **Export Virtual Machine** dialog box, select **Browse**.

e) Select the **C:\COMPTIA-LABS\TEMP** folder. Select the **New folder** button and create a new folder named **VMBACKUP**. With the **VMBACKUP** folder selected, select the **Select Folder** button.

f) In the **Export Virtual Machine** dialog box, select **Export**. Wait for the **Status** column to clear.

Obviously, you could have performed a backup of the VM by doing this in the first place, but the point of this exercise is to demonstrate approximately how image backup would work on a physical machine. The procedure to mimic the rescue disc is a bit more convoluted because you don't have a VM that can burn DVDs, and there's no simple option to create a file-based ISO rescue disc.

This will take about 10 minutes to complete.

7. Create a new VM, and attach the exported BACKUP virtual disk file as a second disk.

   a) In Hyper-V Manager, in the **Actions** pane, select **New**→**Virtual Machine**.
   b) On the **Before You Begin** page, select **Next**.
   c) In the **Name** box, type *RESTORE*
   d) Check the **Store the virtual machine in a different location** box. In the **Location** text box, type *C:\COMPTIA-LABS\TEMP\VMBACKUP* and then select **Next**.
   e) Select **Generation 2** and select **Next**.
   f) Select **Next** to accept the default memory allocation.
   g) From the **Connection** list box, select **vLOCAL**. Select **Next**.
   h) Select **Next** to accept the default disk configuration.
   i) Select **Install an operating system from a bootable image file**. Select the **Browse** button and select **C:\COMPTIA-LABS\win10.iso** or a file location and name as suggested by your instructor. Select **Open**.
   j) Select **Finish**.
   k) In Hyper-V Manager, right-click the **RESTORE** VM and select **Settings**.
   l) Select the **SCSI Controller** node and then, with **Hard Drive** selected in the box, select the **Add** button.
   m) Select the **Browse** button. Select **C:\COMPTIA-LABS\TEMP\VMBACKUP\PC1\Virtual Hard Disks\BACKUP.vhdx** and then select **Open**.
   n) In the **Settings for RESTORE** dialog box, select **OK**.

8. Use the product disc to boot the new VM, and then use the Recovery Environment to restore the image from the BACKUP drive.

   a) Double-click the **RESTORE VM** icon to open a connection window.
   b) In the **Virtual Machine Connection** window, select the **Start** button.
   c) When you see the message **Press any key to boot from CD or DVD**, press a key. If you miss this, press **Ctrl+Alt+End** to reboot and try again.
   d) In the **Windows Setup** dialog box, select **Next**.
   e) Select **Repair your computer**.
   f) In the **Windows Recovery Environment**, select **Troubleshoot**.
   g) Select **System Image Recovery**.
   h) With **Use the latest available system image** selected, select **Next**.

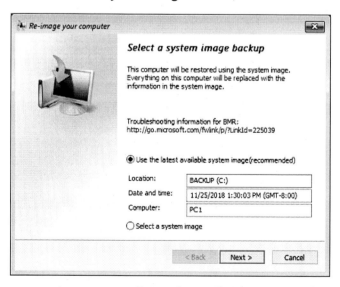

Performing a system image restore. (Screenshot used with permission from Microsoft.)

   i) Do not change any restore options. Select **Next**.
   j) Select **Finish** and then confirm the prompt by selecting **Yes**.

This will take about 5 minutes.

k) When the **Re-image your computer** process is complete, the VM will reboot. Select **Restart** now if necessary.

l) In the **Connect to RESTORE** dialog box, select an appropriate screen resolution and then select the **Connect** button.

m) Sign in as **Admin** with the password *Pa$$w0rd*. Open the **Documents** folder, and verify that the files you created are present. You could also check that File History is still configured.

A system image backup preserves the exact configuration of the OS system and boot drives as they are at the time the image was created. You have included some "personal" data files in this image. This isn't really best practice. Keep the tasks of maintaining system images and using file-level backup separate.

9. You need to revert the changes you made and delete the VM you created. Please complete these steps carefully to ensure the other activities continue to function as expected.

a) On the **RESTORE VM**, from the connection window, select **Action→Revert**. If you are prompted, select the **Revert** button to confirm.

b) In Hyper-V Manager, right-click the **RESTORE VM** and select **Delete**. In the confirmation dialog box, select **Delete**.

c) Select **PC1**. In the **Checkpoints** pane, right-click the **Initial Config** checkpoint and select **Apply**. In the confirmation dialog box, select **Apply**.

d) In the **Checkpoints** pane, right-click the dated checkpoint and select **Delete Checkpoint**. In the confirmation dialog box, select **Delete**.

e) Open File Explorer and delete the contents of the **C:\COMPTIA-LABS\TEMP** folder.

Topic E

Basic Scripting Concepts

 EXAM OBJECTIVES COVERED
1002-4.8 Identify the basics of scripting.

Many IT support tasks are quite straightforward but repetitive. Whenever people are called upon to perform repetitive tasks, there is quite a high chance that they will make mistakes. Developing scripts to automate these repetitive tasks means that they can be performed with greater consistency. Also, if you want to change something about the configuration, it is easier to tweak the script than to adjust a large number of desktops or user accounts manually. As a CompTIA A+ technician, you are highly likely to work in environments that make use of scripting. You should understand the basics of how a script is written and executed.

 Show Slide(s)

Script Files

 Teaching Tip

Determine learners' current level of knowledge about programming, and in particular about scripting, so you have an idea on how deeply to cover this information.

 Show Slide(s)

Scripting Languages (7 slides)

 Interaction Opportunity

Ask learners if anyone has experience with any of the scripting languages listed.

 Teaching Tip

Point out that Java (a compiled programming language) is different than JavaScript (an interpreted scripting programming language).

SCRIPT FILES

A **script file** is a text document containing commands. The commands might be operating system commands that are run in the order they are listed in the script file. In other cases, the script file lists instructions from a particular **scripting language** that are **interpreted** by a **command interpreter** designed for that particular scripting language. When you access a script file, if the appropriate interpreter is installed on the computer, the instructions contained in the file are run or **executed**. You can also open the script file in any text editor, such as Windows **Notepad**.

> *Note: You can modify any script in a basic text editor such as **Notepad**, but using a text editor with script support is more productive. Script support means the editor can parse the syntax of the script and highlight elements of it appropriately. For complex scripts, you might use an **Integrated Development Environment (IDE)**. This will provide autocomplete features to help you write and edit code and debugging tools to help identify if the script is executing correctly.*

SCRIPTING LANGUAGES

In computer programming, there are several types of instruction sets.

*   One is a **compiled program**, in which the instructions are performed by the computer processor. Examples of compiled language programs are Perl, Java™, C, and C++®.
*   The second type is a script, in which the instructions are interpreted and carried out by another program such as the operating system or a command interpreter.
    *   Examples of script languages include Visual Basic®, Python®, and JavaScript® scripts. These are general purpose scripting languages.
    *   Batch files and PowerShell® in Windows® operating systems and shell scripts in the Linux® operating system are also considered script files. These languages support the automation and configuration of a particular operating system.
*   Most languages can call (or "wrap") system commands as part of the code and can therefore also be used for scripting.

File extensions for each of these scripting languages are shown in the following table.

Scripting Language	File Extension
Windows batch file	.bat
PowerShell	.ps1
Linux shell script	.sh
VBScript	.vbs
JavaScript	.js
Python	.py

Whatever language is used to create it, a script is *usually* a smaller piece of code than a program. A script is generally targeted at completing a specific task, whether that task is based within a web-based application or is used by a network administrator to perform a repetitive administrative task. Although a program usually provides some sort of unique functionality, anything a script does could usually be performed manually by a user.

Writing scripts is a good place to learn the basics about programming. They are usually simpler to learn, require no compiling, and are well documented on the Internet should you require guidance or samples.

BATCH FILES

Batch files are a collection of command-line instructions that you store in a .BAT file. You can run the file by calling its name from the command-line, or double-clicking the file in File Explorer. Generally, batch file scripts run from end to end, and are limited in terms of branching and user input.

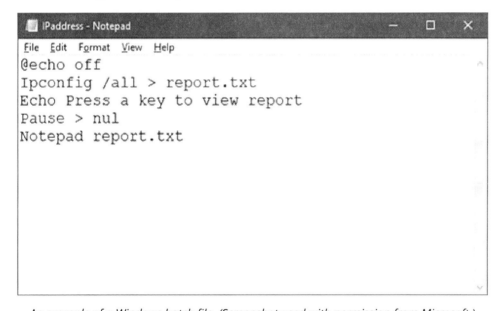

An example of a Windows batch file. (Screenshot used with permission from Microsoft.)

WINDOWS POWERSHELL

Windows PowerShell enables you to perform management and administrative tasks in Windows 7 and later. It is fully integrated with the operating system and supports both remote execution and scripting. To help create and manage your Windows PowerShell scripts, Microsoft provides the Windows PowerShell Integrated Scripting Environment (ISE).

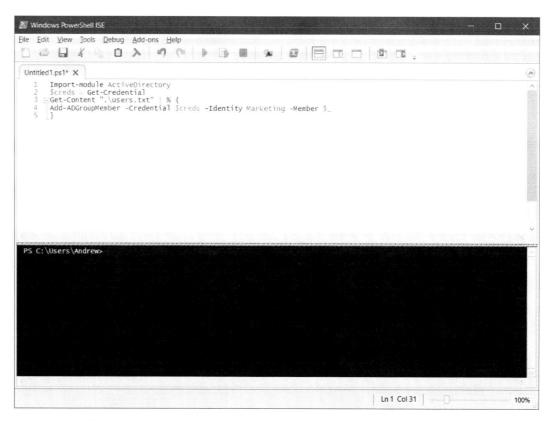

Windows PowerShell ISE. (Screenshot used with permission from Microsoft.)

LINUX SHELL SCRIPT

In Linux, a **shell script** is the equivalent of a Windows batch file. A shell script is a file that contains a list of commands to be read and executed by the shell. Frequently used commands can be stored in a shell script for repeated use. Every shell script starts with a line that designates the interpreter. This line instructs the operating system to execute the script. Shell scripts allow you to perform various functions. These functions include automation of commands and tasks of system administration and troubleshooting, creation of simple applications, and manipulation of text or files.

An example of a Linux shell script open in a text editor.

VBScript

VBScript is a scripting language based on Microsoft's Visual Basic programming language. VBScript is often used by network administrators to perform repetitive administrative tasks. With VBScript, you can run your scripts from either the command-line or from the Windows graphical interface. Scripts that you write must be run within a host environment. Windows 10 provides Internet Explorer, IIS, and Windows Script Host (WSH) for this purpose.

```
test - Notepad                                    —   □   ×
File Edit Format View Help
highnumber = 50
lownumber = 10
count = 0
Title = "Number count"
for i = 1 to 10
    randomize
    displaynumber = int((highnumber - lownumber + 1) * rnd + lownumber)
wscript.echo displaynumber
if displaynumber > 25 then
    count = count+1
End If
Next
Msg = Cstr(Count) + " numbers are greater than 25"
msgbox Msg,vbok,Title
```

Visual Basic Script in Windows 10. (Screenshot used with permission from Microsoft.)

 Note: *You would now normally use PowerShell for Windows automation tasks. You might need to support legacy VBScripts, though.*

JavaScript

JavaScript is a scripting language that is designed to create interactive web-based content and web apps. The scripts are executed automatically by placing the script in the HTML code for a web page, so that when the HTML code for the page loads, the script is run.

An example of JavaScript code.

PYTHON

Python is a general-purpose programming language that can be used to develop many different kinds of applications. It is designed to be easy to read and program using much fewer lines of code when compared to other programming languages. The code runs in an interpreter. In Windows, a default interpreter called CPython is installed with the Python development tools supplied by the Python Software Foundation (**python.org**). Python is preinstalled on many Linux distributions.

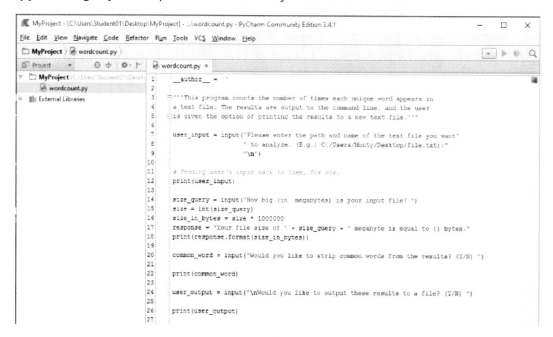

An example of Python code.

Show Slide(s)
Basic Script Constructs

BASIC SCRIPT CONSTRUCTS

In order to write a script in a particular language, you must first understand the structure and syntax of the language. Most scripting languages share similarities in their structure and syntax, but it is important to use the specific syntax correctly as any errors will cause the code to not run.

Show Slide(s)
Comment Syntax

COMMENT SYNTAX

It is important to use comments in code to assist with maintaining it. A comment line is ignored by the compiler or interpreter. A comment line is indicated by a special delimiter, such as double forward slash (//), hash (#), or apostrophe ('). The following table identifies the syntax used to add comments to various languages.

Scripting Language	Comment Syntax
Windows batch file	Rem Comment text is added here
	or
	:: Comment text is added here
PowerShell script	# Comment text is added here
Bash shell script	# Comment text is added here
VBScript	' Comment text is added here
JavaScript	// Comment text is added here
Python	# Comment text is added here

IDENTIFIERS

An **identifier** is used in a program to access a program element, such as a **stored value**. For example, you might assign the identifier FirstName to a stored value that contains a user's first name. In essence, an identifier is a label for something within your program. If your identifier stores data, then it will be either a **variable** or a **constant**.

Show Slide(s)

Identifiers

Type	Description
Variable	A variable contains a value that can change during the execution of the program. This value might be a text string, a number, or any other data type.
	Variables are usually **declared**, defined as a particular **data type**, and given an initial value at the start of the **routine** in which they are used. It is often possible to use **undeclared variables**, but this can make code harder to read and more prone to errors.
	Using the example of a first name, it's important to understand that although a person's name might not change, if you use a programmatic technique to reference a user's name without knowing which user you're referring to, then, as far as the program is concerned, that is a variable. You can assign a value to a variable using fairly simple code. For example, the following **pseudocode** declares the FirstName variable to store a string value with an initial value Andy, then sets it to a value from a data store:
	``` declare FirstName as String = "Andy" FirstName = find LastLoggedOnUser and get Forename print FirstName ```
	Running this code might produce the following output:
	James
Constants	A constant is a specific identifier that contains a value that cannot be changed within the program. For example, you might want to reference the numerical value for the screen dimensions or resolution.

ENVIRONMENT VARIABLES

An **environment variable** is a storage location in the environment of the operating system's command shell. For example, when you are entering directory paths as arguments in a script automating some task in Windows, you may not know exactly which locations were chosen for installation. The shell recognizes some system variables and replaces the correct path when one of these is used. Some of the common variables include:

Show Slide(s)

Environment Variables

- %SystemDrive%—for example, "C:"
- %SystemRoot%—for example, "C:\Windows"
- %UserName%—for example, "George"
- %HomeDrive%—for example, "C:"
- %HomePath%—for example, "\Users\George"

In Windows, you can view the full list of variables by using the `set` command (without switches) at the command prompt. `set` also lets you create and modify new variables. You can also view variables through the **Advanced** page of the **System Properties** dialog box by selecting the **Environment Variables** button.

In Linux, you use the `printenv` or `env` commands to view and change environment variables. However, in Linux, each shell can use additional variables, configured by using the `set` command.

 Note: *If you need to use environment variables outside of a batch file or shell script, each language will have a different syntax for reading them.*

Show Slide(s)
Branches and Loops

BRANCHES AND LOOPS

A script contains one or more statements. In the normal scheme of execution, each statement is processed in turn from top to bottom. Scripts are used for tasks that are too complex to be completed as a simple series of statements, though. In this case, you can change the order in which statements are executed based on logical conditions evaluated within the script. There are two main types of conditional execution: branches and loops.

BRANCHES

A script runs from the start to the end unless you instruct it to deviate from this path. One way of doing so is to create a **branch**, which is an instruction to your computer to execute a different sequence of instructions. You use branches to control the flow within your program.

For example, you might create a branch based on a condition; you might verify that a number has been entered correctly. If it has, then one thing happens, and if it has not, then something else happens. This is a conditional branch.

For example, in the following pseudocode, the value of a variable called `DisplayNumber` is compared to 25. If `DisplayNumber` is greater than 25, then a variable called Count is incremented by 1. If `DisplayNumber` is less than 25, no action occurs and the variable `Count` remains the same.

```
If DisplayNumber > 25 Then
      Count = Count+1
End If
```

LOOPS

Loops are similar to branches in as much as they deviate from a linear sequence of statements according to some sort of logic condition. However, with a loop, you instruct your computer to perform, or repeat, a task until a condition is met. For example, you might create a loop that continues until a certain amount of time has elapsed or until a counter reaches a certain level. Then, a predetermined action might occur, depending upon what you want. In the following example, the program loops around until the value of `i` is 5. Then the program proceeds to the next statement.

```
For i = 1 to 5
      print i
Next
```

As well as "For" structures, loops can also be implemented by "While" statements:

```
Do While i <= 100
      i = i + 1
      print i
Loop
```

Note: *Make sure your code does not contain unintended or infinite loops. Without the statement to increment i in the Do loop example, the loop would continue forever. An infinite loop will make the process hang.*

OPERATORS

Looping and branching structures depend on logical tests to determine whether to continue the loop or the branch to follow. A logical test is one that resolves to a TRUE or FALSE value. You need to be familiar with basic **comparison operators**:

- **==**—is equal to (returns TRUE if both conditions are the same).
- **!=**—is not equal to.
- **<**—less than.
- **>**—greater than.
- **<=** and **>=**—less than or equal to and greater than or equal to.

You might also want to test more than one condition at the same time. The **logical operators** are as follows:

- **AND**—if both conditions are TRUE, then the whole statement is TRUE.
- **OR**—if either condition is TRUE, then the whole statement is TRUE.
- **XOR**—if either condition is TRUE but not both, then the whole statement is TRUE.

You can also use the negation operator NOT to reverse the truth value of any statement.

BASIC DATA TYPES

It is important to understand the different data types that a script can use. The CPU and storage devices in a computer only process data as ones and zeros. These hardware components have no conception of what the data mean. When it comes to writing scripts, though, **data types** are very important because they determine what sort of operations can be performed. For example, the characters "51" can be treated as a number value, in which case you can use the data in addition and subtraction, or they can be treated as a text string (representing a house number, for instance). If "51" is stored as a string, it must be converted before it can be used in a mathematical operation.

There are different types of number values and a variety of text forms. These include:

 Show Slide(s)

Basic Data Types (2 slides)

 Teaching Tip

Ensure learners understand the difference between integers and strings. Provide examples or ask learners to provide examples.

Data Type	Description
Integers	These are whole numbers. For example: 5, 21, or 65536. An integer data type consumes 1 to 8 bytes of computer storage.
Floating point numbers	This type can support decimal fractions such as 4.1, 26.4, or 5.62. A floating point number (or just "float") consumes between 4 and 8 bytes of storage. Note that the floating point type could store a whole number too (4.0, for instance).
Boolean values	These are a special numeric data type indicating that something is either TRUE or FALSE (with a 1 or 0). They consume a single bit of storage.

Data Type	Description
Characters	A character (or char) is a single textual character, and can be a letter of the alphabet, a symbol, or, indeed, a numerical character. For example: a, D, 7, $, @, #. These consume one byte of storage. Note that when a number is entered as a character data type, you cannot perform any mathematical operations on it.
Strings	A string is a collection of text characters. For example: XYZ, Hello world. There is no real limit on the amount of storage that can be used by a string. Generally, you define the string length when you define the data type.

When single or double quotes can be used to delimit a string ("Hello World"), the quotes are NOT part of the string itself. If you want to represent a quote character (or other delimiter) within a string, you have to use an **escape character**. For example, the string "John said \'Hello World\' then left again." contains two single quotes, escaped using the backslash character (\\).

Note: *Different languages have different escape characters, but the backslash is often the syntax used.*

Scripting Language	Escape Character
Windows batch file	%%
PowerShell	There are different escape characters for different circumstances. --% ` \\
Linux Bash shell script	\\
VBScript	To escape a single quote, enter two single quotes: '' To escape a double quote, enter two double quotes: "" Use the `Escape(charString)` function to encode a string so that the string contains only ASCII characters. Any other characters are replaced with %##, where ## is the hexadecimal equivalent to the character.
JavaScript	\\
Python	\\

Note: *To learn more, check the **Video** tile on the CHOICE Course screen for any videos that supplement the content for this lesson.*

Activity 18-6
Discussing Scripting

Show Slide(s)
Activity: Discussing Scripting

SCENARIO
Answer the following questions to check your understanding of the topic.

1. **What is the file extension for Python script files?**

   `.py.`

2. **Which batch or scripting language is represented here?**

   VBScript.

3. **What are the characteristics of a variable?**

   A variable is a construct within programming code for some sort of value that can change during the execution of the script. The variable must be given a name. A variable also has a data type, such as string or integer. The data type can be explicitly declared or set when the variable is initialized (given its first value). It is good programming practice to declare variables before they are used.

4. **What command can you use to define an environment variable?**

   In Windows, environment variables are defined using `set`. In Linux, there are not only environment variables (`env` and `printenv`), but also variables specific to the current shell. Shell variables are configured with `set`. The syntax of `set` is different between Windows and Linux

5. **What type of script construct is "For ... Next" an example of?**

   The `For ... Next` statement is one kind of loop. The script will execute statements within the loop repetitively until a logical condition is met.

6. **What is a string?**

   A string is a data type that represents a series of text characters.

Activity 18-7
Using Windows PowerShell

Show Slide(s)
Activity: Using Windows PowerShell

BEFORE YOU BEGIN
Complete this activity using Hyper-V Manager and your HOST PC.

SCENARIO
In this activity, you will customize a PowerShell script to help you better understand basic code constructs.

---

1. Start the PowerShell ISE as an Administrator, use the help system, and set the execution policy to unrestricted.

   a) Click in the **Instant Search** box, type *powershell* and then right-click **Windows PowerShell ISE** in the search results and select **Run as administrator**. Confirm the UAC prompt by selecting **Yes**.

   In the Integrated Scripting Environment (ISE), you write your code in the top pane and then use the prompt in the lower pane to run it or to execute ad hoc PowerShell cmdlets.

Teaching Tip
Optionally, demonstrate or point out that Tab completion is available.

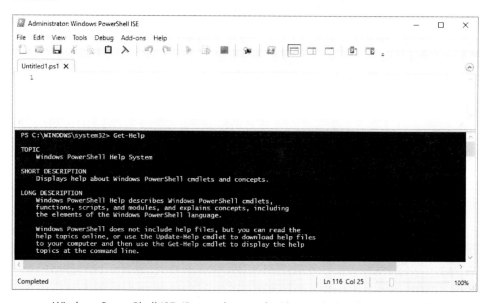

Windows PowerShell ISE. (Screenshot used with permission from Microsoft.)

   b) At the prompt, type `Get-Help` and press **Enter**. If you are prompted to update the help file, select **Cancel**. Read the help file.

   c) Run this cmdlet: `Get-ExecutionPolicy`

   The execution policy determines whether scripts need to be signed or not.

   d) For this activity, if the result was anything other than **Unrestricted**, run this cmdlet:
   `Set-ExecutionPolicy -Unrestricted`

   e) If you needed to run the cmdlet in the last sub-step, confirm the prompt by selecting **Yes to All**.

As you can see, cmdlets are the basis of PowerShell. Each cmdlet is composed of a verb-noun phrase and can take various optional parameters.

2. Open the script **C:\COMPTIA-LABS\LABFILES\VM1.ps1**, and identify the code constructs. Once you understand how the script works and what it is going to do, run the script.

a) On the Window PowerShell ISE toolbar, select the **Open Script** button. and browse to select **C:\COMPTIA-LABS\LABFILES\VM1.ps1**. Select **Open**.

Examining the first version of the VM script. (Screenshot used with permission from Microsoft.)

b) Look at line 1 in the script.

This is a comment describing the function of the script. Such preceding comments might also include the date of last revision, identify the responsible developer, explain the use of any parameters the script takes, and so on.

c) Look at the other comment lines, noting the green highlighting.

These contain code, but this code will not execute while the lines are commented.

d) Look at lines 2 through 4.

These lines declare variables. Each variable name is preceded by $ (this is a PowerShell convention) and is set to an initial value by using the equals sign (=). Each variable is set to a string value, enclosed in single quotes. Note the color-coding for the variables and the strings.

e) Look at lines 13 through 17.

These five statements contain the code that will execute. Various cmdlets are used to create a new Hyper-V VM, assign the Windows setup ISO file to its emulated DVD drive, and then start the VM.

f) In line 13, observe the way the parameters are set and the color coding for the different values. Note the use of a variable plus a literal string to identify the path for the virtual disk.

This parameter uses double quotes to allow the variable to be substituted during execution.

g) At the prompt, run `Get-Help New-VM` to see all the parameters that could have been used.

h) In line 16, observe that a parameter is set by using another cmdlet within parentheses.

i) In line 17, observe that the result of the `Get-VM` cmdlet is piped to the `Start-VM` cmdlet.

j) Select the **Run Script** button.

Teaching Tip

If the path to your Windows 10 setup disc ISO is different, ask learners to update the `$bootdisc` variable now and then save the script file.

k) Open Hyper-V Manager and verify that **VM** is present and running.

l) Open a connection window for this new VM, press **Ctrl+Alt+End**, and then when you see the prompt, press a key to boot from the setup disc.

If you needed to create a large number of VMs, using a script would save a lot of time compared to completing the **New VM** wizard over and over.

m) Close the connection window, but leave the VM running.

3. Try to run the script again, and see if you can resolve the error.

a) In the ISE window, select the **Run** button ▶ and observe the error messages.

One of the greatest challenges in developing effective scripts is to anticipate and account for errors. There are two ways you could approach this one.

- You could change the value of the $vmname variable so that the script creates a different VM.

- Or you can enable the Try code block to check whether a VM of that name exists already.

You'll take the second approach for this activity.

b) For each line of code in 6 through 12 and 18, remove the # comment character from the start of the line. As you uncomment each line, observe how the ISE highlights errors in the structure of the code. When you uncomment the last line, the errors will be resolved.

c) Save the file and then run it again.

d) Verify that the VM thumbnail in Hyper-V Manager is back to the boot sequence.

This is a new version of the VM.

The Try block is one example of branching code. It is specifically designed to catch an error. In this script, if Get-VM cannot return a VM object with the name declared by $vmname, the other statements within Try { ... } to stop the VM and remove it are not executed. The statements within the Finally { ... } block to create the new VM are executed in either case, however.

4. This script might be considered a little bit destructive if you ran it without understanding what it could do. What if you had spent hours installing Windows and third-party applications to VM and then another tech ran this script? Linux users might be quite happy with no opportunity to cancel, but Windows users are accustomed to having the chance to think about whether they really want to run a command. To accommodate this, you will add a prompt to the script. You will probably need to follow the guided steps and use the sample provided to accomplish this task.

a) Close the vm1.ps script and open **vm2.ps1**.

Examining the second version of the VM script. (Screenshot used with permission from Microsoft.)

b) Position the cursor in line 6, and select the **Run Selection** button.

c) Select **OK** at the prompt.

Running portions of your code is a useful way to check that what you have added works.

d) Look at the code in line 6.

It defines a variable that gets its value from a system-generated prompt dialog box. The parameters control the text in the dialog box, the type of buttons, the icon used, and so on.

e) In the lower prompt window, run `write $prompt`

The value is set to **OK**. The value of the variable persists even though you only ran a portion of the code. Its value will stay the same in this PowerShell session, unless it is changed again by some code.

f) Look at line 7.

This version of the script wraps the previous code within an `If` block. The earlier code will run only if the user selects **OK** at the prompt.

g) Observe the `-eq` operator used to test the condition.

Most languages would use `==` as the operator for "is equal to," but PowerShell uses its own system of operators. Note also the parentheses used to enclose the condition. While many of the code constructs are similar between languages, each language has its own syntax. To develop code, you need to understand both the general use of code constructs *and* the syntax of particular languages.

h) Look at line 21.

This bracket closes the `If` block. When you start nesting control structures, it becomes very, very easy to make mistakes in the code syntax. Using different indents for these blocks can help you to keep track of the code structure.

i) Use the Arrow keys to move the cursor between the curly brackets in lines 20 and 21. Observe how the matching bracket is highlighted in the earlier code (line 21 matches with line 7, while line 20 matches with line 14).

j) Run the whole script again to test it. At the prompt, select **Cancel**.

k) Run the script again, selecting **OK** at the prompt.

5. Now, what if you want to create more than one VM? Can you suggest what sort of control structure you could add to the script to accomplish that? View the **vm3.ps1** script for a solution.

    a) Close the vm2.ps script and open **vm3.ps1**.

Examining the third version of the VM script. (Screenshot used with permission from Microsoft.)

    b) In lines 6 and 7, observe that a different method is used to open a dialog box.

        This script uses a form with a control that can capture input. The script leverages a built-in Visual Basic form to do this.

    c) Look at line 7. Can you see the difference in the way the variable is declared, compared to the previous version of the script?

        PowerShell demonstrates more flexibility than most programming languages when it comes to variable data types. The execution engine will try to dynamically change (or cast) a variable to fit the use to which it is being put. This can lead to unexpected results, however. If the script uses a variable in a way that depends on a certain data type, it is much better to explicitly declare the variable as that type. In PowerShell, you can set the type explicitly by using square brackets and the type, such as [Int] or [String].

    d) In line 8, observe that the If block is now testing an integer, rather than a string.

        The -le operator means "less than or equal to."

    e) In line 9, observe the use of a For block to create a looping structure within the code.

        The variable $i is used to count the number of iterations, starting at 1. The use of $i++ within the condition causes the value of $i to increase by 1 for each iteration of the loop. When $i exceeds the value of $prompt, the loop exits.

    f) Observe the use of $i in the cmdlet parameters to change the name used for each VM.

    g) Run the script a few times, entering different values to test that it works reliably. Note that there is a limit to the number of VMs that you can create.

        Each VM uses memory. If the user were to enter *100* and the script were to try to run the loop that number of times, the HOST computer would be quickly overloaded. When you are developing scripts, try to anticipate what could go wrong, as well as what you want to achieve.

6. To finalize this activity, you need to delete the VMs you created.

    a) Close the PowerShell ISE window.

b)   In Hyper-V Manager, **Shift-click** to select all the **"VM"** VMs. Right-click the selection and select **Turn Off**. In the confirmation dialog box, select **Turn Off**.

c)   Right-click the selection and select **Delete**. In the confirmation dialog box, select **Delete**.

d)   Open File Explorer and delete the contents of the **C:\COMPTIA-LABS\TEMP** folder.

Topic F

Professionalism and Communication

EXAM OBJECTIVES COVERED
1002-4.7 Given a scenario, use proper communication techniques and professionalism.

On almost every service call, you will need to interact with users who are experiencing problems. In this topic, you will identify best practices for PC technicians to use to communicate appropriately with clients and colleagues and to conduct business in a professional manner.

You are a representative of your profession, as well as your company. Working with customers is a fundamental job duty for every A+ technician. How you conduct yourself will have a direct and significant impact on the satisfaction of your customers, and your level of professionalism and communication skills can directly affect whether or not you will do business with them again.

CUSTOMER SERVICE ATTITUDE

Customer Service Attitude

A service technician should not only understand technical issues but must also be a good communicator. It is easy to pick up facts and information but it can be much harder to use this information in a troubleshooting scenario requiring customer interaction, whether face-to-face or over the telephone.

Learning how to deal with customers, interpret the information they give you, and respond to their queries can be difficult but logical problem diagnosis and successful techniques for working with customers go hand-in-hand. A person with poor customer contact ability is not likely to impress as a professional customer service technician, even if he or she is competent at technical problem solving.

Remember that "customer" need not refer to someone who buys something; it can include any users or clients of a support service.

Three golden rules can be applied to good customer service:

- Be positive—project confidence, be in control, and drive the issue towards resolution.
- Be clear, concise, and direct.
- Be consistent, fair, and respectful.

COMMUNICATION SKILLS

Show Slide(s)
Communication Skills

There are many things that contribute to the art of communication: the words you use, listening effectively, and giving feedback are particularly important.

USING PROPER LANGUAGE

When you greet someone, you should be conscious of making a good first impression. When you arrive onsite, make eye contact, introduce yourself and your company, and shake hands. When you answer the phone, introduce yourself and your department and offer assistance.

When you speak to a customer, you need to make sense. Obviously, you must be factually accurate, but it is equally important that the customer understands what you are saying. Not only does this show the customer that you are competent, but it also proves that you are in control of the situation and gives the customer confidence in your abilities. You need to use clear and concise statements that avoid jargon, abbreviations, acronyms, and other technical language that a user might not understand. For example, compare the following scenarios:

Scenario 1	Scenario 2
"Looking at the TFT, can you tell me whether the driver is signed?"	"Is a green check mark displayed on the icon?"

The first question depends on the user understanding what a TFT is, what a signed driver might be, and knowing that a green check mark indicates one. The second question gives you the same information without having to rely on the user's understanding.

While you do not have to speak very formally, avoid being over-familiar with customers. Try not to use very informal language (slang) and do not use any language that may cause any sort of offense. For example, you should greet a customer by saying "Hello" or "Good morning," rather than "Whassup?" or "Hey!"

LISTENING AND QUESTIONING

You must listen carefully to what is being said to you; it will give you clues to the customer's technical level, enabling you to pace and adapt your replies accordingly. **Active listening** is the skill of listening to an individual so that you give them your full attention and are not trying to argue with, comment on, or misinterpret what they have said.

With active listening, you make a conscious effort to keep your attention focused on what the other person is saying, as opposed to being distracted by thinking what your reply is going to be or by some background noise or interruption. Some of the other techniques of active listening are to reflect phrases used by the other person or to restate the issue and summarize what they have said. This helps to reassure the other person that you have attended to what they have to say. You should also try to take notes of what the customer says so that you have an accurate record.

Listening carefully will help you to get the most information from what a customer tells you. (Image by goodluz © 123RF.com.)

It is important to understand that you must not interrupt customers when they are speaking. Also, do not ignore what they have said. If you are rude in this sort of way, the customer will form a poor opinion of you and may become less willing to help with troubleshooting.

There will inevitably be a need to establish some technical facts with the customer. This means questioning (or probing) the customer for information. There are two broad types of questioning:

- **Open**—a question that invites the other person to compose a response, such as "What seems to be the problem?"
- **Closed**—a question that can only be answered with a "Yes" or "No" or that requires some other fixed response ("What error number is displayed on the panel?" for instance).

The basic technique is start with **open questions**. You may try to guide the customer towards what information will be most helpful. For example, "When you say your printer is not working, what problem are you having—will it not switch on?" However, be careful about assuming what the problem is and leading the customer to simply affirming a guess. As the customer explains what they know, you may be able to perceive what the problem is. If so, do not assume anything too early. Ask pertinent closed questions that prove or disprove your perception. The customer may give you information that is vague or ambiguous. Clarify what they mean by asking questions like "What did the error message say?," or "When you say the printout is dark, is there a faint image or is it completely black?," or "Is the power LED on the printer lit?" If a customer is not getting to the point or if you want to follow some specific steps, take charge of the conversation at the earliest opportunity by asking closed questions. For example, compare the following scenarios:

Scenario 1	Scenario 2
"It's been like this for ages now, and I've tried pressing a key and moving the mouse, but nothing happens."	"It's been like this for ages now, and I've tried pressing a key and moving the mouse, but nothing happens."
"What does the screen look like?"	"OK, pressing a key should work normally, but as it isn't I'd like to investigate something else first. Can you tell me whether the light on the monitor is green?"
"It's dark. I thought the computer was just resting and I know in that circumstance I need to press a key, but that's not working and I really need to get on with..."	
	"No, there's a yellow light though."

In the first example, the technician asks an open question, which just lets the user focus on what they perceive as the problem, but which isn't producing any valuable troubleshooting information. Using a closed question, as in the second example, allows the technician to start working through a series of symptoms to try to diagnose the problem.

Do note that a long sequence of closed questions fired off rapidly may overwhelm and confuse a customer. Do not try to force the pace. Establish the customer's technical level and target the conversation accordingly. A customer with little technical knowledge will be confused by technical information; conversely, a knowledgeable customer may know exactly what the problem is and will not appreciate being treated like a novice. On the other hand, don't assume that the customer has diagnosed the problem correctly. Sometimes a little knowledge is worse than no knowledge at all.

GIVING FEEDBACK

When you give the customer instructions—for example, if you want them to try to complete a series of troubleshooting steps—be clear and concise. This is where having a good "mental map" of the sequence of steps to any particular configuration option demonstrates its value. Always confirm that the customer has taken the correct step.

Also, you must be patient; remember that the customer probably has little idea of what they are doing and will proceed quite slowly.

Firing question after question at a customer can be off-putting, especially if the customer does not understand what he or she is being asked to do or check.

Technical support depends on good customer relationships. A good understanding between you and a customer also makes troubleshooting that much easier. This sort of understanding is often referred to as rapport.

React to what you learn about the customer's technical ability, and develop the conversation in a positive manner to help resolve the issue. Try and form a partnership with the customer. Avoid using the pronoun "you," as it can imply blame and push the customer away from you. Consider the following:

Scenario 1	Scenario 2
"Have you checked that the printer is turned on?"	"Let's make sure the printer's turned on."

The first statement implies blame and signals that you are not prepared to accept responsibility for troubleshooting the problem. The second emphasizes you are willing to share responsibility for solving the problem and provide assistance at every step.

PROFESSIONALISM

Professionalism means taking pride in one's work and in treating people fairly. Several techniques and procedures can be used to develop an effective support service. You should understand these and the personal qualities that you should develop.

PROPER DOCUMENTATION

One of the key points of providing an effective support service is making it easy for customers to contact it. Most support takes place either over the telephone or through an email/web contact form. More advanced options include text messaging and Remote Assistance-style desktop sharing.

Whatever the method used, the contact information and hours of operation should be well advertised, so that the customer knows what to do. The service should have **proper documentation**, so that the customer knows what to expect in terms of items that are supported, how long incidents may take to resolve, when they can expect an item to be replaced instead of repaired, and so on.

PROBLEM MANAGEMENT

Problem management means tracking and auditing support requests. Whatever the tools and resources used to implement problem management, the basic process of receiving a support request, resolving the problem, and verifying the solution remains much the same.

On receiving the request (whether it is a call, email, or face-to-face contact), acknowledge the request and set expectations. For example, repeat the request back to the customer, then state the next steps, such as "I have assigned this problem to David Martin. If you don't hear from us by 3pm, please call me." The customer may have a complaint, a problem with some equipment, or simply a request for information. It is important to clarify the nature of these factors:

- The customer's expectations of what will be done and when to fix the problem.
- The customer's concerns about cost or the impact on business processes.
- Your constraints—time, parts, costs, contractual obligations, and so on.

Show Slide(s)

Professionalism (3 slides)

Interaction Opportunity

Ask learners if they have been in situations where they had to refuse a request. What are some good ways of saying "No"?

It is important not to allow the customer to form unrealistic expectations of how long the problem will take to solve. On the other hand, you should focus your attention on resolving the customer's concerns (if they are valid). Consider this exchange for example:

Customer	A+ Technician
"I have to get a job application printed today—you must send a technician around immediately."	"Do you have another print device that you could use?"
"No, I only have one printer and it's not working."	"Do you have email? You should be able to send the job application to a copy shop and they'll print it for you for a small fee."
"Yes, but I'm sure I don't know about any stores like that."	"There's actually a location a short distance from your house. If you have a pen and paper ready, I can give you the details and arrange an appointment for a technician to come and inspect your printer..."

The course of action that you agree on must be realistic and achievable.

Acknowledge the request and set expectations. (Image by goodluz © 123RF.com.)

Each request must be logged as an **incident** or **ticket** so that progress on resolving it can be documented. Most support departments use a Call Management or Problem Management System for this.

As with any communications, job tickets should be completed professionally, with due regard for spelling, grammar, and clarity. Remember that other people may need to take action using just the information in the ticket and that analysis of tickets will take place as part of quality assurance procedures. It is also possible that tickets will be forwarded to customers as a record of the jobs performed.

If possible, the request should be resolved in one call. If this is not possible, the call should be dealt with as quickly as possible, and escalated to a senior support team if a solution cannot be found promptly. What is important is that you drive problem acceptance and resolution, either by working on a solution yourself or ensuring that the problem is accepted by the assigned person or department.

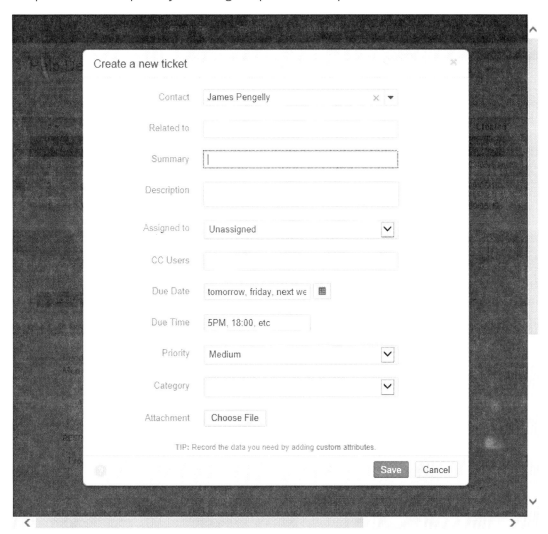

Creating a ticket in the Spiceworks IT Support management tool. (Screenshot courtesy of spiceworks.com.)

If a problem cannot be resolved within the course of a single call, it is imperative to manage the customer's expectations of when the problem will be resolved. Customers should not feel the need to call you to find out what's happening. This is irritating for them to do and means time is wasted dealing with an unnecessary call.

If have resolved the problem, and tested that the system is operating normally again, you should give the customer a general indication of what caused the problem and what you did to fix it plus assurance that the problem is now fixed and unlikely to reoccur. On leaving or on ending the call, thank the customer for their time and assistance and show that you have appreciated the chance to help them.

When the solution has been tested and verified and the customer has expressed satisfaction with the resolution of the problem, log the problem as closed. Record the solution and send verification to the customer via email or phone call.

PRIORITIZING WORK

Time is an invaluable factor in the service industry because workload usually outweighs staff resources. Time management practices impact the level of service you are able to provide to your customers.

Anybody who requests support will hope that their problem can be resolved immediately. However, this is not always possible for a number of reasons, and the customer's idea of an acceptable response time may vary greatly from your own. A formal call management system will usually allow a priority code to be assigned to a call. Open tickets can be monitored and re-prioritized to ensure that they do not fail to meet the agreed on service and performance levels.

PUNCTUALITY AND ACCOUNTABILITY

If a customer expects a visit—or call or email—from a service technician at a certain time, it is reasonable to assume that the technician will respond as promised. If it becomes obvious that the technician is not going to be on time, then the customer should be informed as soon as possible. A customer may make special arrangements to be with the technician at the allotted time and changes can be very annoying.

Be accountable for your actions, both before you arrive on site and while on site. This usually means being honest and direct about issues, but make sure this is done in a positive manner. For example:

- "I'm sorry I'm late—show me this faulty PC and I'll start work right away."
- "The printer needs a new fuser—and I'm afraid that I don't have this type with me. What I will do is call the office and find out how quickly we can get one..."
- "I've not seen this problem before, but I have taken some notes and I'll check this out as soon as I get back to the office. I'll give you a call this afternoon—will that be OK?"

FLEXIBILITY AND COMPROMISE

As a service technician, you want to ensure your customer receives the best possible attention at all times but, unfortunately, saying no is sometimes inevitable:

- The customer may ask that you do something beyond your control or perhaps beyond the terms of the service contract.
- The customer may ask you to confirm a fact or detail beyond your control.
- The customer may demand a replacement when a repair option is the only one merited by your company's procedures.

Consider the following examples; which approach is better?

Customer	A+ Technician
"My printer is broken again—I want a replacement."	1. "I'm sorry, we can't do that..."
	2: "I can arrange for a technician to be with you first thing tomorrow, and I'll mention to my supervisor that this is the second time this has occurred."
"Can you guarantee that the technician will be with me before 3 pm?"	1: "Sorry, I can't guarantee a specific time."
	2: "I'll ask the technician to try and visit before 3 pm if possible, and I'll call you around 2 pm if it looks like the technician will be later than that—is this OK?"

Note: The key to saying "no" in a positive way is to offer an alternative.

RESPECT

Respect means that you treat others (and their property) as you would like to be treated. Respect is one of the hallmarks of professionalism. At a bare minimum, respect means not being rude or offensive. Some of the other elements are listed below.

Show Slide(s)

Respect

- **Avoid Distractions**. Do not allow interruptions when you are working at a customer's site. Do not take calls from colleagues unless they are work related, urgent, and important. Do not take personal calls or respond to texts or posts on social media.

  If you are speaking with a customer on the telephone, always ask their permission before putting them on hold or transferring their call.
- **Respect for Property and Confidentiality**.
  - Do not treat customers' property carelessly. Do not use equipment or services such as PCs, printers, web access, or phones without permission and never for personal use.
  - If you are visiting someone's home or office do not help yourself to food or drink, ask before using the bathroom, and do not attempt to snoop around other areas. Do not be tempted to snoop around data files on someone else's PC either!
  - If you find printed copies of confidential materials while performing some support task (bank statements or personal letters for instance), do not look at them, make the customer aware of them, and allow time for them to be put away.
  - If you are making a site visit, keep the area in which you are working clean and tidy and leave it as you found it.
- **Cultural Sensitivity**.
  - **Cultural sensitivity** means being aware of customs and habits used by other people. It is easy to associate culture simply with national elements, such as the difference between the way Americans and Japanese greet one another. Within each nation, there are many different cultures, however, created by things such as social class, business opportunities, leisure pursuits, and so on. For example, a person may expect to be addressed using a professional title, such as a doctor or a judge; other people may be more comfortable speaking on a first name basis. It is safer to start on a formal basis and use more informal language if the customer signals that they are happier speaking that way.
  - You need to realize that though a person may be influenced by several cultures, their behavior is not determined by culture. Customer service and support requires consideration for other people. You cannot show this if you make assumptions about their cultural background without treating them as an individual (stereotyping).
  - Accent, dialect, and language are some of the crucial elements of cultural sensitivity. These can make it hard for you to understand a customer and perhaps difficult for a customer to understand you. When dealing with a language barrier, use questions, summaries, and restatements to clarify customer statements. Consider using visual aids or demonstrations rather than trying to explain something in words.
  - Also, different cultures define personal space differently, so be aware of how close or far you are from the customer.

CUSTOMER COMPLAINTS

Show Slide(s)
Customer Complaints

Teaching Tip

Ask learners if they have experienced customer complaints in their jobs, either in computer support or another area, or if they ever complained about a service or experience.

All customer complaints, whether they are valid or not, should be treated with equal seriousness.

MAINTAIN A POSITIVE ATTITUDE

Understand that an angry customer is usually frustrated that things are not working properly or feels let down (perhaps the technician arrived late). Empathizing with the customer is a good way of developing a positive relationship towards resolving their problem. Saying you are sorry does not necessarily mean you agree with what the customer is saying, just that you can understand their point of view.

"I'm sorry you're having a problem with your new PC. Let's see what we can do to sort things out..."

Arguing with the customer, denying that a problem exists, or being judgmental (assuming that the problem is of the customer's making because they do not understand the system properly) will only tend to lower the customer's impression of the service you offer. Do not try to dismiss a problem out of hand or minimize its importance. If the customer has taken it to the point of complaining, then clearly they feel that it is important; whether you consider the matter trivial is not the issue.

Listen while the customer explains the problem and let them know that you are listening. On the phone, use confirmatory phrases such as "Yes," "I see," and "Uh-huh" from time to time to make sure the customer knows you are paying attention. Do not just repeat the same phrase every few seconds—the customer may think you are mocking them.

If you are face-to-face with the customer, maintain eye contact and nod your head frequently but watch your body language. Do not fold your arms as this puts up a barrier.

BE ACCURATE AND HONEST

A common problem when dealing with customer complaints is feeling that you have to defend every action of your company or department. If the customer makes a true statement about your levels of service (or that of other employees), do not try and think of a clever excuse or mitigating circumstance for the failing; you will sound as though you do not care.

If you have let a customer down, it is probably best to empathize while including some positive actions:

"You're right—I'm sorry the technician didn't turn up. I guarantee that a technician will be with you by 3pm and I'll let my supervisor know that you have had to call us. Shall I call you back just after 3 to make sure that things are OK?"

On the other hand, if the customer is incorrect in their understanding of the situation, empathy and correction is in order:

"I'm sorry the replacement disk hasn't arrived, but I know it was put in the mail. Would you be happy to wait to see whether it arrives tomorrow or should I mail another one to you?"

If the customer had a valid cause to complain about levels of service or any aspect of your company's operation, resolve the problem and then investigate what can be done to ensure this type of problem never occurs again.

DEALING WITH A DIFFICULT CUSTOMER

It is never easy to talk to someone who is being unreasonable, abusive, or shouting down the telephone but it is important to be able to deal with these situations professionally.

1. Identify signs that a customer is becoming angry early (for example, raised voice, speaking too quickly, interrupting, and so on). Try to calm the situation down by using a low voice, soothing language, and focusing on positive actions.

2. Do not take complaints personally—provided that you haven't deliberately caused the problem about which the customer is complaining, they are using you as a representative of your organization and any anger expressed in your direction is not personal but a symptom of their frustration.

3. Listen and let the customer explain the problem—draw out the facts and use them as a positive action plan to drive the conversation forward.

4. Hang up—if a customer is persistently abusive or threatening, issue a caution, then warn them about their behavior, then end the call or contact if they do not act reasonably.

Let the customer vent. (Image by Wang Tom © 123RF.com.)

BE PROFESSIONAL

Everyone has bad days when they feel the need to get some difficult situation off their chest. Perhaps a customer has been particularly obtuse or foolish or perhaps someone has treated you unpleasantly. Find a colleague for a private face-to-face chat but under no circumstances should you ever disclose these types of experiences via social media outlets. Remember that anything posted to social media is very hard to withdraw and can cause unpredictable reactions. Tweeting some mistake made by someone you have supported is a sure way to get yourself and your company in trouble.

GUIDELINES FOR COMMUNICATING WITH CUSTOMERS

Here are some guidelines to follow to help you communicate effectively with your customers.

Show Slide(s)

Guidelines for Communicating with Customers (2 slides)

INTERACT WITH CUSTOMERS

Consider these guidelines when interacting with customers:

• Use proper language and avoid jargon, acronyms, and slang whenever possible.
• Maintain a positive attitude and project confidence.
• Actively listen, take notes, and avoid interrupting the customer.
• Be culturally sensitive.
• Use appropriate professional titles, when applicable.
• Be on time, and if you will be late, be sure to contact the customer.

- Avoid distractions, including:
  - Personal calls
  - Texting
  - Accessing social media sites
  - Talking to coworkers while interacting with customers
  - Personal interruptions
- When dealing with difficult customers or situations:
  - Do not argue with customers or be defensive.
  - Avoid dismissing customer problems.
  - Avoid being judgmental.
  - Clarify customer statements by asking open-ended questions to narrow the scope of the problem, restating the issue, or asking questions to verify understanding.
  - Do not disclose experiences via social media outlets.
- Set and meet expectations, adhere to the prescribed timeline, and communicate status with the customer.
  - If necessary, offer different repair or replacement options.
  - Provide proper documentation on the services provided.
  - Follow up with customers and users at a later date to verify satisfaction.
- Deal appropriately with customers' confidential and private materials. This includes items located on a computer, desktop, printer, and in their workspace.

Activity 18-8

Discussing Customer Service and Communication Skills

SCENARIO

Answer the following questions to check your understanding of the topic.

Show
Slide(s)

Activity: Discussing
Customer Service and
Communication Skills

1. **How would you cope with a user who is struggling to explain the problem that they are experiencing?**

   Use closed questions that allow the user to give simple yes or no answers.

2. You have received an off-site service call to service a network printer at a customer location. When you arrive, the user is at the printer and starts talking about how the printer is not working properly, and he cannot get his reports handed in on time.

   How should you approach this user?

   Demonstrate empathy with the customer's situation and use active listening skills to show that you understand the importance of the issue and make the customer confident that you can help. Then use closed questioning techniques to start to diagnose the problem.

3. **How would you deal with a customer who is becoming abusive because you have taken three separate calls to deal with their problem?**

   Explain why the problem is taking so long to resolve, and get them to focus on helping you, rather than hindering you. If the abuse continues, warn them that it cannot be tolerated and that you will have to end the call if it persists.

4. You are trying to troubleshoot a problem over the phone and need to get advice from your manager.

   How should you handle this with the customer?

   Advise them that you will put them on hold while you speak to someone else or arrange to call them back.

5. You are troubleshooting a print problem, which turned out to be caused by user error. The user is not confident that the problem is solved and wants more reassurance. You have already explained what the user was doing wrong in some detail.

   What should you do?

   Run through the print process step-by-step to show that it works. It is very important to get a customer's acceptance that a problem is "closed."

6. A user known to your department as a "frequent flyer" with regard to support requests calls in with a genuine but non-urgent problem. You are in the middle of another important job that is urgent.

   What would be the best approach?

   Confirm that the problem is not impacting their work and get them to email a support request, which you will attend to within 48 hours.

7. **What should you be wary of if a customer phones in with a problem you think you have solved already?**

   Do not assume—allow the customer to describe the problem fully then make a proper assessment.

8. You are working on the training documentation for new A+ technicians in the organization.

   What should you include for dealing with difficult customers or situations?

   Answers will vary, but might include the following. Do not argue with customers and/or be defensive. Avoid dismissing customer problems and do not be judgmental. Try to calm the customer and move the support call towards positive troubleshooting diagnosis and activity, emphasizing a collaborative approach. Do not disclose experiences via social media outlets.

Summary

In this lesson, you implemented operational procedures, including dealing with environmental impacts and controls, documentation, change management, disaster prevention and recovery, scripting, and communication skills. With the proper tools, awareness of safety and environmental issues, basic communication skills, and a solid method to use when troubleshooting, you are prepared to do your job in a safe, effective, and professional manner.

Which of the best practices discussed in this lesson apply in your workplace?

A: Answers will vary, but may include silencing phones and pagers, using active listening techniques, and treating clients with respect.

How do you think the scripting concepts discussed in this lesson will help you at your workplace?

A: Answers will vary, but may include the ability to automate repetitive, tedious tasks.

 Practice Question: Additional practice questions are available on the CompTIA CHOICE platform within the Assessments tile.

Course Follow-Up

Congratulations! You have completed *The Official CompTIA® A+® Core 1 and Core 2 (Exams 220-1001 and 220-1002)* course. You have acquired the essential skills and information you will need to install, configure, optimize, troubleshoot, repair, upgrade, and perform preventive maintenance on PCs, digital devices, and operating systems.

What's Next?

Become a CompTIA A+ Certified Professional!

CompTIA A+ certified professionals are proven problem solvers. They support today's core technologies from security to cloud to data management and more. CompTIA A+ is the industry standard for launching IT careers into today's digital world. It is the only industry recognized credential with performance-based items to prove pros can think on their feet to perform critical IT support tasks in the moment. It is trusted by employers around the world to identify the go-to person in end point management and technical support roles. CompTIA A+ is regularly re-invented by IT experts to ensure that it validates core skills and abilities demanded in the workplace.

In order to become a CompTIA A+ Certified Professional, you must successfully pass both the A+ Core 1 exam (Exam Code 220-1001) and A+ Core 2 exam (Exam Code 220-1002).

In order to help you prepare for the exams, you may want to invest in CompTIA's exam prep product, CertMaster Practice for A+.

CertMaster Practice is an online knowledge assessment and certification training companion tool specifically designed for those who have completed The Official CompTIA A+ Core 1 and Core 2 course. It helps reinforce and test what you know and close knowledge gaps prior to taking the exam.

CertMaster Practice features:

- Adaptive knowledge assessments with feedback, covering all domains of the A+ Core 1 or Core 2 exams.
- Practice tests with performance-based questions.
- Question-first design and smart refreshers to get feedback on the questions you get wrong.
- Learning analytics that track real-time knowledge gain and topic difficulty to help you learn intelligently.

Taking the Exams

When you think you have learned and practiced the material sufficiently, you can book a time to take the test.

Preparing for the Exams

We've tried to balance this course to reflect the percentages in the exam so that you have learned the appropriate level of detail about each topic to comfortably answer the exam questions. Read the following notes to find out what you need to do to register for the exam and get some tips on what to expect during the exam and how to prepare for it.

Questions in the exam are weighted by domain area as follows:

CompTIA A+ Core 1 (Exam 220-1001) Certification Domain Areas	Weighting
1.0 Mobile Devices	14%
2.0 Networking	20%
3.0 Hardware	27%

CompTIA A+ Core 1 (Exam 220-1001) Certification Domain Areas	Weighting
4.0 Virtualization and Cloud Computing	12%
5.0 Hardware and Network Troubleshooting	27%

CompTIA A+ Core 2 (Exam 220-1002) Certification Domain Areas	Weighting
1.0 Operating Systems	27%
2.0 Security	24%
3.0 Software Troubleshooting	26%
4.0 Operational Procedures	23%

For more information about how to register for and take your exam, please visit the CompTIA website: **https://certification.comptia.org/testing**

Mapping Course Content to CompTIA® A+® Core 1 (Exam 220-1001)

Achieving CompTIA A+ certification requires candidates to pass exams 220-1001 and 220-1002. This table describes where the exam objectives for Core 1 (Exam 220-1001) are covered in this course.

Domain and Objective	Covered in
Domain 1.0 Mobile Devices	
1.1 Given a scenario, install and configure laptop hardware and components.	
• Hardware/device replacement	Topic 15B
• Keyboard	Topic 15B
• Hard drive	Topic 15B
• SSD vs. hybrid vs. magnetic disk	Topic 15B
• 1.8in vs. 2.5in	Topic 15B
• Memory	Topic 15B
• Smart card reader	Topic 15B
• Optical drive	Topic 15B
• Wireless card/Bluetooth module	Topic 15B
• Cellular card	Topic 15B
• Video card	Topic 15B
• Mini PCIe	Topic 15B
• Screen	Topic 15B
• DC jack	Topic 15B
• Battery	Topic 15B
• Touchpad	Topic 15B
• Plastics/frames	Topic 15B
• Speaker	Topic 15B
• System board	Topic 15B
• CPU	Topic 15B
1.2 Given a scenario, install components within the display of a laptop.	
• Types	Topic 15B
• LCD	Topic 15B
• OLED	Topic 15B
• Wi-Fi antenna connector/placement	Topic 15B
• Webcam	Topic 15B
• Microphone	Topic 15B
• Inverter	Topic 15B
• Digitizer/touchscreen	Topic 15B
1.3 Given a scenario, use appropriate laptop features.	
• Special function keys	Topic 15A
• Dual displays	Topic 15A
• Wireless (on/off)	Topic 15A
• Cellular (on/off)	Topic 15A
• Volume settings	Topic 15A

Domain and Objective	Covered in
• Screen brightness	Topic 15A
• Bluetooth (on/off)	Topic 15A
• Keyboard backlight	Topic 15A
• Touchpad (on/off)	Topic 15A
• Screen orientation	Topic 15A
• Media options (fast forward/rewind)	Topic 15A
• GPS (on/off)	Topic 15A
• Airplane mode	Topic 15A
• Docking station	Topic 15A
• Port replicator	Topic 15A
• Physical laptop lock and cable lock	Topic 15A
• Rotating/removable screens	Topic 15A

1.4 Compare and contrast characteristics of various types of other mobile devices.

• Tablets	Topic 16A
• Smartphones	Topic 16A
• Wearable technology devices	Topic 16A
• Smart watches	Topic 16A
• Fitness monitors	Topic 16A
• VR/AR headsets	Topic 16A
• E-readers	Topic 16A
• GPS	Topic 16A

1.5 Given a scenario, connect and configure accessories and ports of other mobile devices.

• Connection types	Topic 16B
• Wired	Topic 16B
• Micro-USB/Mini-USB/USB-C	Topic 16B
• Lightning	Topic 16B
• Tethering	Topic 16B
• Proprietary vendor-specific ports (communication/power)	Topic 16B
• Wireless	Topic 16B
• NFC	Topic 16B
• Bluetooth	Topic 16B
• IR	Topic 16B
• Hotspot	Topic 16B
• Accessories	Topic 16B
• Headsets	Topic 16B
• Speakers	Topic 16B
• Game pads	Topic 16B
• Extra battery packs/battery chargers	Topic 16B
• Protective covers/waterproofing	Topic 16B
• Credit card readers	Topic 16B
• Memory/MicroSD	Topic 16B

Domain and Objective	Covered in
1.6 Given a scenario, configure basic mobile device network connectivity and application support.	
• Wireless/cellular data network (enable/disable)	Topic 16C
• Hotspot	Topic 16C
• Tethering	Topic 16C
• Airplane mode	Topic 16C
• Bluetooth	Topic 16C
• Enable Bluetooth	Topic 16C
• Enable pairing	Topic 16C
• Find a device for pairing	Topic 16C
• Enter the appropriate pin code	Topic 16C
• Test connectivity	Topic 16C
• Corporate and ISP email configuration	Topic 16C
• POP3	Topic 16C
• IMAP	Topic 16C
• Port and SSL settings	Topic 16C
• S/MIME	Topic 16C
• Integrated commercial provider email configuration	Topic 16C
• iCloud	Topic 16C
• Google/Inbox	Topic 16C
• Exchange Online	Topic 16C
• Yahoo	Topic 16C
• PRI updates/PRL updates/ baseband updates	Topic 16C
• Radio firmware	Topic 16C
• IMEI vs. IMSI	Topic 16C
• VPN	Topic 16C
1.7 Given a scenario, use methods to perform mobile device synchronization.	
• Synchronization methods	Topic 16D
• Synchronize to the cloud	Topic 16D
• Synchronize to the desktop	Topic 16D
• Synchronize to the automobile	Topic 16D
• Types of data to synchronize	Topic 16D
• Contacts	Topic 16D
• Applications	Topic 16D
• Email	Topic 16D
• Pictures	Topic 16D
• Music	Topic 16D
• Videos	Topic 16D
• Calendar	Topic 16D
• Bookmarks	Topic 16D
• Documents	Topic 16D
• Location data	Topic 16D
• Social media data	Topic 16D

Domain and Objective	Covered in
• E-books	Topic 16D
• Passwords	Topic 16D
• Mutual authentication for multiple services (SSO)	Topic 16D
• Software requirements to install the application on the PC	Topic 16D
• Connection types to enable synchronization	Topic 16D

Domain 2.0 Networking

2.1 Compare and contrast TCP and UDP ports, protocols, and their purposes.

• Ports and protocols	Topic 8F
• 21 – FTP	Topic 8F
• 22 – SSH	Topics 8F, 9D
• 23 – Telnet	Topics 8F, 9D
• 25 – SMTP	Topic 8F
• 53 – DNS	Topic 8F
• 80 – HTTP	Topic 8F
• 110 – POP3	Topic 8F
• 143 – IMAP	Topic 8F
• 443 – HTTPS	Topic 8F
• 3389 – RDP	Topics 8F, 9D
• 137-139 – NetBIOS/NetBT	Topic 8F
• 445 – SMB/CIFS	Topic 8F
• 427 – SLP	Topic 8F
• 548 – AFP	Topic 8F
• 67/68 – DHCP	Topic 8F
• 389 – LDAP	Topic 8F
• 161/162 – SNMP	Topic 8F
• TCP vs. UDP	Topic 8F

2.2 Compare and contrast common networking hardware devices.

• Routers	Topic 8E
• Switches	Topic 8B
• Managed	Topic 8B
• Unmanaged	Topic 8B
• Access points	Topic 8C
• Cloud-based network controller	Topic 11B
• Firewall	Topic 9C
• Network interface card	Topic 8B
• Repeater	Topic 8B
• Hub	Topic 8B
• Cable/DSL modem	Topic 8D
• Bridge	Topic 8B
• Patch panel	Topic 8A
• Power over Ethernet (PoE)	Topic 8B
• Injectors	Topic 8B

Domain and Objective	Covered in
• Switch	Topic 8B
• Ethernet over Power	Topic 8B
2.3 Given a scenario, install and configure a basic wired/ wireless SOHO network.	
• Router/switch functionality	Topic 9B
• Access point settings	Topic 9B
• IP addressing	Topic 9A
• NIC configuration	Topic 9A
• Wired	Topic 9A
• Wireless	Topic 9A
• End-user device configuration	Topic 9A
• IoT device configuration	Topic 9F
• Thermostat	Topic 9F
• Light switches	Topic 9F
• Security cameras	Topic 9F
• Door locks	Topic 9F
• Voice-enabled, smart speaker/digital assistant	Topic 9F
• Cable/DSL modem configuration	Topic 9B
• Firewall settings	Topic 9C
• DMZ	Topic 9C
• Port forwarding	Topic 9C
• NAT	Topic 9C
• UPnP	Topic 9C
• Whitelist/blacklist	Topic 9C
• MAC filtering	Topic 9C
• QoS	Topic 9A
• Wireless settings	Topic 9B
• Encryption	Topic 9B
• Channels	Topic 9B
• QoS	Topic 9B
2.4 Compare and contrast wireless networking protocols.	
• 802.11a	Topic 8C
• 802.11b	Topic 8C
• 802.11g	Topic 8C
• 802.11n	Topic 8C
• 802.11ac	Topic 8C
• Frequencies	Topic 8C
• 2.4Ghz	Topic 8C
• 5Ghz	Topic 8C
• Channels	Topic 8C
• 1–11	Topic 8C
• Bluetooth	Topic 9F
• NFC	Topic 9F
• RFID	Topic 9F

Domain and Objective	Covered in
• Zigbee	Topic 9F
• Z-Wave	Topic 9F
• 3G	Topic 8D
• 4G	Topic 8D
• 5G	Topic 8D
• LTE	Topic 8D
2.5 Summarize the properties and purposes of services provided by networked hosts.	
• Server roles	Topic 8F
• Web server	Topic 8F
• File server	Topic 8F
• Print server	Topic 8F
• DHCP server	Topic 8F
• DNS server	Topic 8F
• Proxy server	Topic 8F
• Mail server	Topic 8F
• Authentication server	Topic 8F
• syslog	Topic 8F
• Internet appliance	Topic 8F
• UTM	Topic 8F
• IDS	Topic 8F
• IPS	Topic 8F
• End-point management server	Topic 8F
• Legacy/embedded systems	Topic 8F
2.6 Explain common network configuration concepts.	
• IP addressing	Topic 8E
• Static	Topic 8E
• Dynamic	Topic 8E
• APIPA	Topic 8E
• Link local	Topic 8E
• DNS	Topic 8E
• DHCP	Topic 8E
• Reservations	Topic 8E
• IPv4 vs. IPv6	Topic 8E
• Subnet mask	Topic 8E
• Gateway	Topic 8E
• VPN	Topic 8E
• VLAN	Topic 8E
• NAT	Topic 8E
2.7 Compare and contrast Internet connection types, network types, and their features.	Topic 8E
• Internet connection types	Topic 8D
• Cable	Topic 8D
• DSL	Topic 8D

Domain and Objective	Covered in
• Dial-up	Topic 8D
• Fiber	Topic 8D
• Satellite	Topic 8D
• ISDN	Topic 8D
• Cellular	Topic 6C
• Tethering	Topic 16B
• Mobile hotspot	Topic B
• Line-of-sight wireless Internet service	Topic 8D
• Network types	Topic 8A
• LAN	Topic 8A
• WAN	Topic 8A
• PAN	Topic 8C
• MAN	Topic 8A
• WMN	Topic 8C

2.8 Given a scenario, use appropriate networking tools.

• Crimper	Topic 8A
• Cable stripper	Topic 8A
• Multimeter	Topic 8A
• Tone generator and probe	Topic 8A
• Cable tester	Topic 8A
• Loopback plug	Topic 8A
• Punchdown tool	Topic 8A
• WiFi analyzer	Topic 9E

Domain 3.0 Hardware

3.1 Explain basic cable types, features, and their purposes.

• Network cables	Topic 8A
• Ethernet	Topic 8A
• Cat 5	Topic 8A
• Cat 5e	Topic 8A
• Cat 6	Topic 8A
• Plenum	Topic 8A
• Shielded twisted pair	Topic 8A
• Unshielded twisted pair	Topic 8A
• 568A/B	Topic 8A
• Fiber	Topic 8A
• Coaxial	Topic 8A
• Speed and transmission limitations	Topic 8A
• Video cables	Topic 3A
• VGA	Topic 3A
• HDMI	Topic 3A
• Mini-HDMI	Topic 3A
• DisplayPort	Topic 3A
• DVI (DVI-D/DVI-I)	Topic 3A
• Multipurpose cables	Topic 2C

Domain and Objective	Covered in
• Lightning	Topic 2C
• Thunderbolt	Topic 2C
• USB	Topic 2C
• USB-C	Topic 2C
• USB 2.0	Topic 2C
• USB 3.0	Topic 2C
• Peripheral cables	Topic 2C
• Serial	Topic 2C
• Hard drive cables	Topic 4B
• SATA	Topic 4B
• IDE	Topic 4B
• SCSI	Topic 4B
• Adapters	Topic 3A
• DVI to HDMI	Topic 3A
• USB to Ethernet	Topic 15A
• DVI to VGA	Topic 3A
3.2 Identify common connector types.	
• RJ-11	Topic 2C
• RJ-45	Topic 2C
• RS-232	Topic 2C
• BNC	Topic 8A
• RG-59	Topic 8A
• RG-6	Topic 8A
• USB	Topic 2C
• Micro-USB	Topic 2C
• Mini-USB	Topic 2C
• USB-C	Topic 2C
• DB-9	Topic 2C
• Lightning	Topic 2C
• SCSI	Topic 2C
• eSATA	Topic 2C
• Molex	Topic 2C
3.3 Given a scenario, install RAM types.	Topic 4A
• RAM types	Topic 4A
• SODIMM	Topic 4A
• DDR2	Topic 4A
• DDR3	Topic 4A
• DDR4	Topic 4A
• Single channel	Topic 4A
• Dual channel	Topic 4A
• Triple channel	Topic 4A
• Error correcting	Topic 4A
• Parity vs. non-parity	Topic 4A

Domain and Objective	Covered in
3.4 Given a scenario, select, install and configure storage devices.	
• Optical drives	Topic 4C
• CD-ROM/CD-RW	Topic 4C
• DVD-ROM/DVD-RW/DVD-RW DL	Topic 4C
• Blu-ray	Topic 4C
• BD-R	Topic 4C
• BD-RE	Topic 4C
• Solid-state drives	Topic 4B
• M2 drives	Topic 4B
• NVME	Topic 4B
• SATA 2.5	Topic 4B
• Magnetic hard drives	Topic 4B
• 5,400rpm	Topic 4B
• 7,200rpm	Topic 4B
• 10,000rpm	Topic 4B
• 15,000rpm	Topic 4B
• Sizes	Topic 4B
• 2.5	Topic 4B
• 3.5	Topic 4B
• Hybrid drives	Topic 4B
• Flash	Topic 4C
• SD card	Topic 4C
• CompactFlash	Topic 4C
• Micro-SD card	Topic 4C
• Mini-SD card	Topic 4C
• xD	Topic 4C
• Configurations	Topic 4D
• RAID 0, 1, 5, 10	Topic 4D
• Hot swappable	Topic 4D
3.5 Given a scenario, install and configure motherboards, CPUs, and add-on cards.	
• Motherboard form factor	Topic 2B
• ATX	Topic 2B
• mATX	Topic 2B
• ITX	Topic 2B
• mITX	Topic 2B
• Motherboard connector types	Topic 2B
• PCI	Topic 2B
• PCIe	Topic 2B
• Riser card	Topic 2B
• Socket types	Topic 2B
• SATA	Topic 2B
• IDE	Topic 2B

Domain and Objective	Covered in
• Front panel connector	Topic 2B
• Internal USB connector	Topic 2B
• BIOS/UEFI settings	Topic 5B
• Boot options	Topic 5B
• Firmware updates	Topic 5B
• Security settings	Topic 5B
• Interface configurations	Topic 5B
• Security	Topic 5B
• Passwords	Topic 5B
• Drive encryption	Topic 5B
• TPM	Topic 5B
• LoJack	Topic 5B
• Secure boot	Topic 5B
• CMOS battery	Topic 2B
• CPU features	Topic 5A
• Single-core	Topic 5A
• Multicore	Topic 5A
• Virtualization	Topic 5A
• Hyperthreading	Topic 5A
• Speeds	Topic 5A
• Overclocking	Topic 5A
• Integrated GPU	Topic 5A
• Compatibility	Topic 5A
• AMD	Topic 5A
• Intel	Topic 5A
• Cooling mechanism	Topic 5A
• Fans	Topic 5A
• Heat sink	Topic 5A
• Liquid	Topic 5A
• Thermal paste	Topic 5A
• Expansion cards	Topic 3A
• Video cards	Topic 3A
• Onboard	Topic 3A
• Add-on card	Topic 3A
• Sound cards	Topic 3C
• Network interface card	Topic 2C
• USB expansion card	Topic 2C
• eSATA card	Topic 2C

3.6 Explain the purposes and uses of various peripheral types.

• Printer	Topic 17A
• ADF/flatbed scanner	Topic 17F
• Barcode scanner/QR scanner	Topic 17F
• Monitors	Topic 3A

Domain and Objective	Covered in
• VR headset	Topic 3A
• Optical drive types	Topic 4C
• Mouse	Topic 2D
• Keyboard	Topic 2D
• Touchpad	Topic 2D
• Signature pad	Topic 2D
• Game controllers	Topic 2D
• Camera/webcam	Topic 3C
• Microphone	Topic 3C
• Speakers	Topic 3C
• Headset	Topic 3C
• Projector	Topic 3A
• Lumens/brightness	Topic 3A
• External storage drives	Topic 4C
• KVM	Topic 2D
• Magnetic reader/chip reader	Topic 2D
• NFC/tap pay device	Topic 2D
• Smart card reader	Topic 2D

3.7 Summarize power supply types and features.

• Input 115V vs. 220V	Topic 5C
• Output 5V vs. 12V	Topic 5C
• 24-pin motherboard adapter	Topic 5C
• Wattage rating	Topic 5C
• Number of devices/types of devices to be powered	Topic 5C

3.8 Given a scenario, select and configure appropriate components for a custom PC configuration to meet customer specifications or needs.

• Graphic/CAD/CAM design workstation	Topic 5E
• SSD	Topic 5E
• High-end video	Topic 5E
• Maximum RAM	Topic 5E
• Audio/video editing workstation	Topic 5E
• Specialized audio and video card	Topic 5E
• Large, fast hard drive	Topic 5E
• Dual monitors	Topic 5E
• Virtualization workstation	Topic 5E
• Maximum RAM and CPU cores	Topic 5E
• Gaming PC	Topic 5E
• SSD	Topic 5E
• High-end video/specialized GPU	Topic 5E
• High-definition sound card	Topic 5E
• High-end cooling	Topic 5E
• Network attached storage device	Topic 5E
• Media streaming	Topic 5E

Domain and Objective	Covered in
• File sharing	Topic 5E
• Gigabit NIC	Topic 5E
• RAID array	Topic 5E
• Hard drive	Topic 5E
• Standard thick client	Topic 5E
• Desktop applications	Topic 5E
• Meets recommended requirements for selected OS	Topic 5E
• Thin client	Topic 5E
• Basic applications	Topic 5E
• Meets minimum requirements for selected OS	Topic 5E
• Network connectivity	Topic 5E
3.9 Given a scenario, install and configure common devices.	
• Desktop	Topic 5E
• Thin client	Topic 5E
• Thick client	Topic 5E
• Account setup/settings	Topic 5E
• Laptop/common mobile devices	Topic 15A
• Touchpad configuration	Topic 15A
• Touchscreen configuration	Topic 15A
• Application installations/configurations	Topic 16D
• Synchronization settings	Topic 16D
• Account setup/settings	Topic 16D
• Wireless settings	Topic 16C
3.10 Given a scenario, configure SOHO multifunction devices/printers and settings.	
• Use appropriate drivers for a given operating system	Topic 17D
• Configuration settings	Topic 17D
• Duplex	Topic 17D
• Collate	Topic 17D
• Orientation	Topic 17D
• Quality	Topic 17D
• Device sharing	Topic 17D
• Wired	Topic 17D
• USB	Topic 17D
• Serial	Topic 17D
• Ethernet	Topic 17D
• Wireless	Topic 17D
• Bluetooth	Topic 17D
• 802.11(a , b, g, n, ac)	Topic 17D
• Infrastructure vs. ad hoc	Topic 17D
• Integrated print server (hardware)	Topic 17D
• Cloud printing/remote printing	Topic 17D
• Public/shared devices	Topic 17D

Domain and Objective	Covered in
• Sharing local/networked device via operating system settings	Topic 17D
• TCP/Bonjour/AirPrint	Topic 17D
• Data privacy	Topic 17D
• User authentication on the device	Topic 17D
• Hard drive caching	Topic 17D

3.11 Given a scenario, install and maintain various print technologies.

• Laser	Topic 17A
• Imaging drum, fuser assembly, transfer belt, transfer roller, pickup rollers, separate pads, duplexing assembly	Topic 17A
• Imaging process: processing, charging, exposing, developing, transferring, fusing, and cleaning	Topic 17A
• Maintenance: Replace toner, apply maintenance kit, calibrate, clean	Topic 17A
• Inkjet	Topic 17B
• Ink cartridge, print head, roller, feeder, duplexing assembly, carriage, and belt	Topic 17B
• Calibrate	Topic 17B
• Maintenance: Clean heads, replace cartridges, calibrate, clear jams	Topic 17B
• Thermal	Topic 17C
• Feed assembly, heating element	Topic 17C
• Special thermal paper	Topic 17C
• Maintenance: Replace paper, clean heating element, remove debris	Topic 17C
• Impact	Topic 17C
• Print head, ribbon, tractor feed	Topic 17C
• Impact paper	Topic 17C
• Maintenance: Replace ribbon, replace print head, replace paper	Topic 17C
• Virtual	Topic 17D
• Print to file	Topic 17D
• Print to PDF	Topics17D
• Print to XPS	Topic 17D
• Print to image	Topic 17D
• 3D printers	Topic 17C
• Plastic filament	Topic 17C

Domain 4.0 Virtualization and Cloud Computing

4.1 Compare and contrast cloud computing concepts.

• Common cloud models	Topic 11B
• IaaS	Topic 11B
• SaaS	Topic 11B
• PaaS	Topic 11B
• Public vs. private vs. hybrid vs. community	Topic 11B
• Shared resources	Topic 11B

Domain and Objective	Covered in
• Internal vs. external	Topic 11B
• Rapid elasticity	Topic 11B
• On-demand	Topic 11B
• Resource pooling	Topic 11B
• Measured service	Topic 11B
• Metered	Topic 11B
• Off-site email applications	Topic 11B
• Cloud file storage services	Topic 11B
• Synchronization apps	Topic 11B
• Virtual application streaming/cloud-based applications	Topic 11B
• Applications for cell phones/tablets	Topic 11B
• Applications for laptops/desktops	Topic 11B
• Virtual desktop	Topic 11B
• Virtual NIC	Topic 11B
4.2 Given a scenario, set up and configure client-side virtualization.	
• Purpose of virtual machines	Topic 11A
• Resource requirements	Topic 11A
• Emulator requirements	Topic 11A
• Security requirements	Topic 11A
• Network requirements	Topic 11A
• Hypervisor	Topic 11A
Domain 5.0 Hardware and Network Troubleshooting	
5.1 Given a scenario, use the best practice methodology to resolve problems.	
• Always consider corporate policies, procedures, and impacts before implementing changes	Topic 1B
• 1. Identify the problem	Topic 1B
• Question the user and identify user changes to computer and perform backups before making changes	Topic 1B
• Inquire regarding environmental or infrastructure changes	Topic 1B
• Review system and application logs	Topic 1B
• 2. Establish a theory of probable cause (question the obvious)	Topic 1B
• If necessary, conduct external or internal research based on symptoms	Topic 1B
• 3. Test the theory to determine cause	Topic 1B
• Once the theory is confirmed, determine the next steps to resolve problem	Topic 1B
• If theory is not confirmed re-establish new theory or escalate	Topic 1B
• 4. Establish a plan of action to resolve the problem and implement the solution	Topic 1B
• 5. Verify full system functionality and, if applicable, implement preventive measures	Topic 1B

Domain and Objective	Covered in
• 6. Document findings, actions, and outcomes	Topic 1B
5.2 Given a scenario, troubleshoot problems related to motherboards, RAM, CPUs, and power.	
• Common symptoms	Topic 5D
• Unexpected shutdowns	Topic 5D
• System lockups	Topic 5D
• POST code beeps	Topic 5D
• Blank screen on bootup	Topic 5D
• BIOS time and setting resets	Topic 5D
• Attempts to boot to incorrect device	Topic 5D
• Continuous reboots	Topic 5D
• No power	Topic 5D
• Overheating	Topic 5D
• Loud noise	Topic 5D
• Intermittent device failure	Topic 5D
• Fans spin – no power to other devices	Topic 5D
• Indicator lights	Topic 5D
• Smoke	Topic 5D
• Burning smell	Topic 5D
• Proprietary crash screens (BSOD/pin wheel)	Topic 5D
• Distended capacitors	Topic 5D
• Log entries and error messages	Topic 5D
5.3 Given a scenario, troubleshoot hard drives and RAID arrays.	
• Common symptoms	Topic 4E
• Read/write failure	Topic 4E
• Slow performance	Topic 4E
• Loud clicking noise	Topic 4E
• Failure to boot	Topic 4E
• Drive not recognized	Topic 4E
• OS not found	Topic 4E
• RAID not found	Topic 4E
• RAID stops working	Topic 4E
• Proprietary crash screens (BSOD/pin wheel)	Topic 4E
• S.M.A.R.T. errors	Topic 4E
5.4 Given a scenario, troubleshoot video, projector, and display issues.	Topic 3B
• Common symptoms	Topic 3B
• VGA mode	Topic 3B
• No image on screen	Topic 3B
• Overheat shutdown	Topic 3B
• Dead pixels	Topic 3B
• Artifacts	Topic 3B
• Incorrect color patterns	Topic 3B
• Dim image	Topic 3B

Domain and Objective	Covered in
• Flickering image	Topic 3B
• Distorted image	Topic 3B
• Distorted geometry	Topic 3B
• Burn-in	Topic 3B
• Oversized images and icons	Topic 3B

5.5 Given a scenario, troubleshoot common mobile device issues while adhering to the appropriate procedures.

• Common symptoms	Topic 15C
• No display	Topic 15C
• Dim display	Topic 15C
• Flickering display	Topic 15C
• Sticking keys	Topic 15C
• Intermittent wireless	Topic 15C
• Battery not charging	Topic 15C
• Ghost cursor/pointer drift	Topic 15C
• No power	Topic 15C
• Num lock indicator lights	Topic 15C
• No wireless connectivity	Topic 15C
• No Bluetooth connectivity	Topic 15C
• Cannot display to external monitor	Topic 15C
• Touchscreen non-responsive	Topic 15C
• Apps not loading	Topic 15C
• Slow performance	Topic 15C
• Unable to decrypt email	Topic 15C
• Extremely short battery life	Topic 15C
• Overheating	Topic 15C
• Frozen system	Topic 15C
• No sound from speakers	Topic 15C
• GPS not functioning	Topic 15C
• Swollen battery	Topic 15C
• Disassembling processes for proper reassembly	Topic 15B
• Document and label cable and screw locations	Topic 15B
• Organize parts	Topic 15B
• Refer to manufacturer resources	Topic 15B
• Use appropriate hand tools	Topic 15B

5.6 Given a scenario, troubleshoot printers.

• Common symptoms	Topic 17E
• Streaks	Topic 17E
• Faded prints	Topic 17E
• Ghost images	Topic 17E
• Toner not fused to the paper	Topic 17E
• Creased paper	Topic 17E
• Paper not feeding	Topic 17E
• Paper jam	Topic 17E

Domain and Objective	Covered in
• No connectivity	Topic 17E
• Garbled characters on paper	Topic 17E
• Vertical lines on page	Topic 17E
• Backed-up print queue	Topic 17E
• Low memory errors	Topic 17E
• Access denied	Topic 17E
• Printer will not print	Topic 17E
• Color prints in wrong print color	Topic 17E
• Unable to install printer	Topic 17E
• Error codes	Topic 17E
• Printing blank pages	Topic 17E
• No image on printer display	Topic 17E
• Multiple failed jobs in logs	Topic 17E

5.7 Given a scenario, troubleshoot common wired and wireless network problems.

• Common symptoms	Topic 9E
• Limited connectivity	Topic 9E
• Unavailable resources	Topic 9E
• Internet	Topic 9E
• Local resources	Topic 9E
• Shares	Topic 9E
• Printers	Topic 9E
• Email	Topic 9E
• No connectivity	Topic 9E
• APIPA/link local address	Topic 9E
• Intermittent connectivity	Topic 9E
• IP conflict	Topic 9E
• Slow transfer speeds	Topic 9E
• Low RF signal	Topic 9E
• SSID not found	Topic 9E

Mapping Course Content to CompTIA® A+® Core 2 (Exam 220-1002)

Achieving CompTIA A+ certification requires candidates to pass exams 220-1001 and 220-1002. This table describes where the exam objectives for Core 2 (Exam 220-1002) are covered in this course.

Domain and Objective	Covered in
Domain 1.0 Operating Systems	
1.1 Compare and contrast common operating system types and their purposes.	
• 32-bit vs 64-bit	Topic 1A
• RAM limitations	Topic 1A
• Software compatibility	Topic 1A
• Workstation operating systems	Topic 1A
• Microsoft Windows	Topic 1A
• Apple Macintosh OS	Topic 1A
• Linux	Topic 1A
• Cell phone/tablet operating systems	Topic 1A
• Microsoft Windows	Topic 1A
• Android	Topic 1A
• iOS	Topic 1A
• Chrome OS	Topic 1A
• Vendor-specific limitations	Topic 1A
• End-of-life	Topic 1A
• Update limitations	Topic 1A
• Compatibility concerns between operating systems	Topic 1A
1.2 Compare and contrast features of Microsoft Windows versions.	
• Windows 7	Topic 1A
• Windows 8	Topic 1A
• Windows 8.1	Topic 1A
• Windows 10	Topic 1A
• Corporate vs. personal needs	Topic 1A
• Domain access	Topic 1A
• BitLocker	Topic 1A
• Media center	Topic 1A
• BranchCache	Topic 1A
• EFS	Topic 1A
• Desktop styles/user interface	Topic 1A
1.3 Summarize general OS installation considerations and upgrade methods.	
• Boot methods	Topic 6C
• Optical disc (CD-ROM, DVD, Blu-ray)	Topic 6C
• External drive/flash drive (USB/eSATA)	Topic 6C
• Network boot (PXE)	Topic 6C
• Internal fixed disk (HDD/SSD)	Topic 6C

Domain and Objective	Covered in
• Internal hard drive (partition)	Topic 6C
• Types of installations	Topic 6C
• Unattended installation	Topic 6C
• In-place upgrade	Topic 6C
• Clean install	Topic 6C
• Repair installation	Topic 6C
• Multiboot	Topic 6C
• Remote network installation	Topic 6C
• Image deployment	Topic 6C
• Recovery partition	Topic 6C
• Refresh/restore	Topic 6C
• Partitioning	Topic 1E
• Dynamic	Topic 1E
• Basic	Topic 1E
• Primary	Topic 1E
• Extended	Topic 1E
• Logical	Topic 1E
• GPT	Topic 1E
• File system types/formatting	Topic 1E, 6A, 6B
• ExFAT	Topic 1E
• FAT32	Topic 1E
• NTFS	Topic 1E
• CDFS	Topic 1E
• NFS	Topic 6A
• ext3, ext4	Topic 6A
• HFS	Topic 6B
• Swap partition	Topic 6A
• Quick format vs full format	Topic 1E
• Load alternate third-party drivers when necessary	Topic 6C
• Workgroup vs. Domain setup	Topic 6C
• Time/date/region/language settings	Topic 6C
• Driver installation, software, and Windows updates	Topic 6C
• Factory recovery partition	Topic 6C
• Properly formatted boot drive with the correct partitions/format	Topic 6C
• Prerequisites/hardware compatibility	Topic 6C
• Application compatibility	Topic 6C
• OS compatibility/upgrade path	Topic 6C
1.4 Given a scenario, use appropriate Microsoft command line tools.	
• Navigation	Topic 1D
• dir	Topic 1D
• cd	Topic 1D
• ..	Topic 1D

Domain and Objective	Covered in
• ipconfig	Topic 9E
• ping	Topic 9E
• tracert	Topic 9E
• netstat	Topic 9E
• nslookup	Topic 9E
• shutdown	Topic 1C
• dism	Topic 6C
• sfc	Topic 7C
• chkdsk	Topic 6D
• diskpart	Topic 1E
• taskkill	Topic 7A
• gpupdate	Topic 10C
• gpresult	Topic 10C
• format	Topic 1E
• copy	Topic 1D
• xcopy	Topic 1D
• robocopy	Topic 1D
• net use	Topic 10B
• net user	Topic 10A
• [command name]/?	Topic 1C
• Commands available with standard privileges vs. administrative privileges	Topic 1C

1.5 Given a scenario, use Microsoft operating system features and tools.

• Administrative	Topic 1C, 1F, 7A, 7B, 7C, 9C, 9D, 10A
• Computer Management	Topic 1C
• Device Manager	Topic 1F
• Local Users and Groups	Topic 10A
• Local Security Policy	Topic 10A
• Performance Monitor	Topic 7B
• Services	Topic 7A
• System Configuration	Topic 7C
• Task Scheduler	Topic 6D
• Component Services	Topic 7A
• Data Sources	Topic 7A
• Print Management	Topic 7A
• Windows Memory Diagnostics	Topic 7C
• Windows Firewall	Topic 9C
• Advanced Security	Topic 9C
• Event Viewer	Topic 7C
• User Account Management	Topic 1C
• MSConfig	Topic 7C
• General	Topic 7C
• Boot	Topic 7C

Domain and Objective	Covered in
• Services	Topic 7C
• Startup	Topic 7C
• Tools	Topic 7C
• Task Manager	Topic 7A
• Applications	Topic 7A
• Processes	Topic 7A
• Performance	Topic 7A
• Networking	Topic 7A
• Users	Topic 7A
• Disk Management	Topic 1E
• Drive status	Topic 1E
• Mounting	Topic 1E
• Initializing	Topic 1E
• Extending partitions	Topic 1E
• Splitting partitions	Topic 1E
• Shrink partitions	Topic 1E
• Assigning/changing drive letters	Topic 1E
• Adding drives	Topic 1E
• Adding arrays	Topic 1E
• Storage spaces	Topic 1E
• System utilities	Topic 1C, 1D, 1F, 6D, 7A, 7C
• Regedit	Topic 1C
• Command	Topic 1C
• Services.msc	Topic 7A
• MMC	Topic 1C
• MSTC	Topic 9D
• Notepad	Topic 1C
• Explorer	Topic 1D
• Msinfo32	Topic 1F
• DxDiag	Topic 1F
• Disk Defragmenter	Topic 6D
• System Restore	Topic 7C
• Windows Update	Topic 6D
1.6 Given a scenario, use Microsoft Windows Control Panel utilities.	
• Internet Options	Topic 9C
• Connections	Topic 9C
• Security	Topic 9C
• General	Topic 9C
• Privacy	Topic 9C
• Programs	Topic 9C
• Advanced	Topic 9C
• Display/Display Settings	Topic 1F

Domain and Objective	Covered in
• Resolution	Topic 1F
• Color depth	Topic 1F
• Refresh rate	Topic 1F
• User Accounts	Topic 1C
• Folder Options	Topic 1D
• View hidden files	Topic 1D
• Hide extensions	Topic 1D
• General options	Topic 1D
• View options	Topic 1D
• System	Topic 7B
• Performance (virtual memory)	Topic 7B
• Remote settings	Topic 7B
• System protection	Topic 7B
• Windows Firewall	Topic 9C
• Power Options	Topic 1F
• Hibernate	Topic 1F
• Power plans	Topic 1F
• Sleep/suspend	Topic 1F
• Standby	Topic 1F
• Credential Manager	Topic 10A
• Programs and features	Topic 7A
• HomeGroup	Topic 10B
• Devices and Printers	Topic 1F
• Sound	Topic 1F
• Troubleshooting	Topic 1F
• Network and Sharing Center	Topic 9A
• Device Manager	Topic 1F
• BitLocker	Topic 13B
• Sync Center	Topic 10B
1.7 Summarize application installation and configuration concepts.	
• System requirements	Topic 7A
• Drive space	Topic 7A
• RAM	Topic 7A
• OS requirements	Topic 7A
• Compatibility	Topic 7A
• Methods of installation and deployment	Topic 7A
• Local (CD/USB)	Topic 7A
• Network-based	Topic 7A
• Local user permissions	Topic 7A
• Folder/file access for installation	Topic 7A
• Security considerations	Topic 7A
• Impact to device	Topic 7A
• Impact to network	Topic 7A

Domain and Objective	Covered in
1.8 Given a scenario, configure Microsoft Windows networking on a client/desktop.	
• HomeGroup vs. Workgroup	Topic 10B
• Domain setup	Topic 10C
• Network shares/administrative shares/mapping drives	Topic 10B
• Printer sharing vs. network printer mapping	Topic 10B
• Establish networking connections	Topic 9A
• VPN	Topic 9A
• Dial-ups	Topic 9A
• Wireless	Topic 9A
• Wired	Topic 9A
• WWAN (Cellular)	Topic 9A
• Proxy settings	Topic 9C
• Remote Desktop Connection	Topic 9D
• Remote Assistance	Topic 9D
• Home vs. Work vs. Public network settings	Topic 9C
• Firewall settings	Topic 9C
• Exceptions	Topic 9C
• Configuration	Topic 9C
• Enabling/disabling Windows Firewall	Topic 9C
• Configuring an alternative IP address in Windows	Topic 9A
• IP addressing	Topic 9A
• Subnet mask	Topic 9A
• DNS	Topic 9A
• Gateway	Topic 9A
• Network card properties	Topic 9A
• Half duplex/full duplex/auto	Topic 9A
• Speed	Topic 9A
• Wake-on-LAN	Topic 9A
• QoS	Topic 9A
• BIOS (on-board NIC)	Topic 9A
1.9 Given a scenario, use features and tools of the Mac OS and Linux client/desktop operating systems.	
• Best practices	Topic 6D
• Scheduled backups	Topic 6D
• Scheduled disk maintenance	Topic 6D
• System updates/App Store	Topic 6D
• Patch management	Topic 6D
• Driver/firmware updates	Topic 6D
• Antivirus/Anti-malware updates	Topic 6D
• Tools	Topic 6B, 6D
• Backup/Time Machine	Topic 6D
• Restore/Snapshot	Topic 6D
• Image recovery	Topic 6B

Domain and Objective	Covered in
• Disk maintenance utilities	Topic 6D
• Shell/Terminal	Topic 6B
• Screen sharing	Topic 6B
• Force Quit	Topic 6B
• Features	Topic 6B
• Multiple desktops/Mission Control	Topic 6B
• Key Chain	Topic 6B
• Spot Light	Topic 6B
• iCloud	Topic 6B
• Gestures	Topic 6B
• Finder	Topic 6B
• Remote Disc	Topic 6B
• Dock	Topic 6B
• Boot Camp	Topic 6B
• Basic Linux commands	Topic 6A
• ls	Topic 6A
• grep	Topic 6A
• cd	Topic 6A
• shutdown	Topic 6A
• pwd vs. passwd	Topic 6A
• mv	Topic 6A
• cp	Topic 6A
• rm	Topic 6A
• chmod	Topic 6A
• chown	Topic 6A
• iwconfig/ifconfig	Topic 6A
• ps	Topic 6A
• su/sudo	Topic 6A
• apt-get	Topic 6A
• vi	Topic 6A
• dd	Topic 6A
• kill	Topic 6A

Domain 2.0 Security

2.1 Summarize the importance of physical security measures.

• Mantrap	Topic 12C
• Badge reader	Topic 12C
• Smart card	Topic 12C
• Security guard	Topic 12C
• Door lock	Topic 12C
• Biometric locks	Topic 12C
• Hardware tokens	Topic 12C
• Cable locks	Topic 12C
• Server locks	Topic 12C

Domain and Objective	Covered in
• USB locks	Topic 12C
• Privacy screen	Topic 12C
• Key fobs	Topic 12C
• Entry control roster	Topic 12C
2.2 Explain logical security concepts.	
• Active Directory	Topic 10C
• Login script	Topic 10C
• Domain	Topic 10C
• Group Policy/Updates	Topic 10C
• Organizational Units	Topic 10C
• Home Folder	Topic 10C
• Folder redirection	Topic 10C
• Software tokens	Topic 13A
• MDM policies	Topic 12A
• Port security	Topic 12A
• MAC address filtering	Topic 12A
• Certificates	Topic 12A
• Antivirus/Anti-malware	Topic 12A
• Firewalls	Topic 12A
• User authentication/strong passwords	Topic 13A
• Multifactor authentication	Topic 13A
• Directory permissions	Topic 13B
• VPN	Topic 12A
• DLP	Topic 13B
• Access control lists	Topic 12A
• Smart card	Topic 12C
• Email filtering	Topic 14B
• Trusted/untrusted software sources	Topic 12A
• Principle of least privilege	Topic 12A
2.3 Compare and contrast wireless security protocols and authentication methods.	
• Protocols and encryption	Topic 9B
• WEP	Topic 9B
• WPA	Topic 9B
• WPA2	Topic 9B
• TKIP	Topic 9B
• AES	Topic 9B
• Authentication	Topic 13A
• Single-factor	Topic 13A
• Multifactor	Topic 13A
• RADIUS	Topic 13A
• TACACS	Topic 13A
2.4 Given a scenario, detect, remove, and prevent malware using appropriate tools and methods.	

Domain and Objective	Covered in
• Malware	Topic 14A
• Ransomware	Topic 14A
• Trojan	Topic 14A
• Keylogger	Topic 14A
• Rootkit	Topic 14A
• Virus	Topic 14A
• Botnet	Topic 14A
• Worm	Topic 14A
• Spyware	Topic 14A
• Tools and methods	Topic 14A
• Antivirus	Topic 14A
• Anti-malware	Topic 14A
• Recovery console	Topic 14A
• Backup/restore	Topic 14A
• End user education	Topic 14A
• Software firewalls	Topic 14A
• DNS configuration	Topic 14A

2.5 Compare and contrast social engineering, threats, and vulnerabilities.

• Social engineering	Topic 12B
• Phishing	Topic 12B
• Spear-phishing	Topic 12B
• Impersonation	Topic 12B
• Shoulder surfing	Topic 12B
• Tailgating	Topic 12B
• Dumpster diving	Topic 12B
• DDoS	Topic 12B
• DoS	Topic 12B
• Zero-day	Topic 12B
• Man-in-the-middle	Topic 12B
• Brute force	Topic 12B
• Dictionary	Topic 12B
• Rainbow table	Topic 12B
• Spoofing	Topic 12B
• Non-compliant systems	Topic 12B
• Zombie	Topic 12B

2.6 Compare and contrast the differences of basic Microsoft Windows OS security settings.

• User and groups	Topic 10A
• Administrator	Topic 10A
• Power user	Topic 10A
• Guest	Topic 10A
• Standard user	Topic 10A
• NTFS vs. share permissions	Topic 1D, 10B

Domain and Objective	Covered in
• Allow vs. deny	Topic 10B
• Moving vs. copying folders and files	Topic 10B
• File attributes	Topic 1D
• Shared files and folders	Topic 10B
• Administrative shares vs. local shares	Topic 10B
• Permission propagation	Topic 10B
• Inheritance	Topic 10B
• System files and folders	Topic 1D
• User authentication	Topic 10A
• Single sign-on	Topic 10A
• Run as administrator vs. standard user	Topic 1C
• BitLocker	Topic 13B
• BitLocker To Go	Topic 13B
• EFS	Topic 13B
2.7 Given a scenario, implement security best practices to secure a workstation.	
• Password best practices	Topic 13A
• Setting strong passwords	Topic 13A
• Password expiration	Topic 13A
• Screensaver required password	Topic 13A
• BIOS/UEFI passwords	Topic 13A
• Requiring passwords	Topic 13A
• Account management	Topic 13A
• Restricting user permissions	Topic 13A
• Logon time restrictions	Topic 13A
• Disabling guest account	Topic 13A
• Failed attempts lockout	Topic 13A
• Timeout/screen lock	Topic 13A
• Change default admin user account/password	Topic 13A
• Basic Active Directory functions	Topic 10C
• Account creation	Topic 10C
• Account deletion	Topic 10C
• Password reset/unlock account	Topic 10C
• Disable account	Topic 10C
• Disable autorun	Topic 12A
• Data encryption	Topic 13B
• Patch/update management	Topic 12A
2.8 Given a scenario, implement methods for securing mobile devices.	
• Screen locks	Topic 16E
• Fingerprint lock	Topic 16E
• Face lock	Topic 16E
• Swipe lock	Topic 16E
• Passcode lock	Topic 16E

Domain and Objective	Covered in
• Remote wipes	Topic 16E
• Locator applications	Topic 16E
• Remote backup applications	Topic 16E
• Failed login attempts restrictions	Topic 16E
• Antivirus/Anti-malware	Topic 16E
• Patching/OS updates	Topic 16E
• Biometric authentication	Topic 16E
• Full device encryption	Topic 16E
• Multifactor authentication	Topic 16E
• Authenticator applications	Topic 16E
• Trusted sources vs. untrusted sources	Topic 16E
• Firewalls	Topic 16E
• Policies and procedures	Topic 16E
• BYOD vs. corporate-owned	Topic 16E
• Profile security requirements	Topic 16E

2.9 Given a scenario, implement appropriate data destruction and disposal methods.

• Physical destruction	Topic 12C
• Shredder	Topic 12C
• Drill/hammer	Topic 12C
• Electromagnetic (Degaussing)	Topic 12C
• Incineration	Topic 12C
• Certificate of destruction	Topic 12C
• Recycling or repurposing best practices	Topic 12C
• Low-level format vs. standard format	Topic 12C
• Overwrite	Topic 12C
• Drive wipe	Topic 12C

2.10 Given a scenario, configure security on SOHO wireless and wired networks.

• Wireless-specific	Topic 9B
• Changing default SSID	Topic 9B
• Setting encryption	Topic 9B
• Disabling SSID broadcast	Topic 9B
• Antenna and access point placement	Topic 9B
• Radio power levels	Topic 9B
• WPS	Topic 9B
• Change default usernames and passwords	Topic 9B
• Enable MAC filtering	Topic 12A
• Assign static IP addresses	Topic 9B
• Firewall settings	Topic 9C
• Port forwarding/mapping	Topic 9C
• Disabling ports	Topic 9C
• Content filtering/parental controls	Topic 9C
• Update firmware	Topic 9B

Domain and Objective	Covered in
• Physical security	Topic 9B
Domain 3.0 Software Troubleshooting	
3.1 Given a scenario, troubleshoot Microsoft Windows OS problems.	
• Common symptoms	Topic 7C
• Slow performance	Topic 7C
• Limited connectivity	Topic 9E
• Failure to boot	Topic 7C
• No OS found	Topic 7C
• Application crashes	Topic 7C
• Blue screens	Topic 7C
• Black screens	Topic 7C
• Printing issues	Topic 7C
• Services fail to start	Topic 7C
• Slow bootup	Topic 7C
• Slow profile load	Topic 7C
• Common solutions	Topic 7C
• Defragment the hard drive	Topic 7C
• Reboot	Topic 7C
• Kill tasks	Topic 7C
• Restart services	Topic 7C
• Update network settings	Topic 9E
• Reimage/reload OS	Topic 7C
• Roll back updates	Topic 7C
• Roll back devices drivers	Topic 7C
• Apply updates	Topic 7C
• Repair application	Topic 7C
• Update boot order	Topic 7C
• Disable Windows services/applications	Topic 7C
• Disable application startup	Topic 7C
• Safe boot	Topic 7C
• Rebuild Windows profiles	Topic 7C
3.2 Given a scenario, troubleshoot and resolve PC security issues.	
• Common symptoms	Topic 14B
• Pop-ups	Topic 14B
• Browser redirection	Topic 14B
• Security alerts	Topic 14B
• Slow performance	Topic 14B
• Internet connectivity issues	Topic 14B
• PC/OS lockup	Topic 14B
• Application crash	Topic 14B
• OS updates failures	Topic 14B
• Rogue antivirus	Topic 14B

Domain and Objective	Covered in
• Spam	Topic 14B
• Renamed system files	Topic 14B
• Disappearing files	Topic 14B
• File permission changes	Topic 14B
• Hijacked email	Topic 14B
• Responses from users regarding email	Topic 14B
• Automated replies from unknown send email	Topic 14B
• Access denied	Topic 14B
• Invalid certificate (trusted root CA)	Topic 14B
• System/application log errors	Topic 14B

3.3 Given a scenario, use best practice procedures for malware removal.

• 1. Identify and research malware symptoms.	Topic 14A
• 2. Quarantine the infected systems.	Topic 14A
• 3. Disable System Restore (in Windows).	Topic 14A
• 4. Remediate the infected systems.	Topic 14A
• a. Update the anti-malware software.	Topic 14A
• b. Scan and use removal techniques (safe mode, pre-installation environment).	Topic 14A
• 5. Schedule scans and run updates.	Topic 14A
• 6. Enable System Restore and create a restore point (in Windows).	Topic 14A
• 7. Educate the end user.	Topic 14A

3.4 Given a scenario, troubleshoot mobile OS and application issues.

• Common symptoms	Topic 16F
• Dim display	Topic 16F
• Intermittent wireless	Topic 16F
• No wireless connectivity	Topic 16F
• No Bluetooth connectivity	Topic 16F
• Cannot broadcast to external monitor	Topic 16F
• Touchscreen non-responsive	Topic 16F
• Apps not loading	Topic 16F
• Slow performance	Topic 16F
• Unable to decrypt email	Topic 16F
• Extremely short battery life	Topic 16F
• Overheating	Topic 16F
• Frozen system	Topic 16F
• No sound from speakers	Topic 16F
• Inaccurate touch screen response	Topic 16F
• System lockout	Topic 16F
• App log errors	Topic 16F

3.5 Given a scenario, troubleshoot mobile OS and application security issues.

• Common symptoms	Topic 16F

Domain and Objective	Covered in
• Signal drop/weak signal	Topic 16F
• Power drain	Topic 16F
• Slow data speeds	Topic 16F
• Unintended WiFi connection	Topic 16F
• Unintended Bluetooth pairing	Topic 16F
• Leaked personal files/data	Topic 16F
• Data transmission over limit	Topic 16F
• Unauthorized account access	Topic 16F
• Unauthorized location tracking	Topic 16F
• Unauthorized camera/microphone activation	Topic 16F
• High resource utilization	Topic 16F
Domain 4.0 Operational Procedures	
4.1 Compare and contrast best practices associated with types of documentation.	
• Network topology diagrams	Topic 18B
• Knowledge base/articles	Topic 18B
• Incident documentation	Topic 18B
• Regulatory and compliance policy	Topic 18B
• Acceptable use policy	Topic 18B
• Password policy	Topic 18B
• Inventory management	Topic 18B
• Asset tags	Topic 18B
• Barcodes	Topic 18B
4.2 Given a scenario, implement basic change management best practices.	
• Documented business processes	Topic 18C
• Purpose of the change	Topic 18C
• Scope of the change	Topic 18C
• Risk analysis	Topic 18C
• Plan for change	Topic 18C
• End-user acceptance	Topic 18C
• Change board	Topic 18C
• Approvals	Topic 18C
• Backout plan	Topic 18C
• Documentation changes	Topic 18C
4.3 Given a scenario, implement basic disaster prevention and recovery methods.	
• Backup and recovery	Topic 18D
• Image level	Topic 18D
• File level	Topic 18D
• Critical applications	Topic 18D
• Backup testing	Topic 18D
• UPS	Topic 18A
• Surge protector	Topic 18A
• Cloud storage vs. local storage backups	Topic 18D

Domain and Objective	Covered in
• Account recovery options	Topic 18D
4.4 Explain common safety procedures.	
• Equipment grounding	Topic 2A
• Proper component handling and storage	Topic 2A
• Antistatic bags	Topic 2A
• ESD straps	Topic 2A
• ESD mats	Topic 2A
• Self-grounding	Topic 2A
• Toxic waste handling	Topic 2A
• Batteries	Topic 2A
• Toner	Topic 2A
• CRT	Topic 2A
• Cell phones	Topic 2A
• Tablets	Topic 2A
• Personal safety	Topic 2A
• Disconnect power before repairing PC	Topic 2A
• Remove jewelry	Topic 2A
• Lifting techniques	Topic 2A
• Weight limitations	Topic 2A
• Electrical fire safety	Topic 2A
• Cable management	Topic 2A
• Safety goggles	Topic 2A
• Air filter mask	Topic 2A
• Compliance with government regulations	Topic 2A
4.5 Explain environmental impacts and appropriate controls.	
• MSDS documentation for handling and disposal	Topic 18A
• Temperature, humidity level awareness, and proper ventilation	Topic 18A
• Power surges, brownouts, and blackouts	Topic 18A
• Battery backup	Topic 18A
• Surge suppressor	Topic 18A
• Protection from airborne particles	Topic 18A
• Enclosures	Topic 18A
• Air filters/mask	Topic 18A
• Dust and debris	Topic 18A
• Compressed air	Topic 18A
• Vacuums	Topic 18A
• Compliance to government regulations	Topic 18A
4.6 Explain the processes for addressing prohibited content/activity, and privacy, licensing, and policy concepts.	
• Incident response	Topic 13C
• First response	Topic 13C
• Identify	Topic 13C

Domain and Objective	Covered in
• Report through proper channels	Topic 13C
• Data/device preservation	Topic 13C
• Use of documentation/documentation changes	Topic 13B
• Chain of custody	Topic 13C
• Tracking of evidence/documenting process	Topic 13C
• Licensing/DRM/EULA	Topic 13B
• Open-source vs. commercial license	Topic 13B
• Personal license vs. enterprise licenses	Topic 13B
• Regulated data	Topic 13B
• PII	Topic 13B
• PCI	Topic 13B
• GDPR	Topic 13B
• PHI	Topic 13B
• Follow all policies and security best practices	Topic 13B
4.7 Given a scenario, use proper communication techniques and professionalism.	
• Use proper language and avoid jargon, acronyms, and slang, when applicable	Topic 18F
• Maintain a positive attitude/ project confidence	Topic 18F
• Actively listen (taking notes) and avoid interrupting the customer	Topic 18F
• Be culturally sensitive	Topic 18F
• Use appropriate professional titles, when applicable	Topic 18F
• Be on time (if late, contact the customer)	Topic 18F
• Avoid distractions	Topic 18F
• Personal calls	Topic 18F
• Texting/social media sites	Topic 18F
• Talking to coworkers while interacting with customers	Topic 18F
• Personal interruptions	Topic 18F
• Dealing with difficult customers or situations	Topic 18F
• Do not argue with customers and/or be defensive	Topic 18F
• Avoid dismissing customer problems	Topic 18F
• Avoid being judgmental	Topic 18F
• Clarify customer statements (ask open-ended questions to narrow the scope of the problem, restate the issue, or question to verify understanding)	Topic 18F
• Do not disclose experiences via social media outlets	Topic 18F
• Set and meet expectations/timeline and communicate status with the customer	Topic 18F
• Offer different repair/replacement options, if applicable	Topic 18F
• Provide proper documentation on the services provided	Topic 18F
• Follow up with customer/user at a later date to verify satisfaction	Topic 18F
• Deal appropriately with customers' confidential and private materials	Topic 18F
• Located on a computer, desktop, printer, etc.	Topic 18F

Domain and Objective	Covered in
4.8 Identify the basics of scripting.	
• Script file types	Topic 18E
• .bat	Topic 18E
• .ps1	Topic 18E
• .vbs	Topic 18E
• .sh	Topic 18E
• .py	Topic 18E
• .js	Topic 18E
• Environment variables	Topic 18E
• Comment syntax	Topic 18E
• Basic script constructs	Topic 18E
• Basic loops	Topic 18E
• Variables	Topic 18E
• Basic data types	Topic 18E
• Integers	Topic 18E
• Strings	Topic 18E
4.9 Given a scenario, use remote access technologies.	
• RDP	Topic 9D
• Telnet	Topic 9D
• SSH	Topic 9D
• Third-party tools	Topic 9D
• Screen share feature	Topic 9D
• File share	Topic 9D
• Security considerations of each access method	Topic 9D

Glossary

*aaS
(Something as a Service) An ownership model for cloud services where the "something" can refer to infrastructure, network, platform, or software.

2-step verification
When a user connects to a service using a device that was not previously registered with the service, the authenticator application sends a **one time password** to a smartphone or alternate email address that the user then enters to complete the authentication process.

2D barcodes
See **QR codes**.

3D modeling software
Software that creates a model of a physical object using polygons, spline curves, and bezel curves.

3D print process
A printing process that builds a solid object from successive layers of material.

3D printer
Hardware device capable of small scale manufacturing. 3D printers use a variety of filament media (typically plastic) with different properties.

3D scanner
A scanner that can gather data about the shape and appearance of a physical object and save that information to a computer.

3D slicing software
Software in a 3D printer or in 3D modeling software that takes a 3D model and creates multiple horizontal layers of the model.

802.3af
PoE powered devices can draw up to about 13 W over the link. Power is supplied as 350mA@48V and limited to 15.4 W, but the voltage drop over the maximum 100 feet of cable results in usable power of around 13 W.

802.3at (PoE+)
PoE powered devices can draw up to about 25 W. PoE+ allows for a broader range of devices to be powered such as cameras with pan/tilt/zoom capabilities, door controllers, and thin client computers.

absolute path
The specific location, including the domain name, irrespective of the working directory or combined paths.

AC
(alternating current) When electricity is produced by a generator at the power station, the rotational movement of the magnetic coils causes the current produced to oscillate like a sine wave (it is said to alternate). Computers require direct current (at a constant voltage). A transformer is used to convert AC from the power outlet into the 3.3, 5, and 12 V DC supply required by the computer.

AC adapter
An external power supply used to power laptops and other portable devices.

accelerometer
Mobile technology that can determine the orientation of a device with a sensor that measures the acceleration of the device direction.

accelerometer/gyroscope
Components used in mobile devices to detect motion (accelerometer) and rotation (gyroscope). As well as switching screen orientation, this can be

used as a control mechanism (for example, a driving game could allow the tablet itself to function as a steering wheel).

access time
The speed at which memory or a disk drive can be addressed and utilized (opened, read from, or written to).

accident
Any instance where a person is injured or computer equipment is damaged.

accounting
In security terms, the process of tracking and recording system activities and resource access. Also known as auditing.

ACE
(access control entry) Within an ACL, a record of subjects and the permissions they hold on the resource.

ACL
(Access Control List) The permissions attached to or configured on a network resource, such as folder, file, or firewall. The ACL specifies which subjects (user accounts, host IP addresses, and so on) are allowed or denied access and the privileges given over the object (read only, read/write, and so on).

ACPI
(Advanced Configuration and Power Management Interface) An open standard to communicate between the operating system and hardware to enable power management features.

active listening
The skill of listening to an individual so that you give them your full attention and are not trying to argue with, comment on, or misinterpret what they have said.

ActiveX
Microsoft's software framework for browser plug-ins that allow users to run software components accessed from the Internet.

AD DS
(Active Directory Domain Services) The database that contains the users,

groups, and computer accounts in a Windows Server domain.

ad hoc network
A peer-to-peer network created for the current print session.

ad-hoc mode
A temporary network mode in which devices connect to each other directly without an intermediary networking device.

adapter card
Circuit board providing additional functionality to the computer system (video, sound, networking, modem, and so on). An adapter card fits a slot on the PC's expansion bus and often provides ports through slots cut into the back of the PC case. Different cards are designed for different slots (PCI or PCIe).

add-on card
An adapter card installed in a PCIe slot.

additive color printing
A color printing method that combines differently colored transmitted light to form different shades.

ADF
(Automatic Document Feeder) Device that feeds media automatically into a scanner or printer.

Administrative Templates
Group Policy files for registry-based policy management. The files have the .ADM file extension.

Administrator account
A Microsoft Windows user account that can perform all tasks on the computer, including installing and uninstalling apps, setting up other users, and configuring hardware and software.

ADSL
(Asymmetrical DSL) A consumer version of DSL that provides a fast downlink but a slow uplink. The upstream rate is between 64 Kbps and 1 Mbps and the downstream rate it 500 Kbps to 8 Mbps.

Adult account
Any Microsoft Windows user account that is not configured as a **Child account**.

AES
(Advanced Encryption Standard) Modern encryption suite providing symmetric encryption (the same key is used to encrypt and decrypt). AES is a very strong cipher with many applications, including being part of the WPA2 Wi-Fi encryption scheme.

AFP
(Apple Filing Protocol) Protocol supporting file sharing on macOS networks. AFP works over TCP port 548.

agent
A process running on an SNMP compatible network device that sends information to an SNMP manager.

AHCI
(Advanced Host Controller Interface) A logical interface used by SATA drives to communicate with the bus.

air or dust filters
Polyester sheets that cover fan inlets to trap dust on their surface, preventing the dust from getting into a computer or other device.

airborne particles
Dust and other small items that can be blown about and carried on air currents, that if they get inside computers, can prevent effective heat dissipation.

airplane mode
A toggle found on mobile devices enabling the user to disable and enable wireless functionality quickly.

all-in-one unit
A desktop computer in which all the computer components, except the keyboard and mouse, are contained within the monitor case.

ALU
(Arithmetic Logic Unit) A circuit in the CPU that performs integer-based calculations and performs bit-wise logical calculations.

AMD-V
Extensions in AMD-based systems that allow hardware virtualization.

AMD64
AMD's 64-bit instruction set that was also adopted by Intel for its 64-bit desktop and mobile line. Intel refers to it as EM64T or Intel 64.

analog display
A computer monitor that accepts continuously varying signals. CRT monitors use analog signals and are capable of supporting several output resolutions without losing quality.

Android
An open-source operating system supported by a wide range of hardware and software vendors.

Android application package
(APK) Third-party or custom programs that are installed directly through an APK file, giving users and business the flexibility to install apps directly on Android devices.

Android Auto
An Android phone feature that allows users to interact with their phone using voice commands and a vehicle's built-in display.

answer file
An XML text file that contains all of the instructions that the Windows Setup program will need to install and configure the OS without any administrator intervention, including the product key.

anti-malware software
A software program that scans a device or network for known viruses, Trojans, worms, and other malicious software.

antiglare cover
A display cover to deal with ambient lighting issues on the display.

antistatic bag
A packaging material containing anti-ESD shielding or dissipative materials to protect components from ESD damage.

antivirus
Software capable of detecting and removing virus infections and (in most cases) other types of malware, such as worms, Trojans, rootkits, adware, spyware, password crackers, network mappers, DoS tools, and so on. antivirus software works on the basis of both identifying malware code (signatures) and detecting suspicious behavior (heuristics). antivirus software must be kept up to date with the latest malware definitions and protect itself against tampering.

AP
(Access Point) A device that provides connectivity between wireless devices and a cabled network. APs with Internet connectivity located in public buildings (cafes, libraries, and airports, for instance) are often referred to as hotspots.

APIPA
(Automatic Private IP Addressing) A means for Windows clients configured to obtain an address automatically that could not contact a DHCP server to communicate on the local subnet. The host randomly selects an address from the range 169.254.x.y. This is also called a link-local address.

app scanner
A class of security software designed to monitor the permissions allocated to apps and how they are using (or abusing) them.

App Store
The online site where Apple users can purchase or get free apps have been submitted to and approved by Apple before they are released to users.

Apple CarPlay
An iPhone feature that allows users to interact with their phone using voice commands and a vehicle's built-in display.

Apple ID
A user account on an Apple device based on the sign-in email address that is used to sign-in to the App Store, access iCloud, and other Apple features and functions.

Application protocols layer
In the TCP/IP suite, numerous protocols used for network configuration, management, and services reside at this level. Application protocols use a TCP or UDP port to connect the client and server.

application virtualization
Rather than run the whole client desktop as a virtual platform, the client either accesses a particular application hosted on a server or streams the application from the server to the client for local processing.

apps
Installable programs that extend the functionality of the mobile device, that must be written and compiled for a particular mobile operating system (Apple iOS, Android, or Windows).

apt
A tool for maintaining packages on Debian-based Linux systems.

AR
(augmented reality) Using software and smartphone cameras or headsets to interact with real-world objects and images or change the way they appear in some way.

arguments
Values supplied to the command for it to operate on, supplied in the correct order required for the command's syntax.

ARP
(Address Resolution Protocol) When two systems communicate using IP, an IP address is used to identify the destination machine. The IP address must be mapped to a device (the network adapter's MAC address). ARP performs the task of resolving an IP address to a hardware address. Each host caches known mappings in an ARP table for a few minutes. It is also a utility used to manage the ARP cache.

ARP poisoning
(Address Resolution Protocol poisoning) Injecting a false IP:MAC lookup into the victim's ARP cache. This can be used to perform a variety of attacks, including DoS, spoofing, and Man-in-the-Middle.

array
See **RAID**.

ASF
(AutoSheet Feeder) In an inkjet printer, the paper pickup mechanism to feed paper into the printer.

aspect ratio
A characteristic of display devices that indicates the ratio of width to height.

asset
A thing of economic value. For accounting purposes, assets are classified in different ways, such as tangible and intangible or short term and long term.

asset management
Asset management means identifying each asset and recording its location, attributes, and value in a database.

attended installation
A software or operating system installation where the installer inputs the configuration information in response to prompts from a setup program.

ATX
A standard PC case, motherboard, and power supply specification. Mini-, Micro-, and Flex-ATX specify smaller board designs.

audio subsystem
Made up of a sound card and one or more audio input and output devices.

auditing
See **accounting**.

AUP
(Acceptable Use Policy) A policy that governs employees' use of company equipment and Internet services. ISPs may also apply AUPs to their customers.

authentication
A means for a user to prove their identity to a computer system. Authentication is implemented as either something you know (a username and password), something you have (a smart card or key fob), or something you are (biometric information). Often, more than one method is employed (2-factor authentication).

authentication factor
Information used to identify a user from one of several categories (something the user knows, has, or "is," or the user's location).

authenticator application
An app that requires, when using a new computer or device to access a service, a code to be sent in the form of a **one time password**.

authorization
In security terms, the process of determining what rights and privileges a particular entity has.

autodiscover
The ability of a mobile device to determine connection settings based on the user entering their email credentials.

availability
The fundamental security goal of ensuring that systems operate continuously and that authorized individuals can access data that they need.

back haul
A link or transit arrangement with another ISP to connect each Point of Presence to their core network infrastructure and one or more IXPs.

backdoor
A remote administration utility providing a means of configuring a computer. Remote admin software may be installed intentionally, in which case it must be properly secured. Backdoors may also be installed by malware.

backed up print queue
A problem situation where there are lots of jobs pending but not printing.

background
A process that runs without a window and does not require any sort of user interaction.

backlight
Fluorescent lamp illuminating the image on a flat panel (LCD) screen. If the backlight or inverter fails, the screen image will go very, very dark.

backout plan
A plan defined ahead of making any moves, adds, or changes so that in case unforeseen problems arise when the change is made, there is a plan to put things back as they were before making the change.

backup
Recovery of data can be provided through the use of a backup system. Most backup systems provide support for tape devices. This provides a reasonably reliable and quick mechanism for copying critical data. Different backup types (full, incremental, or differential) balance media capacity, time required to backup, and time required to restore.

backup power generator
A Standby Power Supply fueled by diesel or propane. In the event of a power outage, a UPS must provide transitionary power, as a backup generator cannot be cut-in fast enough.

barcode label
A label containing a UPC code. Can be affixed to tangible assets for identification in an **asset management** system.

barcode scanner
A barcode reader is a handheld or pen-shaped device designed to scan barcodes. A barcode is a pattern of different sized parallel bars, typically representing a product number, such as an ISBN, EAN, or UPC. The reader uses a sensor mechanism (typically either a photo diode, laser, or CCD) to read the intensity of light reflected back by the barcode. The reader then reports the number back to application software, which links it to a product database.

baseband update
Modification of the firmware of a cellular modem.

baseline
The point from which something varies. A configuration baseline is the original or recommended settings for a device, while a performance baseline is the originally measured throughput.

battery backup
See **UPS**.

BCD
(Boot Configuration Data) Windows stores information about operating systems installed on the computer in a boot configuration data store, located in \boot \bcd on the system partition. The BCD can be modified using the bcedit command-line tool or MSCONFIG.

BD
(Blu-ray Disc) The latest generation of optical disc technology that uses a 405 mm blue laser for high density storage, with disc capacity of 25 GB per layer. Transfer rates are measured in multiples of 36 MBps.

biometric devices
Peripherals used to gather biometric data for comparison to data stored in a database.

biometrics
Identifying features stored as digital data can be used to authenticate a user. Typical features used include facial pattern, iris, retina, or fingerprint pattern, and signature recognition. This requires the relevant scanning device, such as a fingerprint reader, and a database of biometric information (template).

BIOS
(Basic Input/Output System) Firmware that contains programs and information relating to the basic operation of PC components such as drives, keyboard, video display, and ports. It also contains specific routines to allow set-up configuration to be viewed and edited and it contains the self-diagnostic Power-On Self-Test (POST) program used to detect fundamental faults in PC components. BIOS can also be used to secure components not protected by the OS by specifying a supervisor password (to prevent tampering with BIOS settings) and a user password (to boot the PC).

BIOS setup
(Basic Input/Output System setup) Another name for the setup program used to configure system firmware settings. Also known as CMOS setup or UEFI setup.

bitmap image data
A pixel-by-pixel image sent to a printer to print a file.

blacklisting
An address added to the black list is prohibited from connecting to any port.

blackout
A complete loss of electrical power.

blanking plate
Metal strips that cover unused adapter slots in the case so that proper air flow is maintained within the system case.

blaster
See **IR**.

BLE
(Bluetooth Low Energy) A radio-based technology designed for small battery-powered devices that transmit small amounts of data infrequently. BLE is not backwards-compatible with "classic" Bluetooth, though a device can support both standards simultaneously.

Blu-ray drive
An optical drive for reading, and if so equipped, writing to Blu-ray disc media. Most drives can also read CD and DVD discs.

Bluetooth
Short-range radio-based technology, working at up to 10 m (30 feet) at up to 1 Mbps used to connect peripherals (such as mice, keyboards, and printers) and for communication between two devices (such as a laptop and smartphone).

bookmark
A record of a website or web page that you visited.

Boolean values
Data type supporting 1-bit storage, representing FALSE and TRUE. Boolean logic is a statement that resolves to a true or false condition and underpins the branching and looping features of computer code.

boot device priority
See **boot sequence**.

boot partition
In Microsoft terminology, the partition that contains the operating system (that is, the \WINDOWS folder) is referred to as the boot partition. This is typically a different partition to the system partition (the partition containing the boot files).

boot sector
See **Volume Boot Record (VBR)**.

boot sequence
The order in which the system firmware searches devices for a boot manager.

botnet
A network of computers that have been compromised by Trojan, rootkit, or worm malware. Providing the botnet can also subvert any firewalls between the controller (or herder) and the compromised computers (zombies), so that they can be remotely controlled and monitored using covert channels.

branch
Used to control the flow within a computer program or script, usually based on some type of logic condition. Often implemented with If or Goto statements.

BRI
(Basic Rate Interface) A class of ISDN service that provides two 64 Kbps (B channels) for data and one 16 Kbps (D channel) for link management control signals

bridge
A bridge can be used to divide an overloaded network into separate segments. Intrasegment traffic (traffic between devices on the same segment) remains within this segment and cannot affect the other segments. A bridge works most efficiently if the amount of intersegment traffic (traffic between devices on different segments) is kept low. Segments on either side of a bridge are in separate collision domains but the same broadcast domain. The function of bridges is now typically performed by switches.

broadband
The technical meaning of broadband is a transmission that divides the available media bandwidth into a number of

transmission paths or channels. WAN signaling generally uses this form of transmission and consequently the term is used generally to refer to 2 MBps+ Internet links such as DSL or cable.

broadcast address

A packet sent to all hosts on the local network (or subnet). Routers do not ordinarily forward broadcast traffic. The broadcast address of IP is one where the host bits are all set to 1; at the MAC layer, it is the address ff:ff:ff:ff:ff:ff.

brownout

A brownout occurs when the power that is supplied by the electrical wall socket is insufficient to allow the computer to function correctly. Brownouts are long sags in power output that are often caused by overloaded or faulty mains distribution circuits or by a failure in the supply route from electrical power station to a building.

BSOD

(Blue Screen of Death) A condition that indicates an error from which the system cannot recover (also called a stop error). Blue screens are usually caused by bad driver software or hardware faults (memory or disk).

BSSID

(Basic Service Set Identifier) The MAC address of the access point.

Bubblejet

The term used by the Canon company to refer to their **thermal inkjet print method.**

burning

In optical discs, the process of using a special laser used to transform the dye to mimic the pits and lands of a premastered CD.

bus

Buses are the connections between components on the motherboard and peripheral devices attached to the computer. Buses are available in industry standard formats, each with its own advantages and disadvantages. The standard functions of a bus are to provide data sharing, memory addressing, power supply, and timing. Common bus types include PCI, PCI Express, and USB.

bus mastering

Feature of a bus allowing devices to communicate with one another without going through the CPU. Bus mastering is supported by most bus types, including PCI, SCSI, and ATA (in "Ultra DMA" modes).

BYOD

(Bring Your Own Device) Security framework and tools to facilitate use of personally owned devices to access corporate networks and data.

CA

(Certificate Authority) A server that can issue digital certificates and the associated public/private key pairs.

CAB

(Change Advisory Board) In change management, the team responsible for approving or denying RFCs.

CAC

(Common Access Card) An identity and authentication smart card produced for Department of Defense employees and contractors in response to a Homeland Security Directive.

cache

A small block of high-speed memory that enhances performance by pre-loading (caching) code and data from relatively slow system memory and passing it to the CPU on demand.

CAD

(Computer-Aided Design) Software that makes technical drawings and schematics easier to produce and revise.

CAL

(Client Access Licenses) Licenses required for clients accessing software services from a server, purchased per server (with a limited number of simultaneous users) or per seat (specifying each unique device or user).

calibration (printer)

The process by which the printer determines the appropriate print density or color balance, or how much toner to use.

CAM
(Computer Aided Manufacturing) Software that can control machine tools found in manufacturing environments.

CAM
(Content Addressable Memory) See **MAC address table**.

CAN
(Campus area network) A network that spans multiple nearby buildings.

capacitor
An electrical component that stores electrical energy and is often used to regulate voltages. It can hold a charge after the power is removed.

capacity
The amount of space available on storage media.

CATV
(Cable Access TV) Access to television stations over a coaxial cable connected to a TV, set-top box, or computer.

CCD
(Charge Coupled Device) A type of microchip widely used as a digital image sensor. Each element in a CCD converts light captured by a photodiode into a proportional electric charge, which is then amplified, sampled, and stored as a digital value. The number of elements determines the resolution.

CCFL
(Cold Cathode Fluorescent Lamp) A type of lamp providing a bright, clear light source. CCFLs are used for LCD backlights and scanners.

CD drive
An optical drive consisting of a spindle motor to spin the disc, a laser and lens to read the disc, and a tracking system to move the laser and lens assembly.

CD-R
Compact disks containing a layer with photosensitive dye in which a laser

transforms the dye to mimic the pits and lands of a premastered CD.

CD-ROM
(Compact Disc - Read Only Memory) An optical storage technology. The discs can normally hold 700 MB of data or 80 minutes of audio data. Recordable and re-writable CDs (and DVDs) are a popular backup solution for home users. They are also useful for archiving material. Unlike magnetic media, the data on the disc cannot be changed (assuming that the disc is closed to prevent further rewriting in the case of RW media). This makes them useful for preserving tamper-proof records.

CD-RW
Compact disks containing a heat sensitive compound whose properties can be changed between crystalline and amorphous by a special laser.

CDMA
(Code Division Multiple Access) Method of multiplexing a communications channel using a code to key the modulation of a particular signal. CDMA is associated with Sprint and Verizon cellular phone networks.

cellular data
Connecting to the Internet via the device's cell phone radio and the handset's cellular network provider.

cellular radio
A component in a mobile device that is capable of switching frequencies automatically when moving between network cells without losing the connection.

chain of custody
Documentation attached to evidence from a crime scene detailing when, where, and how it was collected, where it has been stored, and who has handled it subsequently to collection.

challenge question
Questions asked, usually through software but sometimes from a help desk staff member, that only the end-user can answer. A feature of multifactor authentication or for account recovery.

change management
A means of putting policies in place to reduce the risk that changes to information and communications technology infrastructure components could cause service disruption.

channels
Paths between PATA drives and motherboard, called IDE1 and IDE2, or primary (PRI IDE) and secondary (SEC IDE).

character
Data type supporting storage of a single character.

charms
Commands displayed in a vertical bar on the right side of a Windows 8 Start Screen. The commands are Search, Share, Start, Devices, and Settings.

chassis
See **system case**.

Child account
A Microsoft Windows user account that is a standard user account with the **Family Safety Settings** enabled.

chip creep
Cards can work free from a slot over time, though this is not common.

chipset
The chipset provides communications between different components by implementing various controllers (for memory, graphics, I/O, and so on). Historically, "fast" controllers (memory and video) were part of a "northbridge" chipset, placed close to the CPU and system memory. Slower buses were part of a "southbridge" chipset. In modern PC architecture, video and memory controllers are part of the CPU (on-die), the northbridge would mostly handle PCI Express adapters, and the southbridge would host SATA, USB, audio and LAN functions, plus PCI/PATA legacy bus support.

Chrome OS
Chrome OS is derived from Linux, via an open source OS called Chromium. Chrome OS itself is proprietary. Chrome OS is developed by Google to run on specific laptop (chromebooks) and PC (chromeboxes) hardware.

CI
(configuration item) In change management, an asset that requires specific management procedures for it to be used to deliver the service. Each CI is identified with a label and defined by its attributes and stored in a **CMDB**.

CIFS
(Common Internet File System) Another term for **SMB**.

CIRT/CSIRT
(Cyber Incident Response Team/Computer Security Incident Response Team) Team with responsibility for incident response. The CIRT must have expertise across a number of business domains (IT, HR, legal, and marketing, for instance).

CIS
(Contact Image Sensor) A type of digital imaging sensor. An array of LEDs strobing between red, blue, and green light are used to illuminate an object. The reflected light is captured through a lens onto an image sensor.

clean install
Installing the OS to a new computer or completely replacing the OS software on an existing computer, and in the process, deleting existing applications, user settings, and data files.

cleaning blade
See **cleaning unit**.

cleaning unit
Parts such as a blade, roller, or brush that rest on the surface of a laser printer's photosensitive drum that are used to clean excess toner and remove residual charge from the photoconductor.

CLI
(Command Line Interface) A textual interface based on the operating system, where a user typically enters commands at the command prompt to instruct the computer to perform a specific task.

client-side virtualization
Any solution designed to run on desktops or workstations in which the user interacts with the virtualization host directly.

clock battery
See **RTC battery**.

closed network
A network where the elements of the network are all known to the system vendor and there is no connectivity to wider computer data networks.

cloud computing
Any environment where software (Software as a Service and Platform as a Service) or computer/network resources (Infrastructure as a Service and Network as a Service) are provided to an end user who has no knowledge of or responsibility for how the service is provided. Cloud services provide elasticity of resources and pay-per-use charging models. Cloud access arrangements can be public, hosted private, or private (this type of cloud could be onsite or offsite relative to the other business units).

cloud-based network controller
A cloud-based management system that enables registering and monitoring all of the organization's networks, clients, and servers.

clusters
Disk sectors are grouped in clusters of 2, 4, 6, 8, or more. The smaller the cluster size, the lower the data overhead in terms of wasted space, but larger clusters can improve performance.

CMDB
(Configuration Management Database) In change management, the database in which **configuration items** are stored, identified using a label and defined by their attributes.

CMOS
(complementary metal oxide semiconductor) A type of integrated circuit with a wide range of applications, including static RAM (for firmware and flash memory) and imaging sensors.

CMOS battery
(complementary metal oxide semiconductor battery) A battery designed to last 5 to 10 years to maintain CMOS settings.

CMOS setup
(complementary metal oxide semiconductor setup) Another name for the setup program used to configure system firmware settings. Also known as BIOS setup or UEFI setup.

CMP
(chip-level multiprocessing) Multiple processors combined on the same die.

CMS
(Configuration Management System) The tools and databases that collect, store, manage, update, and present information about **CIs**.

CMTS
(Cable Modem Termination System) Equipment used by cable companies to allow computers to send and receive IP packets by inserting the packets into MPEG frames over an RF signal and reverses the process for data coming from a cable modem.

CMYK Color Model
(Cyan Magenta Yellow Key [Black] color model) Subtractive color model used by print devices. CMYK printing involves use of halftone screens. Four screens (or layers) of dots printed in each of the colors are overlaid. The size and density of the dots on each layer produces different shades of color and is viewed as a continuous tone image.

coaxial cable
Cable type using two separate conductors that share a common axis (hence the term co-axial). Coax cables are categorized using the Radio Grade (RG) "standard". Coax is considered obsolete in terms of LAN applications but is still widely used for CCTV networks and as drop cables for cable TV (CATV).

collated
A print job where all pages of the first copy are printed, followed by all pages of the next copy.

collision domain
The network segment in which contention collisions occur.

color calibration
The process of adjusting display and scanner settings so that color input and output are balanced.

color depth
Each pixel in a digital image can be one of a number of colors. The range of colors available for each pixel is referred to as the color depth. Providing a greater range of colors requires more memory. If 1-bit is allowed for color depth, two colors (white and black) are allowed. A VGA video system supports 4-bit color (16 possible colors). SVGA supports 8-bit (256 colors), 16-bit (65,536 colors), 24-bit (16,777,216 colors), and 32-bit (deep color).

COM port
(communications port) Windows' representation of a computer's serial port(s), numbered sequentially (COM1, COM2...).

COM+
(Component Object Model plus) Microsoft's object-oriented programming architecture and operating system services for developing applications. See also **Component Services**.

command interpreter
The portion of an operating system or script language that is able to read and implement commands entered by a user or from a **script file**.

command mode
In Linux vi editor, the mode that allows users to perform different editing actions using single keystrokes.

comparison operator
A relationship evaluation between two variables to determine whether they are equal, not equal, less than, greater than, less than or equal to, or greater than or equal to each other.

compiled program
An instruction set in which the programming instructions are performed by the computer processor.

Component Object Model
(COM) Microsoft's object-oriented programming model specification.

Component Services
Windows applications use various component (COM) models and APIs to share data. Component Services in Administrative Tools allows configuration of component servers.

compressed air blaster
A can of air packaged under pressure that is used to remove dust and debris from inside printers and other computing devices.

conductor
A material that is good at conducting electricity, such as gold, copper, or tin. These are used for wires and contacts.

confidentiality
The fundamental security goal of keeping information and communications private and protecting them from unauthorized access.

configuration baseline
The original or recommended settings for a device.

configuration management
A means of identifying all components of the information and communications technology infrastructure, including hardware, software, and procedures, and the properties of those items.

connections
The physical access points that enable a computer to communicate with internal or external devices.

constant
Identifier for a value that is fixed before program execution and does not change.

contact
A record with fields for name, address, email address(es), phone numbers, notes, and other information related to the entity defined in the record.

container virtualization
A virtualization method that doesn't use a hypervisor and instead enforces resources

separate at the operating system level with isolated containers for each user instance to run in with its own allocated CPU and memory resources, but all processes are run through the native OS kernel.

contention
A media access method in which nodes compete or cooperate among themselves for media access time. Also called competitive media access.

contrast ratio
A measure of the ratio of luminance (brightness) of whites to blacks, indicating the color performance of a display or scanner. A device supporting a higher contrast ratio is able to display a wider range of colors and deliver "true" black.

Control Center
An iOS feature that is accessed by swiping up from the bottom of the display to access iOS feature settings.

Control Panel
Management interface for configuring Windows settings. In Windows 8 and later, the touch-enabled app PC Settings/Windows Settings is used for many options previously configured via Control Panel.

core clock speed
The speed at which the CPU runs internal processes and accesses L1 and L2 cache.

corona
An assembly within a laser printer that contains a wire (the corona wire), which is responsible for charging the paper.

corporate mail gateway
A connection between mail servers that use different communications protocols or between two networks that use the same or different protocols.

counter logs
Windows log files that allow you to collect statistics about resources and can be used to determine system health and performance.

cover
The removable portion of the system case that allows access to the motherboard and internal components.

CPU
(Central Processing Unit) The principal microprocessor in a computer or smartphone responsible for running operating system and applications software.

CPU form factor
(central processing unit form factor) The size, shape, and connection method of the CPU.

critical update
A widely released, non-security update to fix a critical issue.

CRM
(Customer Relationship Management) Software designed to manage an organization's customer (and potential customer) relationships and interactions.

cron
A Linux/Unix daemon that runs in the background and executes specified tasks at a designated time or date.

cron table
The file (crontab) in Linux that contains instructions defining the tasks to be executed by a cron.

crossover cable
A twisted pair cable wired as T568A on one end and as T568B on the other end.

cryptographic hash
A hashed value from which it is impossible to recover the original data.

CSV
(Comma Separated Values) A file format in which data is stored using commas or another character to separate fields in the data. Typically, data has been exported from a spreadsheet or a database.

cultural sensitivity
Being aware of customs and habits used by other people.

current
The actual flow of electrons, measured in Amps (I).

current working directory
In Linux, the location on the file system that you are accessing at any point in time.

cyber warfare
The use of IT services and devices to disrupt national, state, or organization activities, especially when used for military purposes.

cylinder
The aggregate of all tracks that reside in the same location on every disk surface.

DAC
(Digital-to-Analog Converter) A sound card component that converts the digital signals generated by the CPU to an analog electrical signal that can drive the speakers.

data backup
A system maintenance task that enables you to store copies of critical data for safekeeping as protection against loss of data due to disasters such as file corruption or hardware failure.

Data Collector Sets
Windows log files that record information for viewing in real time or at a later date.

data restoration
A system recovery task that enables you to access and restore the backed-up data.

Data Sources
Windows applications can import data from various data sources. The links to different data files and database drivers can be configured from Administrative Tools.

data transmission overlimit
When apps, especially malware or rogue apps, trying to collect data in the background use excessive amounts of data on a mobile device.

data type
The way the data is intended to be used in a program such as character or string, integer, real number, logical, or Boolean.

daughter board
A circuit board that connects to the motherboard to provide extra expansion slots or connectors. Typically, these are used in slimline case designs so that adapter cards can be installed parallel to the motherboard, reducing the height of the case.

DB-9
Although the original serial port used a 25-pin male D connector, most PCs today use a male DB-9 (9-pin) port. (See also **serial port**.)

DC
(direct current) PCs and most computer components function by using power supplied in the form of direct current. This is normally at low voltage and is produced by stepping down the voltage from the building supply. Direct current, unlike alternating current, does not oscillate between positive and negative states.

DCOM
(Distributed COM) Microsoft's interface that allows a client program object to request services from server program objects.

DDoS
(Distributed Denial of Service) A **DoS** attack that uses multiple compromised computers (a "botnet" of "zombies") to launch the attack.

DDR SDRAM
(Double Data Rate Synchronous Dynamic Random Access Memory) A standard for SDRAM where data is transferred twice per clock cycle (making the maximum data rate 64x the bus speed in bps). DDR2/DDR3/DDR4 SDRAM uses lower voltage chips and higher bus speeds.

declared variable
A variable for which the data type, possibly the size, and optionally an initial value have been specified within the script or program file.

default gateway
The default gateway is an IP configuration parameter that identifies the location of a router on the local subnet that the host can use to contact other networks.

default mask

In the early days of IP addressing, the network ID was determined automatically from the first octet of the address. When subnet masks were introduced, the "default" masks (255.0.0.0, 255.255.0.0, and 255.255.255.0) that corresponded to treating the first octet as classful were commonly described as "class A", "class B", and "class C" masks. The Internet no longer uses classful addressing but many LANs use the private IP address ranges and the default masks.

defense in depth

Configuring security controls on hosts (endpoints) as well as providing network (perimeter) security, physical security, and administrative controls.

defragmentation

See **disk defragmentation**.

degaussing

Exposing the disk to a powerful electromagnet to disrupt the magnetic pattern that stores data on the disk surface.

desktop

The desktop is at the top of the object hierarchy in Explorer, containing the Computer, Documents, Network, and Recycle Bin objects. The desktop also stores shortcuts to programs, files, and system objects.

desktop computer

A computing device designed to be placed on or near a user's desk.

desktop style

Computers designed for stationary use come in various styles including tower, slimline, and all-in-one.

detac corona

A strip that removes the charge to prevent paper curl in a laser printer.

developer roller

A magnetized roller to which toner adheres during the printing process. See also **developer unit**.

developer unit

Assembly that applies toner to areas of the photoconductor where charge has been removed by the laser. The main components are a toner hopper, transfer roller, waste toner hopper, a screw or blade to stir the toner, and a doctor blade to ensure the correct level of toner on the developer roller.

device driver

A small piece of code that is loaded during the boot sequence of an operating system. This code, usually provided by the hardware vendor, provides access to a device, or hardware, from the OS kernel. Under Windows, a signing system is in place for drivers to ensure that they do not make the OS unstable.

DHCP Server

(Dynamic Host Configuration Protocol server) A networking service that allows a client to request an appropriate IP configuration from a server. The server is configured with a range of addresses to lease. Hosts can be allocated an IP address dynamically or be assigned a reserved IP address, based on the host's MAC address. The server can also provide other configuration information, such as the location of DNS servers. DHCP utilizes UDP ports 67 and 68. It is important to monitor the network to ensure that only valid DHCP servers are running on the network.

diagram

A drawing that captures the relationships between network elements and identifying the location of items on the network.

dial-up

A remote network access method that utilizes the local telephone line (Plain Old Telephone System [POTS]) to establish a connection between two computers fitted with modems. Dial-up is a legacy method of Internet access. It may still be deployed for special administrative purposes or as an emergency backup connection method. Configuration is generally a case of setting the telephone number, username, and password.

die
The area on a silicon chip containing millions of transistors and signal pathways created by the hoping process.

digital assistant
A voice interface designed to respond to natural language commands and queries.

digital camera
A version of a 35mm film camera where the film is replaced by light-sensitive diodes (an array of CCDs [Charge Coupled Devices]) and electronic storage media (typically a flash memory card). The sensitivity of the array determines the maximum resolution of the image, measured in megapixels.

digital certificate
An X.509 digital certificate is issued by a Certificate Authority (CA) as a guarantee that a public key it has issued to an organization to encrypt messages sent to it genuinely belongs to that organization. Both parties must trust the CA. The public key can be used to encrypt messages but not to decrypt them. A message can only be decrypted by the private key, which is mathematically linked to the public key but not derivable from it. This is referred to as asymmetric encryption. Part of the CA's responsibility is ensuring that this private key is known only to the organization owning the certificate. This arrangement is referred to a Public Key Infrastructure (PKI).

digital display
A computer monitor that accepts a digital signal. Flat-panel monitors use digital signals and only support lower resolutions by interpolating the image, which can make it appear fuzzy.

digitizer
As part of a touchscreen assembly, the digitizer is a touch-sensitive glass panel covering the LCD. The panel converts touch events to digital signals that can be interpreted as different types of input.

dim display
When a mobile device has the **backlight**set to its lowest setting and the automatic light adjustment is disabled, or the phone is set to conserve power by auto-dimming the light.

DIMM
(Dual In-line Memory Module) The standard packaging for system memory. There are different pin configurations for different RAM types (DDR SDRAM [184], DDR2/3 SDRAM [240], and DDR4 SDRAM [288]).

diode
A valve, allowing current to flow in one direction only. These are used in a computer's power supply and as protection for components.

direct thermal printer
A thermal printer that uses heated pins to form images directly onto specially coated thermal paper.

Disaster Recovery Plan
A documented and resourced plan showing actions and responsibilities to be used in response to critical incidents. The recovery plan may also provide for practice exercises or drills for testing and to familiarize staff with procedures. As well as facilitating a smooth transition in the event of disaster, plans must stress the importance of maintaining secure systems.

disk defragmentation
Fragmentation occurs when a data file is not saved to contiguous sectors on a disk. This decreases performance by making the disk read/write heads move between fragments. Defragmentation is a software routine that compacts files back into contiguous areas of the disk. The process can be run from a command-line using the defrag utility, but it is more often run from Windows.

disk mirroring
See **mirroring**.

disk striping
A disk array access pattern where data is written in stripes to two or more disks sequentially, improving performance. Note that a RAID 0 striped volume provides no redundancy, and if any of the physical disks in the set fails, the whole volume will be lost.

disk thrashing
A state in which the main memory is filled up, pages are swapped in and out of virtual memory—which needs to be written to the hard disk—in rapid succession, leading to possible early drive failure.

disk wiping
Using software to ensure that old data is destroyed by writing to each location on the media, either using zeroes or in a random pattern. This leaves the disk in a "clean" state ready to be passed to the new owner.

DisplayPort
Digital A/V interface developed by VESA. DisplayPort supports some cross-compatibility with DVI and HDMI devices.

distended capacitors
Capacitors that are swollen or bulging or emitting residue indicates that they have been damaged or could have failed due to a manufacturing defect.

distinguished name
A unique identifier for any given resource within the LDAP directory.

distribution
A complete Linux implementation, including kernel, shell, applications, and utilities, that is packaged, distributed, and supported by a software vendor.

distribution frame
A device that terminates cables and enables connections with other devices.

distro
See **distribution**.

DLP (loss prevention)
(Data Loss/Leakage Prevention) Software that can identify data that has been classified and apply "fine-grained" user privileges to it (preventing copying it or forwarding by email, for instance).

DLP (video)
(Digital Light Processing) Mirror-based projector technology developed by Texas Instruments.

DMZ
(Demilitarized Zone) A private network connected to the Internet must be protected against intrusion from the Internet. However, certain services may need to be made publicly accessible from the Internet (web and email, for instance). One solution is to put such servers in a DMZ. The idea of a DMZ is that traffic cannot pass through it. If communication is required between hosts on either side of a DMZ, a host within the DMZ acts as a proxy. It takes the request and checks it. If the request is valid, it re-transmits it to the destination. External hosts have no idea about what (if anything) is behind the DMZ. A DMZ is implemented using either two firewalls (screened subnet) or a single three-legged firewall (one with three network ports).

DNS
(Domain Name System) A network service that provides names to IP address mapping services on the Internet and large intranets. DNS name servers host the database for domains for which they are authoritative. Root servers hold details of the top-level domains. DNS resolvers perform queries or lookups to service client requests. The DNS protocol utilizes TCP/UDP port 53.

dock
macOS feature for managing applications from the desktop, similar to the Windows taskbar.

docking station
A sophisticated type of port replicator designed to provide additional ports (such as network or USB) and functionality (such as expansion slots and drives) to a portable computer when used at a desk.

DOCSIS
(Data Over Cable Service Interface Specification) A global telecommunications standard that enables data to be sent over cable modems in a CATV system.

domain controller
Any Windows-based server that provides domain authentication services (logon services) is referred to as a domain controller (DC). Domain controllers

maintain a master copy of the database of network resources.

domain name
The unique and officially registered name that identifies a company, organization, or individual.

domain network
A group of computers which share a common accounts database, referred to as the directory.

domain user account
In a corporate environment, an account that is part of a domain, so the user account settings are controlled by the domain administrator.

DoS
(Denial of Service) A network attack that aims to disrupt a service, usually by overloading it.

dot matrix printer
A type of impact printer that uses a set of pins to strike the ribbon to create printed characters and images using combinations of dots.

dotted decimal notation
32 bit addresses displayed in human readable format using base-10 numbering.

DRAM
(Dynamic Random Access Memory) A type of volatile memory that stores each bit of data as a charge within a single transistor. Each transistor must be refreshed periodically. Standard DRAM is the lowest common denominator of the DRAM types. Modern PCs use a DRAM derivative to store data (Double Data Rate **SDRAM**).

drive controller
The controller is the circuitry in the disk unit that allows it to put data on the bus, which the HBA shuttles to the CPU or RAM.

drive enclosure
An external case that holds one or more disks and typically connects to the computer through USB or Thunderbolt ports.

drive encryption
The entire contents of the drive (or volume), including system files and folders, are encrypted.

driver
Software that creates an interface between a device and the operating system. It may also include tools for configuring and optimizing the device.

DRM
(Digital Rights Management) Copyright protection technologies for digital media. DRM solutions usually try to restrict the number of devices allowed for playback of a licensed digital file, such as a music track or ebook.

drop cable
Solid cables used for permanent links such as cable running through walls.

DSL
(Digital Subscriber Line) A technology for transferring data over voice-grade telephone lines. DSL uses the higher frequencies available in a copper telephone line as a communications channel. The use of a filter prevents this from contaminating voice traffic with noise. There are various "flavors" of DSL, notably S(ymmetric)DSL, A(symmetric)DSL, and V(ery HIgh Bit Rate)DSL.

DSLAM
(DSL Access Multiplier) A network device at the telecommunications central office that connects subscribers with the Internet.

DSLR
(Digital Single Lens Reflex) A digital camera that replicates the features of compact 35mm film cameras, preserving the traditional viewfinder method of picture composition and supporting replaceable lenses and manual adjustments.

DSP chip
(Digital Signal Processor chip) The basis of a sound card containing one or more DACs. It also provides functions for playing digital sound (synthesis) and driving MIDI compatible devices.

DTLS
(Datagram Transport Layer Security) TLS used with UDP applications, such as some VPN solutions.

DTP
(Desktop Publishing) An application similar to word processing but with more emphasis on the formatting and layout of documents than on editing the text.

dual heat pipe
Two **heat pipe** tubes to provide better cooling.

dual rail
A power supply with two +12 V rails.

dual-channel memory
Memory controller with two pathways through the bus to the CPU so that 128 bits of data can be transferred per transaction.

dumpster diving
A social engineering technique of discovering things about an organization (or person) based on what it throws away.

duplexing assembly
A device that enables a printer or scanner to use both sides of a page automatically.

DVD
(Digital Video/Versatile Disk) An optical storage technology. DVDs offer higher capacities (4.7 GB per layer) than the preceding CD-ROM format. As with CDs, recordable and re-writable forms of DVD exist, though there are numerous competing formats (notably ±R and ±RW and DVD-RAM).

DVD drive
An optical drive similar to a CD drive, but with a different encoding method and a shorter wavelength laser. Typically can read and burn CD and DVD media.

DVI
(Digital Video Interface) A video adapter designed to replace the VGA port used by CRT monitors. The DVI interface supports digital only or digital and analog signaling.

dye sublimation printer
See **thermal dye transfer printer**.

e-ink
(electrophoretic ink) Micro-encapsulated black and white particles, electronically manipulated to create images and text on an **e-reader**.

e-magazine
A digital magazine that can be read on an electronic device such as an **e-reader**, smartphone, tablet, or computer.

e-newspaper
A digital newspaper that can be read on an electronic device such as an **e-reader**, smartphone, tablet, or computer.

e-reader
A tablet-sized device designed for reading rather than general-purpose computing.

EAP
(Extensible Authentication Protocol) Framework for negotiating authentication methods, supporting a range of authentication devices. EAP-TLS uses PKI certificates, Protected EAP (PEAP) creates a TLS-protected tunnel between the supplicant and authenticator to secure the user authentication method, and Lightweight EAP (LEAP) is a password-based mechanism used by Cisco.

EAPoL
(Extensible Authentication Protocol over LAN) Another term for EAP. See **EAP**.

early-life failure rate
A method of calculating how quickly a device will fail through accelerated testing.

EAS
(Exchange ActiveSync) Microsoft's synchronization protocol that enables mobile devices to connect to an Exchange Server to access mail, calendar, and contacts.

eavesdropping
Some transmission media are susceptible to eavesdropping (listening in to communications sent over the media). To secure transmissions, they must be encrypted.

ebook
A digital book that can be read on an electronic device such as an **e-reader**, smartphone, tablet, or computer.

ECC
(Error Checking and Correcting [or Error Correcting Code]) System memory (RAM) with built-in error correction security. It is more expensive than normal memory and requires motherboard support. It is typically only used in servers.

EDR
(Enhanced Data Rate) An option in the Bluetooth specification that allows faster data rates and potentially better battery life.

effective group ID
In Linux, the group ID used by the kernel in determining the group permissions a process has when accessing files and shared resources.

EFS
(Encrypting File System) Under NTFS, files and folders can be encrypted to ensure privacy of the data. Only the user who encrypted the file can subsequently open it.

EIR database
(Equipment Identity Register database) A database where **IMEI** numbers are stored. A lost or stolen device IMEI is marked as invalid.

Electrostatic discharge
See **ESD**.

electrostatic latent image
Representation of the image to be printed created as a series of raster lines with charge/no-charge areas.

email filtering
Techniques to prevent a user being overwhelmed with spam (junk email). Spam can be blocked from reaching an organization using a mail gateway to filter messages. At the user level, software can redirect spam to a junk folder (or similar). Anti-spam filtering needs to balance blocking illegitimate traffic with permitting legitimate messages. Anti-spam techniques can also use lists of known spam servers (blacklists).

embedded system
A computer system that is designed to perform a specific, dedicated function, such as a microcontroller in a medical drip or components in a control system managing a water treatment plant.

EMF
(Enhanced MetaFile) When using EMF, the software application and GDI quickly produce a partial print job. Control is then released back to the user while spooling continues in the background (GDI and the print driver are called to complete the processing of the job).

enclosure
A container with its own air filters and fans to protect computers or other devices in dirty or dusty environments.

encryption
Scrambling the characters used in a message so that the message can be seen but not understood or modified unless it can be deciphered. Encryption provides for a secure means of transmitting data and authenticating users. It is also used to store data securely. Encryption uses different types of cipher and one or more keys. The size of the key is one factor in determining the strength of the encryption product.

encryption key
A specific piece of information that is used with an algorithm to perform encryption and decryption in cryptography.

end of life system
A system that is no longer supported by the developer or vendor.

Endpoint Management Server
Facilitates the defense in depth process by identifying computing devices running on the network and ensuring that they are securely configured. This can include applying OS and antivirus updates automatically, cataloging software applications installed on each device, applying security policies, retrieving and analyzing log files, and monitoring performance and other status alerts.

energy
The amount of power consumed by a device over time, measured in Watt-hours (or more typically Kilowatt-hours [kWh]).

entry control roster
Sign-in sheet for managing access to premises.

environment variable
A storage location in the environment of the operating system's command shell.

environmental power problems
Issues affecting power including **surges**, **brownouts**, and **blackouts** caused by failures in the building power supply.

EP drum
(Electrostatic Photographic drum) The component in a laser printer that carries the electrical charge to attract toner and then to transfer the toner to the paper.

EPD
(Electronic Paper Display) A low-power display using **e-ink** to create a display that mimics the look of text on paper without using a backlight or glossy surface.

EPS specification
(Entry-level Power Supply specification) 8-pin +12 V connectors developed initially for server-class hardware.

EPT
(Extended Page Table) The term used for SLAT extensions by Intel.

erase lamp
See **cleaning unit**.

eSATA
(external Serial Advanced Technology Attachment) An external interface for SATA connections, enabling you to connect external SATA drives to PCs.

eSATAp
A non-standard powered port used by some vendors that is compatible with both USB and SATA (with an eSATAp cable).

escape character
A character used to allow alternate use of a reserved character within a particular programming language. The escape characters vary between programming languages. Often used to allow use of a reserved character within a string.

ESD
(electrostatic discharge) The release of a charge from a metal or plastic surface that occurs when a potential difference is formed between the charged object and an oppositely charged conductive object. This electrical discharge can damage silicon chips and computer components if they are exposed to it.

Ethernet
A family of networking technologies that provide connectivity by using Ethernet network adapters, contention-based media access, and twisted pair, coax, or fiber media.

EULA
(End User License Agreement) The agreement governing the installation and use of proprietary software.

evil twin
In an evil twin attack, the attacker creates a malicious wireless access point masquerading as a genuine one, enabling the attacker to harvest confidential information as users connect via the AP.

Exchange
Microsoft Exchange is a client-based email system that allows mobile devices to sync with the server.

execute
Carry out the command entered by a user or as read from a script file.

execution control
Logical security technologies designed to prevent malicious software from running on a host and establish a security system that does not entirely depend on the good behavior of individual users.

exFAT
A file system designed for flash memory cards and memory sticks.

expansion bus
The external bus that allows additional components to be connected to the computer.

expansion cards
A printed circuit board that is installed in a slot on a system board to provide special functions for customizing or extending a computer's capabilities. Also referred to as adapter card, I/O card, add-in, add-on, or board.

expansion slots
Connection slots on the motherboard in which adapter cards can be installed to extend the range of functions the computer can perform.

Explorer
See **File Explorer**.

Extended Service Set
Basic service sets can be grouped into an extended service set.

external transfer rate
A measure of how fast data can be transferred to the CPU across the bus.

extranet
A network of semi-trusted hosts, typically representing business partners, suppliers, or customers. Hosts must authenticate to join the extranet.

Face ID
The Apple device feature that uses face lock to grant access to the device.

face lock
A biometric authentication mechanism in which the hash is computed from a picture of the user's face.

factory default reset
Setting a mobile device back to the original factor settings, creating a clean OS, removing all data and apps, and resetting any configuration done by the user.

Factory Recovery Partition
Disk partition accessible via the startup sequence that contains an image of the system partition as produced by the PC vendor. This can be used to recover the PC to its factory state by performing a repair install, but will erase any user data or installed programs.

failed login attempts
A configurable value that specifies how many incorrect login attempts can be used before the device is locked for a specified length of time.

Fair Use Policy
See **AUP**.

false negative
A condition where a system denies entry when it should have granted it.

false positive
A condition where a system grants entry when it should have denied it.

Family Safety Settings
A Microsoft Windows setting that helps protect children by limiting their access to functions and features.

fast charge
A general technology for quickly charging mobile devices using varying voltages to speed up charging times.

FAT
(File Allocation Table) A basic disk format allowing the OS to write data as files on a disk. The original 16-bit version (FAT16, but often simply called FAT) was replaced by a 32-bit version that is almost universally supported by different operating systems and devices. A 64-bit version (exFAT) was introduced with Windows 7 and is also supported by XP SP3 and Vista SP1 and some versions of Linux and macOS. There is also a 12-bit version used to format floppy disks.

FAT16
(File Allocation Table, 16-bit) The 16-bit file system used in the Windows 3.1 and DOS operating systems with 128 K sectors that only allowed very small partitions (about 32 MB) with later Windows versions employing 512 K sectors allowing for 2 GB partitions.

FAT32
(File Allocation Table, 32-bit) The 32-bit file system that allows approximately 4 GB partitions.

FDE
(full disk encryption) Encryption of all data on a disk (including system files, temporary files, and the pagefile) can be accomplished via a supported OS, third-party software, or at the controller level by the disk device itself. Used with a strong authentication method, this mitigates against data theft in the event that the device is lost or stolen. The key used to encrypt the disk can either be stored on a USB stick or smart card or in a Trusted Platform Module.

FDM
(fused deposition modeling) See **FFF**.

feature updates
Semi-annual updates to the Windows operating system that include enhanced features that are installed in multiple phases, requiring a reboot after each phase of the update installation. Compare with quality updates.

federated identity management
An agreement between enterprises to allow users to authenticate using the same information to all networks within the agreed upon group.

feed assembly
In a thermal printer, a stepper motor turns a rubber-coated roller to feed the paper through the print mechanism using friction feed.

feed roller
Roller that works with a separation roller or pad to feed just one sheet of paper (or other media) into the printer mechanism.

female port
A port that has hole connectors.

FFF
(fused filament fabrication) A 3D printing method which lays down each layer of filament at high temperature, and as layers are extruded, adjacent layers are allowed to cool and bond together before additional layers are added to the object.

filament
In 3D printing, the spool of plastic or other material used to create the three-dimensional object.

file attribute
A characteristic that can be associated with a file or folder that provides the operating system with important information about the file or folder and how it is intended to be used by system users.

File Explorer
A Microsoft Windows tool that offers a single view of all the resources and information that you can access from a computer.

file extension
A series of characters at the end of a file name; used by an OS to identify the software application that is associated with a file.

file system hierarchy
In Linux, the directory structure starting with the root directory (/) with directories and subdirectories below it to store files.

Finder
The file management GUI in macOS.

fingerprint sensor
A device, usually integrated into a mobile device, that reads the user's fingerprint to determine whether to grant access to the device.

firewall
Hardware or software that filters traffic passing into or out of a network. A basic packet-filtering firewall works at Layer 3 (Network). Packets can be filtered depending on several criteria (inbound or outbound, IP address, and port number). More advanced firewalls (proxy and stateful inspection) can examine higher layer information, to provide enhanced security.

firewall apps
Mobile device firewall app that can monitor app activity and prevent connections to particular ports or IP addresses.

firmware
This refers to software instructions stored semi-permanently (embedded) on a hardware device. Modern types of firmware are stored in flash memory and can be updated more easily than legacy

programmable Read Only Memory (ROM) types.

flash memory
Flash RAM is similar to a ROM chip in that it retains information even when power is removed, but it adds flexibility in that it can be reprogrammed with new contents quickly. Flash memory is used in USB thumb drives and memory cards for removable storage and in Solid State Drives (SSDs), designed to replicate the function of hard drives.

flatbed scanner
A type of scanner where the object is placed on a glass faceplate and the scan head moved underneath it.

floating point numbers
Data type supporting storage of floating point numbers (decimal fractions).

folder redirection
A Microsoft Windows technology that allows an administrative user to redirect the path of a local folder (such as the user's home folder) to a folder on a network share, making the data available to the user when they log into any computer on the network where the network share is located.

fonts
The display and word processing programs can make use of any typeface designs (fonts) installed on the local system. Most Windows fonts are OpenType (replacing the earlier TrueType) but some design programs and printers also use Adobe Type 1 fonts.

footprinting
An information gathering threat, in which the attacker attempts to learn about the configuration of the network and security systems through social engineering attacks or software-based tools.

force stop
An Android option to close an unresponsive app.

forensics
The process of gathering and submitting computer evidence to trial. Digital evidence is latent, meaning that it must be interpreted. This means that great care must be taken to prove that the evidence has not been tampered with or falsified. The key points in collecting evidence are to record every step and action, to gather appropriate evidence, and to bag evidence. To preserve evidence correctly, it should be stored securely. Any investigation should be done on a copy of the digital files, not the originals. Each piece of evidence must be accompanied by a chain of custody form, detailing when, where, and how it was collected, where it has been stored, and who has handled it subsequently to collection.

formatter board
In a laser printer, the unit that exposes and processes all of the data received from the computer and coordinates the steps needed to produce the finished page.

FPU
(Floating Point Unit) A math co-processor built into the CPU that performs calculations on floating point numbers.

FQDN
(Fully Qualified Domain Name) The full name of any host which reflects the hierarchy from most specific (the host) to the least specific (the top level domain followed by the root).

fragmentation
Occurs when a data file is not saved to contiguous sectors on a disk. This decreases performance by making the disk read/write heads move between fragments.

frame rate
The number of times the image in a video stream changes per second. This can be expressed in Hertz or Frames per Second (fps).

freeware
Software that is available for download and use free of charge.

frequency response
The volume that can be produced at different frequencies.

friction feed
An impact printer mechanism that uses two rolls placed one on top of the other to force individual cut sheets of paper or envelopes through the paper path.

front panel
The portion of the system case that provides access to removable media drives, power switch, and LEDs to indicate driver operation.

FRU
(field replaceable unit) An adapter or other component that can be replaced by a technician on-site. Most PC and laptop components are FRUs, while the components of smartphones are not.

FTP
(File Transfer Protocol) A protocol used to transfer files across the Internet. Variants include S(ecure)FTP, FTP with SSL (FTPS and FTPES), and T(rivial)FTP. FTP utilizes ports 20 and 21.

FTTC
(Fiber to the Curb/Cabinet) A fiber optic solution which places the connection on a pole or cabinet at the curb, then coax or twisted pair cables carry the signal from this point to the home or business.

FTTH
(Fiber to the Home) A fiber optic solution which places the connection inside the home or residence.

FTTN
(Fiber to the Node) A fiber optic solution which places the connection within one mile of customers with the final connections made using existing phone or cable lines.

FTTP
(Fiber to the Premises) A fiber optic solution which places the connection inside the premises.

fuse
A circuit breaker designed to protect the device and users of the device from faulty wiring or supply of power (overcurrent protection).

fuser assembly
The part of a laser printer that fixes toner to media. This is typically a combination of a heat and pressure roller, though non-contact flash fusing using xenon lamps is found on some high-end printers.

game pad
A controller containing multiple buttons and toggles, each of which controls a different action in a video game or program, typically held and manipulated with two hands.

gaming rig
A computer used for standalone or online gaming, often connected to surround sound speakers or headphones, sometimes integrated with virtual reality goggles. May use specialized gaming equipment such as gaming controllers, joysticks, gaming mouse, and keyboard.

GDI
(Graphics Device Interface) The Windows XP component responsible for drawing graphics objects. Cheaper printers use GDI as the print processor. Windows Vista and later have a redesigned display/print architecture called Windows Presentation Foundation, but retain compatibility with GDI applications.

generator
See **backup power generator**.

geolocation
The process of identifying the real-world geographic location of an object, often by associating a location such as a street address with an IP address, hardware address, Wi-Fi positioning system, GPS coordinates, or some other form of information.

geotagging
The process of adding geographic location metadata to captured media such as pictures or videos.

geotracking
Determining the location of a person or object using the GPS data from a GPS-enabled device.

gestures
Finger movements on a trackpad or mouse that enable a user to scroll, zoom, and navigate desktop, document, and application content.

global address
In an IPv6 address, an address that is unique on the Internet (equivalent to public addresses in IPv4).

gloss coating
A display coating that helps the display appear richer, but reflects more light, which can cause problems with screen glare and reflections of background objects. Compare with **matte coating**.

gloves
Latex hand coverings to protect the technician when they are working around a toner spill.

Gnome
A popular Linux GUI desktop.

GNU
A recursive acronym standing for "GNU is Not UNIX."

Google account
An account from Google used to access an Android device and related online services.

Gov Cloud
A Google cloud service that can be used by branches of the U.S. government, but is not available to other consumers or businesses.

GP registers
(General Purpose registers) Registers that store data from the CPU's basic instruction set. 32-bit processors have 32-bit GP registers for the x86/IA-32 instruction set; 64-bit processors are so-called because they have 64-bit GP registers. CPUs also support larger registers to optimize graphics processing.

GPO
(Group Policy Object) On a Windows domain, per-user and per-computer settings can be deployed through Group Policy Objects attached to Active Directory containers, such as domains and Organization Units. Group policy can be used to configure security settings such as password policy, account restrictions, firewall status, and so on.

gpresult
A command line tool that displays the **RSoP** for a computer and user account.

GPS
(Global Positioning System) Means of determining a receiver's position on the Earth based on information received from GPS satellites. The receiver must have line-of-sight to the GPS satellites.

GPT
(GUID Partition Table) A modern disk partitioning system allowing large numbers of partitions and very large partition sizes.

GPU
(Graphics Processing Unit) a Type of microprocessor used on dedicated video adapter cards or within a CPU with integrated graphics capability.

gpupdate
A command line tool to apply a new or changed **policy** immediately. When used with the /force option, it causes all policies (new and old) to be reapplied.

graphics adapter
See **video card**.

grounded
An equipment ground provides a safe path for electrical current to flow away in the event that a device or cable is faulty. Self-grounding removes any static potential difference between a technician's clothes and body and a device they are handling, reducing the risk of damaging the component through Electrostatic Discharge (ESD).

GSM
(Global System for Mobile Communication) Standard for cellular radio communications and data transfer. GSM phones use a SIM card to identify the subscriber and network provider. 4G and later data standards are developed for GSM.

Guest account
A Microsoft Windows user account with limited capabilities, no privacy, and is disabled by default.

GUI
(Graphical User Interface) An easy to use, intuitive interface for a computer operating system. Most GUIs require a pointing device, such as a mouse, to operate efficiently. One of the world's first GUI-based operating systems was the Apple Mac OS, released in 1984. Thereafter, Microsoft produced their Windows family of products based around their GUI. In fact, recognizing that GUI covers a whole range of designs, the Windows interface is better described as a WIMP (Windows, Icons, Menus, Pointing [device]) interface.

guideline
Used for areas of policy where there are no procedures either because the situation has not been fully assessed or because the decision making process is too complex and subject to variables to capture it in a procedure.

gyroscope
Mobile device technology that can determine the rotation of a device with a sensor that measures the rotation of the device. (See also **accelerometer/ gyroscope**).

hacker collective
A group of hackers, working together, to target an organization as part of a cyber warfare campaign.

haptic feedback
Tactile response on a touchscreen device, typically a slight vibration of the surface, although the entire device can vibrate in certain responses.

hard copy
Printer output of electronic documents onto paper.

hardening
A security technique in which the default configuration of a system is altered to protect the system against attacks.

hardware RAID solution
A method of creating volumes from an array of physical disks by using a plug-in controller card or the motherboard, independently of the installed OS.

hash
The value that results from hashing encryption as a short representation of data. Also called a hash value or message digest.

hash function
A variable length string (text) is taken as input to produce a fixed length value as output.

HAV
(Hardware Assisted Virtualization) Instruction set extensions (Intel VT-x and AMD-V) that facilitate the operation of virtual machines.

HBA
(host bus adapter) A component allowing storage devices to exchange data with a computer system using a particular interface (PATA, SATA, SCSI, and so on). Motherboards will come with built-in host adapters and more can be added as expansion cards if necessary.

HCL
(Hardware Compatibility List) Before installing an OS, it is vital to check that all the PC components have been tested for compatibility with the OS (that they are on the Hardware Compatibility List [HCL] or Windows Logo'd Product List). Incompatible hardware may not work or may even prevent the installation from completing successfully.

HDD
(Hard Disk Drive) A device providing persistent mass storage for a PC (saving data when the computer is turned off). Data is stored using platters with a magnetic coating that are spun under disk heads that can read and write to locations on each platter (sectors). A HDD installed within a PC is referred to as the fixed disk. HDDs are often used with enclosures as portable storage or as Network Attached Storage (NAS).

HDMI
(High Definition Multimedia Interface)
High-specification digital connector for
audio-video equipment.

head unit
In a car, the unified hardware interface for
the audio system and related components.

headset
A device that combines headphones and
microphone in a single device.

health policy
Policies or profiles describing a minimum
security configuration that devices must
meet to be granted network access.

heat pipe
A sealed tube containing water or ethanol
coolant. The liquid close to the heat source
evaporates then condenses at a cooler
point in the pipe and flows back towards
the heat source.

heat sink
A passive heat exchanger that dissipates
heat from a source such as a CPU and
transfers it, normally via an enlarged
surface area, to another medium such as
air or water.

heat spreader
Similar to a **heat pipe** except it is a flat
container rather than a pipe.

heating element
In a thermal printer, the component within
the printer that is heated to react to
chemicals in **thermal paper** to change
color, creating images on the thermal
paper.

heuristic
Monitoring technique that allows dynamic
pattern matching based on past
experience rather than relying on pre-
loaded signatures.

HFC Cable
(Hybrid Fiber Coax cable) A cable Internet
connection is usually available along with a
cable telephone/television service (Cable
Access TV [CATV]). These networks are
often described as Hybrid Fiber Coax (HFC)
as they combine a fiber optic core network
with coax links to consumer premises

equipment, but are more simply just
described as "cable." Consumers interface
with the service via a cable "modem"
(actually functioning more like a bridge).

HFS+
(Extended Hierarchical File System) The file
system used by Apple Mac workstations
and laptops.

HIDs
(Human Interface Devices) Peripherals that
enable the user to enter data and select
commands.

high resource utilization
When apps, especially malware or rogue
apps, use excessive processor cycles (often
trying to collect data in the background)
and overwhelm a mobile device.

hives
The Windows Registry is made up of hives.
Each hive contains a discrete body of
configuration data corresponding to an
aspect of the system; for example; the
SOFTWARE hive contains all the software
configuration information. The files
comprising the hives are stored in the
%SystemRoot%\System32\Config folder.

home directory
A directory where you are placed when
you log in to a Linux system. It is typically
represented by the ~ symbol.

home folder
A private network storage area located in a
shared network server folder in which
users can store personal files.

home server PC
Either a **home theater PC (HTPC)** with a
slightly expanded role or a repurposed
desktop or low-end PC server used
primarily for file storage, media streaming,
and printer sharing.

homegroup
Windows networking feature designed to
allow Windows 7 and later home networks
to share files and printers easily through a
simple password protection mechanism.
Earlier versions of Windows are not
supported. Support for homegroups was
discontinued in later versions of Windows
10.

host controller
A hardware component of the USB subsystem responsible for recognizing when a USB device is attached or removed from the system, monitors the device status, provides power to the USB devices, and controls the flow of data between the USB host and USB devices.

host firewall
See **personal firewall**.

host ID
In an IP address, the portion of the address that uniquely identifies a host on a particular IP network

host name
The description name assigned to a computer.

host-hinted mode
A SATA standard (version 3.2) that defines a set of commands to allow the host computer to specify how the cache should be used.

hot swappable
A device that can be added or removed without having to restart the operating system.

hotfix
A hotfix is a software update designed and released to particular customers only, though they may be included in later Service Packs.

hotspot
A location served by some sort of device offering Internet access via Wi-Fi.

HT
(HyperThreading) Intel CPU architecture implemented on many Pentium 4 models. HT exposes two or more logical processors to the OS, delivering performance benefits similar to SMP.

HTPC
(Home Theater PC) A PC used in place of consumer appliances such as Personal Video Recorders (PVRs) to watch and record TV broadcasts and play movies and music.

HTT
(HyperThreading technology) Intel's term for HyperThreading.

HTTP
(HyperText Transfer Protocol) The protocol used to provide web content to browsers. HTTP uses port 80. HTTPS(ecure) provides for encrypted transfers, using SSL/TLS and port 443.

HTTPS
(HTTP Secure) A protocol that provides for encrypted transfers, using SSL/TLS and port 443.

hub
An OSI layer 1 (Physical) network device used to implement a star network topology on legacy Ethernet networks. Hubs may also be known as "multiport repeaters" or concentrators. They are the central points of connection for segments and act like repeaters so that every segment receives signals sent from any other segment.

HVAC
(Heating, Ventilation, and Air Conditioning) The building environmental heating and cooling services and the control of those systems.

hybrid drive
A drive in which a portion is SSD, which functions as a large cache, containing frequently accessed data and a magnetic disk portion which is only spun up when non-cached data is accessed.

I/O addresses
(Input/Output addresses) Input/output peripherals have a special area of memory in the range 0000-FFFF set aside to allow data reading and writing functions. This is normally configured by Plug-and-Play but can be set manually using Device Manager.

I/O port
A device connection through which data can be sent and received.

IA-32
See **x86-32**.

IA-64
The 64-bit instruction set developed by Intel for its Itanium server CPU platform that never gained acceptance in the PC market.

IaaS
(Infrastructure as a Service) A cloud computing service that enables a consumer to outsource computing equipment purchases and running their own data center.

IC
(integrated circuit) A **silicon chip** embedded on a ceramic plate.

iCloud
Cloud storage service operated by Apple and closely integrated with macOS and iOS.

iCloud Keychain
A **Keychain** feature that makes the same passwords securely available across all macOS and iOS devices.

ICM
(information content management) The process of managing information over its lifecycle, from creation to destruction.

ICMP
(Internet Control Message Protocol) IP-level protocol for reporting errors and status information supporting the function of troubleshooting utilities such as ping.

IDE
(Integrated Development Environment) A programming environment that typically includes a code editor containing an autocomplete feature to help you write code, a debugger to help you find coding errors, and an **interpreter** that translates the **script file** code into machine readable code the computer can **execute**.

identifier
A computer programming component used to access program elements such as a stored value, class, method, or interface.

IDF
(Intermediate Distribution Frame) A cable rack that interconnects the telecommunications wiring between an MDF and any end-user devices.

IDS
(Intrusion Detection System) Software or security appliance designed to monitor network traffic (NIDS) or configuration files and logs on a host (HIDS) to record and detect unusual activity. Many systems can automatically take preventive action (Intrusion Prevention System [IPS]). Detection is either signature-based or anomaly-based (or both). IDS software typically requires a lengthy period of configuration and "training" to recognize baseline "normal" activity.

IEEE 802.11
A series of Wi-Fi standards used to implement Wireless Local Area Networks.

illuminance
The light projecting power. Compare with **luminance**.

image
A duplicate of an operating system installation (including installed software, settings, and user data) stored on removable media. Windows makes use of image-based backups and they are also used for deploying Windows to multiple PCs rapidly.

image level backup
Backup of a virtual machine which captures all of the information required to run the VM.

imaging drum
See **EP drum**.

IMAP
(Internet Message Access Protocol) A TCP/IP application protocol providing a means for a client to access email messages stored in a mailbox on a remote server. Unlike POP3, messages persist on the server after the client has downloaded them. IMAP also supports mailbox management functions, such as creating subfolders and access to the same mailbox by more than one client at the same time. IMAP4 utilizes TCP port number 143.

IMEI number
(International Mobile Equipment Identity number) A number that uniquely identifies a mobile device on a GSM network.

impact printer
Typically, a dot matrix printer, this uses pressure to transfer ink from a ribbon onto paper in a particular pattern, similar to the mechanism of a typewriter.

impersonation
An approach in which an attacker pretends to be someone they are not, typically an average user in distress, or a help-desk representative.

implicit deny
Implicit deny is a basic principle of security stating that unless something has explicitly been granted access it should be denied access. An example of this is firewall rule processing, where the last (default) rule is to deny all connections not allowed by a previous rule.

IMSI number
(International Mobile Subscriber Identity number) A number that uniquely identifies a mobile subscriber.

in-place upgrade
Installing the OS on top of an existing version of the OS, retaining applications, user settings, and data files.

incident
Something that is not normal and disrupts regular operations in the computing environment.

incident management
A set of practices and procedures that govern how an organization will respond to an incident in progress.

Incident Response Policy
Procedures and guidelines covering appropriate priorities, actions, and responsibilities in the event of security incidents. The stages will generally be notification, investigation, remediation, and follow-up. Incident response is often handled by a special group—the Computer Security Incident Response Team—made up of staff with both technical skills and decision-making authority.

incineration
Exposing the disk to high heat to melt its components.

infrastructure mode
Wi-Fi network configuration in which each client device or station is configured to connect to the network via an access point.

ink cartridge
In an inkjet printer, a cartridge containing an ink reservoir and sensors to detect the amount of remaining ink, typically with separate cartridges for cyan, magenta, yellow, and black ink. Most ink cartridges also contain the print head for the printer.

ink dispersion printer
Better known as inkjets, this is a type of printer where colored ink is sprayed onto the paper using microscopic nozzles in the print head. There are two main types of ink dispersion system: thermal shock (heating the ink to form a bubble that bursts through the nozzles) and piezoelectric (using a tiny element that changes shape to act as a pump).

ink jet printer
See **ink dispersion printer**.

input voltage
A PSU setting to set North American power supplies to 115 V and UK power supplies to 240 V.

insert mode
In Linux vi editor, the mode that allows users to insert text by typing.

installation boot method
The way in which the installation program and settings are loaded onto the PC.

instruction set
The machine language code and commands the CPU can process.

insulator
A material that does not conduct electricity, such as rubber or plastic.

integer
Data type supporting storage of whole numbers.

integrated GPU
(integrated graphics processing unit) A graphics adapter built into the motherboard or the CPU.

integrity
The fundamental security goal of ensuring that electronic data is not altered or tampered with.

interface
The point at which two devices connect and communicate with each other.

internal transfer rate
A measure of how fast read/write operations are performed on the disk platters. Also known as data or disk transfer rate.

Internet backbone
The major infrastructure of the Internet.

interpreted
A command language in which the commands in a **script file** are performed without being compiled into a machine-level set of instructions. In interpreted languages, the code must be read and evaluated each time the script is run, making it slower than compiled instructions.

intranet
A network designed for information processing within a company or organization. An intranet uses the same technologies as the Internet but is owned and managed by a company or organization.

inventory management
An inventory is a list of things, usually stored in a database. Inventories are usually compiled for assets.

iOS
Mobile OS developed by Apple for its iPhone and iPad devices.

IoT
(Internet of Things) The global network of personal devices (such as phones, tablets, and fitness trackers), home appliances, home control systems, vehicles, and other items that have been equipped with sensors, software, and network connectivity.

IP
(Internet Protocol) The network (Internet) layer protocol in the TCP/IP suite providing packet addressing and routing for all higher level protocols in the suite.

IP scale
(ingress protection) An international standard to determine how well electrical enclosures are sealed against dust, water, moisture, and other intrusive materials from entering the enclosure. The ratings scale is defined in the British EN60529:1992 and European IEC 60509:1989 standards.

IPS
(in-plane switching) An LCD panel technology designed to resolve the quality issues inherent in TN panel technology, including strong viewing angle dependence and low-quality color reproduction.

IPS
(Intrusion Protection System) Systems that can automatically take preventive action using signature-based or anomaly-based detection. Also known as network IDS (NIDS).

IPS
(Indoor Positioning Systems) A system that works out a device's location by triangulating its proximity to other radio sources, such as Wi-Fi access points or Bluetooth beacons.

IPSec
(Internet Protocol Security) Layer 3 protocol suite providing security for TCP/IP. It can be used in two modes (transport, where only the data payload is encrypted, and tunnel, where the entire IP packet is encrypted and a new IP header added). IPsec can provide confidentiality and/or integrity. Encryption can be applied using a number of hash (MD5 or SHA) and symmetric (DES or AES) algorithms. Key exchange and security associations are handled by the Internet Key Exchange Protocol. Hosts can be authenticated by a shared secret, PKI, or Kerberos.

IR
(Infrared) Infrared Data Association (IrDA) was a wireless networking standard supporting speeds up to about 4 Mbps. Infrared (IR) sensors are used in mobile devices and with IR blasters to control appliances.

IRQ
(Interrupt Request) A communications channel between a hardware device and the system processor. Originally, when hardware was added to the computer it had to be manually configured with a unique interrupt number (between 0 and 15). Plug-and-Play compatible systems configure resources automatically. The PCI bus introduced IRQ steering, which allowed IRQs to be shared. Modern computers use programmable interrupt controllers, allowing for hundreds of interrupts.

ISDN
(Integrated Services Digital Network) A digital phone/fax/data service used to provide Internet connectivity. There are two classes of ISDN: Basic Rate Interface (BRI) provides two 64 Kbps (B channels) for data and one 16 Kbps (D channel) for link management control signals; Primary Rate Interface (PRI) provides either T1 or E1 capacity levels (23B or 30B) channels, depending on location in the world, and one 64 Kbps D channel.

ISO file
A file that contains all of the contents from an optical disc in a single file which can be mounted to the file system as though it were a physical optical drive.

ISP
(Internet Service Provider) An organization that provides a connection to the Internet and other web- and email-related services. A connection to the ISP's Internet routing equipment can be made using a variety of methods.

ITIL
(IT Infrastructure Library) An IT best practice framework, emphasizing the alignment of IT Service Management (ITSM) with business needs. ITIL was first developed in 1989 by the UK government and the ITIL v3 2011 edition is now marketed by AXELOS.

IXPs
(Internet eXchange Points) High bandwidth trunks that connect to the Internet backbone.

jailbreaking
Removing manufacturer restrictions on a device to allow other software, operating systems, or networks to work with a device. Typically refers to iPhone devices.

jamming
In wireless networking, the phenomenon by which radio waves from other devices interfere with the 802.11 wireless signals used by computing devices and other network devices.

jitter
A variation in the time it takes for a signal to reach the recipient. Jitter manifests itself as an inconsistent rate of packet delivery. If packet loss or delay is excessive, then noticeable audio or video problems (artifacts) are experienced by users.

joystick
A pivoting stick or lever attached to a base that is used to control movement on a device.

jumper
A small plastic clip containing a metal conductor that fits over two contacts to complete a circuit that configures the motherboard or adapter card one way or another.

KB
(Knowledge Base) A searchable database of product FAQs (Frequently Asked Questions), advice, and known troubleshooting issues. The Microsoft KB is found at support.microsoft.com.

kernel
A low-level piece of code responsible for controlling the rest of the operating system.

key exchange
Two hosts need to know the same symmetric encryption key without any other host finding out what it is.

key fob

A chip implanted in a plastic fob. The chip can store authentication data (such as a digital certificate) that can be read when put in proximity to a suitable scanner. Another use for fobs is to generate a One Time Password, valid for a couple of minutes only and mathematically linked to a code generated on a server.

keyboard

The oldest PC input device and still fundamental to operating a computer. There are many different designs and layouts for different countries. Some keyboards feature special keys.

Keychain

macOS app for managing passwords cached by the OS and supported browser/web applications.

keyed port

A port with physical attributes that prevent a connector from being inserted into the port the wrong way around.

kill switch

Another term for **remote wipe**.

KVM switch

(Keyboard Video Mouse switch) A switch supporting a single set of input and output devices controlling a number of PCs. KVM are more typically used with servers but 2-port versions allow a single keyboard, mouse, and display to be used with two PCs.

LAN

(Local Area Network) A network in which all the nodes or hosts participating in the network are directly connected with cables or short-range wireless media.

lands

In optical storage media, raised areas on the disk.

lanes

In PCIe, two wire pairs (four wires in total) using low voltage differential signaling, with one pair used to transmit and the other pair to receive (bi-directional).

laptop

A portable computer offering similar functionality to a desktop computer. Laptops come with built-in LCD screens and input devices (keyboard and touchpad), and can be powered from building power (via an AC adapter) or by a battery.

laser printer

A type of printer that develops an image on a drum using electrical charges to attract special toner then applying it to paper. The toner is then fixed to the paper using a high-heat and pressure roller (fuser). The process can be used with black toner only or four color toner cartridges (Cyan, Magenta, Yellow, and Black) to create full-color prints. Monochrome laser printers are the "workhorses" of office printing solutions.

latency

The time it takes for a signal to reach the recipient. A video application can support a latency of about 80 ms, while typical latency on the Internet can reach 1000 ms at peak times. Latency is a particular problem for 2-way applications, such as VoIP (telephone) and online conferencing.

latent

Evidence that cannot be seen with the naked eye and instead must be interpreted using a machine or process.

LC

(Lucent Connector) Small Form Factor version of the SC push-pull fiber optic connector; available in simplex and duplex versions.

LCD panel

(Liquid Crystal Display panel) A display technology where the image is made up of liquid crystal cells controlled using electrical charges. LCD panels are used on laptops and have replaced CRT monitors as the main type of computer display screen.

LDAP

(Lightweight Directory Access Protocol) Standard for accessing and updating information in an X.500-style network resource directory. LDAP uses port 389. Unless secure communications are used,

LDAP is vulnerable to packet sniffing and Man-in-the-Middle attacks. It is also usually necessary to configure user permissions on the directory. LDAP version 3 supports simple authentication or Simple Authentication and Security Layer, which integrates it with Kerberos or TLS.

least privilege
Least privilege is a basic principle of security stating that something should be allocated the minimum necessary rights, privileges, or information to perform its role.

LED
(Light Emitting Diode) Small, low-power lamps used both as diagnostic indicators, LCD backlights, and (as Organic LEDs) in high-quality flat panels.

LED printer
(light emitting diode printer) A type of printer that uses LEDs to print.

legacy system
A computer system that is no longer supported by its vendor and so no longer provided with security updates and patches.

LGA
(Land Grid Array) A CPU form factor used by Intel where the pins that connect the CPU and socket are located on the socket.

life expectancy
The length of time for which a device can be expected to remain reliable.

light sensors
Sensors in a mobile device used to dim and brighten the display based on ambient conditions.

Lightning ports
Proprietary connector and interface for Apple devices.

line conditioner
A device that adjusts voltages in under-voltage and over-voltage conditions to maintain a normal output.

link
Point-to-point connections in PCIe.

link-local address
Addresses used by IPv6 for network housekeeping traffic. Link-local addresses span a single subnet (they are not forwarded by routers).

Linux
An open-source operating system supported by a wide range of hardware and software vendors.

Linux processes
An instance of a running program that performs a data processing task.

literal
A match to the exact string.

load roller
In an inkjet printer, a roller that turns against the paper stack to move the top sheet, while a separation roller prevents more than one sheet from entering the printer.

local account
An account that is only associated with the computer on which it was created.

local bus
The internal bus that links components directly to the processor, resulting in the highest possible data speed as required by components such as the video display.

Local Security Accounts database
A local (non-network) database where local system account information is stored. In Windows systems, this is the **SAM** database, and in Linux systems the information is stored in the /etc/passwd or /etc/shadow file.

Local Security Policy
A set of policies relating to log on, passwords, and other security issues that can be enforced or disabled on the local machine. On domains, security policy is configured centrally using Group Policy Objects (GPO).

locally installed printer
A printer that Windows communicates with directly over the relevant port.

locator applications
An app installed on mobile devices that identifies the device location to help locate a lost or stolen device.

locked out
When a user is unable to access a device because the device has been disabled either by means of the user forgetting the passcode too many times or remotely using an app that locks the device if it is reported lost or stolen.

lockout policy
A policy designed to restrict failed login attempts.

logical operator
A comparison of more than one condition at the same time by using AND, OR, or XOR.

logical security
Controls implemented in software to create an access control system.

logon script
A text file that runs when the user logs on. The file contains commands and settings to configure a user's environment.

LoJack tracking software
"Rootkit"-style software that enables a stolen laptop to be traced or remotely locked down or wiped in the event of theft.

loop
Like a **branch**, a loop deviates from the initial program path to some sort of logic condition. In a loop, the computer repeats the task until a condition is met. Often implemented with For or While statements.

loopback plug
A special connector used for diagnosing network transmission problems that redirects electrical signals back to the transmitting system.

LoS
(Line of Sight) A wireless connection method using ground-based microwave antennas aligned with one another.

low level format
A "proper" low level format creates cylinders and sectors on the disk. This can generally only be done at the factory. The disk utilities just clean data from each sector; they don't re-create the sector layout.

LTE
(Long Term Evolution) A packet data communications specification providing an upgrade path for both GSM and CDMA2000 cellular networks. LTE Advanced is designed to provide 4G standard network access.

LTE-A
(LTE Advanced) LTE Advanced is designed to provide 4G standard network access

luminance
The perceived brightness of a display screen, measured in candelas per square meter (cd/m²).

MAC address
A unique physical hardware address for each Ethernet network adapter that is composed of 12 hexadecimal digits.

MAC address table
The table on a switch keeping track of MAC addresses associated with each port. As the switch uses a type of memory called Content Addressable Memory (CAM), this is sometimes called the CAM table.

MAC filtering
(media access control filtering) Applying an access control list to a switch or access point so that only clients with approved MAC addresses can connect to it.

MAC flooding
Overloading the switch's MAC cache using a tool such as Dsniff or Ettercap to prevent genuine devices from connecting and potentially forcing the switch into hub or flooding mode.

Mac OS
The name of the Apple operating system from launch to 2001.

Machine to Machine (M2M)
Internet of Things feature that allows objects to communicate and pass data

between themselves and other traditional systems like computer servers.

macOS
Operating system designed by Apple for their range of iMac computers, Mac workstations, and MacBook portables. macOS (previously called OS X) is based on the BSD version of UNIX. macOS is well supported by application vendors, especially in the design industry.

MACs
(Moves, adds, changes) A record of any requested moves, adds, or changes to computers, devices, users, or related policies.

Magic Mouse
An Apple mouse with a touchpad surface that supports **gestures**.

Magic Trackpad
An Apple trackpad with a larger work surface than the Magic Mouse.

main board
See **motherboard**.

main connector
The adapter from the power supply that supplies power to the motherboard.

maintenance kit
A set of replacement feed rollers, new transfer roller, and a new fuser unit for a laser printer.

male port
A port that has pin connectors.

managed_switch
Works as an **unmanaged switch** out-of-the-box but an administrator can connect to it over a management port, configure security settings, and then choose options for the switch's more advanced functionality.

mantrap
A secure entry system with two gateways, only one of which is open at any one time.

MAPI
(Message Application Programming Interface) A Windows messaging interface used primarily by the email client software

Outlook to communicate with an Exchange mail server.

mask
A face covering, usually made of cloth, plastic, or rubber, that fits over your mouth and nose should be worn when you are using a compressed air canister, working around toner spills, or working in an otherwise dusty environment. A mask minimizes the risk of inhaling damaging airborne particles.

mass storage device
Non-volatile storage devices that are able to hold data when the system is powered off.

matte coating
A display coating that is best suited to office work. Compare with **gloss coating**.

MBR
(Master Boot Record) A sector on a hard disk storing information about partitions configured on the disk.

MD5
(Message Digest Algorithm v5) The Message Digest Algorithm was designed in 1990 by Ronald Rivest, one of the "fathers" of modern cryptography. The most widely used version is MD5, released in 1991, which uses a 128-bit hash value.

MDF
(Main Distribution Frame) A cable rack that interconnects external communication cables and the cables that comprise the internal network.

MDM
(Mobile Device Management) Software suites designed to manage use of smartphones and tablets within an enterprise.

measured service
A provider's ability to control and bill a customer's use of resources such as CPU, memory, disk, and network bandwidth through metering.

media center
A computer used for media streaming, often connected to surround sound

speakers, and capable of recording TV shows.

media guides
In a paper tray, the movable components that can be adjusted to hold the paper in the proper position for feeding through the printer.

megapixels
A unit of measure for the number of pixels a digital camera is capable of producing.

MEID
(Mobile Equipment ID) A number that uniquely identifies a mobile device on a CDMA network.

member server
Any Windows-based server computer configured into a domain but not maintaining the Active Directory database (authenticating users) is referred to as a member server. Servers in a workgroup are referred to as standalone servers.

memory card
Flash drives typically used for digital cameras and smartphones; typically small and flat.

memory card reader
A device containing one or more slots to accommodate reading (and writing) memory cards.

memory module
A printed circuit board that holds a group of memory chips that act as a single unit.

message digest
See **MD5**.

metadata
Data about data, typically one set of data summarizes information about the original set of data.

MFD
(multifunction device) Any device that performs more than one function. This typically refers to either SOHO Internet routers/access points or print devices that can also scan and fax.

MIB
(Management Information Base) A database used by SNMP in which agents maintain configuration and usage data and identifies what information the managed system offers.

microATX
Introduced in late 1997, and is often referred to as μATX, and has a maximum size of 9.6 inches by 9.6 inches.

microprocessor
A programmable **integrated circuit (IC)**.

microsegmentation
Each switch port is a separate collision domain. In effect, the switch establishes a point-to-point link called a virtual circuit between any two network nodes.

Microsoft account
The type of account required to get apps from the Microsoft Store, to sync data between devices, access OneDrive, and work with parental controls for a Child account.

Microsoft Windows
Windows started as version 3.1 for 16-bit computers. A workgroup version provided rudimentary network facilities. Windows NT 4 workstations and servers (introduced in 1993) provided reliable 32-bit operation and secure network facilities, based around domains. The Windows 9x clients (Windows 95, 98, and Me) had far lower reliability and only support for workgroups, but were still hugely popular as home and business machines. Windows 2000 and Windows XP workstations married the hardware flexibility and user interface of Windows 9x to the reliability and security of Windows NT, while the server versions saw the introduction of Active Directory for managing network objects. The subsequent client releases of Windows (Vista and Windows 7) featured a substantially different interface (Aero) with 3D features as well as security improvements. The latest client versions—Windows 8 and Windows 10—are designed for use with touchscreen devices.

MIDI
(Musical Instrument Digital Interface) Allows a computer with a sound card to

drive MIDI compatible musical instruments, such as synthesizers, samplers, and drum machines (or [vice versa] for a synthesizer to drive a computer audio application [such as a sampler]).

MIME
(Multi-purpose Internet Mail Extensions) A protocol specifying Internet mail message formats and attachments.

MIMO/MU-MIMO
(Multiple Input Multiple Output/Multiple User MIMO) Wireless technology used in 802.11n/ac and 4G standards. MIMO is the use of multiple reception and transmission antennas to boost bandwidth. A Multi-user MIMO (MU-MIMO)-capable access point can use separate streams to connect multiple MU-MIMO-capable stations simultaneously, providing the stations are not on the same directional path.

mini-ITX
A small compact board that fits the same form factor as the ATX and the micro-ATX boards. They have a maximum size of 6.7 inches by 6.6 inches.

mirroring
Mirroring is a type of RAID (RAID 1) using two hard disks, providing the simplest way of protecting a single disk against failure. Data is written to both disks and can be read from either disk.

Mission Control
App facilitating multiple desktops in macOS.

MitM
(Man-in-the-Middle) Where the attacker intercepts communications between two hosts.

MMF
(Multimode Fiber) A category of fiber optic cable. Compared to SMF, MMF is cheaper (using LED optics rather than lasers), but supports shorter distances (up to about 500 m).

mobile device synchronization
Copying data back and forth between a mobile device and another device such as another mobile device, tablet, laptop, PC,

or cloud service to keep the information up-to-date on all of the devices.

mobile hotspot
See **tethering**.

mobile VPN
A **VPN** that can maintain the VPN link across multiple carrier networks, where the IP address assigned to the mobile device may change often.

mobile VR headset
(mobile Virtual Reality headset) A VR device designed to be used with specific smartphones.

mobo
See **motherboard**.

modem
(modulator/demodulator) A network device that is used to interface a computer with the telephone network for data and fax communications, modulating digital data for transmission as an analog signal and demodulating incoming analog transmissions. Broadband modems are used to transmit signals over telephone (DSL) or cable TV networks.

Molex connector
A power connector that is used to supply power to Parallel Advanced Technology Attachment (PATA) drives, optical drives, and SCSI drives.

motherboard
The computer motherboard, also called the system board, provides the basic foundation for all of the computer's hardware, including the processor, RAM, firmware, and expansion cards. Several motherboard standards are available, each with a different layout and associated advantages.

mount point
A partition or volume mapped to a folder in another file system rather than allocated a drive letter.

mouse
The essential device to implement a WIMP GUI, a mouse simply controls the movement of a cursor that can be used to select objects from the screen. All

Windows mice feature two click buttons, which are configured to perform different actions. Many mice also feature a scroll wheel.

MSDS
(Materials Safety Data Sheet) Information sheet accompanying hazardous products or substances explaining the proper procedures for handling and disposal.

MTBF
(Mean Time Between Failures) The rating on a device or component that predicts the expected time between failures.

multiboot system
Installing multiple operating systems on a single computer. Each OS must normally be installed to a separate partition.

multifactor authentication
Strong authentication is multifactor. Authentication schemes work on the basis of something you know, something you have, or something you are. These schemes can be made stronger by combining them (for example, protecting use of a smart card certification [something you have] with a PIN [something you know]).

multimedia
Multimedia refers to PC components that can playback and record sound and video (or to sound and video files). There are numerous sound and video file formats, including legacy Windows-specific formats such as WAV (for audio) or AVI (for video and audio). The preferred file format for Windows Media Player is ASF (Advanced Systems Format), which is usually compressed (WMA or WMV). Other file formats include those used for Apple's QuickTime player (MOV and QT), Apple's iTunes format (AIFF), and RealNetworks player (RA or RAM). The most popular standards-based format is MPEG.

multimeter
An electrical meter capable of measuring voltage, resistance, and current. Voltage readings can be used to determine whether, for example, a power supply unit is functioning correctly. Resistance readings can be used to determine whether a fuse or network cable is functioning correctly.

multiple desktops
A feature that enables users to set up one or more desktops with different sets of apps, backgrounds, and so on. See **Mission Control**.

multiport repeater
See **hub**.

multitasking
The ability of an operating system to run multiple programs, or tasks, at one time. DOS was a single tasking operating system. Windows 3.x was a cooperative multitasking operating system, while Windows 9x and higher provide preemptive multitasking. Cooperative multitasking relies on the applications to share CPU cycles with one another and to voluntarily relinquish the processor to other tasks, which has reliability implications.

multithreaded
Software that runs multiple parallel threads within a process.

multitouch
A touchscreen or touchpad capable of interpreting gestures, such as pinching or swiping.

mutual authentication
Typically a client authenticates to a server. In many circumstances, it may be necessary for the server to authenticate to the client also (to prevent Man-in-the-Middle attacks, for instance). This is referred to as mutual authentication.

mutual authentication for multiple services
(SSO [Single Sign On]) One service accepts the credentials from another service. Also known as **federated identity management**.

NAC
(Network Access Control) A means of ensuring endpoint security—ensuring that all devices connecting to the network conform to a "health" policy (patch level, antivirus/firewall configuration, and so on). NAC can work on the basis of pre- or post-

admission control. The core components are an agent running on the client, policy enforcers (network connection devices such as switches and access points), and policy decision points (NAC policy server and AAA/RADIUS server).

NAPT
(Network Address Port Translation) Similar to NAT, it (or PAT or NAT overloading) maps private host IP addresses onto a single public IP address. Each host is tracked by assigning it a random high TCP port for communications.

NAS
(Network Attached Storage) A storage device with an embedded OS that supports typical network file access protocols (TCP/IP and SMB, for instance). These may be subject to exploit attacks (though using an embedded OS is often thought of as more secure as it exposes a smaller attack "footprint"). The unauthorized connection of such devices to the network is also a concern.

NAT
(Network Address Translation) A network service provided by router or proxy server to map private local addresses to one or more publicly accessible IP addresses. NAT can use static mappings but is most commonly implemented as Network Address Port Translation (NAPT) or NAT overloading, where a few public IP addresses are mapped to multiple LAN hosts using port allocations.

native resolution
The fixed resolution for LCD or other flat panel display devices.

Negative Acknowledgement
(NACK) On a TCP/IP network, when using TCP and the data is delivered in a damaged state, a NACK packet is sent back to the sender to force retransmission of the data.

NetBEUI
A proprietary Microsoft network transport protocol typically found in non-routed networks. Fast and efficient, but not widely supported by third parties. Largely forgotten in these days of TCP/IP.

NetBIOS
NetBIOS is a session management protocol used to provide name registration and resolution services on legacy Microsoft networks. WINS provides NetBIOS name resolution. See also **NetBEUI**.

NetBT
(NetBIOS over TCP/IP) NetBIOS that was re-engineered to work over the TCP and UDP protocols.

network
Two or more computer systems linked together by some form of transmission medium that enables them to share information.

network drive
A local share that has been assigned a drive letter.

network firewall
A firewall placed inline in the network that inspects all traffic that passes through it.

network ID
In an IP address, the portion of the address that is common to all hosts on the same IP network.

Network Interface layer
In the TCP/IP suite, the layer responsible for putting frames onto the physical network.

network mapping
Tools used to gather information about the way the network is built and configured and the current status of hosts.

network topology
The shape or structure of a network is commonly described as its topology. Topologies may be either physical (the actual appearance of the network layout) or logical (the flow of data across the network). In a star topology, nodes are connected to a single point while in a hub topology, all nodes connect to the same media and share bandwidth. A ring topology means that communications travel from node-to-node in a loop. In a full mesh network, each node is linked to every other node, but partial meshes are far more common. A hybrid topology uses

elements of different topologies, such as a logical bus but physical star.

NFC
(Near Field Communications) A Standard for peer-to-peer (2-way) radio communications over very short (around 4") distances, facilitating contactless payment and similar technologies. NFC is based on RFID.

NFS
(Network File System) A remote file access protocol used principally on UNIX and Linux networks.

NIC
(Network interface Card) An expansion card that enables a PC to connect to a LAN. Also referred to as a network adapter.

NIST
(National Institute of Standards and Technology) Develops computer security standards used by US federal agencies and publishes cybersecurity best practice guides and research.

NLA
(Network Level Authentication) An RDP technology requiring users to authenticate before a server session is created.

non-parity
System memory that does not perform error checking (except for the startup memory count).

notification shade
An Android feature that is accessed by swiping down from the top of the display to access Android OS feature settings.

NTFS
(NT File System) A Windows file system that supports a 64-bit address space and is able to provide extra features such as file-by-file compression and RAID support as well as advanced file attribute management tools, encryption, and disk quotas.

NVMe
(Non-volatile Memory Express) An interface for connecting flash memory devices, such as SSDs, directly to a PCI

Express bus. NVMe allows much higher transfer rates than SATA/AHCI.

NVMHCI
(Non-Volatile Memory Host Controller Interface Specification) A logical interface used by PCIe-based SSD drives to communicate with the bus.

objects
A data structure in Windows that represents system resources.

OCP
(Overcurrent Protection) A power supply rail safety feature that cuts the circuit if the power exceeds a safe limit.

OCR
(Optical Character Recognition) Software that can identify the shapes of characters and digits to convert them from printed images to electronic data files that can be modified in a word processing program. Intelligent Character Recognition (ICR) is an advanced type of OCR, focusing on handwritten text.

octet
32 bit addresses subdivided into four groups of 8 bits (1 byte).

ODBC Data Sources
See **Data Sources**.

offline files
Files (or folders) from a network share that are cached locally. The Offline Folders tool handles synchronization between the local and remote copies.

OLED display
(organic light emitting diode display) A type of LED flat panel display device that uses organic compounds that emit light when subjected to an electric current.

on-access
A type of antivirus scan where the AV software intercepts OS calls to open files, so that it can scan the file before allowing or preventing the file from being opened.

onboard adapter
A low-end adapter included with the motherboard or as part of the CPU itself.

onboarding
The process in which MDM software logs use of a device on the network and determines whether to allow it to connect or not, based on administrator-set parameters.

online social lives
An online way to interact with other people using sites such as Facebook, Twitter, and Instagram.

open questions
Questions that guide the customer to telling you what will be most helpful in resolving their issue.

open source
Open source means that the programming code used to design the software is freely available.

operating system
A software package that enables a computer to function. It performs basic tasks, such as recognizing the input from a keyboard, sending the output to a display screen or monitor, and controlling peripheral devices such as disk drives and printers.

options
The modifiers used with Linux commands to make a command more versatile.

OS X
The name of the Apple operating system from 2001 through 2016.

OSD
(on-screen display) Display configuration menus that show up on the monitor and that you interact with by using buttons on the monitor case.

OTP
(one time password) A password that is generated for use in one specific session and becomes invalid after the session ends.

OU
(Organizational Unit) In Windows Active Directory, a way of dividing the domain up into different administrative realms.

overclocking
Manually setting the CPU and chipset to run at a faster speed than advised by the manufacturer. Some CPUs are better suited to overclocking than others and the system will generally need a better cooling system to cope with the increased thermal output.

PaaS
(Platform as a Service) A cloud computing service that enables consumers to rent fully configured systems that are set up for specific purposes.

packet filtering
A type of firewall that inspects the headers of IP packets and can perform filtering on IP address, protocol type, and port numbers.

page description language
(PDL) A high-level computer language used to describe the contents and the layout of the information to be printed on a page through PDL commands.

pagefile
See **virtual memory**.

PAN
(Personal Area Network) Close range networking (usually based on Bluetooth or NFC) allowing communications between personal devices, such as smartphones, laptops, and printers/peripheral devices.

paper jam
Occurs when paper does not feed through the printer properly, resulting in pages that are stuck within the paper feed mechanism, often crumpled or torn.

parent directory
A directory that is one level above your current working directory.

parity checking
An error checking method where each byte of data in memory is accompanied by a ninth bit used to check for corrupted data.

partitioning
The act of dividing a physical disk into logically separate storage areas, often referred to as drives.

passive cooling device
A CPU generates a large amount of heat that must be dissipated to prevent damage to the chip. Generally, a CPU will be fitted with a heatsink (a metal block with fins) and fan. Thermal compound is used at the contact point between the chip and the heatsink to ensure good heat transfer. The PSU also incorporates a fan to expel warm air from the system. Modern motherboards have temperature sensors that provide warning of overheating before damage can occur. Very high performance or overclocked systems or systems designed for quiet operation may require more sophisticated cooling systems, such as liquid cooling. Cooling systems that work without electricity are described as passive; those requiring a power source are classed as active.

password policy
A weakness of password-based authentication systems is when users demonstrate poor password practice. Examples include choosing a password that is too simple, reusing passwords for different tasks, writing a password down, and not changing a password regularly. Some of these poor practices can be addressed by system policies; others are better approached by education.

PAT
(portable appliance testing) In the UK, Australia, and New Zealand, the process for inspecting and testing electrical equipment to ensure its safety.

PAT
(port address translation) Another term for NAT overloading or NAPT.

PATA
(Parallel Advanced Technology Attachment) Used to be the main disk interface for PCs. The interface was very commonly called IDE (Integrated Drive Electronics) or Enhanced IDE (EIDE). Each PATA adapter supports two devices, commonly called master and slave. A drive is connected to the bus by a 40-pin ribbon cable. The PATA interface has been replaced by SATA.

patch
A fix or update for a software program or application, designed to eliminate known bugs or vulnerabilities and improve performance.

Patch Management
Identifying, testing, and deploying OS and application updates. Patches are often classified as critical, security-critical, recommended, and optional.

Patch Tuesday
The second Tuesday of every month when Microsoft releases updates.

pattern lock
To access a locked device, the user must trace a predetermined pattern on screen, or join the dots.

PCI bus
(Peripheral Component Interconnect bus) Introduced in 1995 with the Pentium processor, it connects the CPU, memory, and peripherals to a 32-bit working at 33 MHz. PCI supports bus mastering, IRQ steering, and Plug-and-Play. Later versions defined 64-bit operation and 66 MHz clock but were not widely adopted on desktop PCs.

PCI DSS
(Payment Card Industry Data Security Standard) Information security standard for organizations that process credit or bank card payments.

PCIe
(PCI Express) An expansion bus standard using serial communications. Each device on the bus can create a point-to-point link with the I/O controller or another device. The link comprises one or more lanes (x1, x2, x4, x8, x12, x16, or x32). Each lane supports a full-duplex transfer rate of 250 MBps (v1.0), 500 MBps (v2.0), or 1 GBps (v3.0). The standard is software compatible with PCI, allowing for motherboards with both types of connectors.

PDU
(power distribution unit) A device designed to provide power to devices that require power, and may or may not support remote monitoring and access.

peer-to-peer network
In peer-to-peer networks there is no dedicated server, but instead, each computer connected to the network acts as both a server and client (each computer is a peer of the other computers). These types of networks were originally developed as a low-cost alternative to server-based systems for use in smaller companies and organizations where there are up to about ten users. A major drawback to this type of network is a comparative lack of security whereby each user must control access to resources on his/her machine.

permissions
To access files and folders on a volume, the administrator of the computer will need to grant file permissions to the user (or a group to which the user belongs). File permissions are supported by NTFS-based Windows systems.

personal firewall
A firewall implemented as applications software running on the host. Personal software firewalls can provide sophisticated filtering of network traffic and also block processes at the application level. However, as a user-mode application they are more vulnerable to attack and evasion than kernel mode firewalls or network firewall appliances.

PGA
(Pin Grid Array) A CPU socket form factor where pins are located on the bottom of the processor to fit in the matching holes in the motherboard socket. PGA-type sockets are still used by AMD but Intel has switched to Land Grid Array (LGA), where the pins are located on the socket rather than the chip.

PGP
(Pretty Good Privacy) Email encryption product providing message confidentiality and integrity using web of trust PGP certificates.

pharming
Similar to phishing, this type of social engineering attack redirects a request for a website, typically an e-commerce site, to a similar-looking, but fake, website. The

attacker uses DNS spoofing to redirect the user to the fake site.

PHI
(Protected Health Information) Information that identifies someone as the subject of medical and insurance records, plus associated hospital and laboratory test results.

phishing
Obtaining user authentication or financial information through a fraudulent request for information. Phishing is specifically associated with emailing users with a link to a faked site (or some other malware that steals the information they use to try to authenticate). Pharming is a related technique where the attacker uses DNS spoofing to redirect the user to the fake site. Vishing refers to phishing attacks conducted over voice channels (VoIP), while spear phishing or whaling refers to attacks specifically directed at managers or senior executives.

photopolymer
A polymer material that is sensitive to light, and changes its properties when exposed to a light source.

pickup roller
Roller that turns above a stack of paper to feed a sheet into the feed roller.

PID
See **Process ID**.

piezoelectric printing
Ink delivery system in an **inkjet** printer that uses a tiny element that changes shape to act as a pump used in Epson printers.

PII
(Personally Identifiable Information) Data that can be used to identify or contact an individual (or in the case of identity theft, to impersonate them). A Social Security number is a good example of PII. Others include names, date of birth, email address, telephone number, street address, biometric data, and so on.

pipe symbol
A vertical bar typed between commands to pipe or redirect the results or output of

one command as the input to another command.

pits
In optical storage media, recessed areas on the disk.

PIV Card
(Personal Identification Verification card) Smart card standard for access control to US Federal government premises and computer networks.

pixel
The smallest discrete element on a display. A single pixel is composed of a red, a blue, and a green dot.

PKI
(Public Key Infrastructure) Asymmetric encryption provides a solution to the problem of secure key distribution for symmetric encryption. The main problem is making a link between a particular public-private key pair and a specific user. One way of solving this problem is through PKI. Under this system, keys are issued as digital certificates by a Certificate Authority (CA). The CA acts as a guarantor that the user is who he or she says he or she is. Under this model, it is necessary to establish trust relationships between users and CAs. In order to build trust, CAs must publish and comply with Certificate Policies and Certificate Practice Statements.

plenum
An air handling space, including ducts and other parts of the HVAC system in a building.

plenum cable
A grade of cable that does not give off noxious or poisonous gases when burned. Unlike PVC cable, plenum cable can be run through the plenum and firebreak walls.

Plug and Play
See **UPnP**.

PNAC
(Port-based Network Access Control) An IEEE 802.1X standard in which the switch (or router) performs some sort of authentication of the attached device before activating the port.

PoE
(Power over Ethernet) Specification allowing power to be supplied via switch ports and ordinary data cabling to devices such as VoIP handsets and wireless access points. Devices can draw up to about 13 W (or 25 W for PoE+).

pointing device
A peripheral used to move a cursor to select and manipulate objects on the screen.

policy
A subset of a security profile, and a document that outlines the specific requirements and rules everyone must meet.

PoP
(Point of Presence) The equipment that allows a location, facility, home, or other point-of-access to connect to the Internet.

POP 3
(Post Office Protocol) A TCP/IP application protocol providing a means for a client to access email messages stored in a mailbox on a remote server. The server usually deletes messages once the client has downloaded them. POP3 utilizes TCP port 110.

port (logical)
In TCP and UDP applications, a port is a unique number assigned to a particular application protocol (such as HTTP or SMTP). The port number (with the IP address) forms a socket between client and server. A socket is a bi-directional pipe for the exchange of data. For security, it is important to allow only the ports required to be open (ports can be blocked using a firewall).

port (physical)
A hardware connection interface on a personal computer that enables devices to be connected to the computer.

port forwarding
Port forwarding means that a router takes requests from the Internet for a particular application (say, HTTP/port 80) and sends them to a designated host on the LAN.

port number
The number between 0 and 65535 assigned to each type of network application so that the transport layer can identify it.

port replicator
A simple device to extend the range of ports (for example, USB, DVI, HDMI, Thunderbolt, network, and so on) available for a laptop computer when it is used at a desk.

port scanning
Software that enumerates the status of TCP and UDP ports on a target system. Port scanning can be blocked by some firewalls and IDS.

port triggering
Port triggering is used to configure access through a firewall for applications that require more than one port. Basically, when the firewall detects activity on outbound port A destined for a given external IP address, it opens inbound access for the external IP address on port B for a set period.

POST
(Power-On Self-Test) A hardware checking routine built into the PC firmware. This test sequentially monitors the state of the memory chips, the processor, system clock, display, and firmware itself. Errors that occur within vital components such as these are signified by beep codes emitted by the internal speaker of the computer. Further tests are then performed and any errors displayed as on-screen error codes and messages.

POTS
(Plain Old Telephone System) Parts of a telephone network "local loop" using voice-grade cabling. Analog data transfer over POTS using dial-up modems is slow (33.3 Kbps). DSL technologies make better use of the bandwidth available, but are not accessible over all of the network.

power
The rate at which electricity is drawn from the supply by the device using it, measured in Watts.

power drain
When apps, especially malware or rogue apps, use excessive power and quickly drain the battery of a mobile device.

power injector
Used when an existing switch does not support PoE. When a device is connected to a port on a PoE switch, the switch goes through a detection phase to determine whether the device is PoE-enabled. If not, it does not supply power over the port and therefore does not damage non-PoE devices. If so, it determines the device's power consumption and sets the supply voltage level appropriately.

power management
Computers and hardware supporting a power management specification such as ACPI (Advanced Configuration Power Interface) can enter power-saving or standby modes that can be reactivated from the host.

power rating
The maximum power output available from a PC power supply, measured in watts, calculated as voltage multiplied by current.

power redundancy
A duplicate power source to be used in case one power source is unavailable.

power supply tester
A type of meter designed to test PC Power Supply Units.

PPP
(Point-to-Point Protocol) Dial-up protocol working at layer 2 (Data Link) used to connect devices remotely to networks. Often used to connect to an ISP's routers and out to the Internet. PPPoE (PPP over Ethernet) or PPPoA (PPP over ATM) are used to provide broadband connections (over DSL or cable Internet, for instance).

PPPoA
(PPP over ATM) The PPP protocol is used with the ATM transport protocol by DSL providers.

PPPoE
(PPP over Ethernet) PPP packets are encapsulated within Ethernet frames for transport by DSL providers.

PRI
(Preferred Roaming Index) An index that works with the PRL to provide the best data/voice quality to a phone while roaming.

PRI
(Primary Rate Interface) A class of ISDN service that provides either T1 or E1 capacity levels (23B or 30B) channels, depending on location in the world, and one 64 Kbps D channel.

primary charge roller
See **cleaning unit**.

primary group
In Linux, users can be members of one primary group and multiple supplemental groups.

print driver
Software that provides an interface between the print device and Windows.

print head
In a dot matrix printer, pins that are fired by solenoids are secured to a moving carriage that sweeps across the paper and the pins make contact with the **ribbon** to press it against the paper to create images. In an inkjet printer, the print head is typically contained in the **ink cartridge** although Epson inkjet printers include the printhead as part of the printer instead.

print job
The output produced by an application and passed to the printer, and then to the print device via a print monitor and port.

print languages
The language used by printers to interpret output from the computer as printable text and images. Some printers can use multiple print languages.

print monitor
In Windows, the print monitor is a process that checks the print queue (%SystemRoot%\System32\Spool\Printers\) for print jobs. When they arrive, they are processed, if necessary, then passed via a print port to the print device.

printer
An output device that produces text and images from electronic content onto physical media such as paper or transparency film.

printer technology
The mechanism used in a printer to create images on paper. It determines the quality, speed, and cost of the output.

printer type
The mechanism used to make images on the paper. Also referred to as printer technology.

privacy filter
A filter to fit over a display screen so that it can only be viewed straight-on.

privacy screen
A filter to fit over a display screen so that it can only be viewed straight-on.

private address
IP addresses in ranges defined by RFC1928 which are not allowed to route traffic over the Internet, with those addressed being confined to private LANs.

PRL
(Preferred Roaming List) A database built by CDMA service carriers to indicate which radio bands should be used when connecting to a cell tower.

problem management
A method of identifying, prioritizing, and establishing ownership of **incidents**.

procedure
An inflexible, step-by-step listing of the actions that must be completed for any given task.

Process ID
Also PID. The number assigned to a process.

processor
See **CPU**.

professionalism
Taking pride in one's work and in treating people fairly.

profile of security requirements
A set of policies to apply for different employees and different site areas within a site.

program
Software that provides functionality such as word processing, graphics creation, database management, or other productivity or entertainment uses.

proper documentation
A record of what will be done so that the customer knows what to expect in terms of items that are supported, how long incidents may take to resolve, when they can expect an item to be replaced instead of repaired, and so on.

prosumer
A combination of the words professional and consumer, typically referring to an amateur user who uses professional level devices.

protocol
Rules and formats enabling systems to exchange data. A single network will involve the use of many different protocols. In general terms, a protocol defines header fields to describe each packet, a maximum length for the payload, and methods of processing information from the headers.

protocol suite
A collection of several protocols used for networking are designed to work together.

proxy server
A server that mediates the communications between a client and another server. The proxy server can filter and often modify communications as well as provide caching services to improve performance.

PSE
(Power Sourcing Equipment) Network switches that provide power through the Ethernet cable to connected devices.

pseudocode
Writing out a program sequence using code blocks but without using the specific syntax of a particular programming language.

PSK
(Pre-shared Key) Symmetric encryption technologies, such as those used for WEP, require both parties to use the same private key. This key must be kept a secret known only to those authorized to use the network. A pre-shared key is normally generated from a passphrase.

PSTN
(Public Switched Telephone Network) National telecommunications systems have evolved and combined over the years to create a global (and indeed extra-terrestrial) communications network This is referred to as the Public Switched Telephone Network (PSTN) but it is capable of carrying more than simply voice-call services. The basis of PSTN is a circuit-switched network, but the infrastructure can also carry packet-switched data services.

PSU
(Power Supply Unit) Transformer that converts AC mains power into 3.3 V, 5 V, and 12 V DC to power components on the motherboard. The type of PSU must match the case and motherboard form factor.

PVR
(personal video recorder) Software installed on a **home theater PC (HTPC)** to record and watch TV broadcasts.

PXE
(Preboot Execution Environment) A feature of a network adapter that allows the computer to boot by contacting a suitably configured server over the network (rather than using a local hard disk).

QC
(Quick Charge) A Qualcomm **fast charging** technology that also has a second chip for power management that allows higher wattage than is allowed by the USB standard without overheating.

QoS
(Quality of Service) Systems that differentiate data passing over the network that can reserve bandwidth for particular applications. A system that cannot guarantee a level of available bandwidth is often described as Class of Service (CoS).

QR codes
(Quick Response codes) A 2D barcode created of black and white squares used to store information that can be read using a barcode scanner or the camera on a smartphone that has a barcode scanning app installed.

quality updates
Windows updates that are typically released each Tuesday designed to address security vulnerabilities, usually installed in one group of patches and requiring a single reboot. Compare with feature updates.

Quick Response codes
See **QR codes**.

radio firmware
An operating system that is separate from the end-user operating system in a mobile device.

RADIUS
(Remote Authentication Dial-in User Service) Used to manage remote and wireless authentication infrastructure. Users supply authentication information to RADIUS client devices, such as wireless access points. The client device then passes the authentication data to an AAA (Authentication, Authorization, and Accounting) server, which processes the request.

RAID
(Redundant Array of Independent/ Inexpensive Disks) A set of vendor-independent specifications for fault-tolerant configurations on multiple-disk systems.

rainbow table
Tool for speeding up attacks against Windows passwords by precomputing possible hashes.

RAM
(Random Access Memory) The principal storage space for computer data and program instructions. RAM is described as being volatile in the sense that once power has been removed or the computer has been rebooted, data is lost.

range extender
See **wireless range extender**.

ransomware
A type of malware that tries to extort money from the victim, by appearing to lock their computer or by encrypting their files, for instance.

rapid elasticity
The ability to scale cloud computing resources quickly to meet peak demand and just as quickly remove resources if they are not currently needed.

raster
A bitmap image of a page for printing. See also **Raster Image Processing**.

RAW
When applied to a print job, RAW means the job is fully rendered and ready to be passed to the print device without further processing.

RDPRA Mode
(RDP Restricted Admin Mode) A method of mitigating the risk of using Remote Desktop.

real time
The date and time that are maintained by the Real Time Clock.

rear panel
The portion of the system case with cut-out slots aligned with the position of adapter card slots.

recovery disc
OEM recovery media enabling the user to reset the system to its factory configuration.

recovery image
A custom image that contains the current state of the operating system files, plus all of the desktop applications installed to the boot partition.

redirection
When the user tries to open a web page but is sent to another page (which may or may not look like the page the user was attempting to access).

reference machine
The process of Windows deployment to multiple computers by using disk imaging software to clone an installation from one PC to the rest.

refresh rate
The picture displayed on a CRT monitor is updated (by vertical refreshing) many times per second. The more times the image is refreshed, the more stable and flicker-free the picture. On flat panels, there is no flicker as each pixel is not redrawn but only updated. Flat panels can suffer from motion blur and ghosting, however, and better refresh rates can reduce these issues.

regex
(regular expressions) Strings of characters that denote a word, a set of words, or a sentence.

register
Registers are temporary storage areas in the CPU that can hold data prior to processing by the Arithmetic Logic Unit (ALU) and other components of the processor. A CPU can incorporate a number of different registers, but the most important are the **General Purpose (GP) registers**.

registration roller
Roller equipped with a sensor that feeds paper into the print engine.

relational operators
See **comparison operator**.

relative distinguished name
In an LDAP directory, the most specific attribute in the distinguished name that uniquely identifies the object within the context of successive (parent) attribute values.

relative path
The path relative to the current working directory.

remnant removal
Data that has nominally been deleted from a disk by the user can often be recovered using special tools. The best way to shred data without physically destroying a disk is to ensure that each writable location has been overwritten in a random pattern.

Remote Assistance
A Windows remote support feature allowing a user to invite a technical support professional to help them over a network using chat. The user can also grant the support professional control over their desktop. Remote Assistance uses the same RDP protocol as Remote Desktop.

Remote Credential Guard
A method of mitigating the risk of using Remote Desktop.

Remote Desktop
The Windows feature that allows a remote user to initiate a connection at any time and sign on to the local machine using an authorized account.

remote wipe
Software that allows deletion of data and settings on a mobile device to be initiated from a remote server.

removable storage
A storage device that can be removed from the computer, or the removable media that can be inserted in a drive, to store portable data.

repeater
A repeater is a layer 1 device that takes a signal and repeats it to the devices that are connected to it. Repeaters can be used to maintain signal integrity and amplitude across a connection or a network.

replay attack
Where the attacker intercepts some authentication data and reuses it to try to re-establish a session.

rescue disk
See **recovery disc**.

reserve
In DHCP servers, particular IP addresses are set aside for and assigned to specific

devices so that those devices receive the same IP address each time.

resistance
Resistance (R) describes the property of a material to prevent electrical flow through itself. Metals have little electrical resistance whereas plastics and rubber have very high resistance and in most cases will not allow electrical current to pass through them. The resistance of a body to electrical current is measured in Ohms (Ω or R) and is related to potential difference (V) and current (I) by the equation V=IR.

resistor
A component that opposes the flow of current without blocking it completely and is used to manage electronic circuits.

resolution
A measure of the number of picture elements (pixels) that an imaging device can use to sample or display the image, measured in pixels per inch (ppi). On a digital printer, the resolution is the number of toner or ink dots that the print engine can put on paper (measured in dots per inch [dpi]). Note that sometimes dpi is used interchangeably with ppi to describe scanner or monitor resolution, but image pixels and printer dots are not equivalent, as multiple print dots are required to represent a single image pixel accurately.

resolution (digital camera)
The number of megapixels a digital camera is capable of producing.

resource pooling
A cloud provider's data center hardware is not dedicated or reserved for a particular customer account, allowing the provider to provision more resources through management software rather than physically altering hardware to allocate or deallocate resources for a customer.

respect
Treating others and their property as you would like to be treated.

response rate
The time taken for a pixel to change color, measured in milliseconds (ms).

restore points
System Restore takes a snapshot of the system configuration and enables rollbacks to these restore points.

RF
(Radio Frequency) Radio waves propagate at different frequencies and wavelengths. Wi-Fi network products work at 2.4 GHz or 5 GHz.

RFC
(Request for Change) In change management, the formal document submitted to the **CAB** that has the details of the proposed alteration.

RFID
(Radio Frequency Identification) A chip allowing data to be read wirelessly. RFID tags are used in barcodes and smart cards.

RFID badge
(Radio Frequency Identification badge) An ID badge containing a chip allowing data to be read wirelessly.

RFID tag
A tag containing an RFID chip programmed with asset data.

ribbon
In an impact printer, the inked medium against which pins press to create the image.

RIP
(Raster Image Processing) The component responsible for converting instructions in the Page Description Language (PDL) to instructions that control the print engine (an inkjet's ink dispersion nozzles or a laser printer's developer laser, for instance). A PDL might contain instructions for printing vector graphics and fonts; the RIP translates these instructions into a pattern of dots (raster) at the required resolution.

riser card
A space-saving feature of some motherboards, a riser card puts the PC's expansion slots on a separate board installed at right-angles to the main board. This allows the system components to fit within a slimline case.

risk
The likelihood and impact (or consequence) of a threat actor exercising a vulnerability.

RJ connector
(Registered Jack connector) A connector used for twisted pair cabling. 4-pair network cabling uses the larger RJ-45 connector. Modem/telephone 2-pair cabling uses the RJ-11 connector.

RJ-11 connector
A six-position connector that uses just one pair of wires. It is used in telephone system connections.

RJ-45 connector
An eight-position connector that uses all four pairs of wires. It is usually used for network connectivity.

roaming profile
A Microsoft Windows technology that redirects user profiles to a network share so that the information is available when the user logs into any computer on the network where the network share is located.

rogue access point
An unauthorized wireless access point on a corporate or private network, which allows unauthorized individuals to connect to the network.

rogue VM
(rogue virtual machine) A virtual machine that has been installed without authorization.

root directory
Top of the file directory structure on a drive.

root user
A user who has access rights to all files and resources on the system and is the default administrative account on a Linux system.

rooting
Gaining privileged level or root level access to an Android device to enable modifying code or installing software not intended for the device.

rootkit
A class of malware that modifies system files, often at the kernel level, to conceal its presence.

rotational latency
The time it takes for the read/write head to find a sector location.

router
A network device that links dissimilar networks and can support multiple alternate paths between locations based upon the parameters of speed, traffic loads, and cost. A router works at layer 3 (Network) of the OSI model. Routers form the basic connections of the Internet. They allow data to take multiple paths to reach a destination (reducing the likelihood of transmission failure). Routers can access source and destination addresses within packets and can keep track of multiple active paths within a given source and destination network. TCP/IP routers on a LAN can also be used to divide the network into logical subnets.

routine
A section of code within a program to be used repeatedly for a specific task and is usually independent from the rest of the code within the program.

rpm
(Red Hat Package Manager) A tool for maintaining packages in Red Hat Linux systems.

RPO
(Recovery Point Objective) The amount of data loss that a system can sustain, measured in time. See also **recovery time objective**.

RS-232
A serial port that uses a 25-pin male D connector. (See also **serial port**).

RSA
(Rivest Shamir Adelman) The first successful algorithm to be designed for public key encryption. It is named for its designers.

RSoP
(Resultant Set of Policies) In Windows systems, a Group Policy report showing all

of the GPO settings and how they affect the network. It can also be used to show how GPOs affect user and computer combinations with the local security policy in effect.

RSSI
(Received Signal Strength Indicator) For a wireless signal, an index level calculated from the signal strength level.

RTC
(real time clock) Part of the system chipset that keeps track of the date and time. The RTC is powered by a battery so the PC keeps track of the time even when it is powered down. If the computer starts losing time, it is a sign that the battery is failing.

RTC battery
(real time clock battery) The battery that powers the chipset that keeps track of date and time for the system.

RTO
(Recovery Time Objective) The period following a disaster that a system may remain offline. See also **recovery point objective**.

RTOS
(real-time operating system) An OS that is optimized for use in embedded or real-time apps.

RVI
(Rapid Virtualization Indexing) The term used for SLAT extensions by AMD.

S.M.A.R.T.
(Self Monitoring Analysis and Reporting Technology) Technology designed to alert the user to possible hard disk failures before the disk becomes unusable.

S/MIME
(Secure Multipurpose Internet Mail Extensions) Email encryption standard (Cryptographic Message Standard) using PKI (X.509) certificates for confidentiality (digital envelopes) and integrity (digital signatures). S/MIME provides extensions for standard MIME headers.

S/PDIF
(Sony/Phillips Digital Interface) A high-quality audio port that uses coax cabling with RCA connectors or fiber optic cabling and connectors. S/PDIF supports surround sound speakers.

SaaS
(Software as a Service) A cloud computing service that enables a service provider to make applications available over the Internet.

sag
A sag can occur when the power supply entering a computer's components dips briefly below that which is required. Sags are commonly caused when heavy machinery or other high power appliances are started.

SAM
(Security Account Manager) The Windows local security account database where local system account information is stored.

sample
A sound pattern stored in a wave table.

Samsung account
An account created for Samsung Android devices used to access the Samsung devices and related online services.

SAS
(Serial Attached SCSI) Developed from parallel SCSI, SAS represents the highest performing hard disk interface available.

SATA
(Serial ATA) The most widely used interface for hard disks on desktop and laptop computers. It uses a 7-pin data connector with one device per port. There are three SATA standards specifying bandwidths of 1.5 Gbps, 3 Gbps, and 6 Gbps, respectively. SATA drives also use a new 15-pin power connector, though adapters for the old style 4-pin Molex connectors are available. External drives are also supported via the eSATA interface.

SC
(Subscriber Connector) Push/pull connector used with fiber optic cabling.

scalable fonts
Fonts that are **vector based**.

scanner
A type of photocopier that can convert the image of a physical object into an electronic data file. The two main components of a scanner are the lamp, which illuminates the object, and the recording device, an array of CCDs (Charge Coupled Devices). There are flatbed and sheet-fed versions, with sheet-fed versions typically being incorporated with a printer and fax machine into a multifunction device. Scanners can output images directly to a printer or to a suitable file format (such as JPEG, PNG, or TIFF). Scanners can also interface with applications software using one of several interfaces (TWAIN, WIA, SANE, or ISIS).

schematic
A schematic is a simplified representation of a system. Physical network diagrams or schematics can show the general location of components and their identification. Logical network diagrams show the organization of the network into subnets and zones.

screen lock
A way to prevent unauthorized access to a computer or mobile device. Configuring a screen lock requires the user to enter a passphrase, complete a pattern, or enter a PIN to access the device.

script file
A text file containing commands or instructions that are performed by a program on the computer rather than by the computer itself.

scripting language
A programming language that is **interpreted** rather than compiled.

SCSI
(Small Computer Systems Interface) A legacy expansion bus standard allowing for the connection of internal and external devices. SCSI 1 defines the original 8-bit bus with a transfer rate of 5 MBps. SCSI 2 features a 16-bit data bus implementation (Wide SCSI) and a faster transfer rate (Fast SCSI) while maintaining backward compatibility with most of the original devices. SCSI 3 introduces further data rate enhancements (Ultra SCSI) and a serial SCSI standard (Firewire). Each device on a SCSI bus must be allocated a unique ID. The bus must also be terminated at both ends.

SDK
(Software Development Kit) A set of resources provided by a platform vendor for programmers to use when creating software to work with the vendor's platform.

SDN
(Software Defined Networking) Application Programming Interfaces (API) and compatible hardware allowing for programmable network appliances and systems.

SDRAM
(Synchronous Dynamic Random Access Memory) A variant on the DRAM chip designed to run at the speed of the system clock, thus accelerating the periodic refresh cycle times. SDRAM can run at much higher clock speeds than previous types of DRAM. Basic SDRAM is now obsolete and has been replaced by DDR/DDR2/3 SDRAM.

sector
The regularly sized subdivision of a drive track. During low-level formatting, the size and position of the sectors is written to the disk so that the data can be placed into uniform spots that the drive head can easily access.

secure boot
A security system offered by UEFI that is designed to prevent a computer from being hijacked by malware.

security control
A technology or procedure put in place to mitigate vulnerabilities and risk and to ensure the Confidentiality, Integrity, and Availability (CIA) of information. Control types are often classed in different ways, such as technical, operational, and management.

security group
A collection of user accounts that can be assigned permissions in the same way as a single user object.

security template
Settings for services and policy configuration for a server operating in a particular application role (web server, mail server, file/print server, and so on). In Windows, the current configuration can be compared to the baseline defined in a security template using the Security Configuration and Analysis tool.

seek time
The time it takes for the read/write head to locate a particular track position.

self-grounding
Manual dissipation of static buildup by touching a grounded object prior to touching any electronic equipment.

semiconductor
A material that can act as both a conductor and an insulator, which provides switch-like functionality, where a circuit can be opened and closed, used to represent binary (on/off) digits.

separation pad
A stationary pad in a paper tray that pushes the stack of paper back, allowing only a single sheet of paper to be fed into the printer.

separation roller
A roller in a paper tray that pushes the stack of paper back, allowing only a single sheet of paper to be fed into the printer.

serial port
Asynchronous serial transmission (RS-232) is one of the oldest PC bus standards. A serial port is a legacy port that can be used to connect devices such as modems, mice, and Uninterruptible Power Supplies (UPS). Serial ports transmit data bit-by-bit using a single data line at a speed of up to about 115 Kbps. Although the original serial port used a 25-pin male D connector, most PCs today use a male DB9 (9-pin) port. The serial port is now little used but does provide an "out-of-band" means of configuring network appliances such as switches and routers.

server consolidation
Using virtual servers, make more efficient use of system resources and hardware since most servers' capacity is not fully utilized.

server-side virtualization
A solution in which one or more virtual servers are created on a physical server in which each virtual server acts like it was a separate computer.

service
Windows machines run services to provide functions; for example, Plug-and-Play, the print spooler, DHCP client, and so on. These services can be viewed, configured, and started/stopped via the Services console. You can also configure which services run at startup using msconfig. You can view background services (as well as applications) using the Processes tab in Task Manager.

SFF
(Small Form Factor) Motherboards and connectors that are designed to take up less space.

SHA
(Secure Hash Algorithm) A cryptographic hashing algorithm created to address possible weaknesses in MDA. The earlier SHA-1 has been superseded by SHA-2.

shareware
Software that you can install free of charge usually for a limited time of use or with limited functionality. To continue using it or to access additional features, the user will need to register and often pay for the software.

sheet-fed scanner
A scanner in which the paper is passed over a fixed scan head.

shell
An OS component that interacts directly with users and functions as the command interpreter for operating systems.

shell script
A Linux file that contains a list of commands to be read and executed by the shell.

shoulder surfing
A human-based attack where the goal is to look over the shoulder of an individual as he or she enters password information or a PIN.

shredding
Grinding a disk into little pieces.

sideload
See **Android application package**.

silicon chip
A wafer of purified silicon doped with a metal oxide (typically copper or aluminum).

SIM
(Subscriber Identity Module) A small chip card that identifies the user and phone number of a mobile device via an International Mobile Subscriber Identity (ISMI). A SIM card also provides a limited amount of local storage for contacts.

single-channel memory
Memory with one 64-bit bus between the CPU and RAM.

SLA
(stereolithography) A 3D printing method which uses a resin or **photopolymer** to create objects which are cured using an ultraviolet laser.

SLAT
(Second Level Address Translation) A feature of virtualization software designed to improve the management of virtual (paged) memory.

slicing
Creating horizontal layers to use in 3D modeling and 3D printers.

slipstreamed media
A disc-based installation that has all of the various updates, patches, and drivers included along with the original installation files.

SLS
(selective laser sintering) A 3D printing method which fuses layers together using a pulse laser, creating the object from a plastic or metal powder with the model

being lowered into a tank as each layer is added.

smart card
A card with a chip containing data on it. Smart cards are typically used for authentication, with the chip storing authentication data such as a digital certificate.

smart card reader
A device, either built-in or attached as a peripheral, that uses a slot or NFC to interact with a smart card.

SMB
(Server Message Block) A protocol used for requesting files from Windows servers and delivering them to clients. SMB allows machines to share files and printers, thus making them available for other machines to use. SMB client software is available for UNIX-based systems. Samba software allows UNIX and Linux servers or NAS appliances to run SMB services for Windows clients.

SMF
(Single Mode Fiber) A category of fiber optic cable. SMF is more expensive than MMF (using high quality cable and optics) and supports much longer distances (up to about 70 km).

SMP
(symmetric multiprocessing) A condition where two or more physical CPUs that share a common OS and memory execute instructions simultaneously.

SMT
(Simultaneous Multithreading) Processing of multiple threads simultaneously.

SMTP
(Simple Mail Transfer Protocol) The protocol used to send mail between hosts on the Internet. Messages are sent over TCP port 25.

SNMP
(Simple Network Management Protocol) A protocol for monitoring and managing network devices. A management system collates data sent by agents running on each device. The agents maintain a Management Information Base of

configuration and usage data. An agent can also generate a trap, alerting the management system of some notable event (such as a printer being out of paper). SNMP works over UDP ports 161 and 162 by default.

Snort
An intrusion detection program.

SNR
(Signal-to-Noise Ratio) A sound measurement that is expressed in decibels that compares the signal power with the noise power.

social engineering
A hacking technique, widely publicized by Kevin Mitnick in his book "The Art of Deception," whereby the hacker gains useful information about an organization by deceiving its users or by exploiting their unsecure working practices. Typical social engineering methods include impersonation, domination, and charm.

SODIMM
(Small Outline Dual In-line Memory Module) Memory that is half the size of DIMMs, are available in 32- or 64-bit data paths, and are commonly found in laptops and iMac systems.

soft reset
Power cycling a mobile device in an attempt to resolve issues the user is experiencing.

SOHO network
(small office/home office network) A small network that provides connectivity and resource sharing for a small office or home office.

solid state storage
Any type of persistent digital storage technology that does not use mechanical parts.

SOP
(Standard Operating Procedure) See **procedure**.

sound card
An add-on card or built-in adapter to process audio signals and provide interfaces for connecting audio devices.

spam
Junk messages sent over email (or instant messaging [SPIM]). Filters and blacklists are available to block spam and known spam servers. It is also important to ensure that any mail servers you operate are not open relays, allowing a spammer to leverage your server to distribute spam and making it likely that it will be blacklisted.

spear phishing
See **whaling**.

spike
A spike can occur when electrical devices are turned off or when electrical storms are happening. Normally, spikes and surges are not sufficient to cause problems but occasionally big fluctuations may lead to the system crashing or hanging.

spoofing
Where the attacker disguises their identity. Some examples include IP spoofing, where the attacker changes their IP address, or phishing, where the attacker sets up a false website.

Spotlight
File system search feature in macOS.

spyware
Software that records information about a PC and its user. Spyware is used to describe malicious software installed without the user's content. Aggressive spyware is used to gather passwords or financial information such as credit card details.

SSD
(solid state drive) A personal computer storage device that stores data in non-volatile special memory instead of on disks or tape.

SSH
(Secure Shell) A remote administration and file copy program that is flexible enough to support VPNs too (using port forwarding). SSH runs on TCP port 22.

SSID
(Service Set ID) Identifies a particular Wireless LAN (WLAN). This "network name"

can be used to connect to the correct network. When multiple APs are configured with the same SSID, this is referred to as an E(xtended)SSID.

SSL
(Secure Sockets Layer) A security protocol developed by Netscape to provide privacy and authentication over the Internet. It is application independent (working at layer 5 [Session]) and can be used with a variety of protocols, such as HTTP or FTP. Client and server set up a secure connection through PKI (X.509) certificates (optionally, both client and server can authenticate to one another). The protocol is now being developed as Transport Layer Security (TLS).

SSO
(Single Sign-on) Any authentication technology that allows a user to authenticate once and receive authorizations for multiple services. Kerberos is a typical example of an authentication technology providing SSO.

SSTP
(Secure Socket Tunneling Protocol) Uses the HTTP over SSL protocol and encapsulates an IP packet with an SSTP header.

ST Connector
(Straight Tip connector) Bayonet-style twist-and-lock connector for fiber optic cabling.

standard
A measure by which to evaluate compliance with a policy.

standard client
A business computer that performs most or all computing functions on its own. Also referred to as a thick client or a fat client.

Standard User account
A Microsoft Windows user account recommended for day-to-day operations, which has much more limited capabilities than the Administrator account, and is able to run installed programs.

standoffs
Used to firmly attach the motherboard to the case, ensuring no other part of the motherboard touches the case.

static eliminator
See **detac corona**.

storage bus
A special type of expansion bus dedicated to communicating with storage devices.

stored value
The area where programs keep variable and constant values while the program is running.

STP
(Shielded Twisted Pair cabling) A type of network cabling used where protection from interference is required. Insulation is installed around all four pairs of twisted cables.

string
Data type supporting storage of a variable length series of characters.

structured cabling system
The use of patch cords, permanent links, and patch panels.

subnet mask
An IP address consists of a Network ID and a Host ID. The subnet mask is used in IPv4 to distinguish these two components within a single IP address. The typical format for a mask is 255.255.0.0. Classless network addresses can also be expressed in the format 169.254.0.0/16, where /16 is the number of bits in the mask. IPv6 uses the same /nn notation to indicate the length of the network prefix.

subtractive color printing
A color printing method that uses the reflective properties of inks.

superpipelining
Superscalar architectures feature longer pipelines with multiple stages but shorter actions (micro-ops) at each stage.

superscalar architecture
CPUs process multiple instructions at the same time (for example, while one instruction is fetched, another is being

decoded, another is being executed, and another is being written back to memory).

superuser
Another term for the root user.

supplicant
Under 802.1X, the device requesting access.

surge
An abrupt but brief change in the value of the voltage, lasting from a few billionths of a second (a transient) to a few thousandths of a second.

surge protector
A simple device intended to protect electrical devices against the damaging effects of a power spike.

Suricata
An intrusion detection program.

surround sound
Placement of multiple speakers positioned around the listener to provide a cinematic audio experience.

SVGA
(Super VGA) A variant of the VGA standard that supported 800x600 pixel resolution with 4-bit or 8-bit color.

swap partition
A portion of the hard disk that is formatted with a minimal kind of file system and used in situations when Linux runs out of physical memory and needs more of it. It can only be used by the memory manager and not for storage of ordinary data files.

Swift
Apple's programming language for developing mobile apps.

swipe lock
Another term for unlocking a device by tracing a predetermined on screen pattern or joining dots on screen.

switch
Ethernet switches are at the heart of most local networks. A switch receives incoming data into a buffer, then the destination MAC address is compared with an address table. The data is then only sent out to the

port with the corresponding MAC address. In a switched network, each port is in a separate collision domain (microsegmentation). Advanced switches perform routing at layers 3 (IP), 4 (TCP), or 7 (Application). Switches routing at layer 4/7 are referred to as load balancers and content switches.

switches
See **options**.

syslog
Used in UNIX and Linux, log files that allow for centralized collection of events from multiple sources.

system board
See **motherboard**.

system case
A plastic and metal box that houses components such as the motherboard, Central Processing Unit (CPU), memory, adapter cards, disk drives, and power supply unit. System units are also often referred to as boxes, main units, or base units.

system clock
The computer's timing mechanism that synchronizes the operation of all parts of the computer and provides the basic timing signal for the CPU; measured in MHz or GHz.

system files
The files necessary for the operating system to function properly.

system firmware
Low-level code to allow the computer components to be initialized and load the main operating system software.

system memory
The main storage area for programs and data when the computer is running.

system partition
In Microsoft terminology, the system partition is the bootable partition on the hard disk. This is usually, but not always, separate to the boot partition, which contains the operating system. The system partition is usually hidden from File Explorer (no drive letter is assigned to it).

system resources
Settings that enable a device to communicate with the CPU and memory without the device conflicting with other devices.

system restore
See **restore points**.

T568A
A legacy twisted pair standard that was used in commercial buildings and cabling systems that support data networks, voice, and video. It further defines cable performance and technical requirements.

T568B
A twisted pair standard that defines the standards for preferred cable types that provide the minimum acceptable performance levels for home-based networks.

TA
(Terminal Adapter) An external appliance or a plug-in card for a PC or compatible router that facilitates an ISDN connection.

tab completion
A feature in Linux that facilitates auto completion of commands and file names by pressing Tab.

TACACS+
(Terminal Access Controller Access Control System) An alternative to **RADIUS** developed by Cisco. The version in current use is TACACS+; TACACS and XTACACS are legacy protocols.

tailgating
Social engineering technique to gain access to a building by following someone else (or persuading them to "hold the door").

Task Scheduler
The Task Scheduler is a Windows program that enables the user to perform an action (such as running a program or a script) automatically at a pre-set time or in response to some sort of trigger.

TB
(Thunderbolt) It can be used as a display interface (like DisplayPort) and as a general peripheral interface (like USB 3). The latest version uses USB-C connectors.

TCO
(total cost of ownership) The cost of a device over its lifetime, including the cost of replacement components and consumables.

TCP
(Transmission Control Protocol) A protocol in the TCP/IP suite operating at the transport layer to provide connection-oriented, guaranteed delivery of packets. Hosts establish a session to exchange data and confirm delivery of packets using acknowledgements. This overhead means the system is relatively slow.

TCP/IP Suite
(Transmission Control Protocol/Internet Protocol suite) The network protocol suite used by most operating systems and the Internet. It is widely adopted, industry standard, vendor independent, and open. It uses a 4-layer network model that corresponds roughly to the OSI model as follows: Network Interface (Physical/Data Link), Internet (Network), Transport (Transport), Application (Session, Presentation, Application).

telnet
TCP/IP application protocol supporting remote command-line administration of a host (terminal emulation). Telnet is unauthenticated and has therefore been superseded by SSH or graphical remote configuration utilities. Telnet runs over TCP port 23.

terminal window
In Linux, a computer interface for text entry and display, where information is displayed as an array of preselected characters.

tethered VR headset
(tethered Virtual Reality headset) A self-contained VR device.

tethering
Using the cellular data plan of a mobile device to provide Internet access to a laptop or PC. The PC can be tethered to the mobile by USB, Bluetooth, or Wi-Fi (a mobile hotspot).

TFT Active Matrix Display
(Thin Film Transistor active matrix display)
The TFT display provides the best
resolution of all of the currently available
flat-panel Liquid Crystal Display (LCD)
designs, although they are also the most
expensive. TFT displays offer very high
image clarity, contrast ratios of between
150:1 to 200:1, fast refresh rates, and wide
viewing angles.

THD
(Total Harmonic Distortion) A sound
measurement that is expressed as a
percentage that compares input and
output audio signals, which indicates the
amount of distortion in the output signal.

thermal dye transfer printer
A sophisticated type of color printer that
uses heat to diffuse dye from color
ribbons onto special paper or
transparency blanks to produce
continuous-tone output similar in quality
to a photographic print. Also called dye
sublimation printer.

thermal inkjet print method
Ink delivery system in an inkjet printer that
uses **thermal shock**.

thermal paper
Paper that contains a chemical designed to
react with the heating element of a
thermal printer to create images on paper.

thermal paste
A paste that is used to connect a heat sink
to a CPU to provide a liquid thermally
conductive compound gel that fills any
gaps between the CPU and the heat sink to
permit a more efficient transference of
heat from the processor to the heat sink.

thermal printer
A type of printer that uses a thermal (high
heat) print head to fuse or transfer wax-
based ink onto paper or selectively heats
specially treated paper to form the image.
Most thermal printers are handheld
devices used for printing labels or receipts.

thermal shock
An ink delivery system where the ink is
heated to form a bubble that bursts
through the nozzles.

thermal wax transfer printer
A printer that uses a thermal printhead to
melt wax-based ink from a transfer ribbon
onto the paper.

thick client
A business computer that performs most
or all computing functions on its own. Also
referred to as a standard client or a fat
client.

thin client
A business computer that relies heavily on
another system, typically a server, to run
most of its programs, processes, and
services.

thrashed
See **disk thrashing**.

thread
A stream of instructions generated by a
software application. Most applications
run a single process in a single thread.

threat
Any potential violation of security policies
or procedures.

threat actor
See **threat agent**.

threat agent
A person or event that triggers a
vulnerability accidentally or exploits it
intentionally.

three-factor authentication
An authentication scheme that requires
validation of three authentication factors.

throttling
Technology that allows the CPU to slow
down if thermal output reaches a critical
level or to improve power performance.
Intel's throttling technology is called
SpeedStep; AMD's is called PowerNow!.

ticket
A record created when an incident occurs,
or move, add, or change is requested, so
that progress on resolving or completing
the task can be documented.

Time Machine
App facilitating backup operations in
macOS.

TKIP
(Temporal Key Integrity Protocol) Mechanism used in the first version of WPA to improve the security of wireless encryption mechanisms, compared to the flawed WEP standard.

TLS
(Transport Layer Security) A security protocol that protects sensitive communication from eavesdropping and tampering by using a secure, encrypted, and authenticated channel over a TCP/IP connection.

TN
(Twisted Nematic) An LCD panel technology where the panel is black when no electric current is running through the liquid crystal cells because the cells align themselves in a twisted state. When an electric current is applied, the liquid crystal cells untwist, allowing light to pass through, resulting in a white display screen.

tone generator and probe
The tone generator is an electronic device that sends an electrical signal through one set of UTP cables. The tone probe (or tone locator) is an electronic device that emits an audible tone when it detects a signal sent by the tone generator in a set of wires.

toner
Specially formulated compound to impart dye to paper through an electrographic process (used by laser printers and photocopiers). The key properties of toner are the colorant (dye), ability to fuse (wax or plastic), and ability to hold a charge. There are three main types of toner, distinguished by the mechanism of applying the toner to the developer roller: dual component (where the toner is mixed with a separate magnetic developer), mono-component (where the toner itself is magnetic), and non-magnetic mono-component (where the toner is transferred using static properties).

Top Level Domains
(TLD) In the DNS hierarchy, the level immediately below the root.

Touch ID
The Apple device feature that uses fingerprint biometric information to grant access to the device.

touchpad
Input device used on most laptops to replace the mouse. The touchpad allows the user to control the cursor by moving a finger over the pad's surface. There are usually buttons too but the pad may also recognize "tap" events and have scroll areas.

touchscreen
A display screen combined with a digitizer that is responsive to touch input.

tower case
A desktop computer designed to sit vertically on a surface so that it is taller than it is wide. Tower cases come in four basic sizes: full, mid, mini, and slim line.

TPM
(Trusted Platform Module) A specification for hardware-based storage of digital certificates, keys, hashed passwords, and other user and platform identification information. Essentially, it functions as a smart card embedded on a motherboard.

trace logs
Windows log files that allow you to collect statistics about services, including extensions to Event Viewer to log data that would otherwise be inaccessible.

traces
Wires etched on to the motherboard to provide electrical pathways.

track
When data is written onto a drive, it is stored as magnetic changes in the structure of the disk. These alterations are written as concentric rings as the disk spins. Each of these rings is termed a track.

tractor feed
An impact printer mechanism that uses pairs of wheels with pins evenly spaced around the circumference at a set spacing to feed continuous roll paper with matching holes that fit over the pins.

transfer belt
In a color printer, combining colors to print in one pass.

transfer roller
See **transfer unit**.

transfer unit
Roller, corona wire, or belt assembly that applies a charge to the media (paper) so that it attracts toner from the photoconductor. A detac strip then removes the charge to prevent paper curl. On a color laser printer, the transfer unit is usually a belt.

transistor
In computers, semiconductor switches used to create logic devices.

trickle charge
Charging a device that has been fully charged at the rate at which the charge discharges, keeping the device fully charged without overcharging the battery.

trip hazard
Any object placed in pathways where people walk.

Trojan Horse
A malicious software program hidden within an innocuous-seeming piece of software. Usually the Trojan is used to try to compromise the security of the target computer.

trusted app source
A source for apps that is managed by a service provider.

tunneling
A tunneling (or encapsulation) protocol wraps up data from one protocol for transfer over a different type of network. For example, PPP can carry TCP/IP data over a dial-up line, enabling a remote computer to communicate with the LAN.

TWAIN
Standard "driver" model for interfacing scanner hardware with applications software.

two-factor authentication
An authentication scheme that requires validation of two authentication factors.

Type 1 hypervisor
A bare metal hypervisor in which you install directly on the server's hardware.

Type 2 hypervisor
A host-based hypervisor in which you install the host operating system first, then install the hypervisor.

UAC
(User Account Control) A security system in Windows designed to restrict abuse of accounts with administrator privileges. Actions such as installing hardware and software can be performed without changing accounts but the user must authorize the use of administrative rights by clicking a prompt or re-entering user credentials.

UDP
(User Datagram Protocol) A protocol in the TCP/IP suite operating at the transport layer to provide connectionless, non-guaranteed communication with no sequencing or flow control. Faster than TCP, but does not provide reliability.

UEFI
(Unified Extensible Firmware Interface) A type of system firmware providing support for 64-bit CPU operation at boot, full GUI and mouse operation at boot, and better boot security.

UEFI setup
(Unified Extensible Firmware Interface setup) Another name for the setup program used to configure system firmware settings. Also known as BIOS setup.

unattended installation
A software or operating system installation where the configuration information is derived from an input file.

unauthorized account access
When someone other than an authorized user gains access to an online account.

unauthorized camera and microphone usage
When an attacker gains access to the camera and microphone on a mobile device and uses it to cause a security breach of sensitive data.

unauthorized location tracking
Giving away too much sensitive information to third parties.

unauthorized root access
When an attacker gains root access which allows the attacker to have system-level access to every process running in the OS.

uncollated
A print job where all copies of page 1 are printed first, followed by all copies of page 2, and so on.

undeclared variable
A variable that is used without first identifying the data type.

undocumented feature
A software feature or function that is not included in the official documentation and is typically unsupported, and can be removed or modified without users' knowledge. Also used as a derogatory term for a software bug.

unicast addressing
A packet addressed to a single host. If the host is not on the local subnet, the packet must be sent via one or more routers.

unified file system
Everything available to the Linux OS is represented as a file in the file system, including devices.

UNIX
UNIX is a family of more than 20 related operating systems that are produced by various companies. It can run on a wide variety of platforms. UNIX offers a multitude of file systems in addition to its native system. UNIX remains widely deployed in enterprise data centers to run mission critical applications and infrastructure.

unmanaged_switch
Performs microsegmentation without requiring any sort of configuration.

updates
Updates are made freely available by the software manufacturer to fix problems in a particular software version, including any security vulnerabilities. Updates can be classified as hotfixes (available only to selected customers and for a limited problem), patches (generally available), and service packs (installable collections of patches and software improvements).

UPnP
(Universal Plug-and-Play) A protocol framework allowing network devices to autoconfigure services, such as allowing a games console to request appropriate settings from a firewall.

UPS
(Uninterruptible Power Supply) An alternative AC power supply in the event of power failure. A UPS requires an array of batteries, a charging circuit, an inverter to convert DC to AC current, a circuit to allow the system to take over from a failing power supply, and some degree of spike, surge, or brownout protection (possibly including a line conditioner).

UPS sizing
The process of determining the appropriate size UPS to protect the load from a given system.

URL
(Uniform Resource Locator/Identifier) An application-level addressing scheme for TCP/IP, allowing for human-readable resource addressing. For example: protocol://server/file, where "protocol" is the type of resource (HTTP, FTP), "server" is the name of the computer (www.microsoft.com), and "file" is the name of the resource you wish to access.

USB
(Universal Serial Bus) The main type of connection interface used on PCs. A larger Type A connector attaches to a port on the host; Type B and Mini- or Micro-Type B connectors are used for devices. USB 1.1 supports 12 Mbps while USB 2.0 supports 480 Mbps and is backward compatible with 1.1 devices (which run at the slower speed). USB devices are hot swappable. A device can draw up to 2.5 W of power. USB 3.0 and 3.1 define 5 Gbps (SuperSpeed) and 10 Gbps (SuperSpeed+) rates and can deliver 4.5 W of power.

USB 2.0 (HighSpeed) standard
A USB standard that operates at up to 480 Mbps.

USB hub
A device that connects to a USB port to allow additional USB devices to be connected to the PC, essentially increasing the number of USB ports available.

USB On the Go (OTG)
A USB standard that allows a port to function as either a host or as a device.

USB SuperSpeed
The USB 3.0 standard that operates at up to 5 Gbps and makes the link full duplex.

USB SuperSpeed+
The USB 3.1 standard that operates at up to 10 Gbps.

user account
Each user who wishes to access a Windows computer will need a logon ID, referred to as a user account. Each user will normally have a local profile, containing settings and user-created files. Profiles are stored in the "Users" folder or can be redirected to a network folder.

UTM
(Unified Threat Management) All-in-one security appliances and technologies that combine the functions of a firewall, malware scanner, intrusion detection, vulnerability scanner, Data Loss Prevention, content filtering, and so on.

UTP
(Unshielded Twisted Pair cabling) The type of cabling typically used for computer networking, composed of eight insulated copper wires grouped into four pairs with each pair twisted to reduce interference between wires.

variable
Identifier for a value that can change during program execution. Variables are usually declared with a particular data type.

VBR
(Volume Boot Record) Loads the boot manager, which for Windows is **bootmgr.exe**.

vCard
The digital equivalent of a business card.

VDE
(Virtual Desktop Environment) A virtual environment in which users can customize and update the environment as if it was a physical environment.

VDI
(Virtual Desktop Infrastructure) Hosting user desktops as virtual machines on a centralized server or cloud infrastructure. The desktop OS plus applications software is delivered to the client device (often a thin client) over the network as an image.

VDSL
(Very High Bitrate DSL) A high speed version of DSL with an upstream rate between 1.5 Mbps and 2.5 Mbps and a downstream rate between 50 Mbps and 55 Mbps.

vector font
A font that consists of a description of how each character should be drawn that can be scaled up or down to different font sizes.

vector graphics
Scalable images that are created from vectors which describe how a line should be drawn.

VGA
(Video Graphics Array). A standard for the resolution and color depth of computer displays. VGA specifies a resolution of 640x480 with 16 colors (4-bit color) at 60 Hz.

VGA Connector
(Video Graphics Array connector) A 15-pin HD connector has been used to connect the graphics adapter to a monitor since 1987. The use of digital flat-panel displays rather than CRTs means that as an analog connector, it is fast becoming obsolete.

video card
Provides the interface between the graphics components of the computer and the display device. A number of connectors may be provided for the display, including VGA, DVI, and HDMI. Most adapters come with their own processor (Graphics Processing Unit [GPU]) and onboard memory.

video projector
A large format display in which the image is projected onto a screen or wall using a lens system.

virtual application streaming
Just enough of an application is installed on the end user device for the system to recognize that the application is available to the user, and when the user accesses the application, additional portions of the code are downloaded to the device.

virtual assistant
Another term for a **digital assistant**.

virtual file system
A layer that sits between the actual file system and the kernel. It identifies the location of the persistent root partition from the appropriate storage device and loads the file system stored on the disk.

virtual memory
An area on the hard disk allocated to contain pages of memory. When the operating system doesn't have sufficient physical memory (RAM) to perform a task, pages of memory are swapped to the paging file. This frees physical RAM to enable the task to be completed. When the paged RAM is needed again, it is re-read into memory.

virtual switch
A software application that enables communication between VMs.

virtualization
Software allowing a single computer (the host) to run multiple "guest" operating systems (or Virtual Machines [VMs]). The VMs are configured via a hypervisor or VM Monitor (VMM). VMs can be connected using virtual networks (vSwitch) or leverage the host's network interface(s). It is also possible for the VMs to share data with the host (via shared folders or the clipboard, for instance). VT is now used as major infrastructure in data centers as well as for testing and training.

virus
Code designed to infect computer files (or disks) when it is activated. A virus may also be programmed to carry out other malicious actions, such as deleting files or changing system settings.

VLAN
(Virtual LAN) A logically separate network, created using switching technology. Even though hosts on two VLANs may be physically connected to the same cabling, local traffic is isolated to each VLAN so they must use a router to communicate.

VM
(Virtual Machine) A guest operating system installed on a host computer using virtualization software (a hypervisor), such as Microsoft Hyper-V or VMware.

VM escaping
(virtual machine escaping) Malware running on a guest OS jumping to another guest or to the host.

VM sprawl
(virtual machine sprawl) The uncontrolled development of more and more virtual machines.

VNC
(Virtual Network Computing) Remote access tool and protocol. VNC is the basis of macOS screen sharing.

volatile
A type of memory where data cannot be stored without power being supplied.

voltage
The potential difference between two points (often likened to pressure in a water pipe) measured in Volts (V). In the US, grid power is 114-126 VAC. In Europe, grid power is referred to as mains electricity and is supplied at 220-240 VAC.

voltage regulators
Voltage Regulator Modules ensure that the motherboard delivers the voltage required by the CPU. When CPUs changed from 5 V to 3.3 V operation, VRMs were provided as plug-in modules. Most modern CPUs use around 1.5 - 2 V and the voltage regulators are built into the motherboard.

VPN
(Virtual Private Network) A secure tunnel created between two endpoints connected via an unsecure network (typically the

Internet). VPNs are typically created using SSL/TLS or IPsec. Encryption software is used to ensure privacy of data as messages transit through the public network.

VR
(Virtual Reality) A computer-generated, simulated environment experienced via a headset connected to a PC or powered by a smartphone.

VR headset
(Virtual Reality headset) A headset worn like goggles to interact with images displayed in the headset.

VSAT
(Very Small Aperture Terminal) A microwave antenna aligned to an orbital satellite that can either relay signals between sites directly or via another satellite.

VT-x
Extensions in Intel-based systems that allow hardware virtualization.

vulnerability
Any weakness that could be triggered accidentally or exploited intentionally to cause a security breach.

walled garden
A closed software system in which the user's access to content and services is controlled by the user's mobile carrier or by a service provider.

WAN
(Wide Area Network) A network that spans multiple geographic locations.

wear leveling
Routines used by flash drives to prevent any single storage location from being overused and to optimize the life of the device.

web server
HTTP servers host websites. A basic website consists of static HTML pages but many sites are developed as front-end applications for databases. Web servers are popular targets for attack, particularly DoS, spoofing, and software exploits. Many companies use hosted web servers but if not, the server should be located in a DMZ. Web servers are also commonly used for intranet services, especially on Microsoft networks.

webcam
A webcam can be used to stream and record video. There are many types, from devices built into laptops to standalone units. While early devices were only capable of low resolutions, most webcams are now HD-capable.

WEP
(Wired Equivalent Privacy) A mechanism for encrypting data sent over a wireless connection. WEP is considered flawed (that is, a determined and well-resourced attack could probably break the encryption). Apart from problems with the cipher, the use and distribution of a pre-shared key (effectively a password) depends on good user practice. WEP has been replaced by WPA.

whaling
A form of phishing that targets individuals who are known or are believed to be wealthy.

whitelisting
An address added to the white list is permitted to connect to any port.

Wi-Fi
IEEE standard for wireless networking based on spread spectrum radio transmission in the 2.4 GHz and 5 GHz bands. The standard has five main iterations (a, b, g, n, and ac), describing different modulation techniques, supported distances, and data rates.

Wi-Fi analyzer
A Wi-Fi spectrum analyzer used to detect devices and points of interference, as well as analyze and troubleshoot network issues on a WLAN or other wireless networks.

Wi-Fi Direct
Technology that enables two mobile devices to connect to each other without a wireless access point.

WIA
(Windows Image Acquisition) Driver model and API (Application Programming Interface) for interfacing scanner hardware with applications software on Windows PCs.

wiki
A website that is configured so users can view, enter, and share information about a subject.

wildcard
A special character that is used to substitute characters in a string.

Windows Certified Products List
A searchable database of hardware devices that have been tested to ensure they are compatible with the Windows 10 operating system.

Windows Explorer
See **File Explorer**.

Windows LPL catalog
(Windows Logo'd Product List catalog) A catalog of devices and drivers that have been tested to ensure they are compatible with the Windows 7 operating system.

Windows Media Center
An obsolete program included with Windows Vista and Windows 7 that included a broadcast TV schedule that allowed computers equipped with a TV tuner card to view and record TV programs. It also acted as a playback interface for optical discs.

Windows Resource Protection
A Windows feature that prevents essential system files, folders, and registry keys from being replaced to help prevent application and operating system failure.

Windows Server
A network operating system typically used for private network servers and Internet servers running web, email, and social networking apps.

Windows Settings
Windows 10 app for configuring and managing the Windows 10 computer.

Wireless Range Extender
Designed to repeat the signal from an access point to extend the range of a WLAN.

WISP
(Wireless Internet Service Provider) An ISP offering Internet access over ground-based Line of Sight (LoS) microwave transmitters.

WMN
(Wireless Mesh Network) Wireless network topology where all nodes—including client stations—are capable of providing forwarding and path discovery. This improves coverage and throughput compared to using just fixed access points and extenders.

WoL
(Wake on LAN) Where a host has a compatible network card, a network server can be configured to transmit a "magic packet" that causes the host to power up.

work instruction
Detailed documents that contain step-by-step tasks needed to perform a specific task.

workgroup
A small group of computers on a network that share resources in a peer-to-peer fashion. No one computer provides a centralized directory.

working directory
See **current working directory**.

workstation
Client devices connecting to the network represent one of the most vulnerable points as they are usually harder to monitor than centrally located equipment, such as servers and switches. As well as secure configuration of the OS and applications, workstations should be protected with anti-malware software. Users should be trained in security best practices and educated about common threats.

worm
A type of virus that spreads through memory and network connections rather than infecting files.

WoWLAN
(Wake-on-Wireless LAN) A wireless version of WoL that is not widely implemented.

WPA
(Wi-Fi Protected Access) An improved encryption scheme for protecting Wi-Fi communications, designed to replace WEP. The original version of WPA was subsequently updated (to WPA2) following the completion of the 802.11i security standard. WPA features an improved method of key distribution and authentication for enterprise networks, though the pre-shared key method is still available for home and small office networks. WPA2 uses the improved AES cipher, replacing TKIP and RC4.

WPF
(Windows Presentation Foundation) In Windows, handles the display and print functions for compatible applications.

WPS
(Wi-Fi Protected Setup) Mechanism for auto-configuring a WLAN securely for home users. On compatible equipment, users just have to push a button on the access point and connecting adapters to associate them securely.

WWAN
(Wireless Wide Area Network) A large wireless network, such as a cellular data network or line-of-sight microwave transmission.

WYSIWYG
(What You See Is What You Get) The screen and print output are supposed to be the same.

x64
See **x86-64**.

x86-32
The instruction set used by IBM PC compatible CPUs.

x86-64
Another term for the **AMD64** instruction set.

Xcode
Apple's **SDK** for macOS and iOS software development.

XML
(eXtensible Markup Language) A system for structuring documents so that they are human- and machine-readable. Information within the document is placed within tags, which describe how information within the document is structured.

XPS
(XML Print Specification) A file format based on **XML** that describes one or more pages and how the information should appear on the page.

yum
A tool for maintaining packages on Fedora-based Linux systems.

Z-Wave
Low-power wireless communications protocol used primarily for home automation. Z-Wave uses radio frequencies in the high 800 to low 900 MHz range and a mesh topology.

zero day exploit
An attack that exploits a vulnerability in software that is unknown to the software vendor and users. Most vulnerabilities are discovered by security researchers and the vendor will have time to create a patch and distribute it to users before exploits can be developed, so zero day exploits have the potential to be very destructive.

ZIF socket
(Zero Insertion Force socket) A processor socket type allowing the chip to be placed in the socket with as little risk of damaging the pins on the processor chip as possible.

Zigbee
Low-power wireless communications open source protocol used primarily for home automation. Zigbee uses radio frequencies in the 2.4 GHz band and a mesh topology.

zombie
Unauthorized software that directs the devices to launch a DDoS attack.

Index

D

DACs *196*
data backup *1020*
Data Collector Sets *443*
Data Loss Prevention, *See* DLP
Data Over Cable Service Interface Specification, *See* DOCSIS
data policies *764*
data restoration *1020*
Data Sources *418*
data types *1037*, *1039*
daughter boards *125*
DC *289*, *682*
DCOM *418*
DDoS attack *741*
DDR SDRAM *207*
declared variables *1037*
default gateway *528*
default masks *526*
defense in depth *547*, *729*
defragmentation *390*
Degaussing *749*
Demilitarized Zone, *See* DMZ
Denial of Service, *See* DoS
Denial of Service attack, *See* DoS attack
desktop *3*
desktop computers *115*
Desktop Publishing, *See* DTP
desktop style *2*
detac corona *926*
developer roller *925*
device drivers *2*
DHCP *528*
dial-up connection *566*
die *262*
digital assistants *642*
digital cameras *201*
digital certificates *727*, *808*
digital displays *171*
Digital Light Processing, *See* DLP
Digital Rights Management, *See* DRM
Digital Signal Processor chips, *See* DSP chips
Digital Single Lens Reflex, *See* DSLR
Digital Subscriber Line, *See* DSL
Digital-to-Analog Converters, *See* DACs
digital versatile discs, *See* DVDs
Digital Visual Interface, *See* DVI
digitizer *830*
DIMM *209*
diode *290*

Direct Current, *See* DC
direct thermal printers *940*
Disaster Recovery Plan, *See* DRP
disk defragmentation *252*
disk images *78*
disk mirroring *242*
disk striping *241*
disk thrashing *248*
disk wiping *749*
DisplayPort *176*
distended capacitors *308*
Distinguished Name *546*
Distributed COM, *See* DCOM
Distributed DoS attack, *See* DDoS attack
distributions *328*
    See also distros
distros *328*
DLP *170*, *770*
DMZ *600*
DNS *528*, *539*
dock *354*
docking stations *823*
DOCSIS *516*
domain accounts *682*
domain controllers *682*
domain names *540*
Domain Name System, *See* DNS
domains *378*, *682*
DoS *711*, *915*
DoS attack *741*
dot matrix printers *938*
dotted decimal notation *525*
Double Data Rate SDRAM, *See* DDR SDRAM
DRAM *207*
drive controllers *221*
drive enclosures *238*
drive encryption *284*
drivers *162*
drives
    hot swappable *246*
DRM *772*
drop cables *487*
DRP *1020*
DSL *515*
DSL Access Multiplier, *See* DSLAM
DSLAM *515*
DSLR *202*
DSP chips *196*
DTP *317*

ISBN-13 978-1-6427-4174-2
ISBN-10 1-6427-4174-4